TEEN MOVIE HELL
A Crucible of Coming-of-Age Comedies from Animal House to Zapped!
by Mike "McBeardo" McPadden

Second printing, published in 2021 by

Bazillion Points
New York | USA
WWW.BAZILLIONPOINTS.COM

Produced for Bazillion Points by Ian Christe
Cover painting by Andrei Bouzikov
Layout and design by Bazillion Points
Quality control by Polly Watson

"Dedication" and "Condemned to Teen Movie Hell" illustrations by Scott R. Miller
"Booger," "Madonna," "Teen Mike," "Blow Me," and "Rush Tape"
illustrations by Corinne Halbert

In loving memory of William Michael McPadden

A bazillion thank-yous to Rachel McPadden, Lisa Carver, Liz Mason, Christina Ward, Greg Fiering, Aaron Cantor, Sam Henderson, Derek Yip, Jeffrey J. Jensen, Ian Marshall, Anne Marshall, Max Nichols, Dianna Dilworth, Roman Fox, Vivienne Isa, Carole Ann Christe, Kris Durso, Christiane F., the Callicoon Theater, and drive-in theaters, video rental stores, and basic cable channels everywhere.

Library of Congress Control Number: 2019932426
Library of Congress Cataloging-in-Publication Data is available upon request

ISBN 978-1-935950-23-3

Printed in the United States

TEEN MOVIE HELL

A CRUCIBLE OF COMING-OF-AGE COMEDIES FROM ANIMAL HOUSE TO ZAPPED!

MIKE "McBEARDO" McPADDEN

Bazillion Points

Late to the party, Heavy Metal Summer *(1988) delivers the* Teen Movie Hell *archetypes.*

DEDICATION

FOR THE XEROX-AND-STAPLES PUBLISHING MAGNATES WHO FIRST ALERTED ME TO WHAT CAN BE POSSIBLE WHEN YOU DO IT YOURSELF

RICK SULLIVAN [*GORE GAZETTE*]
LISA CARVER [*ROLLERDERBY*]
MICHAEL WELDON [*PSYCHOTRONIC*]
BILL LANDIS & JIMMY MCDONOUGH [*SLEAZOID EXPRESS*]
GERARD COSLOY [*CONFLICT*]
AARON LEE [*BLUE PERSUASION*]

BUZZ
BEER
FART CONTEST
TONITE
ODDBALLS
HARDBODIES
PORKY'S
PORKYS
VHS
TMH
HAMBURGER
TOUCHDOWN!
PAC MAN

Table of Contents

Illustration by Scott R. Miller

Mike "McBeardo" McPadden, photo by Rachel McPadden

All the Kids Are Doing It!

Porno movies watered down for thirteen-year-olds—that's is what this book is about. The teen sex comedies reviewed here are what once served preadolescents in lieu of X-rated access during the couple of decades after 1968. In that year, Hollywood's new "R" rating arrived, allowing for nudity and profanity in mainstream productions. From then until the arrival of America Online subscription CD-ROMs twenty-five years later, anything labeled "adults only" remained genuinely difficult to access for anyone except, indeed, *adults*.

The R rating brought a fresh array of sensations within orbit of a planet of hormone-inflamed teens. As always, exploitation filmmakers seized the opportunity to profit via a new film genre: the teen sex comedy. Such films combined familiar teenage settings—mostly schools and summer camps—with fantasies of freedom, juvenile humor, and hyped-up erotic content. To a thirteen-year-old in the 1970s, 1980s, and early 1990s, topless females proved titillating enough to monumentally propel this cottage industry, much to the substantial benefit and enrichment of the otherwise marginal operators of drive-in movie theaters, ma-and-pa video stores, and lower-tier pay cable television channels.

Meanwhile, at the mall multiplex, theater owners were nominally mandated to restrict admission to R-rated movies to patrons over age seventeen. Sneaking into such attractions became an adolescent rite of passage. Everyone did it! This struggle became almost moot after the advent of the VCR, as renting R-rated tapes seldom posed the same kind of problem. Children were shooed away from curtained-off X-rated sections at the backs of video stores, but the entire remainder of the premises was up for grabs. And thirteen-year-olds got plenty grabby when it came to teen sex comedies.

A couple of megaton 1970s box office monsters established the value of this cash-flush adolescent audience when it came to movies loaded with sex, pranks, and, sometimes, real-life bummers. In the beginning came *American Graffiti* (1973), which, against a budget of $770,000, grossed $140 million ($795 million today). Five years later, *Animal House,* which cost $3 million to make, earned back $141.6 million. Both *Graffiti* and *House* were set in 1962 and trafficked in nostalgia for the time when baby boomers, the power generation of the 1970s, actually experienced puberty. Producers only expected middle-aged audiences; the teens who flocked to the sticky seats were pure gravy.

Following the money, countless teen exploitation knockoffs soon filled drive-ins and grindhouses in the wake of *Graffiti* and *House*, many taking place in some vague Eisenhower-era vapor. Poodle skirts, pompadours, and pom-poms dominated the imagery between gross-out pranks and prominent T&A. With that formula, it was difficult to flop. Not every B movie was a grand slam on the order of *Graffiti* and *House*, but many were solid singles that turned into inside-the-park home runs.

In 1981, Universal opted to distribute the independently made *Private Lessons* and scored the year's most profitable hit. The nerdy-teen-cracks-the-croissant-of-his-hot-French-tutor romp grossed ten times its *petite* $2.8 million investment. Backed by Universal's muscle, *Private Lessons* penetrated mainstream consciousness. The public perceived it as a just another entertainment option at the multiplex, right alongside *On Golden Pond* and *Raiders of the Lost Ark*. Universal rushed an official follow-up into production (that evolved two years later into *Private School*), and the other major studios caught teen-flick fever fast.

Most monolithically, 20th Century Fox mined the motherlode when it scooped up the $5 million, Canadian-made *Porky's*. Test audiences in Colorado and South Carolina in November 1981 nearly rioted with elation. Fox made *Porky's* its big spring release, and unleashed the boys and boobs of Angel Beach High nationwide in March 1982. Sticking in theaters for more than a year, *Porky's* earned $105 million in North America, and, according to some estimates, another $100 million worldwide. Dollar-for-dollar, *Porky's* was only bested that year by *E.T. the Extra-Terrestrial*.

The summer of 1982 brought forth *The Last American Virgin* and *Fast Times at Ridgemont High*. Both films turned healthy profits in theaters, but truly etched themselves into the teen experience by way of cable TV and videocassette rentals. These movies filled a unique adolescent niche that could not have been designed better for the emerging media of the times; the role of teen sex comedies in getting the cable broadcasting and home video industries off the ground can never be underestimated.

Teen sex comedy numbers remained huge throughout the first half of the '80s. Typical tenfold return ratios blessed not only behemoths such as *Risky Business* (1982; $6.2 million budget/$63 million gross) and *Revenge of the Nerds* (1984; $6 million budget/$60 million gross) but also rock-solid underdogs like *Joysticks* (1983; $300,000 budget/$4 million gross) and *Hot Dog... The Movie* (1984; $2.5 million budget/$17.1 million gross).

At first blush, *Sixteen Candles* (1984)—with its naked shower peeping, panty pilfering, and Long Duk Dong—probably appeared to be just another teen sex cash calf, turning a $6.5 million investment into a $27.1 million return. But writer-director John Hughes changed the playing field by cannily shifting focus to a female perspective, shooting for a PG rating, and reuniting everyone the following year for *The Breakfast Club*. Rated R, but solely for dirty words, *The Breakfast Club* cost Universal a scant $1 million and reaped $51.5 million in ticket sales.

Alas, much like puberty itself, the teen sex comedy in its classic form soon petered out. Little by little, the PG-13 rating, initiated in 1984, enticed studios to further tone down what would have been R-rated material in order to initiate an ever-younger audience into multiplexes. Lots of talking about getting it on remained on-screen, but lots of *showing* "getting it on" no longer did. The situations depicted on-screen were no longer as adult in emotional content either. Instead of making films about adult themes for teens, distribution companies notched down and began producing teen films for pre-teens.

Then in the 1990s, pop culture grew self-aware, trafficking in irony and sarcasm. Teenagers of the time followed suit. The inherent naiveté that enabled *The Pom-Pom Girls* (1976) or *Porky's* to seem "naughty" came off as anachronistic and even embarrassing. Increasingly, a tsunami of cheap videos and ever-increasing modem speeds meant actual X-rated materials were no longer beyond the reach of audiences technically too young to get their hands on them. Kids were not about to get funny feelings watching *Hot Dog...The Movie* after having their eyes opened wide by *Cherry Poppers Vol. 17*. The teen sex comedy, as it had been from *The First Time* (1969) on up to, say, *Hamburger: The Motion Picture* (1986), graduated into oblivion, without honors.

Teen sex comedies were relatively innocent, and the adolescents of the 1970s and 1980s really were the last American virgins. Total twenty-four-hour media interconnectedness has made everything instantly available—and yet nothing equivocally replaced what was gone. Right or wrong, thirteen-year-olds no longer have their very own entertaining sex movies, complete with a smattering of morality lessons about binge drinking, teen pregnancy, and finding true love in the middle of a massive food fight.

Come now. Let us gather and celebrate a cinematic era when kids could imagine themselves behaving as adults, at least for one last summer before being kicked out into the real world and becoming fuddy-duddy parents, gym coaches, and local sheriffs themselves. Prepare to party with three decades of freaks, jocks, geeks, cheerleaders, and more beer-drinking dogs on surfboards than anyone could ever imagine possible.

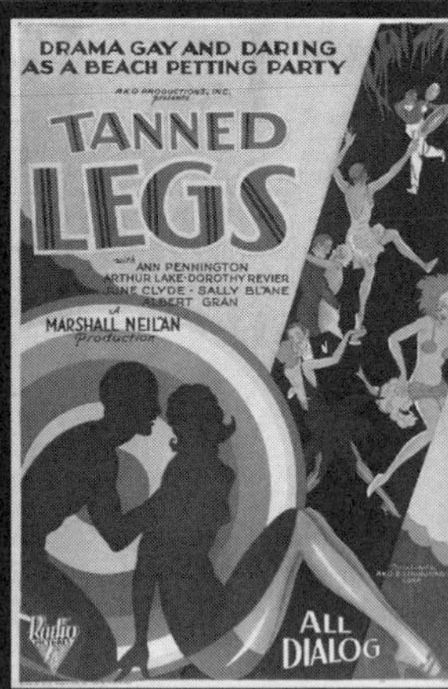

Taglines and titillation in the 1930s, before the Hays Code pooped Hollywood's party. Clockwise from top left: *Loretta Young bares back in* Born to Be Bad *(1934)*; *Nancy Carroll sweats out* Hot Saturday *(1932)*; White Woman *(1933), white heat*; *Clara Bow flaunts "It" in* The Saturday Night Kid *(1929)*; Call Her Savage *(1932) had prudes writing the censors*; Tanned Legs *(1929)—what a concept!*; *devilish Mae West declares* I'm No Angel *(1933)*; *Eddie Cantor's orgy of laughs* Roman Scandals *(1933)*; *Tallulah Bankhead, fingered as* The Cheat *(1931)*. Center: *James Cagney goes* Blonde Crazy *(1931)*.

The Ellinger Code

Teen Sex Comedies in the Age of #MeToo and for All Eternity

by Kat Ellinger

Without wanting to begin with the usual clichéd "so honored to be here" business, the fact is, I am very honored to be part of a balls-out celebration of the most raucous, sleaziest, grossest teen comedies of the Golden Age; films representing an era when anarchy and teen culture ruled. These movies and their moment present the opportunity for some sublime commentary, particularly on the topic of sex. Let's face it, who doesn't want a piece of that?

Apparently, some people don't share my excitement. The author of a *USA Today* article "In the Era of #MeToo, Is it Still OK to Laugh at 'Animal House'?" published on July 27, 2018, is perplexed that the seminal classic *Animal House* (1978), an, *ahem*, "toxic showcase of racism, homophobia, and jokes about sexual assault" could end up in the U.S. National Film Registry at the Library of Congress, alongside *Casablanca*, *Gone with the Wind*, and *Titanic*.

I had a little laugh to myself at the ignorant assessment that a film like *Animal House* has no cultural value. As for whether it is sullying pristine vestal gems of cinema past, I would like to refer the *USA Today* writer to Meg Elison's article "How I Bought Into *Gone with the Wind*'s Mythology of Whiteness," published on *Electric Lit*, just to see them do a complete about-face and enter another spontaneous burst of overwrought virtue signaling, complete with self-flagellation for being so awfully wrong in previous assumptions over what makes a "film great" and so on. I say I *would like to* show this to the *Animal House* detractor, but I won't—these people are doing a good enough job on their own of finding things that offend them.

I think *Animal House* is culturally significant, and in my opinion that extends to the entire cycle of teen sex comedies. We need to stop looking to films to give us a moral compass. We can just enjoy things for what they are, without feeling the need to eradicate entire shelves of film reels and VHS tapes just because they don't comply with today's concept of "wokeness," requiring everything to be dissected, pored over, criticized, and ultimately rejected.

Take, for example, another film listed as "culturally, historically, or aesthetically significant" by the National Film Registry: *Breakfast at Tiffany's* (1961). Like *Animal House*, the film is a comedy that centers around sex, and has also been criticized in recent times for being problematic. Turning again to the dubious realm of pop magazine think pieces, here comes "3 'Breakfast at Tiffany's' Problems No One Ever Talks About," published by *Glamour* in 2016. Problem one, according to the piece, is that Holly Golightly (Audrey Hepburn) is a "call girl." Um, no shit, Sherlock—why is this a bad thing?

Says the writer: "Maybe she was empowered for her time, but she's also operating almost completely as a cipher for men's desires; so can we put the mantle of early feminist role model on slightly less coquettish shoulders, please?" Woe to viewers possessing a more dexterous sense of nuance or subversion, because the screen is now blocked by a blanket judgmental attitude. God forbid we let these things breathe and then have rational adult conversations beyond a Twitter hashtag and 140 characters.

Hollywood has been stifled and silenced before. For the most part, people haven't learned those lessons, and they simply join the condemnation chorus. Everybody knows racism and sexism are bad, and nobody wants to be socially excluded for trying to argue a middle ground. That's a disturbing state of affairs that will have a major impact on film culture if we don't stop. Naturally, then, any book that goes against the—hopefully fleeting—popular negation of the American teen sex comedy is an incredibly crucial text.

Even teen comedy queen Molly Ringwald rang the bell of the *New Yorker* in 2018, arriving with a portfolio of her own elaborate issues with the genre. Her personal history "What About 'The Breakfast Club'" read like a strange open letter to herself, speaking aloud in a room where she forgot other people were present as she explored how exploitative the films where, asking herself if these films supported systemic sexism under which figures like Harvey Weinstein could flourish?

Unlike other commentators on the subject, Ringwald provided thoughtful commentary, acknowledging that, while she saw some problems, director John Hughes often took her creative input in certain areas. She had some autonomy in the situation, and her voice, some of the time, was heard. Her article opened matters up into an adult arena for further discussion—but many of her so-called adult readers ran straight to the vortex of Twitter, ripping out the juiciest sound bites and using her quotes to fuel the ongoing hysteria surrounding these films.

Make no mistake, that hysteria is not just any hysteria; it's hysteria about sex. Sex-related worries spew from these think pieces across the board. We've been here before, and the consequences of America's first puritanical cinematic cleansing resulted in one of the biggest crimes committed against American movies since the dawn of the medium: the adoption in 1930 of the Hays Code. After suffering under its maddening contraints for decades, filmmakers like Billy Wilder, Alfred Hitchcock, Otto Preminger, Ida Lupino, and many others later put their careers on the line to fight for creative liberty free of rigid moral policing. Those rights now stand to be taken away again—or given away, even.

Enforced between 1934 and 1967, the Hays Code bears an outsize impact on most of what are considered the classic Hollywood films, and as a result is rarely recognized as the aberration that it is. Prior to 1934, as the Hollywood studio system flourished under the likes of Adolph Zukor at Paramount and Darryl F. Zanuck at Fox, the name of the game was sin, sex, and subversion. In fact, the more lurid the poster and its tagline, the better the box office—does that sound at all familiar?

In the earliest days of cinema, pioneering filmmaker Lois Weber not only gave us the first incidence of female full-frontal nudity in American film (*Hypocrites,* 1915), she also tackled social issues like abortion in pictures like *Where Are My Children?* (1916). Weber was a Christian evangelist with a moral agenda, but she was allowed to express her ideas in a truly adult way, portraying "sinful" topics on-screen in order to encourage discussion.

Top-earning studio pictures starting in the 1920s almost always featured sex or violence. James Cagney gangster pictures flourished, and bold sophisticated bedroom farces, such as those by Ernst Lubitsch (*Trouble in Paradise* [1932]), thrived. Often these older films are dismissed as outdated and boring, but this simply isn't true. Films were much more progressive and sexually liberated in the late 1920s and early 1930s—look at *Smarty* (1934), where Joan Blondell plays a husband-hopping, smart-mouthed woman with a penchant for S&M; or *Baby Face* (1933), where Barbara Stanwyck literally sleeps her way to the top of the corporate ladder.

During the 1920s, the so-called Jazz Age, society experienced a new cultural permissiveness, especially as far as sex, drugs, and generally decadent behavior was concerned. Women found a feeling of freedom they had never known before. They were emboldened to think about careers, sex before marriage, cutting their hair short, and ripping off their Victorian corsets. Hollywood embraced every last beautifully sordid minute, and the public swooned over stories of celebrity excess pumped out by the media.

Soon scandal after scandal started to hit the press. Much-loved comedian Fatty Arbuckle was charged with rape and manslaughter following the death of twenty-six-year-old actress Virginia Rappe at the St. Francis Hotel in San Francisco. Soon the court of public opinion was baying for his blood, and Hollywood's, too. Women's groups and church groups began picketing movie theaters. All of Arbuckle's films were withdrawn, but that wasn't enough.

Then high-profile director William Desmond Taylor was murdered, and the shit really hit the fan. Actress Mabel Normand—a pivotal figure in founding the Keystone Studio, and a mentor to actors like Charlie Chaplin—was accused of killing him. Normand had already had a few previous drug scandals, and her reputation suffered even after she was found innocent. The deaths of other actors were put down to suicide or drug overdose, and the moralistic drums started to bang louder and louder, screaming that something must be done about Hollywood's licentious films!

Studio heads decided to unveil the biggest public PR exercise known to man, and they instituted the Hays Code, otherwise known as the Motion Picture Production Code.

This set of general principles and specific taboos forbade the portrayal of sex, sinful behavior—unless justified and duly punished, all kinds of supposedly deviant sexualities, and stories about rape, childbirth, violence, crime, and just about any other adult and ungodly theme imaginable.

Initially, the Hays Office really was a public relations gimmick not to be taken seriously. Things changed for the worse as a new regime actually began to enforce the code in 1934, and for more than thirty years afterward nothing could go into production or be shown at theaters without Code Office approval. Actors were required to sign contracts containing morality clauses to ensure they behaved decently at all times. Basically, a gang of grandmothers were put in charge of the world's video collection.

Depressing as all that sounds, Fatty Arbuckle wasn't guilty in the first place. After three trials, his innocence was proven, but his name and career were wrecked. He ended up on skid row directing one-reel comedy shorts under a false name. So much for due process—he had already been condemned by the public before ever stepping foot in a courtroom.

These sad tales from a hundred years ago might seem irrelevant, but here we are, back there again. The lack of morality in Hollywood—whether embodied by actual criminal acts or tweets in bad taste—is lighting up social media every day. Careers and reputations are dangling in the balance, and, just like in Arbuckle's time, films of questionable content are being roundly condemned as morally dangerous.

The irony in all of this, of course, is that women's groups who fought so hard to get the Hays Code implemented did so with the naïve idea that they were protecting women. People actually thought that women could be morally corrupted by seeing others of their sex acting indecently on film. Yet the code oppressed female sexuality far above anything else. Women became somewhat infantilized, and, aside from some sly subversion, viewers grew used to seeing women represented as wives and mothers. Sexual women had to pay a price, as according to the code rules.

All of which brings us back at last to the dawn of teen sex comedies. The Hays Code ended in 1967, and even afterward puritan values still hung around in film for a little while longer. Once America came out from under the haze of Hays during the 1970s, the aftereffects were glorious. Comedy and horror exploded into new, transgressive, daring, and sexy territory. Kids lapped up every outrageous frame of film.

Teen sex comedies opened up a discussion about sex with brutal honesty. Despite the displays of acres of supple skin, these films were very rarely erotic in a traditional sense. Instead, they were open about how painful the entire experience of losing your virginity can really be. For teenagers, romantic relationships are fleeting, and tied to social pressure, social acceptance, and the drive to prove maturity. Sexual relationships are difficult to negotiate at the best of times, especially for the inexperienced.

Teen sex comedies aren't even solely about sex—but, come on, teenagers are obsessed with the subject, whether they are doing it or not. These movies are innately anti-establishment, featuring kids (I use that word loosely, as a lot of the actors clearly weren't) striving for independence in a world governed by archaic adult rules. The genre celebrates outsiders, and the themes of looking for love, acceptance, and individuality rang true for a generation of young people confused by the sexual revolution happening a few years out of their reach. For kids growing up in Britain, the films had an extra exotic American allure. The amount of nonstop parties and proms these kids were apparently having was honestly exciting. Such is the magic of Hollywood.

In order to find all the wonderful things in these films, you have to look beyond whether or not the boys are properly punished or rebuked for sneaking a peek at someone's tits. You have to consider nuance, and what these films actually meant at the time of their release to millions of young people. Nobody ever looked to Abbott & Costello for moral guidance, so why is *Animal House* expected to provide this? Surely everyone knows certain behavior is bad, regardless of whether they saw it in a film.

Teen Movie Hell is a beautiful celebration of what makes these films so great, and yes, so important. With that in mind, and with loving admiration for the devotion and heart that went into creating this wonderful guide, I urge the public to bury the Hays Code forever, and to replace it immediately with the four righteous tenets of the Ellinger Code. Now tap a beer keg and party on!

1. WE ARE ALL INTERESTED IN SEX ON SOME LEVEL, AND COMEDY IS THE PERFECT VEHICLE TO EXPLORE THE ABSURDITY OF IT ALL.

Some people really don't like sex at all, and that's all good. Whatever floats your boat—as long as those involved are consenting, and everyone else minds their own damned business—is all good in my book. Regardless, humans are fascinated by two things: sex and death.

Not by coincidence, then, sex comedies and horror films continue to be hugely popular. Comedy in particular is the perfect arena in whcich to explore sexual issues. The very act of pursuing a mate and then wiggling around in a dark room is all quite ludicrous and silly. Bodies and their functions are largely grotesque, and, dare I say it, *funny*, even—or maybe especially—during intimate times.

Shakespeare knew that—just take a look at some of the sexual innuendo in his plays. Boccaccio knew it when he wrote *The Decameron* in the fourteenth century, unknowingly making perfect fodder for Italy's sexy *Decameron* genre; an early-1970s group of films with a lot in common with American teen sex comedies. Sex is a universal dramatic theme that has played for laughs for centuries, and there's no reason to stop now.

2. YOUNG WOMEN IN TEEN SEX COMEDIES USUALLY OWNED THEIR SEXUALITY.

Unlike in the violent slasher films, which exhibit certain puritan sexual anxiety according to formula, bad girls in teen sex comedies are rarely punished for getting high or getting laid. Mainly, when it comes to these things, young women, just as much as the men, are active participants in the sex game. What's more, the women rule it.

This directly contrasts with many of the classic Hays Code comedies focused on sex, which, no matter how funny they were, usually featured women who were obsessed with settling down and getting married. The name of the game there was tricking, coercing, or enchanting men into marriage, thus curtailing the freedom of the previously liberated bachelors.

Teen sex comedies didn't do this; the protagonists are years away from even the faintest thought of marriage.

Teen sex comedies were the first movies where I saw young women talking freely about sex without shame; and not in a deliberately awkward or overly cinematic erotic way. I also saw young women having sex without feeling sorry about it afterward. Subjects like abortion and STDs cropped up, but those are exactly the kind of things you need to hear about when you are learning about sex.

Young women want to talk about sex at least as much as young men do with their peers. As ever, the adults sure as hell are not going to tell a kid anything. This is why characters like Molly Ringwald's Samantha Baker in *Sixteen Candles* (1984) or Phoebe Cates and Jennifer Jason Leigh in *Fast Times at Ridgemont High* (1982) were so liberating. These young women were obsessed with boys, but they didn't pretend to want to marry the first dreamboat they set eyes on. They had more important things to do, like going to college and getting careers.

3. COMEDIES HAVE SOCIOLOGICAL AND CULTURAL VALUE.

I am fascinated by people and the way in which culture evolves. I think film, all film, has a unique sociological value when it comes to looking back on the cultural climate in any given era. While cinema doesn't reveal absolute truths about society, movies do give us a guide to the prevailing ideology of any era. When it comes to revealing fears and anxieties, comedy and horror are the sociological motherlode.

Male anxiety in film as a reflection of cultural changes in response to feminism is especially intriguing. From the late 1950s into the 1960s, many sex-focused comedies exposed how the gradual rise of women's liberation felt for men. A new form of masculinity was coming forth; nuanced, sensitive. Billy Wilder addressed this initially in films such as *The Apartment* (1960); the cinematic square-jawed, all-American hero was replaced to a certain extent by a flawed "everyman," who was largely confused and powerless. All of a sudden, men could be insecure, selfish, silly, childish, and all these other wonderful things that are so perfect for comedy.

The American teen sex comedy is the extension of this progression. Even Scott Baio, a boy nearly universally responsible for the fluttering of teen girl hearts in the 1970s, had trouble getting laid in the genre. In *Zapped!* (1982), he finds himself having to resort to accidental ESP to even get a look at a girl's boobs.

Across the board, young men in *Teen Movie Hell* are shown as insecure, frail, and coming up short on love and acceptance. Not every teenager will be successful, and the pressure may drive young men to extremes—even to telekinesis. Contrasted with the 1980s dominance of materialism, hypermasculinity, and yuppie greed, the vulnerability and sexual desperation make perfect relatable sense.

4. THIS IS A GENRE FOR OUTSIDERS.

The American teen sex comedy is a genre for outsiders, regardless of gender. In films like *Revenge of the Nerds* (1984) or *Weird Science* (1985), suddenly the dork becomes a hero. In context, these films were made just as hordes of kids broke with conformity en masse and embraced punk and heavy metal. In most cases, the teen comedy probably matched music culture as a voice for the marginalized.

Small wonder that these highly anarchic comedies had so much resonance with teen audiences. Parents were largely absent or peripheral figures on a landscape where kids had infinite freedom; and truly, at the time, many in the audience were members of the first and last generation of latchkey kids. These films represented the ultimate teen fantasy, an exciting place where rules were made to be broken. Left to their own devices, the kids came up with some pretty wild ways to entertain and enrich themselves; these insane plots were uplifting. Not by accident, the snooty rich bullies and the beautiful people are frequently carved out as villains, and kids from the fringes get the last laugh.

Coming full circle back to *Animal House*, the film represents the punk spirit inherent in the era, the art of not giving a fuck, and of taking back power when society gives you none. Beautifully constructing an archetype that will be repeated in hundreds of movies to follow, the plots pits against each other two frat houses—the revoltingly snobbish Omega Theta Pi, and the much more exciting misfit haven Delta Tau Chi. Throughout the film, foes try and tie the Deltas down with rules. The Delts persevere and overcome their class disadvantage, which may be unrealistic but remains a beautiful fantasy nevertheless. For that reason, no matter how much the movies in *Teen Movie Hell* are written off as being in poor taste or worthless, I will always be batting for team Delta—all the way.

Girl talk, on the real, at the mall and in the hall, from Fast Times at Ridgemont High (1982).

The Free Clinic Isn't Free

and Other Insights from That One Scene in *Fast Times at Ridgemont High*

by Wendy McClure

Pretty much the first thing I knew about abortion as a kid in the early 1980s was that hardly anyone could manage to even say the word *abortion* without losing their shit. Clergymen hissed it on *60 Minutes;* Ronald Reagan sputtered it in speeches. My right-to-life grandmother tried to say it in a matter-of-fact way in sentences such as, "The local *abortionist* here in Albuquerque looks *just* like Lucifer!" Considering she made these utterances almost randomly and apropos of nothing in every conversation, she only came off as crazy.

I was too young to have seen the abortion episodes of *All My Children* and *Maude* that aired around the time of the *Roe v. Wade* decision in 1973. In those respective TV story lines, Erica Kane and Maude Findlay apparently made calm decisions to exercise their legal right to end their pregnancies. I was old enough, however, to be subjected to viewings of *The Silent Scream*—thanks again, Grandma! That 1984 documentary aimed to convince young women that abortions were the most shameful things imaginable, and that everyone who got one would be doomed to spend the rest of her life followed around by an invisible cloud of ghost-baby screams only they could hear.

I wasn't convinced. As it turned out, I was old enough *and* lucky enough to catch *Fast Times at Ridgemont High* (1982) on cable. I watched the movie in bits and pieces, and I honestly don't remember much of the plot: something about Sean Penn, and he was stoned, and he had a pizza delivered? Something about Judge Reinhold and a pirate hat? The only story line I recall in its entirety is the one where Jennifer Jason Leigh as Stacy Hamilton becomes pregnant. The part where she has an abortion. The part where after her abortion she continues to be the romantic lead, the girl gotten in the end. To paraphrase Jackson Browne in that ubiquitous song on the film's soundtrack, she gets to *be* somebody's baby, not *have* somebody's baby.

Not only was Stacy not haunted by her decision, her story line in *Fast Times* taught me several other things about abortion:

- An unplanned pregnancy is a reasonable topic of discussion during school hours. You can stroll the bleachers, just like a character in *Grease* (1978), and talk about your need for an abortion.
- It *is* possible to say "abortion" matter-of-factly, especially when it is clearly the best option—as it would definitely be after getting knocked up by Mike Damone when you're both still in high school.
- It is possible to get an abortion in the same span of time as an afternoon spent at the bowling alley.
- An abortion is a peril of teen sexuality that rates pretty much on par with being caught jerking off in a bathroom.
- Getting an abortion is a secret, but maybe doesn't have to be an after-school-special *big-deal* secret. It can be a secret just like coming home after curfew is a secret; a don't-tell-mom secret, with just a dash of *are you okay?*
- It is possible to be okay.
- Moreover, there should be humiliating consequences for guys who agreed to pay for half of the procedure and give you a ride to the clinic but then stand you up. And seeing that guy suffer these consequences—aw yeah, "Little Prick" scrawled on Damone's car and locker—can be a deeply entertaining and satisfying spectacle.

Fast Times is not all fun and reproductive rights. Because it's a 1980s film, a strain of cautionary tale lurks beneath the edginess. While Stacy goes after what she wants sexually, losing her virginity to stereo salesman Ron Johnson in a creepy baseball dugout doesn't seem like very much fun. Neither does the mediocre quickie with Mike Damone that gets her into trouble.

As in *Last American Virgin*, also released in 1982, abortion is imaginable as a choice only because of an earlier dubious choice—namely, the decision to hook up with a sketchy player-type guy. All the same, the memory of Stacy's story line stayed with me into my teen and adult years as a strangely reassuring presence, almost as familiar as a best friend's secret, ready to be spilled out into the open if I ever needed it.

Good news travels fast, as Fast Times at Ridgemont High *parties around the world. The German title at upper right ("I think I'm standing in the forest") is only outdone by the Danish dementia at lower left ("Beer, Farts, and Rock Music").*

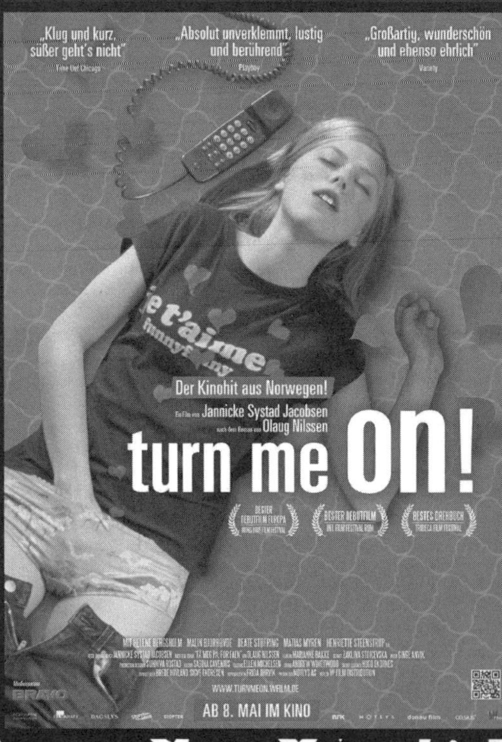

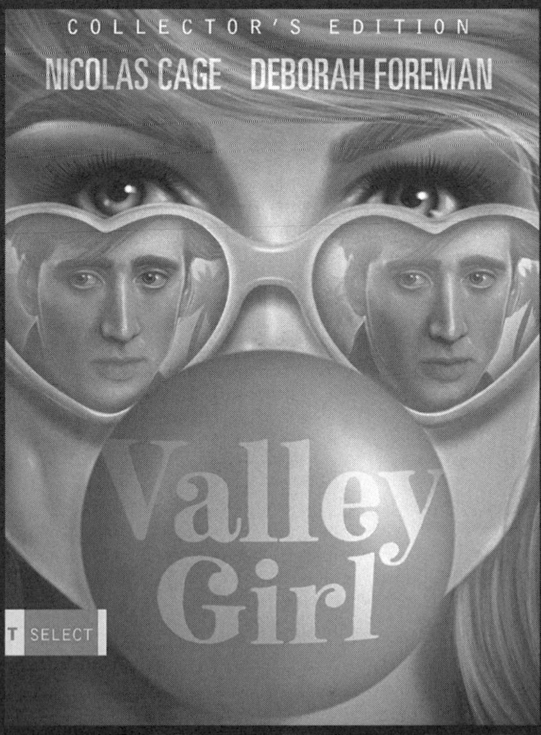

Women at the helm. Clockwise from top left: *Katt Shea's* Poison Ivy *(1992); Deborah Brock's contribution to the woman-directed* Slumber Party Massacre *series; the female gaze gets priority on a 2018 reissue of Martha Coolidge's* Valley Girl *(1983); Jannicke Systad Jacobsen's delightfully titled* Turn Me On, Dammit! *(2011).*

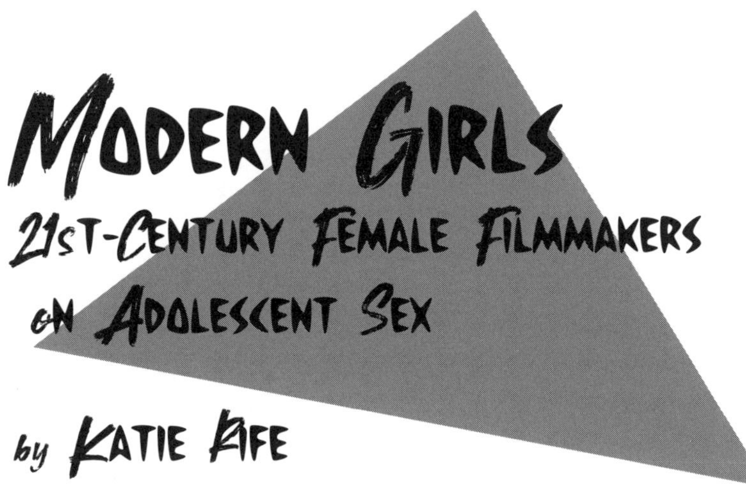

Modern Girls
21st-Century Female Filmmakers on Adolescent Sex

by Katie Rife

Girls have always been ubiquitous on-screen in teen sex comedies. But behind the camera, they're harder to come by, particularly during the genre's golden age in the 1980s. Women directors *were* present; Amy Heckerling depicted both boys' and girls' sexual awakenings in a relatable way in *Fast Times at Ridgemont High* (1982). Lisa Gottlieb made *Just One of the Guys* (1985), which starts with a moment of feminist frustration and ends with one of the most necessary nude scenes in cinema history. Both films pushed boundaries by asking male audiences to relate to their female peers on a human level, but also bent to the social norms of their era by making girls suffer consequences for being sexually active or diverting their stories into a more "appropriate" romantic storylines.

Those same social norms centered horny boys as the audience for all things teen on-screen—which makes sense for *Animal House* (1978) and *Porky's* (1981), but less so for *Valley Girl*. Nevertheless, director Martha Coolidge has since said in interviews that distributor Atlantic Releasing insisted on giving an exploitation edge to her kicky '80s update on *Romeo and Juliet,* telling her that the 1983 rom-com had to include at least four well-lit shots of bare breasts if she wanted to get it into theaters. She agreed. Ironically, Coolidge's attempt at a straight-up sex-comedy romp, *Joy of Sex* (1984), is one of the least remembered in her '80s filmography, paling next to the romance of *Valley Girl* (1983) and geeky sci-fi comedy of *Real Genius* (1985). Also little remembered, but worthy of rediscovery, is Coolidge's feature debut *Not a Pretty Picture* (1976), an ahead-of-its time hybrid of documentary and fiction exploring the aftermath of date rape from an era where many didn't recognize it as rape at all.

Meanwhile, punk auteur Penelope Spheeris and actress-turned-director Katt Shea were working the "consequences" end of the teen-sex equation with *Hollywood Vice Squad* (1986) and *Streets* (1990), both hardscrabble cautionary tales about runaways being lured into lives of squalor and sex work on the streets of L.A. Neither of those films are typical of either woman's filmography, however: Spheeris's teen-focused movies, like *Suburbia* (1982) and *Dudes* (1987), typically have male protagonists. And Shea, who played memorable roles in a number of teen sex comedies in her youth—check out her proto–Paris Hilton in *Preppies* (1984)—is usually unapologetic about her characters' sexuality, although her most famous film, *Poison Ivy* (1992), adds an intriguing hint of angst to the "teen seductress" formula. Shea's career trajectory is remarkably similar to that of San Francisco model-turned-actress-turned-director Valerie Breiman; her path led her to Adam Sandler's big-screen debut in *Going Overboard* (1989). Shea was honored by the Museum of Modern Art, New York, with a retrospective in 1992.

Throughout this period, opportunities for women to direct were just as scarce outside the Hollywood system as within it, with a few notable exceptions. Perhaps the most notable openings were provided by B-movie king Roger Corman, who not only produced the *Slumber Party Massacre* movies (the only slasher franchise directed entirely by women), but had several women in his stable of reliable journeyman—or journeywoman, as the case may be—directors. These were B-movie generalists, capable of delivering films on budget and on time in a variety of genres, including teen sex comedies.

In the 1970s, Barbara Peeters anticipated the '80s teen-sex boom with a pair of campy drive-in comedies, *Summer School Teachers* (1974) and *Carhops* (1978). Toward the tail end of the teen-movie boom, Corman protégé Francis Ford Coppola produced *Seven Minutes in Heaven* (1985), a coming-of-age story written and directed by Linda Feferman, an NYU film school grad and Guggenheim Fellow who had made her directorial debut with a 1974 educational film about menstruation. Although it won a prize at the Sundance Film Festival, and stars a young Jennifer Connelly, *Seven Minutes in Heaven* is nearly forgotten today, perhaps because its naïve sweetness and chaste view of teen romance, while charming, were old-fashioned even in 1985. (The same can't be said for *Slumber Party Massacre II* (1987), whose director, Deborah Brock, also made *Rock 'n' Roll High School Forever* (1991), a sequel to Corman's own *Rock 'n' Roll High School* [1978].)

But unlike male peers—including Jonathan Demme and James Cameron—none of these women made the leap to directing big-budget mainstream fare. Corman gave them a chance, but Hollywood wasn't so open-minded. By the 2000s, Peeters was in semi-retirement making promotional films in Oregon, and Feferman was writing, directing, and producing science documentaries for PBS. Brock is still plugging away on the independent festival circuit. The same is true of Jan Marlyn Reesman, who made her solo directorial debut with coed bikini-car-wash movie *California Hot Wax* back in 1992, before transitioning to more autobiographical material; and also Teresa Sparks, a UCLA grad whose one and only feature film was released on VHS in 1985 as *Over the Summer.* (She prefers the more accurate alternate title, *Appalachian Summer.*)

Of course, not all these women were looking for career longevity in the feature-film world. Teen sex comedies also made a blip on the career radar of Gabrielle Beaumont, a British TV director whose only feature credit is the obscure cross-dressing-teen comedy *He's My Girl* (1987). And Tamar Simon Hoffs? Her main interest in teen comedies was to get her daughter, Susanna Hoffs, a starring role in one. She succeeded with 1987's *The Allnighter,* a genial but generic teen comedy mostly of interest to Bangles fans.

The statistics for women directors remain grim. According to the advocacy group Women and Hollywood, only eighteen percent of the top five hundred films released in 2017 were directed by women. But in the twenty-first century, we've started to see female directors making teen sex comedies with heroines who neither have to suffer for their horniness, nor sublimate it into romance. Maggie Carey's *The To-Do List* (2013), starring Aubrey Plaza as a type-A overachiever who makes a checklist of sexual activities to experience before going away to college, is a unabashedly crude homage to the '80s teen sex comedy. It's clumsily executed at times, but in a way that fans of *Porky's*-style horndog comedy find nostalgically endearing.

Even now, raunchy, hard-R comedies are rarely offered to female directors. But women auteurs have been making headway in the quieter realm of character-based teen dramedies that take a frank look at sex but don't necessarily revolve around it. Greta Gerwig got a lot of well-deserved praise (and an Oscar nomination) for her observant *Lady Bird (*2017), and that same autobiographical streak runs through *The Diary of a Teenage Girl* (2015), for which director Marielle Heller adapted Phoebe Glockner's graphic novel about losing her virginity to her mother's boyfriend in '70s San Francisco.

And while writer-director Kelly Fremont Craig has made clear that nothing about her film *The Edge of Seventeen* (2016)—starring Hailee Steinfeld as a high schooler whose angst reaches critical mass after her best friend starts dating her older brother—is autobiographical, it strikes a similar tone, with a heroine that's troubled, confused, sometimes unlikejable, and always relatable. British director Deborah Haywood, meanwhile, serves up coming-of-age dramedy with a kitschy, crocheted aesthetic and a deep morbid streak in her debut, *Pin Cushion* (2017). True, sex is one of the less traumatic things Iona (Lily Newmark) has to deal with after moving to a small town with her extremely overprotective, clingy mother, but it's still on the list.

One of the most liberated takes on the female-directed, female-led teen sex comedy comes from laissez-faire Norway, via Jannicke Systad Jacobsen's delightfully titled *Turn Me On, Dammit!* (2011). The only problem fifteen-year-old Alma (Helene Bergsholm) has with her sexuality is the way her classmates react to it: Labeled the town slut after a popular boy exposes himself to her at a school dance, Alma calls phone sex lines to try to soothe her burning hormones. Her mother is horrified when she finds out, mostly because she has to pay the phone bill. With much of its seventy-three minutes devoted to Alma's daydreams, the film is a straightforward—and nonjudgmental—look inside the horny teenage mind from a female perspective.

Seven years later, that same refreshing point of view makes its Hollywood debut in the surprise critical favorite *Blockers* (2018), which not only refuses to shame the three teenage girls whose sex pact drives the plot (in fact, it's their parents' attempts to stop them that are portrayed as foolish), it depicts one character questioning her sexual orientation in a positive and open way. Director Kay Cannon doesn't overplay these progressive elements, however, keeping things light with witty dialogue and gobs of dirty jokes. As Cannon, who adapted the script to make the high-school heroines both crasser and more confident—including adding a cunnilingus joke that made her male producers uncomfortable—told *Esquire* shortly after the movie's release: "We are no longer the women of the 1950s, who's prim and proper and wouldn't dare say such a thing... I'm really proud to be a part of a project that shows these young women being who they are." Amen, sister.

Eddie Deezen: Duke of Dorks, Knave of Nerds, God of Geeks

God's Gift to Women

by Eddie Deezen

Skinny, bespectacled, bug-eyed, lanky-limbed, high-strung, and motor-mouthed, with a voice like helium erupting through the world's tightest vocal cords, Eddie Deezen was nailed by film historian Danny Peary as being "like a page of Mad *magazine come to life." Although the* Happy Days *TV series (1974–84) brought the term "nerd" to mass consciousness, Deezen embodied the concept brilliantly as Eugene Felsnic in* Grease *(1978). Adorned with Coke-bottle eyeglasses, plaid high-water pants, a bow tie, and too many pens in his pocket protector, Deezen, through his clueless confidence, flailing pratfalls, and circus seal guffaw, established the DNA for pop culture nerds extending through "Waldo" from Van Halen's "Hot for Teacher" video (1984); Steve Urkel on TV's* Family Matters *(1989–98); and, of course, countless teen sex comedies—including the title characters of the ultimate doofus opus,* Revenge of the Nerds *(1984).*

After attaining goofball god status in Grease *and Steven Spielberg's mega-budget misfire,* 1941 *(1979), Deezen built a gutbusting body of work, including turns in* Zapped! *(1982; in which he wears a "God's Gift to Women" T-shirt), the cult Disney comedy* Midnight Madness *(1980), the young adult sex comedy* The Rosebud Beach Hotel *(1984), and* Surf II *(1984), where he reigned as mad scientist Menlo Schwartz.*

I was a nerd growing up, but kind of a funny nerd. I was mainly popular because I was funny. I was a nerd, but I was also the class clown. There was cruelty there. I was hurt—not physically, but spiritually—more than once because I was a geek. That part was no fun.

Jerry Lewis was absolutely my nerd influence. As a kid, I worshipped the Jerry Lewis and Dean Martin film *That's My Boy* (1951). Jerry's character "Junior" Jackson was me. My nickname with my closest friends is still "Junior." My other comedy influences—Curly Howard of the Three Stooges, Harpo Marx, and Daffy Duck—were not nerds. But Jerry? Definitely. I was also a *Mad* fan. When I was growing up, all the cool kids read *Mad* magazine. It was the only subversive thing we had in those days.

I have had many guys write or tell me in person, "Eddie, you made being a nerd easier!" I really believe I made the nerd character popular in the late '70s and '80s. Nowadays, those guys on *The Big Bang Theory* are so talented, they're much better actors than I ever was. Still, the basic geeky nerd, a clumsy geek with glasses and a high nasal voice—I think I started the curiosity of that character being popular. I was never called a "nerd" in high school. No one knew the word then.

Of course, I was not the first nerd in movies, maybe Harold Lloyd was. The guy in *American*

Graffiti (1973), Charles Martin Smith, also preceded me. At least 100 percent without a doubt I invented the concept of a "computer nerd." My role in *WarGames* (1983) was the very first computer nerd in a movie. This is just a fact, and I am proud of that.

My breakthrough was *Grease* in 1978. I went into a huge cattle call and read for the role. The director, Randal Kleiser, was there. So was Allan Carr, our producer, and the casting director, Joel Thurm. I only had, like, three lines, but as I read, I saw them nudging each other. I saw that nudge, and I knew I did well.

I told my family that I got a role in a John Travolta movie, and, of course, I was ecstatic. Then a few days later, they called my agent and said the Eugene role was written out of the movie! I was devastated.

My agent said, "Let's go to church and pray." I am Jewish, and I never went to church, but we lit candles at an altar and prayed. I swear to God, the next day, they called and told my agent the role of Eugene was put back in the script! It's a religious story, if you believe in spirits. Just a coincidence? Maybe. Whatever.

Grease was like going to the greatest party of your life, and it lasted two months. It was that much fun. The single greatest thing John Travolta, he was a true mensch. He is perhaps the kindest human being and the nicest guy I have ever met. *Grease 2* (1982) was fun, but not as magical as *Grease*. You can't catch lightning in a bottle twice. To me, it is like comparing *The Wizard of Oz* to *The Wiz*!

To work with John Belushi on *1941* (1979), I turned down the roles of Spaz in *Meatballs* (1979) and Eaglebauer in *Rock 'n' Roll High School* (1979). I regret that I never had the chance to work with Bill Murray, who I love and who is a brilliant actor. I wish I could have done all those movies.

Instead, my next movie was *Midnight Madness* (1980). My character Wesley, the White Team Leader, is much like my character in *I Wanna Hold Your Hand* (1978) or *1941*. That was my real character. The Daffy Duck influence is there, you can see it. Yes, my character has a dark side, as do all nerds. They are life's tragic creatures; trying so hard to look cool and to fit in. But it's just not there. They are funny, but tragic. Nerds are devastated creatures.

While *Midnight Madness* was shooting, I used to have lunch with Michael J. Fox. We would play handball together, knocking my Super-Ball against a brick wall at Disney Studios. We both loved *The Twilight Zone*. After the movie wrapped, the next time I saw him was five or six years later on the Universal Studios lot. He was driving a red sports car, I definitely noticed that, but he was the same nice, friendly, great guy, and totally unaffected by his success.

After *Grease 2*, I made *Zapped!* (1982). Scott Baio was a marvelous guy, a great guy. Another guy in the cast was mean, and he picked on me because I was nerdy. I never forgot how nice Scott was, or how mean this other actor was. The T-shirt I wore that said "God's Gift to Women" was my own shirt. I brought it to the set and wore it.

I had a lot of fun filming *Surf II* (1984)—a very crazy film. There were lots of hot girls in bikinis. I loved working with Ron Palillo and Lyle Waggoner, they were great guys. The director, Randall Badat, let me be me. I really enjoyed that, and it was great being myself at the very center of a movie like that. Just the title itself—*Surf II* was the first "sequel" where there was no *Surf I*—that was just one funny concept in a crazy, original film.

Revenge of the Nerds also came out in 1984. Contrary to popular belief, I am not in the movie! I am mistaken for Robert Carradine often, and I have been many times over the years. In 1986, I did a turkey called *The Whoopee Boys* with the *Nerds* producer, Adam Field. I asked why they didn't cast me in *Revenge of the Nerds*? He said, "The joke of the movie was we took regular guys and make them up to look like nerds. You were already a nerd!"

I transitioned over the years from playing nerds on-screen to working as a voice actor on projects like *Dexter's Laboratory* (1996–2003), *The Polar Express* (2004), and *The SpongeBob SquarePants Movie* (2015).

In 2005, I was at the Chiller Theatre Expo in New Jersey, a signing show for fans. I was doing really well, making a ton of money. I was a real hotshot, sharing the spotlight with huge stars and legends like Adam West, Burt Ward, and Barbara Eden. Fans kept telling me how great I was. I was Mister Big Shot.

As I sat at my signing table, I looked up and saw the biggest nerd I have ever seen in my entire life. This guy made me look like Steve McQueen! He looked like Jerry Lewis in *The Nutty Professor*—glasses; messy, greasy hair; gnarly teeth. I swear, he was wearing a white T-shirt with grease stains all over it. I suppressed my laughter as I took his money and signed his photo.

"Don't laugh at him, after all, he's a paying customer," I said to myself.

I have never in my life felt so superior to another human being as I felt toward this geek, this drip, this nerd. But, wait—he wanted to tell me something!

Smirking, I leaned in to hear what this nerd wanted to tell me. He said, "When I was in high school and the other kids wanted to make fun of me, they called me *Eddie Deezen*!"

Clockwise from top left: *The neon nostalgia of* American Graffiti *(1973);* Almost Summer *(1978);* American Drive-In *(1985);* Assault of the Party Nerds *(1989), when the ragers decamped full time to VHS.*

Trailer No. 2

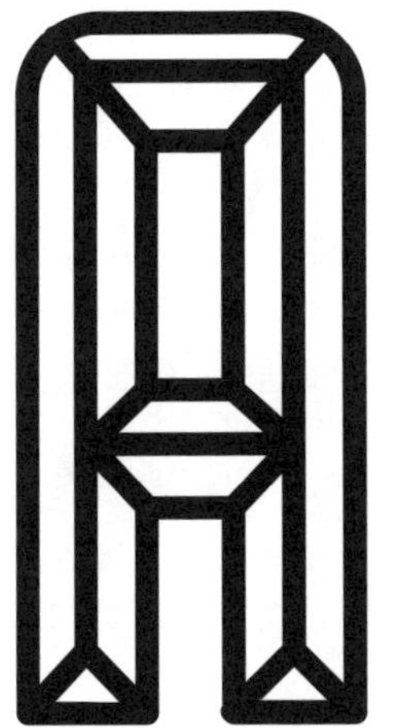

After School [1988]

aka Private Tutor; Return to Eden

DIR. WILLIAM OLSEN; W/SAM BOTTOMS, RENÉE COLEMAN, DICK CAVETT

COLLEGE ▫ GIRLS' BATHROOM ▫ HORNY PRIEST ▫ SARONG-FREE CAVEWOMEN

In one of the most dastardly of all VHS-box bait-and-switch scams, *After School* lit up video rental shelves with a buxom blonde in a slinky swimsuit sneaking a sulty bite from a forbidden apple. Behind her, palm trees gleam and amorous couples suck face. It's party time, right? Wrong-o, padre!

After School turns out to be an earnest drama about a college campus priest, Father Michael McCarren (Sam Bottoms), forced to question his chastity vows as he longs for comely coed September Lane (Renée Coleman). To convey the eternal nature of the reverend's ongoing dark night of the cassock, *After School* intermittently flashes back to prehistoric times, where a noble caveman must contend with the timeless temptations of naked cave babes. When symbolism becomes that bare and blatant, you can beat yourself with your own club.

Erudite talk show host Dick Cavett also turns up along the way. He plays talk show host Dick Cavett—eruditely.

The Allnighter [1987]

DIR. TAMAR SIMON HOFFS; W/SUSANNA HOFFS, DEDEE PFEIFFER, JOAN CUSACK, PAM GRIER

GRADUATION ▫ BEACH HOUSE ▫ BIKINIS ▫ SURFERS ▫ MOPEDS ▫ UNDERWEAR DANCING

This big-screen vehicle for Bangles lead singer Susanna Hoffs has three things working for it. First is Joan Cusack as a college senior ready to whoop it up seaside on graduation eve. Second is Simon Hoffs, Susanna's mother, who directed the film. Third and best is the *Allnighter*'s tagline, promising, "*Rock star* Susanna Hoffs in her movie debut!" The awkward advertising, with its emphasis on "rock star," fail to mention the Bangles, universally loved at the time for their "Walk Like an Egyptian" MTV video. You have to imagine Susanna's fellow Bangles getting one whiff of this PG-13 stinkpot and declaring: "Do not associate us, our sleeveless turtlenecks, our Hula-Hoop-size earrings, or the name of our big hit music group with this lame puddle of crap!"

Even though blaxploitation queen Pam Grier turns up on-screen as a coed-busting cop who tosses rock star Susanna Hoffs behind bars, the Bangles were right.

Almost Summer [1978]

DIR. MARTIN DAVIDSON; W/DIDI CONN, JOHN FRIEDRICH, TIM MATHESON, BRUNO KIRBY, LEE PURCELL

NERDS 📼 CHEERLEADERS 📼 SKATEBOARDS 📼 SURFERS 📼 BIKINIS 📼 CUSTOM VANS 📼 LAST DAY OF SCHOOL 📼 PROM 📼 VICE COP

A beaming California incoming senior class runs an energetic election for student body president, pitting popular cheerleader Christine Alexander (Lee Purcell) against Daryl Fitzgerald (John Friedrich), the doltish puppet candidate of slick-talking Bobby DeVito (Bruno Kirby). Christine is Bobby's ex-girlfriend and he's primed to use every dirty trick at hand to nix her candidacy. But Daryl didn't expect to fall for Bobby's sister Donna (Didi Conn). When a trio of professional teen skateboarders get up to tricks on campus, and all the vast majority of the adolescent electorate wants to do is hit the beach, everyone has to act fast because it's—can you guess?—*Almost Summer*!

Almost Summer was a minor theatrical hit, although perhaps Universal should have released it closer to the time frame of the title, not in September—right at the end of summer. Such marketing madness had a method, though. *Almost Summer* prominently features both Didi Conn and Tim Matheson, both of whom exploded fame-wise during the summer of 1978; Conn by way of *Grease*, Matheson via *Animal House*.

Conn and Matheson are no closer to being bona fide teenagers here than in the films that made them famous. Similarly, "man-out-of-time" lead Bruno Kirby had already graduated from playing college students in *Superdad* (1973) and *The Harrad Experiment* (1973) to being borderline terrifying and solidly adult as Clemenza in *The Godfather Part II* (1974). So from delivering violent Sicilian justice in cahoots with a young Don Corleone, here he goes right back to high school.

Though original soundtrack by Mike Love of the Beach Boys enjoyed some radio play, *Almost Summer* never made it to VHS or any other home video format. The movie did repeat throughout the '80s on various UHF channels, and continues to replay, decades later, on classic cable channels. For its pioneering efforts, *Almost Summer* surely now rates as a golden oldie.

Alone in the T-Shirt Zone [1986]

DIR. MIKE B. ANDERSON; W/MICHAEL BARRACK, BILL BARRON, JENNIFER ANDERSON

MASTER BAIT-AND-SWITCH 📼 T-SHIRTS

An elite cadre of films can conjure notions of what an electroshock patient must envision while squeezing his eyes shut—re-creating the mental space of a political prisoner during waterboarding. Consider, for example, the obscure celluloid psychoses of Dwain Esper's *Maniac* (1934); Thierry Zéno's *Vase de Noces* (1974), aka *The Pig Fucking Movie*; or Damon Packard's *Reflections of Evil* (2002). Add to that roster Mike B. Anderson's *Alone in the T-Shirt Zone*, an outburst of psychological illness marketed as a pent-up-puberty farce.

The labeling of this movie during its brief VHS lifespan can only be described as misleading. This is not a teen sex comedy at all. Yet the cover image, painted with *Garbage Pail Kids*–style comic detail, depicts a quartet of fluffy blondes in double-entendre T-shirts ("Teachers Do It With Class") emerging from the head of a sweaty, cross-eyed schlemiel. The tagline is true to contents ("Peek into the mind of the most depressed man on earth"), but the visual sales pitch is unmistakably comic in its raunchy dishonesty.

The actual movie is far from comedy. Michael Mikaele (Michael Barrack) works at a T-shirt factory where all the women find him irresistible. Even on the streets around what might be Venice Beach, women can't keep their eyes off of him. His condition induces such stress that the panicky, mouth-breathing lad lands in a mental hospital. There, his female doctor rapes him. More convoluted nonsense occurs that follows the logic of a nightmare fueled by huffing paint thinner. Then it's over. Hopefully, whoever painted those busty T-shirt honeys on the video box got paid more than the director, because they won your money.

Viewers who survived *Alone in the T-Shirt Zone* must have either gone straight to therapy or beaten a path to art school. The entire experience is a stab at homemade surrealism fueled by multiple *Eraserhead* viewings and new wave's angular pop art aesthetics. The final results land in the realm of theatrical porn's simultaneous bizarre onslaught of self-consciously strange, hypnagogic overkill (e.g., *Night Dreams, Café Flesh, Driller, New Wave Hookers*). Even weird shit made weird on purpose can be plenty weird.

American Drive-In [1985]

DIR. KRISHNA SHAH; W/BERNARD WHITE, EMILY LONGSTRETH, ALLISON HEATH

DRIVE-IN ▫ VIRGIN ▫ BIKERS ▫ FAT FAMILY ▫ QUEENS ▫ OUTRAGEOUS ELDERLY

Don't confuse *American Drive-In* with director Rod Amateau's *Drive-In* (1976); they have little in common aside from two-thirds of the title; the basic premise; and the reality that car-bound audiences of both movies must have repeatedly exclaimed, "Can you believe we're watching a *Drive-In* movie at the drive-in movies?"

Krishna Shah's *American Drive-In* is an '80s teen sex comedy flabbergaster highly worthy of rediscovery—even if not at a drive-in. Lured by the big-outside-screen attraction of heavy metal horror opus *Hard Rock Zombies* (also directed by Shah), a traffic jam of genre characters converges at the City Limits Drive-In. Various vehicles respectively contain horny high schoolers attempting back seat orgiastics; a city boy and a country gal on a first date; a family of fatsos; flaming homosexuals; two daffy old ladies; a buttoned-up local politician; a bumbling biker gang; and a dwarf.

The plot is all raunch and romping (sample dialogue: "You pooed on me and I liked it!"), until halfway through. Suddenly, *American Drive-In* shifts gears into an entirely different film category. The bikers stop bumbling and set up a dire denouement that is not entirely unlike that of Peter Bogdanovich's *Targets* (1968) or the needs-no-explanation *I Spit on Your Grave* (1977). Park near the exit if you can't handle a drive-in this American.

American Graffiti [1973]

DIR. GEORGE LUCAS; W/RON HOWARD, CINDY WILLIAMS, RICHARD DREYFUSS, CHARLES MARTIN SMITH

NERD ▫ JOCK ▫ GREASER ▫ VIRGINITY ▫ PROM ▫ GRADUATION ▫ GANGS ▫ DRAG RACE ▫ RADIO ▫ MYSTERY WOMAN

"Where were you in '62?" asked the ad campaign for *American Graffiti*, and the entire baby boomer generation showed up to reminisce through a nostalgic dreamscape of small-town 1962 California teens vividly experiencing their last night of summer after high school. George Lucas's creative and commercial breakthrough left its hot rod tire tracks all over every coming-of-age film for at least the next twenty years. Fortunately, the genre could not have asked for a richer, deeper, or more hilariously heartfelt cinematic role model.

Graffiti's uncannily conveyed Eisenhower-era setting was copied everywhere (*Animal House, Porky's, Mischief*), even when amusingly unnecessary (*Screwballs, Hot Times*). Beyond the era, though, *Graffiti*'s awkward romances, automotive fetishism, comically disastrous attempts at getting laid, pop music obsessions, greasy-spoon hangout, and authority-humiliating pranks set a template that will forever resonate.

Every single *Graffiti* character became a teen movie archetype. Richard Dreyfuss is a nice guy out for a night of kicks, chasing Suzanne Somers as a mystery blonde in a white Thunderbird.

Then Ron Howard and Cindy Williams are high school sweethearts torn asunder by graduation. Add Paul Le Mat as a hell-raising greaser; Mackenzie Phillips as reckless jailbait; Candy Clark as a sweet but "fast" hair-hopper; and Harrison Ford as a scary drag racer. Above all, *Graffiti* serves up Charles Martin Smith as a boilerplate-setting four-eyed nerd named Terry the Toad.

American Graffiti's character icons continue to echo as avatars throughout art, entertainment, and, truthfully, real life as we've all subsequently lived it. Even Mel's Drive-In, the roadside hamburger joint with roller-skating waitresses where all the characters eventually converge, is itself a character for the ages.

Prior films brokered any number of these models, but *Graffiti* got them all right. *American Graffiti* simply gets everything right. Ease back and marvel at the movie's stream-of-consciousness Top 40 soundtrack as it rolls over roadside Americana, while juvenile delinquents loom as both threats to and liberators of the teenage soul. Behind the curtain awaits a wondrous, *Wizard of Oz*–style unveiling of all-powerful disc jockey Wolfman Jack. *Graffiti*'s explosively evocative cartoon poster by master *Mad* magazine illustrator Mort Drucker provided the perfect wrapper.

Graffiti instantly earned critical hosannas and busted box offices worldwide, ultimately banking $171 million on a $777,000 investment. An Academy Award nomination for Best Picture followed—as did dozens, if not hundreds, of rip-offs and variations. *Happy Days*, starring Ron Howard, was TV's unofficial adaptation. The show—which spun off the even more popular *Laverne & Shirley*, starring *Graffiti*'s Cindy Williams—was the biggest one on earth for a time.

More American Graffiti (1979) is an ambitious but jumbled, time-tripping sequel. George Lucas made some other movies after this one, too, but who needs them? The term "work of genius" will be applied to exactly one movie in *Teen Movie Hell*, and you're looking at it right here, right now—filed confidently under *American Graffiti*.

Angel [1984]

DIR. ROBERT VINCENT O'NEILL; W/DONNA WILKES, DICK SHAWN, RORY CALHOUN, SUSAN TYRELL

PREP SCHOOL ▪ TEEN HOOKERS ▪ CROSSDRESSING ▪ SEXY SECRETS

"High school honor student by day...Hollywood hooker by night!" So goes the instant-classic tagline of *Angel*, B-movie maven Roger Corman's trash-flick spelunk into L.A.'s underage sidewalk sex trade. Powered by that truth-in-advertising declaration, *Angel* became a surprise theatrical smash on arrival and endured for a solid spell as a sleepover favorite on home video. Three sequels of sadly diminishing daffiness followed: *Avenging Angel* (1985); *Angel III: The Final Chapter* (1988); and *Angel 4: Undercover* (1993).

An entire half-decade after playing McLean Stevenson's sixteen-year-old daughter on NBC sitcom bomb *Hello, Larry*, twenty-five-year-old Donna Wilkes stars in *Angel* as fifteen-year-old Molly Stewart. She spends her daylight hours earning top grades at a ritzy prep school, but, come sundown, she slaps on booty shorts and straps on f-me pumps to strut the rancid pavement of Hollywood Boulevard; where she earns tuition, rent, and lipstick money by manipulating the pants of pulled-over male motorists.

It's not all intense academia and anonymous STD risks for our heroine, though. While out plying her trade, Angel falls in with a lovable crew of street freaks, colorfully and campily portrayed by cult movie eccentrics including Dick Shawn (*The Producers*) as flamboyant drag queen Mae; Rory Calhoun (*Motel Hell*) as faded movie cowboy Kit Carsonl; and Susan Tyrell (*Forbidden Zone*) as loud lesbian landlady Solly.

Leaving no '80s teensploitation trope unturned, *Angel* taps slasher horror by way of John Diehl as a prostitute-hunting psycho known simply as "the Killer." The Killer stalks our precious Angel, which proves only slightly more stressful than when kids from school catch her turning tricks in front of the gnarly Cave Theater.

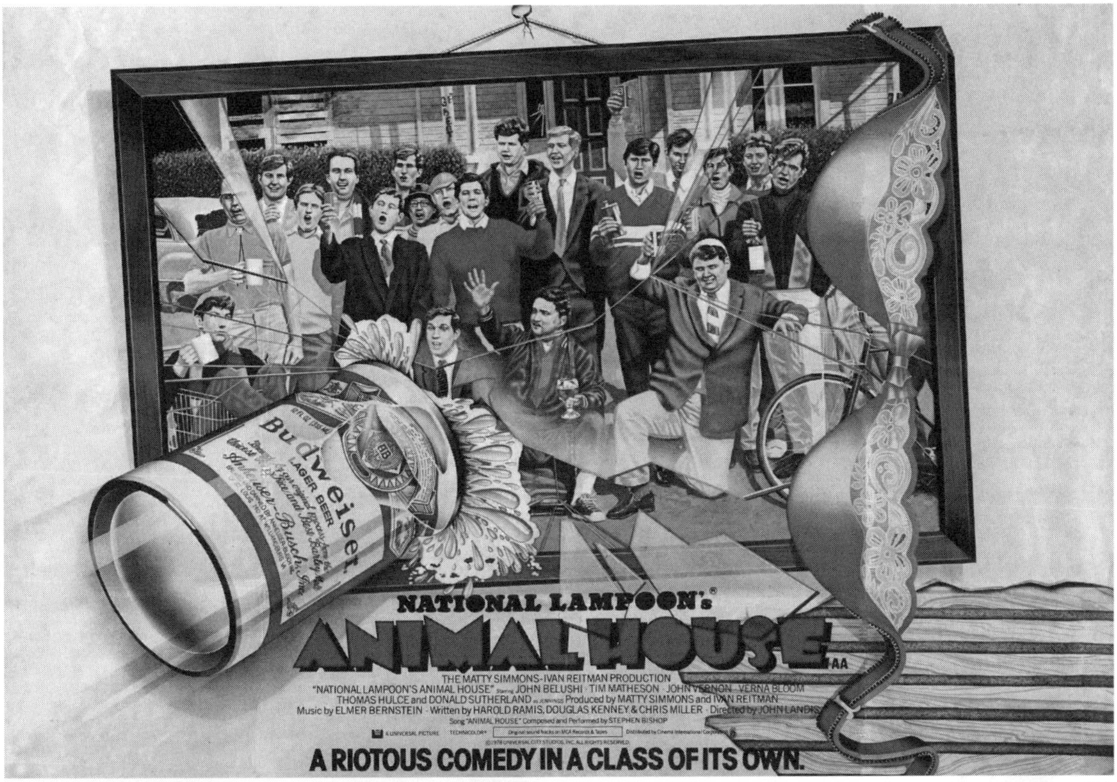

NATIONAL LAMPOON'S®
ANIMAL HOUSE AA
THE MATTY SIMMONS-IVAN REITMAN PRODUCTION
"NATIONAL LAMPOON'S ANIMAL HOUSE" JOHN BELUSHI · TIM MATHESON · JOHN VERNON · VERNA BLOOM
THOMAS HULCE and DONALD SUTHERLAND Produced by MATTY SIMMONS and IVAN REITMAN
Music by ELMER BERNSTEIN · Written by HAROLD RAMIS, DOUGLAS KENNEY & CHRIS MILLER · Directed by JOHN LANDIS
Song "ANIMAL HOUSE" Composed and Performed by STEPHEN BISHOP
A RIOTOUS COMEDY IN A CLASS OF ITS OWN.

Collegiate chaos incarnate, Animal House *(1978) pits Delta House against the rules, and the rules lose. The U.K. poster proves that none of the mayhem is lost in translation. In the war between slobs (John Belushi, lower left, as John "Bluto" Blutarsky) versus snobs (James Daughton, lower right, as Greg Marmalard), the battle still rages. Where do you stand?*

Angel's action, intrigue, and footage of Dick Shawn seeming to *really* enjoy his evening gowns all build to a climax of gutter justice, when the sex workers and back alley weirdoes band together to defeat the Killer. All give some and some give all—Shawn didn't make it back for *Avenging Angel*. The movie works surprisingly well, embracing its own leering attitude and plays its preposterously scuzzy premise straight. Coupled with some wildly hammy performances, that straightlaced treatment of outrageously evil subject matter helps makes *Angel* a laugh riot and an evergreen camp classic.

Far from an aberration in its abhorent subject matter, *Angel* is the exclamation point on a line of sensationalist cinema dating back at least to *The Road to Ruin* (1928), a silent melodrama smash about a high school maiden who hops into a fast jalopy, tastes bathtub gin, and then finances a back alley abortion by gigging in a brothel.

On the silver screen and, eventually, the VCR, professional pubescent sex evolved with what was permissible. By the 1970s, titles such as *The Working Girls* (1974), *Street Girls* (1975), and the bluntly stated *Teenage Prostitution Racket* (1979) prolifically bounced around drive-in bills. Meanwhile, the hyperbolic NBC TV movie *Dawn: Portrait of a Teenage Runaway* (1976), featuring Eve Plumb (Jan Brady herself!) strolling Santa Monica Boulevard looking for johns, proved such a ratings giant that it generated a working-boy follow-up, *Alexander: The Other Side of Dawn* (1977). ABC countered a bit later with Mare Winningham in its own Nielsen juggernaut, *Off the Minnesota Strip* (1980).

Further up the respectability scale, fourteen-year-old Jodie Foster scored a well-deserved Oscar nomination as an East Village hooker in Martin Scorsese's *Taxi Driver* (1976). Her brilliance may have inadvertently ignited an era that first allowed twelve-year-old Brooke Shields to appear naked as a New Orleans whorehouse virgin-for-sale in *Pretty Baby* (1978), leading to Brooke's subsequent several years of shilling Calvin Klein jeans sans underpants (her ad tagline: "Know what comes between me and my Calvins? Nothing!") and losing her virginity at fourteen in the tropical paradise of *The Blue Lagoon* (1980). Still, by the time *Angel* rolled around, the movie stuck out as being in bombastic, glorious bad taste.

Besides its own sequels, *Angel* spawned a rapid-fire East Coast rip-off, *Streetwalking* (1985), with future Academy Award winner Melissa Leo as a too-young lady of the evening. She parades her wares around the spectacularly seedy intersection of 3rd Avenue and 14th Street, right across from the Dugout bar and the Variety Photoplays theater—two real-life, long-gone havens of vintage teenage vice. Exactly when *Angel* and *Streetwalking* were in New York theaters, the Variety Photoplays presented the XXX-rated *New Wave Hookers* (1984) with Traci Lords. Unlike the stars of the other movies, she actually was fifteen. Oops.

Animal House [1978]

DIR. JOHN LANDIS; W/JOHN BELUSHI, TIM MATHESON, JOHN VERNON, KAREN ALLEN

FRATS ▣ TOGA PARTY ▣ FOOD FIGHT ▣ BEER ▣ SNOBS ▣ ANIMAL SACRIFICE

Launched in 1970, *National Lampoon* provided the greatest wits of the Western world with a creative and monstrously successful outlet for their talents, hitting huge first in print, then in live productions, and finally in radio shows whose stars became the de facto farm team for *Saturday Night Live*. In due time, a *National Lampoon* movie had to happen. *Lampoon* staffers Doug Kenney and Chris Miller, accompanied by Second City vet Harold Ramis, came up with an outline for *Laser Orgy Girls*, the concept of which was "Charlie Manson Goes to High School." Although teens aren't what first comes to mind regarding *Animal House* (only the mayor's barely menstrual daughter qualifies), *Charlie Manson Goes to High School* could have been the weirdest teen sex comedy ever.

Realistically considering that prospect's commercial potential, the writers turned instead to *National Lampoon's 1964 High School Yearbook*, a peerless achievement in both nostalgia and literary satire, along with Miller's autobiographical *Lampoon* stories about being a Midwestern schmuck fumbling his way through the deep end of puberty. Kenney, Miller, and Ramis set out to create the ultimate cinematic encapsulation of the American higher-education experience between the Eisenhower '50s and the flower-power '60s. Fucking hell, they achieved that.

After submitting an unfilmable first draft of their script—highlights included a giant papier-mâché JFK head on a parade float being blown apart by flying beer kegs—the cabal got down to business and delivered the finished *Animal House* screenplay to director John Landis. The up-and-coming director had just scored a big stoner hit with his sketch anthology, *The Kentucky Fried Movie*.

As collegiate chaos incarnate, *Animal House* set a teen comedy template followed by the tsunami of hormone-inflamed adolescent laugh riots. The very structure of outrageous Hollywood comedy in general flows from this saga of bedraggled and defeated underdogs upending their oppressors with an mammoth eruption of slapstick disorder. *Animal House* is the movie and the moment from which belched forth the heightened madness and borderline surrealism of all '80s teen sex comedies: the hyperkinetic cartoon poster; the slobs-vs.-snobs construct; food fights; underage inappropriateness; cougar seduction; the nearly biblical undoing of fascist authority figures; and, of course, big fat party animals.

Without *Animal House* there would be no *Porky's*, no *Party Animal*, no *Screwballs*, and definitely no *King Frat*—and who could live in a world without *King Frat*? Humanity remains permanently and profoundly in debt to *Animal House* for its mythic moments, including "Toga! Toga!! Toga!!!", the Deathmobile, Otis Day and the Knights, and the concept of "double secret probation."

The plot points of *Animal House* go beyond familiar. Even someone who has never seen *Animal House*, if such a person exists, would find the experience disarmingly familiar by virtue of the film's endless supply of archetypes. What matters is that there once existed a time before *Animal House*, and now there's now.

The on-screen action follows 1962 Faber College freshman fraternity pledges Larry Kroger (Tom Hulce) and Kent Dorfman (Stephen Furst)—described by one snooty debutante as "a wimp and a blimp"—as they are rejected by every reputable Greek fraternal organization on campus. Finally, the notorious outlaw Delta Tau Chi house welcomes them, dubbing them, respectively, "Pinto" and "Flounder."

Our innocent twosome must contend with the other Deltas, each of whom metastasized into a cultural icon seconds after the film's release: lady-killer Otter (Tim Matheson); crazed biker D-Day (Bruce McGill); passably respectable chapter president Hoover (James Widdoes); freaky dork Stork (co-screenwriter Douglas Kenney); and likeable schlemiel Boone (Peter Riegert). Boone is romantically entangled with coed Katy (Karen Allen), a classy lassie who seems unreasonably reasonable when she's not hooking up with hilariously pretentious, momentarily bare-assed Professor Jennings (Donald Sutherland).

Villainy oozes from the rich, privileged, militaristic gasbags of Omega House, led by Doug Neidermeyer (Mark Metcalf), Greg Marmalard (James Daughton), and toady Chip Diller (Kevin Bacon). Enabling the Omega creeps are mean-girl cheerleaders Mandy Pepperidge (Mary Louise Weller) and Babs Jansen (Martha Smith). Highest atop the bad-guy perch is Dean Wormer (John Vernon), a seething hybrid of Richard Nixon, J. Edgar Hoover, and Benito Mussolini.

Looming larger than lust, loudness, and life itself while lording over them all, of course, is John Belushi as *Animal House*'s animal supreme, John "Bluto" Blutarsky. Performing mostly in pantomime, John Belushi is the heart, soul, guts, and other expulsive, explosive organs of *Animal House*. Director Landis summed up the film's evolution perfectly: "*Animal House* started out as the writers' movie. Then, for a little while, it was my movie. And then, when it got to the public, it was John's movie. And that's how it will always be. And that's how it should be."

Beyond Belushi, *Animal House* is still original, inventive, and sadistically funny while also being layered and heartfelt. Shock of shocks, it is *a real movie*. Above all, Belushi's sporadic appearances elevate *Animal House* to something actual university students have to learn: commedia dell'arte. Go ahead and fill my cheeks with mashed potatoes and squeeze my head like a zit for remembering anything that term from drama class.

Assault of the Party Nerds [1989]

DIR. RICHARD GABAI; W/RICHARD GABAI, LINNEA QUIGLEY, MICHELLE BAUER, TROY DONAHUE

NERDS ▣ FRATERNITIES ▣ GRADUATION ▣ PRANKS ▣ TOGA PARTY ▣ FOOD FIGHT

Writer-director Richard Gabai stars as Ritchie, head "party nerd" in charge of Lambda Alpha Eta, an all-dork fraternity whose four total members are slated to graduate, thereby putting the brotherhood out of business. The "assault" of the movie's title concerns the frat's frantic drive for new recruits during a period of intense rivalry with a jock house populated by bodybuilding bullies. The jocks don't come off as being as convincingly intrigued by the movie's sole selling point—copious exposed female flesh—as they are by '50s heartthrob-with-a-secret Troy Donahue, appearing here as "Sidney Witherspoon."

Assault's marketable components come courtesy of '80s scream queens Linnea Quigley and Michelle Bauer, as well as fetish porn star Mistress Tantala Ray. In light of her previous work in *Beverly Hills Cox* (1985) and *Let Me Tell Ya 'Bout Fat Chicks* (1987), The Mistress is slumming here.

Gabai has boasted that he shot *Assault of the Party* in five days. It makes one wonder what everybody must have been doing for those other four days and twenty-three-and-a-half other hours. Yet if any single film aired more frequently on cable's *USA Up All Night* than *Assault of the Party Nerds*, may Gilbert Gottfried, Rhonda Shear, and God Almighty (who may be a combination of Gilbert and Rhonda) protect us all. Say your prayers to any or all of the above!

Assault of the Party Nerds 2: The Heavy Petting Detective [1995]

DIR. RICHARD GABAI; W/RICHARD GABAI, MICHELLE BAUER, RHONDA SHEAR, ARTE JOHNSON

NERDS ▣ JOCKS ▣ SAVE THE FRAT HOUSE

Richard Gabai's original *Assault of the Party Nerds* (1989) garnered a sufficient following via ceaseless re-re-re-running on USA's *Up All Night* (1989–1998) to warrant not just a sequel, but a full-blown role for *Up All Night*'s luminous cohost, Rhonda Shear. Just as *Revenge of the Nerds* (1984), provided *Party Nerds* an easy template to, um, "absorb," *Ace Ventura: Pet Detective* (1994) supplied the follow-up with similar "inspiration."

Gabai returns as all-grown-up frat-house party nerd Ritchie. He's married to Muffin (Michelle Bauer) and remains in touch with just about all the characters from the first outing. Not surprisingly, those same actors were all available. After graduation, Ritchie has become a private dick. Business tycoon Mr. Randolph (Burt Ward, aka Robin of TV's *Batman*) hires him to spy on shady operator Bud (Christopher Dempsey). Bud is Mr. Randolph's son-in-law, and turns out to also be one of Ritchie's jock bully rivals from the first *Assault* movie. Small world, huh?

Meanwhile, all the original assaulting the party nerds did to save their frat house may come to naught, as the property's deed is about to expire. Old man Witherspoon—originally Troy Donahue, here played by *Laugh-In*'s Arte Johnson—wants nothing but to shut down Lambda Alpha Eta for good. There's even more plot than that, befitting a movie with the hard-to-swallow title *Assault of the Party Nerds 2: The Heavy Petting Detective*. You can learn more on your own anytime.

Bachelor Party ▭ Back To School

Back to the Future ▭ Beach Babes from Beyond

Beach Balls ▭ Beach Fever ▭ The Beach Girls

Beach House ▭ Beach Party ▭ Better Off Dead

Beverly Hills Vamp ▭ The Big Bet

The Big Steal ▭ The Bikini Carwash Company

The Bikini Carwash Company II ▭ Bikini Drive-in

Bikini Summer ▭ Bikini Summer II ▭ Blame It on Rio

Blue Movies ▭ Blue Summer ▭ Boarding School ▭ Body Waves

The Breakfast Club ▭ Breaking All the Rules ▭ Buford's Beach Bunnies

Bachelor Party [1984]

DIR. NEAL ISRAEL; W/TOM HANKS, TAWNY KITAEN, ADRIAN ZMED, WENDIE JO SPERBER, BARRY DIAMOND

WILD PARTY ▭ SEX PROS ▭ STUFFY RICH FOLK ▭ DONKEY SHOW ▭ JAPANESE BUSINESSMEN

Although no teenagers feature in *Bachelor Party*, this R-rated, taboo-shattering, anything-goes film farce is fueled by youthful abandon, no-holes-barred sexual overindulgence, savage intoxication, slapstick debauchery, and deliriously decadent destruction of property and morality—all in the name of having a kick-ass good time.

Tom Hanks transforms from viscerally charismatic sitcom star (his *Bosom Buddies* remains one of TV's all-time funniest half hours) to megawatt movie idol. Here, Hanks plays a joke-machine Catholic school bus driver named Rick Gassko—who *is* a gas, bro. Gassko is about to marry upper-crust-but-cool debutante Debbie Thompson (Tawny Kitaen)—much to the concern of her snooty, mansion-dwelling, servant-abusing parents. Before tying the knot, she plans to have a tasteful bridal shower. The very same evening, Rick's boys celebrate his final night as a free man, blowing it out big-time in a hotel suite.

The following expertly executed squall of excess comes as close to deserving an X rating as any Hollywood release in 1984. The active ingredients avalanche into a laugh riot strung together by comic mixups. For example, interracial lesbian hookers are given the wrong address and perform their dildo show for Debbie's half-virginal, half-matronly guests. A live donkey snorts a yard-long line of cocaine and keels over, four stiff legs up, moments before he was to perform interspecies intercourse with a belly dancer.

Though no characters between twelve and twenty appear in *Bachelor Party*, the movie is the blatant offspring of outrageously potent teen farces chumming audience waters and creating a demand for something as insane, filthy, and unfiltered as *Screwballs* (1983) or *Hardbodies* (1984). This time, actual adults barfed up popcorn laughing and loving the movie.

Bachelor Party was further immortalized when the Beastie Boys' breakthrough 1987 music video for "Fight for Your Right to Party" quoted the se-

Clockwise from top: Bachelor Party (1984), *a squall of cartoonish and grotesque celebratory excess; when in doubt—and completely bereft of ideas—why not make a T&A movie about* Blue Movies (1988); Better Off Dead *(1986) scores with suicide slapstick.*

quence where party animal Barry Diamond spits beer in a guest's face. According to the video's director, Adam Dubin: "When MCA—the amazing Adam Yauch—enters the party, he takes a can of soda out of one kid's hand, pounds it, bounces the can off the kid's head, and then spits the soda into another kid's face. It was only natural that I threw in that gag as an homage to one of my favorite films of my favorite movie genre."

Back to School [1986]

DIR. ALAN METTER; W/RODNEY DANGERFIELD, SALLY KELLERMAN, KEITH GORDON, ROBERT DOWNEY JR.

WILD AND CRAZY OLD GUY ▪ SORORITY ▪ FRAT PARTY ▪ THE BIG DIVING CONTEST

The star of *Back to School* is decades past his teens, but Rodney Dangerfield's classic campus crack-up is built on the fundamental tropes that define coming-of-age farces as a genre. Rodney shows up on the school grounds by mistakenly barging in on a naked sorority girl in the shower (a happy accident for all involved). Sam Kinison loses his shit as a 'Nam vet professor who screams like an air-raid siren directly into Rodney's face. Ned Beatty barely contains his own amusement at playing a college head named "Dean Martin." Dangerfield complains of his shrewish wife, "She gives great headache!"

Tearing up the screen, Rodney Dangerfield is Thornton Melon, billionaire mogul of a "tall and fat" clothing empire. After his uptight son Jason (Keith Gordon) threatens to drop out of Grand Lakes University, Thornton surprises the lad by enrolling in classes himself. He instantly reigns as Head Party Animal on Campus.

William Zabka, as a-hole diving-team star Chaz Osborn, plays the Big Bully with the same punch-inviting perfection he brought to *The Karate Kid* (1984) and *Just One of the Guys* (1986). Burt Young (Paulie from *Rocky*) is a riot in the role of Lou, Thornton's chauffeur and a martial arts expert. As Jason's roommate, Robert Downey Jr. successfully reconnects to the punk drummer energy he showed in *Tuff Turf* (1985). Sally Kellerman positively glows as the English professor who falls for Thornton. *Slaughterhouse-Five* author Kurt Vonnegut puts in one of the funniest cameos in the history of movies—and the obscene payoff is even funnier.

While toned down from *Caddyshack* (1980) and not as uproarious as Rodney's underappreciated *Easy Money* (1983), *Back to School* is still a monster of gut-busts. To reach the movie's climax even once means forever being about to burst out laughing spontaneously upon reliving the faces Dangerfield makes while executing his signature "Triple Lindy" high-dive, and to forever be tempted to tell your bartender, as Rodney does, "Bring us a pitcher of beer every seven minutes until somebody passes out—then bring one every ten minutes!"

Back to the Future [1985]

DIR. ROBERT ZEMECKIS; W/MICHAEL J. FOX, LEA THOMPSON, CHRISTOPHER LLOYD, CRISPIN GLOVER

TIME TRAVEL ▪ NERD ▪ BULLIES ▪ BIG DANCE ▪ MAD SCIENTIST ▪ INCEST HUMOR

Back to the Future is by far the best, funniest, and most substantial film to emerge from the maniacally prolific Steven Spielberg orbit of the mid-1980s. The movie stands out from associated Amblin Productions sump like *Goonies* (1985), *Batteries Not Included* (1986), and *Harry and the Hendersons* (1987) by focusing on teenagers. For perhaps the only time in the Spielberg universe, the film acknowledges the human experience of sex. The line "My mom has the hots for me!" is especially commendable.

Back to the Future's plot specifics have become almost universal knowledge: Marty McFly (Michael J. Fox) pilots a time-traveling DeLorean invented by Doc Brown (Christopher Lloyd) to 1955, in order to ensure that his parents hook up romantically so that his own existence is possible. Complicating matters, big bully Biff Tannen (Thomas F. Wilson) habitually pummels Marty's dad-to-be George McFly (Crispin Glover) into crippling wimpitude. Even worse on a Freudian level, Marty's future mom, Lorraine Baines (Lea Thompson) rapidly develops the "hots" for the mysterious new kid in town—Marty.

The movie's many fish-out-of-water jokes work (everybody thinks Marty's super-1980s down vest is a life jacket). The script's complicated time-space dynamics are easy to follow. And the cast is historically phenomenal, end to end.

If there's a McFly in the ointment, it's *Back to the Future*'s hyper-capitalist, Yuppie-aggrandizing, retro-aggressive "American Dream" ending. Marty's mission to the '50s emboldens George McFly not only to marry Lorraine, but also to successfully pursue his dream of authoring sci-fi novels. That's great. But the bloodcurdling factor is how the movie depicts such success; the McFlys living in a garishly gadget-strewn home, with Marty's previously cynical siblings transformed into emotionless business drones. Bully Biff is publicly humiliated by scrubbing Marty's huge luxury truck in the driveway and endlessly kissing his former rival George's keister for the privilege of being tossed more shit work of that order.

In fact, irrepressible weirdo Crispin Glover famously refused to bring his George McFly role back to the *Future* sequels specifically because he felt sandbagged by the first movie's conclusion. He vehemently disagreed with what he deemed "corporate propaganda." When producers cast another actor in a rubber mask to portray George McFly in *Back to the Future II*, Glover brought a successful legal action, and now takes credit for changes to Screen Actors Guild rules regarding "sampled" performances.

As for those sequels, I prefer the Jules Verne–esque Old West *Part III* (1990) to the noisy and confusing *Part II* (1989). Also, *Part III* has ZZ Top in it. All the *Back to the Future* films work, and given the sci-fi dynamics, limitless possibilities exist that could potentially upend the first movie's figurative "sellout." Doc's big revelation by the end of the run, in fact, is that the future will *always* be Marty's to invent—and that goes for the viewers, too.

Beach Babes from Beyond [1993]

DIR. DAVID DECOTEAU; W/NICOLE POSEY, LINNEA QUIGLEY, BURT WARD, JACKIE STALLONE

SPACE CHICKS · THE BIG BIKINI CONTEST · SURFER · HEALTH NUTS · SKATEBOARDS

Travolta. Stallone. Swayze. Estevez. Those marquee names above the title represent the primary gimmick and only creative moment of note regarding *Beach Babes from Beyond*. Though the household names are real enough, they belong to the relatives of the early-'90s A-list stars. Is it Patrick Swayze?—well, no.

This direct-to-video fake-tit demo reel boasts performances by Joey Travolta (brother of John) as a SoCal health food guru; Jackie Stallone (mother of Sly and, okay, Frank) as space alien Yanna; Don Swayze (brother of Patrick) as her husband, Gork; Nicole Posey as Sola, Yanna and Gork's cosmos-cruising blonde bombshell daughter; and Joe Estevez (brother of Martin Sheen, uncle of Emilio Estevez and Charlie Sheen) as Uncle Bud, a beach bum who lets his cool dude long-boarder nephew Dave (Michael Todd Davis) and fellow hodad Jerry (Ken Steadman) crash at his shorefront hang shack.

Sola and her hot space chick friends Luna (Tamara Landry) and Xena (Sarah Bellomo) crash-land their starship on Venice Beach. They romance the surf buds, befriend local swimsuit designer Sally (Linnea Quigley), and compete in a $30,000 bikini contest sponsored by hammy hamburger stand proprietor Mr. Bun (Burt Ward, aka Robin of TV's *Batman*.)

The whole outing exemplifies the soft-core-loop format that replaced vital and surprising 1970s exploitation films with harshly lit, hard-hootered Cinemax schedule fillers. Director David DeCoteau's similar sci-fi T&A farce follow-up, *Test Tube Teens from the Year 2000* (1994), and his direct sequel, *Beach Babes 2: Cave Girl Island* (1995), may or may not be worse.

Beach Balls [1988]

DIR. JOE RITTER; W/PHILLIP PALEY, HEIDI HELMER, STEVEN TASH, AMANDA GOODWIN

BOARDWALK ▣ BIKINIS ▣ HAIR METAL ▣ ROLLER-SKATES ▣ THE BIG CONCERT

The most important attraction in *Beach Balls* is star Phillip Paley. Paley's only other acting role of note that of Cha-Ka, the monkey-boy on the '70s kiddie-TV schlock-zenith, *Land of the Lost* (1974–1977). Perhaps knowing there'd be no topping Cha-Ka, it seems Paley laid low for a dozen years following *Lost*, then bounced back for *Beach Balls*. Afterward, he immediately signed out of showbiz forever. Career well done!

Paley plays Charlie Harrington, a teenage wannabe heavy metal guitarist who accidentally runs afoul of both law enforcement and lawbreakers. Compounding Charlie's conundrum, his parents have recently converted to record-burning Satanic-panicked Bible zealots. Understandably, Charlie hightails it to a climate that's in some ways hotter yet infinitely cooler.

Hiding out in sunny Santa Monica, Charlie blends in among the surf dogs, skate rats, bikini foxes, and—what with *Beach Balls* coming out the same year *as The Decline of Western Civilization Part II*—a multitude of fully teased-up, mascara-blasted mousse-metal marauders, including Charlie's all-time favorite glam group, Severed Heads in a Bag (played by real-life Sunset Strip hair-bangers D. R. Starr).

Love finds Charlie, slowly, in the form of jilted Gazzarri's groupie Wendy (Heidi Helmer). She finally falls for Charlie after he's able to simultaneously elude the outlaws who come gunning for him, put the cops on the case of the actual bad guys, and successfully mount a Severed Heads industry gig in his own backyard before Mom and Dad get back from a vinyl-torching church shindig.

Throw in some momentarily de-topped bikini contestants, and slinky blonde twins who jam on guitar store instruments and roller-skate during the big concert, and you've got *Beach Balls* in a basket. The soundtrack LP on Metal Blade Records boasts not just Dr. Starr but also Hans Naughty, Temporary Insanity, Puss 'N' Boots, Black Monday, Castle Blak, Mox Nix, and Strut, and was reissued on vinyl in 2013. Cha-Ka lives!

Beach Fever [1987]

DIR. ALEXANDER TABRIZI; W/KATO KAELIN, RODNEY UENO, LISA CARROWAY, AARON BISTON

BIKINI GREEK CHORUS ▣ SURFERS ▣ NERD ▣ LOVE POTION ▣ HEADBANGER

Notorious O. J. Simpson guest =house occupant and 1990s punch line Brian "Kato" Kaelin actually launched his ultimate SoCal douche-bro campaign as early as 1987. That year The Hairdo That Would Not Testify starred in *Beach Fever* as Chat Frederick IV, seemingly a pile of cocaine in suspenders and Jams shorts.

Chat's the slickest dune-dweller on the shore. When horny Japanese geek Sake (Rodney Ueno) hits the sand in pursuit of humanity's single greatest pickup line, guess whose totally rad motorbike he comically tumbles onto while a gong sound rings? As Chat delivers on the, well, *chat*, he and Sake stumble across science dork Ernie (Jeffrey Asch), who has just perfected a bikini-bunny love potion. Party!

Unfortunately, local organized crime strongman Big Daddy (Aaron Biston) poops said celebration when he kidnaps "a hundred" women from the beach, pumps them full of Ernie's aphrodisiac, turns them into zombie sex slaves, and pimps them out from the Surfside Hotel. Sake's father (George Tsaki) swoops in to save the day. He speaks in a karate-movie-dubbed voice and calls his boy "number one son." Mutant-mugged character actor Irwin Keyes, always a welcome sight, appears as a thug who helps our heroes.

Beach Fever even boasts a bona fide bit of originality, a swimsuit-clad singing trio (Erika Nann, Andrea Savio, and Jennifer Asch) who narrate and comment on the action in the manner of a

Greek chorus with girl-group harmonies. Unlike in Aeschylus' Agamemnon, in *Beach Fever* everything works out swell for everybody—well, except for Ron Goldman and Nicole Brown Simpson.

The Beach Girls [1982]

DIR. BUD TOWNSEND; W/DEBRA BLEE, VAL KLINE, JEANA TOMASINA, JAMES DAUGHTON

BEACH HOUSE ▣ LAST DAY OF SCHOOL ▣ BIKINI-SNATCHING DOG ▣ NERD GIRL

The Beach Girls plays like a post-*Porky's* update of the 1960s "beach party" movie craze; one such outing in 1965 was already even titled *The Girls on the Beach*. In both cases, the standard-issue helium-headed plot follows a bunch of high school sun-seekers as they hit the sand and surf. In the 1982 version, however, a crafty canine repeatedly snatches the bikini tops of tanning beauties, leading to elongated ganders at their previously underexposed pale parts.

Bookish, pent-up Sarah (Debra Blee) invites her more decadent pal Ginger (Val Kline) to come along to her uncle's seaside digs on Paradise Beach, where they'll ostensibly be housesitting for the summer. En route to Paradise, the girls pick up *Playboy* centerfold Jeana Tomasina—the actual first character in an '80s teen sex comedy to be named Ducky. (Sorry, Jon Cryer.)

The party starts quick, and Sarah's stress level soars even before a dozen industrial-size trash bags full of marijuana wash up at the front door. From there, things go up in blazes, swimsuits come off in heaps, and Sarah's inhibitions smolder away in smoking interludes of naked liberation. Uncle Carl (Adam Roarke) comes home early and immediately attempts to call *ixnay* on the orgy, but he succumbs in a sweaty hurry the moment topless Ginger and Ducky welcome him home with a reefer the size of a Louisville Slugger.

The Beach Girls ably and amicably adheres to genre tropes both titillating (all those natural nubile naughty bits) and rib-tickling (a karate-chopping Asian limo driver battling with a horndog Mexican gardener). The film played theaters regularly for five years after its initial release, filling out grindhouse and drive-in bills, and proved to be a rental smash in the early days of home video. It remains a party worth revisiting. Bring your dog. Also keep a lookout for the ever-lovely Corinne Bohrer (*Zapped!*, *Joysticks*, *Surf II*), who fills out a purple bikini swimmingly in her role as "Champagne Girl."

Beach House [1982]

aka Down the Shore

DIR. JOHN A. GALLAGHER; W/ILEANA SEIDEL, JOHN COSOLA, KATE MCNEIL, EDDIE BRILL

BEACH HOUSE ▣ BIKINIS ▣ BIG FAT PARTY ANIMAL ▣ PUNKS ▣ NEW WAVERS ▣ BEER

"Goin' down the shore / Down the shore / Won't take time worryin' 'bout the weather / We're too busy, groovin' all together...." As the theme song to *Beach House*—"Down the Shore," by Adam Roth and His Band of Men—promises, groovin' together is what *Beach House* is all about, and never more groovily than when the power-pop trio jams out "I Just Wanna Have Some Fun" on the sand dunes sans amps while the entire cast boogaloos around them. Nobody's worrying about the weather then, for sure—nor is anybody associated with the production worrying about making a professional-caliber motion picture. Still, like the individual letter stickers on the band's bass drum that spell out "Pleasantville Music Shoppe," the whole thing works.

The threadbare plot of *Beach House* chronicles Italian "goombah" kids from Brooklyn sharing their vacation domicile with less ethnically hyper-identifiable youths from Philadelphia. They fuss, they fret, they fall in love, and they even food-fight after tearing apart a roasted turkey, setting up bricolage worthy of "Singin' in the Rain" as the Band of Men drummer uses the bird's legs as drumsticks.

Beach House looks to be shot with handheld 8mm cameras and thus has the immediacy of a home movie. That sense is compounded by the setting in the blue-collar riviera of scenic Ocean City, New Jersey. All the cars and pickup trucks appear to be borrowed from the cast's parents. From there, the checks just keep coming in the plus column.

Adam Roth and His Band of Men perform multiple numbers in the vein of vintage NYC punks the Rattlers. When they take a break, everybody pogos to "Ça Plane Pour Moi" by Plastic Bertrand at Phil's Disco on the boardwalk. The fat guy visibly sweats through each one of his too-tight sleeveless T-shirts—you'll swear you can smell him. Kate McNeil, who went on to a respectable Hollywood career, capably models a series of bikinis.

Regardless of its PG rating, *Beach House* is a gas that probably cost less to make than a tank of gas in 1982. By the time summer ends, whether or not the movie is any good is immaterial. Like the dialogue, this feature is freakin' *awwww-sim!*—please pronounce that word with a proper Ocean City accent. And while we're on the Jersey Shore, let's address the gorilla on the beach: stand-up legend Eddie Brill, the comic who warmed up David Letterman's studio audiences for decades, costars here as a guido named...*Snooky!*

BEACH PARTY [1963]

DIR. WILLIAM ASHER; W/ROBERT CUMMINGS, DOROTHY MALONE, FRANKIE AVALON, ANNETTE FUNICELLO

BEACH ▣ BIKERS ▣ 1960S

In the archetypal storyline of all 1960s beach party movies, teenage mobs assemble seaside to hook up, get down, cut loose, and rock out. Uptight authority figures and comical roughnecks then attempt to poop the party. Pranks are pulled. Faces are sucked. Hearts are broken and hearts are healed. In the end, the kids will win!

This is the core setup introduced by *Gidget* (1959), an adaptation of a popular young adult novel with Sandra Dee as the teenage surf babe of the title. After several years of fairly straightforward post-*Gidget* dune larks, American International Pictures (AIP) upended the surf shack with *Beach Party* (1963), an anything-goes, joke-a-minute hullabaloo headlined by Top 40 heartthrob Frankie Avalon and famously filled-out *Mickey Mouse Club* member Annette Funicello.

While the bikinis and trunks stay put in *Beach Party*, the movie itself twists and howls and nearly cascades over the screen in a tsunami of hormonal overdrive. Robert Cummings plays an anthropologist who hits the shore to examine the "wild mating habits" of Southern California's surf-crazed teenagers. Bombastic slob Harvey Lembeck provides conflict as Eric Von Zipper, the spectacularly inept leader of the idiotic biker gang the Rats—a parody of Marlon Brando's hoodlums in *The Wild One* (1953). Surf rock overlords Dick Dale & His Del-Tones provide a couple of killer on-screen music jams. The perfect formula is all laid out right there.

Young audiences flooded *Beach Party* screenings and an entire genre named for the movie soon swarmed theaters. Frankie and Annette remained the first couple of the form, going on to make *Muscle Beach Party* (1964), *Bikini Beach* (1964), *Pajama Party* (1964), *How to Stuff a Wild Bikini* (1965), and the absolute Big Kahuna of the cycle, *Beach Blanket Bingo* (1965).

Eric Von Zipper's Rats clumsily torment Frankie and Annette in each picture, and a multitude of rock and soul greats all enjoyed a shot at screen stardom, including Stevie Wonder (*Muscle Beach Party*), James Brown (*Ski Party*), the Bobby Fuller Four (*The Ghost in the Invisible Bikini*) and, of course, the Beach Boys (*The Girls on the Beach*).

Other studios rushed to imitate AIP's tidal wave success, much as every film company hurled themselvee into the *Porky's* business two decades onward. Hybrid subgenres emerged, combining the usual antics with monster flicks (*The Horror of Party Beach*), winter vacation (*Ski Party*) and James Bond spoofs with (*Dr. Goldfoot and the Bikini Machine*). Even Elvis Presley responded by starring in *Clambake* (1964) and *Girl Happy* (1965). By the end of 1967, the hippie counterculture pushed the beach party movie out to sea, where it remained until getting sent up in *Surf II* (1984) and *Back to the Beach* (1987), which features the return of Frankie and Annette themselves; along with Paul Reubens as Pee-Wee Herman, squealing out his should've-been-a-hit take on the Trashmen's "Surfin' Bird."

Better Off Dead [1985]

DIR. SAVAGE STEVE HOLLAND; W/JOHN CUSACK, DIANE FRANKLIN, CURTIS ARMSTRONG

VIRGIN ▫ JOCKS ▫ NERDS ▫ RICH JERKS ▫ SKIS ▫ SUICIDE HUMOR ▫ HILARIOUS ASIANS

John Cusack graduates to leading man and nearly human cartoon status in *Better Off Dead*. He stars as Lane Myer, a high school layabout who is unhealthily—to put it mildly—infatuated with his girlfriend, Beth (Amanda Wyss). Lane's bedroom is wallpapered with Beth's photographs; each of his clothing hangers is topped with a headshot of Beth's face. Her name is written on every surface within Lane's reach. Our boy takes it rather hard, then, when Beth ditches him for Roy Stalin (Aaron Dozier), captain of the school ski team. Afterwards, Lane is preoccupied with violent thoughts. Funny stuff, right? *Right!*

In another movie, *Better Off Dead*'s opening could naturally set up stalk-and-slash horror. In less gifted hands, teen suicide might not be played so effectively for button-busting yuks. Welcome to the lovable dementia of *Better Off Dead* and the deft execution of animation-trained writer-director Savage Steve Holland. He and the up-for-anything cast prove perfectly game for the movie's every gravity-splattering task.

The action in *Better Off Dead* "hangs" from Lane's slapstick attempts to off himself, interspersed with extremely amusing interludes involving an onslaught of human oddities. Standouts in the freak parade include Lane's slime-serving wannabe chef mother (Kim Darby); his nuclear hothead old man (David Ogden Stiers); his evil genius kid brother, Badger (Scooter Stevens), who is silently bent on world conquest; and the great Curtis Armstrong as Charles De Mar, Lane's dope-enthused best bud.

Aside from Stalin, villainy persists in the form of psychotic paperboy Johnny (Demian Slade), a menace who maniacally demands two-dollar payment for his window-shattering deliveries. Also occupying the adversary column is Lane's boss Rocko, the cigar-chomping, porcine Pig Burger meat-stand proprietor played by Chuck Mitchell (yes, "Porky" of *Porky's* himself, keeping the oink jokes alive). More cuddly but most repulsive is Ricky Smith (Dan Schneider), Lane's obese, maternally coddled Very Special Boy neighbor who forever tries to force his affections on Monique Junet (Diane Franklin), the lovely French exchange student the Smith family is hosting. The film's action is underlined by the Ree brothers (Yuji Okumoto and Brian Imada), a pair of ever-looming Japanese street racers, one of whom announces every move in a Howard Cosell voice through a massive speaker atop the pair's car.

Lane's surreal escapades unfold against this weirdly populated backdrop. His most celebrated flight of fancy occurs during a kitchen shift at Pig Burger that headbangingly morphs into a stop-motion-animated dancing hamburger fantasia set to "Everybody Wants Some" by Van Halen.

On arrival, *Better Off Dead* certainly warranted the descriptor "in a class by itself." Yet as Savage Steve Holland followed it with *One Crazy Summer* (1986) and *How I Got Into College* (1989), *BOD* proved to be the opening volley in an extremely distinct genre: "Savage Steve Holland Movies." As entire cinematic categories go, *that* very much does remain one-of-a-kind.

Weirder teen sex comedies than *Better Off Dead* do exist (*King Frat, Surf II, Teen Lust*), but not they are not weirder on purpose. Often, such a level of self-aware strangeness devolves fast into smugness or kitsch. Not here. At the end, no one who watches *Better Off Dead* will forget it. Presented as evidence are the sounds of "I want my two dollars!" still echoing across the landscape many decades past 1985.

Beverly Hills Vamp [1988]

DIR. FRED OLEN RAY; W/EDDIE DEEZEN, BRITT EKLAND, TIM CONWAY JR., MICHELLE BAUER

NERDS ▣ **SEXY VAMPIRES** ▣ **FIRST TRIP TO HOLLYWOOD** ▣ **EDDIE DEEZEN**

Eddie Deezen (*Grease, Zapped!, Surf II*), stars in *Beverly Hills Vamp* as wannabe filmmaker Kyle Carpenter. Daffy geek Kyle travels to Hollywood with pals Brock (Tim Conway Jr.) and Russell (Tom Shell), all of them delirious with ambitions of becoming movie moguls. After a rapid rude awakening, the downtrodden trio pop into a brothel for a pick-me-up. Unbeknownst to them, Madame Cassandra ('70s skinema legend Britt Ekland) is a queen-bee bloodsucker. Her luscious array of sensual service providers (Michelle Bauer, Debra Lamb, and Jillian Kesner) is actually composed of full-fanged succubae who just happen to sport recognizably human female nude bodies.

By and large, *Beverly Hills Vamp* is a dim tramp through Tinseltown, primarily notable for its lead casting of Deezen, nerd-dom's all-time nerdiest of nerds. Respect is due the preposterously prolific schlock pumper-outer Fred Olen Ray for knowing a good geek when he saw one.

The Big Bet [1985]

DIR. BERT I. GORDON; W/SYLVIA KRISTEL, LANCE SLOANE, KIM EVENSON, MONIQUE GABRIELLE

OLDER WOMAN ▣ **VIRGIN** ▣ **NEW GIRL** ▣ **MINISTER'S DAUGHTER** ▣ **RICH JERK**

The Big Bet is an obscurity that unites two unlikely cult cinema icons in the otherwise fairly ho-hum saga of a horny suburban teen. Director Bert I. Gordon ("Mr. B.I.G.") is best known for giant monster sci-fi schlock (*Food of the Gods, Empire of the Ants*) and top-billed star Sylvia Kristel is the Dutch soft-core sex sensation from *Emmanuelle* and, later, *Private Lessons*.

Fired-up high-school senior Chris (Lance Sloane) visualizes sex with every woman he sees: the hot mom next door, the hot teenage girl next door, and especially Michelle (Sylvia Kristel), the exotic fortysomething fashion designer down the block.

As Michelle, Sylvia Kristel performs a youth service akin to her work in *Private Lessons*. She educates Chris in the art of seduction so he can win the wager of the title and beat local loudmouth Norman (Ron Thomas) to bedding Beth (September 1984 *Playboy* Playmate Kim Evenson), the new girl in town who also happens to be a clergyman's daughter. December 1982 Penthouse Pet Monique Gabrielle also gets in on the action, after turns in *Bachelor Party* (1984) and *Hot Moves* (1985). Gabrielle also, coincidentally, would go on to take over the title role from Sylvia Kristel in 1987's *Emmanuelle 5*.

Despite what must have obvious temptations presented by a cast of topless centerfolds, *Big Bet* maker Bert I. Gordon opted not to hyper-exaggerate anyone's anatomy in *The Big Bet*. This goes against his previous cinematic reputation, marked most notably by the army colonel who expands to King Kong dimensions in *The Amazing Colossal Man* (1957) and, more specifically, the mountain-proportioned mammary glands that dominate the dream sequences of his previous teen sex effort, *Let's Do It* (1982). Not blowing up Sylvia Kristel to the size of the Eiffel Tower here remains quite the missed opportunity.

The Big Steal [1990]

DIR. NADIA TASS; W/BEN MENDELSOHN, CLAUDIA KARVAN, STEVE BISLEY

EIGHTEENTH BIRTHDAY ▣ **VIRGIN** ▣ **FIRST DATE** ▣ **GEARHEADS** ▣ **USED-CAR SALESMAN**

Character actor Ben Mendelsohn is one of contemporary Hollywood's go-to no-goodniks, drawing jeers in *The Dark Knight Rises, Exodus: Gods and Kings*, and *Rogue One: A Star Wars Story*. *The Big Steal*, an Australian coming-of-age comedy that hit big Down Under, showcases a considerably softer side of Bad Ben. Here he debuts as gawky Danny Clark, a car-obsessed youth failing to impress on his first date.

The human object of Danny's affection is Joanna Johnson (Claudia Karvan, of *Puberty Blues*). His real love, though, is a 1969 dark green Jaguar XJ6, which he acquires by trading in the creaky, ill-repaired 1963 Nissan Cedric his parents gave him upon his turning eighteen. Alas, the best-laid plans of horny dudes go often in the opposite direction of getting laid—especially after cutting an impossibly sweet deal with a slick used-car salesman like Gordon Farkas (Steve Bisley, who played Goose in *Mad Max*). Danny's Jag contains a lemon engine, which explodes shortly after he gets Joanna on the road. Revenge, as it must, will eventually be his—as will Joanna.

The Bikini Carwash Company [1992]

DIR. ED HANSEN; W/KRISTI DUCATI, RIKKI BRANDO, JOE DUSIC, PATRICK WRIGHT

BIKINIS ▪ HICK IN THE CITY ▪ SUMMER JOB ▪ SEX SAVES THE BUSINESS

In a very real sense, *The Bikini Carwash Company* killed the teen sex comedy, buried it, and scorched the corpse to prevent any possibility of res-*erection*. Allow me to state my case: Youth exploitation films from around 1968 (when MPAA instituted the R rating) until the early '90s (when the theatrical B-movie circuit collapsed) had always been designed to hold an audience's attention for the entirety of the feature—no matter how cheap or dumb the movie itself might be. Some degree of perceptible entertainment was required to hold together the ticket-selling "good parts"—the nakedness, sex, and titillating nonsense like bikini car washing.

However, fast-forward to the era of direct-to-video productions, and anything besides the "good parts" no longer stood a chance. Any substance at all became a hindrance. Even the makers of the mildest jiggle movies caught on quick that actual cinematic elements such as plot and character would prevent and delay their incoming flow of cash. The movie itself was now a total slave to the box cover.

The Bikini Carwash Company arrived at this realization first, but no blue ribbons are deserved for anyone involved. The so-called movie is a no-budget compilation of sudsy swimsuit montages wrapped around the barest scintilla of a notion of a story setup. The end product generated titanic profits by way VHS and late-night cable TV, thereby setting in motion tidal waves of "Bikini" knockoff titles. All of them followed the same formula: flesh-filled ersatz music videos separated by wispy interstitials. With that, the proper teen sex comedy was dead—only to rise again in the late '90s in the form of neo-nostalgia pieces like *American Pie* and *Varsity Blues*, not to mention widely respected serious reappraisals like the book you're holding in your hands.

The Bikini Carwash Company II [1993]

DIR. GARY ORONA; W/KRISTI DUCATI, RIKKI BRANDO, NERIAH DAVIS, LARRY DE RUSSY

BIKINIS ▪ PRUDE CRUSADER ▪ SEX SAVES THE BUSINESS AGAIN!

The Bikini Carwash Company II is worthy of inclusion here, but not because it's any closer to being a movie than the first succession of stupid skin-flick montages. This outing may actually be stupider, as the vaporous whisper of a plot includes expanding the swimsuit-centric title business to a new enterprise—lingerie sold over that most 1990s of outlets, a TV shopping network. Worthy of the top-shelf-of-the-bottom-rack status this title inhabits, the filmmakers opted to denote their sequel with Roman numerals, and that's pure class.

Bikini Drive-In [1995]

DIR. FRED OLEN RAY; W/ASHLIE RHEY, RICHARD GABAI, MICHELLE BAUER, SARAH BELLOMO

BIKINIS ▪ CAR WASH ▪ MONTAGE ▪ SEX SAVES THE BUSINESS

Parked at the outermost field of focus of teen sex comedy parameters, Fred Olen Ray's

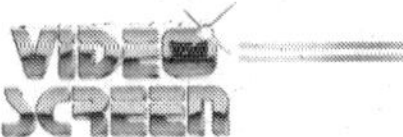

Clockwise from top left: *Dutch* Beach Fever *(1987) video box offers "love potion for sale"; action-packed Euro-release of* The Beach Girls *(1982); more vehicles and swimwear for* Bikini Summer *(1991); go on, blame* The Bikini Carwash Company (1992) *for killing the teen sex comedy genre.*

Bikini Drive-In sees hyper-prolific B-movie maker Ray and his frequent collaborating screenwriter/producer Jim Wynorski still dabbling in the teen sex genre well into the mid-1990s.

In essence, *Bikini Drive-In* combines the music video swimwear montage format pioneered by *The Bikini Carwash Company* (1992) with a self-aware, in-joke plot regarding plucky females saving a business by stripping down to as little as possible. In this case, those pluckster are topless sunbathers Kim (Ashley Rhey) and Carrie (Sarah Bellomo). They take over a collapsing drive-in theater that belongs to Kim's elderly uncle. As always in this archetypal setup, dropped tops raise funds and everybody wins.

Bikini Drive-In is a good example of vintage teen sex cinema's final videotape mutation. Both Fred Olen Ray and Jim Wynorski exude a love of exploitation films that elevates footage that otherwise might best serve as a breast-implant catalogue. In addition to containing cameos by both Ray and Wynorski themselves, *Bikini Drive-In* honors its tawdry cinematic tradition by also featuring *Famous Monsters* publisher Forrest J. Ackerman, legendary B-movie mogul David F. Friedman (*Blood Feast, Scum of the Earth*), sword-and-sandal star Gordon Mitchell, and, in photograph form at least, the late, great fright icon John Carradine. Soon enough, mainstream corporate culture would emulate tail-swallowing nostalgia like via the likes of Steven Spielberg's *Ready Player One* (2018) and guys who beat up actual nerds calling *themselves* "nerds."

Bikini Summer [1991]

DIR. ROBERT VEZE; W/DAVID MILLBERN, KELLI KONOP, MELINDA ARMSTRONG, KENT LIPHAM

BIKINIS ▣ SKINNY-DIPPING ▣ BEACH HOUSE ▣ NERDS ▣ BIG FAT PARTY ANIMAL ▣ RICH TEXAN ▣ EVIL LANDLORD ▣ HEADBANGERS

Bikini Summer beat *The Bikini Carwash Company* to home video by a full year, and therefore falls on the correct side of the line in the Malibu sand in terms of feeling akin to something like a movie. Several elements boost *Bikini Summer*, all of them on the throwback side to vintage shoreline romps dating from the '60s (Frankie and Annette flicks) to the '80s (*Hardbodies, Spring Break*). First are some daffy old folks who leave their beachfront getaway in the hands of party animal Chet (David Millbern). Then there's Jailbait, the all-girl rock group led by dynamic belter Jazz (Shelley Michelle).

Bikini Summer serves up a full house of surfboard-stiff character types: sexy-but-she-doesn't-know-it beachwear designer Renee (Kelli Konop); buxom swimsuit model Cheryl (Melinda Armstrong); rich Texan Brad (Jason Clow); scumbag landlord Max (Ken Davitian); sexy-and-*maybe-she-does-know-it* district attorney Rachel Greene (Rebekah Alfred); surfside nerds Larry (Thom DeLorenzo) and Gary (Tommy Heisler); and an obese beast named Mad Dog (Kent Lipham) who communicates mostly through belching. Right on, Mad Dog.

One stupendously timely touch comes when dune-hippie Moondog (Michael Silverback) tells off mewling tree-hugger Richie (Alex Smith) by saying: "Listen, I spent half the '60s in the slammer. I missed Woodstock. I missed Monterey. I don't plan on missing the '90s!"

The brazen exploitation of fake-tanned, scalpel-sculpted SoCal video vixens preening in swimwear is tempered ever so slightly by having them pose against the driving protest rock backdrop of the band Jailbait. At one point, Jazz wails: "Justice is blind, if you got cash. If you don't, your head they'll bash. Mr. Bush does not tax the rich, isn't that sort of a bitch?" Two sequels of downward spiraling quality followed: *Bikini Summer II* (1992) and *Bikini Summer III: South Beach Heat* (1997). I watched them all.

Bikini Summer II [1992]

DIR. JEFF CONAWAY; W/JEFF CONAWAY, JESSICA HAHN, MAUREEN FLAHERTY, ROBERT MIANO

BIKINIS 📼 GIRL ROCK BAND 📼 SEXY MAID 📼 BAD PARENTS 📼 SEX SAVES THE BUSINESS

At first glance at the video box, *Bikini Summer II* seems like a must-see. This sequel is directed by and stars Jeff Conaway (Kenickie from *Grease*; Bobby from *Taxi*; Death in Slow Motion from *Celebrity Rehab*), and costars 1980s televangelist scandal queen Jessica Hahn. The plot concerns all-knowing homeless booze-bag Joshua (Robert Miano) raising the consciousness of spoiled rich teen sisters Bridget (Maureen Flaherty) and Vanessa (Melinda Armstrong) by organizing a massive bikini bash. Who could resist? If you have read this far: not you.

Unfortunately, upon succumbing to temptation, you'll find *Bikini Summer II* rapidly downgrades into, "Who could possibly watch this all the way through to that massive bikini bash?"

Sadly, the movie's end sum falls short of its silicone-implanted parts. Hahn essentially cameos as the girls' mother, a delirious housewife with the hots for virile home-shopping-TV pitchman Stu Stocker (Conaway). Their father, Harry (Richard Arbolino), sidelines as a sub for dominatrix Mistress Clarice (Avalon Anders) and a hooded female punisher known only as the Executioner. There's also an unnamed all-girl rock band, an obese black cook, a spicy Latin maid, and an effete Japanese handyman. Bare boobs bounce away throughout the lunacy, but not enough to keep *Bikini Summer II* afloat. *Bikini Summer III: South Beach Heat* is just a total downer.

Blame It on Rio [1984]

DIR. STANLEY DONEN; W/MICHELLE JOHNSON, DEMI MOORE, MICHAEL CAINE, JOSEPH BOLOGNA

SPRING BREAK 📼 TOPLESS BEACH 📼 DIRTY OLD MEN 📼 BAD PARENTS

Stanley Donen directed *Blame It on Rio*. The same Hollywood giant who helmed *On the Town* (1949), *Singin' in the Rain* (1952), *Charade* (1963), and *Bedazzled* (1967) culminated his big-screen career with this jerky pseudo-European sex farce about a horned-up, middle-aged dad cavorting on the sunny shores of Brazil and bedding his daughter's bazooka-bosomed best friend. The daughter's best friend also happens to be fifteen years old. This is the first teen sex comedy for retirees.

Michael Caine plays predatory pop Matthew Hollis. Around the time of *Blame It on Rio*, the great British actor was making movies like this and *Jaws: The Revenge* as a means of getting paid to take island holidays. He has since proudly admitted as much: Cheerio to him for that. Newcomer Michelle Johnson does what's necessary as hefty-chested high school sophomore Jennifer Lyons. She busts out an indisputably attention-grabbing anatomy, but otherwise evaporates as a screen presence. Ms. Johnson was eighteen while filming, not fifteen, so apparently the producers were more scrupulous than the screenwriter.

In contrast, Demi Moore stands out as Matthew's daughter. When you say her name fast, it sounds like a description of her topless scene: "demure." As Demi's dad, Joseph Bologna is a ham.

Back in 1984, a fifty-something lunk "succumbing" to the seductive wiles of a teenage temptress was largely shrugged off in public and high-fived in private. In the years ahead, such cultural attitudes would shift fast and forever. A decade earlier, *Blame It on Rio* might have seemed less like a studio executive's post-cocaine dry-heave and more like a treatise on the sexual revolution. A decade later, it would have featured at least one transgendered bikini booty gag. Skipping three decades ahead, it's hard to find any evidence that this reasonably successful mainstream moneymaker ever existed at all.

Blue Movies [1988]

DIRECTORS: ED FITZGERALD, PAUL KOVAL; W/STEVE LEVITT, LUCINDA CROSBY, LARRY POINDEXTER, RUSSELL JOHNSON

BIKINIS ▣ NAKED AUDITIONS ▣ HAWAIIAN SHIRTS ▣ MOBSTERS ▣ VENICE BEACH

The premise of a couple of young goofs grabbing cameras and aiming to pay the bills and cop cheap thrills by busting into the smut biz is an age-old movie trope. The 1976 cult favorite *The First Nudie Musical* provides one charming example ("Let 'em eat cake / And I'll eat you...."). Kevin Smith's 2008 wallow *Zack and Miri Make a Porno* with Seth Rogen is what you'd expect. Between those extremes lay two '80s teen sex comedy takes on the notion, *Screen Test* (1985) and *Blue Movies*. The latter is a slapdash but surprisingly winning buddy comedy. It runs through the requisite bawdy auditions, slapstick sex-on-the-set mishaps, and mafia money muckups with enjoyable if not memorable style.

Slick-tongued collegiate schemers Buzz (Steve Levitt) and Cliff (Larry Poindexter) conspire to helm their own X-rated movie. Much of the ensuing action sees them hitting Venice Beach to convince various stacked sun-worshippers to strip off bikinis for a shot at stardom. Between expeditions, they continually prostrate themselves to negotiate financing from various nefarious purse-string pullers.

Larry Linville, aka Frank Burns of *M*A*S*H*, plays local scuzz-wad physician Dr. Gladding, while Russell Johnson, aka the Professor from *Gilligan's Island*, musters up a degree of legit danger as a mobster named (to the delight of Italian-American anti-defamation organizations, no doubt) Mr. Martin. He's so convincing viewers will wonder if Gilligan ended up sleeping with the fishes.

Blue Summer [1973]

DIR. CHUCK VINCENT; W/DAVEY JONES, BO WHITE, LILLY BI PEEP

COOL VAN ▣ GRADUATION ▣ LAST SUMMER ▣ ROAD TRIP ▣ HIPPIE CHICKS ▣ BIKER

Review by Heather Drain

Growing up is hard; not as hard as losing a limb while in the middle of guerrilla warfare...or hosting an ugly intervention...or wrangling a rogue Osmond. But still, it can be rough stuff. Injecting hormones into the process of establishing a sense of true self is a mainlined prescription for growing pains. Chuck Vincent's tremendously underrated and surprisingly poignant film *Blue Summer* nails those sentiments. This coming-of-age road-trip movie is heart-smart, funny, and also occasionally somber.

Vincent's impressive filmography includes gems of both the golden age of erotica (*Farewell Scarlett* [1975], *Roommates* [1982], *In Love* [1983]) and R-rated sex comedies (*Sex Appeal* [1986], *Student Affairs* [1987], *Cleo/Leo* [1989]). Of his numerous directorial efforts, *Blue Summer*, aka *The Love Truck*, is one of the more obscure—and unfairly so. The fantastically sleazy promotion of the film as a trashy sexploitation movie about "young bodies on the prowl" that "pay by the mile" didn't help matters.

Blue Summer boasts plenty of nudity and roadside shenanigans to satisfy prurient desires, as its two fresh-outta-high-school protagonists enjoy a last hurrah before heading to college and adulthood. Yet this film's heart is bigger than its groin. Director Vincent injects these characters with nuance and emotion, both rare traits in this critically forgotten film genre.

Good eggs Tracy (Darcey Hollingsworth, aka Davey Jones) and Gene (Bo White) are the best friends at *Blue Summer*'s core. The film begins as Tracy opens the garage door at his parents' house to reveal his newly festooned van, all ready for an epic road trip to Stony Lake. This van looks like it has weathered at least a decade of dust and use.

This is not a pimp van, though Tracy's attempts to make it one are charmingly low-rent. He has rigged together a crude sound system with wooden boards, a tape player, and a loudspeaker secured to the roof. The décor is resplendent with extremely 1970s-looking decals of flowers, Mickey Mouse, and white letters that reveal the vehicle's name: "The Meat Wagon." Before he leaves home, Tracy's doting mom hands him some extra money "just in case," then notices his ride and yells, "Tracy, what the hell did you do to that bus?"

In contrast to Tracy's everymom, Gene's parents are like future true crime fodder. In a cloud of secondhand chain smoke, his parents bitch and moan and nag at their son and each other. They are so absorbed in their dysfunctional cesspool that they don't notice Gene leaving the house with a steaming coffee pot, the toaster, and several bottles of vodka. He meets Tracy outside, saying, "Let's go! The shit's about to hit the fan!!"

Once on the road, the boys toast each other with cold brews: "Here's to incredible feats and chickies we meet!" Drinking and driving were more casual in the 1970s, when no ride to a nearby lake was complete without cranking up Bloodrock and downing a case of Hamm's.

Our heroes' journey is full of local color. They pick up a pair of foxy runaways named Bea (Lilly Bi Peep, a onetime-wonder) and Sparky (Joann Sterling); these young ladies prove to have plenty of moxie—and sticky fingers. Next the full van stops to help a spooky biker (Jeff Allen). Not every small-town roadside traveler in the movie is ripped on cheap speed and wearing swastika patches, though. Tracy and Gene also scoop up a long-winded religious kook, a happy capitalist with a white suit and a toothpaste smile. The man is from the Tabernacle of the Holy Souls, and asks for a ten-dollar entrance donation for "up there."

Stopping to change a flat tire in a wooded area, our lucky lads hear flute music. Following the lilting notes that fill the air, they stumble upon a long-haired guru flanked by two topless lovelies. He greets them like so: "Welcome to my home. Let me introduce you to my women!" The man, simply named "Roger" (Larry Lima), declines their offer of beer, but accepts their cigarettes. As the flute plays, the boys get friendly with redhead Liza (Shana McGran) and dark-haired Deborah (Amy Mathieu). This scene is so warm and playful, with the four all kissing in a group formation. The fact that Gene and Tracy are so comfortable with each other, with zero need for peacocking or alpha-male bigot moves, makes their friendship seem beautiful and admirable.

The journey next leads to a no-name diner in a no-nothing town, where they meet a golden-haired cool cat named Fred (Eric Edwards) He lets them know that the town is bereft of hot action, joking that the local women are locked up at sunset—except for one. What follows is something that could very easily play out in a Charles Bukowski story.

Fred promises the boys that a local lady named Regina (Melissa Evers) will be hot to trot if they bring her two cases of beer.

They grab fresh brews and make their way to a stunningly shitty shack for their fateful encounter. This Regina is the living, dripping definition of a blowsy blonde, and she's really one class act, reeking of cheap booze and snapping bon mots like, "I could dance all fucking night!" She burps and dances badly, gets cranky with the boys, and then proceeds to dance and then some with the happily willing Fred. In no hurry, Tracy and Gene stand around waiting for their turn until a loud gaggle of local redneck bullies shows up, straight out of a scenario by Texas exploitation wonder S. F. Brownrigg. Gunshots ensue, rednecks flee, and Regina may or may not be dead.

Eventually, our travelers reach the idyllic shores of Stony Lake. Tracy leaves to locate an attractive older woman to whom he had given directions earlier. He finds her white cottage, and the two have a touching love scene tinged with pregnant dread. Even the instrumental background music is melancholy compared to rest of the movie's upbeat, lightly rocking score by Sleepy Hollow.

Tracy's postcoital bliss sours fast, as his lover stammers about how she's never done anything like this before. Things get worse when her son stops over, and Tracy realizes they are clearly around the same age. Tracy takes his cue to split.

The episode has shaken poor Tracy, who has seen (and had sex with) the finality of aging and adulthood. All things must pass. Meanwhile, Gene remains innocently transfixed by a kooky, lithe blonde who keeps surprising him around the lake. She refuses to give him her name or any personal details, so Gene calls her "Miss No Name" (Chris Jordan, wife of porn star Eric Edwards). They make love, and Gene clearly wants to spend more time getting to know her. "That's not possible," she quips, and runs off for good.

Driving home so soon after what seemed like a very long trip to get to the lake, Tracy muses, almost hopefully: "There'll be other summers!"

Alas, Gene has also been transformed. He knows better: "No. Not like this one."

Gene is right. Reflecting on their rapidly evaporating youth, the boys hoist more road beers to toast all of the characters they met along the way to Stony Lake. They dedicate a final salute to school and freedom, then the van becomes quiet inside as our two men look glumly resigned to a future not purely their own to claim.

Without revealing Tracy and Gene's fates, *Blue Summer* tells us adult reality will force the pair to sacrifice personal freedom. The moment is sad-eyed gold, with a touch of blue. And then just like that, summer is over.

Boarding School [1978] aka Passion Flower Hotel

DIR. ANDRÉ FARWAGI; W/NASTASSJA KINSKI, GERRY SUNDQUIST, GABRIELE BLUM, FABIANA UDENIO

CATHOLIC GIRLS ▫ VIRGINS ▫ HOOKERS ▫ THE BIG STRIP CONTEST ▫ 1950S

The Swiss-made 1978 sex farce *Boarding School* opens with the one exact shot anyone who ever wanted to watch a Swiss 1978 sex farce specifically wants to see. The screen goes from blackness to—*boom!*—nude boob, landing in tight close-up on a dewy nubile's bare breast. There tit is.... The camera then eases back to show the entire pert pair, and then slowly reveals the soft-lit torso of eighteen-year-old starlet Vérnonique Delbourg as finishing academy student Marie-Louise. She is in a dorm room with about a dozen beds, conducting her "I must, I must, I must increase my bust" exercises.

Marie-Louise's giggling classmates surround her, each clad in a flimsy nightgown of the sort so apparently popular with upper-crust gals in 1956, when the movie is set. A handful of those cohorts have clearly put in their own exercise efforts. *Boarding School*'s first ten seconds, then, set a clear picture of where things are headed.

German ingénue and ascendant international screen star Nastassja Kinski emerges among the chuckling nymphs of St. Clara's Boarding School as Yank troublemaker Deborah Collins, who, while cooing with her gal pals about how antsy they all are to lose their virginity, hatches the world's oldest plot. With a boys' academy right across the lake from their own campus, Deborah reasons, she and the other budding Catholic sprites could charge visiting male students money to exercise the awakening adolescent instincts of all involved. The prospect works, small surprise, but not without a share of kookily comic complications—even smaller surprise.

The girls mount a striptease contest, enabling Nastassja to add a spark of surrealism by peeling out of a full-body alligator costume. Her reptilian artistry foreshadows the iconic 1981 *Vogue* magazine pose in which Nastassja wrapped herself nude in a giant, live python. Costar Fabiana Udenio grew up to portray Alota Fagina in *Austin Powers: International Man of Mystery* (1997). The worked-up and/or sleepless souls who subscribed to Showtime in the early '80s became intimately familiar with *Boarding School* by way of repeated overnight airings. Everybody else kind of saw it that way, too, by squinting through the scrambled channel blurs and monkeying with the cable box after their parents went to bed.

Body Waves [1992]

DIR. P. J. PESCE; W/BILL CALVERT, LEAH LAIL, LARRY LINVILLE, DICK MILLER

NERDS ▣ BIKINIS ▣ SKATEBOARDS ▣ JET SKIS ▣ HEMORRHOIDS ▣ BLOW-UP DOLL

A perfect opportunity to employ the British phrase "too clever by half," *Body Waves* is a deft, witty '80s-style teen sex comedy that somehow didn't appear until after the genre's sell-by date. College-age Rick (Bill Calvert) wants no part of Ano-Recto Cream—the family hemorrhoid ointment business—so his cranky old man (Dick Miller) gives him an ultimatum. In essence, the kid's got three weeks to raise three thousand dollars through any other means besides Ano-Recto Cream peddling, or he's out on the street.

Rick springs his surf-affected buddy Dooner (Jim Wise) from a Gilligan-themed seaside food stand and they order crates of Oil Slick suntan lotion from a parody comic book ad promising prizes or cash. They figure they can peddle the goo while lazing around on the beach. Nobody buys anything, naturally, but three unique nerds (one of whom has the same bizarre affected speech as Humpty Hump from early-'90s hip-hop crew Digital Underground) catch Rick's slick way with the ladies. They offer to pay Rick to impart his pickup wisdom.

This moneymaking scam works. A beach babe reads a calendar in the sun, flipping pages only to indicate when time passes. A call-in radio show includes a clip of the vintage prank-call classic Tube Bar tapes. Ano-Recto Cream proves to be an effective aphrodisiac placebo. The dorkular trio flop as faux-metalheads, but they find freak success as a rap group, the Goo Boys.

The whole cast commits fully to the nonsense, especially Larry Linville (Frank Burns of TV's *M*A*S*H*) as Mr. Himmel, an ersatz right-wing censorship crusader and secret nude-pool-party coke-fiend. He's out to shut down the rock radio station owned by guitar-shredding female lead Stacy (Leah Lail, later of Pam Anderson's *V.I.P.* series). Also look out for *Mad TV*'s young Michael McDonald as head dweeb Squirrely and punk tornado Texas Terri as one of Himmel's party girls. Both performers appear topless during a backyard pool scene. Guess which one has bosom-framing spiderweb tattoos?

The Breakfast Club [1985]

DIR. JOHN HUGHES; W/MOLLY RINGWALD, ANTHONY MICHAEL HALL, JUDD NELSON, EMILIO ESTEVEZ, ALLY SHEEDY

NERD ▣ JOCK ▣ DELINQUENT ▣ RICH GIRL ▣ ART FREAK ▣ VIRGINS ▣ WEED

In our popular consciousness, writer-director John Hughes' talky comedy-drama *The Breakfast Club* stands as the definitive 1980s teen film. You know what happens. Five conflicting high school archetypes are forced to spend an all-day detention together. Anthony Michael Hall is the brain, Emilio Estevez is the athlete, Ally Sheedy is the basket case, Molly Ringwald is the princess, and Judd Nelson is the criminal. Ultimately, all involved discover they have a lot more in common than anybody thought. Ain't that something? Also, these sixteen-year-olds are smarter than anybody else in the entire universe. Ain't that *really* something?

With Hughes so drastically stacking the deck in favor of teenagers versus the whole big bad adult world (Sheedy even emotes at one point, "When you grow up, your heart dies!"), *The Breakfast Club* connected soul-deep with young audiences. How could it not? Teens initially packed theaters to experience *The Breakfast Club* multiple times. Then they watched and rewatched it at home so they would never, ever forget how powerfully it moved them. Kids of a certain age grew up with their hearts on loan to hardscrabble Judd Nelson bemoaning the carton of cigarettes he got for Christmas from his abusive dad: "The old man grabbed me and said, 'Hey, smoke up, Johnny!'" (*Puke!* That complaint does beat Ferris Bueller's birthday lamentation of "I wanted a car; they got me a computer!")

From top: *The gang's all here! Teen movie archetypes—soon to be teen idols—all in a row* (L–R): *Judd Nelson, Emilio Estevez, Ally Sheedy, Molly Ringwald, and Anthony Michael Hall in* The Breakfast Club *(1985); advance marketing for a movie that would soon need no introduction; ...but not everyone takes school so seriously—see Rodney Dangerfield in* Back to School *(1986).*

Undeniably, *The Breakfast Club*'s cast swings for the fences, and each player connects. The teenagers themselves achieved a status beyond the mere iconic, with each performance, however rooted in existing tropes or clichés, effectively establishing a new archetype. In addition, Paul Gleason as chapped-ass Principal Vernon creates a villain of wondrous nostril expressiveness and an arsenal of idiosyncrasies you could resent forever. For example, he signals the number two not with a peace sign but by flashing devilish finger horns. That's a great touch. In addition, radio and MTV airwaves teemed inescapably with Simple Minds' presciently titled smash theme song, "Don't You Forget About Me." Decades later, there's no escape: Simple Minds still rules the store speakers at Walgreens, coloring every purchase of beginner tampons, pocket protectors, and cigarettes.

So criticize all you want how lip gloss and a mom-acceptable hairdo could "cure" creative oddball Ally Sheedy—*The Breakfast Club* stands as a generation-defining classic. Good, bad, indifferent, or nauseating and soul-shattering, Hughes' adolescent magnum opus did for 1980s teens what *Rebel Without a Cause* pulled off in the '50s and *Easy Rider* reinterpreted in the '60s. In the '70s, kids smoked their entertainment, so they were happy with other people's nostalgia via *American Graffiti* and *Animal House*.

Let's not gloss over what *The Breakfast House* cost us as a culture. Just as Walt Disney co-opted and assimilated the thrills of the traveling carnival or the seaside boardwalk, scrubbing away their danger while concocting the megacorporate theme park, John Hughes strip-mined '80s teen sex comedies. Hughes reversed the process of alchemy, transmogrifying these films' inherent madness into middle-of-the-road mush.

Sixteen Candles (1984) and *Weird Science* (1985) may have utilized dominant genre tools such as nudity and racial humor, but for Hughes, lowball tricks like that must have just been the price of doing business. Make no mistake—that guy was into *The Breakfast Club* as a business.

After this $1 million investment brought in $51 million in theaters, the property morphed into a never-ending cash geyser on cable TV and home video. On top of the financial windfall, *The Breakfast Club* also enabled studio executives to boast about scoring a youth hit without having to blush about fart gags, intoxicated dogs, and, if they had any shame, underage flesh.

The Breakfast Club successfully opened the decade's teen movie moment to female viewers. That's admirable. However, he also inspired film companies to stupidly try courting the newly enlarged audience by going mawkish and melodramatic. For an especially heinous example, witness the 1988 Molly Ringwald-Andrew McCarthy snooze *Fresh Horses*. Hughes himself hit the same dead end in 1987 when he remade his previous year's hit, *Pretty in Pink*, as the gender-flipped *Some Kind of Wonderful*.

As Hollywood adjusted its product down for the market-widening PG-13 rating, and teenage boys found bona fide pornography with increasing ease, the result was a post-*Porky's* apocalypse. The monstrous success of *The Breakfast Club* essentially bit off the genitals of the '80s teen sex comedy, chomped them into goo, and spewed forth the froth that steadily evolved into our present eterna-tween monoculture.

When you grow up, your heart may or may not die, but my favorite movie genre and all the liberating promise it contained definitely did, and here's where I lay the blame.

Breaking All the Rules

[1985]

DIR. JAMES ORR; W/CAROLYN DUNN, RACHEL HAYWARD, CARL MAROTTE, THOR BISHOPRIC

PUNKETTE ▫ NEW WAVERS ▫ BUMBLING CROOKS ▫ AMUSEMENT PARK ▫ SUMMER JOB

Spiky blonde teen Debbie (Carolyn Dunn) and her spunky sidekick Angie (Rachel Hayward), the rousing heroines of *Breaking All the Rules*, run wild through an amusement park, thereby distracting a pair smitten young male employees (Carl Marotte and the awesomely named Thor Bishopric) from properly working the premises. Boy oh boy, do rules ever start breaking then. Some clumsy thieves hide stolen jewels in a teddy bear that Debbie wins from a game stand. The crooks will do anything to get the bear back. In a similar way, hot new waver Carolyn will do anything to keep the movie audience interested, repeatedly showing off her panties emblazoned with the words "I Love You."

As a high-energy romp set among cool old carnival rides, *Breaking All the Rules* is okay but counts as some weak (and non-spiked) iced tea considering cowriter Rafal Zielinski previously directed both *Screwballs* (1983) and *Loose Screws* (1985). The hormonally overloaded bowling-ball-boffing character Melvin Jerkovski from *Screwballs* would be sadly disappointed in this PG-13 follow-up.

Buford's Beach Bunnies
[1993]

DIR. MARK PIRRO; W/JIM HANKS, RIKKI BRANDO, MONIQUE PARENT, KITTEN NATIVIDAD

NERD ▣ RACE TO TAKE VIRGINITY ▣ BIKINIS ▣ FAST FOOD ▣ CARTOON SOUND EFFECTS ▣ STRIP-O-GRAM ▣ WAITRESSES IN BUNNY COSTUMES ▣ SURFER DUDE NAMED SURFER DUDE

Jim Hanks stars as Jeeter Buford, a spastic nerd who is terrified of women. Jeeter's crusty old man, Harry Buford (Barrett Cooper), is the founder of Buford's Bunny Hole, a restaurant empire built on barbecued rabbit meat. Harry believes his schmuck son will stop going into psychedelic terrors at the mere glimpse of a female if the dorkus can somehow just get laid. Thus begins our adventure.

To assist viewers unaware that Jim Hanks was the Z-list younger brother of Tom Hanks, his name appears on the video box in the same typeface in which his elder sibling's name appeared on the poster for *Big* (1988). Also hitting viewers over the head with a hammer, the "Bunny Hole" waitresses wear screaming pink rabbit lingerie as uniforms. Yet despite how clearly the movie pushes its assets, everything becomes insanely complicated once Harry promises $100,000 to the Bunny Hole server who plucks Jeeter's cherry. Centerfold-stacked waitresses Boopsie Underall (Suzanne Ager), Amber Dextrous (Monique Parent), and Lauren Beatty (Rikki Brando) agree to the challenge while plus-size new manager Beula Lugosi (Ina Rogers) never quite crams her amplitude into a Bunny Hole costume and disciplines wayward employees by sitting on their faces (fetishists take note, it happens more than once).

En route to naked nerd-vana, Jeeter's journey brings him into the insane orbits of Russ Meyer mamazon Kitten Natividad as a brothel madam; a hypnotist called the Amazing Foreskin (David Robinson); and the horny mortician Dr. Van Horney (Robyn Webb). Even in sleep Jeeter finds no comfort, as his nightmares are populated by celebrity lookalikes of Humphrey Bogart, Clint Eastwood, and Marilyn Monroe. The zany happenings are all quite rib-tickling. Impressively, the movie's batshit contents remain off-the-wall while never entirely flying off the rails.

The title *Buford's Beach Bunnies* is misspelled in the movie's opening credits as: "*Bufford's* Beach Bunnies" with two "f"s. That says a lot—all of it good—about Pirromount Pictures, the production company of writer-director-editor-perpetrator Mark Pirro. Astoundingly, cutting a few corners here and there has allowed Pirromount to survive for four decades now, periodically releasing new gems in the vein of *Buford* and its forerunners *A Polish Vampire in Burbank* (1983) and *Nudist Colony of the Dead* (1991).

CADDYSHACK • CALIFORNIA DREAMING • CALIFORNIA GIRLS • CALIFORNIA HOT WAX • CAMPUS MAN • CAN IT BE LOVE • CAN'T BUY ME LOVE • CAREER OPPORTUNITIES • CAVEGIRL • CHEERING SECTION • CHEERLEADER CAMP • THE CHEERLEADERS • CHEERLEADERS WILD WEEKEND • CHERRY HILL HIGH • THE CHICKEN CHRONICLES • CLASS • CLASS OF '44 • CLASS REUNION • COACH • COMBAT ACADEMY • COMPUTER BEACH PARTY • COOLEY HIGH

CADDYSHACK [1980]

DIR. HAROLD RAMIS; W/MICHAEL O'KEEFE, CHEVY CHASE, BILL MURRAY, RODNEY DANGERFIELD

SUMMER JOB • RICH JERKS • PRANKS • RODENTS • THE BIG GOLF GAME

In popular memory, *Caddyshack* is a movie about a war between old men, elderly combatants Judge Smails (Ted Knight), overlord of the ultra-snooty Bushwood Country Club; and good-time vulgarian Al Czervik (Rodney Dangerfield), a loud, gross glop of new money who invades Bushwood's pristine greens like the proverbial Barbarian gate-crasher. One rung down is thirty-ish smooth shooter Ty Webb (Chevy Chase), a ne'er-do-well Bushwood legacy who has elevated laid-back hedonism to a state of Zen. Ty's through-the-cracked-fun-house-mirror avatar is shambling, shot-to-shit assistant groundskeeper Carl Spackler (Bill Murray), a human trash heap who engages the film's famously pesky golf course gopher in apocalyptic combat.

At its core, though, *Caddyshack* is primarily the story of Michael O'Keefe as seventeen-year-old Danny Noonan, an Irish-Catholic upstart (he looks to be one of about thirteen siblings) who is spending the summer schlepping clubs around Bushwood Country Club to save money for college. Along the way, he almost knocks up an exchange student from the Emerald Isles (Sarah Holcomb), and gets caught sinking his driver into the judge's troublemaking niece Lacey Underall (Cindy Morgan). During the movie's climactic golf contest, in which a scholarship and Danny's soul hang in the balance, he chooses sides in the conflict promised by *Caddyshack*'s poster tagline: *"It's the slobs against the snobs!"*

Caddyshack's background and larger themes gushed directly into the bawdy blowout youth farces of the next five years every bit as its spiritual predecessor, *Animal House* (1978). In some ways, the targets were dialed even more precisely. *National Lampoon* cofounder Doug Kenney, the bona fide genius who cowrote *Animal House*, teamed with writer and performer Brian Doyle-Murray to craft this screenplay based on their teen years working as country club golf caddies in the Chicago suburbs. The original drafts of *Caddyshack*, right up until the shooting

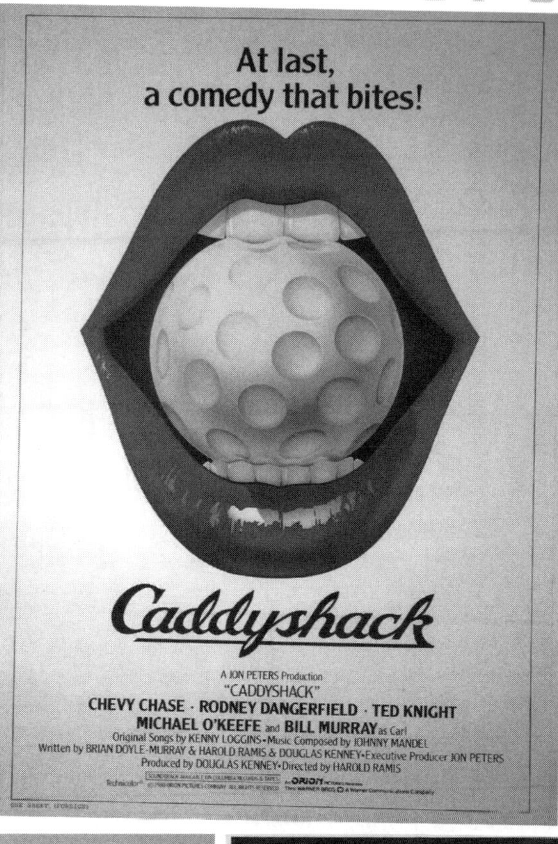

The good news is Jonathan's having his first affair.

The bad news is she's his roommate's mother.

A MARTIN RANSOHOFF Production A LEWIS JOHN CARLINO Film "CLASS"
ROB LOWE JACQUELINE BISSET ANDREW McCARTHY and CLIFF ROBERTSON
Music by ELMER BERNSTEIN Executive Producer CATHLEEN SUMMERS
Written by JIM KOUF & DAVID GREENWALT Produced by MARTIN RANSOHOFF
Directed by LEWIS JOHN CARLINO ORION PICTURES Release

Clockwise from top left: The Cheerleaders *(1973), the smash that injected raw raunch into teen fun; no Bill Murray on this* Caddyshack *(1980) teaser poster*; Cavegirl *(1985), a* cable staple on USA Up All Night; California Girls *(1983), a genuine sunbaked oddity; Class* (1983).

script, focus overwhelmingly on Danny Noonan, in particular his rivalry with fellow caddy Tony D'Annunzio (Scott Colomby), an Italian "guido," making the pair two white ethnic untouchables in Bushwood's WASP garden of exclusivity.

The film transformed when Rodney Dangerfield came aboard, in place of the makers' first choice, Don Rickles. Rodney's ad-libs and improvisations simply eclipsed all previous plans. Thus, *Caddyshack*'s Bluto Blutarsky—the anarchic, irresistible destroyer-god heart of the film—became a sixty-year-old Borscht Belt comic. For further specimens of gray-haired party animals romping with teens, look no further than Dangerfield's own *Back to School* (1986).

In a very specific way, *Caddyshack* defined the "before" side of a line in '80s teen comedies that is clearly divided by *Sixteen Candles* (1984). The entire John Hughes canon that followed defines the "after" portion. The difference is crucial. Like Doug Kenney, Hughes was a *National Lampoon* editor, but their sympathies are polar opposites. The Noonan family of *Caddyshack* is based on the Chicagoland Murray clan that gave us Bill and Brian Doyle-Murray. They are loud, chaotic, packed into cramped conditions, and driving one another nuts while doing exhaustive labor for every dollar they pocket. These are the "slobs." Consider, by contrast, the family in *Sixteen Candles*. They also live just outside Chicago, but in a million-dollar suburban monument to proper manners and respectable taste. When bustling relatives invade for a special event, the high school protagonist bemoans the toll it takes on her weekend as a tragedy. We're supposed to feel her pain. She has been raised as, and we are being conditioned to revere her as, a snob.

More pointedly: Ferris Bueller would be a member of Bushwood. Danny Noonan would be his servant. John Hughes views—and sells—Ferris Bueller as a hero. *Caddyshack* depicts its Ferris Bueller archetype as Spaulding Smails (John F. Barmon Jr.), a mewling, despicable, entitled slug who properly inspires Rodney Dangerfield to snarl, "Now I know why tigers eat their young!"

So following this varmint down the gopher hole, the battle between the slobs and the snobs was played out in teen sex comedies. Whenever anyone anywhere invokes the John Hughes titles as the definitive coming-of-age films of the 1980s, it's a clarion declaration of victory. The snobs came out on top.

CALIFORNIA DREAMING [1979]

DIR. JOHN D. HANCOCK; W/DENNIS CHRISTOPHER, GLYNNIS O'CONNOR, SEYMOUR CASSEL, TANYA ROBERTS

VIRGIN ▫ BIKINIS ▫ BEACH PEOPLE ▫ SURFERS ▫ THE BIG CORVETTE CHALLENGE

Dennis Christopher stands as one of cinema's most peculiar attempts to mold a leading-man type out of ninety-eight pounds of mewling, squeaky-voiced nimrodism. Even when he stands flawlessly straight, Dennis Christopher seems to embody the very essence of "bad posture."

Christopher's most substantial film, the acclaimed *Breaking Away* (1979), casts him as a Midwestern wannabe-Italian bicycle race champion. The movie's great, but left him no closer to heartthrob status. The curious horror flick *Fade to Black* (1980) is Christopher's most enduring cult success. The movie is terrible, but his Gollum-like ooziness as a cinema-obsessed serial murderer makes everything work. To date, Christopher's best, and most credible, performance occurs in the postapocalyptic sci-fi jaunt *Circuitry Man* (1990), where he plays a sewer-dweller named Leech who chomps and slurps phallic slugs that spew goo.

So the makers of *California Dreaming* must have been nuts to showcase Dennis Christopher as T.T., a Chicago transplant who takes to SoCal sun and surf with totally tubular gusto. Toting around his dead brother's trumpet, T.T. walks off a bus and into a seaside bar owned by gruff guru Duke Slusarski (ace character actor Seymour Cassel). Duke is a former Olympic swimmer who hates himself for getting old. Diving from that high point straight into standard nonsense, T.T. goes gaga for surfer chick Corky (Glynnis O'Connor) and soon loses his virginity to her. Meanwhile, her wave-riding passion provides the movie with a solid twenty minutes of cowabunga B-roll footage. A subplot injects beach-com zaniness as hot-dog hodad Earl (Ned Wynn) accepts a challenge to live inside his car for a month in order to win a snazzy new Corvette.

California Dreaming was one of the very last releases from American International Pictures (AIP). Producer Roger Corman's long-lasting studio had invented the beach party genre on the bathing-suited backs of Frankie Avalon and Annette Funicello in the mid-'60s. The special sensibilities director John D. Hancock gleaned after making the shocker *Let's Scare Jessica to Death* (1971) and the Robert De Niro baseball tearjerker *Bang the Drum Slowly* (1973) amplify this movie's uniqueness.

The *California Dreaming* soundtrack features the title track by the Mamas and the Papas as performed by mellow-rock titans America, as well as multiple originals by Guess Who front man Burton Cummings. Circa 1979, these were all viable music stars, so one wonders what high grade of California dream could have attracted them to this low-budget, mildly seamy project.

California Girls [1983]

DIR. WILLIAM WEBB; W/AL MUSIC, LANTZ DOUGLAS, MARY MCKINLEY, ALICIA ALLEN

RADIO DJ ▣ BIKINIS ▣ MOONING ▣ HOT TUBS ▣ SKATEBOARDS ▣ AEROBICS

This *California Girls* is not the 1985 TV movie starring Robby Benson. The latter is more of a rom-com than a youth sex romp. Another difference is that this *California Girls* is not a fully competent film. Here, grape-shaped radio jock Mad Man Jack (Al Music) spins the rock hits with high Panama-hatted, jowl-bearded, suspenders-and-jeans style. When his buzzkill boss at KRZY-FM announces that ratings have dropped for the third period in a row, the Mad Man remarks: "We need excitement like the way things used to be—before everyone went to country and western!"

Mad Man Jack announces a $10,000 KRZY contest to find "The Most Outrageous Girl in California!" The phones light up, advertisers pledge to sponsor the endeavor, and so begins one of the most mind-liquefying exercises ever mounted on reels of celluloid film holding motion-picture images and Top 40 toe-tappers.

"Hey, Mad Man Jack," the first call-in responder proclaims, "I've got to nominate my sister as the most outrageous girl in California. She's such a fitness fanatic, she *jogs* to her tennis lessons!" Mad Man approvingly roars—he never howls, lest anyone alert the lawyers of a certain Wolfman deejay. "Rapture" by Blondie then accompanies a montage of Golden State beauties running in the sun, followed by still more lovelies volleying on outdoor courts.

In essence, *California Girls* consists almost completely of that one sequence repeated over and over again. A guy calls in and nominates a certain woman or women for the $10K crown based on her favorite Pacific-style physical pastime, then Mad Man reacts, and soon a pseudo-music video plays out depicting ladies engaged in the activity at hand. That's the movie. Female bodybuilders pump iron at Gold's Gym to "Brass in Pocket" by the Pretenders. Mountain gals hang-glide to "I'm Not in Love" by 10cc. Aerobicizers twist and thrust to "De Doo Doo Doo De Da Da Da" by the Police. A martial arts sensei with a predictably anti-p.c. "Joe Jitsu" Asian accent sets up a karate demonstration set to "Knock on Wood" by Amii Stewart. Foxy boxers brawl with giant inflatable gloves to "Ladies Night" by Kool and the Gang. And so on.

Two interstitial gimmicks break up the formula. One is man-on-the-street interviews on the topic of California girls. The other depicts three hotsy-totsy female fans of Mad Man Jack on the street outside his studio window. They conspire to win the contest by way of nude roller-skating—one imitates Lady Godiva while riding naked atop the other two in a horse costume.

You'll either flee screaming from *California Girls* well before Mad Man Jack jokes about a gay midget nicknamed "Sweet-N-Low," or you'll be mesmerized before the movie's every brain-mangling moment. The first reaction would be sensible—the second one was mine.

California Hot Wax [1992] aka Bikini Carwash

DIR. JAN MARLYN REESMAN (AS JAN MARLYN); W/GLORIA NELSON, JODY BRADLEY, ROBIN JAMESON

BIKINIS ▪ EVIL LANDLORD ▪ SEX SAVES THE BUSINESS

Devotees of early-'90s soapy female swimsuit montages set to generic mousse metal definitely do exist. *California Hot Wax* exemplifies that movie ideally, setting up three silicone-soiled SoCal exhibitionists who rescue a struggling car wash by showing off their plastic surgery disasters. And that is all they do.

A half-nod for gumption goes to *California Hot Wax*'s reissue as *Bikini Carwash,* featuring a box-cover logo with a gas pump *sort of* shaped like a "3." That con job hints that this film might be an official sequel to the senseless *The Bikini Carwash Company* franchise. Of course, it's not.

Campus Man [1987]

DIR. RON CASDEN; W/JOHN DYE, MORGAN FAIRCHILD, STEVEN LYON, MILES O'KEEFE

HUNK CALENDAR ▪ GET-RICH-QUICK SCHEME ▪ GROUP SHOWERS ▪ BIKER BAR

Campus Man is one for the ladies—especially ladies who are men that like to have sex with other men. Yes, *Campus Man* is that rarest of '80s teen sex rollicks, a true slab of hunksploitation, where the camera's intensely directed eye is focused exclusively on gorgeous dudes with can-do 'tudes. Though the "PG" rating precludes any real southern pole exposure, devotees of dudely pubis mounds are still in for a hot time.

Arizona State University student and fast-talking opportunist Todd (John Dye), who previously scored a dorm-room publishing hit with a "Girls of ASU" calendar, suddenly finds himself in a $100K back-tuition hole. Gleaning sweaty, exquisitely lit inspiration from his ripped blond swim-team-captain roommate, Brett (Steven Lyon), Todd plots a "Guys of ASU" follow-up. Things quickly take a homoerotic turn.

To print the calendar, Todd secures twelve thousand dollars from Cactus Jack, a loan shark with even more pulsating muscles than handfuls of hair gel in his mega-mullet. Miles O'Keefe, the vine-swinger from 1981 Bo Derek opus *Tarzan the Ape Man*, portrays Cactus Jack, and he fared much better in his earlier nonspeaking role. Cash in hand, Todd barges into the school's shower room to pitch his calendar, while the entire swim team continues soaping, flexing, and supplying what must have been a severe case of the vapors to some desperate single male moviegoers circa 1987.

From there, *Campus Man* erupts into a photo-shoot montage set to Timbuk 3's "The Future's So Bright, I Gotta Wear Shades." One drooling visual testament after another to the grandeur of beefcake is clipped together via dopey subplots such as Morgan Fairchild as a sexy-bitchy fashion-mag editor who accidentally gets Brett kicked off the swim squad (*not* by seducing him, rest assured). Todd and Brett undergo a tearful split before making up at a biker bar. Cactus Jack gets paid. No female anywhere near this movie, the theater, or the video store got laid.

Can It Be Love [1992] aka Spring Break Sorority Babes

DIR. PETER MARIS; W/CHARLES KLAUSMEYER, RICHARD BEAUMONT, MARY ANN MIXON, BLAKE PICKETT

SPRING BREAK ▪ SORORITY ▪ CHEERLEADERS ▪ LOCKER ROOM ▪ WET-T-SHIRT CONTEST ▪ SURFERS ▪ SKATEBOARDS ▪ HAIR METAL ▪ LINGERIE SHOP

Semi-nerdy, semi-cool college-age bro-dudes Tim (Charles Klausmeyer) and David (Richard Beaumont) aim their convertible toward Fort Lauderdale just in time for spring break...

but first they join a detective agency. The sudden gumshoe setup is an inexplicable move on par with the producers of this fake-boobs-and-harsh-lighting soft-core piffle changing its title at some point between the final cut and its arrival in video stores from the bodaciously promising *Spring Break Sorority Babes* to the rom-com-reeking *Can It Be Love*.

The two young dicks take the case of a well-to-do sorority sister who's gone missing among the South Florida's beach bonfires, lingerie outlets, and nudie dancing facilities. Forces that would prefer to keep the heiress vamoosed dispatch a Mohawk-headed mountain of muscle named Pigiron (Wally "the Wall" Mueller) to thwart the rescue effort via half-assed slapstick and quarter-assed punch lines. "I'll be *bock*," he warns in the requisite Terminator accent.

Meanwhile, the thong-drenched production doles out ample examples of how bikini-clad backsides appeared weirdly *long* in early-'90s swimwear. The movie also showcases the final fling of Sunset Strip glam-metal group Dillinger performing the title track while the flick's lovable characters cavort alongside them onstage.

Can't Buy Me Love [1987]

DIR. STEVE RASH; W/PATRICK DEMPSEY, AMANDA PETERSON, COURTNEY GAINES

NERDS 📼 CHEERLEADER 📼 SCHOOL DANCE 📼 TEEN HOOKERS

In Disney Studios' neatest feel-good prostitution comedy until the company backed *Pretty Woman* three years later, Patrick Dempsey stars as Ronald, a high-school nebbish who offers a cool grand earned by mowing lawns to radiant cheerleader Cindy Mancini (Amanda Peterson) if she'll pretend to be his girlfriend for a month. Lucky for young Ron, budding glamour-puss Cindy needs fast cash to repair her mom's fur coat after splattering it with red wine at a party. Also, she's sort of cool with being a hooker.

True to the film's working title, *Boy Rents Girl*, Ronald and Cindy's deal is made in a flash, but the john soon falls hard for his purchase. Eventually, the heart of gold beating within the glowingly blonde, suburban cousin of Jodie Foster in *Taxi Driver* succumbs to her customer's messianic impulses. In the end, while the familiar Beatles tune swells before the closing credits, the buyer and the seller sail off to a happy tomorrow onboard the very riding mower that made their transaction possible. Ain't commerce grand?

Appalling premise aside, *Can't Buy Me Love*'s best feature is the dork cabal with whom Ronald hangs out prior to learning that, yes indeed, you *can* buy yourself love. Leading the loser parade is the perpetually stupendous Courtney Gaines (Rag in *Hardbodies*, Malachi in *Children of the Corn*) as Kenneth Wurman. Gaines emotes for the Oscar—and goddammit, he should have gotten one. He breaks down in a video arcade, explosively revealing his hurt after Ronald ditched him to join with the jocks in pulling cruel pranks on former nerd pals. Particularly galling was when football goons pressured Ron into hurling dog feces at Kenneth's home. "*You shit on my house!*" Kenneth rages, slamming his former friend up against a Centipede machine. Choking back tears, he whispers: "You…*shit*…on…my…*house*."

Dempsey, Gaines, Seth Green, and a number of other young stars from *Can't Buy Me Love* went on to high-profile acting careers. Sadly, the same didn't happen for Amanda Peterson, who exuded more natural screen power than the rest of the cast combined. Like Joyce Hyser in *Just One of the Guys*, Amanda was essentially one-and-done after *Can't Buy Me Love*. Still, audiences never forgot her or the movie. Sadly, Amanda died at age forty-three in 2015 under what seemed to be unhappy circumstances. Meanwhile, *Can't Buy Me Love*, like the profession that serves as its plot device, will continue to transact forever.

CAREER OPPORTUNITIES [1991]

DIR. BRYAN GORDON; W/FRANK WHALEY, JENNIFER CONNELLY, DERMOT MULRONEY, JOHN CANDY

TEENAGE DEADBEAT ▪ RETAIL JOB ▪ RICH GIRL ▪ BUMBLING CROOKS

Shaking off his first-wave conquest of pop puberty, John Hughes broke ground on a new cinematic empire in 1990 by penning *Home Alone*. He promptly cashed in that clout by revamping his successful slapstick invasion fantasy for teenagers in the form of *Career Opportunities*. He later aged down the formula to infant level for *Baby's Day Out* (1994). Weirdo.

In the teenager version of Hughes' favorite tale, Jim Dodge (Frank Whaley) is a youthful, working class layabout whose ballbuster old man orders him to get a job at the local Target store. Through happenstance, Jim is locked overnight in the store with Josie McLellan (Jennifer Connelly), the vision of loveliness upon whom he had crushed silently throughout his high school years.

Josie is a stacked stunner beyond reason, *and* she's carrying $52,000 in her purse that she pilfered from her jerky, big-shot biz-exec dad (Noble Willingham). While at first she doesn't quite see Jim as the knight-in-a-shining-red-Target-vest of her dreams, things progressively change after two bumbling burglars (Dermot and Kieran Mulroney) crash through the ceiling and enliven Jim and Josie's wee-hours bonding session. Plenty of product placement and poignant pauses ensue.

Despite endless claims to the contrary, the original *Dawn of the Dead* (1979) never struck me one bit as satirical commentary on consumer culture by creator George Romero; I maintain that the plot of that zombie classic was an excuse for Romero and his buddies to live the dream of using all the stuff in a shopping mall for free and gleefully wrecking the joint in the process. *Career Opportunities* essentially serves the same function in teen comedy form. But where *Dawn of the Dead* delivers on the blood and guts, Jim and Josie take no advantage of Target's inflatable mattresses and lingerie department. That's pure Hughes. He could never forgo an opportunity to run screaming from sex and instead hurl everything in the direction of slam-bam Rube Goldberg–esque booby-trap gags. One more time, for lasting effect, then—what a weirdo.

CAVEGIRL [1985]

DIR. DAVID OLIVER; W/DANIEL ROEBUCK, CYNTHIA THOMPSON, DARREN YOUNG, MICHELLE BAUER

NERD ▪ VIRGIN ▪ BULLIES ▪ PEEPING ▪ LOCKER ROOM ▪ HOLLYWOOD PARODY

In *Cavegirl,* leading lump Daniel Roebuck has a face like the heel of a bloated foot with a couple of Ping-Pong-ball eyes set deep inside the fleshiest part of the instep. His inherent hulking discomfort is terrifically off-putting for his role as girlfriend-killer Samson "John" Tullet in the headbanger tragedy *River's Edge* (1987). As science geek adventurer Rex here, though, Roebuck and his face fade into the background of his pseudo-Neanderthal tribe of dolled-up B-movie bimbos-before-time wearing faux-mammoth-fur bikinis.

As *Cavegirl* opens in a SoCal high school, Rex could easily and logically be mistaken for a teacher. He's a lumbering dolt an ill-fitting Indiana Jones outfit, nastily harassed by hooligans and failing to charm female students even as he spies on their locker room. The idea that nobody likes this zero is easy to believe.

On a class trip to a desert cave, however, Rex rubs a couple of crystals and is transported back to prehistoric times. There he finds a passel of dopey comedy-standard cave folk, the most highly evolved of whom is blonde bombshell Eba (Cynthia Thomson). Rex's initial come-on is pretty blunt: "I'm lost, and you don't speak any English, would you like to sit on my face?"

The remainder of *Cavegirl* mainly consists of Rex attempting to bed Eba by dazzling her with advanced technological tricks, such as making a fire and building a comfy love nest. The other cavepeople supply slapstick gags and fling their boogers around. Intentionally weak action sequences depict Rex fending off a mountain lion, a bear, a volcano, and cannibals.

USA Up All Night aired *Cavegirl* routinely, to the delight of unaccompanied minors with basic cable everywhere. Fans of the film celebrate that warm memory. Nostalgia really can be a club with which to beat all sense out of one's self like a Neanderthal whomping a mammoth.

Cheering Section [1977]

DIR. HARRY KERWIN; W/RHONDA FOX, TOM LEINDECKER, PATRICIA MICHELLE

CHEERLEADERS ▫ JOCKS ▫ BIKINI CAR WASH ▫ VANS

Almost entirely forgotten now, the coming-of-age college basketball drama *One on One* was one of 1977's biggest hits. *Tiger Beat* pinup Robby Benson became a star afterward, and the movie temporarily created the trope of the noble young player enduring sadistic trials at the command of a coach out to break him. Launched in 1978 for bookworms and the elderly, the TV series *The Paper Chase* presented the Harvard law school variation as evidence in this case.

High school football cheapie *Cheering Section* seized upon this trend quickly and ran for the goalposts. When jock star Corey (Tom Leindecker) falls on impact for new-blonde-on-campus Melanie (Rhonda Fox), he instantly forsakes chasing all other pom-pom hotties. Nonetheless, Melanie turns out to be the daughter of a freshly imported hard-ass football coach. That conflict plays out as expected—lots of laps, push-ups, and shouting.

Cheering Section is breezy and peppered with cute nudity. Two standout elements project the sexual politics of the time. First, the football players decorate their custom vans by slapping a pussycat sticker on rear bumpers for each mattress-in-the-back conquest. Also, the home team wagers their cheerleading squad against that of their rivals just prior to the big game. There's a reason "women's lib" took off in the 1970s, you know.

Cheerleader Camp [1988] aka Bloody Pom Poms

DIR. JOHN QUINN; W/BETSY RUSSELL, LEIF GARRETT, LUCINDA DICKEY, GEORGE "BUCK" FLOWER

CHEERLEADERS ▫ MASCOT ▫ PRANKS ▫ NERD GIRL ▫ SEX TAPE ▫ MAD SLASHER

The spoofy horror splat-comedy *Cheerleader Camp* takes place at Camp Hurrah, summertime training ground for Lindo Valley College's pom-pom shakers. Sounds like a gas, except that a psycho killer is seriously pooping their pep squad party.

Ruling the assembled rah-rah roost are pom-pom power couple Alison Wentworth (Betsy Russell), head cheerleader supreme; and Brent Hoover (Leif Garrett), her cool-dude boyfriend—well, as cool as balding Leif Garrett in white ball-hugger shorts could be in 1988.

Also taking up tent space are the blubber-coated barrel-of-laughs Timmy (Travis McKenna); potential pyramid-topper Pam (Teri Weigel); and quiet Cory (Lucinda Dickey), who is ragged on repeatedly for being the (completely hot) loser wearing the furry mascot costume. Prissy fuss Miss Tipton (Vickie Benson) runs the camp in cahoots with handyman Pop (George "Buck" Flower) and local lawman Sheriff Poucher (Jeff Prettyman). We get to know a few other cheerleaders just enough to slightly miss them after a mysterious figure begins slaughtering them with garden tools.

Cheerleader Camp has held up commendably. Director John Quinn and the capable cast deliver good gross-out kills that are not diminished by a jokey atmosphere rooted in classic teen sex comedy traditions. For example, Brent swaps a recording of the practice cheer routines with a sex tape of Miss Tipton and the sheriff enjoying football-themed fornication.

Some points deserve extra cheers. Travis McKenna, the fat guy, is a contender for fattest guy in the whole fat history of teen movie fat guys.

When he hangs a bare-assed full moon out of a van window toward Miss Tipton, it looks like NASA could land a manned rocket on that dimpled white mass. Lucinda Dickey, the messed-with mascot, shows nice range after her historic turn as the white chick in both *Breakin'* (1984) and *Breakin' II: Electric Boogaloo* (1985). Teri Weigel believably embodies bikini-tossing temptress Pam. Teri was the first *Playboy* Playmate (April 1986) to become a hardcore porn star, taking one or more for the home team in *American Bukkake 7* (1999).

THE CHEERLEADERS [1973] aka RETURN TO MONTCLAIR HIGH

DIR. PAUL GLICKLER; W/STEPHANIE FONDUE, DENISE DILLAWAY, JOVITA BUSH, RICHARD MEATWHISTLE

CHEERLEADERS ▫ JOCKS ▫ VIRGIN ▫ THE BIG GAME ▫ GROUP SHOWERS ▫ PEEPING ▫ WATERBED ▫ SEXY CAR WASH

Any celebration of over-the-top(less), hard-raunch high school T&A comedies should begin with *The Cheerleaders.* Surely some pre-game excitement emerged in grindhouses and drive-ins prior to *The Cheerleaders* and its history-making 1973 coast-to-coast rollout, but this movie blew the whistle for the kickoff of the ethos, aesthetics, and light-blue-movie blueprints for every ensuing big-screen puberty burlesque from *Porky's* (1981) to *American Pie* (1999).

The spritely spirit-boosters of Amarosa High School run things with a cocksure coolness that surpasses even that of the football jocks for whom they jump, split, and shake a tit. Squad leader Claudia (Denise Dillaway) benevolently lords over tawny-hued rhyme-dropper Bonnie (Jovita Bush), redheaded fornication fiend Debbie (Brandy Woods), curly-topped casaba-flasher Suzie (Clair Dia), and bouncy blonde bosom-barer Patty (Kimberly Hyde). Punky-coifed freshman—and virgin—Jeannie (Stephanie Fondue) eyeballs the pom-pom posse while they change outfits in the gym locker room amidst Donny Osmond and Engelbert Humperdinck pinups. She *really* longs to join their ranks. As long as Jeannie is capable of taking her clothes off, it's just a matter of time.

Once the roster is introduced, *The Cheerleaders* leaps into sexual set pieces equally as graphic as the nudie magazines of its era—which is more than audiences expected back then *or* today. The bulk of these carnal encounters twinkle with comic elements, such as when Claudia bangs Amarosa High hustler Jon (Richard Meatwhistle) while they ride through the Big Beaver Car Wash.

Jeannie's initiation into the pep squad requires her to take a shower with the entire naked football team. The jocks pile on Jeannie repeatedly, filling the screen with soap suds, studly butts, and heaps of hairy, flapping penises. Ultimately, the athletes' seeming embrace of sudden homoeroticism spares Jeannie the complications of being deflowered in so populous a setting as everybody just sort of group-gropes and the movie moves on to the next bit.

Along the way, the cheerleaders strut, strip, and partake in private parts belonging to (among others) an anal-intercourse-obsessed head football coach, a horny hamburger slinger, a lesbian gym teacher, and a school bus driver who indulges while driving his school bus. Also spotted around campus: an all-nude water slide; a creep janitor who spies on the girls through peepholes; and a midget who gives miniature-golf lessons.

The night before Amarosa's big game against gridiron rivals Central City High, the cheerleaders bust up their own see-through-nightie slumber party with a brilliant plan to go fuck the Central City players to the point of exhaustion so Amarosa can run roughshod over them in the morning. The mass seduction takes a self-defeating turn when members from both teams show up for what explodes into a mass orgy among impressively experienced high school students. In the end, everybody is wiped out come game time, except for the Central City quarterback and somehow-still-virginal Jeannie, who promptly get to work on the twist ending.

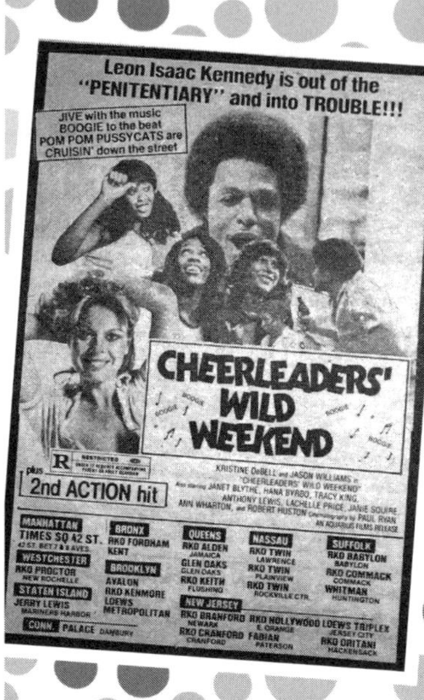

Clockwise from top left: Cheerleader Camp *(1988);* Computer Beach Party *(1987); newspaper ad for the 1982 rerelease of* Cheerleaders Wild Weekend *(1979) highlighting Leon Isaac Kennedy in* Penitentiary II *(1982);* The Chicken Chronicles *by Paul Diamond, adapted for Steve Guttenberg in 1977;* Combat Academy *(1986);* Cooley High *(1975), aka "The Black* American Graffiti.*"*

The Cheerleaders rocks like a droll, crazy, and unforgettable pep squad hottie doing a cartwheel to reveal she forgot her panties. Director Paul Glickler drew inspiration from the long-running 3-D girls-out-of-uniform smash *The Stewardesses* (1969) and built something even better. He cast *The Cheerleaders* with nude models, first-attempt actors, and real recently graduated football players (one of whom turned out to be future Los Angeles Ram Carl Ekern). Even ballsier, Glickler shot *The Cheerleaders* on and around the campus of Cupertino, California's Monta Vista High School, creating a situation for which some real-life school administration types most likely had to answer later.

The Cheerleaders' celebration of explicit sexuality among underage characters garnered the movie an X rating. In 1973, however, "X" really just meant "adults only," not specifically full-penetration pornography. (Though *The Cheerleaders*' concurrent off-Hollywood blockbuster, *Deep Throat* would soon change that). Running in theaters worldwide for the better part of a decade, *The Cheerleaders* grossed the modern equivalent of well over $100 million against an investment of $153,000. Occasionally, a small-town prosecutor would rumble about pressing obscenity charges against the film, but the rise of real sex on camera usually meant the forces of morality had bigger fish to fry. (Again, thank *Deep Throat*.)

The Swinging Cheerleaders (1974) and *Revenge of the Cheerleaders* (1976), each a classic in its own right, are official follow-ups. Unofficially, every film covered in this compendium from 1973 onward owes the original a debt. *The Cheerleaders* is the Book of Genesis of slapstick adolescent cherry-pop nut-and-gut-busters. Praise be!

Cheerleaders Wild Weekend [1979]

aka The Great American Girl Robbery; Bus 17 Is Missing

DIR. JEFF WERNER; W/KRISTINE DEBELL, JASON WILLIAMS, MARILYN JOI, LEON ISAAC KENNEDY

CHEERLEADERS ◘ FLASHING ◘ SCHOOL BUS ANTICS ◘ TOPLESS BEAUTY CONTEST ◘ LESBIAN BATH ◘ GIRL-ON-GIRL WRESTLING ◘ RACE RELATIONS ◘ BIG CHEER COMPETITION

Cheerleaders Wild Weekend commingles seemingly disparate drive-in genres into one intoxicating concoction. The saga of rival high school pep squads who are captured by thugs and held for ransom fortifies its impressive base of a typical T&A pom-pom comedy with women-in-prison flicks à la *Caged Heat* (1974); hard-boiled female grindhouse action à la *Bonnie's Kids* (1973); race relations exploitation à la *Black Mama, White Mama* (1973); and even a dash of psycho kidnap terror on the order of *Last House on the Left* (1972). Abduction and carnal assault have seriously never come off as so much fun.

The wildness commences with three rival factions of cheerleaders forced to share a single yellow school bus en route to the state championships. Snooty private school prisses, eternally annoyed urban homegirls, and well-scrubbed suburban blondes immediately throw down in a competition to see who can sufficiently distract a redneck into driving his pickup off the road. Lisa (Wally Ann Wharton) ultimately wins by dropping a double-D bomb, pressing her exposed gazongas against the bus's back window.

The raw teen girl anger and salacious games of spite continue, until a cabal of armed, multiracial, mixed-gender insurgents diverts the bus to an isolated woodland cabin and takes the girls hostage, demanding $2 million to fund their radical front, the National American Army of Freedom. This very much out-of-nowhere turn evokes the real-world 1974 events involving heiress Patricia Hearst and the Symbionese Liberation Army, thereby adding yet one more '70s genre component to *Cheerleaders Wild Weekend*: Pattysploitation. More direct entries in that field include *Abduction* (1975); *Tanya* (1976), and even *Ilsa, Harem Keeper of the Oil Sheiks* (1976).

Once inside the unsafe-house, a bit of crazy human drama unfolds as we come to understand the kidnappers' backstories. In between pistol-whippings, rape implications, scaring the gals with attack dogs, and threatening local radio disc jockey Joyful Jerome (Leon Isaac Kennedy) into negotiating on air with the young ladies' panicked parents, the movie still offers plenty of laughs. Not to mention that the assembled pep squad members include Kristine DeBell, a *Playboy* Playmate and star of the XXX-rated 1976 *Alice in Wonderland* (the same year *CWW* was released, Kristine also counseled campers in *Meatballs*); black bombshell B-flick actress Marilyn Joi, who was most memorable as Cleopatra Schwartz in *The Kentucky Fried Movie* (1977); and libidinous knockout Lenka Novak, another *Playboy* centerfold, who costarred in *Vampire Hookers* (1978).

Head cheerleader Debbie (DeBell) succumbs to Stockholm syndrome and melts in her pleated skirt for chief bad guy Wayne (Jason Williams, a formidable hunk who cowrote the screenplay and, in 1975, played the title role in *Flesh Gordon*). Fair-haired, buoyant-bosomed kidnapper Frankie (Courtney Sands) shares tender lesbian bath bubbles with nubile Jeanne (Novak). While waiting for cash to be delivered, almost all the girls compete in an impromptu beauty contest, where every division is "Talent" with a focus on variations of traditional categories such as "Swimsuit" and "Evening Gown," except minus any actual garments. An escape plot that incorporates a girl-on-girl-wrestling diversion and a getaway rope of everyone's tied-together panties actually flirts with genius.

Produced by exploitation emperor Bill Osco, who also oversaw the previously mentioned adults-only *Alice in Wonderland* and *Flesh Gordon*, this whole insane undertaking actually adds up to more than the sum of its parts. Even the movie's evolving promotions kicked ass. Filmed as *Bus 17 Is Missing* and originally tested as *The Great American Girl Robbery*, the stunningly wonderful *Cheerleaders Wild Weekend* enjoyed a healthy initial theatrical run. After kidnapper Leon Isaac Kennedy hit big with *Penitentiary* (1979), the film returned to screens. Updated ads billed Kennedy as the main star, and showed his smiling visage next to a flurry of musical notes and hype text declaring, "*Jive* with the music! *Boogie* to the beat! Pompom pussycats are cruisin' down the street!" Thus *Cheerleaders Wild Weekend* is so cool it could successfully sell itself as a blaxploitation musical. So, yes—*boogie*!

CHERRY HILL HIGH [1977]

DIR. ALEX E. GOITEIN; W/LINDA MCINERNEY, GLORIA UPSON, STEPHANIE LAWLOR

VIRGINS ▣ HOT TEACHER ▣ LESBIAN EXPERIMENTATION ▣ BICYCLE SEATS

Cherry Hill High's opening credits appear as yearbook pages being flipped by giddy graduates. In voice-overs (a low-budget technique used heavily in this movie) they simultaneously celebrate freedom from their all-girl institution while wondering why they signed up for a post-commencement two-week bicycle trip with uptight Miss Woodruff (Linda McInerney). Good question!

Clad in bikini tops and short-shorts, five of Cherry Hill High's finest mount their ten-speeds. Soon, each cyclist confesses to being a virgin. Miss Woodruff overhears the sex talk and announces that she is simply appalled...that all these hot chicks have never been laid! Off come Miss Woodruff's eyeglasses, undone goes her spinster hairdo, and down goes a gauntlet she throws for her charges. Each young lady will not only spill her maiden chalice during the course of their trip, but the maidens will also compete for originality of (s)execution.

Kippy (Carrie Olsen) sets a high bar straight away by banging Abalone (Ray Sherry), a muscle-head shark wrangler, while underwater. The presence of Hustler, Abalone's pet shark, is worth a kinky mention. ("He's a pool shark, so I named him Hustler!"), especially when blood from Kippy's freshly penetrated hymen drives Hustler into a frenzy. What a terrifically disgusting touch, only made heavier when Abalone then frantically stabs his shark friend into submission.

Peaches (Gloria Upson) eases back for a butch biker who, upon removing gang leathers, proves to be a busty lesbian. Miss Woodruff applauds her shedding of psychological virginity, but her peers nonetheless urge her to properly penis herself with a demolition derby driver during an actual car-trashing tournament.

Fabulously fake French-accented Michelle (Lynn Hastings) takes a stake in a coffin from a guy done up as a ghostly Dracula. Sarah (Nina Carson) gets clucked by a goof in a chicken suit. A stop at a vineyard along the bike trail allows Miss Woodruff to enjoy a roll in the grapes with a local vigneron while the other lasses doff their tops and splash each other's topless goblets with pinot noir. Wine fight!

Throughout this madness, a luckless schmuck named Larry (Stefan Melnikoff) woos Allison (Stephanie Lawlor) while donning different disguises. The last one works. He lands a flying saucer and, in space alien garb, the couple conjoins in blastoff. Post-coitus, Larry reveals himself to be a scientific genius and the son of the billionaire who owns the winery. Can you relate?

Boasting one of the absolute best monikers in the teen sex comedy canon, *Cherry Hill High* is brisk but loaded with off-the-wall touches. It's fun to imagine the creators logistically mapping out locales by calling in favors and stealing shots where they could ("I know a guy who can maybe let us film a game show in a supermarket parking lot!"). Director Alex E. Goitein went on to make *Cheerleaders Beach Party* with Chuck Vincent a year later, then disappeared. His work was done.

The Chicken Chronicles

[1977]

DIR. FRANCIS SIMON; W/STEVE GUTTENBERG, PHIL SILVERS, LISA REEVES, RAVEN DE LA CROIX

VIRGIN · CHEERLEADERS · RICH KIDS · WEED · PRANKS · LAST DAY OF SCHOOL

Novelist Paul Diamond faithfully adapted his own 1969-era coming-of-age breakthrough *The Chicken Chronicles* to the screen, resulting in a pretty good teen comedy with dramatic elements that seemed unique at the time and later garnered a solid cult following.

Steve Guttenberg (*Police Academy*, *3 Men and a Baby*) stars as Dave Kessler. He's a track star at Beverly Hills High School, a hyper-confident campus troublemaker, and a part-time employee of Chicken in the Basket—owned by lovable penny-pinching grump Old Man Ober, played by TV comedy legend Phil Silvers. He's also a poor little rich boy whose parents only talk to him through their mansion's intercom system, plus he smokes pot constantly and he's never gotten laid. Catholic cheerleader Margaret (Lisa Reeves) repeatedly leaves him with unholy blue balls. Later on, tawdry party girl Tracy (Meridith Baer) promises greater things vis-à-vis popping Dave's cherry. What you'd expect from those specifics is what *The Chicken Chronicles* delivers.

Today, the PG-rated *Chronicles* may come off as bucket of weak batter, but that's only down to how the next decade's high school movie deluge devoured all the tropes laid down here. Among them: virginity as a must-be-cured existential malady (particularly if it involves the prettiest pom-poms in town); madcap pranks (such as pilfering the principal's time clock to counterfeit hall passes) as a way of life; and after-school fast-food employment as a nausea-inducing sack of frustration. Moments of heavy adolescent contemplation linger, as Vietnam looms over any male senior who doesn't get into college.

The Chicken Chronicles didn't flat-out invent all

the above teen-flick ingredients, but it does assemble and deep-fry them into gratifying fare that, say, the makers of *Fast Times at Ridgemont High* must have absorbed, consciously or not. Guttenberg is pretty cluckin' great as *Chronicles'* popular and privileged yet still authority-aggravating hero, and his character would echo everywhere from Robert Wuhl's Newbomb Turk in *The Hollywood Knights* (1980) to Ferris Bueller in that movie everyone but me likes (1986).

Class [1983]

DIR. LEWIS JOHN CARLINO; W/JACQUELINE BISSET, ROB LOWE, ANDREW MCCARTHY, CLIFF ROBERTSON

MILF ▣ VIRGIN ▣ PREPPIES ▣ BOARDING SCHOOL ▣ PRANKS ▣ UNDERAGE DRINKING

In 1981, *Porky's* launched a boobs-and-barf box-office boom that negatively impacted some movies whose makers forced R-rated raunch into what otherwise might have been thoughtful or meaningfully coming-of-age sagas: Among these were *Heaven Help Us* and *Teachers. Class*, on the other gland, works precisely *because* of the nudity, drunkenness, and juvenile idiocy that seems shoehorned in to what otherwise might have been a self-serious meditation on the travails of some poor prepster banging his best buddy's insanely hot British mom.

Andrew McCarthy stars as headlight-eyed Jonathan Ogner, a new senior-year scholarship arrival at a posh suburban Chicago-area boarding school. He immediately feels out of sorts among his cocksure, old-money classmates. Roommate Skip (Rob Lowe) seems cool until he cons Jonathan into dressing only in women's undergarments and locks the newbie outdoors—and there is more initiation hazing to come.

After Jonathan pranks Skip by faking a suicide, the roomies call things even and become fast friends. They bond with dorm dudes Roger (Alan Ruck) and Roscoe (John Cusack), get in trouble with stuffy school administrators, and generally cut up enjoyably...until Jonathan reveals he has never been laid. Skip dispatches his virginal friend to a Chicago pickup bar loaded with loose female opportunists, telling him not to come back until he's earned his fuck wings. There, Jonathan meets Ellen (Jacqueline Bisset), an older Englishwoman. She elegantly deflowers the boy, and only then does he realize the woman is none other than Skip's mother. This leads unavoidably to an awkward confrontation at Skip's family mansion, and, inevitably, to fists meeting faces.

The plot of *Class* is straightforward, even as the tone flops all over the place, bolting from attempts at heartfelt hurt to broad, chaotic burlesque. At one point, the movie goes on a tangent about Skip cheating on the SATs, at which point the always-aces Stuart Margolin (old prison buddy Angel on TV's *The Rockford Files*) arrives to investigate. Virginia Madsen's big star-is-bared moment is also notable. She plays Lisa, a prim student from another prep school out to make a good, formal impression by serving tea and finger sandwiches, but she trips, her blouse is ripped open, and her upper anatomy is exposed—right side only, making her the teen sex comedy genre's all-time champion one-tit wonder.

Class of '44 [1973]

DIR. PAUL BOGART; W/GARY GRIMES, JERRY HOUSER, OLIVER CONANT, DEBORAH WINTERS

HIGH SCHOOL GRADUATION ▣ COLLEGE FRESHMEN ▣ HAZING ▣ 1940S

The dud sequel to *Summer of '42* (1971) tracks the "Terrible Trio" of Hermie (Gary Grimes), Oscy (Jerry Houser), and Benjie (Oliver Conant) as their lives diverge after high school. The first two go to college, while Benjie enlists in the marines to fight Nazis.

Hermie and Oscy join a frat and endure ritualistic paddling and whatnot. Romance blooms, someone's dad dies, and cheating on exams presents a moral quandary. The best evidence of this fun-free film: Oscy gets laid, but then is expelled for having a coed in his room. The most memorable moment of mirth is a few lines muttered by a very young John Candy. If this was life in the 1940s, be grateful for the sexual revolution, television, sugary cereals, rock 'n' roll, and everything that makes life worth living.

CLASS REUNION [1982]

aka NATIONAL LAMPOON'S CLASS REUNION

DIR. MARK MILLER; W/GERRIT GRAHAM, MIRIAM FLYNN, STEPHEN FURST, CHUCK BERRY

HIGH SCHOOL REUNION ▪ HORROR SPOOF ▪ MAD SLASHER ▪ LUNCH LADY

Class Reunion marks the debut of *National Lampoon* editor John Hughes as a screenwriter. Remember that name: He turns up elsewhere in this book. This was also the first *Lampoon* movie to reach wide release in the wake of *Animal House* (1978): The execrable *National Lampoon's Movie Madness* (1980) barely dribbled onto a handful of screens. Hughes had previously written the screenplay for the semi-legendary low-budget comedy *Jaws 3, People 0*, an official *Jaws* spoof to have been directed by the great Joe Dante (*Piranha, Gremlins*) until Steven Spielberg himself reportedly harpooned the silly sequel.

Unfortunately, nothing in *Class Reunion* is as inspired as *Jaws 3, People 0*.

This murky, clunky attempt at satire goofs on Lizzie Borden High's class of '72 graduates confronting their unfinished teenage issues at the event of the film's title. Bizarre but not interesting, that setup is combined with a full-on spoof of '80s slasher movies. Alas, *Student Bodies* (1981)—which *should* have been a NatLamp production—this ain't.

As the classmates reunite, we learn that missing alumnus Walter Baylor (Blackie Dammett, the real-life dad of Chili Pepper Anthony Kiedis) was driven insane by a blow-job-switcheroo senior prank and has spent the prior decade in a psych ward. Walter, naturally, has escaped the nuthouse on reunion night to exact revenge on against the gag's perpetrators, knocking them off in various uninspired fashions. Standard character types on hand include rich jerk Bob Spinnaker (Gerrit Graham, aka Beef from Brian De Palma's *Phantom of the Paradise*), big fat party animal Hubert Downs (Stephen Furst, aka Flounder from *Animal House*), and peppy blonde Cindy Shears (Misty Rowe, aka Junior Samples' handler from TV's *Hee Haw*). One otherwise undistinguished classmate, Delores Salk (Zane Buzby), is possessed by the devil. No explanation is given other than the enduring popularity of *The Exorcist*, but her condition enables chunky-vomit gags and a final showdown involving satanic superpowers.

John Hughes claimed he was fired from *Class Reunion* and that the final film so deviated from his screenplay that he was "shocked" by it. The following year, Hughes scripted *Vacation*, based on his gigantically funny *National Lampoon* short story "Vacation '58." Then he rushed to reinvent teen cinema in his own overprivileged, suburban, conceited adolescent image via *Sixteen Candles* (1984), *The Breakfast Club* (1985), *Pretty in Pink* (1986), and *Some Kind of Wonderful* (1987). All of that worked all too well.

Popular culture has famously championed "the John Hughes Movies." *Class Reunion*, although truly not funny and not good, suggests an unexpected, potentially fascinating path that John Hughes might have taken. Some of us will always prefer it to anything that ever occurred in Shermer, Illinois, regardless.

COACH [1978]

DIR. BUD TOWNSEND; W/CATHY LEE CROSBY, MICHAEL BIEHN, KEENAN WYNN

BASKETBALL ▪ OLDER WOMAN ▪ BIG GAME

Professional tennis player Cathy Lee Crosby first notably switched rackets to acting in a baffling 1974 TV-movie adaptation of *Wonder Woman*. Not only was Cathy blonde in the classically raven-maned comic-book role, but she wore a repulsive zippered jumpsuit instead of WW's signature Amazonian va-va-voom getup. ABC did well by recasting Lynda Carter for the series.

Coach serves Cathy Lee far better. Here, she is a thirtysomething Olympic basketball gold medalist named Randy Rawlings, a dedicated athlete who is hired away from a fat farm to transform a floundering high school boys' basketball team. Turns out the school's main financial underwriter, male chauvinist patron F. R. Granger (Keenan Wynn), had taken "Randy" to be a man's name. Once he discovers that the new coach is a sharp, talented, inspirational, and beautiful woman, he naturally sets out to sabotage the team so he can fire her.

The players initially freeze out Coach Randy, too, but she wins their respect—first by walking in on them while they're naked in the shower, and later by gleefully joining the lads in a dirty sing-along on the school bus. The randy coach also embarks on a full-blown romantic affair with star pupil Jack Ripley (Michael Biehn). Because it's the 1970s, all of this is cool. Even branded with a PG rating, *Coach* shoots and scores when it comes to nudity.

Two years before *Coach*, director Pat "Bud" Townsend made *Alice in Wonderland*: An *X-Rated Musical Fantasy* starring *Meatballs*' Kristine DeBell. Four years later, he helmed *The Beach Girls*. Especially with a name like "Bud," he must have been having the time of his life.

Combat Academy [1986]
aka Combat High

DIR. NEAL ISRAEL; W/KEITH GORDON, WALLY WARD, DANA HILL, GEORGE CLOONEY

MILITARY SCHOOL ▣ NERDS ▣ PRANKS ▣ EXPLODING LOCKERS ▣ COLD WAR RUSSIANS

Rank-and-file TV movie *Combat Academy* casts Keith Gordon (*Christine*; *Back to School*) as Ferris Bueller–esque teen schemer Max Mendelsson. Wally Ward (*Weird Science*; *The Invisible Kid*) appears as Perry Barnett, his stuttering dweeb sidekick. After the pair's sustained prank campaign culminates with fireworks going off in every school locker at once, their enraged principal (Dick Van Patten) threatens to ship them to Kirkland Military Academy. Then he opens his desk and live birds fly up out of the drawer. The hijinks never stop with these two.

Actually, the hijinks do stop momentarily once Max and Perry land at Kirkland. There, they befriend similarly awkward female classmate Andrea Pritchett (Dana Hill) and buff cadet Biff Woods (George Clooney in his TV debut). The new recruits plot to wage joke warfare anew, but headmaster General Ed Woods (Robert Culp), also Biff's dad, crushes their every effort.

Max wants to keep up the fight, Perry says he's going straight, and they both fall in love, though not with each other. Biff and his general dad learn to accept one another during the course of a big character-building war game with Soviet exchange students.

Director Neal Israel (*Bachelor Party*, *Moving Violations*) seems to be sleepwalking his way to a paycheck. Besides featuring Van Patten and Culp, *Combat Academy* also offers off-season employment for other shriveled prime-time TV stars of yore, including Sherman Hemsley (George Jefferson of the recently canceled *The Jeffersons*) as a judge and Richard Moll (Bull of the then-riding-high *Night Court*) as a Kirkland weapons instructor. Jamie Farr, most famous for wearing fancy women's finery as Corporal Klinger on *M*A*S*H*, sticks to standard-issue U.S. Army male dress requirements as an officious colonel. All it took, apparently, was a promotion.

Computer Beach Party [1987]

DIR. GARY TROY; W/HANK AMICO, ANDRE CHIMENE, HUNTER VAIL, STACEY NEMOUR

BIKINI BABES ▣ SAIL-BUGGIES ▣ NERD ▣ TREASURE ▣ HAIR METAL ▣ TALKING DOG

"Open a bag of micro chips, toss around the floppy disc, and interface with a comedy that'll light up your terminal." So declares the back cover of the *Computer Beach Party* video box. This advice is questionable, but *Computer Beach Party* must be interfaced with if only for the watcher to recognize is the pomp and glory of Galveston, Texas, sail-buggy racing in the second half of the 1980s. Forget about Malibu and Daytona, and witness the regal sport of permanently shirtless, semi-buff, vaguely teenage leads played by middle-aged men Andy (Hank Amico) and Dennis (Andre Chimene). Andy wears nerd eyeglasses; Dennis doesn't. Now everyone can tell them apart.

Back to the sail-buggy, a fun-looking, uncool, three-wheeled, plastic-seated vehicle affixed with a nautical-type sail, which whizzes riders along the sand once it catches a breeze. Upon discovering an unspoiled stretch of Gulf of Mexico shoreline, our wind-and-wheels warriors declare the public lands to be theirs alone. The buggy bros claim this dominion upon which to race the shit out of their sail-buggies, while tearing up the terrain with nightly ragers that result in pools of puke and piss, heaps of beer cans and loaded rubbers, and occasional passed-out nude bodies.

The totally righteous sense of manifest destiny is tested after a gold coin turns up in the sand and local authorities become convinced that buried treasure lies just beneath the surface.

Soon the town's greedy mayor wants to oust the sail-buggies and convert the beach into a tourist attraction. Our semi-teen heroes Andy and Dennis combat this development in the style of eco-warrior monkey-wrenchers, plowing down lifeguard stands and other outside intrusions into their sail-buggy runs. The town sends a bumbling cop to bust the boys, too, but he is repeatedly distracted by simple things like a speeding car shaped like a giant chicken. At the mere sight of this wonder, the cop drops everything to chase it while babbling, "Chicken car! Chicken car!"

Fortunately, the mayor's bikini-bunny daughter Allison (Stacey Nemour) sides with the sail-buggy crew. She enlists all her bikini-bunny gal pals and local hair metal sensations Panther to aid and abet the surging, kegger-fueled sail-buggy revolt.

At the same time, a technological revolution is under way—this movie's not called *Computer Beach Party* for nothing! (Close to nothing, though.) Andy, already equipped with dork specs, fires up his giggle-inducing prehistoric PC to print flyers, send party invites via primitive emails, and futz around on something called "the network." "It's like looking at a book," Dennis marvels, "on *TV!*"

Dennis writes "I Love You" to Allison in crappy script on his computer screen, which, in turn, gets Allison into his bed. Many more such miracles of mid-'80s machinery appear in the movie, usually just being as boring and useless as they mostly were back then. Now, though, they look incredibly funny and serve the miraculous purpose of making 1985 look as archaic as the 1800s.

Spoiler alert: *Computer Beach Party* ends with a big sail-buggy race, and doo-wop legends the Drifters immediately appear out of nowhere to perform "Under the Boardwalk" for the winners. The chicken car is never explained, so keep an eye out for that around Texas—it's part of the magnificence of *Computer Beach Party*. Now wrestle up that bag of "micro chips" and tossed-around floppy discs and plug in—*hard*.

COOLEY HIGH [1975]

DIR. MICHAEL SCHULTZ; W/GLYNN TURMAN, LAWRENCE HILTON-JACOBS, CYNTHIA DAVIS, GARRETT MORRIS

BASKETBALL ▪ NERD ▪ GANGS ▪ CHEERLEADERS ▪ HOUSE PARTY ▪ THE BIG EXAM ▪ DOO-WOP ▪ BATHROOM FUN

The familiar poster for *Cooley High* features a colorful, *Mad* magazine–like collection of cartoon depictions of high-energy hijinks of various orders. The tagline matches the images: "Where the student body was a chick named Veronica, the Senior Prom was a 'belly rub,' and the Class of '64 ran a permanent crap game in the Men's Room!"

In reality, Cooley High was a real vocational institute near the Old Town section of Chicago. The movie's promotional one-sheet reflects an assuredly much less titillating reality than the poster, featuring a stark, black-and-white shot of hard-bitten, retro-dressed gangster youths against a barred window scowling at the camera under the words "Meet the Student Welcoming Committee of Cooley High." Of the two marketing plans from opposite sides of the gym, neither paints an accurate picture of this classic of African American cinema. The posters are cool. The movie is endlessly cooler.

In the winter of 1964, bookish and bespectacled "Preach" Jackson (Glynn Turman) and his basketball star best friend "Cochise" Morris (Lawrence Hilton-Jacobs) leave the projects each morning to attend class at Cooley High. Hip history teacher Mr. Morris (Garrett Morris) looks out for the pair as they contend with budding romance (or lack thereof, in Preach's case); back-alley gambling (an emerging problem, in Cochise's case); and the ever-present lure of ditching school for the fast money of street hustling.

After visiting another student's apartment for a "quarter party," where entry costs twenty-five cents (one of *Cooley High*'s many illuminating cultural touches), Preach and Cochise get mixed up joyriding in a stolen Cadillac with rough characters Stone (Rick Stone) and Robert (Norman Gibson). The police give chase, and Stone and Robert are eventually nabbed while Preach and Cochise get away. The movie climaxes in tragedy, but an emotional closing, followed by a "where are they now?" postscript, manages to uplift, even while sticking to realism.

Cooley High's screenwriter Eric Monte also cocreated the touchstone '70s sitcom *Good Times*. Like the show, the movie draws from Monte's own inner-city Chicago youth. *Cooley High* makes good on its promise of being "the black *American Graffiti*." The film's slight B-movie feel and unvarnished edges may well result from it being produced by exploitation powerhouse American International Pictures. Such grit only adds to *Cooley High*'s depth.

In 1976, ABC developed a *Cooley High* sitcom pilot that never successfully jelled. Still, the network stuck with a character based on skinny, poetry-loving, eyeglasses-adorned mama's boy Preach. The network gave the show a contemporary setting in the Watts section of Los Angeles, and focused on a trio of high school pals instead of just a bookworm and a jock. And just like that, *What's Happening!!* came strutting down the block. Hey-*hey*-hey!

Dangerous Curves
Dazed and Confused ▣ Delivery Boys
Dialing for Dingbats ▣ Diner
Don't Tell Mom the Babysitter's Dead
Dr. Alien ▣ Dream a Little Dream
Drive-in ▣ Dutch Girls

Dangerous Curves [1988]

DIR. DAVID LEWIS; W/TATE DONOVAN, GRANT HESLOV, DANIELLE VON ZERNECK, ROBERT STACK

STOLEN PORSCHE ▣ BIKINI CONTEST ▣ SURFER GURU ▣ WETBIKES

Smile-averse business tycoon Louis Faciano (Robert Stack) hires straitlaced college dude Chuck Upton (Tate Donovan) to deliver a Porsche from Los Angeles to his beloved coed daughter in Lake Tahoe. The car is a gift from dad to his darling. Chuck screws up immediately and repeatedly. First, he asks his skirt-chasing party pal Wally Wilder (Grant Heslov) to ride shotgun. Second mistake: Chuck honors Wally's request to hit a bikini contest in San Diego first, where the Porsche is promptly stolen.

Numerous high-speed chases dominate *Dangerous Curves*, the most endearing of which involve two of the most 1980s of all watercrafts, catamarans and Wetbikes. Otherwise, the movie is mostly distinguished by an off-kilter powerhouse cast of showbiz vets, starting with Stack and also including Robert Romanus (Damone of *Fast Times*), Broadway diva Elizabeth Ashley, and MTV VJ Martha Quinn. Funnyman Robert Klein appears as an aging surf philosopher named Bam Bam.

Leslie Nielsen is the pageant host who pilfers the Porsche. After *The Naked Gun* was released three months later, reinventing Nielsen as a comedy brand, international posters for *Dangerous Curves* featured the elderly star dressed in a white tux, aiming a pistol and standing astride a cartoon sports car. See, even an exploitation film can be exploited!

Dazed and Confused [1993]

DIR. RICHARD LINKLATER; W/JASON LONDON, JOEY LAUREN ADAMS, MILLA JOVOVICH, MATTHEW MCCONAUGHEY

LAST DAY OF SCHOOL ▣ KEG PARTY ▣ PRANKS ▣ HAZING ▣ WEED ▣ PINBALL

Writer-director Richard Linklater's last-day-of-school-in-1976 opus ties up the very specific strain of cinematic teen comedies that began bubbling amidst the cowabunga haze of mid-'60s beach party movies, leapt to full life with *American Graffiti* (1973), and peaked at max power just about a decade later with *Fast Times at Ridgemont High* (1982). Like *Graffiti*, Linklater's *Dazed* is a brilliant exercise in nostalgia but also hilarious, pointed, poignant, and universally human. Such traits are only amplified by how the characters' best-laid plans for getting wasted and laid explode into gross-out gags, slapstick abandon, and—more than once—existential disappointment.

In a suburb of Austin, Texas, on the cusp of the American bicentennial, school's out for summer at Robert E. Lee High. Chaos reigns. Randall "Pink" Floyd (Jason London) is the reigning laid-back hippie/stoner-type cool guy, and in this case also the star of the football team. He will be a senior in the fall, and the coach insists Pink sign a pledge that, over the summer, he will not take drugs or in any other way "jeopardize the goal of the championship season." The kid splits campus without delivering his Pink Hancock.

Meanwhile, nervous incoming Lee freshman Mitch Kramer (Wiley Wiggins) frantically tries to head without falling prey to an annual hazing ritual. Each year, new seniors hunt down incoming freshman. If they're boys, the older kids paddle them. If they're girls, they will be covered with ketchup, mustard, eggs, and flour, and forced to ask senior dudes to marry them. Things aren't just bigger in Texas—they also seem insane.

After Mitch gets nailed at a baseball game by paddle-happy asshole O'Bannion (Ben Affleck), Pink gives the sore-keistered kid a ride home. Each comes up with a course of action. Pink plans to cruise by the Emporium, a popular pool hall and teenage hangout, while Mitch calculates revenge. Pink says Mitch can roll with him.

From there, Linklater paints a vivid all-night party portrait of rich and recognizable characters as they bounce from the Emporium to a drive-in burger joint to a climactic kegger under a moonlit tower, one of the luminous structures unique to the Austin area. Viewers spend time with, among others, brainy bombshell Cynthia (Marisa Ribisi), neurotic rocker Newhouse (Adam Goldberg), groovy guitar strummer Michelle (Milla Jovovich), psycho-bitch Darla (Parker Posey), and cannabis-crusading philosopher Slater (Rory Cochrane).

The lifelike storytelling flow echoes Linklater's floating-camera technique from his 1991 breakthrough *Slacker*, only amplified to Hollywood proportions. The movie moves us along quickly with talking, joking, arguing, making out, hooking up, breaking things off, ball busting, and mailbox baseball, all set to the FM-radio anthems of the era. *Dazed*'s indispensable soundtrack tie-in LP proved so successful that it soon generated its own sequel, a feat soon mimicked by every successful teen movie in existence, even, retroactively, *Valley Girl*.

By daybreak, Mitch has sort of triumphed over O'Bannion, and Pink smokes grass on the fifty-yard-line of the football field, where he eschews the coach's straight-edge pledge in favor of scoring Aerosmith tickets. Even after drunken fun and big, stoned laughs have been had by all, as Pink settles into bed with Foghat's "Slow Ride" blaring through his headphones, his earlier declaration remains unshakable: "If I ever start referring to these as the best years of my life, remind me to kill myself."

In his first real role, Matthew McConaughey as David Wooderson is the movie's best, funniest, saddest, and most iconic contribution. Well into his twenties, the character packs a full deck with a muscle car, a pack of smokes rolled up in his tight T-shirt sleeve, a weed-pipe necklace, faded peach jeans, a dank dragon-and-panther forearm tattoo, an oily comb-over, and the same blond mustache that sprouted on his face at age fourteen. Wooderson glides into action outside the Emporium. He surveys the teenage females around him and proclaims: "That's what I love about these high school girls, man. I get older, they stay the same age."

The line is shockingly hilarious, all the more for how it ripples with desperation and grossness. Wooderson is impossible not to love, cheer, and pity at the same time. As the wasted rebel hero of the film that completes the cycle of *American Graffiti* and *Fast Times at Ridgemont High*, Wooderson is the offspring of *Graffiti*'s John Milner (Paul Le Mat), the muscled greaser in a tricked-

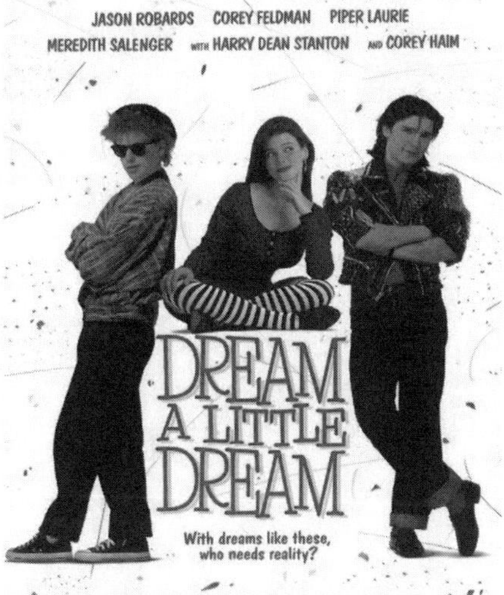

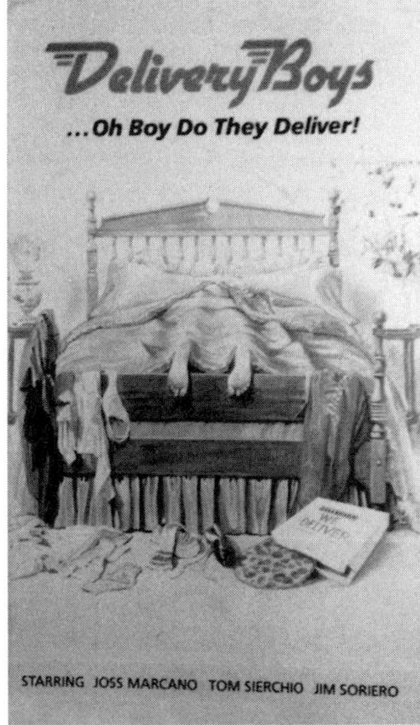

Clockwise from top left: *1-900-TEENMOVIEHELL in* Dialing for Dingbats *(1989); Coreys abound in the nightmarish* Dream a Little Dream *(1989);* Delivery Boys *(1985);* Diner *(1982) stars* (left to right) *Kevin Bacon, Mickey Rourke, Daniel Stern, and Tim Daly.*

out hot rod who tools around with hopped-up teenybopper Mackenzie Phillips; and *Fast Times'* Jeff Spicoli (Sean Penn), the perma-zonked party prophet who insists life can always be a beach.

Wooderson exists at a point where boisterousness turns bleak, and where what was once dazzling goes dim. His furious grip on an idealized past, disguised as loosey-goosey swagger, embodies the title of the Amboy Dukes album cover on his shirt: *Fang, Tooth, and Claw*. As such, the character of David Wooderson celebrates but warns of the intoxication of nostalgia—mission accomplished in the genre-capping coda of *Dazed and Confused*.

Delivery Boys [1984] aka Breakdance Party

DIR. KEN HANDLER; W/MARIO VAN PEEBLES, TOM SIERCHIO, JODY OLIVER, YAYO GONZALEZ

BREAKDANCING ▣ PIZZA ▣ FUNNY NAZI ▣ ACCIDENTAL BESTIALITY ▣ BREAKDANCING

Delivery Boys is a lovably loony snapshot of a quick New York City minute when breakdancing momentarily surpassed its hip-hop soundtrack in teenage popularity. The kinetic action largely goes down at a pizzeria and its adjoining dance stage under the Brooklyn Bridge, where everything is adorned with sponsorship banners from WKTU-FM ("Disco 92").

"Delivery Boys" is the name of a teenage breakdance team that also runs orders for their local pizza parlor. As they practice for a championship break contest, rival crew guru Spider (Mario Van Peebles) threatens them with voodoo. He warns that he successfully worked his mojo on the previous year's winners, then busts out their shrunken heads and shrunken penises right on a pizzeria table.

The sexy toppings to this crust come by way of the delivery customers. One rich kept woman holds a Delivery Boy captive until he escapes by dressing in drag and getting the family's Doberman pinscher to lick its sugar daddy's dick through a jewel-encrusted glory hole. Another Delivery Boy falls prey to mad doctors who use him for erectile implantation experiments that involve stripper nurses and result in him stuck with a slapstick-ready perma-rod. Yet another Delivery Boy is forced to pose as a nude statue. He pisses into champagne glasses that are then happily drained by snooty art-gallery patrons—only in New York! Keep in mind that all this insanity and more takes place in a film that primarily consists of breakdancing. The filmmakers certainly had some fancy moves.

Dialing for Dingbats [1989]

DIR. PETER SLODCZYK; W/JOHN CAPONERA, MARTA DARGHAM, MICHAEL JEFFRIES

NERDS ▣ FOOD FIGHT ▣ SUICIDE COMEDY

If *Dialing for Dingbats* wasn't created expressly to be shown on late-night TV, then the essential wee-hours, basic cable, schlock-flick showcase *USA Up All Night* probably would have spontaneously belched this movie into being. *Dialing for Dingbats* is the first comedy of note to attempt to cash in on the late-'80s craze for 1-900-number phone-chat lines. The non-professional cast talks to one another via one such fictitious service, setting up a series of encounters, but mostly just flapping their yaps. Among the jabberers, "Randy from Redondo" (Michael Jeffries) proves especially irritating. He shows off a bunch of his celebrity impressions, including a dotty Ronald Reagan. Troma Entertainment might have thought he was the real thing issuing an executive order to release *Dialing for Dingbats* on video; that would explain why they did.

Diner [1982]

DIR. BARRY LEVINSON; W/DANIEL STERN, KEVIN BACON, ELLEN BARKIN, MICKEY ROURKE

NOSTALGIA ▣ RECORD-COLLECTOR OBSESSIONS ▣ POPCORN PENIS PRANK

Imagine *American Graffiti* set in 1959 Baltimore instead of 1962 California, as writer-director Barry Levinson guides an outstanding roster of brink-of-stardom talents through a funny, emotionally wrenching farewell to the final vestiges of youth—with fries and gravy on the side.

Five friends in their early twenties converge on their childhood stomping grounds. One of them, Eddie Simmons (Steve Guttenberg), is getting hitched—but only if his bride-to-be can pass a grueling quiz on professional football trivia. Shrevie Schreiber (Daniel Stern) is already married to Beth (Ellen Barkin), though neither of them is too happy. Lady-slaying hairdresser and law student Boogie Sheftell (Mickey Rourke) provides more than a shoulder for Beth to cry on. Fen Fenwick (Kevin Bacon), the emotionally unstable brains of the bunch, tries to booze himself into feeling comfortable, which only makes everyone feel worse.

Diner is more downbeat than *American Graffiti*, and far less epic in scope, sticking to a particular time and place, with pals downing black coffee and cheeseburger platters to fuel their unwinnable fight against oncoming adulthood. The movie opened in the same six-month span that also delivered *Porky's*, *The Last American Virgin*, and *Fast Times at Ridgemont High*, so naturally the film features a dirty prank in which Rourke takes his date to a movie, cuts a hole in the bottom of the popcorn box, bones up, and then bets that, before the flick ends, she will grab his Lil' Mickey. He wins on a ballsy technicality.

Don't Tell Mom the Babysitter's Dead [1991]

DIR. STEPHEN HEREK; W/CHRISTINA APPLEGATE, KEITH COOGAN, KIMMY ROBERTSON, DAVID DUCHOVNY

BABYSITTER ▣ KIDS TAKE OVER ▣ UNDERCOVER TEEN

Don't Tell Mom the Babysitter's *Dead* reveals the movie's basic premise in the title. When their mother splits for a couple of months but the nagging hag she left in charge keels over, Christina Applegate and her four younger siblings are left with an entire summer to themselves. Nineties kids took to the fantasy-fulfillment *Don't Tell Mom* immediately. Unlike other preteen comedies of the era, though, this one continues to find new audiences year after year due in huge part to teenage star Applegate's comic chops and the brash farce involved in keeping mom in the dark.

Keith Coogan, who previously played one of the babysat kids in *Adventures in Babysitting* (1987), plays yet another babysat kid here. This movie's better, because at least *somebody* dies! Keith is also the grandson of Hollywood legend Jackie Coogan, a silent-era child star whose parents squandered his fortune, resulting in a law named after him that protects the earnings of kid actors. Jackie Coogan also, heroically, grew up to play Uncle Fester on TV's *The Addams Family*. Though now middle-aged, hopefully Keith will someday top that high-water mark in the family business.

Dr. Alien [1989]

aka I Was a Teenage Sex Maniac; I Was a Teenage Sex Mutant

DIR. DAVID DECOTEAU; W/JUDY LANDERS, BILLY JACOBY, OLIVIA BARASH, TROY DONAHUE

NERD ▣ VIRGIN ▣ HOT TEACHER ▣ HEAVY METAL ▣ SCI-FI ▣ BRAIN BONER

Billy Jacoby, best known for playing likeable ball-busters in *Just One of the Guys* (1985) and *Party Camp* (1987), does a nerd turn in *Dr. Alien* as Wesley Littlejohn. He's a brazenly bullied high school dweeb who goes from being stuffed into lockers to stuffing himself into lusty ladies after mysterious sex-bomb substitute science teacher Ms. Xenobia (Judy Landers) steps off a UFO and injects his ass-cheek with some glowing, intergalactic sex-mutant serum. We should all be so lucky.

The resulting change in chemistry might be pure bliss for our loser-turned-lothario—except that an erect-penis-shaped flesh antenna sprouts from the top of his head every time he pops a boner. This happens pretty often, too. Even so, what might have been a cursed affliction just becomes a killer gimmick. Wes takes up fronting heavy metal rockers the Sex Mutants, and they play a sold-out concert with all-girl new wavers the Poon Tangs.

The Tangs prove to be a B-movie T&A power trio, comprised of scream queen Linnea Quigley, hardcore porn sweetheart Ginger Lynn Allen, and amply upper-proportioned Laura Albert, who went on to play Mrs. Van Houten in Stephen Sayadian's art-bent *Dr. Caligari* (1990). That last connection proves pertinent, as the Poon Tangs appear here—naked, of course—in a surreal, smoky, neon-scorched dream sequence in which director David DeCoteau effectively rips off/pays homage to Sayadian's brilliant 1982 art-house porn flick hybrid *Café Flesh*.

Nineteen-fifties heartthrob Troy Donahue cameos as biology instructor Dr. Ackerman, named for *Famous Monsters of Filmland* magazine publisher Forrest J. Ackerman. Other such in-jokes abound for vintage sci-fi teen flick fans.

Though she never takes off her clothes, eventually Ms. Xenobia does peel off her fake human face and reveal the blue-skinned, dome-skulled, pointy-eared space alien she is inside. Surely somebody in a galaxy far, far away is hot and bothered at such a sight.

Dream a Little Dream [1989]

DIR. MARC ROCCO; W/COREY FELDMAN, COREY HAIM, MEREDITH SALENGER, JASON ROBARDS

TWO COREYS ▣ BODY SWAP ▣ HIGH SCHOOL

The modern body-swap film genre as we know it commenced in 1976 with kid Jodie Foster and mom Barbara Harris trading minds in the Disney hit *Freaky Friday*. No one imagined how that cute comedy would prove so slow-burningly fertile. Given the deluge of teen-modified *Freaky Friday* flicks just over a decade later, no sane individual would have wished for that, either.

Like Father, Like Son (1987), *18 Again!* (1988), and *Vice Versa* (1988) all paved the way for *Dream a Little Dream*, the most insane imaginable *Freaky Friday* variant, and the only one that dares raise the obvious issue of sex while occupying someone else's physical being. Unfortunately, the grotesquely garish team up of Coreys Feldman and Haim makes for a draining and punishing two hours, no small disappointment given the concept. Plus *Dream a Little Dream* also drags down Hollywood legends Jason Robards (*All the President's Men*) and Piper Laurie (the scary mom in *Carrie*).

The movie begins with high schooler Bobby Keller (Feldman) running through a neighborhood backyard, and accidentally colliding into his eminently lovely classmate Lainie Diamond (Meredith Salenger). At the exact same moment, nearby elderly mystic studies professor Coleman Ettinger (Robards) and his wife Gena (Laurie) attempt a meditative out-of-body experiment that lands their minds in the youthful bodies of Bobby and Lainie, and vice versa. Possibly everyone involved might be stuck in a dream state from which they may never return—the story remains a little skimpy on specifics.

While other entries in this genre play similar setups for slapstick, *Dream a Little Dream* aims for pure incomprehensible irritation. Watch and rage. The only thing more angering would be to actually swap minds with Corey Haim, who somehow allowed himself to be cast as Bobby's colorfully attired class-cutup best bud, "Dinger."

This head-hurting heap, though it bombed hugely at the box office, generated enough lingering interest through cable reruns that a sequel somehow seemed viable. *Dream a Little Dream 2* (1995) reunites the two Coreys after six long years—and, in Haim's case, about sixty extra pounds. Second time around, they found magic sunglasses. Meredith Salenger stayed away, bless her, and audiences followed her cue.

Drive-In [1976]

DIR. ROD AMATEAU; W/LISA LEMOLE, GARY LEE CAVAGNARO, GLENN MORSHOWER, ASHLEY COX

DRIVE-IN MOVIES ▣ CUSTOM VANS ▣ BIKERS ▣ TEEN MARRIAGE ▣ ROLLER RINK

Way better than *Drive-In Massacre* (1976), but not as steadfastly teen intensive as *American Drive-In* (1985) and nowhere near being in the league of *Dead End Drive-In* (1986), the fitfully ambitious *Drive-In* attempts to fuse a miniaturized Robert Altman study of small-town Texas moviegoers at their local outdoor theater (the presciently named Alamo) with a slapstick caper comedy involving inept box-office robbers. Also showing is a full-scale parody of the mega-budget disaster epics that were the rage of Hollywood at the time. Yes, *Drive-In* is something to see.

Veering from okay to pretty good, *Drive-In*'s parking-lot action tells the tale of teenage beauty queen Glowie (Lisa Lemole) ditching Enoch (Gary Lee Cavagnaro), leader of the orange-windbreaker-clad boogie van gang the Widowmakers, to date Ron Howard–esque nice guy Orville (Glenn Morshower). All these various locals have come to the Alamo to see *Disaster '76*, which is a bona fide laugh riot.

We the *real* audience see *Disaster '76* in fits and starts that string together what's going on in the cars. Like a Rube Goldberg concoction directed by Irwin Allen (*The Poseidon Adventure, The Towering Inferno*), *Disaster '76* kicks off with a bomb explosion aboard a 747. The jet crashes into a high-rise building that bursts into flames. That event, in turn, touches off an earthquake that ruptures a massive dam and unleashes a shark-filled flood onto the streets of a major city.

On TV years earlier, heroic *Drive-In* director Rod Amateau forecasted future teen-tertainment via his sharp and subversive CBS sitcom *The Many Loves of Dobie Gillis* (1959–63). In 1984, he returned to the big screen to make the impressively unclassifiable high school rock comedy *Lovelines*, a star vehicle for the sound-effects guy from *Police Academy*. In every sense, then, *Drive-In* makes for a fine midpoint marker in the Amateau oeuvre.

Dutch Girls [1985]

DIR. GILES FOSTER; W/COLIN FIRTH, TIMOTHY SPALL, GUSTA GERRITSEN

JOCKS ▣ SCHOOL TRIP ▣ SEX PROS ▣ UNDERAGE DRINKING ▣ UNDERAGE VOMIT

Dutch Girls tags along with a British boarding school's hockey team as they decamp for the Netherlands in pursuit of high scores and nether glands. Colin Firth stars as the handsome, subtly monikered team captain Neil Truelove. Excellent future bad-guy actor Timothy Spall, possessor of a trademark busted nose and unmistakably English dental finery, costars as boorish Lyndon, the closest one gets to a Belushi-type personage in this milieu.

After a lot of travel footage and wearisome arrival scenes, Neil Truelove goes along with Dutch girl Romelia (Gusta Gerritsen) to a dubious "dance club," i.e., somebody's Dutch basement. Lyndon is on the scene, and dutifully drinks, farts, and vomits.

Eventually, the team's blowhard coach manages to lose the lads in Amsterdam's red-light district. A few flashes of flesh occur, but the film is too good a chaperone to allow these fine British lads any sex. Truelove almost plants his tulip in Romelia's pink wooden shoe, but he ultimately leaves her behind, like the windmills in his mind. Meanwhile, oblivious to proper manners but perhaps more suitable to a movie of this type, Lyndon farts, drinks, and vomits again and again. *Het einde.*

Clockwise from top left: Ferris Bueller's Day Off *(1986), leisure rules, fools drool; rare carrotty cartoon poster for* Fast Times at Ridgemont High *(1982)*; Fast Food *(1989) serves up Jim Varney and Traci Lords*; Feelin' Up (1976) *is a misleadingly marketed hippie dramedy.*

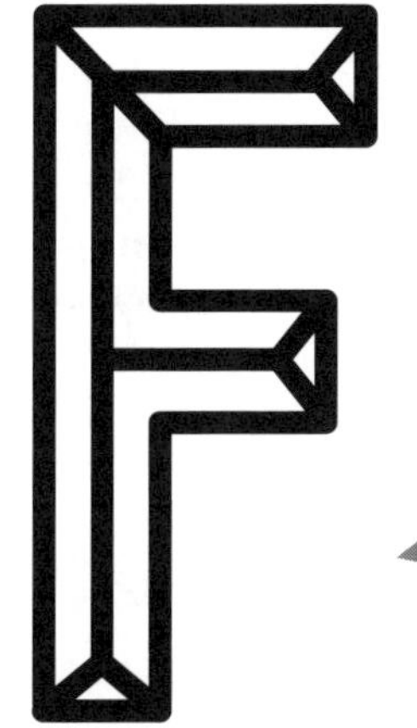

FANDANGO ▪ FAST FOOD
FAST TIMES AT RIDGEMONT HIGH ▪ FEELIN' UP
FERRIS BUELLER'S DAY OFF ▪ THE FIRST TIME
THE FIRST TURN-ON!! ▪ THE FLAMINGO KID
FOR KEEPS ▪ FOXES ▪ FRATERNITY VACATION
FREE RIDE ▪ THE FRESHMAN

FANDANGO [1985]

DIR. KEVIN REYNOLDS; W/KEVIN COSTNER, JUDD NELSON, SAM ROBARDS, ELIZABETH DAILY

GRADUATION ▪ ROAD TRIP ▪ NOSTALGIA

The Groovers, a quartet of UT Austin college buddies, hit the road on a mysterious quest to "dig up Dom" just after graduating with the class of 1971. Gardner (Kevin Costner) aches over losing his sweetheart, referred to only as The Girl (Suzy Amis). ROTC enlistee Phil (Judd Nelson) faces pending shipment to Vietnam. Kenneth (Sam Robards) is already engaged. Seminary student Dorman doesn't say much.

Along the highway, the Groovers mess up their car, meet up with local Texas honey Judy (Elizabeth "E. G." Daily), chow down at a vintage Sonic Drive-In, sack out on the set of James Dean's *Giant*, and, with an impressive degree of comic suspense, narrowly avert being splattered in a skydiving calamity. On a cliff above the Rio Grande, the Groovers finally unearth "Dom"—which turns out to be a bottle of Dom Pérignon champagne they had buried years earlier—and they raise their glasses to "youth and freedom."

In 1984, Steven Spielberg happened upon *Proof*, a short made in 1980 by USC student (and future *Waterworld* director) Kevin Reynolds. Spielberg contacted Reynolds and together they developed *Proof* into the feature-length *Fandango*, which received just enough of a release to generate a cult following. "*Fandango* is one of the best directorial debuts in all of cinema," Quentin Tarantino told *Empire* magazine. "I saw *Fandango* five times at the movie theater and it only played for a fucking *week*, all right?" All right!

FAST FOOD [1989]

DIR. MICHAEL A. SIMPSON; W/JIM VARNEY, CLARK BRANDON, PAMELA SPRINGSTEEN, TRACI LORDS

FRAT ▪ APHRODISIACS ▪ FAST FOOD ▪ SAVE THE BUSINESS

Lunch Wagon (1981). *Hot Dog...The Movie* (1984). *Hamburger: The Motion Picture* (1986). *Fast Food* (1989). One of these over-servings of empty cinematic calories doesn't belong. None of these boner-bait youthful-shenanigans sagas can really claim a sustenance-related plot: *Hot Dog* is actually a ski flick. *Hamburger* is a standalone masterwork of virtuoso lunacy existing on a cracked plane of perfection all its own. However, those movies and *Lunch Wagon* are rated R, and sloppily topped with recommended heaps of nudity and crudity. *Fast Food* isn't just PG-13; it also squanders the one-two casting punch of Jim ("Hey, Vern! It's me, Ernest!") Varney and Traci ("I swear to fucking God, Vern, I'm eighteen!") Lords.

After eight years in college, frat house wheeler-dealer Auggie (Clark Brandon, who played Jo Polniaczek's navy boyfriend on TV's *The Facts of Life*) and his partner-in-campus-scams pal Drew (Randal Patrick) are force-graduated into the real world. They immediately seek employment at Pop's, a gas station owned by Drew's grandfather.

Unfortunately, Pop died and left the place to Drew's pretty cousin Samantha (Tracy Griffith). Now Wrangler Bob (Varney), the stereotypical money-bagged Texan tycoon proprietor of the Wrangler Bob's fast-food chain, wants to purchase Pop's property to put up one of his restaurants. Auggie, Drew, and Samantha don't want to sell, though. They have dreams of converting the crumbling joint into their own burger paradise. Cue the fix-the-place-up music montage, and the rest of the stupid movie.

After Pop's Burgers opens for business, *Fast Food* takes a turn that packs a sack full of plot potential for a teen sex comedy classic. A couple of scientists on campus accidentally invent a liquid aphrodisiac that ends up in Pop's Burgers' secret sauce. From there, the chemically fortified grease pucks are served at a snooty sorority party, where they prove positively transformational for stuck-up Mary Beth (Pamela Springsteen, real-life sister of the Boss, and pep squad leader from *Fast Times at Ridgemont High*).

After this perfect setup, the film's frustration factor only multiplies. A wet-T-shirt contest is announced—but then *never happens*! Traci Lords, working as Wrangler Bob's corporate spy, sets out to seduce Auggie—only to have him stop her when she peels down to her bra and panties. *Fast Food* also wastes the presence of wondrous elfin-faced character actor Michael J. Pollard as a Pop's employee, and same goes for *Invasion of the Body Snatchers* (1956) great Kevin McCarthy as a judge. Director Michael A. Simpson did better by helming the second and third installments of the *Sleepaway Camp* slasher movie series. Those latter films both feature Pam Springsteen sporting a penis—an appendage apparently possessed by no one in *Fast Food*!

Fast Times at Ridgemont High [1982]

DIR. AMY HECKERLING; W/SEAN PENN, PHOEBE CATES, JUDGE REINHOLD, JENNIFER JASON LEIGH, ROBERT ROMANUS, RAY WALSTON

VIRGINITY ▫ SURFERS ▫ MINIMUM-WAGE JOBS ▫ BIG GAME ▫ MASTURBATION ▫ ABORTION

Fast Times at Ridgemont High is both cinema's great American teen sex comedy *and* its great American teen sex drama. This is the one teen movie toward which all previous teen movies led, and from which all have subsequently proceeded. The heart, soul, brains, funny bone, gonads, and remaining vital organs of every other film contained in this book extend, in one way or dozens of others, from *Fast Times at Ridgemont High*.

The movie begins with the book. *Fast Times* is adapted from a 1981 nonfiction novel of the same name by *Rolling Stone* reporter Cameron Crowe. The account details his adventures, at age twenty-four, posing for a semester as a high school student. Weirdly, the *Fast Times* book went out of print almost immediately following the film's release, and has never been reissued. Fortunately, first-time director Amy Heckerling translated the saga into a cinematic vision destined to live—and surf and dance and laugh and cry and party on, dude—forever.

No small credit for *Fast Times*' greatness must be awarded, as well, to casting director Don Phillips. Along with Heckerling, Phillips assembled a peerless squadron of up-and-coming stars to populate the world of Ridgemont High. Right up front, examine the perfection of Jeff Spicoli. Sean Penn creates an archetype from his very first moment on-screen, filtering the "Moondoggie" surfers of the 1960s Frankie-and-Annette beach party flicks through the Cheech-and-Chong '70s and emerging, wholly formed, as a new breed of perma-stoned surfer-mensch that would largely define the '80s. Spicoli rules Ridgemont High, in every sense, and his run-ins with strikingly dedicated history teacher Mr. Hand (Ray Walston) continue to shine as some of the most hilarious comic exchanges in all of cinema.

Fast Times spawned an equally enduring female co-phenomenon, Phoebe Cates. Emerging from a backyard pool in slow motion to the pulsating strains of "Moving in Stereo" by the Cars, she pops her red bikini top open and—*blammo!*—at least two moviegoing generations were rushed straight through puberty. The moment is elevated above mere exploitation, though, by virtue of being a fantasy in the mind of classmate Brad Hamilton (Judge Reinhold). He's watching her swim while he masturbates over a toilet. We see the vision right up to its mutually mortifying and nightmarish implosion when the non-fantasy Phoebe runs inside to use the bathroom and busts in on Judge stroking his gavel. *Blammo!*—puberty comes smashing back down hard in all its uncomfortable, ugly adolescent reality.

The main focus of *Fast Times*' plot is the unhappy sexual awakening of Stacy Hamilton (Jennifer Jason Leigh). She loses her virginity to an older stereo salesman, then drives a wedge between best friends Mark "Rat" Ratner (Brian Backer), a big-hearted nerd who's in love with her, and Mike Damone (Robert Romanus), a slick-talking ticket-scalper who gets her pregnant.

Stacy's awkward, unpleasant pool-house sex with Damone initially earned *Fast Times* an X rating. "There was a very graphic scene in the movie," Leigh told *Entertainment Tonight* in 1982. "It wasn't at all romanticized. It was instead the clumsy, awkward reality of what sex is for young kids. And the teenage audiences, when it was tested, were very uncomfortable with it, I think, because it hit too close to home, you know? It touched on all the anxieties. It's a very anxious time in a girl's life. So the scene was cut.

"So that's sad. The scene is not set up to have fifteen-year-olds go out and do this. My character isn't a role model but, rather, a reflection of fifteen-year-olds in the '80s."

Though the cut to secure an R rating only excised two seconds of film, the loss lingered with director Heckerling. "I had full-frontal nudity," she told *Slant* in 2016. "Because when I grew up, I had read that there was a sexual revolution happening. From what I could see, that meant that women are naked and men aren't. I didn't think that was fair. I thought, 'Well, maybe if there's a female making those movies, men can be naked too. And women will be the ones that are more hidden.' So I had a scene where you saw her from the side and you saw him from the front and then they went at it, and it was a horrible experience. Because I wasn't trying to be sexy.

"And they said, 'No, you can't show the male organ.' I said, 'How come it's okay for an R-rated film to have a naked female from the front, but not a naked guy?' And they said, 'The male organ is aggressive and the female organ isn't.'"

Whether on-screen or not, the coupling of Stacy and Damone results in a pregnancy, leading to an abortion (and some understandably vicious "Little Prick" graffiti revenge). The sympathetic and realistic depiction of the process, including getting a ride to the clinic, was unprecedented.

The film's perfectly conjured brew of mirth and dismay is further embodied by slices of screen life including: disgusted and frustrated cheerleaders (one of whom is Bruce Springsteen's sister) at a pepless pep rally; Ridgemont football sensation Jefferson (Forest Whittaker) assassinating rival players from Lincoln High on the field; Rat's date with Stacy during which he plays the wrong, non-sexy Led Zeppelin album; Damone's fast-jive romantic advice and Cheap Trick sales pitch; demented biology instructor Mr. Vargas (Vincent Schiavelli) gleefully displaying a medical cadaver; and the postscript where we learn that Spicoli went on to save Brooke Shields from drowning and spent all the reward money on hiring Van Halen to play his birthday party.

Behind so much greatness, however, were some real-life hard feelings on the part of actual high schooler Andy Rathbone. Crowe befriended Rathbone while undercover, and evidently based the Mark Ratner character on him. A dozen years later, Rathbone told *People* magazine that the experience hurt him terribly. "All the nerdy things I did [like losing Stacy to his best friend] were attributed to me," he lamented, "but all the cool things I did got attributed to someone else."

The most painful switch, Rathbone said, was that it was *he*—and not the kid who inspired Spicoli—who called for pizza delivery to his classroom. And the teacher loved him for it! Fortunately, Rathbone has been able to console himself by becoming a prominent author of the *... for Dummies* line of books that took over bookstore checkout lines in the '90s, eventually selling over 200 million copies. This coda seems like a character update straight out of the movie.

Oddly, despite the presence of a previously existing hit by the Go-Go's, the *Fast Times* soundtrack is dominated by middle-of-the-road '70s rockers such as Graham Nash, Poco, and every single member of the Eagles. Director Amy Heckerling's intended soundtrack, hand-plucked from L.A.'s neon wellspring of punk, hard rock, and omnipresent KROQ-crammed new wave, would have more accurately matched the teen tastes of the 1980s, but coproducer Irving Azoff didn't manage Oingo Boingo, he managed the Eagles.

Technically, *Fast Times* has two official theme songs: "Fast Times at Ridgemont High" by Sammy Hagar and "Fast Times" (The Best Years of Our Lives)" by Billy Squier. Each rocks mightily, with Squier taking the edge because of the song's prominent placement during a bone-pulping football blowout. For all that, it would seem that the single most out-of-place presence on the *Fast Times* soundtrack has to be Jimmy Buffett. However, his "I Don't Know (Spicoli's Theme)" is a lost classic—a fun, mildly new wave–ish anthem that brilliantly communicates Spicoli's inner life... and you can definitely surf to it. Cowabunga, you Parrot Head. Aloha.

FEELIN' UP [1976]
aka GETTING TOGETHER

DIRECTED BY DAVID SECTER; W/MALCOLM GROOME, KATHLEEN SEWARD, TONY COLLADO

VIRGINS ▪ THREESOME ▪ HIPPIES ▪ SPACE KIDS

Reprehensibly repackaged in the '80s by bait-and-switch schlockhouse Troma as a teen sex comedy, *Feelin' Up* is actually a post-hippie coming-of-age trifle concerning radical politics, avant-garde media, and the shedding of societal mores. Groovy, right? In the case of *Feelin' Up*, the proper descriptor is *grody*.

The feeler-upper who gets felt up in *Feelin' Up* is young, yearning-to-live-life-to-the-fullest filmmaker David (Malcolm Groome). He ditches his fancy things, including a Porsche (WTF?), en route to comingling with a multiracial, pansexual, polyamorous commune of free-loving artists on New York's Lower East Side. Everybody down there is cool, man—though maybe just a little boring.

Feelin' Up hilariously wraps up its long, dull plot with something akin to cosmic transcendence. David and his no-holes-barred cabal all marry one another and we fast-forward to a party atop a downtown rooftop, where they're joined by their brood of many nations, all clad in cheap "space-age" clothing. Some colorful streaks that might be flying cars zoom across the sky. A title on-screen reveals that we're witnessing "1985."

Back to the issue of misrepresentation. The *Feelin' Up* video box showcases an expertly executed photograph of a bugged-eye doofus reaching for an over-the-shoulder squeeze from his chesty movie theater date. The tagline is: "Remember what you felt when you were sixteen?" In this case, you would have felt horribly misled and cheated by Troma.

Ferris Bueller's Day Off

[1986]

DIR. JOHN HUGHES; W/MATTHEW BRODERICK, ALAN RUCK, MIA SARA, JEFFREY JONES

COOL KID 📼 DITCHING CLASS 📼 SWEET RIDE 📼 PRANKS 📼 SCAMS 📼 CHEERLEADER

Ferris Bueller's Day Off is a hugely treasured ode to the notion of kicking back and going your own way. Everybody loves Ferris. Everybody loves his day off. Everybody loves to imitate Ben Stein monotonously droning, "Bueller?...Bueller?... Bueller?" Everybody loves everything about *Ferris Bueller's Day Off*—don't they?

What's *not* to love? Ferris is an endearingly incorrigible scamp, always up to some new scam or other, incorporating the latest crazy technology into his own sweet talk and fancy footwork to blaze his own trail through the course of whatever comes his way. In the course of a single school day, we witness him expertly faking illness to skip class; roguishly liberating his troubled best buddy, Cameron (Alan Ruck); showering affection upon his beautiful cheerleader girlfriend, Sloane (Mia Sara); and socking it to every fascist agent of authority, from a snooty French restaurant maître d' (Jonathan Schmock) to Principal Ed Rooney (Jeffrey Jones). Jones is so hell-bent on busting Bueller's independent streak that he'll stop at nothing short of his own physical ruin to do so.

Ferris is loaded with long green. Dude has *money*, honey! He changes into four different swanky-fresh designer outfits before 11 a.m., with more to come. His musical taste is all about European new wave imports. Through outspoken monologues addressed straight to the camera, Ferris reveals time and again how he is the single most learned, with-it, perceptive, and empirically wise individual regardless of age, life experience, or any other specifics in the entire world as it is defined by the Chicagoland area.

No wonder everybody from his teachers to his fellow students to anyone he encounters anywhere worships Ferris Bueller. He inspires thousands of people of color to spontaneously burst into coordinated dance routines all over downtown Chicago landmarks in honor of his lip-sync rendition of "Twist and Shout" during the Polish Day Parade—bringing the races together in one jubilant swoop. Yes, everyone adores and draws strength from Ferris—well, except his sister, Jeanie Bueller (Jennifer Grey), but she's just jealous. How could she not be?

On top of all this, Ferris Bueller maintains his superhuman level of cool, savvy, and anything-is-possible gumption despite some severe handicaps in life. As Ferris himself reveals what happened on a recent birthday while rigging up his multi-thousand-dollar home PC system and keyboard synthesizer to aid in his latest kooky caper: "I wanted a car. I got a computer. Talk about being born under a bad sign!"

Here comes the breaking news: Everyone does *not* love Ferris Bueller. Seated among cheering audiences everywhere even on its first blockbuster release weekend were those of us who wanted to strangle the beyond-privileged, beyond-obnoxious, beyond-deplorable hegemonic brainwash weapon of class warfare up on the screen that was identifying itself as Ferris Bueller. *Ferris Bueller* makes me upend my popcorn bucket and foam from every head-hole.

With that in mind, I'm also loath to author a book centrally focused on teen comedies of the 1980s and then drone on pompously (like Ben Stein) about how your favorite teen comedy of the 1980s is poisonous garbage.

On the plus side, Hughes finds his footing as a director here, and delivers his takedown of the average putz with confident pacing and effective storytelling. The cartoony moments are especially well mounted, such as when Ferris presumptuously runs home through other people's houses. The acting, across the board, fits the material flawlessly. As Principal Rooney, Jeffrey Jones is an oasis of high comic wattage shining bright beyond his surroundings; just as

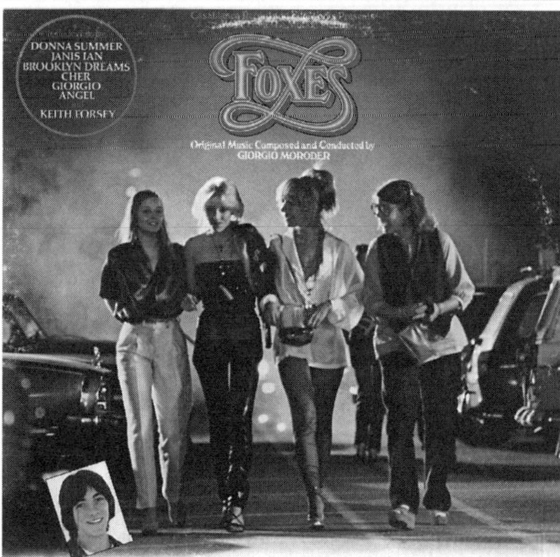

Clockwise from top left: Full Moon High *(1981) howled four years before* Teen Wolf; Free Ride *(1986) doesn't let a language barrier interfere with entry to una película de infierno adolescente;* For Keeps *(1988), Molly Ringwald's teen queen Waterloo; the foxes of* Foxes *(1980) showing slight vinyl ring wear.*

he was the same summer in *Howard the Duck*. Edie McClurg, as Rooney's housewife-caricature secretary, is equally stellar. Jennifer Grey's brain-boiling disgust over Ferris is palpable, but, as you might guess, I'm sympathetic to her point of view. Notably, Charlie Sheen scores a "star-is-born" moment during his quick police station bit as a leather-jacketed bad boy who beguiles Grey and loosens her up.

Still, when it comes to the title figure, my reading of *Ferris Bueller's Day Off* remains pure outrage. First, there's the whole "I didn't get a car" thing. You know what? *Fuck you!* More subtly and infuriating; watch how Ferris interacts with anyone who's not white, not rich, not from an exclusive suburb, not in possession of expensive material items, or, ultimately, not him. Ferris drops wisdom to us in a men's room while a portly old attendant snoozes through his duties at the end of the sink. Regardless, our smartly sweater-vested messiah whips out a brick of pocket cash and drops some in the tip jar anyway, rousing the codger just enough for him to mutter some thanks to his better. Note the swarthy, swollen-nosed, indeterminately ethnic parking garage attendant and his fat black buddy who pull a fast one on Ferris by pretending to park the aforementioned Ferrari before busting it out for a joyride. Don't trust menial cogs in the machine and their minority coconspirators—*that* is the actual message of *Ferris Bueller*.

The world at large sees the movie's tagline, "Leisure rules!", as a joyful taunt, but not me. John Hughes wrote his way into filmmaking via *National Lampoon* humor pieces that were obscene, explosive screeds of anarchic contempt. They were also savagely hilarious, revealing the dark and brutal mind that seethed behind his adorable teen films. *Ferris Bueller* is where Hughes perfectly camouflaged his naked slash-and-burn wit and toxic notions of who should rightfully be in charge of the universe in a cutesy, smirking Trojan horse. So consider that the edict "Leisure rules!" may just a subliminal variation on the overarching command of John Carpenter's 1988 alien-takeover nightmare *They Live*: "OBEY!"

THE FIRST TIME [1969]

DIR. JAMES NEILSON; W/JACQUELINE BISSET, WES STERN, RICKEY KELMAN, WINK ROBERTS

VIRGINS ▫ OLDER WOMAN ▫ HOOKERS

The First Time emerged in 1969 and boasts a *trés* groovy mellow psych-pop soundtrack, but somehow the whole thing looks and feels like it happened ten years earlier. Kenny (Wes Stern), Mike (Rickey Kelman), and Tommy (Wink Roberts) come off like peachy-keen, clean-cut Eisenhower-era sitcom teens, even as they sneak off to the Canadian side of Niagara Falls on a hunt for a house of prostitution. Did Wally Cleaver, the Beav, and Lumpy Rutherford ever trawl for whores?

The assembled Grand Dorks Three never locate a brothel, but they do provide quite a peppy travelogue of Niagara Falls ("Look it's the *Maid o' the Mist*! *The* Maid o' the Mist!"). They also team up with Anna (Jacqueline Bisset), a local woman either deeply troubled or terminally imbecilic, as she believes only these nimrods can help her sneak across the upstate New York border. "I have an English accent!" she frets.

The First Time's tagline cuts both ways: "Funny, nobody thinks about boys when they say the word 'virgin.'" Funny, nobody watching Kenny, Mike, and Tommy will be able to think anything *but* that.

THE FIRST TIME [1983] aka DOIN' IT

DIR. CHARLIE LOVENTHAL; W/TIM CHOATE, KRISTA ERRICKSON, WALLACE SHAWN

VIRGIN ▫ FILM SCHOOL ▫ EVIL PROFESSOR

Freshman film student Charlie Lichtenstein (Tim Choate) chases campus sexpot Dana (Krista Errickson) while enduring the bombastic pretensions of a pompous professor (Wallace Shawn, a hoot as usual) and remaining oblivious to the affection of nerdy-but-wonderful Wendy (Wendy Fulton). *The First Time*'s writer-director-producer shares both a first name and a last initial with his on-screen protagonist, so let's assume we're seeing something autobiographical.

Not quite a sex comedy or a straight coming-of-age saga, this second movie called *The First Time* has not aged especially well. The unusual focus on the specific dynamics of film school, though, and the portrait of the artist as a young nimrod do distinguish this from the post-*Porky's* T&A avalanche.

In hindsight, those atypical factors might explain why highbrow critics went out-of-character bonkers in 1983 for a film marketed to preteens looking for some hijinks and grab-ass. Mainstream critics noticeably gave a bit of overly corrective love to a flick whose poster featured hot-and-bothered coeds gathered around a dazed dude with dropped drawers and altering a chalkboard declaration to read: "Charlie is was the only virgin on campus!"

THE FIRST TURN-ON!! [1983]

DIR. LLOYD KAUFMAN, MICHAEL HERZ; W/GEORGIA HARRELL, MICHAEL SANVILLE, GOOGY GRESS

SUMMER CAMP ▫ VIRGINS ▫ NERDS ▫ WEED ▫ FAT GUY ▫ ITALIAN STUD

For decades, Troma Entertainment honchos Lloyd Kaufman and Michael Herz have piddled the B-flick and midnight movie pool with smug, cutesy-poo, self-aware, self-loathing and sarcasm dressed up as "over-the-top" schlock. *The First Turn-On!!* is a prime grade-Z example. It's goddamned despicable when a filmmaker churns out a "horror comedy" as the obvious result of inability to make a proper horror movie. *The First Turn-On!!* is Troma's "send-up" of raucous summer camp comedies, and festers far beneath even the toilet-sorry levels of *Gorp* (1980) or, worse, *Moonrise Kingdom* (2012).

On the last day of summer at Camp Tee Pee, a counselor leads teen campers on a nature hike. While visiting a cave, the fat dude farts and the resulting rockslide traps everybody inside. Once the hikers settle down, various Tee Pee–ers regale the others with recollections of how they each lost their virginity. The flashbacks play as slapstick with cartoon soundtracks. A softer-than-soft-core orgy climaxes the proceedings.

Vincent D'Onofrio makes his screen debut as the manic musclehead "Lobotomy." Mark Torgl plays the same nerd he would portray as "Melvin Junko" the following year in Troma's signature opus, *The Toxic Avenger*. Troma owners Kaufman and Herz swear that a young Madonna practically beat down the Troma office door to demand a part in *The First Turn-On*, but they passed. I'd say those two are clueless enough for that claim to be credible.

THE FLAMINGO KID [1984]

DIR. GARRY MARSHALL; W/MATT DILLON, HECTOR ELIZONDO, RICHARD CRENNA, JANET JONES

GRADUATION ▫ SUMMER JOB ▫ BIKINIS ▫ THE BIG GAME

The Flamingo Kid served as an ideal and even liberating vehicle for Matt Dillon just as he wrapped up his back-to-back 1983 Francis Ford Coppola "Apocalypse Teen" epics, *The Outsiders* and *Rumble Fish*—two undertakings that immediately conjure Sgt. Hulka's famous line from *Stripes*: "Lighten up, Francis!"

By contrast, *The Flamingo Kid*'s summertime story of recently graduated seventeen-year-old Brooklyn palooka Jeffrey Willis (Dillon) taking a cabana boy job at a swanky Long Island beach club is sunny and spiky, breezy and ready to brawl. *Kid* is as inherently likeable as Dillon himself, and part of his persona's appeal is an obviously rough-hewn good heart, backed by the excitement that at any given moment he also might sock you in the solar plexus.

Jeffrey's blue-collar dad Arthur (Hector Elizondo) hopes his son will go to college, or at least get a gig that will instill in him the virtue of hard work. Jeff starts to think otherwise—immediately and intensely—upon exposure to the surfside Flamingo Club. This place is a paradise full of bikini beauties, an Olympic-size swimming pool, doting members, and enticing gin rummy games lorded over by flashy car dealer and card shark Phil Brody (Richard Crenna). All Jeff wants to do is figure out how to keep his daily scam-in-the-sunshine going all year long.

Romantic tantalization floats Jeff's way in the form of Flamingo club bombshell Carla Samson (Janet Jones), but *The Flamingo Kid*'s core story is about an outer-borough New York street mook choosing between two father figures—his real-life pop, who preaches honest labor, or a gaudy show-off who comes by glitz through unsavory short cuts. Robert De Niro's *A Bronx Tale* (1993) covers the same ground from a different angle. In every sense, though, *The Flamingo Kid* is the day-at-the-beach version. Bask in it and enjoy.

For Keeps [1988] aka Maybe Baby

DIR. JOHN G. AVILDSEN; W/MOLLY RINGWALD, RANDALL BATINKOFF, KENNETH MARS, MIRIAM FLYNN

TEEN PREGNANCY ▫ HIGH SCHOOL NEWSPAPER ▫ GRADUATION

For Keeps is Molly Ringwald's Waterloo—the definitive '80s teen star's final film as a teen star, and, really, her last film as a star, period. Although this nondescript pregnant-during-puberty comedy reportedly made a tidy profit on a tiny budget, the movie came off as a bomb at the time and quickly vamoosed, not even registering as a cable rerun of note. The public seemed to suddenly shrug off the Molly Moment after four fast years, which is, perhaps not coincidentally, the length of your average non-pregnant high school student's entire career.

Molly plays Darcy Elliot, a Kenosha, Wisconsin, school newspaper editor who gets knocked up by Stan (Randall Batinkoff). He's her Captain Dullard boyfriend who plans on studying architecture at Caltech after graduation. The two parents-to-be get married and have the kid. Then Darcy suffers some postpartum depression and they go to college together at the end. As the final credits roll, you'll think, "Wait—the guy who directed *Rocky* and the *Karate Kid* made this? Did he get knocked unconscious on the set while showing off how he used to film fight scenes and nobody noticed until the movie came out?"

Foxes [1980]

DIR. ADRIAN LYNE; W/JODIE FOSTER, CHERIE CURRIE, SCOTT BAIO, SALLY KELLERMAN

SEX ▫ DRUGS ▫ ROCK AND ROLL

Review by Rachel McPadden

Jeanie & Annie & Madge & Deirdre. *Foxes* fleshes out the girl stereotypes more than most movies of the time—including *Little Darlings*, and that's saying something. Jeanie (Jodie Foster) is the clever, smart-alecky, streetwise daughter of an absent British rock manager and an aging blonde divorcee-slash-UCLA undergrad (Sally Kellerman). Jeanie raises herself for the most part, dodging Mom's sleepover guests and Me Generation existential freak-outs. She longs for her own apartment, preferably with her three constant companions. She seems like she would never cry, yet she's always crying.

Annie (Cherie Currie of the Runaways) is the hanging-on-Hollyweird-Boulevard super-doper, the heavy-eyed elephant in the room, a tragedy-to-be, the daughter of a violent cop and a pilled-up zombie punching-bag housewife. The Annies of the world pull us in with charismatic chemical fearlessness, all tube tops and feathered hair. She has the druggy talk of a dude (*maaan*), and friends have to look up Hollywood Huggy Bear pimps to try to find her on a bender. She's always just out of reach, but if you could just save her and re-harness that energy for good, together you'd rule all of SoCal forever and ever.

Madge (Marilyn Kagan) is the normie, the baby. She has sweet, loving married parents, younger siblings, a clean comfortable home, and an unlikely semi-secret thirtysomething music industry graphic designer boyfriend (Randy Quaid). She's shy and nerdy, with big glasses and baggy clothes, and a little softer physically than the other girls. She appears stalled at the threshold of adolescence—except for that older boyfriend.

Foxes offers scarce info on Deirdre (Kandice Stroh), but the stereotype is clear. She embraces spaghetti-strap leotards, wedge heels, and cigarette holders, working over grocery-bagging surfers with a little whoops-I-dropped-my-Tic-Tacs or whatever. She is acutely aware of the power of her sexuality ("I never said I wanna *go* with him, I said I wanna *ball* him"). Even though she breaks down at one point, bemoaning her sophisticate's burden as the group liquor-acquirer, and revealing her mother doesn't know where she is, my guess is Deirdre goes on to get the nose job and pose for *Penthouse*.

These are not teenagers that revel in being teenagers, but "short forty-year-olds" as Jeanie's mother so accurately accuses. They want dinner parties, and they feel the urge to run away to Oregon. They don't want to be tethered to their families of origin, they want to blow everything up. Ruining your own life is a real bittersweet liberation. *Foxes* is the *Sex and the City* prequel for a generation of women who each love their girl gang, but always feel alone, and still live for a horse ranch fantasy dished out by an absentee rock star dad who strokes his daughter's hair, tries to pay her off with clothes-shopping money, and tells her Mom is doing her best.

Foxes offers all these gifts, plus Chachi-era Scott Baio in tuxedo T-shirt on a skateboard, Damone from *Fast Times*, and a young Laura Dern.

FRATERNITY VACATION [1985]

DIR. JAMES FRAWLEY; W/STEPHEN GEOFFREYS, TIM ROBBINS, CAMERON DYE

NERD ▫ JOCKS ▫ PREPPIES ▫ BIKINIS ▫ VIRGIN

"Wendell Tvedt is the ultimate nerd!" proclaims the poster for *Fraternity Vacation*. Below that promising tagline, a lovingly painted scenario depicts Hawaiian-shirted, tube-socked, panic-pussed Wendell flailing into a hotel pool as he fails to wrangle a beach ball, a boom box, scuba gear, an umbrella, a Polaroid camera, a magazine, and a can of Diet Sunkist (a new low in company self-esteem in product placement). In the water, a buxom bikini blonde braces herself for Wendell's impact. Behind the action, a quartet of hunks and hotties crack up.

Fraternity Vacation's poster potently and just about perfectly conveys the on-target calculated nuttiness of this laudably contrived spring-break romp. In fact, its imagery is so flawless that a second tagline was necessary: "Meet Wendell Tvedt. Would you believe he's about to become America's #1 hunk? What happens to him could happen to you!"

Therein lies the inherent promise of *Fraternity Vacation* and, by extension, all other teen sex comedies. Just as the movie's title is a conscious rip of *National Lampoon's Vacation* (1983) and its imagery directly recalls *Revenge of the Nerds* (1984), that final tag almost directly quotes the ads for 1981's *Private Lessons* ("What happened to him should happen to you!"). The reason fans so vividly remember *Fraternity Vacation*, *ROTN*, and *Private Lessons* is that each makes good on its come-on. Here, at last, were movies that really depicted the stuff of which soiled-sock-under-the-mattress dreams were made.

For *Fraternity Vacation*, the greatness begins and ends with Mr. Tvedt, brought to life indelibly by ultra-mega-spaz Stephen Geoffreys while smack in the midst of his history-making 1985 teen movie run. That year he also starred as Evil Ed in *Fright Night* and as Williams, the Catholic school chronic masturbator, in *Heaven Help Us*. Geoffreys is one of his era's great wing-nut screen oddities, and Wendell stands as his finest hour. He is sweet, sincere, naïve, twitchy, horny, and perpetually courting or causing disaster. Given Geoffreys' demented resemblance to a young Jack Nicholson, Wendell also raises the specter of Wilbur Force—Nicholson's maniacally masochistic dental patient in *Little Shop of Horrors* (1960)—and what he might have been like on college break in the mid-'80s in Palm Springs.

Right on par with Geoffreys is Tim Robbins, who fully and with relentless shirtlessness commits to portraying Larry "Mother" Tucker, half of a frat-bro team with Cameron Dye (*Valley Girl, The Joy of Sex*). Together, they're Wendell's very jockish, sort of jerkish, cool-guy best buds who initially use "the ultimate nerd" for his uncle's poolside condo. Eventually, they come around and become enlightened by Wendell's inherent glow.

The rival BMOCs are spoiled business scions Chas Lawlor III and J. C. Springer, douched to maximum obnoxious, respectively, by Leigh McCloskey (Eve Plumb's underage hustler boyfriend in *Dawn: Portrait of a Teenage Runaway*) and Matt McCoy (mental patient Lloyd Braun on *Seinfeld*). Mother and Joe compete with these rich twits to win the affection of Sheree J. Wilson as elegant blonde hardbody Ashley.

Even the movie's "Hi, we're naked" talent is of unique caliber. Bikini tops fly off cult flick starlets Barbara Crampton (*Re-Animator, Chopping Mall*) and Kathleen Kinmont (*Bride of the Re-Animator, Halloween 4*) as party girls who set up a really clunky herpes gag.

The TV backgrounds of director James Frawley (he's helmed everything from *The Monkees* to *Grey's Anatomy*) and screenwriter Lindsay Harrison (*One Day at a Time, Too Close for Comfort*) prove a spot-on fit. After a clever opening that parodies *The Wizard of Oz*, the movie is a well-oiled, mechanically clean dirty-joke machine.

Amanda Bearse plays Nicole Ferret, the well-to-do-lovely who falls in love with our hero and relieves him of his cursed virginity. Later in 1985, Stephen Geoffreys and Bearse went on to even more memorably costar in *Fright Night*. That's not all they share in common. In 1993, while playing Marcy Darcy on the sitcom *Married...with Children*, Amanda Bearse came out, loud and proud, as lesbian. Five years later, just in time for the Internet to make trading such material so fun and easy, keen-eyed male homosexual pornography enthusiasts picked out "power bottom" performer "Sam Ritter" as Wendell Tvedt.

After being pegged as a gay porn star, Geoffreys disappeared for a spell before embracing his past and returning to horror acting in 2007's *Sick Girl*. Since then, Stephen has been a hardworking B-movie presence and a popular guest at the rising tide of fan conventions. Always the hero, that guy. And remember: What happened to him could happen to you!

FREE RIDE [1986]

DIR. TOM TRBOVICH; W/GARY HERSHBERGER, DAWN SCHNEIDER, REED RUDY, MAMIE VAN DOREN

PREP SCHOOL ▪ PEEPING ▪ MOBSTERS ▪ SEXY NURSE ▪ RAMBO

Gary Hershberger, who played a lonesome new kid in town in *Paradise Motel* (1985), does a 180 in *Free Ride*. He stomps onto the screen as prep school coolster Dan Garten, a hot-shit fast-talker who taps the same contemporaneous energy that drove Tom Hanks' early *Bachelor Party* persona and, around the same time, Ferris Bueller.

While trawling a nightclub, Dan lays lines on foxy dancer Jill (Dawn Schneider) about surviving combat in Vietnam. When a valet brings him a snazzy red Ferrari by accident, there's no way he can't "borrow" it. Same goes for the $250,000 in cash he finds stashed under the seats. With this windfall, Dan bribes his way to straight A's; he no longer worries about walking into the girls' shower room while it's occupied; and he ups his a-hole game sufficiently until the mobsters to whom the car and the cash belong take notice and come gunning.

Free Ride's final third entails Dan, Jill, and their cohort dressing up like Rambo (except for one guy in a nun outfit) and sort of proto-*Home-Alone*-ing their way free from the mob—"the Garbagio Family." That section has aged worse than even the *Rambo* afternoon cartoon series. Better is a bit with '50s bosom bombshell Mamie Van Doren as a sex-bomb nurse who lines up the members of the boys' gym class and checks them individually for hernias. "See me in my office later for a full physical," MVD purrs to, of course, to the dorkiest nerdenstein on campus.

Nerrrd! Harold Lloyd is The Freshman *(1925).*

THE FRESHMAN [1925]

DIRS. FRED NEWMEYER, SAM TAYLOR; W/HAROLD LLOYD

NERD ▣ JOCKS ▣ THE BIG GAME ▣ BOOB

With circular eyeglass frames, boater hat, and a wiry body that seemed to defy any laws of physics, funnyman Harold Lloyd is an icon of silent cinema. In his worldwide hit *The Freshman* (1925), Harold Lloyd also begat the very archetype that would evolve into Charles Martin Smith in *American Graffiti* (1973), Robert Carradine in *Revenge of the Nerds* (1984), and Eddie Deezen in absolutely anything. Lloyd was cinema's first big nerd on campus.

Lloyd plays a nervous new college arrival, who, despite being built like a pipe cleaner, attempts to a impress a coed by trying out for the football team. He fails, but the coach agrees to use him as the team's tackling dummy. Naturally, after an array of comical humiliations and spine-bending-slapstick, Lloyd ends up winning the big game.

As the word "nerd" didn't yet exist in the popular lexicon, the term the other students use to describe Lloyd is "boob." So, once again, Harold Lloyd was way ahead of the teen sex comedy formula on every possible curve.

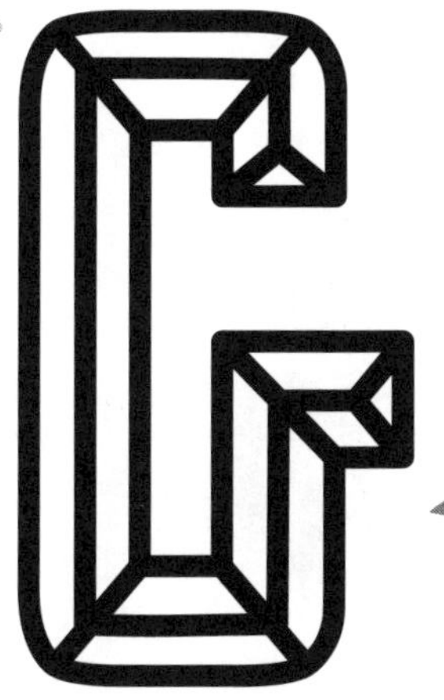

GAS PUMP GIRLS [1979]

DIR. JOEL BENDER; W/KRISTEN BAKER, LINDA LAWRENCE, SANDY JOHNSON

GRADUATION ▫ SUMMER JOB ▫ LOCKER ROOM ▫ MUSICAL NUMBER ▫ OIL FIGHT ▫ RADIO DJ

Gas Pump Girls kicks off with Hometown High's class of 1979 graduation. Unbeknownst to the celebrants, local motorcycle clowns the Vultures (apishly modeled after *Grease*'s second-tier T-Birds) have rigged all the chairs to tear the gowns off female graduates as they rise to accept their diplomas. This being California in the late 1970s, brassieres do not get in the way of what the Vultures' prank reveals. The ribald and chaotic stunt is a fine send-off for the young grads and a righteous start to this movie.

Among the defrocked sheepskin recipients is bouncy blonde June (Kirsten Baker). She soon receives word that her beloved Uncle Joe (Huntz Hall) has been waylaid by cardiac trouble and needs help. The poor old grease monkey has succumbed to the stress of his rinky-dink gas station being squashed by Pyramid Fuels, the corporate behemoth erecting a state-of-the-art service facility just across the road. The ironically named Mr. Friendly (Dave Shelley) lords over the Pyramid outpost, ruling his roost beneath a framed photo of FBI queenpin J. Edgar Hoover.

Nice niece June deigns to single-handedly rescue Uncle Joe's joint. She needs an out-of-nowhere musical number, "I'm Lonely," to get started. Heeding June's distress, bosom pals Betty (Linda Lawrence), April (Sandy Johnson), January (Rikki Marin), and Jane (Leslie King) soon arrive. With pluck, teamwork, and body parts barely packed into tiny halter tops and too-short short-shorts, our heroines ultimately unsaddle Mr. Friendly and his cold capitalist masters.

Uncle Joe is portrayed by Huntz Hall, aka "Satch," second-in-command of that 1940s guttersnipe NYC comedy collective, the Bowery Boys. Mr. Friendly hires a pair of bumbling mobsters, including one played by Joe E. "Ooh-Ooh" Ross, known to TV rerun viewers as Police Officer Gunther Toody on *Car 54, Where Are You?* Meanwhile, manning the local all-knowing, all-commenting radio tower à la Wolfman Jack in *American Graffiti* is Cousin Brucie, primo hairpiece of the New York radio airwaves.

The soundtrack, once available on Blockbuster records and tapes, veers toward sunny soft rock and silken disco—or both, in the case of main theme "Love Is a Gas." The Vultures, in accents that take me home to old Bensonhurst, reconfig-

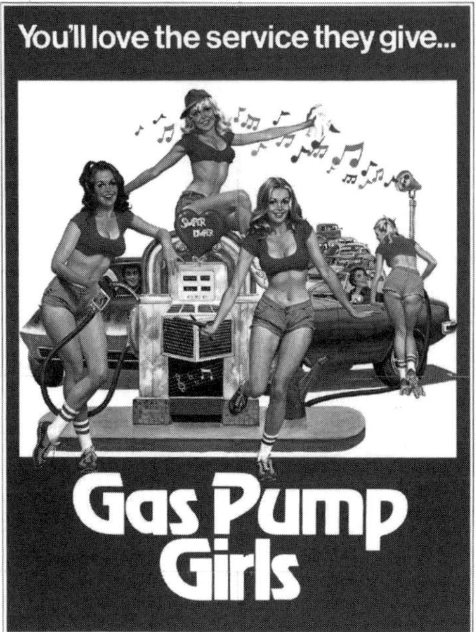

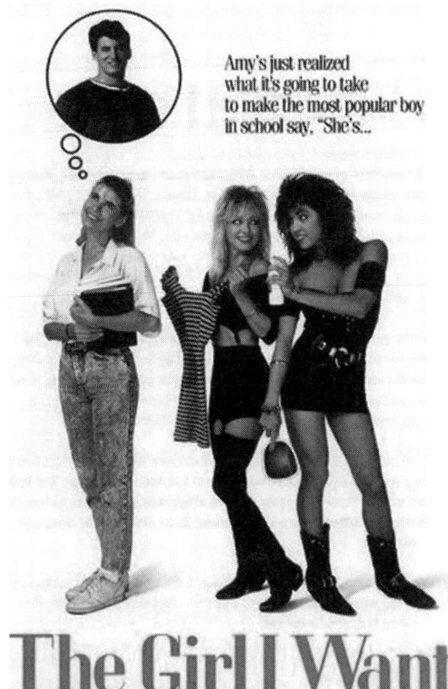

Clockwise from top left: Gas Pump Girls (1979) *turns into a musical, making it a must-see;* Going All the Way *(1982), is right in line with this book;* The Girl I Want *(1990), hangs on another punk reference, this time Devo:* Grandview U.S.A. (1984) *has a funny way, indeed.*

ure the opening "ooh-wah, ooh-wah" of Frankie Lymon & the Teenagers' "Why Do Fools Fall in Love?" singing in proper New York–ese, "Ooh-wah, ooh-wah, ya mutha is a *who-wah*!"

Beyond all that, *Gas Pump Girls* has remarkably endured through the decades, first as a drive-in programmer, then as a pass-along VHS tape, and, kind of strangely, in recent years as a popular video-on-demand feature. Long may these girls, and this gas, continue to pump.

Get Crazy [1983]

DIR. ALLAN ARKUSH; W/DANIEL STERN, MALCOLM MCDOWELL, ALLEN GARFIELD, LOU REED

THE BIG CONCERT ▪ PUNKS ▪ NEW WAVERS ▪ HIPPIES ▪ MAD BOMBER ▪ CLINT HOWARD

Get Crazy is a raucous, anything-goes cult musical comedy that pops rock-and-roll mythology open like a crate of canned champagne during the ultimate New Year's Eve all-star spectacular.

The Saturn Theater, modeled on the legendary Fillmore in San Francisco, stands poised to close unless fortunes change like right now for owner Max Black (Allen Garfield, modeling his role on Fillmore promoter Bill Graham). Saturn staffer Neil (Daniel Stern) calls in favors and rushes together a December 31 blowout, kicking off non-stop beer-shooting-out-your-nose comic chaos.

Directed by Allan Arkush, who also made the Ramones' *Rock 'n' Roll High School*, *Get Crazy* loads every scene like a *Mad* magazine panel while unloading kitchen-sink gags at a rate that makes it *Airplane!* for classic rock obsessives.

Malcolm McDowell achieves comic nirvana as Reggie Wanker, a megastar combination of Mick Jagger, David Bowie, and Caligula. Fear front man Lee Ving hams it up as a revolting punk named Piggy. Real-life AM-radio heartthrobs Fabian and Bobby Sherman parody themselves as uncomfortably aging teen idols Mark and Marv. Howard Kaylan, of the Turtles and Frank Zappa's Mothers, socks it to hippies in the space-case role of Captain Cloud.

Further enriching the *Get Crazy* are Ed Begley Jr. (*This Is Spinal Tap*) as the chief evil real estate schemer; Mary Woronov (Principal Togar from *Rock 'n' Roll High School*) as a high-strung lighting director; Paul Bartel (*Eating Raoul*) as Max Black's physician; Dick Miller (*A Bucket of Blood*) as a concerned parent; Franklin Ajaye (*Car Wash*) as a soul slickster named Cool; Clint Howard (tons of stuff; you know him) as the head usher; and '80s horror scream queen Linnea Quigley (Trash from *Return of the Living Dead*) as a groupie who screams very much indeed.

Get Crazy's genuine shocker is rock's archetypal unsmiling gloom-fiend Lou Reed as Auden, an affectionately savage send-up of Bob Dylan. As the concert wails through the night, Auden orders a taxi driver to just keep driving so he can write a ludicrous song before going onstage. You will not believe you're witnessing Lou Reed actually pull off silliness. Go figure—and *Get Crazy*.

Getting It On! [1983]
aka American Voyeur

DIR. WILLIAM OLSEN; W/MARTIN YOST, HEATHER KENNEDY, JEFF EDMOND, KATHY BRICKMEIER

PEEPING ▪ PROM ▪ PILLOW FIGHT ▪ VIDEO ARCADE ▪ CRAZY PREACHER

With a Noo Yawk accent borrowed from Scott Baio's cousin Jimmy, Alex Carlson (Martin Yost) is an entrepreneurial North Carolina sixteen-year-old in 1983. Here at the dawn of the home video revolution, Alex predicts a rich future in the surveillance industry. He's righter than anyone imagined, of course, but when Alex hits up his dad (Terry Loughlin) for four grand to launch a "security camera" business, his true intentions are simply to modernize his own spy technology from binoculars in order to more effectively peer into the bedroom of luscious classmate and neighbor, Sally (Heather Kennedy).

Alex's best bud, Nick (Jeff Edmund), wants in on the racket. He's a *boner* fide perv with unnerving inner-tube lips, who, in another moment of *Getting It On!*'s uncanny future foresight, "gifts" females all over campus with Polaroid shots of his wang. Together, Alex and Nick secretly film various undressed females, including a group of girls involved in a bra-and-panties sleepover pillow fight featuring full-frontal nudity. The serial snoopers also record the a-hole school principal's hot daughter Marilyn (Kathy Brickmeier) having sex with Jeff's brother, Richard (Mark Alan Ferri). That videotape, as per the rules of movies like this, accidentally gets screened for the entire student body during a school assembly.

The madness hurtles along enjoyably if confusingly. They visit a video arcade, where Nick is clearing playing a machine called Robby Roto that he keeps referring to as "Nuclear Madness." They attend a costume party in which George Washington and Uncle Sam hoover rails of cocaine. At one point, Nick is busted for shoplifting a porno mag at a convenience store. Two seconds later, a little kid sashays into the frame with a monster boom box on his shoulder and asks the camera, "Wanna see my radio?" All this getting it on builds to a sexual blackmail revenge scheme that the boys somehow pull off successfully.

The *Getting It On* soundtrack is a winner, too. Stuffed with local North Carolina acts, the songs are mostly terrible in a manner that fans of these films will love. Of particular goofy coolness is Buddy Causey's "(Watching My) Video," an idiotically sincere ode to doing just what the title says. In the film the song underscores a thrilling montage of shopping for electronic equipment.

Writer-director William Olsen crafts a whacked-out wet-dream vision where everyone's both a voyeur and an object of voyeurism, and the main function of constantly developing technology is to serve that mutual fetish. Watching this time capsule in the twenty-first century can be disconcerting, as the movie celebrates the genesis of our present snoop society. The erosion of private space all goes down tastily with a likeable handmade, homey Southern flavor, and happy nudes.

Be warned, however: The closing credits bill Amrita Bost as "Nude Girl with Flamethrower," yet *Getting It On!* contains *no* actual flamethrower!

Getting Lucky [1990]

DIR. MICHAEL PAUL GIRARD; W/STEVEN COOKE, LEZLIE Z. MCCRAW, RICK MCDOWELL, GARY KLUGER

VIRGINS ▣ BEER ▣ SEX MAGIC ▣ SKATEBOARD ▣ FRENCH EXCHANGE STUDENT

The pubes are the thing in *Getting Lucky*, crowding out many other bonkers aspects of this hyper-amateur, seemingly shot-on-Scotch-tape, late-night-cable staple. Consider the very premise of *Getting Lucky*: Bullied high school towel boy Bill (Steven Cooke) finds Lepke the Leprechaun (Gary Kluger) trapped in a lucky beer bottle. Bill gains three wishes, which he uses to win over remarkably glum cheerleader Krissi (Lezlie Z. McCraw). Throughout the movie, Bill and Lepke converse by way of the beer bottle. Lepke is about an inch tall, and speaks like Carvel's Cookie O'Puss ice cream cake on a helium jag.

Getting Lucky's villainous jock (Rick McDowell) is named Tony Chanuka (pronounced "cha-NOO-kah"). He repeatedly threatens to sexually assault both his punching bag Bill and his girlfriend Krissi; at least until Lepke zaps him into shoving a tennis racket up his own ass. Further hazards await, however, as the school principal furiously paddles Bill's bare keister over a misuse of magic that makes the lad suddenly appear in the girls' crowded shower room. Lepke responds by hitting the principal with a heart attack spell.

Despite all this malarkey in *Getting Lucky*, the pubes still manage to steal the show. At one point, Bill wishes he could get into Krissi's underpants; but Lepke botches a bewitchment and shrinks the teen down to the size of a baby cockroach or—just maybe—a pubic louse. We see Bill in a room full of billowy, pale pink balloon walls intended to depict Krissi's thighs, from which spring a patch of long, wavy, black ropes, which are supposed to be the hairs around her vulva. Krissi is sitting in history class when this spell goes down. Bill, crawling all over her *mons veneris*, frantically scrambles to crawl up the grotesque black ropes of Krissi's pubes. He waves his arms and legs all about in an effort to avoid getting sucked up inside her moistening vagina. Due to all his spastic kicking, stroking, and pawing about her clitoral area, Bill delivers Krissi into massive orgasm right at her desk. He is immediately doused with geysers of feminine discharge. This really happens. Though all we actually see is a jackass among blowsy sheets with black ropes attached to them, *Getting Lucky* makes a *Ben Hur* production out of its hero being consumed by the heroine's genitalia.

After the pubes scene, writer-director Michael Paul Girard must have figured he could literally pull off anything, so that's what he tried to do. The sprightly paced and easygoing *Getting Lucky* then erupts in a climax involving attempted sex crimes, kidnapping, vice detectives named Faukett and Nubbs, shish-kebab swordplay, Genghis Khan appearing from nowhere, and the two underage leads getting married.

Lezlie Z. McCraw's embattled pom-pom heroine Krissi not only looks like a high school student, she acts like one—not in the manner of a teenaged thespian; just like a kid with a camera pointed at her, and she does *not* seem happy. Not surprisingly, she never made another movie. Auteur Michael Paul Girard, however, went on to craft, among other gems, *Bikini Med School* (1994), *Witchcraft IX: Bitter Flesh* (1997), and the Dana Plato bisexual soft-core potboiler *Different Strokes* (1998). He never did top *Getting Lucky*'s pubes scene, but neither has anyone else.

GETTING WASTED [1980]

DIR. PAUL FRIZLER; W/BRIAN KERWIN, STEPHEN FURST, WENDY RASTATTAR

MILITARY SCHOOL ▪ SMOKING BANANA PEELS ▪ EXPLODING TOILET

Getting Wasted is a good description of a fine setup for a teen sex comedy featuring a primo cast that includes fresh-off-*Animal House* Stephen Furst ("Flounder") and ramping-up-to-*Repo Man* Tracey Walter (the shrimp-fixated "Miller"). All the promise gets wasted.

Longtime character actor and nobody's idea of a leading man Brian Kerwin stars as a Brad Carson, an unruly 1967 high schooler who is shipped to an all-boys' military academy for corrective molding. The movie makes little effort to convey a time setting, just a few party store hippie costumes and a vintage soundtrack featuring "Psychotic Reaction" by the Count Five. Sometimes such a dereliction of movie duty is charming (*Screwballs* might take place in the 1950s or the 1980s, does it matter?) Not this time—*Getting Wasted* fundamentally misunderstands fun.

One interlude depicts a youthful David Caruso lighting gasoline-soaked tires on fire and rolling them onto a busy highway at night. Another sees the gang attempting to derail a passenger train. One last knee-slapper depicts a little dog being murdered in a microwave oven. I hope every character in *Getting Wasted* was drafted and died in the invasion of Grenada.

GIMME AN F [1984]

DIR. PAUL JUSTMAN; W/STEPHEN SHELLEN, JENNIFER COOKE, JOHN KARLEN

CHEERLEADERS ▪ CAMP ▪ LOCKER ROOM ▪ JAPANESE BUSINESSMEN

Gimme an F boasts one of the greatest titles in *Teen Movie Hell*. By the end of this limp cheerleader romp's long 100-minute run time, however, the movie's more fitting moniker might be *Gimme an "F This!"* This R-rated mid-1980s film about a cheerleader camp contains no naked hijinks; not a pom-pom, not a nay-nay, not even a thong underneath a vertical-striped skirt. Yet it all starts with a bang!

Various booster teams arrive at Camp Beaverview (where the dining hall is labeled "Beaverteria"), cleverly setting up rah-rah archetypes to combat one another during a climactic competition that is, as such things always were back in 1984, broadcast live on prime-time network TV. (Note: That never happened, and nobody should blame camp cheer competitions for the collapse of network television.) Clean squeaksters the Moline

Ducks ally themselves with the ersatz heavy metal troupe the Demons to combat the fascist Falcons of Fudge Academy.

Buff jock Stephen Shellen, who previously starred in the sexless bait-and-switch stinkpot *Spring Fever* (1982), plays the Ducks' camp coach. Shellen's sweaty, schlong-centric gymnastic workouts seem to be a running gag—except none of those segments totally seem to be jokes.

At one point, Beaverview proprietor Bucky Berkshire (John Karlen, who played Harv on TV's *Cagney and Lacey*) takes a piss balloon—*pow!*—right in the kisser. Anyone who went to see *Gimme an F* and reasonably expected R-rated raunch will identify at that moment with exactly how Bucky Berkshire feels.

The Girl I Want [1990]

DIR. DAVID DECOTEAU (AS ELLEN CABOT); W/LINNEA QUIGLEY, KAREN RUSSELL, LYLE WAGGONER, KITTEN NATIVIDAD

JOCK ▫ NERD GIRL ▫ HOT CHICK MAKEOVER

The Girl I Want consists almost entirely of '80s scream queen Linnea Quigley (*Return of the Living Dead*) and robustly ebullient Karen Russell (*Hell High*) jumping up and down on a bed in slow motion to the movie's semi-rocking theme song, "Teen Bimbos" by Susan Justin.

The little non-jiggling that does occur in *The Girl I Want* comes when nerdy knockout-to-be Amy (Elizabeth Kaitan) is sexily made over by her fellow thirtysomething high school classmates Teri (Quigley) and Lisa (Russell). A football jock named Scott (Steven Craig Daugherty) can't dissuade his father (Burt Ward) from accusing the lad of gayness ("Holy homosexual!" Dad exclaims, in a nod to Ward's late-1960s past as Robin on TV's *Batman*).

Victoria Nesbitt (*Linnea Quigley's Horror Workout*) struts her stuff as a seductive mom, as does bazooka-bosomed Russ Meyer starlet Kitten Natividad (*Beneath the Valley of the Ultra-Vixens*) as a *muy caliente* Spanish instructor. All of that, as expected, entails more jiggling.

Girls Just Want to Have Fun [1985]

DIR. ALAN METTER; SARAH JESSICA PARKER, LEE MONTGOMERY, HELEN HUNT, JONATHAN SILVERMAN

DANCE CONTEST ▫ GYMNASTICS ▫ ARMY DAD

Review by Liz Mason

Even before the 1980s—the era viewed by many as *the* dance battle decade—folks between twelve and twenty had long been settling differences on the dance floor after some kind of instigative argument. Years prior to *Flashdance* (1983), *Footloose* (1984), or *Beat Street* (1984), the Technicolor spectaculars *Seven Brides for Seven Brothers* (1951) and *West Side Story* (1961) boasted story lines about young people dance battling. Dance battling is historic!

Characters dance on-screen to battle for turf, for street cred, or for a position on a team, a show, or a crew. Sometimes the battle can be a healthy, friendly, even flirty, form of competition. Sometimes kids battle to prove they are adults. No matter how easy dance battles look on-screen, "easy" is the one thing that a dance battle is not.

Though I prefer pretty much any kind of street dance scene involving B-boys and B-girls, the dance-off that sticks out the most in my mind is in a movie with pretty traditional aerobics-flavored moves: *Girls Just Want to Have Fun* (1985). Throughout the second half of the 1980s, *Girls Just Want to Have Fun* played on cable TV for what seemed like every second of every day, sometimes on multiple different channels at once. The ubiquitous background noise of the movie lent itself to catching sequences from one day to the next in random order, with details falling differently and reassembling in ever-changing order, molding my brain patterns into a nonlinear, scatterbrained way of thinking. *Girls* was also in heavy rotation at slumber parties, because nothing has ever been more fun than putting on music and dancing with friends.

The heroines of *Girls Just Want to Have Fun*, played by Sarah Jessica Parker and Helen Hunt, long to be featured on *Dance TV*, a hit series that combines *American Bandstand, Soul Train, Solid Gold*, and the still ascending MTV. Their quest leads soon enough to an epic dance battle. Parker and Hunt are so young, but they act circles around the other actors. The dancing is nice but lacks character. One concern that did not affect fourteen-year-old me: Why do filmmakers seem to treat dance movies like porn, assuming the audience is thinking, *Who cares about the plot? We want some moves!*

Girls delivers a surprising amount of plot. The story hinges on the pivotal moments where the teenagers prove themselves to be independent thinkers. For Sarah Jessica Parker in *Girls*, that happens when she lands a "real" office job, just as her parents demanded, but also a regular on-camera *Dance TV* gig—in direct defiance of her parents. Kids, please note: In real life, there isn't just one moment where we prove that we are capable adults. We have to *continually* dig ourselves out of the shithole filled with our own fuckups.

Weirdly, the dancing in *Girls* is *not* interesting. What puts the "winners" over the top is that they can do backflips. Especially in the era that revolutionized break dancing, flips don't deserve "last word" status. Let's have some love for the acrobatic difficulty involved in windmills, jackhammers, air flares, and backspins. Even elementary moves like popping and locking requires intense muscle isolation and endless practice. How come those are never the closing moves?

Lest you think I'm going "snobs vs. slobs" here, in both *Breakin'* movies the big dance battles end also end with flips and roundoffs. Often the ladies are doing them, which is cool. My point is that to dance battle properly, you've got to utilize everything you've got, including some sense of personality and character. Or, as Ice-T put it, "Use every move you've learned in life / Dance is your weapon, not a knife!"

Growing up in real life is much harder than in the movies. If you have to save the rec center by dancing, do it with style. Your dance moves require more than prowess, or leftover agility from maybe a few years of gymnastics classes. The true victory in a dance battle, and everywhere else, is always in the details.

GOIN' ALL THE WAY [1982]

DIR. ROBERT FREEMAN; W/DAN WALDMAN, EILEEN DAVIDSON, JOE COLLIGAN

VIRGIN ▪ MALT SHOP ▪ AEROBICS ▪ ROLLER RINK ▪ MUD WRESTLING

Gangly, unlikeable horndog Artie Mulligan (Dan Waldman) hounds his frigid best gal Monica about doing like the title of the movie says. His best friend, the sawed-off, even *more* unlikeable Reggie Weis (Joe Colligan, who looks like Dudley Moore if he joined the Bay City Rollers) works as an old-timey soda jerk. Short stuff Reggie boasts of ruling their high school's sex roster as a stud supreme, and, as such, he gets the movie's gnarliest line: "Wendy's late with her period again. Looks like I'm going to have to break up with her!"

These two are prickly ninnies. So are the young ladies in orbit of their orgasmic schemes. Yes, making good on its inherently prurient promises, *Goin' All the Way* offers naked shower-room peeping, female mud wrestling, and even an unforeseeable encounter with a couple of topless party girls who, on the path to bottomlessness, reveal themselves to be—not girls.

Such scenes and supporting characters are meatier than the main course. The jerky jock on campus is a frequently near-nude fat prick named Bronk (Joshua Cadman). Boom Boom (Rachel Spooner) is a pure-beef female weightlifter who, after being humped and dumped by a cad, organizes her testosterone-tower gym-hulk gal pals into a head-shaving revenge posse. Best of all is arch-eyebrowed sex-ed instructor Mr. Stephens (James R. Sweeney). Even when doling out the most even-keeled lessons on love and lust, that guy exudes the seedy aura of first-generation Church of Satan clergy. Hail him.

It's the war of the waiters…they capture the kitchen, demolish the dining room, and leave Camp Oskemo in ruins.

GORP*

*a bunch of fruits, nuts and flakes.

SAMUEL Z. ARKOFF presents
A JEFFREY KONVITZ PRODUCTION
"GORP" MICHAEL LEMBECK
DENNIS QUAID • PHILIP CASNOFF
FRAN DRESCHER • DAVID HUDDLESTON
Story by JEFFREY KONVITZ and MARTIN ZWEIBACK
Screenplay by JEFFREY KONVITZ
Produced by JEFFREY KONVITZ and LOUIS S. ARKOFF
Directed by JOSEPH RUBEN Color by MOVIELAB
A PICTURE BY AMERICAN INTERNATIONAL

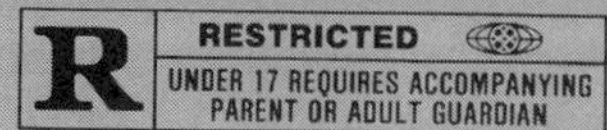

Clockwise from left: Gorp *(1980), "fruits, nuts, and flakes";* Getting It On *(1983), a prescient peek at techno-voyeurism;* Gotcha! *(1985), offers a different kind of school shooting.*

GOING OVERBOARD [1989]

DIR. VALERIE BREIMAN; W/ADAM SANDLER, LISA ZANE, BURT YOUNG, MILTON BERLE

CRUISE SHIP ▣ BEAUTY QUEENS ▣ PUNK ROCKER ▣ GREEK GODS

After MTV's *Remote Control* (1987–1990) and before his stint on *SNL*, Adam Sandler starred in *Going Overboard* as Schecky Moskowitz, a cruise ship waiter and wannabe stand-up comic. He's a natural. Schecky addresses the camera nonstop while serving a giggling gaggle of beauty queens, contending with a hyper-venomous heckler (Billy Bob Thornton), butting heads with a hostile punk rocker (Adam Rifkin), learning joke tips in a dream from old-school comedy giant Milton Berle, and ultimately rescuing Miss Australia (Lisa Zane) from Nicaraguan despot General Manuel Noriega (Burt Young) with an assist from the great god of the sea, King Neptune (Billy Zane). Whoever titled this slapdash outburst of mental illness *Going Overboard* was not exaggerating. It floats.

GORP [1980]

DIR. JOSEPH RUBEN; W/MICHAEL LEMBECK, PHILIP CASNOFF, DENNIS QUAID, FRAN DRESCHER

SUMMER CAMP ▣ SELF-LOVE ▣ LOW-WAGE JOB

To the best of my knowledge in the 1970s, at least according to Pops McBeardo, a "gorp" was someone who "bites the bubbles in the bathtub." Imagine my frenzied delight when that fantastically disgusting title turned up as the name of a teen sex comedy in an HBO programming guide. Sadly, *Gorp* contains nothing close to a mouth-popper of underwater flatulence.

Regardless, the premise is promising. *Gorp* opens at the Jewish-oriented Camp Oskemo, setting up a crew of collegiate mess hall waiters for what should end up being *Kosher Meatballs.* A dull mix of cutout types—fat dude, party girl, chronic pud-puller, etc.—orbit around nice guy Bergman (Philip Casnoff), studly pseudo-Italian Kavell (Michael Lembeck), and the excellently named but underdeveloped lunatic military enthusiast Mad Grossman (Dennis Quaid).

Also wandering Camp Oskemo are Fran Drescher as a counselor, and Rosanna Arquette, as a camp worker with apparently no time for topless sunbathing. Several ace character actors cop their SAG/AFTRA scale paychecks, including David Huddleston (the Big Lebowski himself) as camp owner Walrus Wallman and blaxploitation heavy Julius Harris as Fred the Chef.

Gorp was the final film released by Samuel Z. Arkoff and James H. Nicholson's legendary exploitation house, American International Pictures. A.I.P. was the studio that primarily built itself by launching the teen sex comedy genre through Frankie Avalon and Annette Funicello's beach party movies of the 1960s. From there, A.I.P. kept abreast of youth exploitation film trends with an extremely specific audience in mind, narrowed down by the studio's publicity department using the following formula:

- A younger child will watch anything an older child will watch.
- An older child will not watch anything a younger child will watch.
- A girl will watch anything a boy will watch.
- A boy will not watch anything a girl will watch.

Thus to catch your greatest audience, you zero in on the nineteen-year-old male. By such logic, this movie should have been A.I.P.'s last great, gross triumph. Instead, *Gorp* comes off as cluttered, chaotic, and rushed to the point that the studio seems to have been literally crumbling during production. The soundtrack is especially rough, as dialogue, audio effects, music, and set noise run relentlessly from the first frame to the last.

Star Michael Lembeck is the son of Harvey Lembeck, a comedic TV mainstay who also played beach-party-hating biker gang leader Erich Von Zipper in all those Frankie-and-Annette romps for A.I.P. Michael's previous greatest claim to pop culture notoriety was portraying Kaptain Kool, leader of the ersatz Kiss bubblegum-metal band Kaptain Kool and the Kongs on ABC's Saturday morning live-action and cartoon omnibus *The Krofft Supershow* (1976–78). Those rock 'n' roll clowns deserved their own movie.

GRAD NIGHT [1981]

DIR. JOHN TENORIO JR.; W/JOE JOHNSON, SUANNE FAGAN, CAROLYN BATES

GRADUATION 📼 FLASHING 📼 PRANKS

"Shoestring" is used to describe some movie budgets. In the case of *Grad Night*, the term could be upgraded to "mortarboard tassel"—but not by many strands. The poster conveys the movie's feel; an *Animal House*–style cavalcade of campus chaos that looks like what somebody goofing off in class would doodle on a sheet of loose-leaf paper. That depiction is accurate.

As usual, actors in their late twenties pretend to be high schoolers. On the night before graduation, they navigate through pranks, rivalries, dumb authority figures, and pretty suburban Sacramento scenery to a musical score of pleasingly generic light rock. The movie virtually evaporates as you watch it—pleasantly. Upon release, *Grad Night* must have been an absolute bottom dweller in terms of cheap-date theatrical programming, but it worked as a mid-1980s Saturday-afternoon movie on regular TV, and it still works now.

GRANDVIEW, U.S.A. [1984]

DIR. RANDAL KLEISER; W/JAMIE LEE CURTIS, C. THOMAS HOWELL, PATRICK SWAYZE, JENNIFER JASON LEIGH

VIRGIN 📼 OLDER WOMAN 📼 HIGH SCHOOL GRADUATION 📼 BIG RACE

A swing and a miss for director Randal Kleiser (*Grease, The Blue Lagoon, Summer Lovers*), *Grandview, U.S.A.*, also lets down its '80s über-cast. C. Thomas Howell is wayward high school senior Tim Pearson. Jamie Lee Curtis is Michelle "Mike" Cody, a tough, sexy broad who works at a demolition derby track. Patrick Swayze is Earl "Slam" Webster, the track's star driver. Guess who ends up in a love triangle?

The story covers Tim's last summer in rural, corn-y Grandview, Illinois, before he departs to study oceanography at college. Scuba jokes abound. Tim hangs around Mike and the track. Nothing happens that is as interesting as watching dudes crash old junker cars into one another.

Many fellow Grandview residents are equally underutilized heavyweights, including Jennifer Jason Leigh, M. Emmet Walsh, Michael Winslow (the sound-effects guy from *Police Academy*), pioneering Chicago radio shock jock Steve Dahl, and both John *and* Joan Cusack. Glowingly tanned '50s heartthrob Troy Donahue amuses as a recklessly amorous washing machine repairman. The most energetic aspect of the movie is its maniacally chipper theme song, "Take Me Home to Grandview, U.S.A.," by Air Supply.

GREGORY'S GIRL [1981]

DIR. BILL FORSYTH; W/JOHN GORDON SINCLAIR, DEE HEPBURN, CLARE GROGAN

HIGH SCHOOL SOCCER 📼 TOUGH GIRL

The charm of *Gregory's Girl* spilled out of Scotland and into art-house theaters worldwide during the early 1980s. The film's gross of nearly $40 million on a $200,000 investment qualifies it, pound for pound (in Scottish sterling), as a blockbuster. Times were different then—and hard not to say *better*—for moviegoing.

John Gordon Sinclair stars as Gregory, a loose-limbed teen soccer player. Dee Hepburn is Dorothy. She's the *Girl*—or is she? Dorothy tries out for the boys' team and sets in motion a series of wittily dorky dates and honest moments that pluck like magic the viewer's smile reflex.

Audiences connected deeply and warmly with *Gregory*'s heartfelt and very funny adolescent awkwardness in regard to sports and romance. The young cast looked destined for international stardom, even if they weren't. Director Bill Forsyth loomed as one of the decade's most promising filmmakers. His *Local Hero* (1983) was a little masterpiece, but, after that, he stumbled. Alas, *Gregory's Girl* is the one that got away.

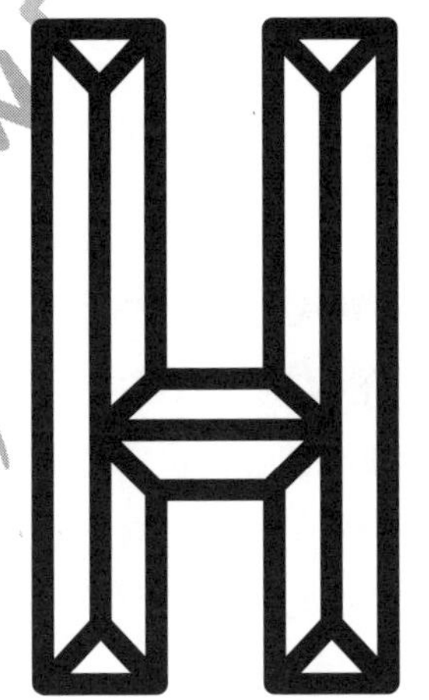

Hamburger: The Motion Picture ▫ Happy High School
Hardbodies ▫ Hardbodies 2 ▫ The Harrad Experiment
The Harrad Summer ▫ He's My Girl ▫ Heathers
Heaven Help Us ▫ The Heavenly Kid
Heavy Metal Summer ▫ Hiding Out
High School U.S.A. ▫ High Test Girls
Higher Education ▫ Hog Wild ▫ Hollywood Dreaming
Hollywood High ▫ Hollywood High Part II
Hollywood Hot Tubs ▫ Hollywood Hot Tubs 2: Educating Crystal
Hollywood Zap ▫ Hometown U.S.A. ▫ Homework ▫ Hot and Bothered
Hot Chili ▫ Hot Dog...the Movie ▫ Hot Moves ▫ Hot Pursuit
Hot Resort ▫ Hot Splash ▫ Hot Times ▫ Hot Times at Montclair High
H.O.T.S. ▫ Hot T-Shirts ▫ House Party ▫ How I Got Into College ▫ Hunk

Hamburger: The Motion Picture [1986]

DIR. MIKE MARVIN; W/LEIGH MCCLOSKEY, DEBRA BLEE, DICK BUTKUS, CHUCK MCCANN

FAST FOOD ▫ PEEPING ▫ SHOWERS ▫ NERD ▫ BAD TEACHERS ▫ NUN ▫ PARTY DOLL

Sex sizzles juicily among the hot meat, fresh buns, and squirting sauce in *Hamburger: The Motion Picture*. College lady killer Russell (Leigh McCloskey) opens the movie being busted while getting it on with a coed in a crowded female dorm shower room. As a last resort to get him educated, the adults in charge (as opposed to the adults playing horny teenagers) ship him to Buster Burger University, the training academy of the Buster Burger fast-food chain. Their motto: "A Lotta Bull in Every Bite!"

BBU is owned by cadaverous Lyman Vunk (Charles Tyner) and run by drillmaster Sgt. Drootin (Dick Butkus), a human buzz cut. Viennese-accented junk-food scientist Dr. Mole (Chuck McCann) heads the faculty. Russ rooms with wannabe stud Fred (Sandy Hackett, son of comedian Buddy), and their class members include slurring nerd Nacio (Jack Blessing), Latin sex bomb Conchita (Maria Richwine), nervous nun Sister Sara (Barbara Whinnery), bombastically blobular fat guy Prestopopnick (John William Young), and one of the movie's most unique and uproarious creations, Magneto Jones (Chip McAllister), an African American pop performer who seems to combine Rick James, Michael Jackson, pioneering disco drag queen Sylvester, and an anthropomorphic bottle of curl activator. Once assembled, those characters cook up a recipe for hilarity.

As with an actual special order of fast food, the details matter in *Hamburger: The Motion Picture*. And they are exquisite. This is a cartoonish, borderline surreal "anything goes" burlesque in the tradition of *Screwballs* (1983) and *The Party Animal* (1984)—i.e., mostly a collection of outrageous, nigh-obscene gags hung on an agreeably idiotic plot. There alone, the movie is delicious. The dialogue contains at least one-third puns, and outlandish imagination crops up repeatedly.

Consider each deluxe topping: A classroom instructor chops the balls off a model bull; they roll down the aisle, and famished fat fuck Prestopopnick grabs one, sprinkles salt on it from the shaker in his shirt pocket, and takes a bite. Bespectacled chump Nacio submits to experimental fried chicken treatments, sprouts feathers, takes to clucking, and eventually is dragged into a mysterious shower room by heavyset scrubber women; he returns in triumph after laying an egg. In one of the grandest, most magnificently go-for-broke slob comedy climaxes ever, an "eating team" of exclusively quarter-ton-plus circus-sideshow-size large folk (including the identical twin sisters from 1980's *Midnight Madness*) invades a Buster Burger for our team's final training. The party consumes everything in sight and is struck with a collective gas attack. In a panic, the overweight Americans pile into a bathroom where a Japanese businessman is reading a huge-boob nudie magazine on the toilet, and they proceed to fart the entire building into explosive oblivion. It's so funny you can *smell* it.

Hamburger is top-of-the-menu laughs, elevated to premium-item status by the effort (and, for once, the budget) that went into the art direction. For example, Russ and Joe finding themselves "in a pickle" by getting locked inside punishment sweatboxes shaped like giant, smiling, anthropomorphic gherkins. Likewise, the movie offers jokes such as dorm rooms stocked with beds built to resemble multilayer Buster Burgers; a campus church called "The Chapel of the Immaculate Bathroom"; a working "Burgercopter,"; and Sister Sara's Buster Burger uniform being a red-and-gold adaptation of her penguin-style nun's habit. *Hamburger* is a delectable gourmet banquet of grease cinema, seasoned to perfection with utter tastelessness.

Happy High School [1986]

aka Las Colegialas Se Divierten

DIR. FERNANDO SIRO; W/SUSANA TRAVERSO, GUILLERMO FRANCELLA, IGNACIO QUIROS, MARCELLA LUPPI

MEAN GIRLS ▪ BAD TEACHERS ▪ HOT AUNT ▪ FLASHING

Happy High School, sold around the world as "the Argentinian *Porky's,*" takes place at the learning institution of the title. The students there, in keeping with their counterparts up north, all look to be in their mid-twenties, and the whole bunch of them get naked—or rather, *desnudo.*

The principal of Happy High suspects his pupils have grown too libidinous and libertine, as evidenced by the utter lack of female undergarments anywhere and one monster-knockered test-taker copying from crib notes she scribbled all over her exposed upper body. A state inspector is brought in to analyze the carnal chaos. She is knocked out and kidnapped by a passel of popular hotties, and they replace her with one girl's aunt, who happens to be a sexy stripper.

Las Colegialas Se Divierten, the movie's original Spanish title, means "The Schoolgirls Have Fun." Less fun is the work of tracking down a version of *Happy High School* anywhere *en el mundo* with English subtitles, let alone dubbed dialogue. *Así es la vida!*

Hardbodies [1984]

DIR. MARK GRIFFITHS; W/GRANT CRAMER, COURTNEY GAINES, TEAL ROBERTS, SORRELLS PICKARD

SURFERS ▪ HAIR METAL ▪ PUNKS ▪ VANS ▪ BIKINI-SNATCHING DOG

Hardbodies is the one. It is the T&Alpha and the Big O-mega. It is the Titterdämmerung. It is *the* actual *ultimate* 1980s teen sex comedy. This over-the-topless, beyond-the-tail kaleidoscopic overload of SoCal summertime madness throws cool dudes and hot babes against endless waves of untamed fun, a volcanic sugar rush of bared boobs and dick jokes, surf slang, beer and weed, rock 'n' roll, skateboarders, muscleheads, aerobicizers, pranksters, puns, all-night ragers, and a dog trained to snatch bikini tops. The entire day at the beach at the movies is riotously funny and near-soft-core salacious from its first frame to the last. *Hardbodies* is the no-holds-barred bacchanal to out-bash all others in humanity's collective almost passed-out consciousness, and it's raging right now—dive in anywhere!

After a fit-inducing montage of Venice Beach sights, sounds, and squeezable appendages, *Hardbodies* introduces smooth-talking local Scotty (Grant Cramer) right as he receives the boot from his seaside hellhole apartment. Scotty may be homeless, but he has an uptight girlfriend named Kristi (Teal Roberts) and a keen sense of when opportunity knocks.

Scotty also has the greatest sidekick of all time in Rags (Courtney Gaines, redheaded cult killer Malachi in *Children of the Corn*), a surf-goof supreme who convulses in outbursts of obscene gestures as he "flips you off in forty-seven languages!" As Gaines explains the origin of his indecent parlor trick: "I asked everybody I could find to show me how to say 'F.U.' with their hands from every different country they could think of. I wrote them all down and ended up with twenty, and I actually ran through everything twice to get to forty."

A trio of middle-aged, recently divorced bachelors rents a "fancy"—or fantastically gaudy—mid-1980s beach house near the action. Once they catch sight of Scotty in action with local bikini bunnies, they hire him to tutor them in the language of sex along the shoreline. The hilarious sad sacks are wannabe lady-slayer Hunter (Gary Wood), pointedly named rotund quipster Rounder (Michael Rapport), and, most curiously, Ashby (Sorrells Pickard), a bald, gray-bearded cowboy with an authentic Southern drawl and strange natural acting ability. Immediately, the party is on and no, it does not stop.

Local female rock trio Diaper Rash plays the guys' first shindig. Scotty is so impressed, he convinces steaming-skulled Italian gym owner Rocco (Anthony Ponzini) to hire the group to perform while his coterie of spandex-encased bodybuilders and aerobicizers pump up and sweat it out. One caveat: Diaper Rash must change their name to Hardbodies. In real life, the band is up-and-strumming hair metal powerhouse Vixen; they absolutely slay a number titled "Computer Madness."

Sticky romantic entanglements arise as Scotty's disapproving girlfriend Kristi catches wind of his budding attraction to party babe Candy (Crystal Shaw). Meanwhile, Ashby wins the heart of good-time hottie Lana (Roberta Collins) when he shows up in a Western hat made of individual marijuana joints. Unlike the Erich Von Zipper–led motorcycle baddies of '60s beach party flicks, *Hardbodies*' troublemakers travel in a van with "Dirtbag" painted on the side. They're led by an oaf in a "Boogie 'Til You Puke" T-shirt who pumps 45 Grave out of his boom box.

The real villainy, though, comes from discouraged Hunter when he attempts to force himself on Candy, just to be quickly foiled by Scotty. Maybe for the first time in one of these movies, date rape is portrayed as 100 percent *not* cool, asshole! Before the end, Scotty takes off on a motorized surfboard to commune with seals for a bit before returning, entirely enlightened.

Like the same year's *Preppies, Hardbodies* was created to air on cable on the newly launched Playboy Channel, but was judged too funny, outrageous, and larger-louder-and-loonier-than-life to be confined to the small screen. Ultimately, *Hardbodies* made a brief but lucrative theater run, then went on to a larger-than-life dominion over cable and VHS lasting nearly a decade.

If any film could ever argue "bigger is better," this is it. In 1984, *Entertainment Tonight* asked playwright David Mamet how he felt after recently winning the Pulitzer Prize for *Glengarry Glen Ross*. Mamet said he'd recently seen a preview for a movie called *Hardbodies* that pled, "If you see one movie this year, see this one, too." Mamet smiled and added, "so if you see one play this year, see *Glengarry Glen Ross*, too."

Hardbodies 2 [1986]

DIR. MARK GRIFFITHS; W/BRAD ZUTAUT, FABIANA UDENIO, BRENDA BAKKE, JAMES KAREN

ISLAND RESORT ▪ CRUISE SHIP ▪ MOVIE SHOOT ▪ SURFBOARDS

How could anyone follow the creation of a perfect thing, beloved by the world, worthy of exploding adoration, and a milestone, a juggernaut, a marker by which the public measures its lives? This conundrum and resulting pressure famously faced down artists ranging from J. D. Salinger to Kurt Cobain to Quentin Tarantino. For Mark Griffiths, writer-director of *Hardbodies* (1984), the absolute unhinged pinnacle of '80s teen sex comedy madness, the solution was simple. He just figured, "Fuck it, I'll get a movie studio to pay for my Greek island vacation!"

Griffiths returns to his auteur seat for *Hardbodies 2*, and right away jets off to party in the Mediterranean. The two main beach bum buddies from the first film have since taken up acting. Right away they find themselves starring in a movie about—what else?—two beach bum buddies who jet off to party in the Mediterranean. Complicating this meta-narrative, two new actors portray the beloved *Hardbodies* characters: Brad Zutaut steps in for Grant Cramer in the lead as suave mover Scotty Palmer; Sam Temeles replaces Courtney Gaines as wildman Rags. (Gaines says he was underage and presented a fake ID to obtain his passport, and so was detained by the FBI.) The casting is a downgrade on both counts, *severely* so in the latter case. Nobody gets flipped off in *one* language, let alone forty-seven of them.

Scotty and Rags perform for mad-dog filmmaker Logan (James Karen from *Return of the Living Dead*) as he shoots a soft-core sex flick titled *Foreign Affairs*. That scenario requires lots of nudity on the movie sets, which are mostly just clothing-optional beaches. Next, Scotty and Rags accidentally mix up their luggage with that of the son of a billionaire. His bags happen to be packed with bales of cash and boarding passes to a cruise ship full of college coeds on a "semester at sea." Soon nudity turns the boat into a clothing-optional luxury liner.

Scotty recruits stunning local waitress Cleopatra (Fabiana Udenio) to star with him in *Foreign Affairs*, even though her Mount Vesuvius–tempered father bellows, "No love scenes!" Naturally, she films a love scene. She is also kidnapped and rescued, but, as with many scenes on the screen here, viewers will be hard-pressed to determine if the kidnap is part of *Hardbodies 2* or the movie within *Hardbodies 2*. Not that it really matters.

Nakedness abounds in quantities that dwarf even *Hardbodies'* tits-and-astronomical figures. Aside from Mark Griffiths, the only actual flesh-and-blood connection between the films is a cameo by Sorrells Packard, returning as Southern-drawling cowpoke Ashby, and B-movie sexpot Roberta Collins again playing real estate broker Lana. The two characters are married in the sequel and, quite amusingly, Ashby has somehow become the captain of the semester-at-sea ship. Like everything else in *Hardbodies 2*, you just go with the sun, sand, and sex in the Greek Isles.

The Harrad Experiment [1973]

DIR. TED POST; W/DON JOHNSON, LAURIE WALTERS, BRUNO KIRBY, TIPPI HEDREN

HIPPIES ▪ FREE LOVE ▪ VIRGINS ▪ NERD ▪ COED DORMS ▪ WEED ▪ NUDE YOGA

The Harrad Experiment, a 1966 novel by Robert H. Rimmer, ruled as the single most dog-eared, underlined, and passed-around best seller in the history of junior high schoolyards until *Forever* by Judy Blume dropped in 1975. Winking at being based on "true events," *The Harrad*

Experiment lays bare a cutting-edge New England college program where the secret curriculum pairs computer-matched male and female students as roommates; recommends public nudity as often as possible; and encourages sexual interaction among the participants. Groovy!

The movie version of *The Harrad Experiment* sticks close to the book's essential plot, following relatively prim and plain Sheila (Laurie Walters) as she arrives on campus under the tutelage of group-marriage-espousing husband-and-wife professors Phillip and Margaret Tenhausen (James Whitmore and Tippi Hedren). Sheila is matched with resident hunk Stanley (Don Johnson), who runs wild with the school's do-who-thou-wilt policy before comprehending that even free love comes at a price. Fellow collegiate seekers Harry (Bruno Kirby) and Beth (Victoria Thompson) live, lust, learn, skinny-dip, and perform nude yoga with them.

The straightforward and mostly unremarkable *The Harrad Experiment* is loaded with extracurricular points of intrigue. First comes the opportunity to ogle Don Johnson's superstardom in first bloom, and Laurie Walters just prior to her familiar TV gig as Joanie Bradford on the ABC dramedy *Eight Is Enough*. Johnson began dating his future wife, Melanie Griffith, on the *Harrad* set, when he was twenty-four and she was fourteen. Compound that with the movie's bra-and-panties near-sex scene between Johnson and Tippi Hedren, who was Griffith's mother and Don's future mother-in-law. *Harrad* co-screenwriter Ted Cassidy, who cameos as a cigarette-puffing diner patron, is beloved zombified butler Lurch on TV's *The Addams Family*.

THE HARRAD SUMMER [1974]

DIR. STEVEN HILLIARD SMITH; W/LAURIE WALTERS, ROBERT REISER, RICHARD DORAN, VICTORIA THOMPSON

HIPPIES · SKINNY-DIPPING · POOL PARTY

The core foursome of *The Harrad Experiment* returns for *The Harrad Summer*, but no need to break out the nude-yoga mat in celebration. Laurie Walters and Victoria Thompson reprise their respective roles as free-love university students Sheila Grove and Beth Hillyer. Their computer-matched partners have been recast, however. Robert Reiser replaces Don Johnson as Stanley Kolasukas, magically transforming the character from stud to dud. Richard Doran steps in for Bruno Kirby as lovable schnook Harry Schacht. Doran, who costarred in some good Roger Corman flicks (*The Student Teachers, Hollywood Boulevard*) isn't half bad, but he isn't half Bruno Kirby, either.

The Harrad Summer tracks the two couples across their hot-weather college break, whereupon we meet their various bombastically ethnic or WASPtastically chilly families. On the upside, 1950s TV funnyman Bill Dana (best known for his hapless Hispanic character José Jiménez) brings Borscht Belt brio to the part of Harry's thunderously grumpy Jewish dad. In addition, wild-haired, anarchic comedic curiosity Marty Allen slips into a suburban pool party, but he's freakishly subdued for a movie about cross-country collegiate swinger sex.

HE'S MY GIRL [1987]

DIR. GABRIELLE BEAUMONT; W/T. K. CARTER, DAVID HALLYDAY, JENNIFER TILLY, DAVID CLENNON

CROSS-DRESSING · ROCK STAR · SASSY WAITRESS

Somewhere between Flip Wilson as Geraldine (hilarious) and Martin Lawrence as Shanaynay (not hilarious), T. K. Carter contributed Reggie/Regina to the canon of African American cross-dressing comedy in *He's My Girl*.

Reggie (Carter) is a young, hard-hustling music manager whose sole client, singer-songwriter Bryan (David Hallyday), wins a trip to Hollywood with the odd stipulation that he must accompanied by a "girlfriend." Reggie shaves his legs, slips into a prom dress, dons a bouffant wig, and—*voilà!*—he is Regina, Bryan's hastily created better half. The usual stupid stuff happens from there, except no situation arises that forces

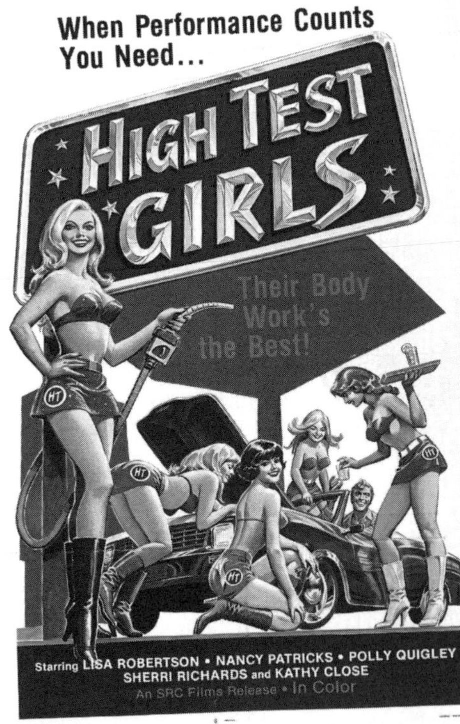

Clockwise from top left: *Hard-hearted hit* Heathers *(1988)*; The Harrad Experiment *(1973)—"based on the bestselling book" is a rare phrase in this book*; Heaven Help Us *(1985), hallowed by Catholic kids*; High Test Girls, *aka Six Swedes on a Pump (1980).*

the two dudes to uncomfortably fuck or at least pretend to fuck, which would have really saved the day and twisted some things around. Tyler Perry's Madea would rightly sass all this nonsense.

One point of amusement: Just as *The Allnighter* touted itself as featuring "rock star Susanna Hoffs," the *He's My Girl* poster proudly announces "the debut of Europe's #1 rock star, David Hallyday," the sports-car racing scion of the great man Johnny Hallyday. Couldn't we have gotten a movie with Falco, or even Baltimora, instead?

HEATHERS [1988]

DIR. MICHAEL LEHMAN; W/WINONA RYDER, CHRISTIAN SLATER, SHANNEN DOHERTY

HIGH SCHOOL ▪ EVIL JOCKS ▪ NERDS ▪ WEED ▪ TEEN UPRISING

A serrated, post-punk commingling of the pitch-black teen sex satire *Lord Love a Duck* (1966) and the sneaky suspense-horror political allegory *Massacre at Central High* (1976), *Heathers* shook the world as a cult phenom with big, nasty laughs and deep-sinking teeth. There is comical teen sex in *Heathers,* but, like the rest of the movie, it hurts.

Winona Ryder stars as Veronica Sawyer, a nearly popular hall-walker at Westerberg High, where she's alternately tormented by and attracted to a gaggle of magnificently malevolent mean girls who rule the school—Heather Chandler (Kim Walker), Heather Duke (Shannen Doherty), and Heather McNamara (Lisanne Falk).

Enter Christian Slater as teenage demolitionist J.D. Dean (as in James Dean, but also as in "juvenile delinquent"). Armed with industrial explosives, knowledge of how to use them, and a sick secret, J.D. enacts a series of lethal ideas about how to settle cafeteria comeuppances. Naturally, Veronica can't resist.

Heathers is brutal satire for the ages; the movie's overall tone is acidly indicated by its most quoted line: "Fuck me gently with a chainsaw!" Other enduring pop-cult contributions include overweight bully-target Martha Dumptruck (Carrie Lynn); the on-screen pop hit "Teenage Suicide" (Don't Do It)" by Big Fun; and the very first codification of the modern concept of "mean girls." Also vividly memorable (and incredibly nervy even at the time) is J.D. and Veronica murdering a couple of heartless football thugs and then attempting to make it look like a lovers' suicide. When the scheme backfires, and the dead jocks are seen as martyred victims of homophobia, the movie pulls off one of its meanest gags as a grieving dad weeps, "I love my dead gay son!"

Bare-knuckled mockery of mass eating disorders, mass public humiliation, and ultimately mass slaughter pack a rattling wallop unimaginable today—outside of the sort of tweets that get people kicked off Twitter. Still, Heathers never teeters into cartoonish or show-offy overload, even when the (anti?-)hero goes boom at the end.

Heathers debuted to fanfare in Italy in 1988, opening slowly in the U.S. in March of 1989 and generating stunned reviews and buzzy word-of-mouth. The cult swelled via home video and cable, and, from there, became a generation-spanning phenomenon. In 2010, an Off-Broadway musical adaptation of *Heathers* began a five-year run, and it remains a popular touring production.

An attempted TV series spin-off of *Heathers* was pulled twice before its premiere, once due to sensitivity after the February 2018 Stoneman Hill High School shooting, and again later that year due to general concerns over "content."

Anger arose over the show's reinvention of the original rich, white, hetero Heathers as being gay, trans, overweight, racially mixed, and fitting other traditionally marginalized descriptors. Yesterday's victims turning into today's victimizers does seem to be one of the movie's main thrusts, so that update would make an interesting spin. Alas, we willl never know. Our media guardians have "protected" us again. Hooray for somebody.

HEAVEN HELP US [1985]
aka CATHOLIC BOYS

DIR. MICHAEL DINNER; W/ANDREW MCCARTHY, KEVIN DILLON, MARY STUART MASTERSON, DONALD SUTHERLAND

CATHOLIC SCHOOL ▣ SODA SHOP ▣ PRANKS ▣ SCHOOL DANCE ▣ CLERGY

Heaven Help Us is the story of four Brooklyn palookas who attend an all-male Catholic high school that requires them to wear blazers and ties to class and religious services. That describes my own educational experience (Xavier High School, class of 1986), as well as that of the three other papist Kings County cutups with whom I saw *Heaven Help Us* on opening night. The main differences between us and the guys on-screen is that the movie takes place in 1965, and that we studied under Jesuits, the church's philosophical left-wing fringe. The guys in the movie suffer at the hands and ass-paddles of what appear to be Christian Brothers, as queer a cabal of man-nuns as you'll come across, Catholic-wise.

Heaven Help Us focuses mostly on nice guy Michael Dunn (Andrew McCarthy), the new kid at St. Basil's Prep. There he meets Caesar (Malcolm Danare), the fat kid, along with hilarious semi-hoodlum Rooney (Kevin Dillon), wishy-washy Corbet (Patrick Dempsey), and near-mute chronic masturbator Williams (Stephen Geoffreys). As happens at all-boys' schools, the gang pulls a prank that goes awry, a couple of them get into a fistfight, and they then bond deeply while being punished harshly. This being the mid-1960s, the punishment is of humiliating variety. Throughout the movie we see the boys subjected to weird kneeling tortures, forced to clean bird shit off a statue with toothbrushes, and whipped bare-assed on an exercise horse by psycho almost-out-of-the-closet sadist Brother Constance (Jay Patterson). Blessed are the saints!

Sensitive Dunn takes up with tomboyish Danni (Mary Stuart Masterson), who runs the soda shop where the boys hang out and dance to the jukebox with girls from nearby Virgin Martyr Academy. Danni also takes constant care of her cripplingly depressed widower father and his expression of "melancholia"—sitting immobile and frowning at the kitchen table with his head in his hands. Hilarious.

Dunn and Danni fall deeply in love. The gang attend a high school dance where Father Abruzzi (Wallace Shawn) roars forth a thunderous, fist-pounding edict against the perils of lust—or, as he puts it through his yellow teeth and his unmistakable lisp, *"LUTHT!"* Pope Paul VI comes to town, but the dudes skip the scene to catch a screening of Elvis in *Blue Hawaii*. In the movie's funniest scene, chronic palm-yanker and altar boy Williams goes into a trance watching Virgin Martyr girls stick out their tongues for Holy Communion. He collapses like an epileptic into spontaneous orgasm—what a mind he has. Brother Thaddeus continues to dole out miseries that in turn escalate the gang's escapades until they decapitate the statue of St. Basil in the school's courtyard.

Heaven Help Us is a fine nostalgia effort, gritty in spots and moving in others. In the wake of *Porky's*, et cetera, the movie does feel a little choppy and inconsistent. Luckily, as a result, the studio injected some distracting and unnecessary slapstick and raunch to even the score. Ten years earlier, *Heaven* would have been more like the goyish equivalent of *Summer of '42* (1971) or *The Apprenticeship of Duddy Kravitz* (1974). Though essentially flawed, *Heaven Help Us* is rife with goodness and packed with potential for a greatness it could never possibly achieve—perfect for a Catholic teen sex comedy.

THE HEAVENLY KID [1985]

DIR. CARY MEDOWAY; W/JASON GEDRICK, LEWIS SMITH, NANCY VALEN, RICHARD MULLIGAN

NERD ▣ GREASERS ▣ THE BIG DRAG RACE ▣ GUARDIAN ANGEL

The Heavenly Kid opens with a title card that reads, "The Late 1960s," priming viewers for hippies, gurus, acid-heads, hopefully some free love, probably a psychedelic rock band, and maybe a Vietnam War protest if things get serious. Instead, the movie settles right away on leather-jacketed greasers in the mass-production 1950s *Grease* or *Happy Days* mold. These alleged members of Woodstock Nation are engaging in that most popular Age of Aquarius pastime, a *Rebel Without a Cause*–style "chicken run" drag race. Each pompadoured participant pilots a hot rod toward the edge of a cliff, and the first one to bail loses, which sounds much more James Dean than Wavy Gravy.

Hoodlum Bobby Fontana (Lewis Smith) wins the chicken run but plummets to his death, leaving behind an infant dweeb. Sixteen years later, Bobby returns to earth looking none worse for the years in limbo, to act as guardian angel and "cool instructor" to his bully-bait son Lenny (Jason Gedrick). If Bobby succeeds, he will take an ethereal escalator to "Uptown." If not, he burns in hellfire for all eternity. Bobby is successful. He goes to heaven, Lenny gets laid, and we in the audience are released from our own limbo as the end credits roll.

Heavy Metal Summer [1988] aka State Park

DIR. KERRY FELTHAM, RAFAL ZIELINSKI; W/KIM MYERS, ISABELLE MEJIAS, JENNIFER INCH, TED NUGENT

CAMPERS ▪ HEADBANGERS ▪ EVIL CAPITALIST ▪ THE BIG RACE ▪ BEAR COSTUME

Set at highly fictional and frictional Weewankah Park, *Heavy Metal Summer* was codirected by Rafal Zielinski, the filmmaker who previously unleashed *Screwballs* (1983), *Loose Screws* (1985), and *Valet Girls* (1987). This heavy metal–themed outing is a Canadian tax write-off production set in the U.S.A., following the trails blazed by *Pinball Summer* (1980), *Porky's* (1981), and *Oddballs* (1984).

The movie begins, and a guy in a bear costume is running amok all over a construction site, a promising beginning to a boobs-beers-and-barf brouhaha. Sorry to say, however, that the volume never goes up to eleven. In fact, *Heavy Metal Summer* is more aptly described by its bland alternate title, *State Park*. This is an almost gentle, female-focused comedy centered on the weekend camping plans of redheaded environmentalist Eve (Kim Myers), soon-to-be college freshman Linnie (Jennifer Inch), and sassy fashionista Marsha (Isabelle Mejias).

While staking ground in Weewankah, the lasses pal up with headbanging "heavy metalers" (as they're constantly referred to) Johnny Rocket (Peter Virgile) and Louis (Louis Tucci), both of whom look very Mötley Crüe; the latter even paints his face with Nikki Sixx–style stripes under his eyes. We meet the guy in the bear suit, who turns out to be Truckie (James Wilder), owner of the park's general store. His ursine antics were an effort to thwart industrialist Mr. Rancewell (Walter Massey) from converting Weewankah into a pesticide plant. Eco-warrior Eve is all about people power, as long as it doesn't distract from the upcoming Wilderness Challenge, a suspiciously Canadian-sounding contest offering a $5,000 prize for swimming, kayaking, and "orienting."

Jennifer Inch, as Linnie, earns *Heavy Metal Summer* its R rating in a unique fashion. In lieu of cheating on her boyfriend while she's hot and bothered from the great outdoors, Linnie compromises by giving haircuts to boys she likes while she's naked above the waist. A little off the top, indeed!

Hiding Out [1987]

DIR. BOB GIRALDI; W/JON CRYER, ANNABETH GISH, KEITH COOGAN

UNDERCOVER IN HIGH SCHOOL ▪ STUDENT ELECTION ▪ KINDLY JANITOR

"Jon Cryer is *Hiding Out*!" That's what the poster tells us. In fact, he's hiding out in high school, a prospect marketed as "more frightening than murder." Maybe. In this hybrid mobster movie–slash–teen comedy, Cryer plays a boyish-faced Boston stockbroker waiting to testify against a Mafia boss. He goes into witness protection disguised as a teenage student, but soon attracts attention by spazzy dancing and winning the election for class president.

Much to its good fortune, *Hiding Out* hit cable TV when HBO and Showtime often relentlessly aired the same movie at the exactly the same time. Turning on either channel between 1988 and 1989, viewers were likely to uncover *Hiding Out*. Such saturation resulted in a generation of repeat viewers embracing an otherwise lackluster picture and its stool pigeon stockbroker star as their own.

The movie's mostly alt-rock soundtrack boasts an early employment of the Public Image Limited favorite "Seattle," and made a non-Mafia hit out of the obnoxious skull-thumper "Catch Me (I'm Falling)" by dance club stars Pretty Poison. Was everyone in America high on amyl nitrate poppers in 1987 when that 45 reached the *Billboard* Top 10?

High School U.S.A. [1983]

DIR. ROD AMATEAU; W/MICHAEL J. FOX, NANCY MCKEON, DANA PLATO, CRISPIN GLOVER

PREPPIES ▪ NERDS ▪ JOCKS ▪ RICH JERKS ▪ ROBOT ▪ ROLLER DERBY ▪ THE BIG RACE

NBC's gimmick with its TV movie *High School U.S.A.* was to cast the young stars of present hit sitcoms as students and have grown-up former teen TV idols play their teachers. Lining the classroom seats are Michael J. Fox (*Family Ties*), Nancy McKeon (*The Facts of Life*), and Dana Plato and Todd Bridges (*Diff'rent Strokes*). Crispin Glover (*Back to the Future, What Is It?*) and Michael Zorek (*Private School, Hot Moves*) make a fine skinny-and-fatty nerd combo. Anthony Edwards, who later costarred on NBC's *E.R.*, a-holes it up as an arrogant preppy overlord in an ironic warm-up for where he went the following year as Gilbert in *Revenge of the Nerds*.

Among the faculty members are Dawn Wells (*Gilligan's Island*), Dwayne Hickman (*The Many Loves of Dobie Gillis*), Elinor Donahue (*Father Knows Best*), and Tony Dow and Ken Osmond (*Leave It to Beaver*). Gilligan himself, Bob Denver, plays a dad who passes out drunk and is tricked into thinking he wrecked his car in a blackout (really, his dopey kid did it).

The plot is some senseless network boardroom bullshit. The new kid (Fox) falls for the moneyed creep's heart-of-gold girlfriend (McKeon). A genius kid (Bridges) builds a guy-in-a-robot-suit robot. Pranksters prank. Nerds nerd. The rich dick gets what's coming to him.

After the bell rang for *High School U.S.A.*, NBC saw the potential for a weekly series that would keep those old sitcom fogies working. *Mystery Science Theater 3000* creator Joel Hodgson says the network offered him the Michael J. Fox part for the show, but he turned it down as the material was beneath him. The one-hour pilot aired on Memorial Day weekend in 1984, with Crispin Glover alone returning from the student actors, finding himself overwhelmed by the addition of even more ghosts from the golden age of television, including Barbara Billingsley and Jerry Mathers from *Leave It to Beaver*.

High Test Girls [1980]
aka Six Swedes on a Pump

DIR. ERWIN C. DIETRICH; W/BRIGITTE LAHAIE, JANE BAKER, NADINE PASCAL

SWEDES ▪ SUMMER JOBS ▪ IDIOT POLITICIAN

Humanity demanded a sequel to *Six Swedes on a Campus* (1979) and Euroshlock exploitation maven Erwin C. Dietrich (*Barbed Wire Dolls*) came through again. Somehow, this Swiss dignitary managed to blast out *High Test Girls*, aka *Six Swedes on a Pump*, in 1980, while the very same year writing, directing, and producing the sexploiters *Come Play With Me 2*, *Ballgame*, and *Gefangene Frauen* (*Women Prisoners*).

This go-around, Greta (Brigitte Lahaie), Inga (Nadine Pascal), Kerstin (France Lomay), Lil (Danielle Troger), Astrid (Kathleen Kane), and Selma (Elsa Maroussia), the not-all-that-Swedish sextet that stormed boarding school in the original film, take over a gas station. Lube jobs, rim work, dipsticks, tailpipes, and the like provide inevitable humor; a pair of news anchors on TV stopping their broadcast to declare that they can see the girls at home getting it on is a nice attempt at a chuckle. Also, the mayor's wife is a nympho.

Pump a little love toward *Six Swedes* super-starlet Brigitte Lahaie. The French bombshell kicked off her movie career at age fifteen in 1971's *Africa Exotica* (*excusez-moi* if you know it as *Jungle Erotique*.) The moment her homeland legalized hardcore sex on-screen in 1976, twenty-one-year-old Brigitte put on her best birthday suit and spent four years as the single most exquisite Euro-star to ever don the crown of porn queen.

By 1980, Brigitte had switched to soft sex romps, such as anything *Six Swedes*–related, and extreme horror, notably in Jean Rollin's psychedelic splatterfest *Fascination* (1979). Her roles became more mainstream as the years passed. Today, Brigitte is a popular talk radio host in France. She should invite the other five faux Swedes up to her studio for a pillow fight.

HIGHER EDUCATION [1988]

DIR. JOHN SHEPPARD; W/KEVIN HICKS, ISABELLE MEJIAS, LORI HALLIER, STEPHEN BLACK

NEW ON CAMPUS ▫ FRENCH TEACHER ▫ PUNKS ▫ RACE RELATIONS

Rural Ontario farm boy Andy Cooper (Kevin Hicks) hops a bus to university to grab himself some *Higher Education*. Andy's roommate is a lady-chasing party animal, punk rockers carom through the dorm hallways on scooters, and everything sure is different than life back home (though not any less Canadian, to be honest).

Andy falls fast and hard for comely fellow first-year student Carrie (Isabelle Mejias), but spends Canadian Thanksgiving weekend in bed with Mademoiselle Hubert (Lori Hallier), his zesty French art professor. The necessary complications percolate and fizz all over the place.

North-of-the-border tax write-off youth comedies don't come much more generic than *Higher Education*, but given the same funding system's high-water marks of *Porky's* (1981), *Screwballs* (1983), and *Oddballs* (1984), who can blame a poor boy from the country for trying?

HOG WILD [1980]

DIR. LES ROSE; W/MICHAEL BIEHN, PATTI D'ARBANVILLE, TONY ROSATO

BIKERS ▫ NERDS ▫ JOCKS ▫ BIG FAT PARTY ANIMAL ▫ ▫ PROPERTY DESTRUCTION ▫ THE BIG RACE

Canadian-made motorcycle youth comedy *Hog Wild* reunites Spaz (Jack Blum) and Fink (Keith Knight) from *Meatballs*. To recap, this is scrawny, bespectacled Spaz, the champion teacup stacker, paired again with obese, omnivorous Larry "Fink" Finkelstein, who in *Meatballs* beats "the Stomach" in a weenie-eating contest. Naturally, Blum and Knight play variations here on their signature roles, which makes *Hog Wild*—a hoot on its own terms—all that much better if you imagine it's a chronicle what happens after Spaz and Fink go home from Camp Northstar.

Elsewhere in the movie, just shortly before he filled a Belushi-esque slot on *SCTV* and then the actual Belushi slot on *Saturday Night Live*, Tony Rosato exhibits heightened comedic chops as a highly Bluto-like biker named Bull in *Hog Wild*. Bull leads the Rustlers, a motorcycle gang whose members raise hell at their crash pad by night, then attend the local public high school by day. They look like neither high school students nor bikers, adding to movie's fun.

After a mix-up, clean-cut Tim (Michael Biehn) is expelled from a military academy, landing square on the Rustlers' turf—specifically the school cafeteria, where the roughnecks dump plates of chow on seemingly everyone's head. Tim catches the eye of Bull's biker babe Angie, played by Patti D'Arbanville, she of cinema's most skyward-pointing upturned nose and a veteran of David Hamilton's uneasy 1977 soft-core frolic, *Bilitis*.

Since Bull is most definitely and understandably the jealous sort, the Rustlers dump wet cement into Tim's beloved convertible and then literally run it up the campus flagpole. Nobody salutes. Hijinks escalate when a local screening of the 1972 bikesploitation saga *Angels Hard as They Come* so excites the Rustlers that they strip Tim and his mild-mannered crew down to their tighty-whities and force them to walk home, handcuffed.

Tim fights back through elaborate vandalism. His counterterrorism so fires Angie with desire that she ditches Bull to roll with her fresh honey in a vat of actual fresh honey. As with other ludicrous movie scenarios, I have to imagine that some tech guy, script girl, or other lackey on the crew knew somebody who could come up with a vat of honey, prompting an eleventh-hour script revision.

All this back-and-forth brouhaha leads to one big motorcycle race that will determine who leads the school. As to who wins, figure that out by calculating the difference between how many Hells Angels bought tickets to teen sex comedies in 1980 versus how many dorks who looked like Spaz and Fink would likely be in the *Hog Wild* audience. So—hooray for Tim it is!

Sarcasm aside, *Hog Wild* is pretty damn funny. Rosato is very, very good as Bull. He impressively expands on the Harpo Marx pantomime aspects of John Belushi's *Animal House* performance by having the gang leader speak in unintelligible grunts and snarls that only the other bikers can interpret. Biehn and D'Arbanville look lovely, and pull off what needs pulling off.

Canadian cult hero Keith Knight—also Barnyard in *Class of 1984*—rips shit up as Vern Jones, a tubby, schlubby wannabe Rustler who amuses the hard-asses he idolizes. Both he and Jack "Spaz" Blum as nerd's nerd Gil Lasky will amuse you. Too bad they didn't carry on their act elsewhere in the way that *Zapped!* (1982) launched the timely comedy team of Scott Baio and Willie Aames.

Beyond the incredibly great movie poster art by *Mad* magazine master Jack Davis and its tagline, "The comedy that's pure bullsh...!", *Hog Wild* was also promoted via a short, crazy TV spot that parodied *Close Encounters of the Third Kind* by showing a cartoon pig face looming over a cartoon Devil's Tower. Keep washing the skies!

Hollywood Dreaming [1986]
aka Smart Alec, The Movie Maker

DIRECTOR JIM WILSON; W/BEN GLASS, NATASHA KAUTSKY, KERRY REMSEN, ORSON BEAN, ZSA ZSA GABOR

SLEAZY PRODUCERS • SEXY STARLETS • HEIRESS • HORSE JOCKEY

Young moviemaking hopeful Alec Carroll (Ben Glass) quits college to pitch his screenplay around Hollywood. Once he's there, seemingly every character Alec meets, both male and female, wants to produce or finance his movie, so long as he sleeps with them first. Just like in real life!

Alec embarks on a succession of slapstick near-carnal negotiations with potential backers. The funniest is with veteran actor Orson Bean (Dr. Lester in *Being John Malkovich*), as loopy financier Arthur Fitzgerald. For a real hoot, pick up Bean's 1971 orgasm-therapy memoir, *Me and the Orgone: The True Story of One Man's Sexual Awakening.*

Fitzgerald will go all in on Alec's film, so long as it stars famous-for-being-famous Hungarian pop culture curiosity Zsa Zsa Gabor. The real Zsa Zsa shows up, and so does her real pet lion. There's some nudity, too, but not from anyone mentioned here by name, except Zsa Zsa's lion.

Hollywood High [1976]

DIR. PATRICK WRIGHT; W/MARCY ALBRECHT, SHERRY HARDIN, SUSANNE SEVEREID

BIKINIS • CHEERLEADERS • WEED • SURFERS • FOOD FIGHT • HUNG DWARF

Some films you watch. Others, you smoke. Pack *Hollywood High* tight into the bong of the

Clockwise from top left: *Everyone likes* H.O.T.S. *(1979), Honey (Susan Kriger), O'Hara (Lisa London), Terri (Pamela Jean Bryant), and Samantha (Kimberly Cameron);* Hollywood High *(1976);* Hollywood Zap *(1986)* Hollywood Hot Tubs 2 *(1990).*

latter category and light up. Radiant, dewy, and possessing not one standard-functioning human brain cell between them, best buds Jan (Susanne Severeid), Candy (Sherry Hardin), Monica (Rae Sperling), and Bebe (Marcy Albrecht) open *Hollywood High* by cruising sunny L.A. in a Cadillac with the top down. The gals announce they're students at the title institution as they drive past. They all look dandy in see-through string bikinis, which they doff upon hitting the beach to get naked and wasted with a van full of male classmates.

That above describes much of what happens in *Hollywood High*. Various eccentrics pop into the action between the beach bits. The school scenes also introduce flamingly exuberant Greek-history teacher Mr. Flowers (Hy Pyke; billed as "Hy Camp") and purringly sultry French instructor Ms. Crotch (Kress Hytes).

After class, the girls take their jalopy to a dwarf mechanic named Big Dick (Mark Lawhead). At Big Dick's gas station, they meet cigar-puffing vintage Hollywood sex bomb June East (Marla Winters), who invites them to crash at her mansion whenever they want. Doing a nonstop—and terrible—Mae West impression, Marla naturally says, "Come *down* and see me some time!"

An ersatz Wolfman Jack howls zit-cream commercials out of the convertible's radio. A spastic cop called "Policeman" (director Patrick Wright) attempts to break up the gang's food fight, but comes away coated in whipped cream with a pickle protruding from each nostril. A mildly psychedelic soft rock soundtrack eases us through the frequent use of handheld cameras, employed to capture all the endless jiggling and giggling in the manner of Vietnam combat photography.

Hollywood High's greatest contribution to the motion-picture arts and sciences is "Fenzie," aka "the Fenz" (Kevin Mead). An absolutely wretched parody of the Fonz from TV's *Happy Days*, Fenzie exists to give thumbs-up and exclaim "Aaayyy!" when not spouting third-person declarations on the order of "There can only be one Fenz!" and "Fenz needs another beer!"

All this delirium culminates with the core female foursome topless and running in fast-motion to the frantic pounding of a silent-movie piano. The girls stop short, look up into the camera, and announce, one at a time, "This!" "Is!" "The!" "End!"

Hollywood High Part II [1981] aka Los Muchachos de Hollywood

DIRS. CARUTH C. BYRD, LEE THORNBURG; W/NICOLE SCENT, BRAD COWGILL, ALISA ANN HULL, CON COVERT

BIKINIS • BEER • WEED • PRUDE • BAD COP • HOLLYWOOD BOULEVARD

Five long years passed between *Hollywood High* installments, nearly an eternity leapfrogging the entire disco era, the birth of punk, and countless other key events in teen history. Come the 1980s, randomly assembled beach romps and pool parties peppered willy-nilly by bad behavior and naked bodies no longer passed lowball trash movie muster. Whereas the dazed sloppiness of first film intoxicated and beguiled, in *Part II* those aspects just seem like a bummer hangover.

Hardboiled character actor Con Covert (*Repo Man, Flesh Gordon*) provides conflict as "Cop." He nastily frisks the bikini girl heroines and gets caught sans uniform in the lustful embrace of class prude Chessie (Alisa Ann Hull). That's what *Hollywood High Part II* passes off as fun. Grody to the max.

Hollywood Hot Tubs [1984]

DIR. CHUCK VINCENT; W/PAUL GUNNING, REMY O'NEILL, JEWEL SHEPARD, EDY WILLIAMS

HOT TUBS • SUMMER JOB • VALLEY GIRLS • BIKERS • KINKY GRANDMAS • NAKED SOCCER

Hollywood Hot Tubs kicks off with the greatest teen prank in the annals of teen prank cinema. Amidst a dark, confusing first few minutes, we hear and partly see high school hooligan Shawn (Paul Gunning) and a pair of his pals bitching, scrambling, and semi-panicking as they sneak up a hillside. After some visual hints that they are high above Los Angeles, the camera pulls back as dawn breaks to reveal that they've altered the iconic Hollywood sign to read "Holly*weed*." Clear helicopter footage reveals that it's no camera trick or special effect: the *Hollywood Hot Tubs* production team physically vandalized the landmark, at least temporarily, to get their opening gag. Take that, John Wayne!

Shawn's parents keep their troublemaking teen out of jail by sending him to work for his cranky uncle's hot tub repair service. Once properly dispatched, the horny apprentice happens upon a merry succession of mammary-and-muff-studded misadventures, servicing the coitus cauldrons of Asian massage parlors, Tinseltown hedonists, lusty limousine occupants, and the sex spa of the title. The Hollywood Hot Tubs facility is best described as a hetero version of a gay bathhouse; not to be confused with the standard actual gay bathhouse that come into play later. That's where Shawn's jerky parole officer tries to spy on him and falls victim to forced anal copulation—turns out the pig loves it!

Tough-talking MILF Pam Landers (Remy O'Neill) runs Hollywood Hot Tubs with her brassiere-averse, torpedo-torsoed Valley Girl daughter Crystal (Jewel Shepard) acting as receptionist and human embodiment of the word *jiggle*. An impromptu family reunion occurs with the arrival of Butch (Jeff Austin), Pam's bad-motherfucker of a biker brother, and his hog-straddling cohorts Aquarius (Danny Wong) and Warbaby (Michael Ragsdale). These toughs will be looking for asses to stomp and they will find them.

Fleshing out the amorous antics around hot tubs are encounters with eccentric horror star Edgar Blood (Victor Marko); outdoor intercourse enthusiast Dee Dee (Katt Shea); and matronly knockered nympho Desiree (Russ Meyer glamazon Edy Williams). At its peak, the bacchanal overflows with nude nubiles, a mariachi band, a brew-chugging chimpanzee, and a Burt Reynolds look-alike played by Sasha Gabor, mainly known as the as the hardest-working Burt Reynolds look-alike in 1980s porn.

At one point, a female soccer team visits the spa to celebrate a win, stripping nude and gang-banging the film's youthful hot-tub-repair hero. Among the dozen or so completely naked female athletes, one blonde keeps her white T-shirt on as the orgy rages around her. In his excitement, Shawn hurls a soccer ball against a wall and it bounces back full force, slamming the T-shirted nubile smack in the kisser. Nobody stops what they are doing.

Hollywood Hot Tubs reigned as a "hard-R" cable TV favorite for years before going into the heaviest of rotations on *USA Up All Night*. What truly keeps *Hot Tubs* afloat is Jewel Shepard's boobs-to-the-tube performance as Crystal. Clad in tops that maddeningly tantalize by just barely containing her bobbling bosom, Jewel crafts a SoCal airhead character to out-puff all others. The 1990 sequel, *Hollywood Hot Tubs 2: Educating Crystal*, is essentially a solo showcase for Shepard in that role.

Hollywood Hot Tubs 2: Educating Crystal [1990]

DIR. KENNETH RAICH; W/JEWEL SHEPARD, REMY O'NEILL, PATRICK DAY, BART BRAVERMAN

HOT TUBS • VALLEY GIRL • NERDS • PHONE SEX • RANDY ARAB SHEIK • ROCK BAND

Six years separate *Hollywood Hot Tubs* (1984) and *Hollywood Hot Tubs 2: Educating Crystal*. During that stretch, cheap T&A movies didn't get less schlocky—in fact, quite the crap-leaning contrary—but B-flick bombshell Jewel Shepard continually honed her formidable skills as a savvy, witty actress who would un-shirt a couple of times per picture. Jewel's A-caliber effort overall elevates this production to a D-plus ranking.

Shepard reprises her role here as Crystal, the Valley girl to out-gag-with-a-spoon all pretenders to her totally tubular throne. Remy O'Neill also returns as Pam, Crystal's mom and the proprietor of Hollywood Hot Tubs, a health spa of sorts—if you believe rampant and random banging of naked party babes within the confines of bubbling wooden sin-soakers is healthy. Pam wants Crystal to take over but, like, Crystal, like, comes off, like, maybe like functionally brain-damaged, as evidenced by, like, how often she says "like."

Our ambitious airhead enrolls in business school. Her jackass classmate Jason (Patrick Day) attempts to mold Crystal into his idea of a proper young lady—hence the subtitle *Educating Crystal*, a reference to the now-forgotten 1983 British rom-com *Educating Rita*. Arab huckster Prince Ahmet (Bart Braverman) woos Pam in hopes of swindling her. Struggling novelist Gary (David Tiefen), the sheik's chauffeur, also goes gaga for Crystal. Yet another boob-interrupting subplot involves maintenance man and secret guitar ace Darby (J. P. Bumstead) joining an ersatz hair-metal ensemble called Brain Dead.

Hollywood Zap [1987]

DIR. DAVID COHEN; W/BEN FRANK, IVAN E. ROTH, DE WALDRON, CHUCK "PORKY" MITCHELL

NERDS ▪ VIDEO GAMES ▪ ROAD TRIP ▪ PUNKETTE ▪ DWARF

A handful of things about *Hollywood Zap* are simply magnificent—all of them aspects of the movie's VHS box cover. The pastiche of images fondling your eyes includes a skinny-tied, new wave nerd with taped-up eyeglasses; a bikini blonde; a hard-bodied punk rock guy firing a pistol; and an obese, poultry-snarfing greaseball, all superimposed over an oncoming car and what looks like a tidal wave of quarters. The painting itself is a righteously tubular onslaught of shoddy skills.

Pull quotes made from thin air with no attribution whatsoever boast: "[Three Stars] Absolutely, Unbelievable...." The back cover headline reads: "*Hollywood Zap* is the best 'buddy' picture I've seen in a long, long time!" Also notable on the back cover is that Chuck Mitchell, who plays Porky himself in the *Porky's* movies, is officially billed as Chuck "Porky" Mitchell.

That any movie would fall short of such an amusing package is a foregone conclusion. The Troma Entertainment logo ices the deal: *Hollywood Zap* does suck. Ivan Roth from *Repo Man* (the "7 Up" dude) stars as Downer. After ditching his lingerie shop gig in the Deep South (bogus "hey y'all" accents are the tip-off), Downer hits the road to find his AWOL dad. Hitchhiker Nash (Ben Frank) shits his pants as soon as he gets in the car. *Hollywood Zap* thereafter becomes a buddy picture, though far short of the billing promised by another phantom testimonial on the video box: "Not since Laurel and Hardy, Abbot and Costello, or Martin and Lewis has any comedy team been so hilarious!"

Ben heads to L.A. to confer with Kong, an arcade guru who knows all regarding the 3-D headache-inducing video game Zaxxon. After the inevitable Hollywood Boulevard montage, Chuck "Porky" Mitchell turns up as a private investigator who will accept payment in fried chicken, but not "sweet taters." Too bad, since those are all Downer has on hand to offer. Next Downer's motelier Uncle Lucas (Claude Earl Jones) attempts to molest his young adult nephew. The supermodel punkette from the video box cover turns out to be lumpy Zaxxon freak Tee-Tee (De Waldron), while Kong is a kung fu dwarf (Tony Cox, Billy Bob Thornton's elf partner from *Bad Santa*). Blonde beach honey Debbie (Anne Gaybis) is on hand to flash flesh.

In the big payoff, Downer's dad reveals himself to be living as a transsexual nun. The dipshit we've followed through all this crap instantly beats the holy fuck out of his mom's husband, who is now a Bride of Christ. In case this description makes the movie sound interesting, let that be a testament to the value of this book, because the execution never rises to the level of the video box. Ivan Roth did bring with him a little of the eccentricity of *Repo Man* minus the charm, the cohesion, and the zap.

HOMETOWN U.S.A. [1979]

aka CALIFORNIA GRAFFITI

DIR. MAX BAER JR.; W/GARY SPRINGER, PAT DELANEY, DAVID WILSON, JULIE PARSONS

NERD ▣ VIRGINS ▣ NOSTALGIA ▣ HOT RODS ▣ CRUISING ▣ 1950S

Max Baer Jr. stomped a permanent place for himself in TV history as lovably possum-brained swamp-hunk Jethro Bodine (and his female cousin, Jethrine) on the 1960s hayseeds-with-heaps-o'-money sitcom, *The Beverly Hillbillies*. During the following decade, Baer reinvented himself behind the camera as a drive-in mini-mogul.

In 1972, Baer wrote and produced *Macon County Line*, a brutal redneck potboiler that grossed the present-day equivalent of more than $100 million. In 1976, he directed *Ode to Billy Joe*, another relative blockbuster, inspired by Bobby Gentry's spooky 1967 hit ballad. Both those Baer efforts are downbeat Deep South period pieces set in 1953. For *Hometown U.S.A.*, Baer's last directorial effort to date, the setting switches to Covina, California, and the timeline jumps to 1957. At last, the dunderheads on-screen get to loosen up, have a grand ol' time, and possibly even get laid far from the specter of Southern Gothic doom. This is a film Jethro Bodine himself would love.

Nothing goes right for bloat-faced, burr-headed high school nerd Rodney C. Duckworth, known to all on campus as "the Rodent." He is constantly pranked and picked on, and sees no possible future for himself involving the concept of "cherry pop" that isn't soda-related. All that changes after the Rodent borrows his brother-in-law's totally bitchin' red convertible hot rod. He hits the streets, and slowly but surely he absorbs some of the car's swagger. Local smooth movers T. J. Swackhammer (Brian Kerwin), a wannabe James Dean, and Recil Calhoun (David Wilson), a wannabe Elvis Presley, take the Rodent under their respective red-windbreaker and black-leather-jacket wings. The new friends rechristen Rodent "Rod Heartbender," and the three of them embark on all-night quest for female action.

The resulting botched booty call gags include a sex pro who suddenly turns terrifying, and a fantasy sequence involving the cast getting it on in front of everybody at school. In addition, Messrs. Swackhammer and Calhoun turn out to be as inexperienced as Mr. Heartbender, and everybody has a bunch of gut-busting guffaws to the tune of a wall-to-wall oldies soundtrack.

Afterward, Max Baer was able to equip his real-life Beverly Hills mansion with at least one more "see-ment pond" courtesy of *Hometown U.S.A.*'s enormous box office haul. Having said his piece and made his piece of cash, he has since lived in comfort, never again picking up a director's beret and megaphone.

HOMEWORK [1982]

DIR. JAMES BESHEARS; W/JOAN COLLINS, MICHAEL MORGAN, SHELL KEPLER

VIRGIN ▣ MILF ▣ PEEPING ▣ MILITARY DAD ▣ 1950S

In 1982, British actress Joan Collins was pushing fifty years of age and spectacularly pushing up her classic physique as bustier-favoring prime-time soap mega-bitch Alexis Carrington on the ABC smash *Dynasty*. Joan's late-blooming superstardom landed her front and center on the poster for the just-weird-enough-to-remember teen sex romp *Homework*.

Literally, this movie is "dreamy." Both teenage Tommy (Michael Morgan) and Diane (Collins), the hot mom of Tommy's swim-team-fixated girlfriend, spend much of *Homework* drifting into heady reveries that we watch on-screen. While Tommy imagines himself as a spy or the super-stud of his high school, Diane thinks back to her Eisenhower-era deflowering. Each variation uses the most obvious props and costumes *Homework*'s budget will allow; watch for the mismatched white polyester tuxedo and a poodle skirt with a glued-on poodle.

Healthy heaps of nudity help pass the time, with top-notch topless turns from scream queen Michelle Bauer, and also Barbara Beckinpaugh, a power-topped beauty who figures crucially in the evocatively titled 1984 documentary *Best Chest in the West.* Body double Joy Michael supplies Joan's juicy bits, and strips down during the '50s flashbacks. Nobody who bought a ticket to *Homework* in 1982 was distressed by such D-cup deception; neither were late-night viewers exploring the possibilities of Showtime and Cinemax programming after midnight over the following years.

One-and-done director James Beshears enjoyed a prolific career as a highly respected Hollywood sound editor before and after this film. The same year as *Homework,* Beshears also coscripted the Neil Young freak-fest *Human Highway.* So 1982 would really have been the best time to party with that dude.

Hot and Bothered [1974]

aka High School Girl

DIR. SERGIO MARTINO; W/SUSAN PLAYER, RICCARDO CUCCIOLLA, ROSALBA NERI, ALFREDO PEA

VIRGIN ▪ INCEST ▪ HOOKERS ▪ DIRTY OLD MAN ▪ BRALESS IN CHURCH

"She was hot. He was bothered." To perfection, that tagline explains the title of *Hot and Bothered.* The movie itself is a *molto Italiano* spree into adolescent heavy breathing and boner gags from Sergio Martino, one of the premier craftsmen of lusty and leering bedroom farces produced in the land of the Pope.

The "she" who is hot is Sonia (Susan Player), a teen blonde troublemaker who is dropped off from Rome to finish her studies at her aunt's scenic countryside villa. The "he" who is bothered is Celio (Riccardo Cucciolla), the villa's resident frustrated virgin. Sonia gallivants about in sheer tops and miniskirts sans undergarments, and sunbathes nude no matter who's around. That *is* hot. Celio takes it all in and contends with the fact that Sonia is his first cousin, so you see why he's bothered.

In fine Italian sex romp tradition, the men are all ass-pinching fuck machines and the women are all either face-slapping prudes or happy-to-be-ass-pinched machine-fuckers in return. Celio's papa Nico (Alfredo Pea), for example, beds the villa's horny housekeeper (Rosalba Neri), as well as the loosest young lass among the kids' classmates (Loredana Fabriani). When he's tired, he watches his mistresses enjoy some bubbly lesbian bath time together.

Don't worry, Nico notices that his niece Sonia is one hot 'n' spicy meatball, too. Yet the joyful honor of transgressing that particular incest taboo is left to Celio. We never get to the bottom of how Sonia finishes her studies.

Hot Chili [1985]

DIR. WILLIAM SACHS; W/CHARLES SCHILLACI, ALLAN KAYSER, JOE RUBBO, LOUISA MORITZ

SUMMER JOBS ▪ RESORT ▪ PARTY ANIMAL ▪ SKINNY-DIPPING ▪ HORNY HOUSEWIFE

Cannon Films made *Hot Chili* in a fever rush on the heels of *Hot Resort.* Both boisterous youth farces follow the boobs-out boilerplate established by the company's founding global smash, *Lemon Popsicle* (1978). As always, a cadre of high school pals manically scrounge for sex and comically suffers slam-bang consequences. The formula is most familiar from *The Last American Virgin* (1982), which was Cannon's Americanization of the Israeli-made *Popsicle.*

Interestingly, both *Hot Chili* and *Hot Resort* adjust the elemental *Lemon Popsicle* recipe to expand from three main male pals to four. Each movie also dispatches its quartet to a warm-weather resort for delightfully disastrous summer jobs. We start here with three essential Cannon teen archetypes: smooth operator Ricky (Charles Schillaci), vulnerable romantic Jason (Allan Kayser), and gargantuan good-time glutton Arney (Joe Rubbo, returning from *The Last American Virgin* and still possessing the greatest fat-guy name in the history of fat guys). Due to *Revenge of the Nerds* scoring socko box office the previous year, *Hot Chili* also adds bow-tied, bespectacled dweeb Stanley (Chuck Hemingway), who rages over his hard-to-shuck virginity by repeatedly screaming, “When is it *my* turn? I wanna *fuck*! I *just* wanna *fuck*!”

While on summer break, the lads staff the Tropicana Cabana, a Mexican resort lorded over by despot Esteban (Jerry Lazarus). Unlike *Hot Resort* and its big rowing race, though, *Hot Chili* foregoes much plot in favor of stringing together zany episodes dominated by naked female guests and sped-up chases punctuated with “boing” sound effects. In a weird flash of elegance, the Tropicana Cabana’s music instructor (Bea Fielder) plays the cello naked. Much like our main manatee Joe Rubbo, Louisa Moritz essentially re-creates her *Last American Virgin* role as Chi Chi, a nymphomaniac Latin sex bomb who offers her gangbang services to the boys—only to be thwarted by the sudden appearance of her fury-foaming husband Bruno (mutant-mugged *Maniac Cop* star Robert Z’Dar).

Noticeably cheaper than *Hot Resort* and impossible to follow in the fashion of a normal film, *Hot Chili* takes on the air of a ’70s European soft-core comedy, the exact sort of late-night cable filler that movies like this largely replaced. Despite that, the movie is highly watchable, and its end-credit sequence is a fiesta in itself. While various names and pseudonyms roll, Joe Rubbo runs away from angry hotel guests, locals, and mad beasts escaped from the bullfighting arena. He hightails it through the streets and toward the camera for three spectacular minutes of sweat and gasps and hard-flopping body-parts, resembling a melting, refrigerator-shaped lava lamp melting under the south-of-the-border sun. Apparently, he never recovered, as *Hot Chili* remains Joe Rubbo’s last film.

Hot Dog...The Movie [1984]

DIR. PETER MARKLE; W/PATRICK HOUSER, TRACY SMITH, DAVID NAUGHTON, SHANNON TWEED

RADICAL SKI DUDES ▣ SKI BUNNIES ▣ HOT TUB ▣ THE BIG SNOWBALL FIGHT

There’s a lot of skiing in *Hot Dog...The Movie*—much more than anyone remembers. *Hot Dog* boasts so much ski footage, in fact, that it borders on being one of those Warren Miller winter sports documentaries interrupted on occasion by a zippy youth sex farce.

Slaloming over to the zippy parts, pretty blond boy Patrick Houser stars as ski champ hopeful Harkin Banks. He picks up pretty blonde girl hitchhiker Sunny (Tracy Smith) en route to a freestyle competition at California’s Squaw Valley Ski Resort. As the fair flaxen friends fall for one another, Harkin falls in with the lodge’s resident gonzo, booze-guzzling cutups. David Naughton, as smart-ass New Yorker Dan O’Callahan, leads the pack, which also includes kamikaze snow dog Kendo (James Saito); roadkill-for-brains Squirrel (Frank Koppala); rad punk Slasher (George Theobald); and Dan’s ace ski squeeze, Michelle, aka Bananapants (Lynn Wieland).

Teutonic slope bully Rudolph Garmisch (John Patrick Reger) and his pompous Gestapo hangers-on stack the deck against the white-powder wildmen with ringer judges schlepped over from *der Vaterland*. Shannon Tweed transforms from the 1982 *Playboy* Playmate of the Year into a naked *Hot Dog* hot tub hottie who seduces young Harkin and severely harshes his otherwise smooth run with Sunny.

Harkin and Sunny make up before the end, just as surely as Harkin beats the big bad Bavarian guy during *Hot Dog*’s climactic “Chinese Downhill” race.

Despite all the skiing—again, there is a huge, heaping, mountainload of skiing in this movie—the most fun parts of *Hot Dog* take place off the slopes. Guest stunner Crystal Smith impresses as a naked hotel clerk thirteen years after she posed for *Playboy*, the same year the average *Hot Dog* viewer was born, most likely. The best overall sequence involves a wet-T-shirt contest at a mountain town shit-kicker tavern, where a rollicking country-rock band blasts out a booty-stomping boogie soundtrack for bouncing boobs, flying beer bottles, and good ol' boys raising high hell. Those local guys seem like the real hot dogs—where's their sequel?

HOT MOVES [1985]

DIR. JIM SOTOS; W/MICHAEL ZOREK, ADAM SILBAR, JILL SCHOELEN, MONIQUE GABRIELLE

SUMMER BREAK ▣ PARTY ANIMAL ▣ HEAVY METAL ▣ DWARF ▣ HOLLYWOOD BOULEVARD

Hot Moves begins just moments before classes end for summer break, with a close-up on the front door of a high school. A female voice of authority, obviously belonging to a real sack-buster of a teacher or a vice principal, intones, "So what do you hope to accomplish in the next three months?"

"Well, Mrs. Harrison," answers Barry, still unseen, "my friends and I have decided to do something to enhance our personal growth and self-awareness this summer—we're gonna get *laid*!" The bell rings, the student body pours forth into sun-soaked liberation, and the movie smash-cuts immediately to a barrage of seaside SoCal hijinks. String bikinis! Oiled-up bodybuilders! Skateboards! Breakdancers! BMX bikes! Roller-boogiers! Roller-*booties*! Bikers! Punks! Chain-saw juggling! Dogs wearing sunglasses! That's the picture, and meanwhile New Wave of British Heavy Metal marauders Raven deliver the "athletic rock" title track. So far, every move is coming up plenty *hot*.

When we finally see him, Barry is played by Michael Zorek, beloved by genre devotees as Bubba "The Ultimate Party Animal" Beauregard in *Private School* (1983). He and buddies Michael (Adam Silbar), Joey (Jeff Fishman), and Scotty (Johnny Timko) hit the beach and pledge to pop their cherries before senior year starts in the fall. Proceedings threaten to cool after Michael is shot down by longtime sweetheart Julie Ann (Jill Schoelen, who, in *The Stepfather*, performs the single most gratuitous shower scene in cinema history). No matter. His fellow hot movers have more hot moves in store.

Joey scopes out legendarily scuzz-strewn Hollywood Boulevard, eyeballing streetwalkers and popping into a realistically rash-inducing sex shop to buy a condom. The sleaze beast behind the counter advises him to try an edible jock strap. ("This one's penis flavored!") Barry manages to go home with an amusingly teddy-bear-fixated waitress, but he accidentally sets her house on fire. While delivering newspapers, Joey comes across a sophisticated vixen in gauzy lingerie who invites him inside for a morning meal. Alas, her wig falls off, revealing that *she* is a *he*, and Joey opts out of chowing breakfast sausage.

Before long, the gang find themselves on a group mini-golf date with real live girls that include *Penthouse* Pet and B-flick bombshell Monique Gabrielle as Babs, and Miss California 1975 Debi Richter as Heidi, topped off by a cameo from dapper little person Jerry Maren, the last surviving Munchkin from *The Wizard of Oz*, who, alas, went over the rainbow himself in 2018.

Whether or not our boys putt their way to senior year after sinking their colored balls—well, that's your *hot move* to watch the movie and find out.

HOT PURSUIT [1987]

DIR. STEVEN LISBERGER; W/JOHN CUSACK, WENDY GAZELLE, KEITH DAVID, JERRY STILLER

PREP SCHOOL ▣ CARIBBEAN VACATION ▣ RASTAFARIANS ▣ WEED ▣ MOBSTERS

John Cusack's mid-'80s teen classic hot streak (*Better Off Dead, The Sure Thing, One Crazy Summer*) didn't exactly screech to a halt with *Hot Pursuit*, but he likely remains grateful that *Tapeheads* (1988) and *Say Anything* (1989) came through the pipeline soon after, so nobody noticed this wrong turn. Cusack does his thing

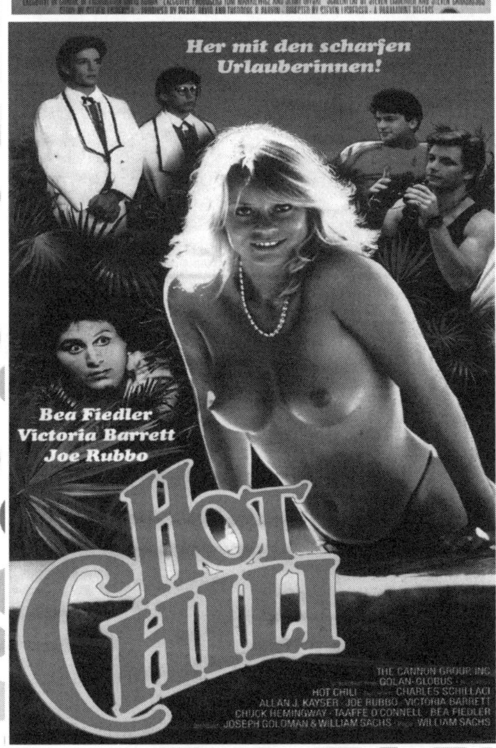

Hot movies. Clockwise from top left: Hot Pursuit *(1987) is lesser John Cusack;* Hot Moves *(1985) is major Michael Zorek;* Hot Splash *(1988) is early Andrea Thompson;* Hot Chili *(1985) is absolutely timeless Joe Rubbo.*

as Burnham Prep student Dan Bartlett. He is amped to do some Caribbean island hopping with his girlfriend Lori Cronenberg (Wendy Gazelle) and her blue-blood family, but, shockingly, nothing goes according to plan.

Hot Pursuit is a paint-by-numbers tropical-getaway comedy with a very limited amount of colors. Some splashes of inspiration keep things conga-lining, starting with a couple of inspired casting choices. Robert Loggia (*Scarface*) crusts it up as salty old sea captain Mac, while Keith David (*They Live*) peaceably puffs his way to enlightenment as Rastafarian groovester Alphonso.

Jerry Stiller and Ben Stiller can't help but amuse as father-and-son thugs out to shake down moneyed old man Cronenberg. Once they kidnap Lori, though, *Hot Pursuit* degenerates into a creaky action farce for the final third. Relax, mon, your mind will erase this movie from memory in less time than it takes to be kind and rewind.

HOT RESORT [1985]

DIR. JOHN ROBINS; W/BRONSON PINCHOT, DAN SCHNEIDER, MARCY WALKER, FRANK GORSHIN

SUMMER JOB ▣ RESORT ▣ NERD ▣ FAT GUY ▣ IVY-LEAGUE SNOBS ▣ THE BIG RACE

Like *The Last American Virgin* and *Hot Chili, Hot Resort* is yet another *Lemon Popsicle*–rooted teen summer sexcapade from the peerless Cannon Films. This one flips the script on the core formula by adding a fourth main dude to the mix.

Previously, offshoots of *Lemon Popsicle*, the 1978 Israeli film, focused on a trio of hormonal high school archetypes: a suave ladies' man, a sensitive romantic, and a thunderously blubbery bucket-of-guffaws fat guy. *Hot Resort* whips out those figures fast: slickster Marty (Tom Parkesian), nice guy Kenny (Michael Berz), and party blob Chuck (Dan Schneider, just prior to playing Dennis on TV's *Head of the Class*). Enter the fourth wheel, take-no-guff ballbuster Brad (Bronson Pinchot, right after *Beverly Hills Cop* and right before Cousin Balki), who makes it clear he's from "Noo Yawk" every time he speaks. Brad acts like a stunningly perfect fusion of all four Sweathogs from *Welcome Back, Kotter*.

Hot Resort drops this awesome foursome into summer jobs at a tropical resort loaded with sex-starved female guests, snobby blue-blood rivals, and bumbling bosses. The adults in charge are tubby schlub Mr. Bray (David Lipman), effervescently effete Bobby (Stephen Stucker), and African American hard-ass Mr. Martin (playwright Samm-Art Williams). The topper, as the opening credits declare, is a special guest appearance by "Mr. Frank Gorshin."

The assembled snobs are pretty interesting villains. An Ivy League rowing team called the Typhoon has been flown to St. Kitt's to film a soup commercial. Each member speaks with clench-jawed contempt and openly disdains the outer-borough New York hotel staff heroes as subhuman schleppers and fetchers. The exposition is a good setup for the inevitable pluck-vs.-privilege rowing race.

Overall, *Hot Resort* starts strong and then meanders to a predictable payoff. The refreshingly harsh insult humor includes Schneider asking a black customs agent if he's the Caribbean guy with the booming laugh in the 7 Up "uncola" ads. The customs agent's deadpan reply: "Give me your passport, fatso." Schneider consoles himself through a non sequitur sex tumble with a naked island nympho.

Mr. Frank Gorshin, the Riddler from TV's *Batman*, plays a rich guest who gives the boys dodgy advice. Famed funnyman Gorshin couldn't be more clearly milking a free vacation from film producers Menachem Golan and Yoram Globus—and that is admirable. Even better if he was already on-site, milking a vacation from some other producers, and decided to double dip.

For a change, the hapless resort bosses get *Hot Resort*'s best laughs. Lumpy dump David Lipman first perfected his character's balding über-nebbish persona in late '70s Miracle Whip commercials. He made a supremely well-fitting fileted pedophile in *The Exterminator* (1980). In various *Law and Order* episodes, he is a recurring, hectoring judge. Stephen Stucker, unforgettable as prancing control tower prankster Johnny in *Airplane!* (1980), works that same fabulously funny shtick here. *Hot Resort* is the last film Stucker made before dying in 1986. At least he got one Caribbean getaway with Mr. Frank Gorshin before he croaked.

HOT SPLASH [1988]

DIR. JAMES INGRASSIA; W/RICHARD STEELE, ANDREA THOMPSON, JAMES MICHAEL HALL, JEREMY WHELAN

SURFERS ▪ BIKINIS ▪ THE BIG CONTEST ▪ HOT TUB ▪ BLOW-UP DOLL

As a title, *Hot Splash* is really rather—er, *evocative* of something, isn't it? That turn of phrase comes as close as any to properly conjuring this mad patchwork of competitive surfers, aspiring new wave songbirds, batty gangsters, and Miami Beach vacation footage. The surfers are Matt (Richard Steele), Woody (Richard Steinmetz), and Jimbo (James Michael Hall—not Anthony). The singer is Jimbo's girlfriend, Jennifer (Andrea Thompson), whom he essentially abuses, clinching her Stockholm syndrome–stricken affections. Jennifer realizes Jimbo has lifted cash from her purse, and a friend asks why she puts up with such treatment. She answers, "Don't you understand? That's what I *like* about Jimbo!"

Jennifer belts out quite an array of numbers during the first half of *Hot Splash*. Her recording session, which is horrible, is followed by an extended performance at a genuinely repulsive and severely Floridian nightspot called Jubilations. She is backed by an even more repugnant band led by horror-haired musician Lenny Macaluso, who headed *Hot Splash*'s music department and also composed the mellifluous soundtrack for *Nerds of a Feather* (1990). Their disgusting duet of Spirit's "Got a Line on You" alone is worth the price of bit-torrenting, even if that price means losing Internet access forever.

While Jennifer sings and Jimbo disrespects her repeatedly in myriad ways, Matt dabbles in running cocaine and dating the daughter of mobster T. J. (Richard Whelan). He and a pal hide out in a gaudy, non-fictitious Miami Beach strip club called the Dollhouse II before embarking on a final chase in the awesome actual amusement pier attraction, the Mystery Funhouse. Flaked throughout the film are scenes involving a hot air balloon escape, a much-discussed surf contest, and grimy blasts of cinema verité such as Jimbo violently and credibly duking it out with some doofus on the Jubilations dance floor.

Jimbo and Jennifer also go at it rather explicitly in a hot tub. Andrea Thompson later dared to bare again during her five years on the ABC drama *NYPD Blue*. While watching Andrea in *Hot Splash*, force yourself to accept that this actress would later costar in a professionally made TV series, among the most acclaimed of its day. She really crawled out of a swamp of Florida insanity, when she just as easily could have drowned in the hot tub right alongside Jimbo.

Hot Splash in no way resembles a "movie," let alone a comedy, yet the entertaining picture is a wild ride even during the dull bits. *Hot Splash* is hard to wash off. Maybe—like Jennifer on the subject of her thieving, cheating, insulting boyfriend—that will be what you like about it!

HOT TIMES [1974]
aka A HARD DAY FOR ARCHIE

DIR. JIM MCBRIDE; W/HENRY CORY, GAIL LORBER, AMY FARBER

VIRGIN ▪ PEEPING ▪ HOOKERS ▪ FUNNY INCEST

Is this a movie? Is it a mugging crossed with a flashing? Is it a car crash in a public toilet? Is it...(*gulp*) art? Whatever the final conclusion, standout nil-budget New York City–shot *Hot Times* comes clean with one of cinema's most emphatically blunt-skulled taglines: "It's like *American Graffiti*...but with *sex*!"

Even more than that, *Hot Times* is like a sexed-up *Archie* comic, hence the film's original title,

A Hard Day for Archie. The story details the ins and outs of high school lothario Archie Anders (Henry Cory), his forever-famished pal Mughead (Steve Curry), and arrogant rival Reggy (Rick Ross), as they lust over sweet Bette (Amy Farber) and sassy Ronnie (Gail Lorber).

Just as the Riverdale gang evolved on the comics page to embrace successive youth cultures—i.e., rock and roll, flower power, and punk—their *Hot Times* doppelgängers mash together every aspect of post-WWII teendom into a filthy, funny, borderline fascinating chaotic heap. A doo-wop theme underscores the credits, after which the music tends toward comically exaggerated orchestrations and cartoon sounds. "Boing!" figures prominently. Mughead's narration and the rapid-fire dialogue pull from ethnic New York 1950s slang, akin to *Mad* magazine's original *Starchie* parody. Archie himself, while sporting a Woodstock-friendly Afro, dresses in the bow ties and argyle sweater-vests of a 1940s jazzbo.

Hot Times is explicitly set in 1973, though, the perfect year for Bette to drag Archie to a convergence by Eastern guru Maha-Vishnu. Mughead reads *Screw* magazine. Ronnie kills time doing motel-room porn shoots. Repeated references to sadomasochism abound. At one point a cabdriver has a long sex monologue, punctuated by the loud street cacophony of police chases, screams, car wrecks, machine-gun fire. At no point are these jarring sounds acknowledged. Illicit encounters loom in every abandoned park, shower room, and massage parlor. Archie spies on his naked sister. The movie climaxes with verité footage of Archie wandering Times Square on New Year's Eve as the ball drops to announce 1974.

Writer-director Jim McBride went on to make legit Hollywood movies in the 1980s (*Breathless, The Big Easy, Great Balls of Fire*). Executive producer William Mishkin was already a grindhouse titan after backing multiple efforts from Z-movie anti-talent Andy Milligan (*Gutter Trash, Bloodthirsty Butchers, Fleshpot on 42nd Street, The Rats Are Coming! The Werewolves Are Here!*). Of the actors, only Steve "Mughead" Curry snagged future credits of note; in 1986, he appeared in *The Sexy Secrets of the Kiss-O-Gram Girls*.

Hot Times at Montclair High [1989]

DIR. JOSE ALTONAGA; W/ROSS HAMILTON, KIM VALENTINE, JONATHAN GORMAN, TROY DONAHUE

NERD ▪ JOCKS ▪ SHOWERS ▪ BAD TEACHER ▪ FAKE METAL BAND

The year 1989 has no rival in terms of twelve consecutive months of sheer cultural ugliness. Case in repulsive point: *Hot Times at Montclair High*, a shot-on-video assemblage of snooze-inducing nonsense. The entire budget might have been better splurged on a local phone call that ended with the words, "Nah, let's not make that cockamamie cocaine high school movie."

Jonathan Gorman stars as Ziggy Karpinski, a hunk in nerd drag who enjoys tepid fantasies about his blonde high school teacher before he finally scores with the hottest virgin at Montclair High. Toward that end, he sports a boner the size of a hoagie. Campus bombshell Bridgette is nicknamed "Peanut Butter" because "she spreads for everybody!" Off-campus, a pseudo–*Miami Vice* subplot unfolds about a yacht-based coke cartel scheming to make Montclair High its major stronghold.

Most of *Hot Times at Montclair High* is punishingly dry. We spend a lot of time with the football star hero as he struggles to pass anatomy class, practicing flash cards in real time. Then drug-boat sexual assault and female nudity coupled with male pervert slapstick in the girls' shower room shakes you awake.

Hot Times gets a positive point for the horrendous fake metal band that plays on-screen, and the gloppy hard rock tunes by Dennis Michael Tenney that dot the soundtrack. The music sounds like the movie looks, which is to say exactly like 1989—all just so fuckin' ugly.

H.O.T.S. [1979]

aka T&A Academy, American Teens

DIR. GERALD SETH SINDELL; W/ANGELA AAMES, DANNY BONADUCE, LISA LONDON, PAMELA JEAN BRYANT

SORORITY ▪ CHEERLEADERS ▪ PRANKS ▪ THE BIG STRIP COMPETITION

What do the initials "H.O.T.S." in *H.O.T.S.* mean, anyway? Is it "Hang On to Sex," "Hands Off Those Suckers," or possibly "Help Out the Seals"? The mysterious acronym title of this shenanigan-stuffed flesh-travaganza is revealed only in the film's very last moments. Fittingly, when the real definition is unveiled, it's dopey, but, like every other aspect of *H.O.T.S.*, equally charming and enjoyably dumb.

The nominal plot of *H.O.T.S.* follows college freshman Honey O'Shayne (Susan Kiger), who gets the cold shoulder from every sorority house on campus. Honey responds by teaming with the other female rejects—almost all are actual brick-house 1970s *Playboy* models—to create a hypersexual secret society that will steal all the studs on campus away from those snooty rivals. They call themselves H.O.T.S.!

Mixed into this pubic-hair-brained scheme is a swimming bear in the H.O.T.S. house pool, a clapping seal in the H.O.T.S. house bathtub, bumbling safecrackers in the H.O.T.S. house attic, and Boom-Boom Bangs (Angela Aames) skydiving bare-bosomed into the H.O.T.S. house backyard.

Also, there is Danny Bonaduce. The grown ex–*Partridge Family* kid and future reality-TV hell-raiser is all over this movie, playing guitar, tossing about silk scarves, and incorrectly thinking he has made love to a seal. In general, Bonaduce defines what cocaine itself would look like if it sweated perpetually while silently chanting, "Be cool, be cool, man, be cool," beneath a hard-blown heap of rocked-out fiery red hair.

H.O.T.S. achieves an apex of affable ogling by way of a climactic strip-football game between our heroines and their enemy coeds. The gridiron showdown begins with all comers in bikinis, and then rapidly escalates into a series of topless huddles, with the camera leeringly shoved into the scene of the scrum.

Fascinatingly, all this mammary-fixated mayhem emerged from the mind of *H.O.T.S.* co-screenwriter Cheri Caffaro. An exploitation movie legend in her own right, sultry blonde Caffaro played bisexual super-spy Ginger McAllister in a series of soft-core espionage grindhouse hits: *Ginger* (1971), *The Abductors* (1972), and *Girls Are for Loving* (1973).

H.O.T.S. first emerged as a popular program on the drive-in circuit. The movie also did big business in the early days of home video; big enough to warrant a second theatrical release in 1984 as *T&A Academy,* the title attempting to tap the success of the same year's *Police Academy*. In fact, *H.O.T.S.* became such a video rental brand name that 1974's *The Swinging Cheerleaders* (itself a big-box VHS sensation) was reissued on tape under the moniker *H.O.T.S. II*.

The original film kept its stride as a cable perennial, airing ceaselessly in prime time and the wee hours on pay channels throughout the entire 1980s. For once, nobody complained about too many reruns.

So pervasive was the potency of *H.O.T.S.* that popular legend claims the Hooters breastaraunt chain snagged its waitress uniform design from the movie's signature costume of way-tight white T-shirts and slit-high satin short-shorts. Hooters has never denied the allegations.

By the way, *H.O.T.S.* stands for (BIG-TIME SPOILER! READ NO FURTHER IF YOU DON'T WANT THE CUTE EPILOGUE RUINED!) "Honey, O'Hara, Terri, and Samantha."

Clockwise from top left: Hometown U.S.A. *(1979) works* American Graffiti *affection hard*; Hog Wild *(1980), brings Canadian bikers straight to teen movie hell; Kid 'n' Play launched a dynasty with* House Party (1990), *a movie that spawned at least four official sequels*; Hunk *(1987), aka* El yuppie *en espanol.*

HOT T-SHIRTS [1980]

DIR. CHUCK VINCENT; W/RAY HOLLAND, GLENN MURE, STEPHANIE LAWLOR

WET T-SHIRTS ▣ CHEERLEADERS ▣ SAVE THE BUSINESS

The *Hot T-Shirts* opening credits deliver a wondrous overload of images, the best rejected James Bond title segment ever. Lava-lamp psychedelic images of women gyrating in T-shirts come and go, then flip into negative color. A disco doll wails on the soundtrack: "My body is wet / My body's soaking wet, dripping wet / Wet! Wet! Wet! Wet!"

From there, two mooks enter a strip club. The disco music continues, but the T-shirts are gone. That was quick. Extroverted mook Charlie (Glenn Mure) is all Long Island guido slick. His sidekick Joe (Ray Holland) is lovable lump in an officially licensed New York Yankees jacket. Charlie owns a combination bar and Italian restaurant that looks as dumpy as he is. Together, the boys hatch a plot to save this meatball hut with wet-T-shirt contests—if only they can find competitors.

Nearby, Joe's girlfriend June (Stephanie Lawlor), Harrison College's head cheerleader coach, is working with her squad on their latest chant: "We're gonna roast them, toast them, cover them in spit! / We're gonna maim them, shame them, make them look like shit!" The perfect wet-T-shirt competitors have arrived.

Soon enough, Charlie's joint is the hottest ticket in this crappy suburb. Townie girls heatedly square off against sopped-top cheerleaders. They disco dance like crazy. Uptight blue-hairs picket the place until they are invited inside for cocktails, then they also run wild. Finally, any question of who will be the Queen of All Doused Blouses is settled with the arrival of Judy (Corinne Alphen, 1982's *Penthouse* Pet of the Year, future costar of 1983's *Spring Break*, and onetime wife of *Wiseguy* actor Ken Wahl). She knows her way around a soggy disco floor.

As usual, director Chuck Vincent imbues the doings with wit and flair above and beyond what sanity requires. As portly proprietor Joe, Glenn Mure is as good playing sad sack as he is at going over-the-top animal as an ersatz Belushi. Such range! Everybody involved should have made sequels. Sadly, Chuck Vincent died from AIDS-related complications in Key West in 1991.

HOUSE PARTY [1990]

DIR. REGINALD HUDLIN; W/CHRISTOPHER "KID" REID, CHRISTOPHER "PLAY" MARTIN, ROBIN HARRIS, TISHA CAMPBELL

HOUSE PARTY ▣ THE BIG DANCE CONTEST ▣ RAP BATTLE ▣ ONE WILD NIGHT

House Party ignited a hip-hop revolution in teen cinema, showcasing a cast of dynamic talents at the dawn of their careers and turning theaters—where it ran in urban neighborhoods for more than a year straight—into impromptu versions of the blowout going down up on the screen. Writer-director Reginald Hudlin adapted his Harvard University student film into a feature-length vehicle designed for an up-and-coming rap duo. DJ Jazzy Jeff and the Fresh Prince passed ("We weren't thinking about doing movies back then," Jeff later lamented), so *House Party*'s leads went to popular *Yo! MTV Raps* hitmakers Kid 'N Play (aka Christopher Reid and Christopher Martin)

House Party opens in a high school cafeteria where Play (Martin, the half of the team with the standard 1990 fade haircut) announces his parents are out of town. Consequently, that night he'll be hosting the bacchanalian spectacular of the year. Bilal (Martin Lawrence) will DJ the party, and Kid (Reid, the dude with the trademark high-top Eraserhead coif) says he just has to sneak out past his grumpy pop (Robin Harris, who is uproarious).

Kid easily slips away to Play's house while his pop snoozes in front of a video of *Dolemite* (1975), but he soon runs into the school bully's entire family of goons. He is also nearly shot by a neighbor who thinks he's a burglar. Seeking shelter, Kid ducks into a fraternity party where the disc jockey (George Clinton) scratches old doo-wop records, giving Kid an opportunity to bust out some freestyle rap.

Kid finally arrives at the party, and soon comes flirtation with the lovely Sydney (Tisha Campbell) and Sharane (A. J. Johnson), then a dance contest, a rap battle, and the arrival of the bullies, police officers, and Kid's now fully-awake-and-ain't-having-it pop. More adventures follow, with Kid ultimately easing back into bed and setting up one of the most hilarious parting shots of this movie's era.

House Party is vital, vibrant, and a pure kick of youthful energy from a slice of life that had been underrepresented in the teen comedy genre. On a budget of $2.5 million, the movie returned $26 million in first-run box office receipts alone. Kid 'N Play returned for *House Party 2* (1991) and *House Party 3* (1994), sandwiching their college romp *Class Act* (1992) right in the middle. They also got their own NBC Saturday morning cartoon. In the years ahead, numerous African American youth comedies resulted from *House Party*'s success, including *Hangin' with the Homeboys* (1991), *The Inkwell* (1994), and even *Friday* (1995).

Tragically, comedian Robin Harris, an instant icon as Kid's fed-up father, died nine days after *House Party* hit theaters. This film, along with animated favorite *Bebe's Kids* (1992), based on Harris's stand-up routines, will keep Robin's hilarious memory alive for generations to come.

How I Got into College

[1989]

DIR. SAVAGE STEVE HOLLAND; W/LARA FLYNN BOYLE, COREY PARKER, ANTHONY EDWARDS

COLLEGE · RICH JERKS · VIRGIN · ROTC HARD-ASS · MARCHING BAND MAYHEM

Savage Steve Holland's third big-screen effort (after the classics *Better Off Dead* and *One Crazy Summer*) is also his first work-for-hire directing gig. The difference shows. *How I Got into College*'s script, by the non-prolific Terrel Seltzer (he wrote *One Fine Day* in 1996) filters the basic plot essentials of *Better Off Dead*—wayward high-school zilch pines for dream girl while overcoming comic obstacles—through a university admissions and standard rom-com strainer. Mush comes out the other end.

The cast fares well. As object-of-obsession Jessica Kailo, Lara Flynn Boyle radiates what would make her a triple household name the following year via *Twin Peaks*. Fortunately for the movie, Anthony Edwards (in a poster-touted cameo), Curtis Armstrong (also making a blip appearance), Brian Doyle-Murray, Charles Rocket, and Nora Dunn are funny people, and they don't deviate here from their standards—unlike the director.

How I Got into College is not entirely devoid of Savage Steve flair. A maniacal marching band that follows Marvin all over a campus recruitment event, for example, could only have come from him. Still, the movie snuck into theaters for a single weekend. Despite its pedigree, no amount of years or mystique have ever promoted this picture for rediscovery. No degree of higher learning is necessary to understand why not.

Hunk [1987]

DIR. LAWRENCE BASSOFF; W/JOHN ALLEN NELSON, STEVE LEVITT, DEBORAH SHELTON, JAMES COCO

NERD 📼 HUNK 📼 AEROBICS 📼 PACT WITH SATAN

Hunk remains the only film so far that seems to be a conscious rip-off of the cinematic canon of esteemed exploitation director Chuck Vincent (*Summer Camp, Preppies, Wimps*). *Hunk* misses on every mark—not funny, no nudity—but horns up, at least a little, for trying.

Horns are appropriate, as *Hunk* depicts computer nerd Bradley Brinkman (Steve Levitt) selling his soul to a devil-in-a-bunch-of-dumb-disguises, Dr. D (James Coco). Bradley's wish is delivered, and he is transformed into a buff, blow-dried he-man named "Hunk Golden" (John Allen Nelson).

Hunk becomes famous and gets all the girls. Inside, Bradley becomes oh so sad, as he realizes all he really needed was true love. Now he must suffer in agonizing hellfire for all eternity—what a bummer. Broadway legend and comedy great James Coco died before *Hunk* came out, and thus is stuck for all eternity with this hunk-of-something as his final credit.

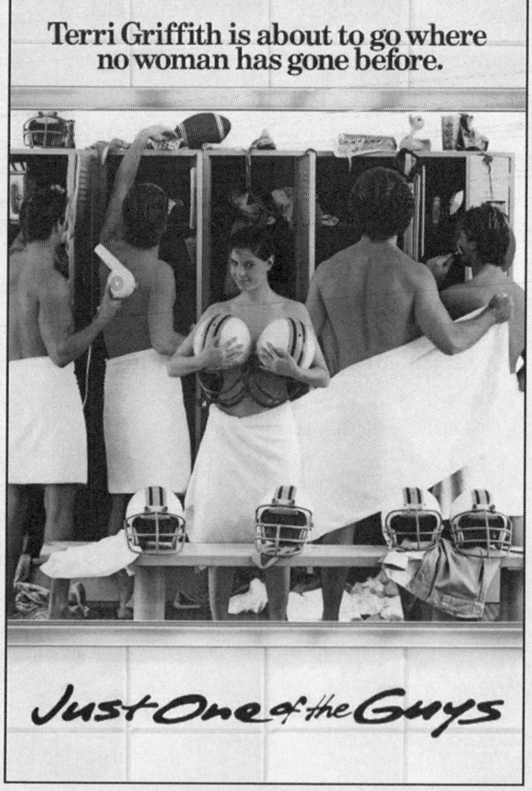

Clockwise from top: *King Vidiot (Jon Gries) disrupts* Joysticks *(1983); this provocative* Just One of the Guys *(1985) poster somewhat misrepresents but sure sold the movie*; The Invisible Kid *(1988)*.

In the Mood ▣ Incoming Freshmen
The Invisible Kid
Jocks ▣ Joy of Sex
Joysticks ▣ Just One of the Girls
Just One of the Guys

In the Mood [1987]

DIR. PHIL ALDEN ROBINSON; W/PATRICK DEMPSEY, BEVERLY D'ANGELO, TALIA BALSAM, MICHAEL CONSTANTINE

OLDER WOMEN ▣ SEX SCANDAL ▣ NOSTALGIA

Patrick Dempsey obnoxiously plays Ellsworth "Sonny" Wisecarver, a real-life fifteen-year-old nicknamed "the Woo-Woo Kid," who distracted America in 1944 from the horrors of World War II by carrying on a series of affairs with older women. Some of these women were married, and he did marry at least one of them. Talia Balsam and Beverly D'Angelo costar as Woo-Woo's main love interests.

My blood pressure skyrockets when I think about Dempsey's repugnant staccato line during a scene requiring comically exaggerated formality, wherein he says, "Good eve-en-ning! I am go-ing to town for ay ham-bur-ger sand-witch; would any-one else care to join me for ay ham-bur-ger sand-witch?" When Beverly D'Angelo jumps up from a crowded boardinghouse table and responds in kind: "Ay ham-bur-ger sand-witch?" it's time to stop.

Incoming Freshmen [1979]

DIR. ERIC LEWALD, GLENN MORGAN; W/ASHLEY VAUGHN, LESLIE BLALOCK, RICHARD HARRIMAN, B. M. CULPEPPER

COLLEGE ▣ VIRGINS ▣ LOCKER ROOMS ▣ PERVERT PROFESSOR ▣ DISCO ▣ TUXEDO-T-SHIRT-WEARING ROCK BAND IN GOAT MASKS

Incoming Freshmen looks, sounds, and feels like a shoddy, muddy 16mm attempt at a female-focused college dramedy shot by University of Tennessee students on and around campus. The lulling action is juiced and goosed every so often by insane insert footage crammed into the cracks by the exploitation geniuses at Cannon Films. Cannon's cacophonous studio cobbling makes *Incoming Freshmen* sufficiently watchable for Showtime to run it late at night for more than a decade. Videotape copies never entirely disappeared from VHS rental shops—until, of course, VHS rental shops themselves disappeared.

Incoming Freshman was described by UT classmates and codirectors Eric Lewald and Glenn Morgan as a drive-in spin on a "women's picture." The plot concerns dewy first-year student Jane McAllister (Ashley Vaughn) learning from her seasoned sophomore roommate Viv (Leslie Blalock) about life, love, and dormitory doings, and dealing with campus-man affections. Learn she does, very slowly, surrounded by authentic Southern accents, unexpected country twanging on the soundtrack, and a tooth-brushing dude basting himself with Crest as he envisions boobs busting out of a tube top in his bathroom mirror.

Cannon's nutzoid additions to *Incoming Freshmen* include the flesh fantasies and voyeuristic fetishes of obscenely obese Professor L. P. Bilbo, played by a mass of humanity going by the colorful moniker B. M. Culpepper. This half-ton teacher repeatedly sees his female classroom charges in the altogether: Among them are an ROTC officer with army stripes painted on her naked ass, a student athlete as a topless boxer, and a pair of cheerleaders stripped of everything but their pom-poms. Professor Bilbo also regularly sneaks peeks into the girls' shower room, setting up long segments of soap-soaked bareness. He dons ludicrous drag for locker-room access prior to getting busted and beaten up by an entire squadron of birthday-suited students.

During a final party with a band that wears goat masks and tuxedo T-shirts, Bilbo shows up in a 15XL white disco suit and declares, "I wanna get down! I wanna get funky! I wanna get up, get out, and get at it! I wanna drink some whiskey, smoke some dope, and *boogie*!" The girls cheer. Later, as they coo around him, Bilbo says, "Let me tell ya—you have not lived until you've made it with a *rotundo* history professor!"

Lewald and Morgan hate the changes Cannon made to their movie. Maybe that's understandable, or maybe they just needed to drink some whiskey, smoke some dope, *boogie*—and, perhaps, make it with a *rotundo* history professor.

The Invisible Kid [1988]

DIR. AVERY CROUNSE; W/JAY UNDERWOOD, CHYNNA PHILLIPS, KAREN BLACK, BROTHER THEODORE

INVISIBILITY ▪ BULLIES ▪ LOCKER ROOM ▪ ALL-GIRL ROCK BAND ▪ FLATULENT PRINCIPAL

Although *School Spirit* (1985) arrived first, was funnier and sexier, and managed to not look shot from the bottom of the La Brea Tar Pits, *The Invisible Kid* does deliver the goods—*and* Brother Theodore.

High school nerd Grover Dunn (Jay Underwood) concocts an invisibility potion and immediately sneaks into the girls' locker room just in time for a naked towel-snapping fight. Good on him. Later, he repeatedly one-ups his bully tormentors and catches the principal farting like a Civil War cannon. Cult '70s actress Karen Black plays Mama Dunn. Outrageous beat-era performance artist Brother Theodore (Uncle Ruben Klopek in *The 'Burbs*) adjusts his sinister persona just enough to portray a psychiatrist named *Dr. Theodore*.

Don't mix up *The Invisible Kid* with *The Invisible Maniac* (1990), despite the classroom setting on the latter's video box. *The Invisible Maniac* is a horror comedy directed by Adam Rifkin (*Detroit Rock City*), starring tragic rock 'n' roll porn queen Savannah. The starring blonde in *The Invisible Kid* is Chynna Phillips, sister of Mackenzie and Bijou; she soon became a highly visible pop star in Wilson Phillips. Why didn't *they* get a movie?

Jocks [1986]

DIR. STEVE CARVER; W/SCOTT STRADER, MARISKA HARGITAY, RICHARD ROUNDTREE, PERRY LANG

TENNIS ▪ LAS VEGAS ▪ THE BIG GAME

"Champions aren't born, they're *made*!" declares the *Jocks* poster, depicting an aerobicized sports babe "making it" with the lucky player she's straddling in a locker room. Get it? Once the movie starts, almost immediately, horror legend Christopher Lee storms on-screen as the president of "Los Angeles College." Hammer Films' Dracula plays a mad dean who comically waves a sword while threatening to cut the school's sports program. Equally against cast against type, Richard Roundtree, the "one bad mutha" blaxploitation bruiser of *Shaft*, plays Los Angeles College's tennis coach, Chip Williams. Unless he can deliver a championship trophy, he's out of a gig and his players will all lose their scholarships.

Chip's team is a deftly assembled roster of archetypes. Perfectly cast and serving on the field of play are cocktail-swigging, lady-killing slickster the Kid (Scott Strader); lead priss Jeff (Perry Lang of *Teen Lust*); cowpoke Tex (Adam Mills); Hispanic powder keg Chito (Trinidad Silva); and rampaging madman Ripper (Donald Gibb, lovably doing his Ogre shtick from *Revenge of the Nerds*). Funniest of all is Andy (Stoney Jackson), a flamingly light-in-his-Nikes Prince imitator who is all Jheri curl, eyeliner, and hilarious affectations. He absolutely spanks all contenders on the tennis court.

Jocks unleashes this crew in Las Vegas for "the playoffs." The boys party, they get ladies topless via strip poker, and Mariska Hargitay turns up as a rare bird among sports groupies—the erotically charged Los Angeles College tennis fanatic. Lots of tennis ends the movie, so what's not to *love*?

JOY OF SEX [1984] aka NATIONAL LAMPOON'S THE JOY OF SEX

DIR. MARTHA COOLIDGE; W/MICHELLE MEYRINK, CAMERON DYE, COLLEEN CAMP, CHRISTOPHER LLOYD

VIRGIN ▫ JOCKS ▫ CHEERLEADERS ▫ FOREIGN EXCHANGE STUDENT

Smack between her towering teen comedy triumphs *Valley Girl* (1983) and *Real Genius* (1985), Martha Coolidge did what she could with the impossible task of making *Joy of Sex* into a movie. The resulting T&A trudge, technically based on Dr. Alex Comfort's gazillion-selling 1972 marriage manual of the same name, ranks low even among the high school flicks of its year. A glaring problem: The mid-'80s teen sex comedy titled *Joy of Sex* contains not a *single* scintilla of anything recognizably sexy—let alone joyful.

Michelle Meyrink (*Revenge of the Nerds*) stars as Leslie Hindenberg, a high school senior wrongly convinced she has just weeks to live. She commits herself to losing her virginity ASAP. Cameron Dye (*Fraternity Vacation*) is Alan Holt, Leslie's haplessly horny classmate. His brother Max (Charles Van Eman) shares the Holt family propensity for bothersome boners. The plot chronicles how their love and lust lives intertwine en route to a school gym masquerade ball. People get laid. Leslie lives. Along the way, there's just one really good gag: Leslie attempts to bed local TV news blowhard Ted Stevens (Paul Tulley), but when she inserts a diaphragm for the first time, the device flies out of her virgin-tense fun-flue and sticks to the ceiling.

Familiar character faces flesh out the cast. Christopher Lloyd plays Leslie's fascist wrestling coach dad. Ernie Hudson is the school principal. Thirty-one-year-old Colleen Camp—fresh from playing the main mom in *Valley Girl*—vamps it up as Liz Sampson, the most hormonally aflame underage vixen on campus. Later, she reveals she's an undercover narc, albeit one willing to toss it all aside for a night of drive-in movie making out with Alan. Unfortunately, in a joke that was dated the moment it was written, he panics when Liz says her real last name is "Reagan."

At least as engaging as anything on the screen is the story of how *Joy of Sex* ended up there. Paramount optioned Dr. Comfort's best seller, a parental nightstand perennial that traumatized kid snoops with its graphic and realistic pencil illustrations of hairy hippies in every conceivable variation of coitus. The studio imagined that the title alone packed enormous box-office potential if applied to the right project. Numerous screenwriters took countless cracks at crafting a script before the studio's rights expired in 1984; even world-class wit Charles Grodin gave it a shot and turned in a script about world-class wit Charles Grodin giving a *Joy of Sex* screenplay a shot (Charlie Kaufman would see this idea through in 2002 with *Adaptation*).

In 1982, Paramount teamed with *National Lampoon* for a *Joy of Sex* script by John Hughes, pitched as an anthology of comic episodes in the mold of Woody Allen's similar 1972 marriage manual adaptation, *Everything You Always Wanted to Know About Sex (but Were Afraid to Ask)*. This John Hughes version reached preproduction with Penny Marshall set to direct and John Belushi in talks to star. Some accounts suggest that Belushi freaked out severely over a segment in which he would don diapers as an adult baby, thus touching off his final, fatal drug spiral.

In the end, Paramount rushed to beat the rights-reversion deadline by slapping both the *National Lampoon* brand and the *Joy of Sex* title onto a half-baked teen flick script that resulted in this lackluster lump. Director Martha Coolidge campaigned to remove her name from the movie, but it stayed there, and she moved on to better things—specifically, *Real Genius.*

JOYSTICKS [1983]

aka VIDEO MADNESS

DIR. GREYDON CLARK; W/JOE DON BAKER, LEIF GREEN, SCOTT MCGINNIS, CORINNE BOHRER, KYM MALIN

VIDEO ARCADE ▪ NERD ▪ PARTY ANIMAL ▪ VALLEY GIRL ▪ PUNKS ▪ AEROBICS

Finally, a movie that beeps, buzzes, clangs, vibrates, and, above all, flashes. *Joysticks* is a lot like the video arcades where it takes place; hyper-stimulating, loud, and bursting with characters that define the mid-'80s adolescent experience. The crucial difference is that the *Playboy* Playmate nudity in the movie is not confined to crumpled-up centerfold pages discarded and mildewing behind a Q*bert machine.

The action starts big. Bespectacled, sweater-vested nerd Eugene (Leif Green) is molested and depantsed by overheated aerobics chicks en route to his first day on the job at the local arcade. Once there, he's confronted by the riotous regulars: preppy lady killer Jefferson (Scott McGinnis); Hawaiian-shirted bag o' blubber McDorfus (Jim Greenleaf); Valley girl airhead Patsy (Corinne Bohrer); bosomy party pals Lola (*Playboy*'s Kym Malin) and Alva (Kim Michel); along with a couple of background bikini-stuffers played by Becky LeBeau and Lynda Wiesmeier.

Overall, *Joysticks* traffics in sublimely funny variations on teen sex comedy archetypes, but King Vidiot (Jon Gries) is a totally original offering. His Majesty is a spike-haired, leather-jacketed, ghoul-eyed punk rocker followed everywhere by a battalion of punkette minions who speak only in chirps. They imitate Pac-Man's chewing motion with every step. You have never seen anything like the King and his comely, jabber-jawed court jesters. Because 1983 only lasted twelve months, you will never see their likes again—although, two decades later, Gries scored cult film stardom anew as Uncle Rico in *Napoleon Dynamite.*

In true 1983 fashion, the arcade becomes a cultural war zone after hosting a pickup strip Pac-Man contest. Patsy's hard-ass old man Joe (Joe Don Baker, magnificently overworking) stumbles into the game room just in time to catch Lola and Alva whooping about topless. Incensed, he vows to, as one picket sign later proclaims, "Nuke the Arcade."

A Super Pac-Man contest is called, and now the arcade itself is at stake. But first McDorfus nabs a high score with Joe's repressed sex-fiend wife (Morgan Lofting). Jeff reveals a past trauma that rendered him Pac-Man-phobic for years. Meanwhile, the bargain-bin power pop theme song repeatedly touts, "Totally awesome video gaaaaames...!" Teen sex comedy reaches an apex when Eugene accidentally flings a hot dog from a pair of kitchen tongs into the abundant cleavage of clueless aerobicizer Alva. "Um," stammers Eugene, "my wiener is in your things."

Director Greydon Clark boasts a gloriously off-the-wall exploitation filmography that plugs into *Joysticks* perfectly. In addition to helming the infernal *Satan's Cheerleaders* (1977), Clark also made the slasher parody *Wacko* (1982), and the non-teen-sexy genre busters *Black Shampoo* (1976), *Angel's Brigade* (1979), *Without Warning* (1980), *Final Justice* (1985), *Skinheads* (1989), and *The Forbidden Dance* (1990). In fact, Clark conceived *Joysticks* while at a test screening for *Wacko.* "I arrived at the theater in Texas," he says, "and in the lobby I noticed lines of teenage boys waiting to put their quarters into video game machines. My first thought was that I should make a movie about videogames and teenagers."

Joysticks opened in around six hundred theaters and topped the box office chart upon its March 4, 1983, release. The movie is a glorious pixel-popping plunge into a sugar-rushing universe where the good guys always win, giddy girls always happily ditch their swimsuit uppers, and nobody ever runs out of quarters. Game over.

JUST ONE OF THE GIRLS [1993] aka ANYTHING FOR LOVE; HE'S MY GIRL 2

DIR. MICHAEL KEUSCH; W/COREY HAIM, NICOLE EGGERT, CAMERON BANCROFT, ALANIS MORISSETTE

GENDER-BENDING ▣ CHEERLEADERS ▣ MUSICALS

Just One of the Girls is absolutely *not* to be confused with *Just One of the Guys* (1985), though the bamboozlers pushing this junk were hoping you would. *Just One of the Girls*, instead, is actually a rerelease of *Anything for Love*, a withered maple leaf of a 1985 Canadian TV movie that was retitled on VHS to promote confusion with the Joyce Hyser cross-dressing favorite. Know your teenage transvestite comedies, people!

Corey Haim stars in *Girls* as Chris, a musically inclined high-school dweeb who trembles in dread of big-bully-on-campus Kurt (Cameron Bancroft). To circumvent Kurt's daily torment, Chris decides to experience the remainder of his secondary education as a female named "Christie." He dresses in his sister's clothes, sashays to class, and even makes the pom-pom squad. Everything's going rah-rah until Kurt gets the hots for "Christie" and Chris falls for Kurt's cheerleader sister Marie (Nicole Eggert).

A round robin of gender and orientation confusion ensues. Chris's parents think he's gay and dating Kurt. The girls' gym teacher discovers the dangling-dong truth about "Christie," and Chris talks his way out of it by claiming to be transsexual. Marie flips when "Christie" comes out as "lesbian" by trying to kiss her. Meanwhile, a multitude of characters in this film are either just plain terrible at telling the difference between a girl and Corey Haim in a skirt, or they're refreshingly accepting of his choices.

As ahead of its time as all this might seem, *Just One of the Girls* is squeakily chaste and almost Disney-esque, except for one lusty interlude. After conning his way out of gym class, Chris-as-Christie gets locker room mop-jockey duties. He lucks into servicing the girls' showers just as they're awash with his fully nude female classmates. In the most credible moment of Corey Haim's acting career, he passes out on the spot.

Everything ends with a splashy song-and-dance performance that features unbilled adolescent Canuck songbird Alanis Morissette, a solid decade before she sort-of discovered irony. Chris reveals the truth about his gender mid–cheer routine, and everybody's cool with all that's gone down, including Kurt, who perhaps could still enjoy an awakening in a far more interesting unmade sequel.

JUST ONE OF THE GUYS [1985]

DIR. LISA GOTTLIEB; W/JOYCE HYSER, CLAYTON ROHNER, BILLY ZABKA, BILLY JACOBY

GENDER-BENDING ▣ SCHOOL NEWSPAPER ▣ BULLY ▣ PROM

When it comes to '80s teen sex comedies, *Just One of the Guys* is just one of the very best! I sincerely hope that sentence ends up on a retro video box, a trailer for a download reissue campaign, or tattooed on the director's bicep. *Just One of the Guys* has knocked back my hair since its April 1985 release. The ad in the *New York Post* movie section showed star Joyce Hyser standing topless in a guy's locker room, two football helmets strategically placed to simultaneously disguise and emphasize her unclothed torso.

"Terri Griffith is about to go where no woman has gone before," announced the tagline.

"Mike McPadden is about to go immediately to see this movie!" I retorted.

As so it comes to pass that teen reporter Terri Griffiths (Hyser) has had enough of the sexism and gender bias at her high school newspaper. When her parents leave town for two weeks, she disguises herself as a dude ("Terry") and enrolls at a school across town to get the scoop on life as a male. Terri's best friend Denise (deadpan Toni Hudson) and jocular kid brother Buddy (Billy Jacobi, screamingly funny in what could have been a nails-on-a-chalkboard role) are aware of her ruse. However, her domineering college boyfriend Kevin (Leigh McCloskey) is not.

When Terri arrives at school decked out in righteous bro drag, smitten student Sandy (Sherilyn Fenn) declares, "Look! What a fox. Dresses like Elvis Costello, looks like the Karate Kid! I'm going to get him." Things later get complicated between Sandy and Terri. Terri-as-Terry more quickly runs afoul of a meathead cafeteria terror squad fronted by Greg Tolan ('80s bully supreme Billy Zabka). She befriends savvy, witty misfit Rick Morehouse (Clayton Rohner).

Tensions arise with Greg, who wants to beat up everybody. Confusion mounts between Terri and Rick, understandable given their blazing adolescent biology. The more confident their friendship makes Rick, the deeper Terri finds herself falling in love. Her predicament worsens he continues to believe her to be—just one of the guys.

Everything blows up at the prom. After Greg tangles with Rick, Terri takes her new best buddy aside, pops open her tuxedo shirt and—*blammo! blammo!*—nakedly reveals she's very much a "Teresa," not a "Terrence." Hurt feelings happen, but Terri wins a scholarship with an article on her gender-swap experience. Rick gets over being duped, and the stage is set for a happy ending.

As Joyce Hyser told *Uproxx* in 2015: "We did not shoot that whole end scene until the very last couple of days. By that time I was completely comfortable in the skin of Terry. We talked about me having a bra on as opposed to nothing, but that seemed less realistic. So [director Lisa Gottlieb] said to me, 'I'll tell you what, let's shoot it both ways and then you will get to decide.'

"I was very comfortable with that and she promised me, pinky swear on the set, that she would never put anything in that I was not comfortable with and I totally trusted her. And that's exactly what we did.

"I can't stand the fact that [in the Internet age] if you go to any porn site or booby site, I'm all over the place. It makes me sad, really, because it's actually a very innocent and desperate moment that drives that scene and drives that reveal."

Just One of the Guys continually makes offbeat and interesting choices. One of the most original is that shy, cynical Rick worships James Brown. He explodes into ecstatic dance moves whenever he hears a song by the Hardest Working Man in Show Business. This surprise detail rings very true to the unexpected discoveries one makes in an actual new friendship. Another real moment happens when "Terry" gets back an English paper marked with nearly the same criticisms she faced as "Terri," forcing her to question her existing assumptions. A lot happens in ten days—and who didn't experience high school that way?

The casting is equaled only by *Fast Times at Ridgemont High* and *Risky Business*, yet somehow Joyce Hyser didn't leap from *Guys* to superstardom. She guested on some TV series—including *L.A. Law*, where she was decapitated and had her head frozen—but she didn't make another movie for five years. Similar big-time fortunes also should have awaited Rohner, Hudson, and Jacoby, all of whom turn in *Ridgemont High*–caliber star-making performances. Zabka did find a place in the pantheon of movie a-holes. Oddly, among the actors in this popular, frequently seen film, only semi-background character Sherilyn Fenn went on to fame. Director Lisa Gottlieb also went on to helm single episodes of *Freddy's Nightmares*, *Dream On*, and *Boy Meets World*, as well as a couple of mid-'90s indie-flick obscurities.

I CAN'T BELIEVE IT! THE WHOLE FAMILY HAVE FORGOTTEN MY BIRTHDAY!
NEVER MIND MAYBE YOU'LL SEE JAKE LATER
SHE MIGHT LIKE JAKE, BUT SHE'S CRAZY ABOUT ME!
OK YOU GUYS GO GET THE CAMERA...YOU'RE NOT GOING TO BELIEVE THIS!
JAKE ALL TO MYSELF... AND A HAPPY BIRTHDAY IT'S TOO MUCH TO HOPE FOR
16 Candles
AND YOU'RE INVITED TO THE PARTY
A JOHN HUGHES FILM • A CHANNEL PRODUCTIONS PRESENTATION
SIXTEEN CANDLES Starring MOLLY RINGWALD PAUL DOOLEY JUSTIN HENRY ANTHONY MICHAEL HALL
Music by IRA NEWBORN Director of Photography BOBBY BYRNE Executive Producer NED TANEN Produced by HILTON GREEN
Written and Directed by JOHN HUGHES A Universal Picture

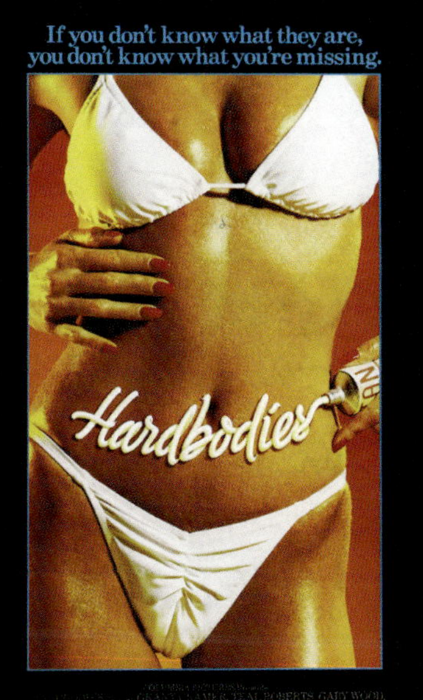

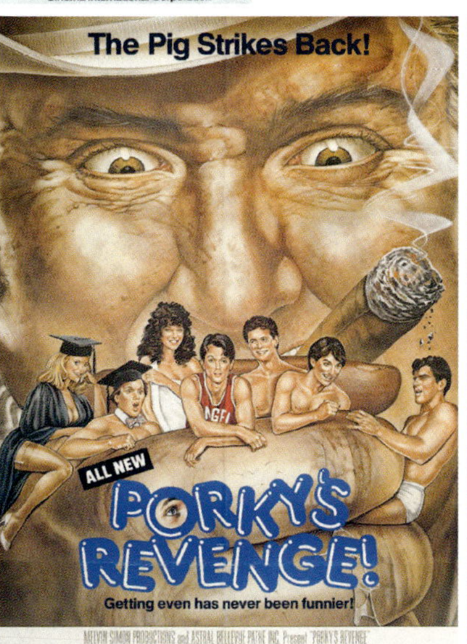

Clockwise from top left: American Graffiti *(1973) en español; a young poster for* Sixteen Candles *(1984);* Midnight Madness *(1980), the scavenger hunt where we find Eddie Deezen and win;* Porky's Revenge *(1985);* Hardbodies *(1984) declares, "If you see one movie this year—see this one, too!"*

Clockwise from top left: King Frat *(1979), J. J. "Gross-Out" Gumbroski (John DiSanti) shows who's "number one"; director Chuck Vincent soaks the wet-T-shirt craze in* Hot T-Shirts *(1980);* The First Turn-On *(1983), a great quad poster for an early Troma product;* Getting Wasted *(1980), a military school bomb;* Puberty Blues *(1981), a sweet, sad, soulful surfer girl saga from Down Under.*

Clockwise from top left: *In any tongue,* The Party Animal *(1984) is "original" and "incredible"; fork over your quarters to King Vidiot, there's no beating* Joysticks *(1983);* Malibu Hot Summer *(1981) showcases young Kevin Costner and seaside roller disco;* Cheering Section *(1977) merits a shake;* Private Lessons *(1981) packed theaters with a lot of help from this intriguing poster.*

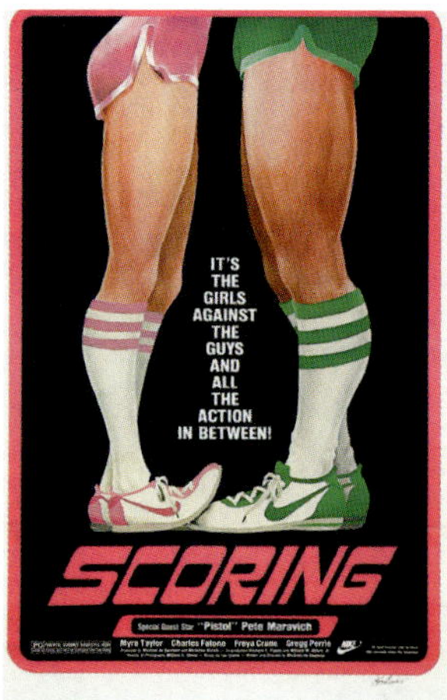

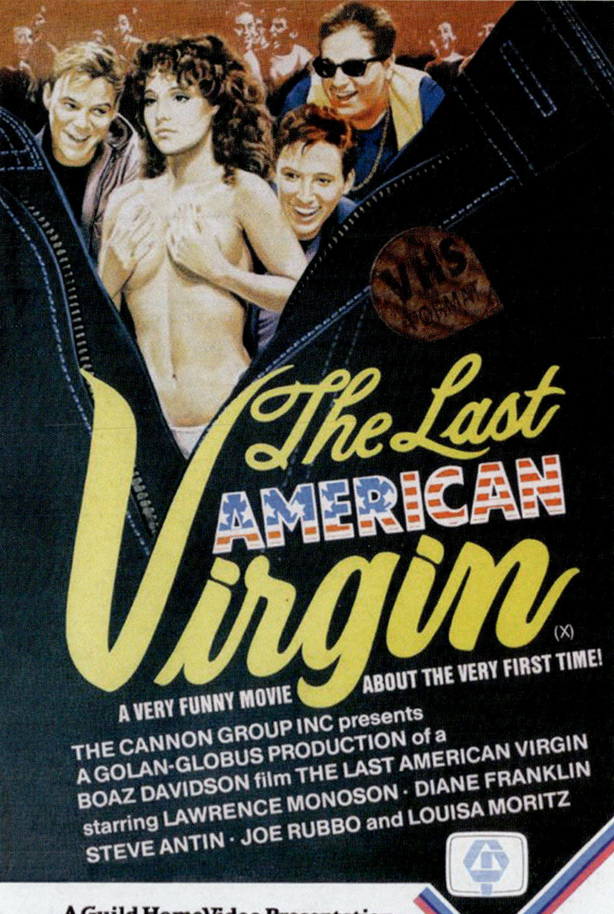

Clockwise from top: *Detail from the genre-defining poster for* Party Camp *(1987)*; The Last American Virgin *(1982) zipper-popping foreign VHS box cover proved inspirational*; Scoring *(1979) was officially sponsored by Nike, then still a growing regional shoe company*; Almost Summer *(1978) has still never received a physical release—Tweet your congressperson!*

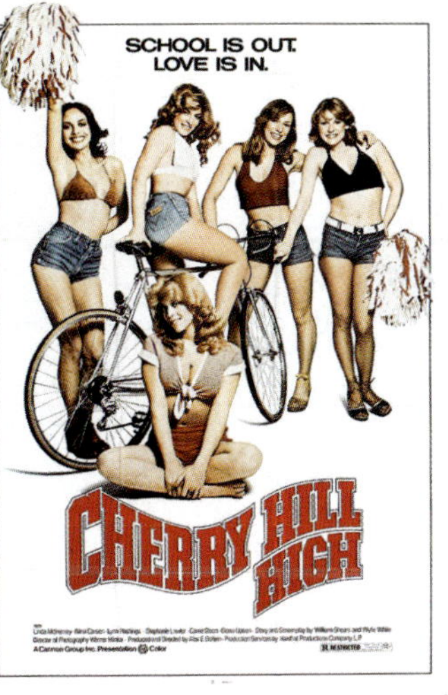

Clockwise from top left: Hamburger: The Motion Picture *(1986); John Cusack does grunt work at Pig Burger for Chuck "Porky" Mitchell in* Better Off Dead *(1985); Tim Matheson (aka Otter), Stephen Furst (aka Flounder), and Dan Monahan (aka Pee Wee) soak the competition in* Up the Creek *(1985); UK quad poster for* Losin' It *(1983);* Cherry Hill High *(1977) delivers sex on two wheels; Glynnis O'Connor has a ball in* California Dreaming *(1979).*

Clockwise from top left: Hardbodies 2 *(1986) in phonetic translation as* Heart Buddies; Summer Camp *(1979), a superb poster for a movie that plays like poison ivy in your underpants;* Fraternity Vacation *(1985) recycles a few* Teen Movie Hell *elements, including the tagline from* Private Lessons; National Lampoon *should have sat out its* Class Reunion *(1982).*

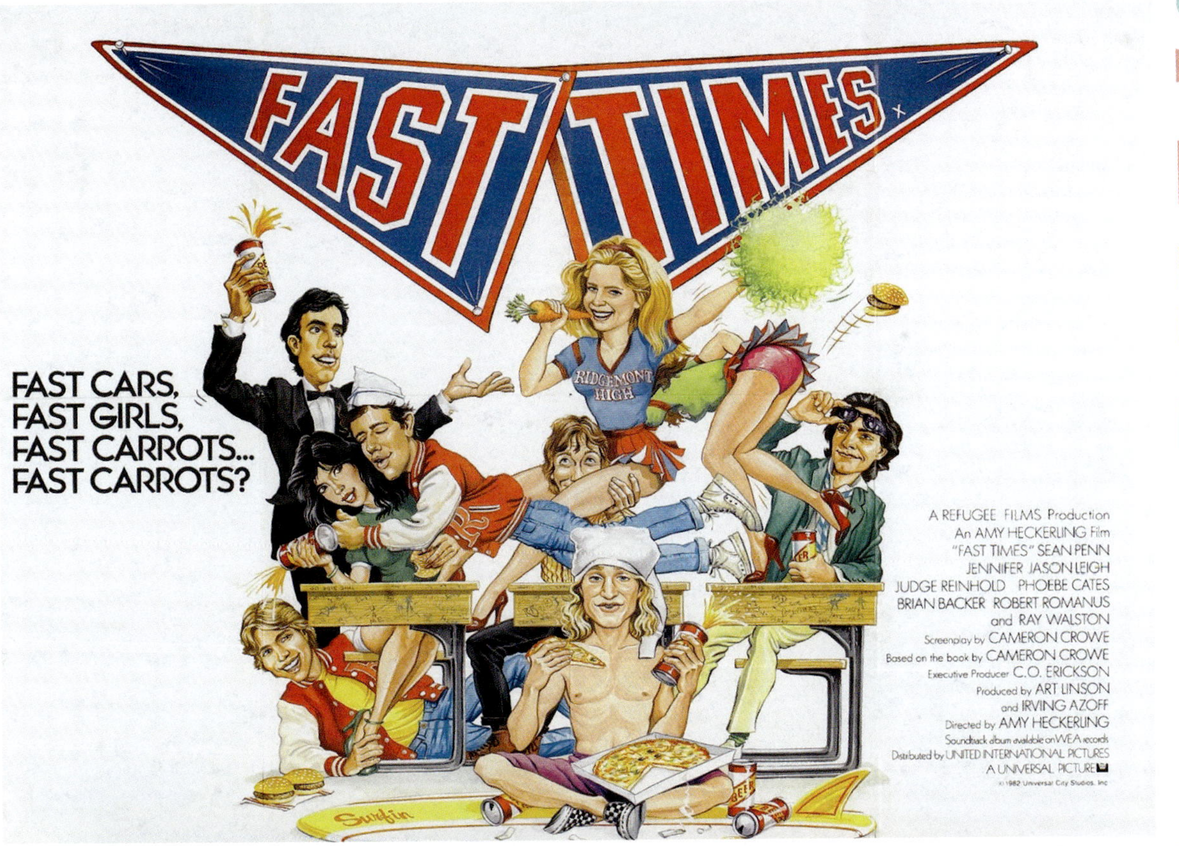

FAST TIMES
FAST CARS,
FAST GIRLS,
FAST CARROTS...
FAST CARROTS?
RIDGEMONT HIGH
A REFUGEE FILMS Production
An AMY HECKERLING Film
"FAST TIMES" SEAN PENN
JENNIFER JASON LEIGH
JUDGE REINHOLD PHOEBE CATES
BRIAN BACKER ROBERT ROMANUS
and RAY WALSTON
Screenplay by CAMERON CROWE
Based on the book by CAMERON CROWE
Executive Producer C.O. ERICKSON
Produced by ART LINSON
and IRVING AZOFF
Directed by AMY HECKERLING
Soundtrack album available on WEA records
Distributed by UNITED INTERNATIONAL PICTURES
A UNIVERSAL PICTURE
© 1982 Universal City Studios, Inc

FREE WHEELING FUN AND ACTION AS
SUPERVAN CREATES SHEER VANDEMONIUM!
SUPERVAN
ONE MEAN MACHINE
STARRING
MARK SCHNEIDER ● KATIE SAYLOR ● MORGAN WOODWARD
Produced by SAL CAPRA ● Directed by LAMAR CARD
SUPER VAN by George Barris
'King of the Kustomisers'
SAV

Spend a weekend with no reservations!
PRIVATE RESORT
They're looking for hot times. And they came to the right place...
Private Resort
TRI-STAR PICTURES Presents A UNITY PICTURES PRESENTATION "PRIVATE RESORT" AN R. BEN EFRAIM PRODUCTION
JOHNNY DEPP EMILY LONGSTRETH TONY AZITO Also Starring DODY GOODMAN LESLIE EASTERBROOK
and HECTOR ELIZONDO as THE MAESTRO Story by KEN SEGALL & ALAN WENKUS and GORDON MITCHELL
Produced by R. BEN EFRAIM and DON ENRIGHT Directed by GEORGE BOWERS
R

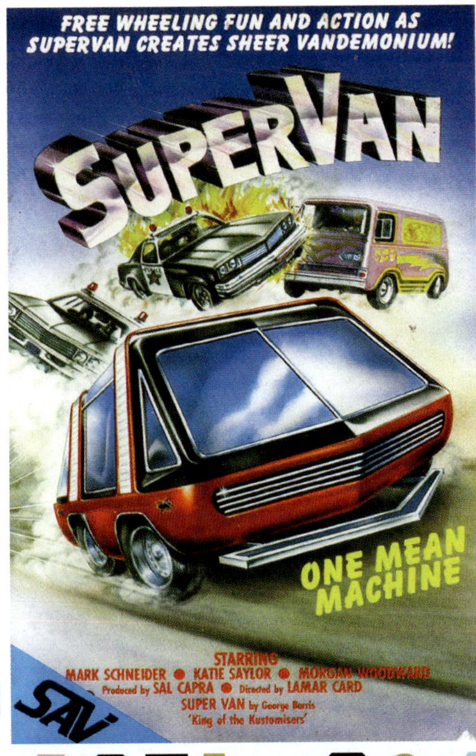

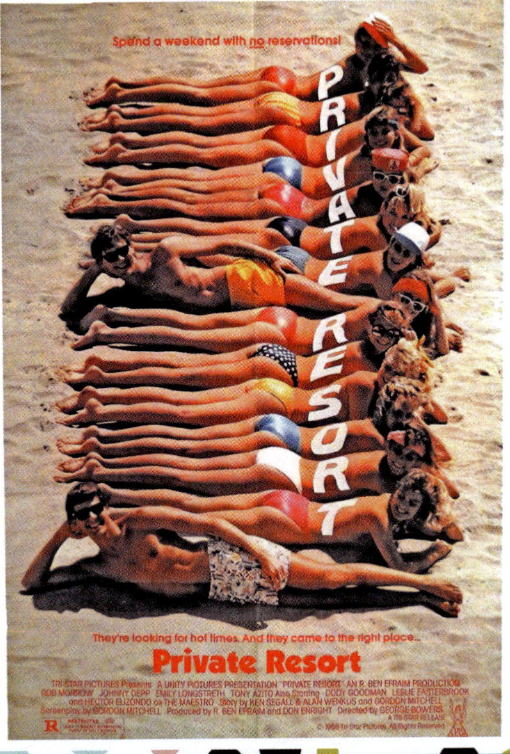

Clockwise from top: Fast Times at Ridgemont High *(1982) survived its rare cartoon poster;* Private Resort *(1985) remains the only costarring vehicle for Johnny Depp and Andrew "Dice" Clay;* Supervan *(1977) costars booze-bag poet Charles Bukowski as "Wet-T-Shirt Contest Water Boy."*

Clockwise from top: *Scott Baio mind-pops Heather Thomas's sweater buttons while Willie Aames ogles in* Zapped! *(1982); the legendary purple pastels of the 1983* Valley Girl *soundtrack; even renowned stoic Lou Reed almost cracks a smile during the infectious uproar of* Get Crazy *(1983).*

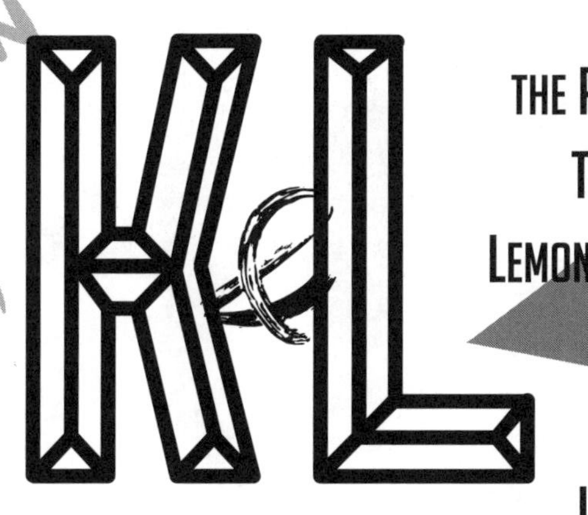

KING FRAT ▭ THE KINKY COACHES AND THE POM-POM PUSSYCATS ▭ LAS VEGAS WEEKEND THE LAST AMERICAN VIRGIN ▭ LAUDERDALE LEMON POPSICLE ▭ LET'S DO IT! ▭ LICENSE TO DRIVE LITTLE DARLINGS ▭ LOOSE SCREWS THE LORDS OF FLATBUSH ▭ LOSIN' IT LOVELINES ▭ LOVERBOY ▭ LUNCH WAGON

KING FRAT [1979]

aka CAMPUS KING; DELTA HOUSE

DIR. KEN WIEDERHORN; W/JOHN DISANTI, CHARLES PITT, ROY SEKOFF, RAY MANN

FRATERNITY ▭ PRANKS ▭ MOONING ▭ BEER ▭ WEED ▭ THE BIG FART CONTEST ▭ LOVE DOLL

When *National Lampoon's Animal House* opened in July 1978, I was just about to turn ten and had been long obsessed with truly tasteless jokes, *Mad* magazine, *Saturday Night Live*, and the ever-popular Three Stooges. *Animal House* promised to combine the best of all those anarchic comedy totems with, yes, *naked ladies*. For the rest of the summer, I could fixate on nothing else and, because I was (sensibly) forbidden to see it, my imagination ran berserk over what extreme insanity *Animal House* must have contained.

The *Animal House* poster alone conveyed an orgy of utter lawlessness, violent scatology, and non-stop obscenity in service to the ultimate party to ever scorch celluloid. No movie—not even *Animal House*—could ever live up to that Roman candle of anticipation and excess; no movie, that is, except *King Frat*.

"Welcome to Yellowstream University." That sign opens *King Frat*, backed by an off-tempo title song by Penny Alemian that sounds like chewed, spit-out, and stepped-on bubblegum pop. It's magnificent. The boys of Pi Delta Kappa patrol their college town in a hearse with a HEY 4Q2 license plate. They crack beers, flip birds, toss trash, belch, fart, and drop their drawers and hang wide, gaping moons out of every window. Among their targets is the university president (Lee Willis), who jogs past the Kappas, catches sight of their crappas, and promptly keels over, having suffered a fatal heart attack.

Soon enough, Belushi look-alike J. J. "Gross-Out" Gumbroski (the *stupendous* John DiSanti) and frat soul-brother Splash (Ray Mann) sneak into the church staging the president's funeral and flood the air vents with marijuana fumes. The gathered mourners laugh hysterically during the eulogy. Eventually, the president's casket rolls

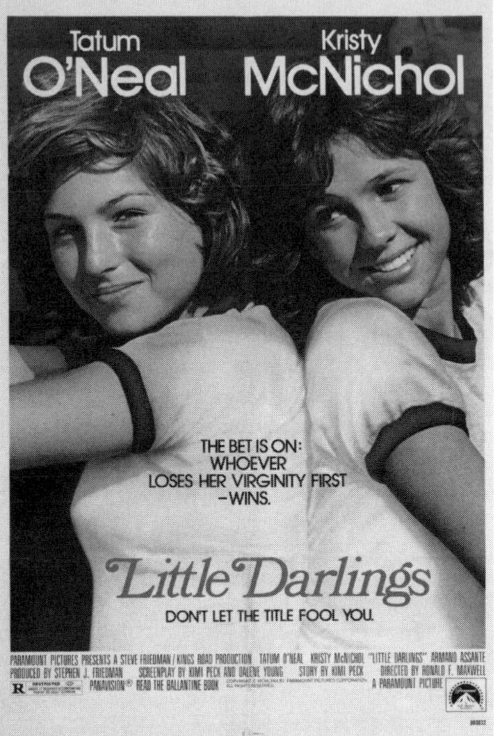

Clockwise from top left: King Frat *(1979), royally outrageous; the fourteen-year-olds of* Little Darlings *(1980)*; The Kinky Coaches and the Pom-Pom Pussycats *(1981), drags Norman Fell into this book*; Loose Screws *(1985), aka* Screwballs 2, *offers teen movie hell on a budget.*

into the back of the Pi Kappa hearse, and his corpse remains a prop for the rest of the movie. This is simply how *King Frat* opens; then it gets *really* nuts.

The showcase centerpiece of *King Frat* is a five-hundred-dollar fart contest conducted at a local theater; the marquee actually reads: FART CONTEST TONITE. Gross-Out thinks he can take the crap-fume crown. Chief Latrine (Dan Chandler), Pi Kap's Native American member (you can imagine the sensitivity with which this stereotype is assembled), brews "Hairy Buffalo Juice." One mug of this stuff enables Gross-Out to fart with such rocket thrust that he crashes headfirst through a wall. The contest itself is a full twenty-minute interlude that only gets more uproarious as it progresses, due to the stunning reality that this eternity of obscenity is actually part of a motion picture theoretically made for commercial consumption.

Equally unbelievable are the power-puking, the intense focus on defecation, Gross-Out's romantic passion for his blow-up doll, a genuinely vomit-inducing scene of meatball preparation, and a visit to Wong's Chinese restaurant. Later on, Pi Kappa lothario Tommy (Roy Sekoff) and a comely coed seek help surgically uncoupling their private parts after banging in the back of a speeding ambulance. Upon their arrival at the emergency room, the attending physician tips his hat to the masters: "It doesn't seem possible! Maybe with animals or in *Mad* magazine."

In the end, the Yellowstream University sign is changed to Kissawong University, in honor of Chief Latrine's tribe. A toddler wearing a "Kissawong Class of 1999" shirt thunder-burps into the camera, capping off a glorious and transformative bout of brain battery, the most impossibly off-the-rails concept of chaotic vice overindulgence that could ever happen in a movie. Whatever this picture owes to *Animal House* for inspiration is repaid in full, because *King Frat* delivers the goods one hundred-point-zero percent.

The Kinky Coaches and the Pom-Pom Pussycats

[1981] aka Heartbreak High; Crunch

DIR. MARK WARREN; W/JOHN VERNON, ROBERT FORSTER, NORMAN FELL, CHRISTINE CATTELL

STRIP POKER · PRANKS · THE BIG GAME

In the most technical sense, *The Kinky Coaches and the Pom-Pom Pussycats* abides by truth-in-advertising laws, but only partially. Coach Alan Arnoldi (Robert Forster) is a nice enough fella who oversees the Johnson High Eagles football program. At one point, he indulges in gridiron-themed foreplay with his wife; that almost qualifies as "kinky" in some states.

The "pom-pom pussycats," then, are the cheerleaders who root for both the Eagles and their crosstown rivals, the City High Moose. The latter play under the raging direction of Coach "Bulldog" Malone (John Vernon, spinning in an anti-intellectual direction from his Dean Wormer in *Animal House*). Wandering to and fro between camps is gonzo sports reporter Jack McGuire, played by delightfully crusty Norman Fell, a crack-up best known as Mr. Roper from the '70s sitcom *Three's Company*.

Sadly, the movie soon proves to be another limp Canadian tax-shelter mish-mosh of genre tropes. The only cliché that clicks is long-haired, buffalo-built linebacker Pigger Peterson (Terry Swiednicki). Whether pummeling opposing players on the field or smashing piled-high trays across the cafeteria, Pigger snorts nonstop like asthmatic boar. Otherwise, even the ball-washing machine could write zingers like, as a cheerleader laughs during a strip-poker game when the dudes drop trou: "Now we'll see who has the joker!"

In 2007, Image Entertainment officially released this movie on DVD as *Heartbreak High*. Later, the Impact cable network ran the film in stunning high definition under the title *Crunch*. Somebody obviously cares about this movie. Odds are this mystery patron has never actually attempted to watch it all the way through, however, as almost the entire final half hour is simply unwatchable footage of a fake football game.

LAS VEGAS WEEKEND [1986]

DIR. DALE TREVILLION; W/BARRY HICKEY, JACE DAMON, VICKIE BENSON, RAY DENNIS STECKLER

NERD ▪ LAS VEGAS ▪ WANG COMPUTER

The bespectacled, bucktoothed, college math whiz lead character of *Las Vegas Vacation* is named Percy Doolittle (Barry Hickey). His story goes like this: Nerd hits the Sin City strip; nerd wins; nerd makes friends; nerd gets girl; nerd loses everything; and nerd wins it all back. The film's PG rating remains intact, even though Percy uses a "Wang" computer to beat the odds at blackjack, because, hey, Wang was an actual computer brand in anything-goes 1986.

One important note: Percy's college professor is played by B-movie auteur Ray Dennis Steckler. It's good to see Steckler in action, but *Las Vegas Weekend* represents a real indignity for the man that brought us *The Incredibly Strange Creatures Who Stopped Living and Became Mixed Up Zombies* (1964), let alone *Rat Pfink a Boo Boo* (1966).

THE LAST AMERICAN VIRGIN [1982]

DIR. BOAZ DAVIDSON; W/ LAWRENCE MONOSON, DIANE FRANKLIN, JOE RUBBO

VIRGINS ▪ ABORTION ▪ COMING OF AGE

For everything to praise about *The Last American Virgin*—and there is much—it must be applauded for its crucial role in establishing an American front for Cannon Films, an Israeli schlock studio supreme lorded over by cousins Menahem Golan and Yoram Globus. Golan and Globus amassed a fortune on the back (and topless fronts) of 1978 teen sex smash *Lemon Popsicle* and its multiple sequels, each of which packed theaters and popped zippers in dubbed language versions just about everywhere in the world—except, curiously, the United States.

So Golan-Globus dreamed up a plan to remake *Lemon Popsicle* for American audiences, ditching the original's ersatz '50s Israel setting for contemporary new wave '80s L.A. Then they amped up the gut-punch twist ending until it ranked with Duane Jones waving at the shooting party in *Night of the Living Dead* (1968) and Edward Woodward's flame-out in *The Wicker Man* (1973).

The chaste horndog of the film's title is teenage pizza delivery driver Gary (Lawrence Monoson). His best pals are Rick (Steve Antin), a slick-talking lady-layer, and David (Joe Rubbo), a big fat party animal. Joe Rubbo deserves a proper salute; the fat guy who plays the fat-guy character in *The Last American Virgin* boasts the single greatest fat-guy name in the history of fat guys.

The Last American Virgin's heroic trio pursues sex through one mayhemic mishap after another. Each set piece delivers big, sonic-boom belly laughs. High points include their passing off Sweet'N Low as cocaine (which everyone snorts and then, naturally, acts like it got them zooted). Equally charming, our heroes line up for round-robin intercourse with a maniacal Mexican nymphomaniac only to have the session interrupted by the return of her furious sailor husband.

Running parallel to the antics, a love triangle arises between Gary, Rick, and gorgeous popular girl Karen (Diane Franklin). This development pays off with out-of-place nudity, shocking gore, and teen cinema's single most ferociously dispatched metaphorical kick in the gonads.

After callous cad Rick impregnates and abandons Karen, Gary swoops in to be of service to her. He spends his pizza salary on getting her an abortion, and then puts her up to recover in his grandmother's unoccupied house. The actual abortion scene is the first signal that *Virgin* is set to veer off in unanticipated directions. The procedure does not go smoothly for Karen, and she bleeds visibly on-screen while crying in wholly credible distress. As she recovers, Karen talks about how grateful she is for Gary and how close she feels to him. Naturally, Gary thinks they're in love.

Virgin cruelly implies that a happy ending awaits. Gary blows the rest of his pizza savings on a ring, proudly telling the pawnshop clerk, "It's for my girlfriend!" He then stops by a holiday party, eager and aglow to share his good fortune. Once inside, he sees Karen in the kitchen—making out with Rick. The smitten couple turn and stare Gary straight in the eye.

Gary is crushed and so are we. He shuffles back to his pizza wagon and starts the engine. "Just Once" by James Ingram swells on the soundtrack, crooning about how "I did my best, but I guess my best wasn't good enough." The camera settles on Gary's face at the steering wheel as he drives away. Slowly, horribly, tears trickle forth. His lip quivers. He cries more. With the shock impact of a thousand horror movies, the end credits begin to roll up alongside the close-up of this weeping, broken teenager.

With that, *The Last American Virgin* defied expectations and became an instant marker of what was possible in even the raunchiest end of the teen sex comedy genre. In hindsight, the movie also slipped in another left-field element that nobody noticed at the time: it's pretty amazingly gay.

Watching *The Last American Virgin* three-plus decades later is to witness it positively percolating with homoeroticism. The film abounds with knowing looks, uneasy glances, cocked eyebrows, lingering gazes, and a camera that heavily objectifies male bodies. The pulsating pinnacle of its strapping-lad fixation is a locker room boner-measuring contest starring an entire male high school class in their tube-tightened tighty-whities. Rear vision being 20/20, it comes as no great shock to learn that lead actors Monoson and Antin, along with prominent costar Brian Peck (the lucky sucker who wins the hard-on contest) eventually leaped out of their closets loud and proud as gay adults. Only Joe Rubbo would have actually enjoyed making out with Diane Franklin—of course, in the movie he has a fat chance of doing that.

Virgin is the crucial middle piece of the teen sex summer comedy onslaught of summer 1982. The picture debuted in July, smack between *Porky's* in March and *Fast Times at Ridgemont High*, which rolled out nationally through August and September. *Virgin* ran in theaters deep into the cold-weather months, and then exploded into true pop culture immortality via VHS and the newcomer pay cable channels.

Golan-Globus also dropped considerable coin on *Virgin*'s soundtrack, and then effectively marketed the movie as a vehicle to hear on-screen music by Journey, REO Speedwagon, and the Commodores. The soundtrack LP is quite the new wave artifact, showcasing hits by Devo, the Police, and the Waitresses. The song "Are You Ready for the Sex Girls?" by Gleaming Spires appeared again two summers later in *Revenge of the Nerds*, never missing a beat. One song that truly stands out in the movie, "I Will Follow," helped lesser-known Irish newcomers U2 break the big time in the United States.

In 2007, horror film kingpin Eli Roth (*Cabin Fever, Hostel*) hosted a *Last American Virgin* screening and cast reunion at the New Beverly theater in Hollywood. Although Lawrence Monoson and Diane Franklin declined, all the other principals appeared and had a great night. Even—make that especially—Joe Rubbo.

LAUDERDALE [1989]
aka SPRING FEVER USA

DIR. BILL MILLING; W/RENEE SHUGART, DARREL GUILBEAU, JEFF GREENMAN, JANINE LINDEMULDER

SPRING BREAK ▫ AEROBICS ▫ ONE-ARMED DWARF ▫ LINGERIE SHOP ▫ BELLY-FLOPS ▫ THE BIG WET-T-SHIRT CONTEST

A pair of hormonally pent-up Florida college pals—skinny oaf Larry (Darrel Guilbeau) and dirigible-proportioned force-of-destruction Animal (Jeff Greenman of *Screwball Hotel*)—open *Lauderdale* by bemoaning their lack of romantic action. The frustrated friends commiserate amidst an expanse of sun-soaked beach, littered end to end with bikini bombshells. "They're everywhere!" Animal babbles. "Mindless hordes of bitchin' bimbos from beyond infinity bent on possessing my mind, with their hot little hands emitting cosmic rays into my mind!" He shovels huge great gobs of sand into his mouth.

Cut to these miserable young men on campus. Larry falls dumbstruck for a glowing blonde passerby named Heather, played by pre-plastic-surgery future porn sensation Janine Lindemulder. Through extreme teen sex comedy happenstance, Larry and Animal suddenly rescue Heather from klutzy, Hawaiian-shirted kidnappers. In time, we learn the goons are brothers Dick Dork (Robert Moss) and Duke Dork (Mark Levine), the underlings of pimpish business tycoon Mr. Geeko (Randy Stevens).

Grateful Heather invites the one of her two saviors who can fit inside a white Rolls-Royce Excalibur and a four-star hotel bubble bath to join her in both locations. After a slapstick liquor store misadventure involving a stocking-masked robber played by porn star Ron Jeremy, the couple settle down and are set to consummate their sex-bomb-and-hero relationship. Then the Dorks barge in and everything goes black.

From there, *Lauderdale*'s plot goes hyperactive. Heather is being held by Mr. Geeko in Fort Lauderdale, Larry learns from Jane (Michelle Kemp), another blow-dried blonde. Jane says she expects to inherit $1 million as soon as she turns eighteen the following week. First, though, Larry and Jane secure an RV and aim it toward Florida, just in time for spring break. They will also, of course, fall in love.

Packing plenty into each merry moment, *Lauderdale* entertainingly builds to an orgiastic final act in the Sunshine State among oceans of bare breasts and beer-injured brains. Along the way, the film's characters check off nearly every imaginable activity for the kind of movie they inhabit: aerobics; oil wrestling; a wet-T-shirt contest; a belly-flop contest; a bikini car wash; a lingerie shop modeling montage; mass flashing; skinny-dipping; even concerts by keytar-equipped hair-metal goofs Fury and surf rockers the Rebel Pebbles. Then Ron Jeremy returns as a biker. At long last, Animal hooks up with Heather.

Lauderdale is laudable, and marred only by the repellent fashions, fake tans, and ludicrously teased-up coifs of the cast, but such were the late 1980s. The movie is still a fine highlight in writer-director Bill Milling's remarkable cult movie career. He handled the grand gross-out special effects on the 1976 worms-in-revolt horror *Squirm*, and helmed a number of well-regarded X-rated productions, including the 1975 coitus-and-karate hybrid *The Vixens of Kung Fu (A Tale of Yin Yang)*.

Lemon Popsicle [1978]

aka Eskimo Limon

DIR. BOAZ DAVIDSON; W/YFTACH KATZUR, ANAT ATZMON, JONATHAN SAGALL, ZACHI NOY

VIRGIN · NERD · ISRAEL · PEEPING · DREAM GIRL · ABORTION · 1950S

If you've seen *The Last American Virgin* (1982), you've almost seen *Lemon Popsicle*. A few differences separate the two films; namely that *Lemon Popsicle* is in Hebrew, the movie takes place in 1958 Tel Aviv, and the soundtrack is end-to-end American oldies instead of new wave hits. Otherwise, *Virgin* is a pretty direct remake from the same director (Boaz Davidson) and same producers (Menahem Golan and Yoram Globus).

Popsicle chronicles a summer during the puberty of three high school pals: sensitive romantic Benzi (Yftach Katzur), studly Momo (Jonathan Sagall), and thunder-blubbered punch line Yudale (Zachi Noy). Together, they ogle female flesh and run wild trying to get laid, until dream girl Nili (Anat Atzmon) comes between smitten Benzi and caddish Momo. Along the way, the trio survive a voluptuous hooker gangbang that goes frantically awry, a boner-measuring contest, an out-of-nowhere downturn into heaviness by way of abortion, and a stupefying kick-in-the-kibbutz heartbreak ending. So, yes, *Lemon Popsicle* is the first draft of *The Last American Virgin*.

The Last American Virgin was the big hit that largely established Cannon Films in America, but *Lemon Popsicle* was a thermonuclear box-office blockbuster everywhere else, generating seven international smash sequels over ten years plus the 2001 *American Pie*-style reboot *Lemon Popsicle 9: The Party Goes On*. Fully *one-quarter* of the entire population of Israel bought a ticket to see *Lemon Popsicle*. The second and third most popular global markets for the movie were Germany and Japan. Didn't those countries team up, just a few decades prior, driven largely by bombastic dislike of the ancestors of the *Lemon Popsicle* team? Clearly, teenage T&A comedies have the power to heal all hatreds.

Let's Do It! [1982]

DIR. BERT I. GORDON; W/GREG BRADFORD, BRITT HEIFER, VICTORIA WELLS, BOBBI VAN EMAN

COLLEGE ▫ ERECTILE DYSFUNCTION ▫ AEROBICS

Not for nothing did schlock-movie maven Bert I. Gordon earn the moniker "Mr. B.I.G." Gordon spent decades churning out horror and sci-fi films that specialized in everyday creatures taking on gigantic proportions, from a sixty-foot-tall army colonel in *The Amazing Colossal Man* (1957) to elephantine barnyard beasts in *Food of the Gods* (1976). In 1985, Mr. B.I.G. crashed the post-*Porky's* teen sex flick party with *Let's Do It!* and *The Big Bet*, and he didn't miss a beat. *Let's Do It!* does for nude boobs what Mr. B.I.G.'s *Empire of the Ants* did for six-legged picnic crashers—blows them up to Hindenburg proportions and turns them into objects of titillation and terror.

Leading to its enlarged lacto-orb climax, *Let's Do It!* chronicles college doof Freddie (Greg Bradford), who has been maniacally mammary-obsessed since he was breastfed too late into childhood. In fact, because Freddie's mom ran that milk train too long, he has somehow become unable to maintain an erection for fear of failing to satisfy any other female. He seeks counsel through sex workers, who prove to be sweet and unflinchingly forthcoming. "I used to be a model," one professional orgasm provider says. When asked in what field she specialized, the ex-model beams, "child pornography!"

Everything builds to a hallucination sequence in which Godzilla-proportioned gazongas fill the screen, while Freddy, appearing to be about the size of an '80s G.I. Joe action figure, bounces between them and swings from nipples the size of big-top circus tents. The moment—like the film—redefines the expression "What a hoot!"

License to Drive [1988]

DIR. GREG BEEMAN; W/COREY FELDMAN, COREY HAIM, HEATHER GRAHAM, JAMES AVERY

TWO COREYS ▫ DRIVER'S ED ▫ CAR CHASE ▫ HIT THEME SONG [LISTED SOMEWHERE?]

License to Drive is funnier than reasonably expected and a nice reminder of how effective Corey Haim had been as a sensitive smarty-twerp in both *Lucas* (1986) and *The Lost Boys* (1987). Costar Corey Feldman, too, was a gut-buster as the Edgar half of the vampire-battling Frog Brothers in that latter effort. They become "the two Coreys" only after this affable car comedy; blame the descent on narcotics and secret Hollywood molestation circles, not on poor *License to Drive*.

Haim stars as sixteen-year-old Dean Anderson, a suburbanite about to take his DMV road test. Should he pass, he will be liberated from bumming rides from his parents (the always great Richard Masur and Carol Kane). Dean aces the test only through a clever series of mishaps. Afterward, he picks up his classmate crush Mercedes Lane (Heather Graham) in his grandfather's "borrowed" 1972 Cadillac Sedan de Ville, a four-wheeled behemoth about the size of a World War II U-boat.

Once the young couple is on the road, Mercedes reveals that she's insanely drunk and just wants to get drunker. Dean pulls over, and Mercedes dents the Caddy's hood by dancing on it. Dean goes to Les (Corey Feldman) for help, thereby setting in motion a succession of high-speed slapstick complications. Dean's severely pregnant mother goes into labor, for example, but finds herself with no way to get to the hospital. The funniest moment involves the lads clumsily stashing comatose Mercedes in the Cadillac's trunk for her own safety.

A happy ending awaits nearly everyone, except, tragically, that gorgeously mammoth Cadillac. Songster Billy Ocean's enjoyed the success of his worldwide number-one smash theme song, "Get Outta My Dreams, Get into My Car," which remains quite the enjoyable accelerator pedal-tapper to this day.

Little Darlings [1980]

DIR. RONALD F. MAXWELL; W/TATUM O'NEAL, KRISTY MCNICHOL, MATT DILLON, ARMAND ASSANTE

SUMMER CAMP ▣ VIRGINITY BET ▣ TEEN MODEL

Reviewed by Rachel McPadden

Along with *Foxes,* starring Cherie Curie and Jodie Foster, *Little Darlings* is one of the two supreme classic teen girl coming-of-age movies. Though higher profile in theaters, *Little Darlings* had music licensing issues and became elusive during the DVD era. For that reason, the impact of *Little Darlings* remains protected in a time capsule of virginal ten-year-old-girl brains.

The *Darlings* are rich girl Tatum O'Neal and poor ruffian Kristy McNichol, who clash at summer camp as they compete to see who can be first to lose her virginity.

Tatum is Ferris, who seems worldly and sophisticated beyond her years. Her clothes are expensive, her manners straight from etiquette school. She also possesses the forethought to go after a grown man for her side of the virginity bet.

Like everyone else at camp, Ferris seems so young. Her airs are clearly a put-on, a child's defense against the life-shaking uncertainty of her parents divorcing and her mother abandoning her. She connects poorly with her fellow campers; she's a daddy's girl who, when separated from her father, goes after grown camp counselor Gary (Armand Assante). He thankfully sets firm boundaries with the Romeo-and-Juliet-jabbering fifteen-year-old.

Kristy McNichol as Angel oozes tough tomboy cool. She struts into camp from the slutty single-mom side of the tracks, and consequently has a more complicated relationship with sex. Perhaps when one feels alone and unprotected, sexuality becomes a threat to use self-destructively and without emotion. That would explain a few things.

Searing, raw, and real characters aside, *Little Darlings* is still a screwball *summer camp* movie, a with elements that could make it a girl-centric *Meatballs.* The supporting cast is filled with brilliant young actors, including super-charming flower child Sunshine, played spectacularly by a teen Cynthia Nixon.

As the virginity bet gets serious, we learn that Angel is only spitefully participating in order to appear "normal." She doesn't know how to react when a snobby catalogue model camper offers her a $100 Tiny Tangles Cream Rinse commercial royalty check as a prize. Ferris wants to be *liked*; Angel wants to be *normal.* Ferris ultimately lies about hooking up with Gary the counselor, telling all the other girls they "did it." In contrast, Angel tells a lie after actually making good on the bet with her look-alike Randy (Matt Dillon) and says they didn't "do it." No longer a virgin and now a fibber, Angel feels overwhelming and verbalized loneliness.

Angel wasn't ready. She got ahead of herself, and learned that while sex and men may be her mother's driving force, they weren't the answer for her. Through the modern-day lens of Kristy McNichol's belated coming-out, it's easy to project some celluloid closeting on her struggling character. Even during the opening challenge that leads to "the bet," the model overtly questions Angel's preference.

Ferris and Angel eventually get vulnerable and become honest with each other, and these enemies-at-first-sight bond and become friends. They talk, which they both need to do more than

Clockwise top left: *A deceptively upbeat 1982 publicity still promoting the palpably painful* Last American Virgin *(1982); thanks to* Lauderdale *(1989), aka* Spring Fever USA, *the number-one spring break destination of the 1980s was only as far as the local video rental hut;* Liar's Moon *(1982) gives Matt Dillon the rough sketch treatment;* Let's Do It *(1982) is a surprisingly sensitive exception to horny teen fare.*

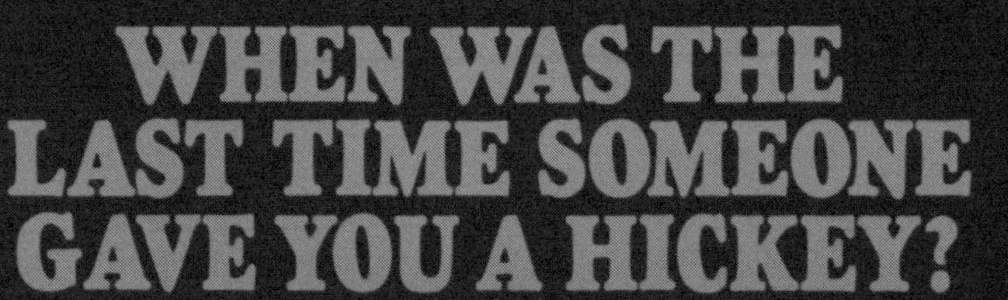

It was 1958 when making love meant "making out."

COLUMBIA PICTURES Presents A VERONA-DAVIDSON Production "THE LORDS OF FLATBUSH"
with SUSAN BLAKELY · RENEÉ PARIS · MARIA SMITH · PAUL MACE · HENRY WINKLER
SYLVESTER STALLONE · PERRY KING · Screenplay by STEPHEN F. VERONA · GAYLE GLECKLER · MARTIN DAVIDSON
Music composed, arranged and conducted by JOE BROOKS
Produced by STEPHEN F. VERONA · Directed by STEPHEN F. VERONA and MARTIN DAVIDSON
COLUMBIA PICTURES / A Division of COLUMBIA PICTURES INDUSTRIES, Inc.
PG

He delivers.

LUNCH WAGON

Music Performed by
MISSING PERSONS

...Where the Tastiest Things Aren't on the Menu!

Seymour Borde and Associates Presents LUNCH WAGON
A Mark Borde Production · An Ernest Pintoff Film
Starring RICK PODELL
AND THOSE PLAYBOY CENTERFOLDS ...
PAMELA BRYANT As MARCY · ROSANNE KATON As SHANNON
JIMMIE VAN PATTEN · CHUCK McCANN · ROSE MARIE
MICHAEL TUCCI CANDY MOORE
COLOR BY DELUXE
R RESTRICTED

Clockwise from left: The Lords of Flatbush *(1974), asking the grossest poster tag-line question of all time;* Loverboy *(1989);* Lunch Wagon *(1981), where comedienne Rose Marie meets new-wavers Missing Persons in food truck nirvana.*

anything else—and what teen girl doesn't? Right there, not on the field of competitive virginity loss, is the real love story.

Loose Screws [1985] aka Screwballs II

DIR. RAFAL ZIELINSKI; W/BRYAN GENESSE, LANCE VAN DER KOLK, ALAN DEVEAU, CYNTHIA BELLIVEAU (AS CYD BELLIVEAU)

SUMMER SCHOOL ▣ PRANKS ▣ AEROBICS ▣ THE BIG WHIPPED-CREAM-BIKINI CONTEST

The mad, magnificent, go-for-broke boobs-and-boners bacchanal *Screwballs* (1983) plays like an R-rated live-action version of a psychedelic X-rated cartoon. Without question, such a whacked-out masterwork warrants a sequel, but whether a second *Screwballs* could even remotely measure up to its predecessor is more daunting. *Loose Screws*, the follow-up to *Screwballs*, comes as close as any round two could hope. The makers didn't even have to call it *Screwballs II*.

Names are crucial in the *Screwballs/Loose Screws* universe, and any possible double entendre *must* be coaxed to full size. *Loose Screws* begins with four main protagonists—tall stud Steve Hardman (Lance Van Der Kolk); hopped-up horndog Brad Lovett (Bryan Genesse); nudity-crazed nerd scientist Hugh G. Rection (Alan Deveau); and breast-obsessed blubber-barrel Marvin Eatmore (Jason Warren). They are told that to graduate from Beaver High they must take summer courses at Coxswell Academy, billed promisingly as "a college for morons."

While *Screwballs* only centered on a contest to expose the naked nay-nays of school prude "Purity Busch," *Loose Screws* tightens up the stakes with a competition to engage in actual intercourse. The wound-up lads work their way toward the ultimate prize, the eyeful towers of French instructor Mona Lott (Cynthia Belliveau). On the road to Mona, the lusting lads don doctor garb to perform breast exams on their female classmates. Soon Brad dresses in drag and calls himself "Bradeen" to penetrate the girls' dorm, a paradise where everyone cavorts in their undies, smokes pot, passes around vibrators, and takes communal baths. Meanwhile, the enormous Mr. Eatmore spies on the ladies' locker room, stuffing his girth into a ceiling vent with the expected "it's raining fat men" results.

Elsewhere, Steve pretends to be an Asian masseuse with a fake Fu Manchu mustache and a first-rate offensive accent. Everyone ends up at a nudie dive called the Pig Pen to enjoy—all in one night—a wet-T-shirt contest, a "best ass" contest, and, fourteen years before *Varsity Blues* (1999), a whipped-cream-bikini contest.

The rest of this movie is rounded out by school expulsion, revenge schemes, and more run-ins with coeds with names like Tracey Gratehead (Liz Green), Nikki Nystroke (Annie McAuley), and Hilda Von Blow (Deborah Lobban). Director Rafal Zielinski doesn't quite ratchet *Loose Screws* up to the superlative stupefaction of *Screwballs*, but *Loose Screws* is still a deserving cinematic home for a character named Hugh G. Rection.

The Lords of Flatbush [1974]

DIR. MARTIN DAVIDSON, STEPHEN VERONA; W/PERRY KING, SYLVESTER STALLONE, HENRY WINKLER, SUSAN BLAKELY

NOSTALGIA ▣ GREASERS ▣ DOO-WOP ▣ TEEN PREGNANCY ▣ SODA SHOP

Bow bow-bow-bow bow-bow-bow-bow/ Doo-doo-doo-doo doo-doo-doo doo / Hey! Hey! Whaddaya say? / Looks like it's gonna be a very fine day

A round of amazingly fake-sounding doo-wop opens *The Lords of Flatbush*. As the music plays, we meet the four numbskulls who comprise the 1957 greaser gang the Lords. We watch as they preen, puff Lucky Strikes, and grunt lustily at poodle-skirted teenagers in front of James Madison High School. This credit sequence promises an agreeable exercise in somebody else's phony nostalgia, and *Lords* delivers.

The Lords themselves are suave leader Chico Tyrell (Perry King); musclehead mook Stanley Rosiello (Sylvester Stallone); secret brain Butchey

Weinstein (Henry Winkler); and Wimpy Murgalo (Paul Mace)—who might as well be an empty black leather jacket. Together, they cut up in class, shoot pool, joyride in a stolen jalopy, rumble with the Avenue J Boys, and croon more fake doo-wop over endless rounds of egg creams at a local soda fountain. Chico romances fancy blonde Jane (Susan Blakely). Stanley raises pigeons and knocks up his squeeze Frannie (Maria Smith). Welcome to Brooklyn, back when the borough's name served as shorthand for white ethnic loudmouths alternately switchblade fighting and gushing love for one another.

Growing up in Flatbush, I knew of Madison High as the place Pops McBeardo always threatened to send me if I didn't raise my grade average above a D-minus. Some adults told me the Lords had been a real gang of Italian-Irish-Jewish no-necks; others denied any knowledge or involvement. While the rest of my generation enjoyed skate parks, solar-powered go-karts, and handheld video games, I really did used to see guys standing on corners over garbage can fires singing doo-wop.

The Lords of Flatbush is easy to enjoy; it's easy to see how such a slapdash nostalgia knockoff ran wild at the box office. Look at the cast. Even while *Lords* was still bouncing around theaters, Sly Stallone became Rocky Balboa at the movies and Henry Winkler took over TV as Arthur Fonzarelli. Cooler than both of them, Perry King starred as Massa Hammond Maxwell in *Mandingo*.

Losin' It [1983]

DIR. CURTIS HANSON; W/TOM CRUISE, SHELLEY LONG, JACKIE EARLE HALEY, JOHN P. NAVIN JR.

ROAD TRIP ▣ TIJUANA ▣ VIRGINS ▣ HOOKERS ▣ SPANISH FLY ▣ DRUNKEN SAILORS

Losin' it! Confusin' it! Cruisin' it! / Havin' the time of our lives / Losin' it! Usin' it! Abusin' it! / Down at the borderline!

The chorus to the nitrous oxide blast of "Losin' It" by the Jeff Alan Band certainly calls it like the movie shows it. Nice work.

In the same 1950s/early-'60s ether occupied by many other R-rated youth comedies, SoCal high school hell-raiser Big Dave (Jackie Earle Haley) rallies good-time jock Spider (John Stockwell) and properly polite Woody (Tom Cruise) for a Tijuana getaway in his red 1957 Chevy Bel Air convertible. The rub is that they have to cart along Big Dave's little brother, Wendell, aka Wimp (John P. Navin Jr.). Nonetheless, Big Dave smiles wide as he promises: "We're going into the mouth of hell!"

The boys pull over to shoplift supplies and step into somebody else's relationship crisis. The married convenience store owners are in the midst of a knockdown drag-out that ends when the wife, Kathy (Shelley Long), hops into Big Dave's ride. Kathy says she saw the dudes pocketing potato chips and such and, unless they want her to call the cops, she'll be tagging along to acquire a Mexican divorce. Just like that, Team *Losin' It* is assembled.

Once the travelers arrive south of the border, adventures occur as expected. A crooked cop shakes them down. Wimp splits to buy fireworks. Big Dave, the crotch-department opposite of Pee-Wee from *Porky's*, hits a strip-bar-*cum*-brothel with Spider and Woody. While naked *mamacitas* strut onstage, late-'70s Long Island comedic pianist sensation John "Dr. Dirty" Valby pounds out the raucous sing-along "Bring Your Mother to the Gangbang."

Big Dave and Spider do manage to "lose it" to professional cherry-pop technicians in a gruesome whorehouse, but one dude also ends up in jail while the other is hung from a crane and menaced with a blowtorch. Woody doesn't have third-world sex tourism in him, so he pounds tequilas at the bar with Kathy until she supplies him with a more romantic memory of his own "losin' it." Wimp finds fireworks, but Big Dave does not find the mythical aphrodisiac Spanish fly. The next challenge becomes how to cross back *north* of the border past the monstrous *federale* (horror giant Joe Spinell) standing guard. Amidst a flurry of chaos—fruit stands, live chickens, and drunken sailors fly—our intrepid squad gets back to the U.S.A., and then that gas-rush Jeff Alan Band number plays again.

Losin' It consistently entertains. Helmed by future Oscar-winner Curtis Hanson (*L.A. Confidential*), the film benefits from efforts to make it a "real" movie; it's canonical. Within a year of its release, Tom Cruise and Shelley Long would be superstars. Still, one crucial question goes unanswered: Where in the braying, kicking, gallon-jizzing *fuck* was the donkey show?

LOVELINES [1984]

DIR. ROD AMATEAU; W/MICHAEL WINSLOW, GREG BRADFORD, MARY BETH EVANS, TAMMY TAYLOR

BATTLE OF THE BANDS ▪ **JOCKS** ▪ **HOUSE PARTY** ▪ **NAKED SWIM TEAM** ▪ **SCI-FI CAR**

In 1983, Los Angeles alt-rock radio powerhouse KROQ launched the hugely popular and long-running late-night call-in relationship advice show *Loveline*. The series hit so big and so fast locally that, a scant year later, a sort-of movie version of the show arrived in theaters. Alas, the film's fate did not mirror that of the radio program—except maybe in a fun-house sense.

The human connection between *Loveline* to *Lovelines* is Jim "Poorman" Trent, an on-air KROQ talent who initially created and cohosted the radio phenomenon. Trent cameos in the movie as "Disk Jockey." However, *Lovelines*' name-above-the-credits star, the guy whose portrait is painted on poster, is Michael Winslow, a gimmick comedian forever cemented in pop culture as "the sound effects guy from *Police Academy*."

Winslow had previously demonstrated his remarkable vocal gymnastics opposite Cheech and Chong in *Next Movie* (1980) and *Nice Dreams* (1981). Still, *Police Academy* truly sent humanity tumbling head over heels in love with Winslow's organic impersonations of garbage trucks, machine guns, and badly dubbed kung fu movies. With all this oddball background info, it's a headscratcher that *Lovelines* can't make good on the weirdness behind it.

The "Lovelines" of *Lovelines* is a curiously explained call-in service through which students at rival learning institutions Malibu High and Coldwater Canyon High spread rumors and announce social happenings. Winslow, as proprietor J. D. Prescott, staffs Lovelines with bikini model operators. On the side, he's a wannabe rock promoter, so soon enough the two schools are embroiled in a battle of the bands.

While all the teens are focused on crosstown rock mania instead of paying attention in English class, an inevitable *Romeo and Juliet* setup develops. Piper (Mary Beth Evans), front-babe of the Firecats, crosses paths with Rick Johnson (Greg Bradford), lead hunk of Racer, her main competition in the musical showdown, and romantic montages do happen.

In the course of the contest, *Lovelines* showcases numerous concert sequences at a place called Charlie's Meet Rack. One group after another performs ersatz arena rock and new wave songs that can only possibly exist in goofwad '80s cinema. One standout combo is party store punkers Dragon and the Flying Phlegm, who likably blast out "Ba Ba Ba Baby" two times. The bandleader Dragon is played by Miguel Ferrer, sporting hair like Adrian Edmondson as Vyvyan Basterd on *The Young Ones*.

Piper's hulking older brother Godzilla (Frank Zagarino) brings the conflict, first by threatening to tamper with the outcome of the battle of the bands through physical violence. Then he bombastically attempts to defend his kid sister's virtue. Turns out he takes the preservation of Piper's hymen *very* seriously.

The heroes deliver comeuppance to Godzilla during a car chase when one member of Racer reveals he's rigged up his vehicle with impossible James Bond gadgets. The only moment more off-the-wall is a prank on the rival school's girls' swim team, which suddenly turns the Coldwater Canyon contestants into skinny-dippers.

Lovelines opened suddenly and with no prerelease ballyhoo in November 1984, ringing in the mid-

1980s with 78 minutes of intoxicating insanity and inanity. The whole endeavor seems a hodgepodge of an existing battle-of-the-bands script crammed with two slightly incongruous "hot property" selling points: the fledgling, pre–Dr. Drew *Loveline* radio show and Michael Winslow mouthing approximations of R2-D2 rolling over Jimi Hendrix's guitar and playing Atari.

Vintage TV sitcom director Rod Amateau (*The Many Loves of Dobie Gillis, My Mother the Car*) made *Lovelines* after having previously helmed *Drive-In* (1976) but prior to bringing us *The Garbage Pail Kids Movie* (1987). The implied lunacy of those credits is irresistibly visible here—insert your own vocal sound effect of approval.

LOVERBOY [1989]

DIR. JOAN MICKLIN SILVER; W/PATRICK DEMPSEY, KIRSTIE ALLEY, CARRIE FISHER, BARBARA CARRERA

PIZZA DELIVERY • COLLEGE SLACKER • COUGARS • GIGOLO

Patrick Dempsey's lanky, nasal, handsome-nerd shtick worked effectively in *Can't Buy Me Love* (1987), but subsequent attempts to cultivate him into a romantic hunk went bust until he reemerged nearly two decades later, all suave and salt-and-pepper-templed, as "Dr. McDreamy" on the TV drama *Grey's Anatomy*. *Loverboy* is one of these joyless misfires.

To recap Dempsey's stale streak; *In the Mood* (1987) stinks on phony nostalgic ice, with Dempsey grossly overselling the 1940s saga of "the Woo-Woo Kid," a fifteen-year-old who scandalized Mr. and Mrs. America by nailing multiple married dames. *Some Girls* (1988) manages to make a boring task of witnessing a hormone-juiced American college student (Dempsey) fall prey to three overheated Canadian sisters (Jennifer Connelly, Sheila Kelley, and Ashley Greenfield). *Loverboy* similarly squanders a solid sex comedy setup in favor of a series of PG-13 anti-payoffs.

Randy Bodek (Dempsey) is a college sophomore who takes a pizza delivery job. His first customer, saucy Italian mama Alexandra Barnett (Barbara Carrera), seduces Randy upon arrival, tips him two hundred dollars, and spreads the word among her sexually famished suburban housewife circle that the new pizza boy really piles on the pepperoni. In short order, Alexandra pimps Randy out to her pals. This highly improbable lady-slayer learns oh so much about life, love, and menopause while turning tricks with clients played by Kirstie Alley and Carrie Fisher.

Screenwriter Robin Schiff went on to pen the great *Romy and Michelle's High School Reunion* (2005). Director Joan Micklin Silver, who started out making the cult romantic drama *Chilly Scenes of Winter* (1979), became a pillar of the movie business. *Loverboy* blows, but it deserves half an okay feeling for sending those two on their way while fulfilling female fantasies of nothing more consequential than casually getting laid.

LUNCH WAGON [1981]

aka COME 'N' GET IT; LUNCH WAGON GIRLS; HAMBURGER GIRLS

DIR. ERNEST PINTOFF; W/PAMELA JEAN BRYANT, ROSANNE KATON, CANDY MOORE, DALE BOZZIO

SAVE THE BUSINESS • NEW WAVE • FIXER-UPPER MONTAGE • PIE FIGHT • MUSCLE BEACH • ANCIENT CELEBRITIES

Lunch Wagon opens on a shot of a poster of new wave chart-toppers the Cars, and only bashes and pops in a more rockingly agreeable direction from there. The main story chronicles three sex-bomb entrepreneurs running a food truck, with comical complications coming from klutzy jewel thieves who lose a diamond in the mustard.

As *Lunch Wagon* gets rolling, bouncy blonde Marcy (Pamela Jean Bryant, *Private Lessons*) and statuesque African American stunner Shannon (Rosanne Katon, *The Swinging Cheerleaders*) quit their garage gig slaving away for lecherous lard-blob Andy (George Memmoli) and buy their favorite kitchen-on-wheels from sweet and suddenly retired Bernie (Dick Van Patten, in a *great* fat-guy '70s disco hat).

Realizing they don't know how to cook, the ladies hightail it to Muscle Beach to recruit Amazonian fitness fiend and expert chef Deidre (Candy Moore). The catch is that she will only whip up healthy dishes. No sweat. Once the Lunch Wagon team stuffs their stupefying physiques into toddler-size mini T-shirts and hot pants, their hopped-up customers will swallow absolutely anything.

The savvy sirens park the wagon outside a construction site, and famished oglers line up. The staff of a rival food truck immediately picks a pie fight with our heroines. Splosh! That cart also turns out to be a front for schmucky mobster Al Schmeckler (Rick Podell), whose hoochie-mama main squeeze Sunshine is played by Latin lust-queen Louisa Moritz (*The Last American Virgin*). His actual mama, Mrs. Schmeckler, is camped up to full Ma Barker hysteria here by vaudeville and *Dick Van Dyke Show* legend Rose Marie (with her signature bow in her hair).

Without ever losing a beat, *Lunch Wagon* also manages to whirl in idiotic diamond heisters Turtle (Chuck McCann) and Ralph (Vic Dunlop), and a recurring amateur talent contest emceed by punky-freaky Danny Death (Michael Mislove). A key subplot involves real-life new wave group Missing Persons, playing the fictitious band Teddy and the Ruff Ryders. Front woman Dale Bozzio is freakily easy to mistake for Lady Gaga, who wasn't born until five years later. Budding romances and botched illegal activities bring all these components together in time for a slap-happy ending.

Lunch Wagon is the work of bona fide Academy Award–winning director Ernest Pintoff, who won an Oscar in 1963 for his animated short *The Critic*. In 1971, he detoured from TV work into counterculture madness with the stoned-hippie midnight movie omnibus *Dynamite Chicken*. The Academy really burned Ernie, though, when they overlooked that film and *Lunch Wagon*.

Mag Wheels [1978]

aka Love Between Four Wheels; Summer School; Wheels of Love

[DIR. BETHEL BUCKALEW; W/JOHN LAUGHLIN, SHELLY HORNER, VERKINA FLOWER, PHOEBE SCHMIDT]

BIKINIS ▫ SKATE PARK ▫ WEED ▫ CUSTOM VANS ▫ C.B. RADIOS ▫ GIRL TRUCK GANG

Once again, a teen movie veers straight to the dark undercurrent of 1970s Southern California teenage life amidst surf, sand, and sun. *Mag Wheels* backs up and unloads plenty of bikinis, beach balls, bonfires, sweet rides, cool dudes, and classroom pranks; but with the good times comes attempted gang rape and contests of luck likely to culminate in multiple casualties.

Mag Wheels' sourness starts right away, as some poor sap works the local beach parking lot, collecting fifty cents per carload. One by one, customers roll up in tricked-out vans, trucks, and hot rods, one and all giving him ferocious grief for doing his job. One female driver flashes her sizable headlights at the dude, and instructs him to buff them for his four bits. When he refuses, she furiously and with ungentle wording questions his sexual orientation (presumptuous, much?).

New bikini babe in town Anita (Shelly Horner) hits the shore sans knowledge of any local nastiness. She's even cool with forking over two quarters to park. Local stud Steve (John Laughlin) cocks an eyebrow in Anita's direction, igniting a nuclear jealousy fit from his psycho-shrew main squeeze, Donna (Verkina Flower). Hell hath no fury like a hot harpy scorned in one of these movies. Fortunately, Anita befriends Jill (Phoebe Schmidt), leader of an all-female squad of custom pickup truck drivers. Steel yourself; within a few minutes the truck chicks are called "lezzies."

As her rage mounts, Donna's concentrated campaign against Anita includes running her off the road; starting a classroom fight that gets Anita expelled; and making it look as though Anita had set up Steve for a drug bust—a frame job within a frame job. As a rational response to the last offense, Steve rallies his fellow custom van enthusiasts (called "vanners") to track down Anita and Jill to dole out justice in the form of a mass sexual assault.

Jill's trucker pals arrive to thwart the forced-penetration party, which prompts the warring factions to declare a "drag out." This is a tug-of-war between vehicles—in this case, vans and pickup trucks—connected by chains over a ravine. The goal is to floor your ride in reverse and drag your opponent over the edge, presumably sending them plunging to a sandy death. Hard stuff for a trifling SoCal bikini flick, even in 1978.

Busting up this act of mutually assured destruction, Anita attempts to martyr herself, piloting her dad's car into the ravine. (That's another pleasant touch: Anita's dad is a screaming asshole who *never* stops yelling at her.) The "lezzie" truckers and rapist vanners unite to rescue their downed object of shared lust. Steve pulls Anita's limp body from the wreckage and shouts, "She's alive!" Then everybody dances.

Mag Wheels is pretty to look at and gurglingly hateful on the inside. All of us have fallen for people who fit that description. In other words, becoming enraptured by *Mag Wheels* could be the beginning of a beautiful relationship, if you survive the carnage.

The Making of Bikini School 3 [1990]

DIR. BOBCAT GOLDTHWAIT; W/TOM KENNY, DAVID SPADE, KATHY GRIFFIN

BIKINIS ▭ SCHOOL ▭ PARODY

Before *Shakes the Clown* (1992), comedian, filmmaker, and *Police Academy* costar Bobcat Goldthwait made his directorial debut with this semi-legendary, extremely hard to find, half-hour mockumentary with his now famously funny friends Tom Kenny (*SpongeBob SquarePants*) and David Spade (*Saturday Night Live*). "It's a parody like *Spinal Tap*," Goldthwait told *The Weekly Week*, "but of bonehead teen comedies."

Unconnected but likewise convinced that the time had come to parody teen sex comedies, *The Simpsons* delivered its own self-aware treatment in 1993. On the episode "Homer Goes to College," the returning freshman bones up for his university adventure by viewing "a program about campus life that I really should watch"—*School of Hard Knockers*, starring teen idol Corey Masterson. On-screen, uptight Dean Bitterman hopes the crazies of Chugalug House won't pull any pranks while he escorts the president of the United States around campus. Of course, Corey sets off Nerdlinger's "bra bomb," which rains down a flurry of undergarments on the authority figures. Delighted, the prez tells a fuming Bitterman to "lighten up!"

Making the Grade [1984] aka The Last American Preppy

DIR. DORIAN WALKER; W/JUDD NELSON, JONNA LEE, DANA OLSEN, ANDREW DICE CLAY

PREPPIES ▭ BOARDING SCHOOL ▭ BIG FAT PARTY ANIMAL

The 1980s *Prince and the Pauper* redo *Making the Grade* almost makes the highest of grades and stands near the upperclassmen of the genre. Smart-mouthed mansion-dwelling rich kid and seventh-year high school senior Palmer Woodrow is told by his way-uncool old-money dad that graduation is now a must, or else Palmer will be disowned and ditched. Meanwhile, in broken-bottles-on-cracked-concrete urban New Jersey, brainy-but-too-dumb-not-to-gamble street dude Eddie Keaton (Judd Nelson) has landed in $3,700 worth of trouble with spine-snapping bookie Dice, palooka'd to perfection by Andrew Dice Clay, making his big-screen debut.

Our protagonists happen upon one another in the locker room of a country club, where Palmer is running up his old man's bar tab and Eddie is running away from Dice's goons. Together, the quick friends concoct a scam good enough to be made into this exact movie: Since no one at Palmer's new school, Hoover Academy, really knows what he looks like, Palmer will pay Eddie ten thousand dollars and a Porsche convertible to move on campus and attend classes in his place.

After Eddie shows up at Hoover hoisting a boom box and wearing a flaming-red pimp suit, Palmer's pal Rand (Carey Scott) offers the newbie some lessons in how to gracefully grease his way into the sea of snooty snobs with green sweaters draped over their pink button-down shoulders. The best tip is a fashion primer, during which Rand displays a succession of golf shirts by logo, saying, "Preppy completely...preppy-come-never..." and then, donning the Izod Lacoste alligator, "Preppy *forever!*"

Making the Grade's mook-among-millionaires scenario runs its natural course. Villainy knocks in the form of handsome, smugly dickish Biff (Scott McGinnis, the arcade owner in *Joysticks*), the boyfriend of equestrian eyeful Tracey (sex-kitteny Jonna Lee). Eddie and Tracey inevitably fall for one another. Just as inevitably, Eddie scrotum-smashingly falls off a horse. Ouch.

Judd Nelson is pretty stupendous in his inaugural lead role. He's very funny and very effectively unaffected as a Garden State guido. Sufficient praise should also be heaped lovingly upon the breakout performance by crazily charismatic Andrew Dice Clay. Busting his "Diceman" shtick out of a comedy club setting for the first time, he is frightening and hilarious.

Making the Grade's secret weapon, however, is Dana Olsen as wealthy ne'er-do-well Palmer Woodrow. Operating out of the young Tom Hanks and Michael Keaton school of irresistibly likeable wiseasses, Olsen sprays every scene he enters with uproarious japes the way Rambo softens up rice paddies with a machine gun. In his only film role of note, Olsen actually comes off as too funny to be a straightforward movie star. After this movie, he switched back to screenwriting full-time. Olsen had previously penned the slasher spoof *Wacko* and the SCTV semi-spin-off *Going Berserk*. Later, he scripted Joe Dante's cult satire starring Tom Hanks, *The 'Burbs* (1989).

One more area in which *Making the Grade* earns high marks is its wealth of funny fat fellows. Gordon Jump, *WKRP*'s Big Guy and *Diff'rent Strokes*' Bicycle Man, makes a terrifically boobish school headmaster. Boisterous blob Walter Olkewicz puts a swell spin on the boozing, smoking, hooker-squiring party animal in the role of gym teacher Coach Wordman. Portraying a student called Blimp, Dan Schneider is his usual affable self, filling the screen to size as he went on to do in *The Sure Thing* (1985) and on TV's *Head of the Class* (1986–1991).

Malibu Beach [1978]

DIR. ROBERT J. ROSENTHAL; W/KIM LANKFORD, JAMES DAUGHTON, SUSAN PLAYER, STEVE OLIVER

CHEERLEADERS • BIKINIS • WEED • SHARK • VANS • BIKINI-SNATCHING DOG

Malibu Beach is the middle installment of Crown International Pictures' definitive, three-volume cinematic statement on late-1970s drive-in teensploitation. Its forerunner is *The Van* (1977), and its successor is *Van Nuys Blvd.* (1979). If only Crown had gone with a consistent title here so we could just call these "The Van Trilogy"—that would have been so great.

By day, athletic blonde Dina (Kim Lankford) works the shores of Malbu Beach as a lifeguard. By night, she romances and skinny-dips with beach bum Bobby (James Daughton). Dina's bubbly best pal Sally (Susan Player) hangs out on the sand and occasionally slips out of her swimsuit with Bobby's buddy Paul (Michael Luther).

Attempting to poop the well-tanned quartet's endless surf party are Bobby's huffy ex-girlfriend Glorianna (Tara Strohmeier) and oily lunkhead Dugan (Steve Oliver). The bad guy from *The Van* gets to jerk it up all over again here, reprising his signature line, "Nobody, but nobody, calls Dugie a turd!"

To its credit and advantage, *Malibu Beach* contains almost no plot. The main characters sit on the beach, party, and look hot. Comical encounters involve misplaced cheerleaders, a dog who

Clockwise from top left: *Far from the fun flick promised by the poster,* Malibu High *(1979) is a psycho freak-out, not to be missed; the underrated* Making the Grade *(1984);* Malibu Beach *(1978) and its bikini-snatching dog;* The Malibu Bikini Shop *(1986), a vision of Skinemax to come.*

steals bikini tops, and a mischievous kid who sprays sleeping female beachgoers with suntan lotion so they'll jump up and show him their boobs. The climax is a swim race between Bobby, Dugan, and stock footage of a shark.

Look for Bill Adler as a van owner who's billed here simply as "Vanner." In *The Van*, he's a supporting character named Steve. In *Van Nuys Blvd.*, Steve is the main protagonist. That makes "Vanner Steve" the element that ties together all three jewels in Crown International's royal triple achievement. He's almost as cool as the dog who makes off with those swimsuits. Judging by a later appearance in *Hardbodies* (1984), bikini-snatching dogs were quite a problem in California in those days.

The Malibu Bikini Shop [1986]

DIR. DAVID WECHTER; W/MICHAEL DAVID WRIGHT, BRUCE GREENWOOD, DEBRA BLEE

MALIBU ▪ BIKINIS ▪ SKATEBOARDS ▪ GRADUATION ▪ DRESSING ROOM MONTAGES

For better or mainly for worse, *The Malibu Bikini Shop* ranks as one of the most prolifically influential films of its era. From the boffo performance of *Malibu Bikini Shop* on VHS and late-night cable arose *The Bikini Carwash Company* movies of the '90s and their myriad imitators, the nadir being 1998's *Bikini Traffic School*. The extinction of properly teen sex comedies followed, in favor of R-rated T&A flicks that emulated hardcore porn's simultaneous elimination of plot and context in favor of just the "good parts"—sex and nudity, horrendous music, and nothing else. *The Malibu Bikini Shop* is better than all that, simply because *some* stuff *sort of* happens in between changing station montages set to songs including "Give Me Your Love to Dream On" by Steve Eaton.

Uptight biz-school grad Alan (Michael David Wright) and his party-hearty brother Todd (Bruce Greenwood) inherit the domicile of the title, which is actually called "Da Bikini Shop." The bros not only take on the store, they move into deceased benefactor Aunt Ida's swanky beach pad with good-time-gal Bikini Shop employees Cathy (Ami Julius), Ronnie (Barbara Horan), and Cindy (Galyn Görg—a name that sounds like a bog from a '70s bigfoot movie).

It's all too much for the bozo brethren to handle, so they spend the rest of the movie attempting to sell the shop to a succession of comic customers. Time-killing montages abound, the most noteworthy of which occurs after the girls fashion bikinis out of surplus surgical scrubs. They put on a *Rambo*-themed fashion show that becomes an ersatz music video for Diana DeWitt's "You Make Me Nervous," one of those bass-popping faux-funk-metal abortions that exist only in shitty movies. Consider such sonic torments the price of fast-forwarding to nudity.

Malibu High [1979]

DIR. IRWIN BERWICK; W/JILL LANSING, STUART TAYLOR, KATIE JOHNSON, PHYLLIS BENSON

BIKINIS ▪ BLACKMAIL ▪ CUSTOM VAN ▪ MOBSTERS ▪ DISCO

Appearances can be deceiving—sometimes gloriously so. *Malibu High* is a rage-driven exploitation sleaze scorch of hatred, cruelty, and violence that Crown International Pictures repackaged as a fun-in-the-sun bikini beach jaunt so the movie would be easily confused with their popular teen frolics, such as *The Pom Pom Girls* (1976), *The Van* (1977), and, especially, *Malibu Beach* (1978). Make no intentionally easy-to-make mistake, though; *Malibu High* is an entirely different beast.

In her one and only movie role on record, Jill Lansing fire-breathes every moment on-screen as high school senior Kim, one of cinema's ultimate hair-trigger psychotic female antiheroes. She is a rage-driven monster somewhere between Elizabeth Berkley in *Showgirls* (1995), Charlotte Gainsbourg at the end of *Antichrist* (2009), and all the Switchblade Sisters combined. She is anything but the broad-grinning swimsuit model surrounded by cartoon suitors on the *Malibu High* poster.

Kim mostly eschews beachwear, in fact, for general nakedness. We meet her stark nude in bed, snarling at her mother's call to wake up for school. She venomously smokes a cigarette at the breakfast table, then blames Mom's appearance for their fatherless household. "You could've looked decent once in a while!" she spits. "Maybe you wouldn't have driven Daddy away. And maybe he wouldn't have killed himself because he couldn't get it up anymore!" *Goooood* morning, *Malibu High*!

Kim's napalm disposition is due to her failing grades and lack of funds, plus she's enraged after being dumped by hunky blond Kevin (Stuart Taylor) in favor of demure Annette (Tammy Taylor). After hitting a disco with her pal Lucy (Katie Johnson), Kim sucks on a bong and guzzles a hooch bottle like she's trying to injure both objects, proclaiming she's officially out for revenge.

The next morning, Kim fucks a teacher on a dirt mound called "High Point," then negotiates a deal to turn tricks under the tutelage of van-driving scum-pimp Uncle Tony (Al Manino). In short order, Kim jumps ship to more elegant love broker Lance (Garth Pillsbury). Alas, when one of her johns gets out of hand with S&M kinks, Kim naturally hacks him to death with an ice pick. Rather than panic or get pissed off, though, Lance likes how Kim handled herself. He upgrades her pay to include cocaine and her assignments to include gangland assassinations. Best of all, the top of the hit list includes her very own high school principal!

The insanity of *Malibu High* is impossible to exaggerate. Intentional comedy or not—and *Malibu High* is *not*—it's necessary to list the movie among the most side-splittingly hilarious of all teen sex films. *Malibu High* looks like a seventh-grade film strip gone rabid, and the music score is a treasure trove of madness. Most scenes end with an electronic "stinger" sound; the same noise was later used between bits on *SCTV*. The big climactic chase, in which the entire surviving population of the film hunts Kim down on a beach, is set to Alan Tew's sizzling, percussive instrumental "The Big One," better known as the theme song from *The People's Court*. In the case of must-see off-the-rails motion pictures based around teenagers, *Malibu High* comes up guilty on all charges—including a few that hadn't been invented yet.

MEATBALLS [1979]

DIR. IVAN REITMAN; W/BILL MURRAY, CHRIS MAKEPEACE, KATE LYNCH, KRISTINE DEBELL

SUMMER CAMP ▪ PRANKS ▪ RICH JERKS ▪ HAWAIIAN SHIRTS ▪ CANADA

Essentially *Animal House* for kids, *Meatballs* is the shorthand title used when describing "all those summer camp movies." That's how things should be. *Meatballs* is the category's defining classic, funny enough to soak your tube socks and codifying all the archetypes for subsequent summer camp cinema. In addition, the movie crystalizes the metamorphosis of Bill Murray into a Superstar with a capital *S*.

Here's how *Meatballs* happened. Canadian moviemaker Ivan Reitman, amped up and rich after producing *Animal House*, sought to imbue a family-friendly romp with just enough of that taboo-smashing blockbuster's unruly behavior and dirty-minded dirty trickery to be effective. As such, *Meatballs* champions the lovable losers of raggedy Camp Northstar, where a hyper-charismatic, whoopee-cushion-on-the-throne-of-authority counselor named Tripper Harrison leads teenage counselors-in-training in overseeing their young charges.

Just as John Belushi's bombastic star power immediately transformed and elevated *Animal House*, the role of Tripper required one exact right mega-talent at the one exact right moment of his upward-racing career. Enter Bill Murray. As Hawaiian-shirted, ukulele-strumming Tripper, Murray explodes hilariousness from the opening moments of *Meatballs*, when he fumbles out of a deep slumber, chomps a half-finished hoagie next to his bed, and dons a makeshift space helmet. Via *Meatballs*, Murray perfects the off-the-cuff, machine-gun wit he developed first with the Second City improv troupe, then on *The National Lampoon Radio Hour*, and, finally, on *Saturday Night Live*.

Murray-as-Tripper makes riotous announcements over the camp's P.A. system: "Tonight's mystery-meat dinner? It was veal!" He coordinates physics-defying pranks against dorkular camp boss Morty Melnick (Harvey Atkin). He rudely romances female head counselor Roxanne (Kate Lynch). Then, in the movie's real, overarching plot, Tripper movingly mentors parentally neglected Rudy (Chris Makepeace), transforming him from silent outcast into champion long-distance runner. ("Wudy da Wabbit da Winner!")

Comically contrasting with the movie's supporting cast of likeable, bloom-of-sexiness counselors-in-training, two giants tower: gregarious blubber-bucket Keith Knight as hot-dog-eating-contest stomach-kicker Larry "Fink" Finkelstein, and Jack Blum as bumbling, bespectacled, archetypal über-nerd Spaz. The cinematic "fatty and skinny" formula that worked for Mack Sennett and Mabel Normand, Laurel and Hardy, Abbott and Costello, and Chris Farley and David Spade hits a deeply lovable apex with the *Meatballs* team of Fink and Spaz. The latter doesn't even need to remove his Coke-bottle eyeglasses to win the heart of adorable jock Jackie (Margaret Pinvidic).

Playboy model Kristine DeBell, who plays counselor-in-training A.L., had starred three years earlier in a hardcore porn version of *Alice in Wonderland* that proved to be a sexploitation smash. After *Meatballs*, Kristine successfully transitioned to a Hollywood career, appearing as Jackie Chan's love interest in *The Big Brawl* (1980), and getting regular TV work on *Eight Is Enough*, *CHiPs*, and *Fantasy Island*, and even landing a long-term soap opera spot on *The Young and the Restless*. She was the first X-rated movie performer to legitimately make it in the mainstream, all thanks to the fuzzy demarcation of *Meatballs*.

Forty-nine minutes into *Meatballs*, the Camp Northstar gang is getting its tail trounced at basketball by the rich jerks from across-the-lake rival Camp Mohawk. Tripper's solution is for the Northstar players on his signal to yank down the shorts of all their opponents at once. Comical chaos results. While most of the Mohawk guys sport tighty-whities, one player wears a jock strap that exposes his bare butt cheeks. Oddly, his naked keister is smeared, scarred, and patched up with gauze and surgical tape, as though he just came from grotesque, splattery sphincter surgery. For gluteus, glorious reasons still unknown after forty years, *Meatballs* hid a horrifically torn-up male tush in plain sight.

The mayhem that is *Meatballs* closes as it opens, with the Camp Northstar Kids' Chorus singing the irresistible, "Are You Ready for the Summer?" That joyful noise brings a summer rush of delight each June as it pitches an earworm tent inside your head. Incredibly, *Meatballs* was the *first* summer camp movie, not a gonzo update of some old Hollywood genre akin to how *Spring Break* and *Hardbodies* took their template from under the sun umbrella of Frankie-and-Annette beach party flicks. The most specific predecessor to *Meatballs* is Allan Sherman's 1963 colossal hit novelty record, "Hello Muddah, Hello Faddah (A Letter from Camp)" and, maybe just a pinch, the single-season NBC sitcom rip-off of that song, *Camp Runamuck* (1965–66).

Meatballs begat *Summer Camp* (1979), *Little Darlings* (1980), *Oddballs* (1984), its own sequel in 1984, and so on. Ultimately, the late 1990s brought the retro send-up *Wet Hot American Summer*, not just a spoof of summer camp movies as invented by *Meatballs*, but a direct confirmation of the singular overwhelming impact of the first summer camp movie that made it all possible.

THE SUMMER CAMP
THAT MAKES YOU
UNTRUSTWORTHY, DISLOYAL,
UNHELPFUL, UNFRIENDLY,
DISCOURTEOUS,
UNKIND, DISOBEDIENT,
AND VERY HILARIOUS.

BILL MURRAY in

MEATBALLS

BILL MURRAY IN AN IVAN REITMAN FILM "MEATBALLS" STARRING HARVEY ATKIN KATE LYNCH RUSS BANHAM KRISTINE DEBELL SARAH TORGOV AND INTRODUCING CHRIS MAKEPEACE AS "RUDY" EXECUTIVE PRODUCERS ANDRE LINK JOHN DUNNING PRODUCED BY DAN GOLDBERG MUSIC BY ELMER BERNSTEIN LYRICS BY NORMAN GIMBEL WRITTEN BY LEN BLUM DAN GOLDBERG JANIS ALLEN, HAROLD RAMIS DIRECTED BY IVAN REITMAN

A PARAMOUNT RELEASE

PG PARENTAL GUIDANCE SUGGESTED

Multiple scoops of Meatballs. *Clockwise from top:* Meatballs *(1979) quad poster;* Meatballs Part II *(1984);* Meatballs III *(1987), about a dead porn star dodging Hell by getting a virgin camper laid; the original 1970s weenie war between The Stomach (Peter Hume, left) and Fink (Keith Knight, right);* Meatballs *star Bill Murray (crouching) and Camp Northstar's male counselors surround director Ivan Reitman (with head in clapboard).*

MEATBALLS PART II [1984]
aka SPACE KID

DIR. KEN WIEDERHORN; W/KIM RICHARDS, JOHN MENGATTI, RICHARD MULLIGAN, MISTY ROWE

SUMMER CAMP ▣ PUNKS ▣ GUIDO ▣ WHEELCHAIR KID ▣ MILITARY JERKS ▣ SPACE ALIEN

Meatballs Part II shares only two common factors with 1979's original *Meatballs*: The film is set at a summer camp, and is a god-damned soil-your-ball-hugger-gym-shorts laugh riot. Originally titled *Space Kid*, a moniker better matched to the movie's plot, *Meatballs Part II* pits the amiable down-and-outers of Camp Sasquatch against the gung-ho military muscleheads across the lake at Camp Patton.

Spicing up the summer are Flash Carducci (John Mengatti), a Brooklyn-accented juvenile delinquent sentenced to do community service as a Camp Sasquatch counselor-in-training; and Meathead (Felix Silla), an uproariously clunky E.T.-knockoff space alien who can move objects with his glowing eyes. His parents talk like Borscht Belt comedians—yes, Meathead's alien parents drop him off at camp.

The stupidity factor in *Meatballs Part II* is astronomical, and exactly equivalent to how funny the movie is. Limb-flailing Richard Mulligan (TV's *Soap*) dials his performance all the way up as Camp Sasquatch's frantic owner. John Larroquette minces magnificently as Lt. Felix Foxglove, Camp Patton's resident closet case. Paul Reubens almost hits Pee-Wee Herman strength as the camp's gonzo bus driver. The film's constant use of "pinky" as a euphemism for "penis" is sublime dumbness, as is the gag of crippled Tommy "Wheelchair" McVee (David Hollander) outracing the camp bus via his own arm power, and then later using his ambulatory device as a tractor and a bulldozer.

Really, *Meatballs Part II* is Meathead's movie. Not one second of Meathead screen time is anything less than incapacitating in idiotic hilarity. When Ted, one of the space kid's human bunkmates, introduces himself by saying, "Me Ted" (à la "Me Tarzan"), the visitor misunderstands and just repeats it as "Meathead." His earth name sticks. While waddling about in a yellow rain slicker, Meathead eats Big Macs and farts like a bicycle horn. He also telekinetically swipes a toke from Flash's lit joint, levitates, and asks, "Flash, will you always be a dork?"

Director Ken Wiederhorn also made the slob romp supreme *King Frat* (1979). The horror movie clip the kids watch in *Meatballs Part II* is from Wiederhorn's 1977 fright flick *Shock Waves*, cinema's one good Nazi zombie movie. *Meatballs Part II* is a triumph all around—onward with the nuttiness!

MEATBALLS III: SUMMER JOB [1986]

DIR. GEORGE MENDELUK; W/PATRICK DEMPSEY, SALLY KELLERMAN, SHANNON TWEED, ISABELLE MEJIAS

VIRGIN ▣ PSYCHO BIKER ▣ DWARF ▣ SUPERNATURAL SEX ▣ SPEEDBOAT GANG ▣ WET T-SHIRT CONTEST

Early on, *Meatballs III: Summer Job* establishes itself as one to watch, as Patrick Dempsey, in nerd glasses, aims the title of the book he's reading right into the camera: *How to Score with Tons of Horny Chicks*. The extra-mile inclusion of the words *Tons of Horny* spells this film's relation to subtlety straight away.

Dempsey is Rudy Gerner, the outcast kid immortalized by Chris Makepeace in 1979's original *Meatballs*. Although eight years separate the films, Rudy looks about twenty now, but he's only supposed to be fourteen. Either way, he has had a rough go after leaving the tutelage of his mentor Tripper (Bill Murray). Superseding even *Meatballs*' own "Spaz" on the nebbish scale, Rudy is a stumbling, bumbling, desperate schlub hellbent on losing his virginity to anyone he deems hotter than his punky-cute best friend Wendy (Isabelle Mejias). She, of course, is in love with him. Thus, Rudy has become a dork *and* a douche.

To escape a town of bullies who construct wagers around Rudy's inability to control his erections, our hero takes a summer gig as at Mean Gene's, a rough-and-tumble biker bar on a party-hearty waterfront. Mean Gene (Canadian pro wrestler George Buza) is the roughest motorcycle maniac on the arena. He chews beer bottles and cracks skulls in defense of his old lady, the Love Goddess (Shannon Tweed), whom he keeps sequestered away from the rabble.

After this primo teen sex comedy setup, *Meatballs III* spices the recipe by stirring in Sally Kellerman as brassy dame Roxy DuJour, a freshly deceased porn star. She succumbed on the set of *E.A.T.-ME: The Sextra-Terrestrial* (could this be a through line to Meathead the Space Kid of *Meatballs Part II*?) but she has been dispatched back to earth as a ghost charged with doing a good deed so she can go to heaven. That good deed, she determines, will come in the form of getting Rudy laid.

Essentially, *Meatballs III* is atrocious, but its faithfulness as a "true" sequel and its smutty supernatural sex setup, bolstered by Sally holding nothing back in her extended Mae West impersonation, render the viewing experience mandatory. The idiotic, quasi-incest attempt at irony when the Love Goddess reveals she's actually Mean Gene's sister, and that he's protecting her from distractions while she studies for her PhD, is a nice, unnecessarily stupid touch.

MEATBALLS 4 [1992]

DIR. BOB LOGAN; W/COREY FELDMAN, JACK NANCE, SARAH DOUGLAS; JOHNNY COCKTAILS

SUMMER CAMP ◘ RICH JERKS ◘ SHOWER PEEPING ◘ THE BIG WATERSKIING CONTEST

Meatballs 4, a sequel-in-licensed-franchise-name only, began life as *Happy Campers*. Then the producers realized that all the film needed was the rights to use history's most beloved and cable-ready summer camp title. Little did they know that they would soon be unleashing history's most Corey Feldmanesque of all Corey Feldman movies.

Feldman stars as Ricky Wade, a Ferris-Bueller-esque wisecracking hotshot who, because he's the World's Greatest Summer Camp Water-Ski Instructor, also seems to have the 1992 version of Monster Energy Drink coursing through his veins. He has razor stubble, he has a closetful of neon Body Glove wet suits, and he has the post-Michael-Jackson-sleepover dance moves. He's got the kind of confidence that lets him just shout, when viewing a girl blow up an inflatable duck pool toy, "[I] wish *I* were a duck!"

Small surprise that Ricky has been hired to pump joie-de-summer into the counselors and staff of Camp Lakeside. The mood is glum, because the beloved dump stands to be swallowed by rich-bitch resort developer Monica Shavetts (Sarah Douglas, back from the Phantom Zone in *Superman II*). Daft, pop-eyed, herky-jerky Neil Peterson operates Camp Lakeside. He's so not willing to sell his beloved facility; he'll stake the deed on a big water-skiing contest. Jack Nance, best known as the lead in David Lynch's *Eraserhead*, plays Mr. Peterson. Is Nance weirder there or here? Like so many Lynchian conundrums, that's a puzzle perhaps not meant to be solved.

Meatballs 4 keeps up with Corey Feldman himself in antic energy, cutting frequently to the Feldster punctuating zingers with Groucho Marx–style eyebrow pumps. The hard, misshapen torso-orbs of its silicone-enhanced and frequently topless female cast parallel the star in overall anti-sexual "sexiness."

Lakeside suffers frequent invasions from Wes and Howie, two excruciatingly unpleasant preppy water-ski jocks from the rich-jerk rival camp, Twin Oaks. Remarkably, the actors portraying Wes and Howie sport real names that would way better fit their roles: Bojesse Christopher and J. Trevor Edmond. Even more amazing is that Victor, *Meatballs 4*'s resident big, fat party animal, is played by a guy named Johnny Cocktails! Five years later, this Hawaiian-shirted blubber bucket was emceeing a Jell-O wrestling night at a Hollywood strip club, and I was there. Imagine if only Johnny had licensed the name, he could have called the event *Meatballs 5* and continued the jubilant degradation of the legacy.

Melvin: Son of Alvin [1984]

aka Foreplay; Girl-Toy

DIR. JOHN EASTWAY; W/GERRY SONT, LENITA PSILLAKIS, GRAEME BLUNDELL

VIRGIN ▣ AEROBICS ▣ DRIVE-IN MOVIES ▣ CUSTOM VANS

The raunchy 1973 Aussie comedy *Alvin Purple*, aka *The Sex Therapist*, proved to be a considerable "Ozploitation" hit, begetting the 1974 sequel *Alvin Rides Again!* and a 1976 TV series spin-off. Following the *Porky's* T&A feeding frenzy, the filmmakers sensed renewed potential and trotted out their franchise for a final go, *Melvin: Son of Alvin*.

Melvin Purple (Gerry Sont), like his old man Alvin (Graeme Blundell), is a lass-magnet supreme, automatically inspiring every woman he meets to hurl herself at him. Knowing how the gift complicated his dad's life—and the previous two movies and TV show—Melvin prefers to avoid human contact. Alas, Mel's best laid plans for not getting laid go kablooey once he comes across Greek glamourpuss Gloria (Lenita Vangellis).

The unique Australian energy that bubbles through the original *Alvin Purple* films (and through Barry Humphries's beer-puking *Barry McKenzie* boot-stompers) elevates *Melvin* to an enjoyably idiotic level. The movie's inherent fun spills out with an infectious and inane title song, bouncy nudity, gross-stuff-to-the-face gags, and the final revelation of Mel's pop as the leader of his own cult—the Purple People.

Midnight Madness [1980]

DIRS. MICHAEL NANKIN, DAVID WECHTER; W/DAVID NAUGHTON, MICHAEL J. FOX, STEPHEN FURST, EDDIE DEEZEN

SCAVENGER HUNT ▣ VIDEO ARCADE ▣ CUSTOM VAN ▣ SWIMMING IN VAT OF BEER

Midnight Madness contains no sex, no nudity, no drugs, and is a production of Walt Disney Studios. Yet here in teen movie hell it firmly belongs, only the second Disney film saucy enough to garner a PG rating—the previous year's *The Black Hole* arrived at the mark first, for its slight violence.

Midnight Madness was a genuine cult sensation in the early 1980s, due to saturation HBO airings that inspired countless kids to imitate the scavenger hunt undertaken in the movie. Many of those same kids would soon escalate to imitating the antics in *Porky's* and *Private School*, so *Midnight Madness* can be considered a gateway to the decade's teen sex comedy obsession.

College gaming maestro Leon (Alan Solomon) devises an all-night treasure hunt around Los Angeles that attracts various color-coordinated teams of teen movie archetypes. Adam (David Naughton) heads up the heroic nice guys (and girl). Harold (Stephen Furst, putting a dark spin on his *Animal House* role as Flounder) leads the cheating villains. Lavitas (Brad Wilkin) fronts the meathead athletes. Donna (Maggie Roswell) captains the sorority sisters, among whom are Peggy and Lulu (Betsy Lynn Thompson and Carol Gwynn Thompson), a pair of obese twins in Dom DeLuise–style "fat-guy hats" (also look for these Thompson twins in *Hamburger: The Motion Picture*). Most importantly, the nerds follow team leader Wesley (Eddie Deezen). Everyone runs around looking for stuff. Along the way they find Michael J. Fox, who makes a charming movie debut as a pipsqueak criminal.

In terms of pacing and zaniness, *Midnight Madness* has aged appallingly. Still, it's near humanly impossible to dislike this film. The cast is irresistible across the board, especially the stunning amped-up nerd archetype Eddie Deezen. Paul Reubens assumes his Pee-Wee Herman persona as the cowboy-suited proprietor of a video arcade. The silky, bass-popping, horn-heavy semi-disco title song is a perfect example of music that only existed in movies at dawn of the 1980s. Anyone with a clue will find this film on their watch list—and, unlike a lot of movies in this book, that decree applies equally here to five-year-olds.

Miracle Beach [1992]

DIR. SKOTT SNIDER; W/DEAN CAMERON, AMI DOLENZ, FELICITY WATERMAN, PAT MORITA

GENIE IN A BIKINI ▫ BEACH HOUSE ▫ BIKINIS ▫ MUSIC MONTAGES

Late-night basic cable channels played the shit out of *Miracle Beach*; not because this home-movie-budget supernatural romantic comedy was anything special, but just because it existed. As a result, a broad captive audience of up-too-late adolescents endured this antimatter in which Dean Cameron (Chainsaw from *Summer School*) plays Scotty McKay, a down-and-out beach bum whose luck changes for the miraculous after he rubs a bottle and frees a genie named Jeannie (Ami Dolenz of *She's Out of Control*).

Any lingering public affection for *Miracle Beach* defies the simple fact that the movie will eat your brain like cancer if watched at less than double speed. Still, nobody should blame the twelve-year-olds of 1992 for loving a film they risked super-maxi grounding to watch at 2 a.m. on a Saturday night. Now that a few decades have passed, though, get to bed!

Mischief [1985]

DIR. MEL DAMSKI; W/DOUG MCKEON, KELLY PRESTON, CHRIS NASH, CATHERINE MARY STEWART

VIRGINS ▫ PEEPING ▫ PRANKS ▫ DRIVE-IN ▫ THE BIG CHICKEN RACE

For some reason, an overwhelming number of R-rated teen sex comedies of the mid-1980s take place in the 1950s. *Mischief* specifically names 1956, while many other examples are content to half-assedly conjure a Eisenhower-era mist, errantly punctured by '60s pop songs (as in *Sweater Girls*) or marred by a simple mistake like a '70s flick on the screen at the drive-in (as in *Screwballs*).

To its 1950s credit, *Mischief* earns points both for soundtrack accuracy and for when the gang goes to the drive-in movies and views *Rebel Without a Cause* (1955). Likewise, the movie's art direction draws spot-on from Norman Rockwell Americana, presenting pristine Nelsonville, Ohio, as a buzz-cut-and-poodle-skirt pastel paradise—filtered for 1985 audience purposes through a fine strainer of *Porky's*-esque filth.

Jonathan Bellah (Doug McKeon), the new kid in Nelsonville, falls hard all over for pointedly named bombshell next door Marilyn (Kelly Preston). He also befriends motorbiking-by-his-own-rules type Gene (Chris Nash), who has a thing for class sweetheart Bunny Miller (Catherine Mary Stewart). Bespectacled Rosalie (Jami Gertz) is a nerdy wallflower who just might remove her glasses by the end to reveal that she's a covert knockout. All these nice people are harassed and bedraggled by town bully Kenny (D. W. Brown).

The drive-in excursion goes along with pickup basketball, horseback riding, bicycle tomfoolery, a state fair double date, backseat groping, and a reenactment of *Rebel Without a Cause*'s "chickie run" car race toward a cliff. Nobody dies, so technically nobody wins the race. Amidst that squeaky cleanliness and potential vehicular homicide, *Mischief* busts out a decidedly R-rated nude scene where Kelly Preston's all-points nakedness sends Doug McKeon flailing backward out her second-story bedroom window. Fortunately, the grass was a lot softer back in 1956.

Clockwise from top left: *Tumbling into some* Mischief *(1985); Teen movie pop art for* Modern Girls *(1986); A very Disneyesque poster variation for* My Bodyguard (1980); *1980s class shows itself for* My Chauffeur *(1986), a debatable hit for Crown International Pictures; School's IN with* My Tutor (1983); My Science Project *(1985), with its unattributed and possibly fabricated pull quote.*

Modern Girls [1986]

DIR. JERRY KRAMER; W/DAPHNE ZUNIGA, VIRGINIA MADSEN, CYNTHIA GIBB, CLAYTON ROHNER

SUNSET STRIP ▪ **NEW WAVE** ▪ **ROCK STAR**

Modern Girls took a bold risk using an ad campaign that suggested its leads—Daphne Zuniga (*The Sure Thing*), Virginia Madsen (*Class*), and Cynthia Gibb (the TV series *Fame*)—would perhaps step beyond the teen material for which they were known. Rendered as an eye-grabbing comic panel in the style of pop artist Roy Lichtenstein, the movie poster depicts three female pulp romance characters with gorgeously rendered flesh: a sultry, preening blonde; a red-lipped redhead kissing a hunk with blue-black hair; and a weeping beauty whose speech bubble decrees: "Never stand in line. Never buy your own drinks. Never stand next to a dweeb."

Zuniga, Madsen, and Gibb play young Sunset Strip club-hoppers who keep their radios tuned to KROQ to catch a whole bunch of Depeche Mode, Icehouse, the Call, and other mid-'80s synth pop. That's realistic. Eventually, they pick up and coerce smart but under-confident Clifford (Clayton Rohner) to soberly drive them from one nightspot after another while they get trashed on free drinks and an excess of Ecstasy, attempting to find any male to have sex with that isn't him. That's even more realistic.

Even with sideways jaunts involving Rohner in a second role as rock star Bruno X, and Gibb comically fleeing for her life after awakening on a pool table surrounded by biker sex criminals, *Modern Girls* is best as a travelogue of Los Angeles at the new wave juncture between Penelope Spheeris's first (punk) and second (metal) *Decline of Western Civilization* documentaries. As Janet Maslin ended her *New York Times* review: "*Modern Girls* isn't notable for anything but its crassness, which is exceptionally complete...it might be worth putting in a time capsule, right beside *Ferris Bueller's Day Off*. Twenty years from now, no one will believe life was ever lived this way."

Morgan Stewart's Coming Home [1987]

DIR. ALAN SMITHEE (PAUL AARON AND TERRY WINSOR); W/JON CRYER, VIVEKA DAVIS, LYNN REDGRAVE, PAUL GLEASON

RICH KID ▪ **HORROR GEEK** ▪ **MUSICAL NUMBER**

Here's the concept of *Morgan Stewart*: Duckie from *Pretty in Pink* plays Ferris Bueller for an audience of no one. Jon Cryer takes on the title role, wailing and flailing as a boarding school wisenheimer. He has been summoned back to the family mansion by his overbearing, frou-frou mom (Lynn Redgrave) to aid with the congressional reelection campaign of his stuffed-shirt old man (Nicholas Pryor).

Materialist wish fulfillment packs the screen in the form of personal helicopters, hallway motorbike rides, and horror fanatic Morgan's mega-awesome warehouse of monster movie memorabilia. When Viveka Davis enters the story as Emily, a cute blonde who Morgan meets in line to get zombie filmmaker George Romero's autograph, the picture tilts over into total fantasy. No girls stood in line for George Romero's autograph back in 1987. Trust me.

Director Terry Winsor, who previously made the U.K. cult fave *Party Party* (1983), abandoned ship mid-filming. Paul Aaron, helmer of Chuck Norris's *A Force of One* (1979) and Wings Hauser's *Deadly Force* (1983), finished the job. Upon completion, he asked for the standard Directors Guild ten-foot-pole "Alan Smithee" credit.

The summer of 1987 proved to be a cruel mistress for Mr. Jon Cryer. Audiences either ignored him as Morgan Stewart, and/or also opted to walk briskly past the open door across the multiplex where he appeared as Lenny Luthor, Lex's daffy nephew, in the nearly (and properly) forgotten *Superman IV: The Quest for Peace*.

Mugsy's Girls [1985]

aka Delta Pi

DIR. KEVIN BRODIE; W/ LAURA BRANIGAN, RUTH GORDON, JOANNA DIERCK, EDDIE DEEZEN

SORORITY ▫ SASSY OLD LADY ▫ MUD WRESTLING ▫ EDDIE DEEZEN

In 1984, at the absolute peak of her musical and cultural superstardom, singer Cyndi Lauper cast her lot with the World Wrestling Federation. A *Newsweek* cover story the previous year had lauded Lauper as a challenging and artistic alternative to her "bimbo" competition, Madonna. Lauper's formula included her creative use of kitsch, such as having wrestling hothead Captain Lou Albano portray her dad in the "Girls Just Wanna Have Fun" video. Then all of a sudden, Lauper seemed to trade MTV for the WWF full time; appearing as a regular foil for Rowdy Roddy Piper and occasionally climbing in the ring alongside Cap'n Lou. Lauper's fans were baffled and she never again kept pace with Madonna.

Around the same time, Laura Branigan, a more conventional Top 40 songbird, scored a number of radio smashes ("Gloria," "Solitaire," "Self-Control") and then also, bizarrely, gambled her burgeoning stardom on the potential of professional wrestling. Rather than hop in with Hulk Hogan and his lot, though, Branigan opted to don the tights herself and play a splattered grappler in the low-blow mud-wrestling sorority farce, *Mugsy's Girls*.

Specifically, Branigan stars in *Mugsy's Girls* as a Delta Pi sorority sister Monica. Beloved zany-old-lady cult star Ruth Gordon (*Harold and Maude, My Bodyguard*) plays Mugsy, the chapter's housemother. Branigan is likeable as an actress and laughably older than, let us say, "college age." Gordon shrieks and whoops and socks it to everybody like she always does, only dirtier than usual given the R rating and her frequent proximity to near nude females clobbering one another in vats of wet soil.

With a loan shark looking to collect on Delta Pi's debts, Monica and Mugsy convince the other coeds to raise funds by way of a whipped-cream wrestling contest. The girls don bikinis, the box office brings in big bank, and among those cheering and leering ringside is Lane, a livewire promoter (to say the least) portrayed to perfection by the mighty Eddie Deezen.

Lane informs the Delta Pi's that if they swap dairy products of earthen glop, he can put them on the road to the international mud-wrestling championship in fabulous Las Vegas. He'll act as their agent, while Mugsy will handle management duties. The Delta Pi's dive deep into their new non-NCAA-sanctioned sport and ultimately have to make a mess against the Nevada Nasties, the crème-de-la-crème of down-and-dirty mud-wrestling cabals.

Amidst numerous knockout slop bouts that indicate *Mugsy's Girls* may well be the passion project of some very singular fetishists, bits of romance bloom on the road, the team gets offered $5,000 to take a dive, and Eddie Deezen shares screen time with Ruth Gordon in a match-up that somehow didn't spontaneously combust the earth what with all that crackpot charisma suddenly coming together.

The tagline of *Mugsy's Girl*'s—"First Mud!"—invokes *Rambo*, but the payoff, as is not likely a spoiler, is pure *Rocky*. It was the Stallone decade, after all, and that very much extended to mud-wrestling.

Alas, despite how enjoyable she and the movie at hand may be, film stardom eluded Laura Branigan. *Mugsy's Girls* went straight to VHS (a rarity at the time, particularly with name stars) and, from there, *American Top 40* radio host Casey Kasem never again uttered Laura Branigan's name in conjunction with a contemporary single.

Tragically, in 2004, Laura Branigan died at age 53 from a cerebral aneurism. One is loath to imagine she was thinking about *Mugsy's Girls* when it hit, but the possibility is just too credible not to rule out—eh, all you *Forensics Files* fans?

My Bodyguard [1980]

DIR. TONY BILL; W/CHRIS MAKEPEACE, ADAM BALDWIN, MATT DILLON, RUTH GORDON

NEW KID 📼 BULLIES 📼 THE BIG FIGHT 📼 WACKY GRANDMA

Heartfelt, funny, powerfully sad in spots, and ultimately uplifting, *My Bodyguard* casts Chris Makepeace (Rudy Gerner from *Meatballs*) as Clifford Peache, a poor little rich high school transplant who relocates to Chicago to live with his single dad (Martin Mull), who manages a luxury hotel, and his zany pepper-tongued grandmother (Ruth Gordon). Instantly upon pulling up to Lake View High School in a stretch limo, Clifford is beset by bullies. Leading the meanies is Melvin Moody (Matt Dillon), and he runs a nifty schoolyard protection racket; kids who suffer his routine abuse and fork over their lunch money to him and his goons will be shielded from Ricky Linderman (Adam Baldwin). Though he keeps to himself, Linderman, Lake View High's resident hulking psychopath, is rumored to have murdered several people, including his own kid brother.

Clifford hatches the novel idea of hiring Ricky to defend him. Ricky initially refuses, but relents as the two become friends. Together, they scour junkyards for a rare cylinder to complete Ricky's motorcycle restoration project. Clifford invites his pal up to meet his dad and grandma, who notices Ricky trying to hide scars on his wrist from a suicide attempt. Grandma gently places her hand on the troubled tough kid's wound and whispers, "You're among friends, Ricky." The moment is both deeply heartfelt and evocative of Gordon's own revelation of a concentration camp tattoo in her best-known work, *Harold and Maude* (1971).

The boys grow close, and after Ricky thwarts a Moody attack, Clifford calls his knight in torn dungarees "my bodyguard." The title sticks.

Unlike the John Hughes movies which also took place in Chicago a few years later, *My Bodyguard* delivers a perception and portrayal of class issues between unlikely partners that feels true and never condescends. Clifford lives in a lakefront penthouse and travels to school by chauffeur, but he is the polar opposite of the too-wise, too-cool Ferris Bueller. Clifford is savvy enough to come up with the bodyguard strategy, but he's also confused, lost, and vulnerable—not to mention that he needs a bodyguard.

Urban "white trash" Ricky is no salt-of-the-friggin'-earth, tell-it-like-it-is noble knuckle-dragger on the order of Judd Nelson's Bender character in *The Breakfast Club*. He's lonely and shattered, burdened by a heartbreaking secret that has pushed him into isolation. He hides from human contact behind a ticking time-bomb image, and we can perceive the hurt that's underneath.

My Bodyguard also comes heavy on the laughs, largely thanks to Matt Dillon. He's truly intimidating as Moody, but ups the comic aspects of blowhard bravado to a flawless fury. Joan Cusack is great as a brainy Moody victim and potential romantic possibility for Ricky. Admirably, the movie leaves that question unresolved. Paul Quandt is the real riot, though. He plays Clifford's stilted, world-weary pal Carson, delivering every deadpan line in a voice that suggests he has never once blown his nose.

Though the film was a hit, *My Bodyguard* came a little early and aimed a little young, and was somewhat buried in public consciousness after the '80s onslaught of high school raunch flicks and less artful John Hughes efforts. Plus the movie was a little too raw, too real, and cut a little too deep to throw on in the background of pizza and smuggled-beer rec room party. You could say *My Bodyguard* was an adult film trapped in an adolescent body, and so didn't fit in with the popular crowd—but what legitimately cool kid ever does?

My Chauffeur [1986]

DIR. DAVID BEAIRD; W/DEBORAH FOREMAN, SAM J. JONES, PENN AND TELLER

MADONNA FASHIONS 📼 OIL SHEIK 📼 GROUPIES 📼 PUNKS 📼 HILLBILLIES

"Some women will, some won't...some men do, some don't. This driver might go everywhere, do anything...for your sizzling backseat pleasure." *My Chauffeur* offers this come-on in its movie poster tagline, typical of claims made by Crown International Pictures. Bless them.

Your chauffeur in question is Casey Meadows, played with antic energy by the former *Valley Girl* herself, Deborah Foreman. She is a restaurant dishwasher given to wearing neon Madonna garb, and is mysteriously recruited to work for a limousine service by a tycoon referred to only as Mr. Witherspoon (E. G. Marshall). Casey's arrival irritates the company's all-male, all-crusty staff of old bastards. No crusty old bastard is more flustered than fleet manager McBride (Howard Hesseman).

My Chauffeur spins Casey into a series of comedic escapades. First, she revives British rock star Cat Fight (Leland Crooke) from a dope-and-groupie-induced stupor to deliver him to his big concert. Later, Casey pilots a backseat orgy involving silent oil sheik Abdul (Teller), his motormouthed assistant Bone (Penn Jillette), and a gaggle of good-time gals. Penn self-reflexively bruises the fourth wall by announcing: "Now it's time for the gratuitous nudity!"—just when the clothes come off.

Writer-director David Beaird (*The Party Animal* [1984]) reveals his classic 1930s screwball comedy ambitions when Casey comes across heartbroken businessman Battle Witherspoon, played by the former Flash Gordon himself, Sam J. Jones. After getting dumped in the back of the limo, Battle gets catastrophically wasted, runs naked in public, and says heinous things to Casey. Later, when the car breaks down and Battle carries our injured heroine through a rainstorm to a mountain cabin, the inevitable falls into place—spiked with a potential incest twist.

After a bit of foundering after *Valley Girl*, real-life high school cheerleader turned model turned actress Deborah Foreman looked poised for big things with the coming of *My Chauffeur*. *Variety* gushed: "Foreman is a real find, fitting into the mold of Goldie Hawn, Carole Lombard, and Claudette Colbert." Similarly, the *Los Angeles Times* deemed Deb "a New Wave Carole Lombard crossed with early Shirley MacLaine." The massive film industry convention ShoWest bestowed on Foreman its award for "Most Promising New Star of 1986." After that, though, her career tanked harder than the limo that sets *My Chauffeur*'s romantic plot in motion.

Considering that all this hoopla occurred during the era when ingénue Pia Zadora's billionaire husband endured rumors of "buying" the 1981 Best New Star Golden Globe Award for her, a scent of skullduggery wafts around all the hubbub. Compounding such suspicions, Crown International Pictures "goofed" in regard to *My Chauffeur*'s opening weekend financial gross in January 1986. According to a July 24, 2017, article on the blog *Film School Rejects*, the company reportedly announced inaccurate numbers that placed the film atop Variety's Monday-morning box office chart, where it usurped the actual number one, Steven Spielberg's *The Color Purple*. The gaffe came to light quickly, but not before *Entertainment Tonight* and coast-to-coast newspaper entertainment pages reported how the little-automotive-sex-farce-that-could had bested a heap of studio blockbusters. While the gall of Crown International Pictures and their wild West attitude to the movie business seems charming in hindsight, *Film School Rejects* reports that the bogus-box-office blowback took a severe toll on Deborah Foreman, as *The Tonight Show* allegedly canceled an appearance she had scheduled. Deborah herself addresses the controversy in an interview included on Vinegar Syndrome's 2017 deluxe Blu-ray release of *My Chauffeur*. Remarkably, she remains chipper.

My Man Adam [1985]

DIR. ROGER L. SIMON; W/RAPHAEL SBARGE, PAGE HANNAH, CHARLIE BARNETT, DAVE THOMAS

NERDS ▫ VALLEY GIRLS ▫ YUPPIES ▫ MALE STRIPPERS ▫ MEMBER'S ONLY JACKETS

In the early 1980s, congenitally hilarious street comedian Charlie Barnett drew massive, convulsive crowds to impromptu midday performances in New York's Washington Square Park. Show business took note of Barnett's abilities, and repeatedly tried to find a place for him. He was cast on *Saturday Night Live*, but quit when it became clear he had trouble reading. Eventually, he starred in *D.C. Cab* (1983), guested on *Miami Vice*, and made *My Man Adam*. Afterward, everything went downhill; Charlie died in 1996 from complications arising from addiction issues.

As twenty-six-year-old high school senior Leroy, Barnett narrates *My Man Adam*. His obscene word choices and jarring use of racial epithets jolt a spark of enjoyably wrongheaded life into this otherwise boring and bewildering muddle. Otherwise, the focus falls on Adam (Raphael Sbarge), the teen of the title, who delivers pizzas for his family business and fantasizes about a dream girl who suddenly becomes flesh in the form of new student Sabrina (Page Hannah).

While attempting to impress Sabrina, Adam is embroiled in a murder conspiracy, resulting in out-of-place violence. A subplot concerning the high school government election pits a teenage black Republican versus a teenage Black Panther, complete with voter intimidation courtesy of a black youth gang that works at an auto chop shop specializing in stolen rides. Not a moment of this out-of-nowhere racial madness is captivating at all, which is a real achievement.

Writer-director Roger L. Simon aims high, wedging '80s cultural satire into a cluttered and confusing 80 minutes. Boy, does this movie ever stick it to Reaganomics, Chippendales dancers, and gourmet pizza! Still, *My Man Adam* wastes not only Charlie Barnett, but also the promising cast, including Dave Thomas, Veronica Cartwright, Austin Pendleton, and, as a detention-happy school administrator, Chris Elliott.

My Science Project [1985]

DIR. JONATHAN R. BETEUL; W/JOHN STOCKWELL, DANIELLE VON ZERNECK, FISHER STEVENS, DENNIS HOPPER

NERDS ▫ COOL TEACHER ▫ AMOK HIGH-SCHOOL SCIENCE EXPERIMENT

My Science Project opened in theaters during summer 1985, smack between *Weird Science* and *Real Genius*. This combination of smart-kid-word titles is actually a Disney movie, and a limp one at that, disguised to resemble those other saucier and sexually aware teen flicks. In this movie, crafty teens accidentally convert their boom box radio into a time portal, bringing post-nuclear mutants and a *Tyrannosaurus rex* to rampage in their school gym. Bill & Ted would handle a similar prospect to properly clever and hilarious effect a few years later.

An uncredited banner declaration proclaimed this "The funniest sci-fi movie of the summer." That bit of gonzo promotion is a fine carny touch, but the liveliest aspect of the film is pre–*Blue Velvet* Dennis Hopper as a hippie science teacher. Not to be outdone on the promotional front, French marketers falsified *My Science Project* as a combination of *Back to the Future* and *Ghostbusters* by renaming it *TimeBusters*.

My Tutor [1983]

DIR. GEORGE BOWERS; W/CAREN KAYE, MATT LATTANZI, KEVIN MCCARTHY, CRISPIN GLOVER

VIRGIN ▫ (FRENCH) TEACHER ▫ AEROBICS ▫ SKINNY-DIPPING ▫ THE BIG EXAM

Two years after *Private Lessons* blasted open the box office path for the teen movie comedy 1980s, *My Tutor* remade essentially the same movie down to the detail of the amorous instructor being hired to boost the virginal student's French class grades. *Ooh-la-la*...whatever works.

The biggest tweak to *My Tutor* from *Private Les-*

sons is that the former's leads are more traditionally "Hollywood hot." Well, that and Crispin Glover arrives to play the main dude's comic relief pal here, jettisoning the wisenheimer fat-ass sidekick from *Private Lessons* and replacing him with...indeed, Crispin Glover.

Matt Lattanzi, baring all the chiseled features and hunkadelic muscles that would make him the boytoy Mr. Olivia Newton-John after appearing with her in *Xanadu* the following year, is just fine as high school senior Bobby Chrystal. He's easy to buy as a kid flunking French, but it's ludicrous to imagine that, as the movie establishes early, he has never gotten laid.

Caren Kaye, on the other hand, is entirely believable as Terry Green. She is precisely the sort of naturally busty, maybe not-so-naturally blonde, raspy-voiced, thirtysomething SoCal aerobics enthusiast who would be hired as a live-in tutor by Bobby's millionaire father (*Invasion of the Body Snatchers* hysteric Kevin McCarthy).

Once Terry is caught within the confines of the Chrystal compound, her midnight backyard pool skinny-dips lead to her boffing Bobby, which leads to him falling for her, which leads to heartbreak. Soon enough, the word "hooker" is angrily shouted, which leads to horny healing and, ultimately, a happy ending for all—even Crispin Glover!

My Tutor is nothing but efficient—and fun. McCarthy is a crackup as the cranky dad. Caren Kaye delivers a star-caliber performance and sex bomb energy to the screen. The following year, Kaye played the mom on the cult NBC series *It's Your Move*, a brilliantly vicious sitcom that pitted scheming teen hustler Jason Bateman against David Garrison as his equally ruthless neighbor/teacher/mom's boyfriend. During *It's Your Move*'s 1984–85 run, *My Tutor* ran relentlessly on cable TV, occasionally even on the same night as the show. As a result, numerous young viewers who changed channels got *quite* an education.

Mystic Pizza [1988]

DIR. DONALD PETRIE; W/ANNABETH GISH, JULIA ROBERTS, LILI TAYLOR, VINCENT D'ONOFRIO

VIRGIN ▣ MINIMUM WAGE JOB ▣ ETHNIC FAMILY ▣ PIZZA

Mystic Pizza takes place entirely in the Connecticut seaport town of Mystic, and mostly in the eatery of the title where the waitresses are the movie's three leads: sisters Kat (Annabeth Gish) and Daisy Araújo (Julia Roberts), and their pal Jojo Barbosa (Lili Taylor).

Kat has been accepted to Yale on a partial scholarship and yearns to travel the world as an astronomer. Daisy is still in high school and she's boy-crazy. Jojo is hot to hop into bed with her fisherman beau Bill (Vincent D'Onofrio), but, being Catholic, he insists they wait until marriage.

Yes, *Mystic Pizza* is an '80s teen movie where a young male refuses to give up his virginity on principal, and not as a gimmick or comical exaggeration. Bill's motivation stems from his and all the other characters being Portuguese-Americans, easily one of the least seen (and thus least stereotyped) immigrant groups in Hollywood.

Beyond this unique sociological aspect of *Mystic Pizza*, the movie caught on quick based on the strength of its cast. Before her iconic breakout in *Pretty Woman* (1990), Julia Roberts was first crowned as a star here. Annabeth Gish adeptly communicates the early 20s burn of having one foot out the door but finding a large, loud family clinging to the other leg. Lili Taylor establishes her enduring on-screen oddball persona.

Mystic Pizza is topped with heaps of extra charm, and peppered with a palpable bit of believable bigotry. (Listen for a crash course in Portuguese slurs.) Best of all, the running time is padded with delicious documentary footage of fresh pies coming out of the hot oven and being expertly sliced. When a snooty TV food critic raves about the pizza at Mystic being "superb," you will believe it. No spoiler alert necessary.

National Lampoon's Last Resort
National Lampoon's Senior Trip
The Naughty Cheerleader
Nerds of a Feather ▫ New Girl
A Night in Heaven
A Night in the Life of Jimmy Reardon
Night of the Comet ▫ No Small Affair

National Lampoon's Last Resort (1994)

DIR. RAFAL ZIELINSKI; W/COREY FELDMAN, COREY HAIM, MAUREEN FLANNIGAN, ZELDA RUBINSTEIN

THE TWO COREYS ▫ TROPICAL ISLAND ▫ NOVELTY BAND ▫ EVIL BUSINESSMAN

National Lampoon's Last Resort unspools as a contest to determine how far the mighty hath fallen—and that goes for the stars, the director, and *National Lampoon*.

First comes the perilous plummet of the mighty Coreys, Feldman and Haim. A very long half decade past their teen heartthrob primes, they play Sam Carver and Dave Eisenhower, fired fast-food employees arriving at an island getaway. There they battle a greedy corporate land developer who wants to snatch paradise away from Sam's Uncle Rex (Geoffrey Lewis, Clint Eastwood's pal and Juliette's dad, accepting payment here for spending a couple weeks in the sun in a pirate costume).

Then comes the downward dive of mighty director Rafal Zielinski, a versatile filmmaker who tapped into teen sex comedy magic via *Screwballs* (1983) and *Valet Girls* (1987). With *Last Resort,* Zielinski is busted down to direct-to-video duty, overseeing Corey Feldman as he struts about in sleeveless black blazers and fedora hatbands—sans hat—around his head.

Next is the tumultuous tumble of *National Lampoon*. The late twentieth century's most important humor wellspring debuted its film division on a note of genius with *Animal House* (1978) and then stumbled repeatedly in the years ahead between *Vacation* movies, until finally, come the dawn of straight-to-tape crapioca, the once venerable name was slapped onto way too many crimes against motion picture technology. In *National Lampoon's Last Resort,* when Dave (Corey Haim) is smooched by sweet and sexy Sonja (Maureen Flannigan), he immediately looks into the camera and says, "Boom!" The movie loops that "Boom!" three times in instant succession before jumping to a quick reaction shot from Sam and Uncle Rex before dropping in a fourth repeat of Haim's "Boom!"

All in all, the big "How Hath the Mighty Fallen?" competition in *National Lampoon's Last Resort* is a tie for last—excepting Corey Feldman. He essentially remade this abhorrence as *South Beach Academy* (1996), and, even today, he still gets to be Corey Feldman. Boom!

National Lampoon's Senior Trip [1995]

DIR. KELLY MAKIN; W/JEREMY RENNER, NICOLE DE BOER, MATT FREWER, TOMMY CHONG

SENIOR TRIP 📼 SEXY NERD GIRL 📼 PRANKS 📼 BEER BASH AT THE PRINCIPAL'S HOUSE

In the timeline of teen movie hell, this is the end point. Scraped from the bottom of a big filthy barrel in the mid-1990s, just as the sounds of 14.4-baud modems began chirping alongside home computers everywhere, *National Lampoon's Senior Trip* is the absolute final vomit-clogged death fart of the theatrically released teen sex comedy's classic R-rated era.

The genre commenced more or less in 1973 with the behemoth success of *American Graffiti* and *The Cheerleaders*; peaked about a decade later by way of *Porky's, Fast Times, Valley Girl,* and *Risky Business*; and finally flamed out on a high note in 1993 via *Dazed and Confused*. Two years after that, *Senior Trip* oozed forth as nothing more—maybe even a lot less—than the classic teen sex comedy era's prom night dumpster baby.

This unfunny nothingness also finally bankrupted the *National Lampoon* brand. The residual cinematic goodwill from *Animal House* (1978)—or even, for fuck's sake, *Class Reunion* (1982)—was finally squandered like a car wash king's inheritance on a spring break road trip. The once mighty satirical magazine's name was doomed forever after to the we-hate-our-audience direct-to-video cellar. (*Van Wilder* [2002] was a different time and place, and even that led nowhere.)

Senior Trip's plot regards an Ohio high school cabal of slackers, misfits, goons, and losers, all given a detention assignment to pen letters to the U.S. president about the state of education. When an essay by the class brain is accidentally mixed among the doodling of the resident droolers, they all win a jaunt to the nation's capital. Matt Frewer (aka Max Headroom) plays the stressed principal. Tommy Chong is the "magic bus" driver. The Kids in the Hall's Kevin McDonald is a harried Trekkie who catches fire after the fat kid farts too close to an eternal flame on J. Edgar Hoover's grave.

Nothing in *Senior Trip* is as clever as the movie's poster, which pictures the seated statue at the Lincoln Memorial wearing sunglasses and holding a can of brew under the words: "Four score and seven beers ago...." And thus the teen sex comedy goes down on history.

The Naughty Cheerleader [1970] aka How Did a Nice Girl Like You Get Into This Business?

DIR. WILL TREMPER; W/BARBI BENTON, BRODERICK CRAWFORD, HUGH HEFNER, KLAUS KINSKI

MAJORETTE 📼 DIRTY OLD MEN

Naughty or not is beside the point, as no cheerleaders at all appear in *The Naughty Cheerleader*. The closest this sexless West German sex comedy gets to pom-poms is when nineteen-year-old *Playboy* empress of 1970 Barbi Benton appears with a marching band as a majorette, twirling a baton. The remainder of the movie is a typical European soft-core lark, with wide-eyed nubile Barbi bumping into one leering letch after another—including freak film legend Klaus Kinski and her real-life benefactor Hugh Hefner.

Please note: Barbi Benton does not appear nude in a motion picture called *The Naughty Cheerleader*! In fact, *The Naughty Cheerleader* is the only theatrically released motion picture in which Barbi Benton appears without getting nude. The film producers of Cold War–era Germany should have been brought before a second Nuremberg tribunal to answer and apologize for this miscarriage of sweaty-palmed expectations.

NERDS OF A FEATHER [1989]

DIRS. GARY GRAVER, ROMEO M.; W/ROMEO M., PAT MCCORMICK, KATHLEEN CONWAY, CHARLES PIERCE

NERDS 📼 VIRGIN 📼 DWARVES

Following the Troma logo, which is never a good sign, this particular fecal heap is a teen sex-adjacent James Bond spoof. Codirector and "Flyaway" theme song cowriter Mario Romeo Milano stars under the billing "Romeo M." Filmed with a possibly broken camcorder on Venice Beach, Mr. M. plays a typical young movie dorkus who becomes transformed into a suave superspy.

Feather's cast includes vintage comedian Pat McCormick (Johnny Carson's longtime head writer); drag legend Charles Pierce (as Granny Greenberg); and a commando squad of "Little Russian Soldiers" that includes Tony Cox (the hench-elf in *Bad Santa* [2003]). That credit is more entertaining than anything in the film.

Lead director Gary Graver is a hyper-prolific exploitation maven. He started as a grindhouse cinematographer (*Satan's Sadists*; *Dracula vs. Frankenstein*; *Grand Theft Auto*), then made interesting theatrical porn films under the name Robert McCallum (*V: The Hot One*; *3 A.M.*; *The Ecstasy Girls*). He also helmed *Texas Lightning*, a PG-rated hicksploitation flick that boasts an on-screen nipple flash from Marcia Brady herself, Maureen McCormick. Graver has remained active in actual sex filmmaking, working in some capacity on hundreds of titles. None could be worse than *Nerds of a Feather*.

NEW GIRL [1985]

DIR. CHARLES ISON; W/BETH ABERNATHY, DUKE RIGHTIOUS, GUY CARSWELL, CRYSTAL DUNN

THE BIG COLLEGE BASKETBALL GAME 📼 FRAT 📼 RICH JERK 📼 COSTUMED EAGLE MASCOT

Be forewarned: The dog dies. He's a pug named Bomber, the mascot of wild-and-stinky frat house PU. He farts and grunts by way of human voice-over dubbing. Granted, he's over fifteen years old, and he dies relatively peacefully, but still—the demise of Bomber sets off the ultra-obscure *New Girl*. How is that not a bummer?

We meet Bomber in the company of his frat-mates: Belushoid beast Wilson (Willie Stratford Jr.); helium-pitched über-nerd Leonard (Tony Elwood); fuzzy-lipped wannabe ladykiller Troy (Shawn Curran); and an unidentified PU brother in full Native American garb. When uptight Beaumont College newspaper editor Chris (played by the improbably named Duke Rightious) happens by PU, Bomber drops a deuce on some important documents, prompting Chris to roar at him like a monster. Bomber drops dead of fright on the spot. Chris stuffs the stiff pug into his briefcase and books out of there.

Now Chris is on the run from the PUs, plus he's under fire after penning an editorial calling for the college to pull the plug on women's basketball. By remarkable coincidence, the team's star players, Julie (Beth Abernathy) and Ginger (Crystal Dunn) catch Chris with Bomber's carcass. Naturally, they blackmail him into dressing in drag and joining their all-female hoops squad as Krystal Katz. As in the 1993 Rodney Dangerfield kiddie soccer favorite *Ladybugs*, the dude in a dress elevates the girls' team to championship status.

New Girl keeps its various balls in the air with amusing amateurishness for a good while. In time, the agreeably idiotic gross-out campus farce flatlines out of sheer sump-skulled stupidity and an irritating lack of humor, nudity, or anything at all that would nullify a PG rating.

African American stand-up comic Kenny Howell supplies needed professional energy as Chris/Krystal's roommate. He really does preface a panicked runaway departure by addressing his shoes and saying: "Feets don't fail me now!" (please note: I'm just the messenger here). The PU alumni's full-scale military operation to recover Bomber with tanks, horses, and helicopters is funny. Stuffed somewhere in there is a swank Schaeffer beer cart

Clockwise from top left: The Naughty Cheerleader *(1970) is actually about a majorette!; the unlikely literary adaptation* A Night in the Life of Jimmy Reardon *(1988);* Night of the Comet *(1984) maintains an intense following;* A Night in Heaven *(1983), sort of an ancestor to* Magic Mike *(2012) where a lot of things went wrong.*

By the end, pug puppies Bomber Jr., and Bomber III join PU—*awwwww, cute*. Furthermore, his Krystal experience enlightens Chris, and all too quickly *New Girl* evaporates into undeserved oblivion. Whoops! There the movie goes now—right back down into the void, just like a cute mutt waiting to be rescued.

A Night in Heaven [1983]

DIR. JOHN G. AVILDSEN; W/CHRISTOPHER ATKINS, LESLEY ANN WARREN, ROBERT LOGAN, DENEY TERRIO

MALE STRIPPERS ▣ BAD TEACHER

With aerobics, mud wrestling, and foxy boxing reinventing female athleticism as dude spectator pastimes in the early 1980s, the simultaneous ascent of male strip clubs for female patrons proved a "turnabout of turn-ons is fair play" riposte. The big blow-dried-coif, silk jockstrap, bow-tie-with-no-shirt fashion fetish truly was a style whose time had come. The 1982 TV movie *For Ladies Only* with Gregory Harrison addressed this hunkadelic cultural hiccup, as did numerous sitcoms, typified by an episode of *Eight Is Enough* where the Bradford girls worry that brother Tommy (Willie Aames) may be moonlighting with a paper bag over his head as "The Unknown Stripper."

Although now dumbfounding to imagine, *A Night in Heaven* began as cinema's serious-minded attempt to examine this potentially loaded gender-swapping phenomenon (the *Magic Mike* movies would finally pull it off two decades later). Joan Tewkesbury, who wrote the brilliant screenplay for Robert Altman's *Nashville* (1975), moved to a Florida town where the phenomenon was exploding as she was penning her script. John G. Avildsen, who made *Rocky* (1976), signed on to direct. These high intentions shine through the final vapid muck of the final cut only in the form of one key character (a cuckolded husband) being a rocket scientist who quits his gig to protest the nuclear arms race. Otherwise, the whole mess is a slapdash of MTV music video editing and nonsensical post-*Flashdance* spandexsploitation.

Christopher Atkins (fresh from impregnating a teenage Brooke Shields in *The Blue Lagoon*) stars as Rick, a college student who struts and peels on stage as "Ricky the Rocket." Lesley Ann Warren is Faye Hanlon, Rick's married speech professor, who catches the Rocket in full bump-and-grind flight. She is transformed by a lap dance, and launches lustily with her pupil behind the back of her spaceship-engineer husband. Ricky then cheats on the cheating teacher, shows his drippy dink in the shower, and ends up nude on a sinking ship after the scientist shoots the hull full of holes. Deney Terrio, host of syndicated television's sensational *Dance Fever*, floats through some of the nightclub scenes, minus his one-two hoochie-mama cohost team, the Motion dancers.

Critics puked at the movie, and audiences stayed away from theaters as though the actual vomit was on every seat. Regardless, *A Night in Heaven*'s soundtrack produced two monster hits; Bryan Adams' instant classic last-dance-at-the-prom ballad "Heaven," and "Obsession," performed here by cowriters Holly Knight and Michael Des Barres. A year later, "Obsession" was retooled as a smash success a year later by the group Animotion. All these decades later, both songs remain in the public consciousness as surely as male strippers continue to wear bow ties with no shirt.

A Night in the Life of Jimmy Reardon [1988] aka Aren't You Even Gonna Kiss Me Goodbye?

DIR. WILLIAM RICHERT; W/RIVER PHOENIX, MEREDITH SALENGER, IONE SKYE, ANN MAGNUSON, MATTHEW PERRY

THE BIG SCHOOL DANCE ▣ MILF ▣ RICH JERKS ▣ BEATNIKS

A Night in the Life of Jimmy Reardon director William Richert adapted the movie's screenplay from his own autobiographical novel, *Aren't You Even Gonna Kiss Me Goodbye?* Despite his double-duty participation, Richert has long maintained that the River Phoenix high school romance romp that eventually bombed in theaters was mangled by the studio beyond the point of recognition.

Nearly a decade earlier, Richert helmed the cult political satire *Winter Kills* (1979), a lost film whose butchery by Hollywood powers-that-stifle is the stuff of legend. That a filmmaker would suffer such a one-two succession of suppressions, coupled with the inherent power of *Winter Kills*, renders Richert an intriguing and tragic figure. Unfortunately, *Jimmy Reardon* is not worth getting agitated over, unless you are an eighth-grade girl living in 1988 and *Tiger Beat* pinup River Phoenix is still five years from spazzing to death on the sidewalk outside the Viper Room on Sunset Boulevard.

The movie is set in 1962, but Phoenix plays the title role like a very late-1980s heartthrob. He is a high-school senior who longs to be a coffeehouse beat poet so he can wax sarcastic about his plastic-fantastic moneyed suburban Chicago surroundings. Hardheaded Pops Reardon (Paul Koslo) wants his son to go to business school instead.

Meanwhile, all the females along Lake Michigan want to screw young Mr. Reardon, including his upper-crust girlfriend Lisa (Meredith Salenger), adorable classmate Denise (Ione Skye), and hot-to-trot neighborhood divorcée Fickett (Ann Magnuson), who actually says the words, "Jimmy, I want to fuck you!" To-the-point dialogue notwithstanding, the movie takes place on just one night, and viewers feel the weight of all eight of those hours during the movie's skimpy 90-minute run time.

In 2016, William Richert released a reedited *Jimmy Reardon* director's cut, retitled after its source novel. Richert was right: his version is a noticeable improvement in terms of pacing and a general air of diminished dumbness. The botch belonged to the studio.

Night of the Comet [1984]

DIR. THOM EBERHARDT; W/CATHERINE MARY STEWART, KELLI MARONEY, ROBERT BELTRAN

STEPMOM ▪ MALL ▪ END OF THE WORLD

Review by Lisa Carver

Here's what happened. One night, a comet hit earth and turned every living thing to dust. A handful of people were unwittingly saved because for some reason they spent the night in a windowless steel building. However, the vents in their building allowed small amounts of corrosive dust inside, so after impact the dozen or so partially protected people are now turning pale and nasty and very slowly dying. They must find healthy survivors and destroy their brain activity, and hook their bodies up to machines to pump for blood transfusions.

Our two heroines—sisters—both survived because they were being bad. One was in a movie projection booth doing it with some gross guy; the other was sulking in a metal shed because she'd slapped her stepmother at a cocktail party in front of everyone. The stepmother full-on punched her in the mouth, so the daughter ran away from home as far as the backyard.

The first sister is a pinball champ and a wisecracker. Think Suzy Quatro. She has a perm and wears blazers or giant sweaters with shoulder pads. The other is rude and silly and Lolita-ish and an old hand at machine guns. Think Pinky Tuscadero. She smacks gum, wears spandex and cheerleader skirts and hooker eye shadow and lip gloss, and she's about fifteen. As for their sleazy stepmother, she was having an affair with the neighbor, and she ridiculed her brave husband, who was off fighting wars. She wore awesome jewelry like the cast of *Dallas*. Still, the comet killed her.

Once the sisters realize everyone around them has turned to dust, what do you think they decide to do? They head to the mall, of course, where everything is marked down to free. Once inside, they crank a beat box up to ten and put on their own fashion show. So far, this all makes sense, because in 1984 we were all shallow and whorey and child-abused and trying on identities and really into music (notably, the girls also go to a radio station).

The unhappy surprise is that the mall is not empty. Three male ghouls in sunglasses also decided that the shopping center was the perfect place for them to spend their remaining hours acting out sadistic psychotic fantasies—first on mannequins, then on our heroines. The guys even put on their *own* fashion show, where they dress up like Kraftwerk meets New Order. Again, young people had fun with identity back then. We didn't require anyone's recognition of who we truly were. Maybe we weren't truly anybody. Maybe we were untruly everybody, in succession.

No mention is made of the age difference between our shoulder-pads heroine and her on-screen *lovahs* in *Night of the Comet*, nor does anyone really care that the other heroine's stepmother punched her full-on in the face—not even the other heroine! As noted, we were whorey in 1984, and not just the white males. The patriarchy was there, and then just a general trickle-down life where most of Gen X got peed on. Like the characters in this movie, we didn't politicize music, fashion, sex, family dynamics, or film. We just did it. All of it. I wouldn't exactly call us happy, but we knew how to have a good time.

Rewatching *Night of the Comet* is a good time. The villains—scientists who tried to protect themselves from the dust but someone forgot to close the vent—are *so bad*. They *laugh* about destroying brain activity and draining blood out of the surviving children so that they can live just a few days more themselves. The cars in the movie are sleek and their owners are dead. All right! I take delight in *Night of the Comet*. I learn nothing. I'm not woke.

I may be the one human being approaching the age of fifty who believes millennials and young SJWs are cool and necessary. They're making their own revolution happen. They're upending it all, and that's more than we Gen Xers can say at this point. I even think destroying someone like Aziz Ansari's career because he doesn't read minds is an overcorrection that needs to happen. But I'd still rather be me. I can just plain like something. It doesn't have to likeable. It doesn't have to be right. It just has to bring me pleasure and delight.

No Small Affair [1984]

DIR. JERRY SCHATZBERG; W/JON CRYER, DEMI MOORE, GEORGE WENDT, ELIZABETH DAILY

NERD ▪ VIRGIN ▪ OLDER WOMAN ▪ BACHELOR PARTY ▪ HOT NERD GIRL

No Small Affair semi-psychically forecasts Demi Moore's role in *One Crazy Summer* (1986). In both cases, Demi plays struggling rock diva who gets a career boost from a high school goof who employs a unique talent to make her famous. In *Summer*, that's John Cusack as a cartoonist; here Jon Cryer is sixteen-year-old shutterbug Charles Cummings.

The affair takes flight when Charles accidentally snaps a shot of twenty-two-year-old songbird Laura Victor (Moore). He becomes obsessed and tracks her down. Indicative of the era's understanding of stalkers and encouragement of creepy Jon Cryer types, the singer is tickled by his youthful affection. Charles soon crosses the line from "cute" to "creep" in Laura's eyes, however, when he spends his college fund on taxicab ads to promote her singing ambitions. Even then, her harshest admonition is, "You're a weird kid, you know that?"

Charles *is* weird, and he's a toolbag. First, he ignores how Mona (gorgeous Jennifer Tilly, whose big eyeglasses and Pac-Man skill indicate she's a "nerdette") pines for him while he pines for his human fetish object. Later, at a bachelor party, he turns down already-paid-for sex with topless Judy Baldwin, appearing as a professional party favor. Throughout it all, Charles also passively accepts bullying from jackass sort-of pal Nelson (Tim Robbins, a top-notch jerk).

Much of *No Small Affair*'s supporting cast performs heroically. George Wendt makes a fine blowhard as a bar owner who consoles Laura with an ass-squeezing hug. Peter Frechette sleazes well as Charles's engaged older brother; Elizabeth "E. G." Daily is sexily bitchy as the intended bride. Better yet are Ann Wedgeworth (lascivious Lana from *Three's Company*) as Charles's dippy mom, and Jeffrey Tambor as Ken, her layabout boyfriend. "Being weird and different is not where it's at," Ken advises Charles. "It takes energy."

No Small Affair is ultimately a piffle about a disagreeable dipshit, but the film is undoubtedly an improvement over the aborted 1981 version that was briefly under way with Matthew Broderick hounding Sally Field.

O. C. and Stiggs
Ocean Drive Weekend
Oddballs ▫ Off the Mark
On the Air Live With Captain Midnight
Once Bitten ▫ One Crazy Summer
One Night Only
Over the Summer ▫ Oxford Blues

O. C. and Stiggs [1987]

DIR. ROBERT ALTMAN; W/DANIEL JENKINS, NEILL BARRY, JON CRYER, MELVIN VAN PEEBLES

RICH KIDS ▫ PRANKS ▫ VANDALISM ▫ ROAD TRIP ▫ MEXICO ▫ VIETNAM VET

O. C. and Stiggs are two suburban Arizona teens created by Todd Carroll and Ted Mann in a series of short stories for *National Lampoon*. They star in the magazine's only single-feature issue ("The Monstrous, Utterly Mind-Roasting Adventures of O. C. and Stiggs," October 1982), as well as this movie. Filmed in 1983, the picture was not released until 1987, when it played a single Manhattan screen for one week to an audience including yours truly.

Baking in Southwestern heat during their summer break, Oliver Cromwell "O. C." Ogilvie (Daniel Jenkins) and Mark Stiggs (Neill Barry) tool around new-money Phoenix in their seismically dangerous muscle car, "The Gila Monster." They glean wisdom and potent potables from sage homeless-man-of-color Wino Bob (Melvin Van Peebles), and creatively torment bigoted, blo-viating local business magnate Randall Schwab (Paul Dooley). The tornado-gale twosome take particular glee in pranks and scams that also snare pissy, mouth-breathing "Horror Child" Randall Schwab Jr. (Jon Cryer).

After Old Man Schwab cuts off an insurance policy belonging to Stiggs's colorfully crusty Gramps (Ray Walston), the lads' psychological warfare escalates from running up intercontinental phone bills to convincing Randall Jr. to fire a machine gun at a wedding reception. They promise the Horror Child it will be the most fun he's ever had. "I don't know, I've had a lot of fun," he responds. "I have Legos, you know!"

Ultimately, O. C. and Stiggs raid a major Schwab family event with armies of Wino Bob's unwashed pals, accompanied by air support from deranged Vietnam vet helicopter pilot Sponson (Dennis Hopper). World music star King Sunny Ade sets up his band and provides a soundtrack for the chaos.

O. C. and Stiggs is generally regarded as the career stink-pit of visionary filmmaker Robert Altman (*Nashville, M*A*S*H, McCabe and Mrs. Miller*). Years later, Altman revealed that he and

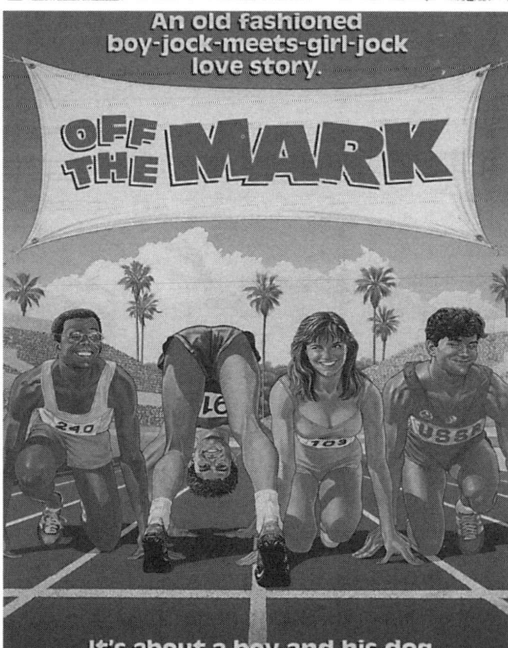

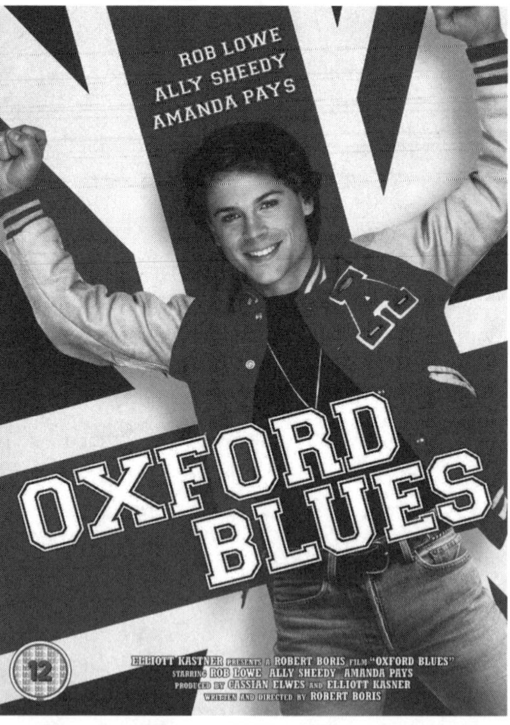

Clockwise from top left: O. C. and Stiggs *(1987) mixes Robert Altman and* National Lampoon; Oddballs *(1984) delivers "ballsploitation" at its bawdy best; Rob Lowe dorks it up for the patriotic UK* Oxford Blues (1984) *DVD*; Off the Mark *(1987), an exercise in outrage.*

the writers despised one another. That tension seems to have burned the edges off the film.

In the original stories, O. C. and Stiggs are psychotic misanthropes who commit atrocities such as pressuring Barbara Bush (then the vice-lady of the United States) to invaginate a banana. Memorably, they also dress in gorilla costumes to sneak into a psychiatric facility and have sex with female inmates; after the fact, who would believe mental patients claiming they were fucked by gorillas? It's nearly impossible to imagine those details working on-screen, even if Altman had attempted at his prime, right after helming the "sick" humor of *M*A*S*H*.

Carroll and Mann's original O. C. and Stiggs adventures are layered, deeply detailed stories of pissed-off children of privilege driven to bored despondency and evil rage by the excess and willful ignorance around them. The characters are the printed-page avatars of the creative minds behind *National Lampoon* during the early-'80s Viking funeral phase, well after the magazine's initial hippie-slaying and *Animal House* heyday.

Understandably, O. C. and Stiggs made ripe candidates for Altman's experiment in the '80s youth-gone-wild movie genre. The film ends up feeling like crabby old Altman flipping the bird to Ronald Reagan's "Morning in America" moment using the era's only mainstream cinema of rebellion. Though unsubtle and not that good, *O.C. and Stiggs* is intriguing and watchable. Devotees of Altman, *National Lampoon*, and post-*Porky's* teen comedies should hop on board this Gila monster at least once.

OCEAN DRIVE WEEKEND [1985]

DIR. BRYAN JONES; W/JOHN ASCHENBRENNER, JEF BAILEY, DAN BYRD, DELLA COLE

1960S ▪ ROAD TRIP ▪ BEACH HOUSE

Ocean Drive Weekend takes place in an early-1960s vapor. A couple of fraternity factions head to the South Carolina shore, where they down booze, dodge the draft, scarf raw steak, and hook up with hotties off-camera. They all shake their swimsuits to shit-hot rock 'n' roll favorites the Rivieras—a local South Carolina bar band, not the slightly better known Rivieras of South Bend, Indiana, who scored a surf classic in 1964 with "California Sun."

Shot and set in the sunny South, *Ocean Drive Weekend* looks and feels like a student film. The Troma studio logo and PG-13 rating would normally automatically warrant an "F," but the green scenery and committed performances muster a passing grade, just by the skin of the movie's teeth—the only skin you'll encounter.

ODDBALLS [1984]

DIR. MIKLÓS LENTE; W/FOSTER BROOKS, KONNIE KROME, MIKE MACDONALD, WALLY WODCHIS

SUMMER CAMP ▪ BIKINIS ▪ PEEPING ▪ FOOD FIGHTS ▪ SPACE KID ▪ RICH JERKS ▪ PUNKER ▪ AEROBICS ▪ PROPELLER BEANIE

"Chicken fat" is the term coined by *Mad* magazine creator Harvey Kurtzman to describe the multitude of sub-gags crammed into each panel of the humor periodical's stories. Crack open any old-school *Mad* issue and you'll see it right off. While the main characters carry on the story in the foreground, all around them are visual puns, crackpot cameos, in-joke graffiti, and other cartoon flourishes that fortify every visible millimeter of the page. In that same sense, the anything-goes Canadian tax-shelter summer camp comedy *Oddballs* could rightly be dubbed *Chicken Fat: The Motion Picture*. Yes, *Oddballs* ranks in a class alongside vintage *Mad* magazine; higher praise exists nowhere.

Built on a standard genre plot—the new kid at camp learns about love and friendship while an evil rich jerk tries to buy the place and shut it down—*Oddballs* leaps beyond *Airplane!*-style gag-a-minute pacing to a new level of stark raving surrealism. Here, an Izod "alligator shirt" is an actual baby alligator stuck on a preppie's chest. Two seconds after that gag, the animal naturally squirms down into the guy's tennis shorts and chomps. That's *Oddballs*.

While *Oddballs* is very much a sex comedy for teenagers, it breaks from tradition with these films of casting twentysomethings as high-schoolers. The lead kids look to be no older than twelve—it's a jarring touch.

New kid Chris Watkins (Wally Wodchis) befriends rotund Jewish hustler Og and black Francophile sophisticate Francois (Ruddy Hall) en route to Camp Bottomout. Their bus is piloted by a blind driver whose seeing-eye guide dog sits next to him and helps steer. The bus immediately plows into an Indiana Jones lookalike and keeps on going. Upon the gang's arrival, new camp owner Hardy Bassett—played by Vegas comedian Foster Brooks doing his signature too-drunk-to-function shtick—reveals how he picked up the facility by *losing* a poker game.

Wrecked cars dot Camp Bottomout's landscape, along with a downed airplane, half-buried WWII bombs sticking up from the dirt, dueling Roman gladiators, and cavemen going at it with clubs. None of these details are even remarked upon, let along explained. One bunk reveals a dusty corpse ("An early arrival!"), while a footlocker contains a little kid vampire complete with a raw sirloin steak on his chest. Meanwhile, Harvey sloshes around with loaded guns, occasionally firing into the air and downing surprise drop-ins on the order of Mary Poppins and the Wicked Witch of the West.

Camp Bottomout's head counselor is wackadoo Laylo Nardeen, portrayed by Mike MacDonald, a stellar Canuck stand-up comic with demonic eyebrows. He also shines very differently in corrupt authority a-hole roles in *Loose Screws* (1985) and *Recruits* (1986). Laylo provides his junior-high charges with a one-dollar sex education course; the tuition includes fake I.D.'s, stick-on *Magnum, P.I.* mustaches, and a field trip to a singles bar called the Meat Rack.

Later, the boys kick one another in the schnuts for an excuse to visit cleavage-in-human-form Nurse Brigitte (Kimberly Brooks). And as Bottomout is an all-boys establishment, repeated raids occur on Camp Bountiful, the female facility across the lake. At least through the lens of a spy telescope, all the girls doing aerobics at dawn appear to be around eighteen—much older than our heroes.

Villainy reigns in the form of corporate lackey Skinner (Donnie Bowes). He runs Camp Bountiful from an office adorned with framed photos of Adolf Hitler and the Crimson Ghost (the same black-and-white horror movie fiend used as the mascot of punk band the Misfits). Skinner dispatches his dipshit son Chadwick (Milan Cheylov) to seduce Harvey's chipper college-age granddaughter Jennifer (Konnie Krome). When their union is sealed, Skinner will buy Bottomout and convert it into a shopping mall. Building a shopping mall way out in the middle of the woods really would be the height of 1980s evil.

Without spoiling much of the plot, *Oddballs'* remaining wonders just partially include the *E.T.*-spoofing Space Kid (Gary Bonfield); the sudden insane appearance of "art film" subtitles; Moses (Bob Liberty) flipping off a succession of burning bushes; convicted child-molester and gym instructor Billy Wanky (Anthony Mason), hired because "he'll work for free"; and the single greatest character in the movie: the adorable, lisping, propeller-beanied Mean Kid (Adam Barratt), a devil child prankster in the vein of Joe Besser's Stinky from *The Abbott and Costello Show*. He repeatedly clocks Harvey in the skull with a brick and maintains perfect deadpan delivery with each blow.

Even up against the movies *Meatballs* (1979), *Screwballs* (1983), *Screwball Academy* (1986), *Fireballs* (1987), *Goofballs* (1987), and *Screwball Hotel* (1988), there is only one *Oddballs*. Nothing else packs as much chicken fat into a summer camp cookout. This movie is the screwiest of them all, balls-down.

Off the Mark [1987] aka Crazy Legs

DIR. BILL BERRY; W/MARK NEELY, TERRY FARRELL, CLARENCE GILYARD JR., DAVID D'ARNAL

JOCKS 📼 GIRLS LOCKER ROOM 📼 VOODOO 📼 SPAZZY DANCING 📼 DWARF

What we have here is a riot, a gem, a revelation, and the fulfillment of this book's aspiration to unearth unfamiliar treasure from familiar territory. Exceeding any remotely rational expectations of excellence, the mega-obscure *Off the Mark*, aka *Crazy Legs*, proves to be a bra-popping, toilet-rupturing surprise milestone of deviously delectable bad taste.

Off the Mark works off a standard sports comedy setup—a college sprinter competes against his own girlfriend and a foreign rival—spiked with *Airplane!*-esque visual puns. When a restaurant diner asks for "a little Russian dressing," famous dwarf Billy Barty appears tableside and dons Cossack garb. The movie also goes heavy on raunchy recklessness, such as when hugely bottom-heavy pro wrestler Queen Kong (of *G.L.O.W.*) cameos as an East German shot-putter whose behemoth bare buttocks force all the other female athletes out of their shower room due to their sheer size.

Rewinding a little, growing boy Howard Markel (Mark Neely) takes an early tumble while exercising and suffers a well-known comic medical condition called "crazy legs." As a result, stress causes Howard's lower extremities to spaz out in fast motion. Alas, stress is all he gets from his Soviet boarding school roommate Dimitri (David D'Arnal). The diabolical Dimitri sells Howard's beloved dog Shep to an animal lab so the pooch can undergo a sex change (Michael Berryman from *The Hills Have Eyes* drives the lab truck). Finding his stride, Howard puts his crazy legs to good use and becomes a champion sprinter. He also grows into a hilariously obnoxious a-hole.

Entering Altered State University, Howard hooks up with foxy fellow runner Jennell Johnson (Terry Farrell) and befriends James B. White (Clarence Gilyard Jr.), an African American über-nerd whose sprinting skill, he tell us, comes from eluding bullies "in the ghetto." Together, the three face off in "The Plutonium Man Triathlon" against Dimitri, who is now a ruthless, Ivan Drago–style Iron Curtain sports drone.

The entire movie is presented as an extended, uninterrupted "Up Close" segment of *Wild World of Sports*. That's a funny concept, and character actors Barry Corbin and Jon Cypher elevate it uproariously as pantsless commentators who psychotically despise one another.

Among all the movie's cartoonish, gag-a-second goof barrages, one segment stands out for sheer gall. James B. White's voodoo attempts to "blackify" his soul would not only be criminally unacceptable today—they were unacceptable back in 1987, too. Hoodoo witch Velma (Virginia Capers) locks James in an all-white apartment where he wears a white cowboy suit and can eat only whitefish, white bread, and white rice until he "overdoses on white." His only means of measuring the blackification process is the friendliness of an albino German shepherd "trained to attack black folk," an out-of-nowhere homage to director Sam Fuller's cult masterwork, *White Dog*.

This spectacular exercise in nonstop outrage has slipped severely through the cultural cracks since it first came out—if it ever even really did come out at all. Even in teen movie hell, there are tormented souls reaching for the heavens. Now on your mark, get set... get *Off the Mark*.

On the Air Live with Captain Midnight [1979]

DIRS. BEVERLY SEBASTIAN, FERD SEBASTIAN; W/TRACY SEBASTIAN, JOHN IRELAND, DENA DIETRICH, JIM LADD

HERO DJ 📼 NERD 📼 VAN 📼 PARACHUTE

A fun trifle from interesting husband-and-wife schlock filmmakers Beverly and Ferd Sebastian (they also made the sexy 1974 bayou action flick *Gator Bait* and the crazy 1984 heavy metal movie *Rocktober Blood*), *On the Air Live with Captain Midnight* seems to have been unofficially and without acknowledgment remade in 1990 with Christian Slater as *Pump Up the Volume*. Technically, *Pump* is the better film, but in terms of conveying the movie's subject—a teenager turned pirate radio star—the Captain rules the high seas all the way.

Tracy Sebastian, son of directors Bev and Ferd, stars as Ziggy, a high schooler who works part-time at a local radio station to make payments on his sweet van. While futzing with the van's CB radio, Ziggy's chubby nerdlinger pal Gargen (Barry Greenberg) accidentally takes over an FM broadcast signal. Ziggy immediately grabs the mouthpiece and launches into a rock-jock rap, introducing himself as "Captain Midnight."

Every kid at school happens to be tuned in at just this moment. Instantly, Captain Midnight becomes a campus mystery and a hero. Ziggy-as-Cap keeps his good thing going, spinning tunes and spewing truths from his mobile outlaw broadcast station, building the legend each time he hits the airwaves.

The FCC catches wind of the Captain and dispatches Agent Pierson (veteran tough-guy actor John Ireland) to stop the madness. Real-life Los Angeles FM legend Jim Ladd, as "Disc Jockey," voices support for the radio renegade.

Ziggy finally deigns to save Captain Midnight by destroying him. He announces he will parachute into Magic Mountain theme park, where devotees will finally get to press flesh with their underground idol. As the climactic scene unfolds, a local news report claims five thousand Cap fans have assembled amidst the amusements. The same locale also welcomed the band Sparks in *Rollercoaster* (1977) and Kiss in *Kiss Meets the Phantom of the Park* (1978). On-screen, the crowd of "thousands" appears to number perhaps a few dozen extras.

Though the movie adventures of Captain Midnight end with the big airborne stunt, his spirit lived until at least until 1986, when a satellite TV tech jammed HBO's Florida signal for five minutes and broadcast a message of outrage against the network's service fee. The video protestor was named John R. MacDougall, but his on-air live handle was Captain Midnight.

Once Bitten [1985]

DIR. HOWARD STORM; W/JIM CARREY, LAUREN HUTTON, CLEAVON LITTLE

VIRGIN ▪ SEXY VAMPIRE ▪ HIGH SCHOOL HORROR ▪ THE BIG HALLOWEEN DANCE

Stand-up comic Jim Carrey and his Plasticman-like powers of contortion undulated on the precipice of stardom several times before he finally hit big in 1990 on TV's *In Living Color*. Before the Canadian funny-freak leapt into the popular consciousness in *Ace Ventura, Pet Detective* (1994), Jim Carrey first had teen sex comedy dues to pay.

Carrey's first crack at the big time happened in 1984, when he won the lead on NBC's *The Duck Factory*, a disconcertingly serious sitcom about a goofy young cartoonist. The rubber-mugged funnyman came closer the following year, playing hapless high schooler Mark Kendall in the popular horror farce *Once Bitten*, a happy harbinger of twenty-million-dollar paydays to come.

Mark's girlfriend Robin (Karen Kopins) continually frustrates him by delaying their mutual loss of virginity. His resulting antsy condition renders him easy prey for a four-hundred-year-old vampire known only as the Countess (Lauren Hutton). To avoid rapidly aging into dust, the Countess must drink the blood of a teenage male virgin three times before Halloween. She complains that it's tough in modern times to find a young dude who hasn't gotten laid. Dorktastic Mark, then, is the answer to her unholy prayers.

The fun of *Once Bitten* comes as Carrey steadily transforms into a knuckleheaded Nosferatu. He mugs, twitches, loses control of his limbs, turns ghost-white, and takes to drinking blood by inserting straws into raw steaks. In one scene, Carrey frightens away kids from his after-school ice cream cart job by flashing his fangs and hissing like a rabid monster. This genuine jump scare is followed by big laughs of relief, which is essentially the best you can ask from a horror comedy. Nobody could possibly deliver it better.

O.G. supermodel Lauren Hutton is satanically sexy as the Countess. Cleavon Little (the sheriff in *Blazing Saddles* [1974) flames it up as the vamp's Liberace-subtle gay assistant. Both bring the funny. So does a literal "gay panic" scene set after gym class in which Carrey's naked school buddies grab him as he washes to see if he's got neck bites. As Carrey struggles, a nearby teen scrubber wails, "Fags in the shower! Fags in the shower!" and a stampede of terrified nude dudes ensues out to the locker room. The joke is clearly directed at the stupidity of hair-trigger homophobia and in 1985—unlike, say, at this book's press time—audiences could grasp that irony and (imagine!) laugh at it. For all that and more, *Once Bitten* is well worth giving at least a once-over.

ONE CRAZY SUMMER [1986]

DIR. SAVAGE STEVE HOLLAND; W/JOHN CUSACK, DEMI MOORE, BOBCAT GOLDTHWAIT

BIKERS ▣ RICH JERKS ▣ NERDS ▣ FREAKY SISTER ▣ THE BIG BOAT RACE

His 1985 smash *Better Off Dead* wrote the check, and with *One Crazy Summer* crackpot creator Savage Steve Holland used his post-hit-making clout to launch all the loony-tune flights of very funny fancy he didn't squeeze into his debut.

John Cusack, ever the dunderheaded De Niro to Savage Steve's slapstick Scorsese, plays college-bound cartoonist Hoops McCann. He accompanies his buddy George Calamari (Joel Murray) on a swelter-season jaunt to Nantucket. Joining them is George's weirdly edgy kid sister Squid, plus her lovable, monstrously ugly canine companion Bosco, about whose looks she is extremely sensitive. Along the way, they pick up fugitive rock diva Cassandra (Demi Moore), and run afoul of a motorcycle gang that functions as the descendants of Harvey Lembeck's Eric Von Zipper motorbike crew from the original Frankie and Annette beach party movies.

Arriving in Nantucket, Hoops and crew add nerdy wisenheimer Ack Ack Raymond (Curtis Armstrong). They are also joined by gloriously dorky handymen the Stork brothers, Egg (Bobcat Goldthwait) and Clay (Tom Villard, beloved as Jaco from *Surf II* (1984), but best remembered for playing the doofus from TV's *We Got It Made* and being the phantom of the grindhouse in 1991's *Popcorn*). The supremely capable young cast at their mid-1980s peak of fearlessness then commits to pursuing comedic chaos. Savage Steve masterfully maneuvers them through a succession of set pieces with directorial confidence and a hit-to-miss joke ratio surprisingly surpassing even that of *Better Off Dead*.

One Crazy Summer's cartoon through-line works perfectly. Hoops draws himself as a lovestruck, animated Rhino who mounts violent combat against malevolent little bunnies who torment him. At one point, Rhino Hoops even blows up rabbits resembling movie critics Gene Siskel and Roger Ebert, who in real life had thumbs-downed *Better Off Dead*.

The monster-movie stuff rocks, too. As a film crew shoots a proto–Syfy channel epic about a radioactive dolphin, Bobcat dons a Godzilla costume and re-creates a miniature Tokyo rampage. The soundtrack is a mix of standard radio oldies (lots of Beach Boys) and contemporary hard rock tracks, the best used of which is Twisted Sister's "Be Chrool to Your Scuel." Also worth noting: "Hoops McCann" originated as a character in the Steely Dan song "Glamour Profession," although that tune does not appear on the soundtrack.

The crazy summer climaxes with a big, island-circling boat race that pits our merry misfits against a pack of rich jerks. You know who wins. Far less predictable, however, is the amusing cameo that brings *One Crazy Summer* to an end with quite the literal bang.

One Night Only [1986]

DIR. TIMOTHY BOND; W/LENORE ZANN, HELENE UDY, TABORAH JOHNSON, HRANT ALIANAK

HOOKERS 📼 HORNY HOCKEY TEAM 📼 BATHTUB PEEPING 📼 LINGERIE STORE 📼 PSYCHO PIMP

Part-time waitress and full-time college student Anne McGraw (Lenore Zann) overhears local hockey coach Mac (Jeff Braunstein) setting up a post-game bacchanal. As she eyeballs Wenko (Hrant Alianak), the oily, switchblade-flicking restaurant manager with whom the coach is negotiating to secure professional party girls, inspiration strikes. Why not cut out the middle-pimp, and organize her sorority sisters to break into the lucrative field of paid orgasm supply? Anne leaps into action and sets up a scenario that she intends to last... *One Night Only*.

After selling her house sisters on the notion with surprisingly little difficulty, Anne hires veteran sex pro Louella (Taborah Johnson) to run the first-timers through a crash course in hooker dynamics. A lingerie shop modeling montage inevitably follows. Trouble arises when Wenko the pimp catches wind that the coeds plan to carnally coopt his economic stronghold.

As the party goes down, plenty of good times come off. Jamie (Geoffrey MacKay), Anne's hockey-goon cousin who incestuously lusts for her, is distracted by nonparticipant Jane (Wendy Lands) as she reads in the bathtub. Their flirty fun halts immediately upon the arrival of the prodigiously pissed-off Wenko, who shows up alongside Wesley (Ken James), Jamie's religious zealot cop dad. In a moment that charmingly points out *One Night Only*'s Canuck origins, Wesley seethes that he had to cross the border to bust up this sick sex soiree, coming "all the way from Plattsburgh!"

From there, slapstick complications spice up the nudity-drenched climax. *One Night Only* wraps up happily—with Anne fucking her cousin and considering changing her major to Advanced Flesh Peddling with a minor in Other People's Vaginas Management.

As with 1984's mighty *Hardbodies* and *Preppies, One Night Only* was created for the Playboy Channel, and then deemed good enough to play in real theaters. The movie seems to have only run on big screens in Canada, and to see it that way would have been worth making the trek up north, even if that meant traveling "all the way from Plattsburgh!" Don't miss the right turn in Potsdam.

Over the Summer [1984]

DIR. TERESA SPARKS; W/LAURA HUNT, CATHERINE WILLIAMS, JOHNSON WEST, WILLARD MILLER

VIRGIN 📼 SUMMER VACATION 📼 HILLBILLIES 📼 GREASERS 📼 SKINNY-DIPPING

Between her junior and senior years of high school, "at risk" city youth Tina (Laura Hunt) is dispatched to her grandparents' Appalachian home. The idea is for her to get some fresh air, do some hard work, and reap the benefits of what really matters in life. After all, nothing bad could possibly happen when a fish-out-of-water sixteen-year-old girl is suddenly surrounded by horny hillbillies—starting with those in her own family.

Tina reunites with her childhood hot-weather pal Rose (Catherine Williams) and falls for local greaser Rich (Johnson West). She loses her virginity to the latter in a graveyard. That sex scene is perhaps most indicative of what makes *Over the Summer* a must-find lost treasure of cinematic wrongness. Grandpa Roy (Willard Miller), the relative over whom Tina gushes the most affection, eerily peeps on her defloration from behind a tombstone!

Add to his file that Grandpa Roy also walks in on Tina while she's changing clothes. He molests a Barbie doll, and plays Russian roulette by himself in the sexy cemetery (he wins). Ol' Gramps is eventually revealed to probably be a murderous arsonist, too, but that's almost an afterthought. While Tina loves creepy Gramps, warts and all, she harbors little fondness for her stepdad, Joe (David Romero)—he must be a complete maniac! Indeed, Joe beats women, tries to

rape Rose, frames Rich for various felonies, and then he mocks a local kid who's developmentally disabled. Joe and the movie end in gunfire. What a *Summer*!

OXFORD BLUES [1984]

DIR. ROBERT BORIS; W/ROB LOWE, ALLY SHEEDY, JULIAN SANDS, AMANDA PAYS

ROWING TEAM ▫ FOREIGN CAMPUS ▫ SEXY ROYALTY ▫ THE BIG RACE

Oxford Blues makes the cut over Rob Lowe's other theatrical college sports flop, the 1986 hockey saga *Youngblood*, simply because this is a rowdy rowing-team comedy, while *Youngblood* begs to be taken as seriously as a slap-shot puck to the windpipe.

Lowe is Nick De Angelo, a teenage Las Vegas hustler turned rowing champ impostor, prone to outbursts like, "Look, I didn't travel over ten thousand miles to spend my first morning in England talking to some wiseass chick from Weehawken, New Jersey!" The wiseass in question is Rona (Ally Sheedy), a fellow American at Oxford who serves as the team's coxswain. "I'm not from Weehawken," Rona snarls back with a grin. "I'm from Lodi!"

Nick's ruse is motivated by his pursuit of snooty-hot Lady Victoria Wingate (Amanda Pays), a globe-trotting young aristocrat who made him lose it when she touched down in Sin City. Once Nick arrives on the Lady's upper-crust UK turf, he discovers her already involved with another row-bro, icy prick Colin Gilchrist Fisher (Julian Sands). The ornery oarsmen assume rival status, and the locals talk down to the hunkily gorgeous ugly American among them. The odds of Nick winning the big race are honestly pretty good, and chances are the wiseass chick from Lodi will win his affections away from the bitchy heiress just in time—right before the credits roll and nobody remembers this movie ever again.

Clockwise from top left: The Party Animal (1984) *raging into the DVD era*; Pick-Up Summer *(1980), better known by its much cooler, way less horny title* Pinball Summer; PCU *(1994) missed its shot at becoming the* Idiocracy *of political correctness*; The Princess Academy *(1987) is Eva Gabor's ticket to* Teen Movie Hell.

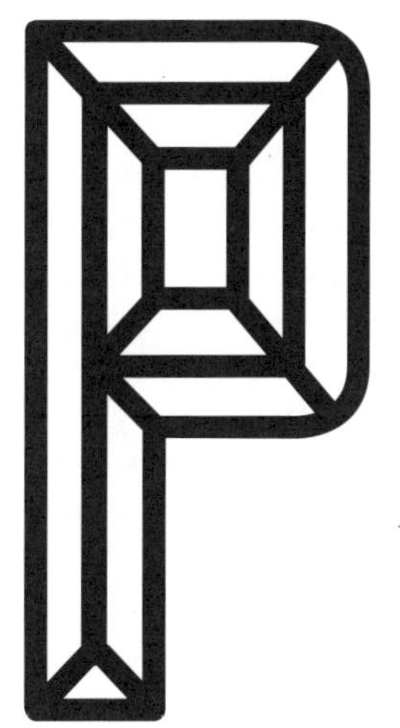

PANDEMONIUM [1982]

DIR. ALBERT SOLE; W/TOMMY SMOTHERS, CAROL KANE, PAUL REUBENS, JUDGE REINHOLD

CHEERLEADER CAMP ▭ STRIP POKER ▭ SLASHER ▭ MUSICAL NUMBER

Shot under the nifty title *Thursday the 12th*, this slasher parody was renamed *Pandemonium* after the Richard Benjamin fright flick sendup *Saturday the 14th* (1981) arrived first in theaters. *Pandemonium* is the better of the two, and in the canon of early-'80s slasher parodies is about on par with Greydon Clark's *Wacko* (1982), way preferable to *National Lampoon's Class Reunion* (1982), but barely a splinter on the horsehead bookend of greatness of *Student Bodies* (1981).

Tommy Smothers and Paul Reubens (aka Pee-wee Herman) star as Royal Canadian Mounted Police who take on a mad killer running roughshod over the cheerleader camp at the local college, It Had to Be U. Judge Reinhold sports really strange-looking platinum-blond hair as a pom-pom boy. Carol Kane does a telekinetic takeoff of *Carrie* (1976). Murder by megaphone occurs, characters break the fourth wall, and the freak-out-inducing "Chicken Man" (David McCharen) from Cheech and Chong's *Nice Dreams* (1981) clucks for the camera. In addition, Smothers's horse named Bob is a world-class charmer. Director Alfred Sole, best known for the incendiary anti-Catholic shocker *Alice, Sweet Alice* (1976), executes the madness admirably.

HBO ran *Pandemonium* nonstop throughout the '80s, and then put it on mothballs for more than a decade before airing it to death on spin-off channels throughout the 2000s. Perhaps the programmers were serving a slow-burning meta-commentary on how the killer constantly reappears in the film after being presumed dead. More likely, *Pandemonium* probably came cheap, just like its highly enjoyable laughs.

Paradise Motel [1985]

DIR. CARY MEDOWAY; W/GARY HERSHBERGER, JONNA LEIGH STACK, ROBERT KRANTZ

NEW KID IN TOWN ▫ TOPLESS SUNBATHING

A small but vibrant cult celebrates actor Gary Hershberger, the rascally redheaded star of *Paradise Motel* and *Free Ride* (1986), referring to him as "the Hersh." As high school senior Sam Kehoe in *Paradise Motel*, the Hersh plays it gawky and low-key. He's a new transplant from stormy Seattle to sunny Southern California, where his seemingly ancient single dad (Bob Basso) has purchased the party-ready, hourly rental motel of the title.

The Paradise Motel attracts its dandy share of randy revelers and bikini busters who sunbathe (sometimes topless) and dip (sometimes skinny) in the shimmering pool. Campus huckster Mick Thurster (Robert Krantz) catches wind that Sam has the keys to the Honeymoon Suite, and he proposes that they rent it behind Sam's dad's back to classmates looking for a hassle-free place to risk teen pregnancy. Conflict arises between Sam and Nick concerning who is a true friend and who will prove more attractive to smiley and sincere Laura (Jonna Lee Stack).

Soon Sam is in the money, the provider of the premier underage nookie haven in the entire Southland area. Eventually, Sam's father figures out the scam, but he's impressed by junior's moxie and tosses his boy the keys to the Honeymoon Suite, effectively saying, "Go ahead, son. Screw your sixteen-year-old girlfriend on my dime!" That's one cool daddy-o.

The Party Animal [1984]

DIR. DAVID BEAIRD; W/MATTHEW CAUSEY; TIMOTHY CARHART, ROBIN HARLAN, JERRY JONES

VIRGIN ▫ NERD ▫ HICK ▫ LOVE POTION ▫ HOOKERS ▫ PUNKS ▫ MALE STRIPPERS

Pondo Sinatra, the party animal of *The Party Animal*, is a teen sex comedy protagonist like no other. He's not only a virgin, a nerd, and a wannabe cool guy who takes love lessons from a ladies' man, he's also a hopeless hayseed—embodying a veritable laundry list of teen comedy archetypes. As portrayed by twitching, sweating Matthew Causey, whose every facial feature appears to be trembling with bipolar disorder, Pondo is an unclassifiable freak for the ages.

The movie itself is an aberration of cinematic nature, scorching the throat with laughter in scene after scene that merrily matches the mind-scrambling mayhem of the lead actor. Shot documentary style, at least some of the time, *The Party Animal* opens with Pondo traveling from Arkansas in the back of a turnip truck. He literally falls out of the truck bed and lands on a college campus. Interview testimonies regarding Pondo perforate his journey. We hear tales from his studly roommate named, yes, Studly (Tim Carhart); soothsaying African American janitor Elbow (Jerry Jones), replete in full Uncle Remus attire with overalls, pipe, and floppy hat; and a coterie of Pondo's female carnal conquests, one of whom growls, "I heard he grew up on a pig farm—and I believe it!"

Arriving on campus, Pondo proves beyond hopeless in the arena of social adjustment. He exclusively wears suspenders and Confederate flag apparel, and his receding-hairline mullet appears to have been combed with an eggbeater. His roommate Studly attempts to educate the new rube on how to get around on campus. None of the advice helps, except to send Pondo away on a succession of set pieces that will soil your shorts with uncontrollable laughter.

For example, Pondo dresses in drag for a sorority strip poker party that soon results in a table full of comely topless lasses; Pondo's resulting boner that sprouts up from his nightgown promptly blows his cover. Pondo also attempts to create a chemistry lab love potion, but the mix turns one of his dates into a gorilla. Another of his concoctions is spiked with "fart pills," and the evening literally combusts upon the lighting of a cigarette.

When Pondo tries to upgrade his personal style, he accidentally wanders into a punk boutique run by sadists. They use power tools to re-render him as a monstrous hunchback, whereupon angry mobs with torches chase him through the streets. In despair, Pondo wanders to a whorehouse, only to have the ladies all rise in disgust, punch their time cards, and leave. (One gripes, "I'd rather fuck my father!")

Pondo also visits a party at a black fraternity. Here's where *The Party Animal*, in 2019 terms, suddenly becomes a dangerous prospect. The revelers, all dressed in dashikis, boogie to a reggae number titled "Kill the White Man" by Gerald Michenaud. Pondo sashays inside, somehow fully bedecked in pimp garb, and immediately drops an N-bomb on his "bruthas." He subsequently comes home with a giant Afro pick slammed deep into his forehead.

Things heat up when Pondo announces he will sell his soul for a piece of ass. Knowing a good deal when he hears one, Satan appears in the form of a mute blonde in red lingerie. Pondo goes to hell, and the filmmakers seize the opportunity to display a pseudo-music video featuring naked she-demons and lots of bug-eyed reaction shots.

After 78 minutes of such carrying on, the madness stops. Pondo becomes the victim of a love potion that works too well. After plowing penis-first through militant lesbians, the sexy college dean, and the entire virginal top floor of the I Phelta Thigh house, Pondo is fucked to death by a half-dozen 400-plus-pound women in a laundromat. He goes out a jittery, glandular legend. Viewers can understand why lead actor Causey never made another movie after starring in *The Party Animal*. Not only would his debut be difficult to top—how could he possibly recover from this experience?

In a movie of endless surprises, acknowledgment also must be paid to *The Party Animal*'s soundtrack, which defies expectations with every note. Almost as a counterbalance, all the brain damage on-screen is underscored by some of the smartest punk and new wave on record. The songs include "Radio Free Europe" by R.E.M., "The General" by the Untouchables, and "No Peace Through Chemistry" by the New Marines, as well as two numbers by the Fleshtones, and no fewer than four greats by the mighty Buzzcocks, including, during one unforgettable interlude, "Why Can't I Touch It?"

PARTY CAMP [1987]

DIR. GARY GRAVER; W/ANDREW ROSS, KERRY WALL, DEAN R. MILLER, JEWEL SHEPARD

SUMMER CAMP ▫ NERD ▫ PRANKS ▫ PEEPING ▫ STRIP POKER ▫ AEROBICS ▫ RAMBO ▫ WEED ▫ THE BIG INTER-BUNK OLYMPICS

Party Camp is a discombobulating concoction, first of all because it has little or nothing to do with parties or camps. While we're all waiting for the lakefront beer-and-boob blasts that don't happen, vast stretches of cranium-rotting sub-Disney PG-rated sap ooze across the screen, jarringly interspersed with spurts of hard-R hormonal antics. It's like somebody spiked only certain sections of the punch bowl, leaving partiers with no option but to just down the whole thing.

Party Camp's schizophrenic whiplashing begins as hungover guttersnipe Jerry Riviera (Andrew Ross) signs up to be a counselor at Camp Chipmunk. He hops aboard a bus piloted by Hunter S. Thompson–costumed motormouth Cody (Dean Miller), and immediately bonds with fellow camper D.A. (Billy Jacoby from *Just One of the Guys*).

Arriving at Camp Chipmunk, the dudes meet the facility's resident adult authority figures, prim matron Mrs. Beadle (Cherie Franklin) and Ramboid disciplinarian Sarge (Peter Jason). We later learn via a broadcast over the camp's PA system that these two indulge in human fly-and-swatter cosplay kinks, so they're cooler than they look.

Muscle-bound bully Tad Whitneyworth (Kirk Cribb) introduces himself as the iron-fisted figurehead of a cabin called the Falcons, while Jerry and D.A. end up overseeing the Squirrels.

Tad, naturally, proves to be even worse than he initially seems, but don't worry, he'll get his. Filling out the requisite *Party Camp* roster are characters like computer nerd Winslow (Corky Pigeon), who rigs up cameras in the girls' poolside locker room. Heather Morris (Kerry Wall) performs multiple functions as a lifeguard, aerobics instructor, and love interest. Nurse Brenda (April Wayne) turns every medical visit into an impromptu dominatrix encounter. Stacked space cadet Dyanne Stein (Jewel Shepard) is unsurprisingly eager to go bust during a round of campfire strip poker.

Party Camp builds less-than-furiously to an über-'80s athletic showdown in which the Squirrels battle the Falcons for what seems like a very long time on skateboards, dirt bikes, and ATV four-wheelers. Every time the *Party* seems completely pooped, some bizarre flourish rises from the campfire ashes, as when the heroes disguise themselves as Darth Vader and the A-Team to negotiate with the camp owners (who believe they're talking to the actual characters). Elsewhere, a pig inexplicably speaks English to Dyanne after she is dumped into his sty. B-movie superstarlet Jewel Shepard shines here, even while suffering a wealth of such indignities.

The *Party Camp* backstory is worth telling over s'mores. Director Gary Graver worked prolifically as an adult filmmaker during theatrical hardcore porn's golden age between roughly 1972 and 1984. Under the name Robert McCallum, he cranked out genre classics including the X-rated *Animal House* knockoff, *Co-Ed Fever* (1980). The presence here of Graver, coupled with that of producer Mark Borde, who previously oversaw *Summer Camp* (1979), *Lunch Wagon* (1981), and *Hollywood Hot Tubs* (1984), would seem to indicate that *Party Camp*'s fun factor would stretch to the most risqué limitations of an R rating. Though the finished film falls full-frontally short on that score, many sources contend that more than twenty-five minutes of sex footage was sheared from *Party Camp*. Among the supposed excised encounters was an explicit BDSM beatdown doled out by Nurse Brenda; producers apparently realized actor Billy Jacoby was seventeen and couldn't wield their editing shears fast enough. For better or worse, they replaced such ridiculous depravity with twenty minutes of mountain-bicycle-racing footage. Pedal faster!

PARTY FAVORS [1987]

DIR. ED HANSEN; W/GEORGE "BUCK" FLOWER, CANDIE EVANS, JEANNIE WINTERS, GAIL HARRIS

STRIPPERS ▣ TOPLESS PIZZA DELIVERY ▣ FRATS ▣ MORAL MAJORITY ▣ PIE FIGHT

Director Ed Hansen and screenwriter George "Buck" Flower (who has a separate career as a cult film actor), are the nightmare team behind the *Bikini Carwash Company* franchise. *Party Favors* is their follow-up to that (unfortunate) success. This movie is an improvement, but still basically a crime against all organic intellect.

Buck Flower himself stars here. He runs a school for strippers, but he's no crusty old dean from a teen sex comedy. After winning a pizza delivery truck while gambling, he rolls with the possibilities. Soon the girls on his staff are driving around delivering pineapple-topped pies—the only kind Buck makes—and peeling down for customers. These teachers-by-day, strippers-also-by-day are all played by X-rated video actresses. The one named Alison (Candie Evans) is supposed to be Buck's daughter.

When a Bible-thumping protestor shuts down his pizza scheme, Buck switches to a strip-o-gram service. Three gals done up as antebellum plantation belles sing in a chorus before skinny-dipping in a backyard pool where somebody dressed as Colonel Sanders floats by on an inflatable alligator. It goes without saying that if a woman appears on the screen at any point, her breasts will soon be bare.

Porn industry bible *Adult Video News* championed *Party Favors* with their 1988 prize for "Best Alternative Video." In a sense, the lack of penetration provides a kind of an "alternative" to the hardcore tapes otherwise touted by AVN. That AVN paid any attention at all is mostly an endorsement of the concept that adult film actresses on their days off would somehow find their way to a "stripper school."

PARTY PARTY [1983]

DIR. TERRY WINSOR; W/DANIEL PEACOCK, PERRY FENWICK, PHOEBE NICHOLLS

HOUSE PARTY ▪ NEW YEAR'S EVE ▪ BULLY ▪ HEART-OF-GOLD ▪ COPS GONE WILD

Though never taking hold stateside, the beautifully titled *Party Party* is a beloved rite-of-passage film in the U.K., ranking high in the hearts and adolescent arousal memories of Brits in the way that John Hughes's movies do in America. Be preparedk, then: This tear-down-the-house comedy is English in the utmost, both culturally and with its language. Viewers outside the British Isles should feel no shame in watching the movie with subtitles enabled.

The specifics of *Party Party* are universal, detailing a teenage New Year's Eve rager that blazes comically out of control at the house of poor slob Larry (Perry Fenwick) while his parents are out on the town. The soirée is masterminded by Larry's suave pals Johnny (Karl Howman) and Toby (Daniel Peacock) and, after an interesting setup involving young police academy recruits Rebecca (Phoebe Nicholls), Sam (Sean Chapman), and Terry (Gary Olsen) getting permission to cut loose, the rest of the action takes place in and around the big bacchanal (fifteen years later, the top-notch Hollywood teen comedy *Can't Hardly Wait* would borrow this formula to excellent effect).

Sam attempts to convince the recently engaged Sharon (Sallyanne Lowe) that a New Year's fling before getting married is a right grand idea and that, more specifically, if she chose him to have it with, that would be bloody brilliant. Toby pitches woo at any and every female attendee, only to amusingly strike out each time. Rebecca and Sam go from partners in crime fighting to partners in canoodling. Terry succeeds in his ambition to get "blotto." Larry can only watch in comedic horror as the revelers relentlessly ravage his parents' previously pristine abode.

The big payoff occurs when Larry's mum (Kate Williams) and Dad (Ken Farrington) come home early and, after evincing the requisite shock, give in to the great time at hand (of course).

The *Party Party* soundtrack, a compilation of cover songs performed by contemporary 1983 artists, made a global splash among record collectors. Among the LP's gifts are the Sex Pistols' "No Feelings" as harmonized by Bananarama; Little Richard's "Tutti Frutti" sung by Sting; and Freda Payne's "Band of Gold" getting a new-wave redo by Modern Romance. Dave Edmunds's take on Chuck Berry's "Run Rudolph Run" became something of a holiday rock radio staple, even in former British colonies. All of a sudden, countries that revolted against England in the pre-VHS era were fighting for their right to *Party Party*.

PCU [1994]

DIR. HART BOCHNER; W/JEREMY PIVEN, CHRIS YOUNG, MEGAN WARD, DAVID SPADE

PREPPIES ▪ HIPPIES ▪ CAMPUS POLITICS ▪ WILD PARTIES

You know you've left the 1980s and entered the 1990s when the name of a fictitious teen sex university actually stands for something—or two things, at that. In this case, *PCU* takes place at Port Chester University, while obviously invoking "Politically Correct University." Yes, the society-upending fervor that has more recently blossomed into safe spaces, trigger warnings, and a terribly concerned Twitter ethicist in 2016 describing *Zapped!* as "a 90-minute sex crime"—all of that seemed like a harmless topic for mockery in the salad days of 1994-era Hollywood.

With the knowledge now of the horrible, slow slide that has led to our current state of paralysis and outrage, *PCU* is amusing but hard to enjoy. The filmmakers had a good amount of funny moments, but if they had hit just a few degrees harder at the initial iteration of today's thought marauders, *PCU* could conceivably have been the academia-attacking equivalent of the mighty *Idiocracy* (2006).

As *PCU* begins, incoming freshman Tom Lawrence (Cliff Young) stumbles onto the Port Chester campus and accidentally offends every conceivable special-interest group of the era. Bashed by eco-warriors, predictably hairy-pitted "womynists," vituperative vegans, and homosexual liberation commandos, Tom ends up crashing with ninth-year senior party animal Droz (Jeremy Piven) and his multiracial, mixed-gender crew. They presently occupy an abandoned frat house in the wake of PCU banning the Greek system. Jon Favreau is quite likeable as dreadlocked burnout Gutter. David Spade, snarking ferociously as snooty blue blood Rand McPherson, is deviously funny.

As that setup hints, however, *PCU* never cashes in on the courage of its ostensible convictions. Even its central cadre of anti-progressive naysayers is unrealistically all-inclusive. None of the pranks or parties or even a performance by George Clinton and Parliament Funkadelic transgresses anywhere beyond a PG-13 rating.

By virtue of its mere existence and endless daytime cable reruns (that PG-13 rating came in handy), *PCU* boasts a cult following. However, in a collegiate comedy context that reaches back not just to *Animal House* (1978) but also to the unholy hilarity of *King Frat* (1979) and *The Party Animal* (1984), the more appropriate title for this missed opportunity to preemptively lambaste a zeitgeist might be just *P.U.* They didn't make fun of overboard PC culture as a point to be satirically skewered, they just did it because they *could*.

In the years between *PCU* and PC now, a savage send-up/takedown of campus speech codes and, say, Halloween costume policing could (and I daresay should) have been made. One tragedy of the bifurcated tribalism that defines contemporary discourse is that any criticism of such mania now would come from an equally totalitarian-minded über-right perspective, steeped in hackneyed clichés en route to the same shit outcome with a different label: some other asshole's idea of utopia where deviation and dissidence are stomped to death, beginning with the decimation and banning of any non-approved notions of fun.

Pick-Up Summer [1980]

aka Pinball Summer

DIR. GEORGE MIHALKA; W/MICHAEL ZELNIKER, CARL MAROTTE, KAREN STEPHEN

BIKINIS ▪ WET T-SHIRTS ▪ VANS ▪ CHEERLEADERS ▪ PRANKS ▪ PINBALL ▪ BIKERS ▪ COOL RADIO DJ ▪ MAYHEM

As is clearer from *Pick-Up Summer*'s more logical and infinitely cooler original moniker, *Pinball Summer*, pinball is the name of the game in this Canuxploitation potpourri. The film opens outside Pete's Arcade, with a sextet of cheerleaders flailing their pom-poms in celebration of the last day of school. A flabby flasher opens his trench coat and sends the pep squad scurrying, revealing that he's wearing panties and dainty garters—a nice touch.

As the ludicrously groovy theme song by semi-pro Beach Boys tribute duo Jay Boivin and Germain Gauthier cranks, "Pinball summer/I'll take you awwwwnnn," the characters bust out of class and hit the road hard to capture those two sweet weeks of summer heat in the Great White North. Greg (Michael Zelniker) and Steve (Carl Marotte) pilot a righteous custom van. Sisters Donna (Karen Stephen) and Suzy (Helene Udy) carom around the lakefront town in a convertible. Bad-news biker Bert (Thomas Kovacs) leads his oily leather goon crew on their motorcycles. Chubby dorkus pinball mechanic and biker wannabe Whimpy (Joey McNamara) tests the tire pressure of his putt-putt moped.

Located between the school and the arcade is OJ's hamburger stand, staffed by eye-popping strawberry blonde Sally (Joy Boushel). Her too-tight work attire consists of a curve-caressing red T-shirt and cheek-peeking short-shorts emblazoned with "Coca-Cola" just above the vulva. Too bad she's wasting her time with biker creep Bert.

Representing the adult world are Hawaiian-shirted arcade proprietor Pete (J. Robert Maze, who exudes the air of a prop comic); fast-talking WDCU radio jock (Marc Denis), who broadcasts from the front half of a car mounted on the wall at Pete's; blowhard local politician Frank Jelnick (Roland Nincheri); and stuffy Mrs. Jelnick (Lyn Jackson), who amusingly takes a blast of tire-flung gutter oil smack in her face.

Pick-Up Summer sends all of its players off in pursuit of hot fun, fast rides, and, ultimately, possession of Pete's Pinball Championship trophy—which comes with the promise of a date with the too-be-determined beauty queen, Miss Pinball.

The movie hops from one archetypal warm-weather teen sex comedy setting to the next—pinball parlor, burger joint, beach, amusement park, swimming pool, discotheque, biker HQ, parent-free house party, and, tellingly, a drive-in movie theater—exactly where most adolescent audiences likely caught this movie at the time of its pre–home video 1980 release. Those open-air park-and-party camps functioned outside of normal watchdogs of authority (parents, teachers, cops) as semi-anarchic hotbeds of smuggled-intoxicant consumption, backseat potential baby-making, and dudes and gals just simply cruising from car to car, making the scene.

The movie debuted in its native Canada and on some low-rent stateside circuits as *Pinball Summer* right on time in 1980. After *Porky's,* another Canadian export, set off the teen sex boom in 1981, distributors rushed any and all related properties back into theaters, with *Pinball Summer* proving to be a newly hot prospect. Alas, *Space Invaders, Asteroids, Pac-Man* and their ilk had rapidly taken a digital dump on pinball's arcade dominance during the intermediate years, thus prompting the switch to *Pick-Up Summer.* The title flip is nearly a "game over," but the re-release's tagline tilts to win with extra balls: "It's the movie that out-'PORKS' them all!"

PINK MOTEL [1982]

DIR. MICHAEL J. MCFARLAND; W/PHYLLIS DILLER, SLIM PICKENS, TONY LONGO, HEIDI HOLICKER

VIRGINS ▣ JOCK ▣ HOOKER ▣ S&M ▣ WACKY OLD PEOPLE

Pink Motel was a mismatched attempt to force a seriocomic, Neil Simon–esque revolving relationship study into the *Porky's* mold of moviemaking. As a result, *Pink Motel* ends up being—like a lot of genuine nuttiness, to be honest—fascinating and boring at the same time.

Veteran screen comics Phyllis Diller and Slim Pickens goose the action with intermittent appearances as Margaret and Roy, the married proprietors of the titular roadside getaway. In keeping with the facility's '50s Western pastel motif, Margaret and Roy wear pink cowboy shirts with white fringe and bolo ties. Talk, however, is really the thing with *Pink Motel,* a movie that begs to be "hushed" itself like a gabby moviegoer. Every character has multiple hyper-dense speeches. Then their partners take turns babbling, until the movie cuts to the next room and the process starts again.

In the first Pink Motel unit, a couple of teenage virgins fuss over birth control. Next door, a muscle-bound jock admits to his hooker date that this will be his kickoff into the world of intercourse. A few rooms down, two wannabe studs sling questionable charm at a pair of suspiciously eager party-girl pickups. Finally—the most talkative of all—an egotistical district attorney dude and his buxom female defense lawyer compare evidence as they ponder the third year of their ongoing extramarital affair. By the end of *Pink Motel,* you will know more about these people than you do about yourself.

Somehow, all this inactivity made it into a movie whose poster depicts a cheerleader pulling down a campus hero's shorts while he shimmies up the motel's glowing signpost. There's some truth in that advertising, as the female nudity that happens here is nowhere near as captivating as the vibrant array of vintage men's underpants on near-constant display. Tiger stripes, tighty-whities, and pop-art patterns all distract the viewer's fatigued mind while the movie pummels with such bombastic diatribes and ace zingers as: "Well, I've been considering suicide...but I don't think I can convince *you* to do it!"

The memorable opening song is a disco diva shriek ("*Piiink* Moe-Tell/Nobody kiss 'n' tell!") blared by a group called Nile, presumably not the veteran death metal ensemble. When the tune is reprised at the end, you'll want to hug every note. Everybody can check out and go home now.

Plain Clothes [1987]

DIR. MARTHA COOLIDGE: W/ARLISS HOWARD, SUZY AMIS, GEORGE WENDT, DIANE LADD

UNDERCOVER COP IN HIGH SCHOOL ▣ BAD TEACHER ▣ BULLIES ▣ NERDS

Director Martha Coolidge enlivened 1980s teen comedies with *Valley Girl* (1983) and *Real Genius* (1985), two of the field's all-time greats. She did what she could with the overly long-in-development, abortive, and impossible *Joy of Sex* (1984). *Plain Clothes*, a PG-rated snoozer, is Coolidge's only real misstep in the realm of high school laffers, and she makes it count.

Playing close to the same essential setup as Jon Cryer's *Hiding Out* (1987), *Plain Clothes* casts Arliss Howard as an undercover cop who poses as a high school transfer student to solve the murder of a teacher. Suzy Amis is the English instructor who believes her feelings for the new kid are inappropriate. Diane Ladd is the senior class sweetheart who also falls for the dick-in-disguise.

Despite the cast, the mystery is way too weak to follow, and the procedural details are too complicated. Beyond Howard, Amis, and Ladd, Coolidge provided paychecks here to luminaries on the order of Abe Vigoda, George Wendt, Robert Stack, Seymour Cassell, Harry Shearer, and Jackie Gayle; yet the movie gives them bupkes with which to work their magic. Besides, endearing as its members are, that roster contains just too many unattractive old men to load into a high school movie that contains no countermeasure of youth gone nakedly wild. As in ballet class, balance is absolutely crucial in these matters.

Playing for Keeps [1986]

DIR. BOB AND HARVEY WEINSTEIN; W/DANIEL JORDANO, MATTHEW PENN, JIMMY BAIO, MARISA TOMEI

HOTEL FOR KIDS ▣ EVIL CORPORATION ▣ MUSICAL NUMBER

The sole directorial credit of Miramax movie mogul siblings Bob and Harvey Weinstein, *Playing for Keeps* is some genuinely dreadful Mira-muck. If only the manner in which this movie bombed had convinced them to abandon showbiz, just think how much happier a Harvey-free society might be (the sacrifice of *Shakespeare in Love* would be worth it; and, really, somebody else would have discovered Tarantino).

Tough-talking, ethnically indeterminate New York City teen Danny d'Angelo (Daniel Jordano) discovers he's inherited the Hotel Majestic, a dilapidated facility in rural Pennsylvania. Danny organizes his streetwise pals into a home-repair posse, and they hightail it to the country. The gang bangs the old joint into shape, an activity not merely meriting a musical montage, but an actual dance number which manages to combine the most seriously cringe-eliciting aspects of lingering *Flashdance*-mania and "The Kids From *Fame*" touring show.

The scrappy squad's goal is to turn the Majestic into "a hotel for kids only, with MTV in every room!" A chemical company wants to scoop up the land and turn it into a waste dump—as opposed to the Weinstein brothers, who used movie screens as a waste dump here. The kids win. Marisa Tomei loses, as her supporting role in *Playing for Keeps* now keeps the movie available on DVD, smack with her kisser all over the cover.

I saw *Playing for Keeps* as a seventeen-year-old as part of a test screening, the first such event I ever attended. Harvey Weinstein sat behind me, and, before the show, I heard him gruffly talking about *Heaven Help Us*, calling the Catholic-school comedy "a very funny movie." I turned to him, nodded, and shot a thumbs-up. He smiled. Of course, I didn't know Harvey was "Harvey" at the time; otherwise I might have been too intimidated to slag *Playing for Keeps* so severely on my post-show commentary card—now, of course, I'm tickled to imagine the dyspepsia my penciled-in teenage outrage much have caused the Monster of Miramax. And if you're reading this now in between legal proceedings, Harvey: I still *really* hate that the graffiti kid's name is "Van Go-Go."

Poison Ivy [1985]

DIR. LARRY ELIKANN; W/MICHAEL J. FOX, NANCY MCKEON, CAREN KAYE, ADAM BALDWIN

SUMMER CAMP ◙ NERD ◙ PRANKS ◙ FAT KID ◙ MILITARY HARDASS

Don't confuse the made-for-NBC 1985 movie *Poison Ivy* with the drippingly lurid 1993 Drew Barrymore potboiler of the same name, directed by *Preppies* costar Katt Shea. This early movie was the first of Michael J. Fox's outings during his whirlwind banner year in 1985. In February, he was on his sitcom's home network, starring in this tepid summer-camp comedy. Come July, *Back to the Future* opened, and in August he planted the flag on his ascent with *Teen Wolf*.

Still a newcomer in *Poison Ivy*, Fox plays a counselor at a waterfront camp for boys. Nancy McKeon, who played biker chick Jo on the teen sitcom *The Facts of Life*, costars as the facility's hard-to-get nurse. Adam Baldwin brings the heavy as the uncool, hard-ass counselor with a military background. Two summers later, Hollywood handed him a rifle and sent him off to Vietnam via *Full Metal Jacket*.

The staff's youthful campers consist of a slick-talking city kid and candy hustler, a wisecracking lil' lardo, and a plucky underachiever desperate to conquer his fear of water. All are motivated to do anything they do by the girls camp residing, as ever, just on the other side of the lake.

Robert Klein proves welcome as boisterous camp owner Big Irv Klopper. Caren Kaye, as Mrs. Klopper, is, just like she was in *My Tutor* (1983), luminous. Still, nothing in *Poison Ivy* rubs off on the viewer on any kind of long-term way. If you have the itch for summer-camp shenanigans, pick any installment of the *Meatballs* franchise at random—yes, that includes Corey Feldman's Jet Ski opus supreme, *Meatballs 4* (1992).

Police Academy [1984]

DIR. HUGH WILSON; W/STEVE GUTTENBERG, KIM CATTRALL, BUBBA SMITH, MICHAEL WINSLOW

BAD COPS ◙ NERDS ◙ FASCISTS ◙ PEEPING ◙ GROUP SHOWERS ◙ PRANKS ◙ GUN NUT

Nobody in *Police Academy* is a teenager, exactly, but this obvious "*Animal House* with cops" blockbuster upended, transformed, and influenced teen sex comedies for the remainder of the 1980s unlike any game changer since the biblically important *Porky's*. *Police Academy* even spawned a parallel workplace-farce genre in which cool dudes, bombshell babes, nerds, slobs, big fat party animals, rich jerks, evil jocks, and other such familiar figures come together under forced circumstances. Here, it's a call for additional law enforcement; in *Basic Training* (1985), it's army recruitment; in *Moving Violations* (1985), it's traffic school; in both *Firehouse* (1987) and *Fireballs* (1989), it's a need for diversified firefighters.

Though technically "adults," the uniformed schmucks on-screen behave exactly like their underage boob-movie counterparts. The message seems to be that high school goes on forever; great news for anybody who never intended to give up on food fights, panty raids, epic pranks, and peeping into female locker rooms. That's bad news in real life for people who want to eat their food, wear their panties, or simply live a life free from fear of being pranked or peeped upon.

The cool dude of *Police Academy* is Cadet Carey Mahoney (Steve Guttenberg), a wisecracking ne'er-do-well who steps up to an unnamed Major

American City's open call for law enforcement recruits. Due to a crisis of diversity and overall staffing, the department's standards have been utterly annihilated and the doors are wide open to new hires. That's good for him, great for viewers, and fantastic for potential criminals.

Joining Mahoney, among others, are sexy smart Karen Thompson (Kim Cattrall); muscle mountain Moses Hightower (Bubba Smith); henpecked nebbish Douglas Fackler (Bruce Mahler); meek mouse Laverne Hooks (Marion Ramsey); firearms freak Eugene Tackleberry (David Graf); and a couple of blowhard SWAT-team wannabes (Andrew Rubin and Brant von Hoffman).

Among the cadets, Larvell Jones proves unique. He's a one-man arsenal of infinite sound effects portrayed by sonically super-gifted stand-up comic Michael Winslow. His performance is so instantly indelible that, thirty years later, Winslow remains immediately identifiable as "the sound effects guy from *Police Academy*."

The actual academy is staffed by cranky hard-ass Lt. Thaddeus Harris (G.W. Bailey); Ilsa-esque amazon Sgt. Debbie Callahan (Leslie Easterbrook); and lovably senile old Commandant Eric Lassard (George Gaynes). You know their types, but *Police Academy* translated and codified the classic teen sex comedy elements into a freshly functioning palette of personalities. Both high school and college comedies would dip from this well repeatedly going forward, as did a plethora of direct *Police Academy* knockoffs.

Loaded with potent personnel, *Police Academy* chronicles the multitude of pranks, mishaps, naked interludes, and slapstick mayhem that goes off during the training process, all of which builds to the trainees getting called into sudden real-world service upon the climactic occasion of a city-wide riot. The best gags involve hiring a hooker (vintage porn queen Georgina Spelvin) to blow addlebrained Commandant Lassard beneath the podium while he's giving an important speech; along with repeatedly sending the pair of gung-ho bully-cops-to-be to be worked over at a gay leather bar called the Blue Oyster.

Police Academy hits all of its marks. Six big-screen sequels, a live-action TV spin-off, an afternoon kids' cartoon, and myriad imitators followed. Steve Guttenberg will be happy to remind you of that. So, too, will Michael Winslow, but he'll do it by perfectly imitating a machine gun, a badly dubbed karate film, and a Jimi Hendrix guitar solo all at once.

The Pom Pom Girls [1976]
aka Palisades High

DIR. JOSEPH RUBEN; W/ROBERT CARRADINE, JENNIFER ASHLEY, MICHAEL MULLINS, RAINBEAUX SMITH

CHEERLEADERS · BIKINIS · CUSTOM VANS · HOT RODS · MOONING · FASCIST COACH · THE BIG GAME · CHICKEN RUN RACE

This character-building movie is a berserk and angry thing. *The Pom Pom Girls* opens with a fit of violence at night on a high school campus, as a football player hanging in effigy explodes into flames while being dangled from a tree limb. Ultimately, the film ends with an actual race toward self-destruction, when the film's ostensible hero jets his souped-up street cruiser off a cliff to win a "chicken run" car race.

The Pom Pom Girls proved to be a massive drive-in hit, and a better-looking, more exuberant cast of Bicentennial-era Golden State young folk may not have ever been assembled. The movie boasts sun-splashed set pieces, a classic jocks-and-cheerleaders romance narrative, an exquisitely groovy soft rock soundtrack, and even a happy ending after the chicken-run crash. Still, *Pom Pom* positively sweats sadism. The experience feels like a locker-room hazing that culminates with jocks holding the audience upside down in the toilet, punching viewers in the crotch for even trying out for the team.

Robert Carradine stars as two-fisted quarterback Johnnie, the diametric opposite of Lewis Skolnick, his signature *dorko-di-tutti-dorki* role in *Revenge of the Nerds* (1984). Witnessing Robert Carradine as the anti–Robert Carradine is a severe blow. He is not a big guy, but he comes off wily, wiry, and strong—even threatening. He throws punches first, he stuffs French fries way up his pal's nose, and he clearly does all his own stunts. These reckless endangerments include stomping around the roof of a zooming car, turning a high-speed dirt bike into an assault weapon, stealing a fire truck, leading a hate-driven tug-of-war over a muddy pit, pissing out a classroom window onto innocent girls below, and crashing down a flight of concrete bleacher steps after being slammed in the skull with a metal trash can.

Writer-director Joseph Ruben must have imagined all this cruising-for-multiple-bruisings would make Johnnie and costar Michael Mullins (as his only slightly less brutality-inclined best bud Jesse) seem likeable. He imagined wrong.

James Gammon, as the coach named "Coach," is a castrating psychopath. He breaks, beats, and belittles the players on and off the field—even, at one uncomfortable point, in the showers. Johnnie transfers this hurt into antisocial outbursts, including relentlessly attempting to spirit away Laurie (Jennifer Ashley), the cheerleader girlfriend of the team's resident gorilla. Jesse, in the meantime, promises romance to pretty pep-rally gal Sally (Lisa Reeves) while, on the side, he's also getting with booster squad beauty Roxanne (the incomparable Rainbeaux Smith).

As with a number of other 1970s-made Southern California cheerleader flicks, (particularly those also issued by Crown International Pictures), the veneer of gorgeous young bodies partying amidst luscious nature, perfect weather, and an anything-is-possible future is commingled with jarring dread and neck-snapping tumult. Agony, panic, and worse seem to lurk with each squeeze of suntan lotion or anytime anybody touches anything in the school cafeteria. *The Pom Pom Girls* pushes its combination of rah-rah spirit and reasons to fear the reaper closer to the surface than practically any other teen sex comedy. Perhaps that was the method to creator Joseph Ruben's madness. In 1987, he changed teams and made the darkly satirical slasher favorite *The Stepfather*.

Aside from remaining in grindhouse and second-run theatrical release for years, *The Pom Pom Girls* caught on as a midnight movie, even running at revival joints in scary, scummy 1970s Manhattan. Upon the early-'80s advent of home video, the film took off anew and genuinely earned its distinction as a triple-threat drive-in/grindhouse/VHS cult classic. This fact is baffling; the movie is not fun, nor overly abundant with exploitable elements like naked cheerleaders—although they are there, Rainbeaux included. After decades of pondering, the *Pom Pom* formula becomes a little more clear; it's "California Dreaming" with a hefty dose of Manson Family values.

Popcorn und Himbeereis

[1978]

DIR. FRANZ JOSEF GOTTLIEB; W/OLIVIA PASCAL, GESA THOMA (AS GESA GABOR), CHRISTINE ZIERL, ZACHI NOY

PEEPING ▣ SEXY NUNS ▣ DRAG ▣ BIKER ▣ HOTEL ▣ FAT GUY ▣ SEXY METER MAID

Popcorn und Himbeereis means "popcorn and red raspberry ice cream," a perfectly evocative salty, juicy, and sweet title for this German teen sexcapade. Randy *mädchen* Vivi (Olivia Pascal) and Bea (Gesa Thoma) store their secret vacation savings in a mattress, which is removed from their apartment without their knowledge. Soon enough, the gals figure out the mattress made it to a madcap hotel downtown—but which room?

In order to locate their missing loot, Vivi and Bea bang away on as many beds as it will take. Along the way, the girls come across fellow hormone-inflamed young women Pamela (Christine Zierl) and Yvonne (Ursula Buchfellner), thereby supplying fat, funny voyeur Jonny (Zachi Noy) with an onslaught of eyefuls on which to peep.

Two years prior to *Popcorn*, Fräulein Pascal stormed the sexploitation circuit at eighteen in the *Emmanuelle* knockoff *Vanessa*. In 1977, the suddenly pink-hot starlet pumped out *The Fruit Is Ripe, The Amorous Miss-Adventures of Casanova, Arrête ton char...bidasse!*, and *Joy of Flying* (whose moniker ingeniously cobbles together the titles of the era's two dominant "dirty books," *The Joy of Sex* and *Fear of Flying*). In 1978, the same year as *Popcorn und Himbeereis*, Olivia also starred in *Behind Convent Walls*, *Summer Night Fever*, and *Triangle of Venus*. Her most popular title, however, brought her back to the confections counter in 1979: *Cola, Candy, and Chocolate*.

PORKY'S [1981]

DIR. BOB CLARK; W/DAN MONAHAN, KAKI HUNTER, CHUCK MITCHELL, SUSAN CLARK

VIRGINS ▫ PEEPING ▫ PRANKS ▫ REDNECKS ▫ HOOKERS ▫ BAD COPS

Porky's is the most archetypal 1980s teen sex comedy, to the point that the movie's title by itself serves as shorthand for the genre. Descriptions of the R-rated, high-school boob farces of the Reagan era inevitably begin with, "You know—like *Porky's*." From there, the scene is set with naked clarity.

From frame one, *Porky's* commingles obscene lust, the notion of virginity as a disease, prostitute mishaps, impossible pranks pulled off to perfection, and the cataclysmic comeuppance of abusive authority figures. Once fully chopped together with the hairy-palmed nostalgia of writer-director Bob Clark, *Porky's* rockets to extremes never imagined in adolescent movies. After sneaking into a screening in 1982, an eighth-grade classmate of mine declared the film report heard around the world: "Dude! *Porky's* shows *everything*!"

Set in fictional Angel Beach, Florida, *Porky's* introduces us, morning-wood-first, to Pee-Wee (Dan Monahan), a high school basketball player nicknamed for his lack of package. He exists in a constant state of erectile fury and carnal dissatisfaction. The action commences when Pee-Wee and teammates Tommy (Wyatt Knight), Meat (Tony Ganios), Mickey (Roger Wilson), Tim (Cyril O'Reilly), and Brian (Scott Colomby) learn of Porky's, a honky-tonk whorehouse situated deep in sweaty, scary Everglades country. The Angel Beach boys' ensuing attempts and repeated failures to gain access to Porky's are the plot tissue connecting the movie's famously outrageous assaults on prudishness and good taste.

Chief among those classic gutbusters is an operatic showdown in the girls' shower room of Angel Beach High. While female classmates soap up after gym, Pee-Wee, Tommy, and Tim assume the position behind a series of strategically placed peepholes to visually drink in every nook and cranny of the young ladies' bodies. Yes, this blatant violation of decency is played for dirty thrills and nasty laughs. Feel free to faint.

The sheer volume and unshaven explicitness of the group shower is shock enough. "There's so much wool you could knit a sweater!" proclaims witty voyeur Tim. What hurls *Porky's* to instant taboo-buster status, though, is the encounter's phallo-terroristic punch line. After Tommy slips his visibly naked penis through a peephole in the wall, hulking female gym matron Miss Beulah Balbricker (Nancy Parsons) enters the shower, clears the girls out, grabs hold of Tommy's exposed organ, and attempts with brute force to pull whoever owns it straight through the solid wall. You can't believe what you're seeing. Then Beulah plants her foot against the wall for tugging leverage and *really* heaves-ho.

The movie's other hilarious high points don't brand on the brain with the same fury, but each is amusing and transgresses ample boundaries to function as rites-of-*Porky's*-passage all their own. Highlights include Kim Cattrall as assistant coach "Lassie," loudly revealing the reason for her nickname by howling as she gets laid within earshot of gym class. Another such episode involves a wild prank in which Susan Clark (Webster's mom on the titular TV sitcom) plays hardscrabble backwoods hooker Cherry Forever.

Also crazily effective are all the rough-and-tumble exchanges with obese, cigar-chomping, gator-raising swamp pimp Porky himself. Character actor Chuck Mitchell makes Porky a frightening and credible villain, yet after his Angel Beach adversaries exact their catastrophic

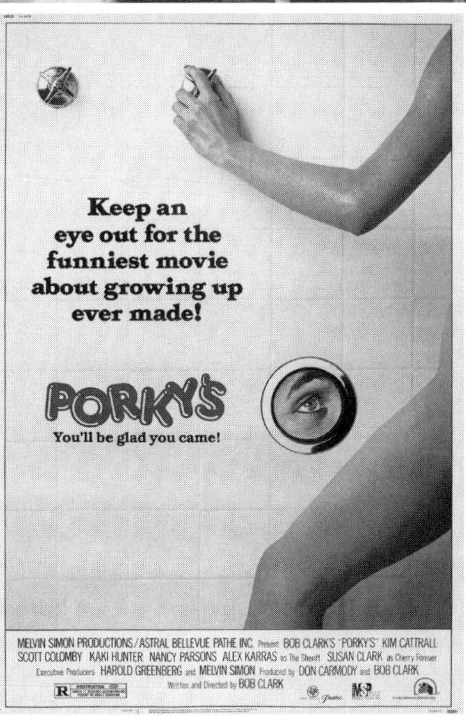

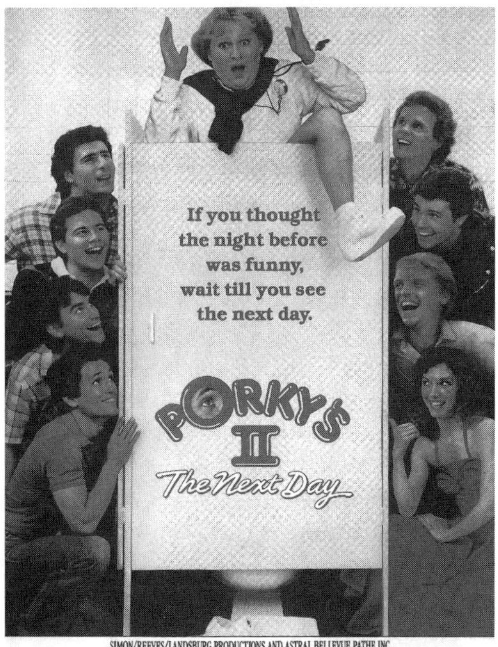

Growing up with Porky's *(1981), a teen movie hell demarcation line like no other.* Clockwise from top: *The gang pushing way past graduation age in* Porky's Revenge *(1985); sprightlier times with Balbricker (Nancy Parsons) in* Porky's II: The Next Day (1983); *peep the original* Porky's *poster.*

revenge, his face grimaces with palpable pathos. At least for that moment, it's impossible not to sympathize with Porky's anguish.

Reaching the end of *Porky's* as a postadolescent, post-1980s viewer, you have to wonder if the punishment doled out by the pampered youth of Angel Beach fits whatever "crimes" may have been committed by this hard, lard-assed hayseed hustler. At the movie's start, Porky and his posse of bog bruisers and professional sex providers keep to themselves. The suburban brats of Angel Beach invade Porky's space, looking to flout the law and do their dirty business over on the poor side of the marsh grass. Porky turns the juveniles away respectfully at first, and then again with some largely harmless lesson dispensation (the kids fall into the water surrounding the nightclub).

When hothead Mickey pushes his luck a third time, Porky's bouncers reach the pivotal point of the code laid out by Patrick Swayze in *Roadhouse*: "It's time to not be nice." Mickey gets roughed up and sent home. For this, the Angel Beach boys ruthlessly destroy Porky, his business, and the central gathering point and economic stronghold of the surrounding community.

To witness the glee that director Clark's camera takes in Porky's pain after the club's undoing is to also suddenly flash back over how many of the film's scenes center on savage and sadistic humiliation, wherein some unfortunate falls for the best-laid plans of one popular jock or another. Quite often, everyone stands around pointing and laughing at whatever stupid sap is getting dorked in public by a giant inflatable condom or running, naked and mortally terrified, from a psychopathic, machete-wielding "negro."

Of course, chin-stroking over class conflict in *Porky's* is as foolish an errand as when the Angel Beachers try to crash the whorehouse; after all, this is a film where a major scene involves getting a waitress to repeatedly and loudly query, "Has anybody seen 'Mike Hunt'?"

On the production side, *Porky's*, the Great American Teen Sex Comedy, was actually a product of Canada. Although the film was shot in Miami, Bob Clark had previously directed his cult horror favorites *Deathdream* (1972) and *Black Christmas* (1974) north of the border, and he made *Porky's* for the Canuck company Astral Media. Such B movies were created en masse to take advantage of specific Canadian tax shelter laws that motivated investments in hundreds of low-budget homegrown films. As a result, *Porky's* held the title as the highest-grossing Canadian film of all time until 2006, when it was surpassed by the crime comedy *Bon Cop, Bad Cop*.

Clark said he labored for years on *Porky's*, grinding away in reaction to TV's *Happy Days* and other pop culture portrayals of 1950s puberty that he felt sanitized his own experience. The juxtaposition is endearingly odd considering Clark's follow-up to *Porky's*: the universally beloved 1983 holiday classic, *A Christmas Story*.

Chuck Mitchell doubled his space in the all-star rogues gallery of teen movie hell by appearing in *Better Off Dead* (1985), where the erstwhile Porky plays Rocko, hothead owner of a restaurant appropriately called Pig Burgers. Mitchell returned for the misbegotten sequel *Porky's Revenge* (1985), after passing on *Porky's II: The Next Day* (1983), as the script called for him to appear on-screen completely naked.

After many, many years of planned remakes, including one to be produced by Howard Stern (who simultaneously sought rights to *Rock 'n' Roll High School*) and another to be directed by Alex Winter (Bill of Bill and Ted), an ultra-obscure official *Porky's* sequel emerged: *Pimpin' Pee-Wee* (2009), aka *Porky's: The College Years*. This hard-to-find curiosity follows different actors as Pee-Wee, Meat, and Tommy in college, where they semi-accidentally open and run a successful whorehouse. They would have done better to let sleeping (undoubtedly in the nude) bodies lie—truly, is nothing sacred?

Porky's II: The Next Day
[1983]

DIR. BOB CLARK; W/DAN MONAHAN, KAKI HUNTER, WYATT KNIGHT, JOSEPH RUNNINGFOX

PRANKS ▫ BELLY DANCER ▫ BAD PREACHER ▫ BOZO POLITICIANS ▫ MALE NUDITY

Porky's II: The Next Day is the low-budget teen sex comedy in which Pee-Wee (Dan Monahan), Wendy (Kaki Hunter), Meat (Tony Ganios) and the rest of the Angel Beach High gang strike out in defense of the Bard of Avon, William Shakespeare. Yes, that really is the premise of *Porky's II*; the school's Shakespeare festival summons the wrath of local fire-and-brimstone preacher Reverend Bubba Flavel (Bill Wiley), who proclaims the Bard's work obscene. Only our worldly boys can make the Sunshine State safe for *Love's Labours Lost*.

Among the Rev. Flavel's flock can be found that tank of a gym teacher, Miss Bula Balbricker (Nancy Parsons), returning from the first movie. Bula bails, though, once the local Ku Klux Klan joins Bubba's movement. The Klan objects to a Seminole student (Joseph Runningfox) playing Romeo opposite a white Juliet. Native American rights are now a priority for the Angel Beach crew.

Pee-Wee and pals wage prank warfare against their foes, a list that grows to include a horny politician and an entire town council addicted to stag films. Much of the action flies by quickly, and, in the moment, it's funny. A scheme involving "Graveyard Gloria, the fuck of death," essentially re-creates the "Cherry Forever" gag from the first movie, and proves to be okay even a second time.

Porky's II is not memorable overall, however. The *Next Day* subtitle literally applies to the timeline of when the on-screen action starts, but also sums up the rushed, slapdash feel of the movie overall. It's as if director Bob Clark and company actually wrote, filmed, and rushed out the finished product within twenty-four hours of wrapping the original *Porky's*.

Porky's touched on redneck anti-Semitism involving Jewish team member Brian (Scott Colomby), but *Porky's II* really goes all out for its activism merit badge. In fact, the bizarre left turn into Shakespeare evokes a previous movie franchise whose sequel aimed to "correct" the excesses of its first installment: *Dirty Harry*.

In *Porky's*, the suburban heroes terrorize and decimate poor, down-home swamp folk who in no way attacked them first. In the original *Dirty Harry* (1971), Clint Eastwood's rogue cop antihero ignores due process and Constitutional rights in .44-caliber pursuit of his own justice. *Porky's II* attempts to redeem the overprivileged Angel Beachers by having them "punch upwards" at the separation of church and state, hypocritical family-values politicians, and that bugaboo-to-beat-them-all, racism.

Liberals and their associated handwringers decried *Dirty Harry* as "fascist" upon arrival. Thus the sequel, *Magnum Force* (1973), pits Harry against *actual* fascists—a secret police squad that functioned as roadside judge, jury, and executioners. Such soul cleansing worked brilliantly in the *Dirty Harry* example and not at all with the *Porky's* movies. *Porky's II*, as a result, stands as a demonstration of *Magnum Force*'s signature line: "A man's got to know his limitations."

Porky's Revenge [1985]

DIR. JAMES KOMACK; W/DAN MONAHAN, KAKI HUNTER, WYATT KNIGHT, CHUCK MITCHELL

PRANKS ▫ CHEERLEADERS ▫ THE BIG GAME ▫ SWEDISH EXCHANGE STUDENT ▫ SHOTGUN WEDDING ▫ PROM

Three long years after *Porky's II: The Next Day*, the allegedly good-natured bad boys of Angel Beach are still on the high school basketball team, still involved in elaborate pranks, and still skirmishing with old-time nemeses, Nazistic gym matron Bula Balbricker (Nancy Parsons) and redneck vice kingpin Porky (Chuck

Mitchell). What they are *not* doing is getting any younger. The returning actors of *Porky's Revenge* look strikingly hard-worn and bedraggled for this third and final romp. Tony Ganios as Meat, in particular, appears as though his nickname is no longer a complimentary reference to his genitals, but a simple observation of his midsection. The movie's dank, dark look and nil energy keeps pace with the easily winded cast.

Porky "strikes back" as the proprietor of an outlaw riverboat casino, and the Angel Beach gang takes on the unlikeable role of high school narcs as they try to get him busted. Have these well-scrubbed pricks not done enough to keep this backwoods entrepreneur down in his place? Of course they have not.

Wendy Feign injects life as nymphomaniacal Blossom, Porky's va-va-voom-bodied, hatchet-faced daughter. By the end, her family's livelihood literally crashes and burns—yet again—when the "good guys" win one more time. Pardon me for not cheering.

PREPPIES [1984]

DIR. CHUCK VINCENT; W/DENNIS DRAKE, STEVEN HOLT, KATT SHEA, JERRY BUTLER

RICH JERKS ▣ PRANKS ▣ HOOKERS ▣ BOOGIE VAN ▣ BREAKDANCING

Polo shirts with upturned collars. Sperry boat shoes. Pastel hues. Khaki pants. Bow ties. Cashmere sweaters tied around waists and shoulders. Stately mansions. Country clubs. Tennis courts. Boarding schools. Ivy League secret societies. "Long Island lockjaw" accents. Snobbery as a constant and enviable state of being. Back in the 1980s, these and other unmistakable signifiers defined everything for which any sane human wanted to pound the pompous, pretentious, overbearing hell out of anybody who defined themselves as a preppy.

The movie *Preppies* turned out to be the lone mitigating factor among all those aesthetic and behavioral transgressions. This Chuck Vincent comedy, initially made for the Playboy Channel, and then (like the same year's *Hardbodies*) deemed theater-worthy, is really goddamned funny and sexy. Believe it, Buffy.

Like *Valley Girl* (1983), *Breakin'* (1984), and *Joysticks* (1984), *Preppies* mines one of the decade's dominant youth moments with a shorthand title, and commits to the premise for its entirety. *Preppies* introduces us to Robert "Chip" Thompson III (Dennis Drake), Bayard Hollingsworth VIII (Steven Holt), and Marc Barrington (Peter Brady Reardon) as university headmaster Dean Flossmore (Leslie Barrett) loudly tears them new a-holes. These young old-money scions face expulsion if they don't pass their economics final the following Monday. When this yelling is happening, it's already Friday.

Lowlife janitor Louie (Anthony Matteo)—aka "the town hump"—eavesdrops, and then rats the lads out to Chip's ne'er-do-well cousin Blackwell (Leonard Haas). That jerk stands to inherit $50 million if Chip flunks the test. Blackwell slips Louie $20,000 cash to make sure Chip and his buddies are too distracted to study over the weekend. As this deal goes down, Blackwell is barely clad in fetish leathers, crawling on all fours, and being walked on a leash by insult-barking Mistress Tanya (Beverly Brown) in a kink dungeon lined with naked real-life porn stars (Little Oral Annie, Annette Heinz, Sharon Kane, and Tish Ambrose).

Louie flags down a sweet black boogie van transporting a quartet of local party girls: feisty Tip (Katie Stelletello), savvy Roxy (Nitchie Barrett), tough-but-sweet Suzy (Jo-Ann Marshall), and towering, toothsome blonde Jo (Cindy Manion). Louie successfully bribes them into fucking Chip, Bayard, and Marc for the next three days to prevent any possibility of studying. Roxy says she's saving her vaginal virtue for TV soap star Dick Foster (peacocking porn stud Jerry Butler). After the ladies spot Dick at a disco on breakdance night, they share a joint in a men's room stall (where, in response to hearing penises spray urine around them, Jo gushes, "This is erotic!").

They coerce Roxy into helping by guaranteeing her a date with the soap stud.

Technically now prostitutes, the van girls don waitress costumes and crash a ritzy soirée at the Thompson estate. They comically run afoul of Chip's skinny, snooty heiress girlfriend Margot (Katt Shea, delivering one of the genre's most hilarious performances) and her bosomy cotillion companion Trini (Lynda Wiesmeier of *Joysticks*, *Private School*, and the July 1982 issue of *Playboy*).

Next, the seductresses-for-hire doll up Roxy in preppette drag and send her inside the Thompson manse pretending she's "Muffy," an old society friend. While Roxy baits the boys with porn videos, the three other gals strip to lingerie and set up an orgy chamber in the swanky living room—only to be banished again by meddling Margot and Trini just prior to penetration.

From there, *Preppies* lurches in an unexpected direction. Margot has her four rivals thrown in the clink on trumped-up charges. Not studying much even without any distractions, the boys head out on a scouting mission to a neighborhood tavern, where they lose their clothes in a drunken backroom poker game. Meanwhile, Margot tells Trini that to win back their men, they'll have to practice the strange feeling of sexual arousal.

With lust in mind, the lean, lanky Margot and curvaceously cushioned Trini peel to their undies, lie next to one another in twin beds, and launch into the sexiest hip thrusts, orgasmic bucks, and moans of ecstasy that could possibly be allowed within the confines of an R rating.

After a few more slapstick crackups, the semiprofessional regular gals with the cool van fall head-over-heels for the prep squad. They decide to switch sides and help the dudes pass their exam. Blackwell busts in with a Thompson submachine gun—a gangster gag about the origins of all the family dough—but he is thwarted by Dick Foster, who thinks the others are shooting a movie. Everybody gets laid at the end, except Blackwell, who gets pummeled, tackled, and kicked. As we already know, for him that beats getting laid in the first place.

I love *Preppies*. Chuck Vincent's energy and imagination peak here, and the performers—a potent mix of New York stage actors, veterans of Chuck's X-rated directorial oeuvre, and reliable exploitation staples—play everything to an uproarious, always engaging hilt. Special commendations go to tall drink of sexily crazy-eyed allure Cindy Manion, as Jo, and Katt Shea, who hits one perfect pitch after another as obnoxiously overprivileged moneybags ballbuster Margot.

Manion legitimately lights up the screen, so it's a shame her only other credits are as "Dancing Coed" in Brian De Palma's *Blow Out* (1981) and as amusingly heartless, nerd-abusing Julie in *The Toxic Avenger* (1984).

Shea, on the other hand, after memorably appearing in *My Tutor* (1983), and in *Hollywood Hot Tubs* (1984), went onto become a maker of stylishly sordid cult thrillers. In addition to writing and directing *Stripped to Kill* (1987) and *Stripped to Kill II: Live Girls* (1989), Katt Shea also created the Christina Applegate runaway saga *Streets* (1990); the franchise-launching Drew Barrymore potboiler *Poison Ivy* (1993); and *The Rage: Carrie II* (1999). In 1994, New York's Museum of Modern Art mounted a retrospective of Shea's work as a writer and director. The high honor was richly deserved, but MoMA somehow omitted *Preppies*. For that particular venue, maybe the subject matter hit a little too close to home.

PRETTY IN PINK [1986]

DIR. HOWARD DEUTCH; W/MOLLY RINGWALD, JON CRYER, ANDREW MCCARTHY, ANNIE POTTS

ARTSY GIRL • NERD • PREPPY • RICH JERKS • RECORD STORE • PROM

Pretty in Pink proves to be the deepest, most heartfelt, and by far most *human* of the John Hughes 1980s teen films. Going against expectation, the movie's star-crossed high school romance dares to end with the smart, genuinely special girl ditching the adoring dork in favor of the rich guy. That's nervy, because that's life, and it *ain't* always "pretty."

The original Hughes screenplay ended with the exact opposite outcome. Andie (Molly Ringwald), the artsy lower-class misfit who makes her own clothes and works at the cool retro–new wave record shop, initially chose her worshipful and flamboyant nerd best friend Ducky (Jon Cryer) instead of privileged, pampered big-money suburbanite Blaine (Andrew McCarthy), who courts her and takes her out for a night to remember.

Test audiences, most of them actual teenagers, bemoaned the forced phoniness of the original "losers are beautiful" wrap-up. They insisted the story should close on the note it reaches so organically and sympathetically. Thus, a quick reshoot rendered the *Pretty in Pink* we all know today.

The plot is familiar. *Pretty in Pink* stands out for how fully realized and multidimensional the characters are, including the ones that, in other Hughes films, would be brittle stereotypes. Andie herself, while courting "dream girl" status, is palpably hurt to her soul by her mother's abandonment. She expresses it through the codependent care she takes of her alcoholic father (Harry Dean Stanton). Her friend Duckie's madness scarily bleeds through when he talks of ritualistically riding his bike past Andie's house, and when with impotent rage he tears down a prom banner and scrambles off to nowhere. Even Blaine is underconfident and confused; he longs for something deeper in life than what he knows is possible; he also knows he's got something coming to him, he just doesn't know what.

Most impressively, *Pretty in Pink*'s villain, Steff (James Spader), is a haughty, wealth-flaunting blowhard who aims to destroy Andie because she rejected him. He is portrayed as being plagued by alternately cruel and inattentive parents. He lashes out at his peers in pursuit of something to fill the hole his parents have dug into him.

Thankfully, the poor kids are not "noble savages" like John Bender (Judd Nelson) in *The Breakfast Club*, neither are the rich kids psychotically arrogant "are-you-having-my-kind-of-fun-yet?" fascists in the mold of Ferris Bueller. Just as thankfully, that's likely because this time screenwriter and executive producer John Hughes ceded the director's chair to Howard Deutch.

Pretty in Pink seems to be aware, especially during the big prom night denouement, that its characters are children. So what we see on-screen *is* life—in the context of what life means as you head toward the senior prom. Everyone involved is about to discover how much bigger they and the world can and inevitably *will* get. Deutch subtly communicates such notions through an important sense of adult distance that Hughes never mustered on his own.

A popular, frequently voiced cross-reading in the years since *Pretty in Pink*'s release insists that Duckie is gay, and that he will find his way out of the closet after high school. I disagree. Ducky just plays like a desperate doofus maniacally trying to inflate the only connection he has to a live female his age into an epic romance, due to paralyzing terror that no other woman will ever be interested in him. Trust me on this one.

The following year's gender-flipped remake, *Some Kind of Wonderful*, also directed by Deutch and written by Hughes, reinstalls Hughes's first feel-good ending, rendering itself inessential.

PRETTY SMART [1987]

DIR. DMITRI LOGOTHETIS; W/TRICIA LEIGH FISHER, PATRICIA ARQUETTE, DENNIS COLE, JULIE K. SMITH

BOARDING SCHOOL ▪ GOTH GIRL ▪ NEW WAVE ▪ PEEPING ▪ PILLOW FIGHTS ▪ EVIL HEADMASTER

Pretty Smart filters the plot specifics—and the nudity—of a tawdry women-in-prison potboiler like *Chained Heat* (1983) through a wholesome sheen and fashion blender of peak 1980s teen chick flicks like *Girls Just Want to Have Fun*

(1985). Remarkably, the twain doth meet here with bizarre effectiveness.

Somehow, this saga—a European girls' boarding school headmaster secretly videotapes fornicating students for profit, then uses them to run drugs—comes off as a sweet coming-of-age tale in which two young sisters learn, at last, that their differences are what makes them such a perfect team. The movie is also loaded with foul language.

In the movie, Ogilvy Academy is a ritzy finishing institution located in a castle on a Greek island. Gothy rebel Daphne "Zigs" Ziegler (Tricia Leigh Fisher, who's great) and her perky blonde sister Jennifer "Jen" Ziegler (Lisa Lörient, who's there) are shipped to this locale by their well-to-do parents. We see their entire life stories play out in still photos while a wondrously bratty synth-pop song plays over the opening credits.

At Ogilvy, Jen quickly finds her place among the fine-scrubbed, bubbleheaded "Preems" (short for "Supremes"), while Zigs falls in with punky new wave multiracial misfits the "Subs." Among the latter is Zero (Patricia Arquette), who explains that the name is thought to stand for "subhumanoids," but they say it's for "subculture." Zero's subculture seems to be that she chain-puffs blue cigarettes.

For a while, some fairly standard sleepover school stuff happens: sex ed, stupid etiquette lessons, impromptu dorm room dance parties, pillow fights, late-night bonding conversations, cafeteria showdowns, and incidental nudity. The supporting cast of stunners includes future B-movie action heroine Julie K. Smith as Samantha Falconwright, a Sub who could pass as a Preem. Lording over them all is headmaster Richard Crawley ('70s TV hunk Dennis Cole), a squinty-eyed prick who gets up to global criminal scuzzery on the side. Crawley looks like a rapidly aged Ricky Schroeder gone rancid, oozing smarmy sleaze with searing villainous impact.

Zigs repeatedly torments Crawley through pranks, such as pretending she's hugely pregnant during a live TV profile of the school. She delivers a crazily elaborate shock rock performance at a fancy benefit soirée. The girls start to suspect that Crawley is not just mean but evil after he fires cool English teacher Miss Gentry (Kim Waltrip) for joining some students in topless sunbathing.

When Crawley's underage pornography and drug trafficking ring comes to light, the Preems and Subs unite and take him down in grand fashion. They show Crawley their own secretly made tape of how they thwarted his cocaine and heroin shipment to Rome; really rubbing it in with a shot of powdery white lines that spell out "No Dope for the Pope." The girls have a good chuckle when an infuriated mobster calls about the missing goods and promises to kill Crawley. A happy ending soon follows, complete with a return from exile of the topless teacher and more of that fabulous theme music.

THE PRINCESS ACADEMY [1987]

DIR. BRUCE A. BLOCK; W/LAR PARK-LINCOLN, LU LEONARD, RICHARD PAUL, EVA GABOR

SWISS BOARDING SCHOOL ▣ VIRGIN ▣ TEXAS GIRL ▣ TEEN FEMINIST ▣ FASCIST AUTHORITIES

Building upon one solid, funny premise after another, *The Princess Academy* sets up a booming teen sex blowout and then busts out all the big guns except the one that matters most: sex.

A cartoon introduces us to an orphan girl who falls in with rough characters before a social reform program ships her off to Von Pupsin Academy in Switzerland. Eighteen-year-old Cindy Cathcart (Lar Park-Lincoln) is a wide-eyed neophyte among her variously snooty and tawdry classmates, each an amusing boarding school stereotype: mafia princess, bawdy Texan, arch French sophisticate, "loony Left" British bra-burner, and so on.

Running the Von Pupsin show are bullish disciplinarian Fräulein Stinkenschmidt (Lu Leonard) and her roly-poly henchman Drago (Richard Paul, who played Jerry Falwell in *The People vs.*

Clockwise from top left: Pink Motel *(1982), a wonderfully weird poster for this woeful film*; Private School *(1983), extra-topless in Germany where teen sexuality was the norm; horizontal advertising for* The Pom-Pom Girls *(1976), a definitive drive-in smash.*

Larry Flynt [1996]). *Green Acres* goddess Eva Gabor portrays Countess Von Pupsin. Her role here, along with Zsa Zsa Gabor's part in *Hollywood Dreaming* (1986), makes complete the contributions of both fabulous Gabor sisters to teen movie hell. Cha-ching, *dahlings!*

Princess Academy sends its cadre of coeds on all the standard adventures—liberating a dorm virgin from her cripplingly intact hymen; busting captives out of a nearby boys' academy; hanging out in swanky European lingerie—and never violates the parameters of a PG rating.

Legendary 1950s comedian Sid Caesar performs the theme song, "Gold Card Rap," in a succession of his signature nonsense-speak foreign dialects. Hail, Caesar!

PRIVATE LESSONS [1981]

DIR. ALAN MYERSON; W/SYLVIA KRISTEL, ERIC BROWN, HOWARD HESSEMAN, PETER PICCININNI

VIRGINS 📼 COUGAR 📼 BIG FAT PARTY ANIMAL 📼 HOMOSEXUAL PANIC

As an all-encompassing come-on, the poster for *Private Lessons* hits a bull's-eye with its pastel rendering of a young boy standing atop a pile of schoolbooks in order to suck face with a taller and presumably older woman. The tagline teases: "What happened to him should happen to you!" At once, the image is cheeky, tawdry, and bogusly innocent—an extremely dawn-of-the-1980s version of "classy."

The "him" that something happens to in *Private Lessons* is poor little rich fifteen-year-old Phillip "Philly" Fillmore (Eric Brown), the motherless scion of an Albuquerque business mogul. His best bud is Sherman (Peter Piccininni), a happy little rich blob next door who loves life and devours entire canisters of whipped cream with boundless brio.

When Philly's pop departs on an extended trip, he leaves the kid in the hands of reptilian chauffeur Lester Lewis (Howard Hesseman, who is hilarious). Also on hand is Nicole Mallow, a newly arrived, thirtysomething live-in French tutor portrayed by international sexploitation superstar Sylvia Kristel (of *Emmanuelle* skinfamy). You don't need to see the poster to know straightaway what's going to happen to *him* and what *should* happen to you.

After a long, intermittently amusing and arousing series of flirtations, Nicole alleviates Philly's unsullied sexual status in a scene of unexpected credibility and resonance, not to mention plenty of the very much expected bare body bits. The older seductress with underage lad coupling sets in motion a wacky caper plot. First, Nicole pretends Philly's sexual prowess killed her. Lester subsequently blackmails the panicked lad. As Philly gets set to pay, Nicole, now in hiding, realizes that her affection for her stupefied student is genuine. (not to mention genuinely against the law, but that's all part of the fun).

Next come some nutty runaround slapstick scenes, highlighted by Ed Begley Jr.'s, amusing attempt to impersonate a police officer. Secrets spill out into the open when Lester's longtime companion is revealed to be the funniest male sex doll ever photographed.

For the generation raised on early-'80s cable TV and the first wave of VHS, viewing *Private Lessons* proved to be a rite of passage—much more so than the actual experiences depicted in the movie. For a nation of preteen virgins, *Private Lessons* delivered the residue of the 1970s sexual revolution in a ball of funny, stressful, uncomfortable, and ultimately rewarding feelings. The action on-screen is repeatedly underscored by two songs—"I Need a Lover" by John Cougar and "Fantasy" by Earth, Wind & Fire. For the rest of Philly's life, we know exactly where his head will go whenever he comes across those nuggets.

Before *Porky's* laid the path for the 1980s teen sex comedy explosion, *Private Lessons* set the table for *Porky's*, both conceptually and in the movie marketplace. Produced for $2.8 million, *Private Lessons* grossed $26.2 million in its long box office run, making it the single most profitable big-screen release of 1981.

Of special literary interest, writer Dan Greenburg adapted *Private Lessons* for the screen, basing it on his own much freakier 1969 novel, *Philly*. The book shares the movie's exact plot, but plays things deadly straight, as a suspense tale flecked with dread and horror. How that particular book became the upbeat, farcical *Private Lessons* on the big screen is a genuine head-scratcher turned crotch-grabber, but happily, somehow it happened. *Lessons*'s success also prompted Universal to hired Greenburg to fire off the script for a sequel. After a couple of years of rewrites, that project evolved into the Phoebe Cates favorite, *Private School* (1983).

TV game show host Jack Barry produced *Private Lessons*. An archetypal "Hairspray Harry"–esque emcee, Barry fell from grace into infamy and industry blackballing during the 1950s quiz show scandals, but then came back a big-time winner in the 1970s by way of *The Joker's Wild*. He really knew how to pull all the right levers.

Private Resort [1985]

DIR. GEORGE BOWERS; W/JOHNNY DEPP, ROB MORROW, HECTOR ELIZONDO, LESLIE EASTERBROOK

VIRGIN ▪ AEROBICS ▪ BUMBLING COP ▪ BUMBLING CROOK ▪ PUNKS ▪ QUAALUDES

Plain and simple, *Private Resort* is a pile of hilarity. Johnny Depp, as Jack, and Rob Morrow, as Ben, are two dudes hanging around a splashy Miami hotel for a weekend, hoping to score some action. They came to the right place; they find plenty, and it's all plenty funny.

Complicating the lads' best let's-get-laid plans are hotheaded jewel heister the Maestro (Hector Elizondo) and his bodacious gun moll Bobbie Sue (Leslie Easterbrook). Jack and Ben also have to contend with the resort's harebrained house detective (Tony Azito) and fascistic barber (Ronald E. House), as well as with a secretly sex-mad snooty old rich lady Mrs. Rawlings (Dody Goodman) and brawny Brooklyn palooka Curt (Andrew Dice Clay). Rounding things out properly are two Japanese sumo wrestlers.

Our boys contend for vacationing young ladies, including glamorous good girls Dana (Karyn O'Bryan) and Patti (Emily Longstreth), who are joined by space cadet Shirley (Hilary Shepard), who nakedly worships a god solely of her understanding that she calls "Baba Ram Donna Madonna." Add to this mix a ten-year-old kid plucking off sunbathers' bikinis with a fishing rod, and a stoned faux-Spicoli surfer with a Mohawk who punctuates each nutty dustup by guffawing, "No waaaaaaaay!"

Depp and Morrow make an instantly winning duo, although the wheels skid when, before a date, Depp tosses Morrow a prescription bottle of "the love drug"—quaaludes— and proclaims: "She'll be *all over* you!" You'll be looking in vain for Bill Cosby's name in the credits, wondering how much else of the "common knowledge" of 1985 was more criminal than comic.

Director George Bowers previously made *My Tutor* (1983). Before that, he honed his teen sex comedy instincts as an editor on *The Pom Pom Girls* (1976), *Van Nuys Blvd.* (1979), and *The Beach Girls* (1982). After *Private Resort*, Bowers returned to editing full-time, reuniting with Depp in 2001 for the Jack the Ripper conspiracy thriller *From Hell*. There the script was off quaaludes and onto laudanum.

Private School [1983]

aka Private School...for Girls

DIR. NOEL BLACK; W/PHOEBE CATES, MATTHEW MODINE, BETSY RUSSELL, MICHAEL ZOREK

GIRLS' SCHOOL ▪ NERDS ▪ PEEPING ▪ TOPLESS HORSEBACK RIDING ▪ AEROBICS ▪ MOONING

"Bubba Beauregard is the ultimate party animal!" proclaimed the ads for *Private School*. Someone vastly misjudged the mark in thinking *Private School*'s primary selling point would be the plus-size neo-Belushi beast played at full force by Michael Zorek. The main attraction, of course, was and is Phoebe Cates, headlining here less than a year after *Fast Times at Ridgemont*

High. Everything about *Private School* promises that Phoebe will get even *more* naked this time.

She doesn't, and Bubba Beauregard is *not* the ultimate party animal of '80s teen sex comedies. Still, Phoebe is lovable and luminous, and both Zorek and the movie itself bust out as many antics as possible in pursuit of good-time over-the-top gold. By the end, everyone involved has earned a T&A-plus for their efforts.

Colloquially known as *Private School...for Girls* due to the poster design, the movie is set at Cherryvale Academy for Women, where Christine Ramsey (Cates) and roommate Betsy (Kathleen Wilhoite) pine for romance and are perpetually annoyed by snooty rich witch Jordan Leigh-Jensen (Betsy Russell). Meanwhile, at the nearby Freemount Academy for Men, aforementioned human wrecking ball Bubba convinces nice guy Jim (Matthew Modine) and nerdburger Roy (Jonathan Prince) to conduct a surveillance run on Cherryvale. They climb on one another's shoulders (with rotund Bubba naturally on top), peep an eyeful of Jordan in the shower, and suffer slapstick injuries.

From there, the game is on! Instead of snooping from afar, the fired-up Freemounters don drag as new female students and take up residency in the girls' dorm. How could this *not* work?

Private School is a blast, fitfully generates out-loud laughter, often over bouts of bona fide sleaze. This is a respectable Hollywood production, which is easy to forget during ogle interludes such as Bubba's expedition to the girls' packed shower room. An outdoor aerobics class set to "The American Girl" by Rick Springfield could be a gynecological training film on the study of spandex-encased female anatomy. The movie's parting shot is a mass all-girl mooning that freezes and then turns into a museum-quality watercolor work of art.

Famously, Betsy Russell doffs her top while astride a galloping horse; she one-ups bareback riding by inventing bare-front riding. The song playing is "How Do I Let You Know," belted out by Phoebe Cates herself. Phoebe also duets with Bill Wray on the soundtrack ballad, "Just One Touch." Since they portray enemies, this is a nice way for the actors to share a happy scene together.

The whole cast rocks. Cates and Zorek are winning protagonists, even more so backed by Modine and Wilhoite. Betsy Russell is one of the genre's best vixen villains. Underappreciated character actress Fran Ryan (Bill Murray's taxi passenger at the beginning of *Stripes* [1981]) makes a perfect prude as headmistress Miss Dutchbok. Ray Walston, arriving directly after playing Mr. Hand in *Fast Times*, does much with his brief turn as a grumpy chauffeur. Martin Mull tickles as always in an unbilled role as a condom-pushing pharmacist. Why a professionally droll wit like Mull remained uncredited on a film like this remains a mystery; maybe he just liked to keep some things *private*.

An educational point: *Private School* began life as a sequel to *Private Lessons* (1981). Universal Pictures made such a cash-heap with that teen sex comedy that the studio hired *Private Lessons* screenwriter Dan Greenburg to pen a follow-up. Just as *Private Lessons* deviated from Greenburg's own source novel *Philly*—which is essentially a horror thriller—*Private School* took two long years to evolve into what it became. The sole connecting point between the two films is costar Sylvia Kristel, who gamely fulfills her contractual obligation to appear in any form of *Private Lessons 2*. In *Private School*, Sylvia plays sex-ed instructor Ms. Copuletta. The lady was a pro.

Puberty Blues [1981]

DIR. BRUCE BERESFORD; W/NELL SCHOFIELD, JAD CAPELJA, JEFFREY RHOE, TONY HUGHES

BEST GIRLFRIENDS ▣ SURFERS ▣ VIRGINS ▣ DRUGS ▣ CUSTOM VANS

Based on a popular, autobiographical young-adult novel and emerging during the late-1970s/early-1980s Australian film explosion, *Puberty Blues* caught on big on its home continent and did well in art-house theaters globally. The film is sweet and a little jarring. It hasn't aged timelessly at all, which makes the movie all the more interesting.

Even during the anything-goes era when *Puberty Blues* was made, the filmmakers felt compelled to age up the main characters from the novel—working-class Sidney and best friends Debbie (Nell Schofield) and Sue (Jad Capelja)—from thirteen to sixteen. That's because, in the course of the girls' attempts to fit in with the socially desirable local "surfie" scene, they drink beer, smoke weed, and have a lot of sex.

The scenes that hit hardest depict Debbie and Sue repeatedly flouncing past their parents while they're freshly sexed and as chemically wasted as any wiped-out surfer. Time and time again, the adults don't notice.

Puberty Blues peaks with our heroines riding waves to an agreeably feminist victory—and becoming fixtures of their national mythology. The source book remains an Australian rite of passage. In 2012, an eight-episode TV adaptation proved so popular that it came back for a second season.

THE RACHEL PAPERS [1989]

DIR. DAMIAN HARRIS; W/DEXTER FLETCHER, IONE SKYE, JAMES SPADER, CLAIRE SKINNER

VIRGIN 📼 SMART GUY 📼 DREAM GIRL

The Rachel Papers, the soulful and sidesplitting 1973 debut novel by Martin Amis, made me guffaw out loud long before the movie. Teenage hero Charles Highway hides a box of Kleenex as he prepares his room for a female visitor, noting, "A box of tissues next to the bed makes the statement, 'You know, the big thing about me is that I wank a devil of a lot.'"

That scene is passively re-created in the film, but, removed from Amis's first-person narration and specific wordplay, the effect is lost. The movie comes off as what writer Rob Sheffield once defined as "medium-funny." You note that you're seeing something clever and amusing, but you never actually laugh.

The plot recounts a heavy end-of-high-school infatuation. Romance forms fast as cuttingly witty, Oxford-bound Charles Highway (Dexter Fletcher) falls for beamingly beautiful American transfer student Rachel (Ione Skye). Charles conspires with friends and family to win Rachel's heart at any cost. He soon steals her away from the frighteningly smug DeForest (James Spader), only to discover that Rachel's not so special after all. Worse than that, and more importantly, Charles comes to realize that maybe he himself isn't so special, either.

The cast is right on the money (not to be confused with *Money*—my favorite Martin Amis book). As Charles, the terribly British, charmin and gawky Dexter Fletcher successfully embodies the young Amis voice. Ione Skye, at once immediately pretty and inwardly distant, perfectly plays Rachel as a teenager who takes things as they come, unaffected by how severely her suitor has idealized her. Spader does his Spader thing to standard perfection. Writer-director Damian Harris performs his tasks ably, too.

The Rachel Papers is not a classic; it's the right movie that simply happened at the very wrong time. Physically, the film resembles the ghastly big-screen abortion of Brett Easton Ellis's *Less Than Zero* from the previous year. Amis's serrated-edge humor stands no chance in so sterile an environment. *The Rachel Papers* is a teen sex comedy that aches to be dirtier, but not in the usual T&A way. Some things just aren't funny enough unless somebody really does get hurt.

Real Genius [1985]

DIR. MARTHA COOLIDGE: W/VAL KILMER, GABRIEL JARRET, MICHELLE MEYRINK, WILLIAM ATHERTON

COOL NERDS ◘ CUTE NERD GIRLS ◘ TECH COLLEGE ◘ SCIENCE PROJECT ◘ PRANKS

Real Genius is the *Risky Business* of '80s science nerd farces. Martha Coolidge's brainy, stylish, pointed collegiate comedy was too often mixed up with its lower-brow cinematic brethren, much the way *Risky Business* tends to be classified as a boob movie about a rich kid trying to pop his cherry with a prostitute. On close inspection, both multilevel classics leverage adolescent struggles to crack open universal and hugely human issues, follies, and foibles.

On the surface, *Real Genius* is all about college science geeks pulling off huge pranks, falling for one another, and socking it to prickly administrators. Even the savagely satiric opening scene indicates larger notions at play. CIA officers watch a video of a space shuttle firing a laser beam toward earth, taking out a single human target on his own front lawn. "Now, gentlemen," beams one agent, "all we have to do is build it!" Nearby in the screening room sits Professor Jerry Hathaway (William Atherton), of the fictional Pacific Institute of Technology, who assures the government folk he already has unpaid, unwitting student talent at his disposal to make this weapon of pinpoint assassination an insanely profitable reality.

Faster than fiber-optic cable, we meet the Pacific Tech attendees that Hathaway will rope into his sinister project. Early high school graduate Mitch Taylor (Gabriel Jarret) moves into a dorm room alongside flashy, cynical, machine-gun-witted physics genius and inveterate prank innovator Chris Knight (Val Kilmer). Overly energetic but endearing motormouth Jordan (Michelle Meyrink) lives across the hall. Somewhere in a lair beyond the very back of Chris's closet dwells legendary engineer turned hairy wraith Lazlo Hollyfeld (Jon Gries). He already cracked years earlier, upon discovering his class theories had been sold to build war machines.

Real Genius sends these complex, credible characters on a labyrinthine adventure fueled by their collective intelligence and talents. In adhering to Knight's guiding principle that work should be always fun, every line is witty and each comedic set piece generates loud laughs—as when the good guys rig a speaker system inside the dental fillings of Hathaway's toady assistant to convince him he's receiving messages from God. The film also assumes the viewer can keep up with the science elements, allowing for better, more devious pranks. Ultimately, the brainiacs invert their own subversion and use the space laser for nothing more nefarious than a peaceful protest that produces tons of fresh-popped popcorn.

Coolidge's direction deftly propels the plot and showcases the performances, each of which ranks among the very best in teen films of this era. Kilmer could not have been better cast; he turns Chris Knight into some very specific cool older-kid hero. Then he spins our perception of the character by gently revealing that we admire him not so much for his attitude as for his brain, and—more important and surprising—his good heart and active conscience.

Atherton's blowhard professor is a great comedic persona that he would tap again on TV's *Murphy Brown* and in the neo-slob comedy *Bio-Dome* (1996). Jarret seems like he could possibly be the prodigy he's playing. Meyrink is a revelation of sharp sweetness and endlessly bubbling depth; her decision a few years later to leave acting and pursue Zen Buddhism full-time comes off as a natural extension of everything she brings here to the screen.

Although up to the minute in its Reagan-era "Star Wars" weaponry and late-Cold War specifics, *Real Genius*'s screenplay, cowritten by erstwhile *Police Academy* collaborators Neal Israel and Pat Proft, comes off like a counterculture lampoon of the 1960s that nobody could pull off back then because they were too stoned.

Revenge of the Nerds also deals with academic overachievers cutting through complications on campus, and it's also extremely funny. On essentially every level, though, *Real Genius* is the better film. It's richer and more fully realized and, when the "vengeance" comes into play, the heroes humiliate the military-industrial complex rather than merely mean-spirited fellow students. They also do it with by making mountains of popcorn rather than creating proto–revenge porn and tricking anybody into sex.

Rebel High [1987]

DIR. HARRY JAKOBS; W/KENNY ROBINSON, HARVEY BERGER, CAROL SHAMY, SHIRLEY MEROVITZ

HIGH SCHOOL RUN WILD • NEW PRINCIPAL • NERDS • PUNKS • BULLIES • SAUNA • FAT GUY • WEED • BEER • HOT TUB • PIE FIGHT

The first image on-screen in *Rebel High* is the director's credit: "A Harry Jakobs Comic Book." Next, a narrator imitating vintage newscaster Walter Cronkite informs us: "This is a story about a high school. It isn't much of a story, but then, this isn't much of a high school. It's full of beer drinkers, dope smokers, hooky players, liars, and assholes...and those are just the teachers." So far, so good. Then we learn the most important aspect of *Rebel High*: The movie happens at a place actually named "Rebel High School." Perfect.

In this Canadian tax-write-off venture, new principal Edwin Swimper (Harvey Berger) arrives at Rebel High School and is stupefied by its post-apocalyptic condition. Boom boxes blare, sludge bubbles from below, fires blaze right and left, dynamite goes bang throughout the day, students attack one another with machine guns, the teachers dress for combat, and the walls literally come crumbling down. To cope, Swimper practices martial arts, hires a weirdly vampiric undercover narc (Shawn Goldwater), and tries to shake up the curriculum with new classes such as archery, leading to more bloodshed.

Chubby class cutup Calvin Hampster (Kenny Robinson) keeps the movie moving through all the anarchy and overall one-hair-above-Troma messiness. In fact, credit is due the entire racially diverse cast; well-integrated schools are a rarity in teen movie hell, needless to say a seeming impossibility in an '80s teen comedy from Canada.

Robinson is a north-of-the-border stand-up comedy institution; many of the other performers were fellow comics from the legendary Toronto club Yuk Yuk's. A documentary on that comedy scene would be cool, and would have no problem fitting all the bits of *Rebel High* worth seeing alongside as much other footage as exists. I also suggest a new movie should come out called *Rebel High* starring Rebel Wilson, a gal who could headline a party animal movie for the ages.

Record City [1978]

DIR. DENNIS STEINMETZ; W/TED LANGE, ED BEGLEY JR., RUTH BUZZI, RICK DEES

RECORDS • COOL DJ • GORILLA ARM

Because the movie is set in a giant 1978 record store heavily patronized by nubile teens in tube tops and short shorts, *Record City* is regularly mistaken for a teen sex comedy. The opening credits alone indicate that nothing young could possibly exist here. Check out this crazy star roster: "Disco Duck" DJ Rick Dees; Frank Gorshin (the Riddler from TV's *Batman*) in multiple roles; Borscht Belt comic Jack Carter; "Ride 'em, Jewboy" country music satirist Kinky Friedman; Ruth Buzzi (*Laugh-In*); Alice Ghostley (*Bewitched*); Larry Storch (Agarn from *F-Troop*) as a deaf crate-digger; Sorrell Booke (Boss Hogg from *The Dukes of Hazzard*); Harold Sakata (Odd Job from *Goldfinger*); Ted Lange (Isaac, Your Bartender, from *The Love Boat*); and young watermelon-slaughtering jokester Gallagher. Ed Begley Jr. turns up as a would-be thief. That isn't a dream cast in teen movie hell, it's a nightmare soup line from retirement home hell.

Record City's plot follows hyped-to-the-gills DJ Rick Dees, wearing one arm of a gorilla suit, throwing a manic variety show in the parking lot of an enormous record store in the L.A. suburbs. Inside the store, the zany cast attempts to connect episodic swings at humor, maintaining a highly flawed hit ratio of zero-point-zero. The real appeal, forty years onward, is the off-the-charts nostalgia factor for anyone who yearns for immersion in 1978-era vinyl LPs by the truckload, complete with promotional standees, mobiles, record flats, and store displays for Nick Drake and ZZ Top in their prime.

Claims that *Empire Records* somehow stole anything from *Record City* are laughable, as the interchangeable barcode-scanning good-looking Lollapalooza drones of the 1990s movie have nothing on the off-show-biz freak-show factor of this extended-play lunacy.

Return to Horror High [1987]

DIR. BILL FROEHLICH; W/LORI LETHIN, BRENDAN HUGHES, MAUREEN MCCORMICK, GEORGE CLOONEY

CHEERLEADERS ▫ MOVIE IN A MOVIE ▫ MAD SLASHER

Horror High (1973), aka *Twisted Brain*, is a blisteringly angry, teenage Jekyll-and-Hyde variation from Texas in which a downtrodden nebbish in a chem lab transforms himself into a bully-slaying beast of vengeance. Now forget everything about *Horror High*, because this movie has nothing to do with that.

Return to Horror High is instead a stand-alone meta-mega-spoof of horror flicks, high school comedies, and some of the low-budget bottom-feeders who make both kinds of movies. This boomeranging return is sometimes funny, not scary, more than a little confusing, and earns a blazing spot in teen movie hell with its awe-inspiring poster of a leaping skeleton in a cheerleader uniform captioned: "Killer to the Left. Killer to the Right. Stand Up. Sit Down. Fright! Fright! Fright!"

Alex Rocco (Moe Green in *The Godfather*) is a scream as always in the role of a scuzzbomb B-flick producer cashing in on real-life high school slayings on the very campus where they happened. George Clooney, hot off his late-seasons replacement role on *Facts of Life*, is the movie-within-the-movie's leading man and dies first. Maureen McCormick plays a cop faced with violence far worse than when a football whomped her in the nose on *The Brady Bunch*.

Revenge of the Cheerleaders [1976]

DIR. RICHARD LERNER; W/DAVID HASSELHOFF, RAINBEAUX SMITH, PATRICE ROHMER, HELEN LANG

CHEERLEADERS ▫ WEED ▫ THE BIG GAME ▫ FOOD FIGHT ▫ TEEN PREGNANCY

David Hasselhoff makes his big-screen debut here, brilliantly embodying a character named "Boner." His nascent star is eclipsed by Cheryl "Rainbeaux" Smith, the most archetypal of '70s pep squad flick starlets, boasting a nine-months-pregnant belly that even the fluffiest and most tassel-heavy of pom-poms fail to conceal. Rainbeaux being Rainbeaux, though, *Revenge*'s makers opted to keep their star working and weave her primed-to-pop condition into the story. The choice to stick with expectantly ripe Rainbeaux benefits both this film and the entire cheerleader movie genre immensely.

Director Richard Lerner, who also cowrote the 1973 drive-in blockbuster *The Cheerleaders* (to which *Revenge* is some sort of cosmic sequel) clearly sports a good, solid head on his shoulders. The vengeance-seeking spirit-boosters of *Revenge of the Cheerleaders* attend Aloha, California's Aloha High School, an institution that, aside from some outdoor footage, consists of a set that might have been rejected as too hokey for

Clockwise from top left: Risky Business *(1983) and the Wayfarers that made Tom Cruise a star;* Real Genius *(1985) en français, Val Kilmer and some old guy swapping what look like Internet-era shirt designs;* Recruits *(1986), a* Police Academy *ripoff from the director of* Screwballs *(1983)—not to be confused evern further with* Screwball Academy *(1986).*

a *Hustler* magazine "Bits & Pieces" shoot.

We meet our multicultural Aloha heroines during the opening credits. The girls freewheel about town in an open-topped convertible, happily changing into and out of their uniforms in broad daylight. Bras do not figure into the required getups in any way. The sweet ride soon arrives on campus, where flaxen-haired preggo Heather (Smith), African American Gail (Jerii Woods), raven-maned Leslie (Helen Lang), Asian babe Tishi (Susie Elene), and bubbly blonde Sesame (Patrice Rohmer) run the show.

Scandal surfaces as the *Aloha Times* runs a front-page story on Heather's knocked-uppedness: MORALITY CRISIS SHATTERS ALOHA HIGH SCHOOL! The town elders attempt to dilute the troublemaking element by merging Aloha with its despised rival, Lincoln High. Should that happen, these cheerleaders will have to claim revenge. First, though, they'll have to get nude in the locker room. Going forward, that intermediary move will be key in the gals setting up their various blows for letter-sweater justice.

Mostly the cheerleaders get even by doing what they already do, just in a slightly more vindictive direction. Specifically, that means shedding clothes and banging the nearest boner—beginning with Hasselhoff, who canoodles with Sesame in a toilet stall. Later make-out maneuvers include a soda jerk getting more than jerked beneath his work counter by Tishi, and an outdoor interlude underneath a roadside brontosaurus attraction during which Sesame and Leslie indoctrinate a mature Boy Scout in the ancient craft of threesomes. Ever energetic, these cheerleaders also dance—frequently, unexpectedly, with mad enthusiasm, and not very well—in a series of crucial time-killing shake-that-booty segments.

Revenge's great attack sequence is a doozy. The girls hold up a Lincoln High class at gunpoint and rob a crime syndicate's worth of drugs, booze, and other intoxicants from their supposedly upright peers. The cheerleaders then dump almost the entirety of their haul right into a pot of spaghetti being prepared for a special school lunch for the Aloha faculty and the Board of Education. After that, the ladies slip off to the gym and smoke what they have left while eyeballing the boys' basketball team. Chaos reigns.

Upon consuming every known inebriant via crappy cafeteria linguini, the uptight lunchroom inhabitants crack up and launch into an explosive food fight. Meanwhile, back at the gym, somebody must have sprinkled nymphomania powder on the cheerleaders' doobage, as they bum-rush the basketball players and hurl them into the shower room for a full-blown, proto-rave soapsuds orgy. The camera cuts back and forth between the two melees, building to a fever pitch that surges with every emergence from below the bubbles of Rainbeaux's inflated-with-impending-motherhood nude form.

The big basketball showdown between Aloha and Lincoln sets all the forces in motion for *Revenge*'s pseudo-action-thriller denouement, the suspense twirled even higher by having a cop pull over and frisk a couple of our extremely unclothed heroines. More dancing happens.

When everybody finally drops to the ground with exhaustion, the credits roll and *Revenge*'s most outstandingly unique moment is revealed. The camera swoops up from behind on Rainbeaux in her cheerleader outfit, whereupon she turns and shows off her real-life baby son, Justin. Both mother and child are beaming and adorable. Reports are that Boner fled the scene in a talking car.

Revenge of the Nerds

[1984]

DIR. JEFF KANEW; W/ANTHONY EDWARDS, ROBERT CARRADINE, CURTIS ARMSTRONG, JULIA MONTGOMERY

NERDS ▫ JOCKS ▫ CHEERLEADERS ▫ FRATS ▫ VIRGIN ▫ PEEPING ▫ PANTY RAID

Revenge of the Nerds long ruled as an iconic 1980s teen sex comedy and one of the best-loved underdog stories in movie history. The film is funny, sweet, inventive, and loaded with clever, original, endearing moments. Many years after its release, it is now clear that the movie is also ripe with moments that, beyond the laughter, deserve some serious reevaluation.

To be sure, *Revenge of the Nerds* is a riot that enriched our culture with its brotherhood of campus outcasts led by über-doofus Lewis (Robert Carradine) and gentledork Gilbert (Anthony Edwards). Among the put-upon compadres are grungy cutup Booger (Curtis Armstrong); English-averse Japanese science major Takashi (Brian Tochi); and flamingly out-and-proud African American Lamar (Larry B. Scott). These geeks are the targets of savage cruelty until they unite and ultimately triumph hilariously over their bullies.

About those bullies—they are the worst. *Revenge* finalized cinematic jock evil in the form of the Alpha Beta asshole frat and its meathead football tools. Handsome dick Stan (Ted McGinley) and brutal beast Ogre (Donald Gibb) lead the offensive in the constant sadistic humiliation of our heroes with vicious Coach Harris (John Goodman) and coldhearted cheerleaders and Pi Delta Pi sorority sisters Betty Childs (Julia Montgomery) and Suzy (Lisa Welch).

Among its beloved comedic highlights, *Revenge of the Nerds* boasts Lewis's uproarious jackass guffaw; Booger claiming ignorance of where his nickname came from while digging in his nostril; Lamar successfully negotiating with black frat Lambda Lambda Lambda to get a campus charter for his mega-pale dork pals; and the nerds' electrifying new-wave techno-rap performance of the tune "They're So Incredible."

Then comes the stuff that once made seemingly millions of viewers laugh long and loud, but now seems difficult to experience with a light heart. When the nerds stage a panty raid, for example, the scene plays as scary. When they install surveillance cameras to watch the sorority girls shower, Booger's victory cry—"We've got bush!"—sounds jarringly ugly. The Lambdas' "vengeance" against head cheerleader Julie involves printing secretly snapped nude photos of her on pie plates and selling them to the public. That kind of revenge soft-porn feels psychotically disproportionate to her offenses: She's really just a very mean girl—no need to screw up the rest of her life. No doubt many obese and ugly fifteen-year-old boys in the audience in 1984 were rooting for that. Gross.

Worst of all is how Lewis "seduces" Julie. During the campus carnival, Lewis dons a Darth Vader mask and convinces Julie he's her boyfriend, Stan. During the deed that ensues, Julie declares it the greatest such encounter of her life, prompting Lewis to reveal his true identity. Rather than respond with horror, the duped cheerleader has an ecstatic epiphany: Jocks are terrible when it comes to sex, because all they ever think about is sports; but nerds are great at sex, because it's all they ever think about.

Four decades ago, these characters came off as cartoony and removed from anyone's actual college experience. Nobody was attempting to fool anybody into having sex in a Darth Vader mask in real life, but of course they were employing even worse methods of manipulation. As with life, though, *Nerds* mixes high and low, good and bad—including in the areas now deemed (sorry for this trite word) "problematic."

Among the charges leveled against the movie at present is that it's racist and homophobic. But although Lamar is a "nerd," because, yes, he's gay and black and therefore at odds with the campus power enforcement thugs, he's also a nerd because the nerds embrace Lamar exactly as he is. He's also technically higher in social status than the rest of the nerds, as without connections to the black fraternity our nerds would never be empowered to stand against their oppressors.

Lamar's funniest moment occurs at the Campus Olympics, when he triumphs by using a javelin "aerodynamically designed to accommodate his limp-wristed throwing style!" It's not just an outrageously amusing idea playing out on-screen in slow motion; it's a tweaking of a stereotype and another example of Lamar using his "otherness" to overcome those who hate him for it.

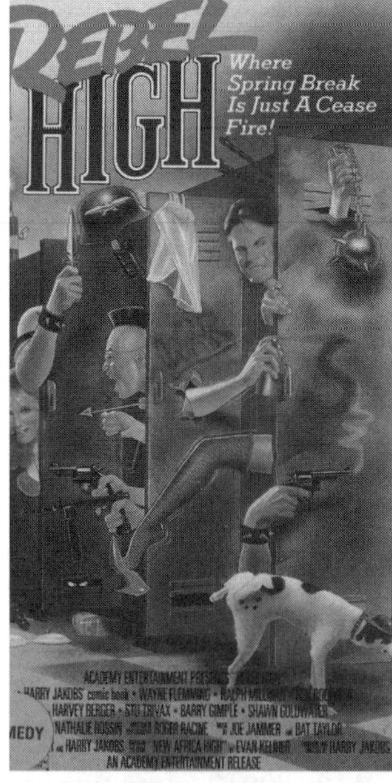

Clockwise from top left: Revenge of the Nerds *(1984), a triumph now tarnished*; Revenge of the Nerds II: Nerds in Paradise *(1987), sunk by PG-13*; Return to Horror High *(1987), slashing for laughs*; Rebel High *(1987)*; Revenge of the Cheerleaders *(1976) with David Hasselhoff as "Boner."*

On the other hand, the film's misogyny is not misunderstood by modern viewers—it's just misogyny. *Revenge of the Nerds* has inspired many teenage rejects to find each other and to live better lives as a result. However, the sexual mayhem aspect of the "revenge" really is damagingly cruel and cannot go unaddressed.

For a long time, both male and female outcasts identified with the movie's nerds and perceived the shower room video peeping and the sex-by-deception plot twist as blows against the sadistic ruling class, regardless of gender. More recently, leading up to and certainly post #MeToo, viewers have come to empathize with the female victims of the nerds' vengeance. The bullied don't just become bullies—they become revenge-porn perpetrators and Lewis even commits a bona fide sex crime. Understanding this now, the film's climactic "We Are the Champions" moment no longer rings universally victorious.

Revenge of the Nerds, it must be noted, has stayed the same—we've changed. Actually, that's presumptuous and bombastic of me: *I've* changed. All this time later, I've come to kind of view *Revenge of the Nerds* in a new light as perhaps the turning point where those who perceived themselves as being oppressed started setting out to become oppressors themselves. This awful turnabout took hold at the dawn of online culture and has since escalated infinitely, bounding from homicidal message board comments, doxxing somebody who disses *Star Wars,* all the way to the vile, violence-expounding nexus of organized alt-right, incel, and antifa groups—all the same manure in different uniforms.

The pursuit of power by those who feel powerless is a mistake when people believe power can only be acquired by making somebody else feel as bad as they once did—or still do. Here's what I know now: Living the life you want without acting like it requires enemies is the best revenge, nerds. Go forth and do that and laugh—or, better yet, bray like Lewis at his best while you can.

Revenge of the Nerds II: Nerds in Paradise [1987]

DIR. JOE ROTH; W/ROBERT CARRADINE, CURTIS ARMSTRONG, COURTNEY THORNE-SMITH

NERDS ▪ FRATS ▪ SPRING BREAK ▪ NATIVE AMERICANS ▪ WET-NIGHTIE CONTEST

Revenge of the Nerds II makes a winning pitch for marketing team and moviegoers alike: the triumphant dork-lords of Lambda Lambda Lamda invade Fort Lauderdale for spring break! Robert Carradine, Curtis Armstrong, and virtually the entire cast return. The Tri-Lambs crash at a place called the Hotel Coral Essex, where the broken neon sign spells out "Hot Oral Sex!" They run afoul of a local Native American tribe that proves to be bogus after not responding to Poindexter (Timothy Busfield) yelling, "Bite my crank!" in fluent Seminole. By the end, one of the initial evil jocks from the first movie charmingly switches sides and proudly forever reigns as the biggest nerd on campus!

Unfortunately, something happened between the hatching of that potential ultimate teen sex comedy and the limp-wick reality of what finally dribbled into multiplexes. Something sucky was the result, cleaning the nads of the definitively R-rated first *Nerds* romp and forcing an acquiescence in tone, humor, and hard-edged content. After all the offenses the first time around, *Nerds II* stumbles whimpering into that most goddamnable of 1980s setbacks: the PG-13 rating.

Revenge of the Nerds III: The Next Generation [1992]

DIR. ROLAND MESA; W/ROBERT CARRADINE, CURTIS ARMSTRONG, JULIA MONTGOMERY

NERDS ▪ JOCKS ▪ FRAT ▪ ELVIS PRESLEY ▪ MORTON DOWNEY JR.

Credit the Fox TV network for lavishing its fresh *Simpsons* income on a fairly elaborate *Revenge of the Nerds* TV movie that doesn't entirely reek like Booger's underwear. *Revenge of the Nerds III: The Next Generation* brings back Robert Carradine as Lewis Skolnick and Curtis Armstrong as Booger, along with OG villains Ted McGinley as Stan and Julia Montgomery as Betty.

Hothead talk show host Morton Downey Jr. is the baddie, an evil tycoon who, after witnessing how nerd-friendly Adams College has become, floods the campus with a fresh wave of dork-torturing jocks. Henry Cho is Steve Toyota, an Elvis-obsessed Tri-Lamb pledge fresh off the boat from Korea, speaking broken English with a Tennessee accent just like his idol. When quizzed how that's possible, Steve says: "I'm from *South* Korea."

Although the declaration that Lewis is "the George Washington of Nerds" might have hurt the feelings of Eddie Deezen somewhere out there in teen movie hell, the honorific is pretty freakin' great and well-deserved.

Revenge of the Nerds IV: Nerds in Love [1994]

DIR. STEVE ZACHARIAS; W/ROBERT CARRADINE, CURTIS ARMSTRONG, CORINNE BOHRER

NERDS ▫ NERDS ▫ MORE NERDS

Revenge of the Nerds IV: Nerds in Love moves the series' familiar reject roster away from Adams College and into adulthood—and it stinks. Lewis Skolnick (Robert Carradine) has long been married to the now-pregnant Betty (Julia Montgomery), the cheerleader queen from the 1984 original. Best friend and über-slob Booger (Curtis Armstrong) plans to tie the knot with upper-crust society cutie Jeannie (Corinne Bohrer of *Zapped!*, *Joysticks*, *Surf II*, and *Stewardess School*). Ogre (Donald Gibb) returns too.

Nobody does anything funny in this TV movie; even Booger's iconic "Who Farted?" T-shirt bows to network standards and is neutered to read, "Who Pooted?"

Compounding the sadness of the *Nerds* movies going out on this note, Fox broadcast the film in 3-D with an Odorama-like gimmick. Imagine the potential glory of the first *Revenge of the Nerds* imbued with such upgrades! Then imagine viewers stuck at home in 1994, equipped thanks to 7-Eleven with 3-D glasses and scratch-and-sniff cards, frowning at *Nerds in Love*. In the end, the system they fought to topple had the ultimate revenge against the *Nerds*.

The Revenge of the Teenage Vixens From Outer Space [1985]

DIR. JEFF A. FERRELL; W/SARAH BARNES, HOWARD SCOTT, EVELYN BISHOP, JULIAN SCHEMBRI

HOT ALIENS ▫ VIRGINS ▫ BEER ▫ ELVIS PRESLEY ▫ COSMIC SEX PLOT

Shot over four years on a budget of $32,000, *The Revenge of the Teenage Vixens from Outer Space* is an efficient slab of regional filmmaking from the Pacific Northwest. Like the top-heavy interplanetary travelers of the title, the movie lands quietly enough, chugs along on its mission with appreciable doltishness, and exudes amateur appeal.

The quartet of teenage Vixens with a capital *V* come to the small earth town of Mayfield because no men exist on their planet. Their entire population has been cosmically horny since 1956, when Elvis Presley captivated humanity on *The Ed Sullivan Show*, despite cameras only showing him from the waist up. The Vixens also received the broadcast, but their version depicted Elvis only from the waist down. Hot stuff.

Having arrived on the planet of the pelvis, the Vixens are soon frustrated by the lackluster fornication skills of inexperienced high school mooks. They angrily turn their sex partners, one by one, into carrots, zucchinis, bell peppers, and other vegetables with Ping-Pong-ball eyes.

One alien stunner had given birth to a local dude when she dropped by Mayfield sixteen years earlier. In a slightly more insane teen sex comedy, the surprised son and sexy space-mom would probably get it on; not in this movie, however. Note that the credits pointedly thank a Seattle-area high school radio station, and be thankful yourself.

RISKY BUSINESS [1983]

DIR. PAUL BRICKMAN; W/TOM CRUISE, REBECCA DE MORNAY, BRONSON PINCHOT, CURTIS ARMSTRONG

VIRGIN ▫ RICH KID ▫ HOOKERS ▫ KILLER PIMP ▫ HOUSE PARTY

One film among the multitude of entries in teen movie hell qualifies as a work of genius—*American Graffiti* (1973). *Risky Business* ranks just below that threshold, still rating alongside George Lucas's most important film in the realm of bona fide art. Had writer-director Paul Brickman's heartfelt sendup of suburban teen stress about sex and success been released at any time in the 1970s, *Risky Business* would rate universally just as critic Roger Ebert perfectly described it: "The greatest American satire since *The Graduate*."

Alas, *Risky Business* emerged during the post-*Porky's* eruption of tits-and-zits mania, and was sold on the undeniable instant-megastar charisma of Tom Cruise. Though the plot doesn't sound that far removed from Cruise's big, dumb screen romp from the previous year, *Losin' It*, do note that *Risky Business* is very much not *Losin' It*.

Future Business Leader of America high school senior Joel Goodsen takes advantage of his parents leaving town. He mixes Jack Daniel's into his dinnertime Coca-Cola; he orders a hot blonde professional virginity extractor; and, most famously, he dances in his socks and underpants to Bob Seger's "Old Time Rock and Roll." When ethereal escort Lana (Rebecca De Mornay) appears, the reality of crossing a definitive Rubicon in life hits Joel like a wave from an ancient myth. Brickman expertly evokes those larger-than-lust feelings by crafting sex scenes as nearly surreal set pieces, flawlessly scored by the electronic musical undercurrents of Tangerine Dream.

Our lonely little rich boy-becoming-a-man falls in love with Lana. She's about his age, and seems to reciprocate his feelings. Of course she does—she's being paid to do exactly that. However, separating the cold capitalism out from carnal brokering proves not so easy for the young folks on either end of this romance-for-hire deal.

Reality crash-lands with terror familiar to anyone who ever really fucked up in high school. Lana makes off with a Steuben glass egg from the Goodsen family fireplace mantel. Joel gives chase to get back his mother's expensive decoration and—amusingly, heartbreakingly—grasp the connection he thought they shared. Lana's manager, "Guido the Killer Pimp" (Joe Pantoliano), stands directly in the way of our hero's badly hatched plan.

While dealing with the sex-worker skullduggery, Joel is also saddled with the brain-boiling social burden of being accepted into an Ivy League college along with his pals Barry and Miles (Bronson Pinchot and Curtis Armstrong, both of whom are great). The agony of the admissions process hits a fever pitch when a Princeton rep (Richard Masur, also stellar) comes to visit the Goodsen home at the peak of the pimp-and-prostitute intrigue.

Risky Business climaxes with Joel turning his parents' lush Chicagoland home into a brothel. He aims to buy his way out of trouble with money, sex, and the species-corrupting power that comes from combining both.

His plan works, just like everything in *Risky Business* works. The funny parts are unforgettably hilarious: Joel sinking his dad's Porsche into Lake Michigan; his schmucky attempts to intimidate Guido with strong language such as "a-hole"; and, yes, the underpants dance. The fang-sinking satire of the greed-is-good '80s still stings today.

Most remarkable are *Risky Business*'s unflinching flashes of naked emotion. Brickman repeatedly lingers on childhood photographs of both Joel and Lana as the young protagonists confront adult perils. The isolation and coldness of the

Goodsen family almost hurts; the characters even consistently walk offscreen in opposite directions. Joel's frantic bicycle ride after absorbing the totality of his deep trouble is punctuated by him wordlessly hugging Lana for dear life and weeping—a great feat of filmmaking.

Cinematographer Bruce Surtees, a frequent collaborator with Clint Eastwood, is as much a star of the film as Cruise and De Mornay. Musically, the aforementioned Tangerine Dream soundtrack stands as one of the decade's most definitive.

The damnedest thing about *Risky Business* is that Paul Brickman, who had previously written Jonathan Demme's Altman-esque *Citizens Band* (1977), aka *Handle With Care*, not to mention *The Bad News Bears in Breaking Training* (1977), basically stopped directing here after demonstrating himself to be a major new talent. His next movie as director was also his last: *Men Don't Leave* (1990), a remake of a French divorce drama with Jessica Lange. He put off studio meetings, turned down the chance to direct *Rain Man* and *Forrest Gump* and, in short order, moved away from Los Angeles forever.

Brickman told *Salon* in 2013 that his alignment with audiences accustomed to *Porky's*-style ribaldry was completely accidental, and that his inspiration for *Risky Business* had instead been Bernardo Bertolucci's *The Conformist* (1970). "I wanted to do a film for young people that was very stylized in a way that I hadn't seen before. I wanted to make the film that if I were in high school I would have wanted to see. I thought, 'Why can't you present that as a film for youth and aspire to that kind of style and still have humor in it?' That was the test: to meld a darker form of filmmaking with humor."

Rock 'n' Roll High School

[1979]

DIR. ALLAN ARKUSH; W/P. J. SOLES, MARY WORONOV, VINCENT VAN PATTEN, THE RAMONES

NERDS ▫ JOCKS ▫ GROUPIES ▫ LOCKER ROOM ▫ WEED ▫ ROCK STARS ▫ CUSTOM VAN ▫ MUSICAL NUMBER ▫ AEROBICS

Viewers in an alternate multiverse are probably right now discussing *Disco High*, the concept initially hatched by B-movie maven Roger Corman that eventually warped into *Rock 'n' Roll High School High School*. Somewhere out there, too, exist alternate versions of the movie titled *Heavy Metal Kids* and *Girls' Gym*, starring the other artists to whom it was offered prior to the Ramones: Todd Rundgren, who wanted the movie to be a drama; Cheap Trick, who were too busy touring; Devo, who were ultimately deemed too conceptual; and even young upstarts Van Halen. Warner Records reps reputedly warned away the filmmakers from that last band of local heroes due to lunatic behavior.

Pogo in glee that we inhabit the realm where the Ramones got the gig, the reality where director Allan Arkush perfectly filtered punk rock through the electric, absurdist pop-splatter he and other contemporary Corman protégés such as Joe Dante (*Piranha*) and Paul Bartel (*Death Race 2000*) had spent the previous few years refining into the greatest drive-in flicks ever made.

P. J. Soles stars as Riff Randall, exuberant semi-student of Vince Lombardi High. She's unmistakably the number one fan of New York punk pioneers the Ramones. *Rock 'n' Roll High School* chronicles her determination to get a song she's written—the movie's title track—to her favorite group. To do so, she must negotiate perils and pitfalls enacted by Vince Lombardi's rock-hating fascist overlord, Principal Togar (Mary Woronov), and her Tweedledim-and-Tweedledump henchmen Fritz Hansel (Loren Lester) and Fritz Gretel (Daniel Davis).

Clockwise from top: *"Hey, we're not students, we're the Ramones"—punk gods enter teen movie hell in* Rock 'n' Roll High School *(1987); Corey Feldman rocks with one eye open in the insulting* Rock 'n' Roll High School Forever *(1991); original John Holmstrom-penned Sire Records full-page print ad for the immortal* Rock 'n' Roll High School soundtrack.

Accompanying Riff on the road to slam-dance salvation are handsome jock and custom-van enthusiast Tom Roberts (Vincent Van Patten); anything-is-scammable wheeler-dealer Eaglebauer (Clint Howard); Riff's mousy best friend Kate Rambeau (Dey Young); and an actual giant mouse (special effects wizard Rob Bottin in a gloriously goofy costume). The mouse is a by-product of an experiment in which kindly music teacher Mr. McGree (Bartel) exposes rodents to Ramones records.

Everything comes together when the Ramones play a local venue (actually the Roxy on the Sunset Strip), and then crash Vince Lombardi High to debut their rendition of Riff's composition. The parting moments light a fuse that even *Massacre at Central High* (1976), *Over the Edge* (1980), and *Heathers* (1989) stomped out before detonating the ultimate declaration against how severely school sucks. It's a blast.

Rock 'n' Roll High School takes nary a false step or wrong move, and doesn't deliver a dull moment. Many of its interludes rank as stand-alone comedy classics: Eaglebauer's fantastically elaborate hustler operation run out of a secretary-equipped stall in the boys' bathroom; Riff's weed-whacked daydream of the Ramones serenading her at home that culminates with fully dressed Dee Dee playing bass under a running shower; the convertible Ramonesmobile piloting the instrument-blaring group into town as they blast "I Just Wanna Have Something to Do"; Joey Ramone sluggishly drawling, "We're not students, we're the Ramones," when the band is challenged on arrival; Principal Togar snarling in disgust, "Does your mother know you're the Ramones?!"; and, of course, the big concert blowout followed by the movie's explosive denouement.

Cult Movies author Danny Peary asserted regarding *Rock 'n' Roll High School* that "if any one film ever screamed out for the 'sick' humor of *National Lampoon's Animal House*, this is it."

Director Allan Arkush disagrees: "It was never consciously thought of as a PG movie. There was no attempt to do that, and yet, there was also no attempt to make it R-rated. It certainly didn't fit that Riff Randall would be walking around naked all the time, that would undermine the veracity of her character.

"But there was a scene where Eaglebauer was selling tickets to look through the window of the girls' locker room. That scene was shot when I was sick in the hospital, on the last day of shooting. Joe Dante shot the scene, and Ron Howard is actually in the scene as a high school kid!

"They peep in the window, and there's screaming, and you can imagine how it goes. But when we saw it in the context of the movie, it was so out of place. When Roger Corman saw the finished cut, he didn't even ask us where that scene had gone. It just didn't fit, you know."

The 1950s-spawned nuttiness and PG-rated sensibility have only compounded the timelessness of *Rock 'n' Roll High School*. Instead of grotesque comedic distortion of high school reality, the movie offers fantasy fulfillment on a phenomenal scale worthy of the Ramones.

Rock 'n' Roll High School Forever [1991]

DIR. DEBORAH BROCK; W/COREY FELDMAN, MARY WORONOV, LARRY LINVILLE

Rock 'n' Roll High School Forever was directed by Deborah Brock, who previously slashed open *Slumber Party Massacre II* (1987). Guess what—here she hacks out another sequel massacre.

In this insulting and even infuriating follow-up to 1979's original *Rock 'n' Roll High School* with the Ramones, none other than Corey Feldman leads the band that drives the kids to rock revolution. Mary Woronov returns, not as Principal Togar but as Vice Principal Doctor Vadar, whose name is one of numerous pandering allusions to *Star Wars*. "The Spirit of Rock 'n' Roll" is just played, nothing more, by Mojo Nixon.

Rock 'n' Roll High School Forever may or may not suck more superlatively than the Howard Stern–produced remake of the initial film that almost happened in 2005—nobody will ever know. Stern also planned to oversee a new *Porky's*, but after he attempted to purchase the rights, those rights became embroiled in a lawsuit between the original owners. Once in a while the lawyers do us all a favor.

Rockin' Road Trip [1985] aka Summertime Blues

DIR. WILLIAM OLSEN; W/MARGARET CURRIE, GARETH MCLEAN, KATHERINE HARRISON, STEVE BOLES

NEW-WAVERS ▪ PUNKS ▪ GROUPIES ▪ CRANKY TAXI DRIVER ▪ BUMBLING CRIMINALS

The surprisingly chaste *Rockin' Road Trip*, directed by William Olsen (*Getting It On* [1983], *After School* [1988]), chronicles Boston new wave band Cherry Suicide, fronted by butch blonde Nicole (Margaret Currie), as they tour the South.

Nicole's sister Samantha (Katherine Harrison) joins the trek, also inviting affable music dork Martin (Garth McLean), a fan she meets at a Cherry Suicide show. Also along for the ride is Wally (Steve Boles), a blind, burly, party-hearty street guru. He inadvertently accepts a stolen diamond in his panhandling cup, thereby attracting a pair of klutzy jewel thieves who chase the caravan all the way to a Christian circus in North Carolina.

Rockin' Road Trip provides loads of pretty scenery and local pit stop travelogues over the course of its tiring hour and forty minutes. The Troma Team logo rolls out before the opening credits, but relax—New York's shittiest anti-studio only picked up the movie for distribution.

Cherry Suicide pantomimes to tracks by indie rockers the Cheryl Wilson Band, but the movie's real prizes are its concert interludes showcasing an array of 1980s college radio stalwarts, including Guadalcanal Diary, Pylon, and Love Tractor. During a club scene, a punk with a big black masking-tape swastika on his T-shirt wanders past the camera. Yeah, that was a thing once.

The Rosebud Beach Hotel [1984]

DIR. HARRY HURWITZ; W/COLLEEN CAMP, PETER SCOLARI, CHRISTOPHER LEE, CHERIE AND MARIE CURRIE, EDDIE DEEZEN

BIKINIS ▪ MIAMI ▪ HOOKERS ▪ HAIR METAL ▪ EDDIE DEEZEN

Another R-rated sort-of-teen farce that was often lumped together with horny high schooler fare, *The Rosebud Beach Hotel* is technically more at home in my *Heavy Metal Movies* book than here. The metal comes from former Runaways vocalist Cherie Currie, who appears in *Rosebud* as a singing maid along with her sister, Marie Currie. The Curries also composed and performed the movie's hard rock soundtrack.

In the lead role as Tracy, Colleen Camp (*The Swinging Cheerleaders* [1974], *Valley Girl* [1983]) inherits the crumbling Miami domicile of the title. Peter Scolari (Henry from TV's *Bosom Buddies*) plays Elliot, Tracy's business-obsessed boyfriend. He hatches a grand scheme to rehab the Rosebud Beach Hotel: The all-female bellhop team will double as hookers! Wouldn't you know it—Elliot's harebrained scheme pays off.

The supporting cast is a crackpot cinema dream team. Horror master Christopher Lee plays Tracy's swordsman-turned-arsonist father. Fran Drescher works her persona effectively as a nasally sex pro. Kiddie-show host Chuck McCann hams it up as the Rosebud's manager. Jonathan Schmock and James Vallely—a legitimately hilarious 1980s stand-up comedy team called the Funny Boys—are fine ne'er-do-well hotel staffers. *Nerdo-di-tutti-nerdi* Eddie Deezen is on board as Eddie Deezen, pressure-treating the screen with the "ooh-ooh" that only he can do to Deezenistic perfection.

Rosebud peaks when the Currie sisters don spandex and perform "Steel" on a seaside bandstand with a hair metal combo. Fran Drescher bops along in a bellhop hat on the lip of the stage, while Deezen, resplendent in Hawaiian shirt and bright orange slacks, shoots the action with a camcorder.

Director Harry Hurwitz is a fascinating character. His way-off Hollywood filmography includes the Chuck McCann star vehicle *The Projectionist* (1971); the Mickey-Rooney-on-acid Nixon satire *Richard* (1972); the uncannily convincing sex mockumentary *Auditions* (1978); the dirty Mother Goose musical *Fairy Tales* (1979); and the self-explanatory *Nocturna: Granddaughter of Dracula* (1979).

THE RUNNIN' KIND [1989]

DIR. MAX TASH; W/DAVID PACKER, PLEASANT GEHMAN, BRIE HOWARD, JULIETTE LEWIS, EL DUCE

PUNKS ▫ HEADBANGERS ▫ GIRL BAND ▫ ROCK CLUB ▫ HICK IN THE CITY

Shaking up the dank cultural doldrums of 1989, *The Runnin' Kind* demonstrates that the Los Angeles punk scene depicted in Penelope Spheeris's landmark *The Decline of Western Civilization* (1982) had not been entirely buried by the commercial hair metal scene depicted in her second documentary *The Decline of Western Civilization, Part II: The Metal Years* (1988).

Ohio hayseed Joey (David Packer) drops by a hardcore music club in his home state, where he is smitten by dangerously glamorous drummer Thunder (Brie Howard). She's headed to L.A., so, after giving it some incredibly empty thought, Joey soon drops all his buckeye business and hightails it west, too. He hopes to track Thunder down and fall in all kinds of rock-and-roll love.

Feisty, vibrant punk vocalist Linda (legendary original Hollywood punk Pleasant Gehman, who cowrote the screenplay) takes a shine to the newly arrived hick-out-of-the-haystacks. Linda's band the Screaming Sirens needs a drummer. When Thunder's band breaks up, the twain doth meet. Rock-and-roll love flutters down among the green liberty spikes and safety-pinned motorcycle jackets.

Gehman, who has since emerged as one of West Coast punk's preeminent historians and raconteurs, is good on-screen. Party scenes and crowded clubs feature flashes of Juliette Lewis, Flea, disc jockey Rodney Bingenheimer, and the late foaming-faced El Duce of shock rockers the Mentors. At one point, the late '80s hair metal incarnation of T.S.O.L. plays "Hit and Run," capping off an ungodly year for pretty much everybody.

Say Anything ▪ School Spirit ▪ Scoring ▪ Screen Test ▪ Screwball Academy ▪ Screwball Hotel ▪ Screwballs ▪ Second Time Lucky ▪ Secret Admirer ▪ Senior Trip ▪ Senior Week ▪ The Seniors ▪ Seven Minutes in Heaven ▪ She's 19 and Ready ▪ She's out of Control ▪ Six Swedes on a Campus ▪ Sixteen Candles ▪ Sizzle Beach U.S.A. ▪ Ski Patrol ▪ Ski School ▪ Ski School 2 ▪ Sky High ▪ Slumber Party '57 ▪ Snowballing ▪ Some Girls ▪ Some Kind of Wonderful ▪ Something Special ▪ Sorority Babes in the Slimeball Bowl-o-Rama ▪ Sorority House Party ▪ Soul Man ▪ Splitz ▪ Spring Break ▪ Spring Fever Squeeze Play ▪ Starhops ▪ Stewardess School ▪ Stitches ▪ The Stöned Age ▪ Student Affairs ▪ Student Bodies ▪ The Student Body ▪ Summer Camp ▪ Summer Job ▪ Summer of '42 ▪ Summer School ▪ Sunset Cove ▪ Supervan ▪ The Sure Thing ▪ Surf II ▪ Swap Meet ▪ Sweater Girls ▪ Swim Team ▪ The Swinging Cheerleaders

Say Anything [1989]

DIR. CAMERON CROWE; W/JOHN CUSACK, IONE SKYE, LILI TAYLOR, JOHN MAHONEY

GRADUATION ▪ KICKBOXING ▪ SMART GIRL ▪ BAD DAD ▪ BOOMBOX

Say Anything presents John Cusack as Lloyd Dobler, a high school underachiever fixated on kickboxing and winning the heart of Ione Skye as Diane Court, the smartest student in their graduating class. Anyone alive since 1989 recognizes the iconic cinematic freeze frame of Lloyd Dobler in an overcoat and a Clash T-shirt, standing in the yard with a boombox raised over his head. This is the context—a rebellion born in teen movie hell.

Lloyd lives with his sister, a single mom, in a walk-up apartment. Diane resides in a fine house where she's doted over by her divorced father Jim (John Mahoney), a pillar of the community who owns and operates a nursing home. Lloyd has no plans beyond the next minute; Diane's life has been mapped out from day one. She will soon go to England, where she will be studying on a scholarship. As the friends and loved ones of the couple meet, sparks fly a little and complications fly explosively.

Over the course of Lloyd and Diane's summer romance, it comes to light that Diane's dad has been embezzling from the nursing home. He's portrayed as a good man shattered by the breakup of his marriage, doing an indefensible thing for selfish reasons. This complicated plot turn would be unusual in any Hollywood movie,

Clockwise from top left: *Say no more, in* Say Anything (1989), *John Cusack speaks softly and carries a large boombox;* Senior Week *(1987) managed to get a real-life high school principal busted; in* Screen Test *(1985), college kids seeking quick cash in blue movies run afoul of the mafia; in* She's Out of Control *(1989) parental discomfort moves to center stage.*

let alone a romance aimed at teenagers (especially during the *Porky's* decade). Therein lies the greatness of *Say Anything*.

This film is defined by uncomfortable, sometimes terrible, always credible details. These all-too-real pieces are mixed with big laughs and lighthearted episodes to create a movie that genuinely *feels* a lot like life. For example, kick-boxing was a highly uncommon sport in the U.S. in 1989. Lloyd's passion for something as offbeat as that begins as unique and becomes believable. Equally convincing is the way Diane waffles in her feelings for Lloyd, not out of pressure from peers or family, but because of her innate, hugely intelligent desire to determine her own destiny.

Say Anything doesn't dodge every cringer and cliché. Lloyd's big speech to Diane's family has always made me wince: "I don't want to sell anything, buy anything, or process anything as a career. I don't want to sell anything bought or processed, or buy anything sold or processed, or process anything sold, bought, or processed, or repair anything sold, bought, or processed. You know, as a career, I don't want to do that."

Then comes the big iconic boombox scene. After Diane gives Lloyd the cold shoulder, he rolls up outside her bedroom window, elevates his battery-powered tape player above his head, and blasts their song, "In Your Eyes" by Peter Gabriel. Though a more contrived Hollywood moment is hard to imagine, the brutal reality is that real-life teens with way less going for them than John Cusack have been serenaded their teen dreams in same fashion ever since—with many of the real lame-asses even using the same song. Hilariously, *Say Anything* provides a savvy female equivalent to Lloyd's desperate musical ploy in the form of Lili Taylor's heartbreaking performance as Lloyd's guitar-strumming friend Corey. Her tormented relationship with a jerk named Joe inspires her to write (precisely) sixty-five songs about him; she bleats them out at every possible opportunity. That detail is awful, true, bravura storytelling.

Fast Times at Ridgemont High (1982) unequivocally proved Cameron Crowe could write a movie, and *The Wild Life* (1984) demonstrated his more-than-okay capabilities as a director. The former teenage *Rolling Stone* correspondent really put it all together, then, for *Say Anything*. Crowe's script creates as rich and tangible an array of characters as any in the entirety of teen cinema. On top of that, as though to bear out the old movie industry saw that "directing is casting," Crowe assembled the ideal actors to bring the story to the screen. *Say Anything* seems to be populated by real people, and they're probably still out there somewhere today.

SCHOOL SPIRIT [1985]

DIR. ALLEN HOLLEB; W/TOM NOLAN, ELIZABETH FOXX, DANIÈLE ARNAUD, LARRY LINVILLE

SUPERPOWERS ▪ PEEPING ▪ EVIL AUTHORITY ▪ GIANT INFLATABLE PIG

The premise of *School Spirit* holds a lot of promise: college kid Billy Batson (Tom Nolan) is fatally creamed by a car while dashing out to buy condoms. He returns to campus as a ghost who can both get laid and turn invisible. He uses his powers to full effect in and out of the girls' shower room. Tight, right?

School Spirit delivers on its potential. The film is funny, comes packed with party babes' bouncing bare flesh, and turns out to be inventive with plot details once graft-minded college head President Grimshaw (Larry Linville) starts trying to swindle $12 million from alluring French alumni donor Madeleine (Danièle Arnaud). The only stone left unturned is why the main character is named after the kid from the *Shazam!* comic books?

Billy's cigar-chomping, film-noir-esque Uncle Pinky (John Finnegan) returns with him from the afterlife to chase nurses and offer sage ghostly guidance. At one point, the spectral path leads straight to an oil-soaked nude slip-and-slide party where the house band is new wave pop fiends Gleaming Spires. Their "Are You Ready for the Sex Girls?" anthem already lit up the soundtracks of both *The Last American Virgin* (1982) and

Revenge of the Nerds (1985), making this a hat trick. Floating over everything is a giant and very visible inflatable pig, so—two hooves up!

SCORING [1979] aka DRIBBLE

DIR. MICHAEL A. DEGAETANO; W/FREYA CRANE, CHARLES FATONE, "PISTOL" PETE MARAVICH

BATTLE OF THE SEXES ▭ THE BIG GAME ▭ CHEERLEADERS

Scoring looks, sounds, and feels like a teen sex sports comedy. In fact, the movie was a promotional vehicle for the Women's Basketball Association (WBA), its Iowa Cornets team, and the "World Champion Cornet International Cheerleaders." When the movie was reissued in 1982, its name was changed from *Dribble* to *Scoring*, and the poster featured a Nike symbol, lengthening the promotional chain by one swooshy link.

NBA superstar "Pistol" Pete Maravich cameos, as does much of the local population of Cedar Rapids, Iowa. Apparently, the movie's local premiere splashed a little Hollywood glitz on Cedar Rapids and Mayor Don Canney. All the excitement far upstaged Iowa's previous claim to cult-cinema glory, the scary *A Thief in the Night* series, an apocalyptic run of movies about the rapture, produced in the outskirts of Des Moines and shown in church basements to terrify Christian kids.

Upending the heartwarming apple cart of the heartland, gay-porn superstar Fred Halsted turns up in *Scoring* as a roughneck trucker named "Highway Psycho," who is knocked out cold by a female basketball coach. Alongside the mayor of Cedar Rapids and other luminaries, Halstad merits a special mention on the movie poster; as he later told gay periodical *The Advocate*: "I got the Rosalind Russell billing!" Maybe this was the result of someone in casting being confused by the film's original moniker, *Dribble*.

SCREEN TEST [1985]

DIR. SAM AUSTER; W/MICHAEL ALLAN BLOOM, ROBERT BUNDY, WILLIAM DICK, MONIQUE GABRIELLE

VIRGIN ▭ NERD ▭ MOBSTERS ▭ SISKEL AND EBERT

The old Mickey Rooney and Judy Garland-era Hollywood trope of "Hey kids, let's put on a show!" has been pornified by exploitation cinema repeatedly since the late 1960s. In terms of R-rated youth takes on the topic, the tradition stretches back to at least the French farce *How to Make a Dirty Movie* (1968), and was embodied in the twenty-first century by the late-night cable TV staple *After School Special* (2003).

The teen sex comedy wave of the 1980s sired two standout examples of the subgenre: *Screen Test* and *Blue Movies* (1988). The former is the more familiar of the two, due to its video store ubiquity. Anyone renting tapes at the time saw this VHS box: a nervous knucklehead in a garish plaid sports coat being embraced on a film set by B-movie bombshell Monique Gabrielle, while her co-sexpot Michelle Bauer feigns surprise in a director's chair. The actual movie inside that busy case isn't half-disappointing, either.

Screen Test follows a somehow familiar gang of horny college-age bumblers who plot to make bank and score chicks by casting and shooting an X-rated production—despite their lack of experience sexually and cinematically. All they know is that they watch a lot of smut, and it looks easy.

The goofs post a casting call, and a parade of potential porn queens rains down upon the suddenly overwhelmed aspiring Gerard Damianos. The bare-babe influx attracts the attention of local porn-controlling mafia figures. Recognizably ethnic representatives of said organization agree to allow the young filmmakers to keep their limbs if they'll accept mob financing and sign over all rights.

The plot is standard for any one of these virgins-filming-vixens sagas. *Screen Test* keeps its energy

high, though, and the sexy bits manage to actually bring some heat, occasionally to a scorching degree. Along with Mademoiselles Gabrielle and Bauer, B-movie scream queens of the most regal order, hardcore starlet Tracey Adams further enriches the entertainment as a topless dancer.

Screwball Academy [1986] aka Loose Ends

DIR. JOHN BLANCHARD (AS REUBEN ROSE); W/COLLEEN CAMP, DAMIAN LEE, PETER SPENCE, CHRISTINE CATTELL

BIKINIS ▣ STRIPPER ▣ PHONY PREACHER ▣ COLLEEN CAMP

In an award-worthy stroke of exploitation ingenuity, the title *Screwball Academy* combines *Screwballs* with all the *Academy* movies (*Up the...*; *Police...*; *Vice...*) The production is even Canadian—just like *Screwballs* and *Oddballs* and *Goofballs* and *Fireballs*. That holds huge promise, eh?

Touted in ads as the movie's star, Colleen Camp had recently been in *Valley Girl* (1983) and *The Joy of Sex* (1984). The VHS box depicts Camp in a pith helmet with a Vegas showgirl coming out of the top of her head. At this point, the potential for mayhem is reaching dangerous levels.

Unfortunately, *Screwball Academy* is actually a repackaged and rather limp made-for-TV (as *Loose Ends*) sendup of religious hucksterism. No screwballs and no academy are anywhere to be found. Bible-banging conman Bishop Wally (Damian Lee) aims to move his bogus church to some beachfront property, and there he crosses paths with Colleen Camp—as a feminist filmmaker. *Screw* this. Right in the *ball*.

Screwball Hotel [1988]

DIR. RAFAL ZIELINSKI; W/MICHAEL BENDETTI, ANDREW ZELLER, JEFF GREENMAN, CORINNE WAHL

MILITARY ACADEMY ▣ HOTEL ▣ VIRGIN ▣ BAD PREACHER ▣ THE BIG COSTUME PARTY

With *Screwball Hotel*, Canadian teen comedy auteur Rafal Zielinski wrapped up a hot streak of hormone-intoxicated idiot farces. He first burst forth like Russ Meyer boobs from a training bra with *Screwballs* (1983), and then continued to bobble beguilingly with *Loose Screws* (1985), *Recruits* (1986), and *Valet Girls* (1987).

Although not officially an offshoot of Zielinski's monumental debut, *Screwball Hotel* honors the titular connection to his masterwork *Screwballs* by opening with surreal sex slapstick by way of a *Wizard of Oz* cosplay kink scene. A doof dressed as the Tin Man and a lady done up as Dorothy respectively turn out to be Mr. Ebell (Kelly Monteith), proprietor of the stately (and soon-to-be *Screwball*-ized) Rochester Hotel, and Miss Walsh (Ishah Laurah Wright), his supremely dedicated assistant. They're blowing off steam because Ebell has five weeks to raise three hundred grand or a bank will reduce the Rochester to rubble.

Right on time, a trio of cutup cadets from East Point Military Academy—tall charmer Herb (Andrew Zeller), nookie nut Mike (Michael Bendetti), and mortally obese agent of good-time mayhem Norman (Jeff Greenman)—get the boot from school and bumble into the hotel looking for jobs. They're hired on the spot, and now everyone can be assured the upcoming Miss Purity teen beauty pageant for churchgoing virgins will not go down without a hitch.

Screwball Hotel near-maniacally maximizes both the comedic and prurient potentials of its sanguine setup. Water-based slapstick gags repeatedly render white clothing translucent, whether worn by a waitress carrying a lobster pot or by the Miss Purity contestants parading through the hotel fountain. The same budding Christian belles are convinced (by our heroes in nun drag) to oil-wrestle for Jesus. Mike initiates foreplay with a partner he believes is a farmer's daughter, but who turns out to be a sheep. Chubby-chasing dominatrix Cherry Amour (Corinne Wahl) takes to stormin' Norman, and the large lad's pals use a hidden earpiece to coach him through his rough-and-tumble cherry-pop procedure.

The Miss Purity Pageant explodes of its own volition into carnal anarchy with dirty poetry recitations, a gospel band going punk, and topless revelry. In all possible senses, it's a hoot.

Though *Screwball Hotel* is a notch down from the decade's greatest addlebrained nip-stravaganzas, that's largely because 1988 was no longer 1983. The cap had been off of the bottle of wrestling oil for quite a while by this point. Running a senselessly long one hour and forty-one minutes, *Screwball Hotel* also strays from its mission a bit. Still, let's all offer a one-armed salute to Zielinski and company for refusing to go quietly into the dying light of teensploitation's dusk.

SCREWBALLS [1983]

DIR. RAFAL ZIELINSKI; W/PETER KELEGHAN, ALAN DEVEAU, LINDA SPECIALE, LINDA SHAYNE, RAVEN DE LA CROIX

VIRGINS ▣ CHEERLEADERS ▣ PRANKS ▣ PREPPIES ▣ PRUDES

Screwballs is utter lunacy—or, keeping with the nature of the movie, "udder lunacy." Opening with an actual image of the word *coming*, accompanied by orgasmic female squeals, the camera pulls back to reveal a pair of teenage nubiles hanging a "COMING SOON" banner outside a hot-dog stand as a giant inflatable wiener pokes them repeatedly to-and-fro in their crotches and butts. Each bump is punctuated, of course, by Three Stooges–style sound effects. From there, the wit just keeps, like the sign says, coming.

Screwballs takes place at Taft and Adams High School, where each cheerleader's sweater is emblazoned in full school spirit with the initials *T&A*. The film's plot rather brilliantly brings together five primary teen sex comedy archetypes by dramatizing, one by one, how each character lands in detention with the others. Following each on-screen transgression, the camera freezes on the protagonist's stunned face, while the sound effect of a metallic door slams and the text DETENTION is stamped across their kissers.

Slickster Rick (Peter Keleghan) impersonates a doctor to administer breast exams in the nurse's office. Inventive nerd Howie Bates (Alan Deveau) rigs a mirror system to spy up cheerleaders' skirts. Tubby orgasm addict Melvin Jerkovski (Jason Warren) can't help but handle himself in a meat locker. Idaho transfer doofus Tim (Jim Coburn) is undeservedly nabbed by school disciplinarians after accidentally wandering into the girls' locker room. Brent Van Dusen III, a kid so profoundly preppy that he even brings his tennis racket into the shower, dashingly convinces a female student to fellate a model Eiffel Tower in French class.

Once united, our heroes set out on a mission of gonad-inflaming glory. Using the homecoming dance as a deadline, their goal is to lay eyes on the naked knockers of campus tight-ass Purity Busch (Linda Speciale). Immediately after school, the gang's manic masturbatory machinations incur the wrath of Principal Stuckoff (Donnie Bowes) and send them on all manner of insane adventures. At a bowling alley meetup, Jerkovski gets his dick stuck in a ball. A swim meet climaxes with Howie creatively snatching bikini tops. During one wild night at a drive-in theater, the entire Taft & Adams faculty and student body (except Purity Busch) are dosed with the mythical aphrodisiac Spanish fly, thereby launching the outdoor theater into a slapstick moonlight orgy.

Rick also dons drag as the girls' sewing teacher; Melvin buries himself in the sand uses a soda straw to spy on sunbathing Purity; and the entire cabal takes in a strip club performance by bazooka-bosomed Russ Meyer glamazon Raven de la Croix.

As fun-time gal Bootsie Goodhead, Linda Shayne makes the most of a van's back window at the drive-in, delivering cinema's greatest "pressed mams" moment this side of Uschi Digard's "Catholic High School Girls in Trouble" shower showcase in *Kentucky Fried Movie* (1977). Multi-talented Ms. Shayne also cowrote *Screwballs* and, akin to Katt Shea of *Preppies* (1984), later went on to direct films herself (including 1988's VHS kiddie curio, *Purple People Eater*). Her cowriter, Jim Wynorski, soon became a one-man exploitation flick machine, helming *The Lost Empire* (1984) and *Chopping Mall* (1986). His subsequent

B-flick frenzy contains more than one hundred titles and heroically continues unabated.

Directed by Rafal Zielinski (*Recruits, Valet Girls*) and produced by exploitation legend Roger Corman, *Screwballs* is a wonder of hormone-driven idiot perfection. It's like *Mad* magazine guest-edited by the staff of *Hustler*—or like *Archie* comics if Jughead ate a Viagra sundae and Betty and Veronica got struck with a case of the nymphos. Like *Porky's*, a likely inspiration, *Screwballs* is a product of Canada; the pinnacle point on the maple leaf of a series of Canuck tax shelter movies whose titles incorporate the term "-balls." The others are *Oddballs* (1984), *Fireballs* (1987), *Goofballs* (1987), *Meatballs III: Summer Job* (1987), and (close enough) *Screwball Academy* (1986) and Zielinksi's own *Screwball Hotel* (1988). The director's own sequel, *Screwballs II* (1984), is more popularly known as *Loose Screws*.

Like *Porky's*, *Screwballs* takes place in a vague, sloppy Eisenhower-esque timeframe. Virtually no element of what's on-screen conveys anything other than the 1980s, from the fashions to the hairstyles to the power-pop-on-the-cheap theme song. As a result, the nonstop anachronisms are a hoot. For one giant film-nerd example: the drive-in marquee touts the fictitious titles *The Big Bust Out* and *Wild Women of Wongo*, but what's actually showing is the Pam Grier ancient Rome potboiler *The Arena*, released in 1974. Later, in disguise as "Dr. Pepper," Rick cites the "Be a Pepper" jingle, a product of the late 1970s. In addition, Melvin credits his spy gear inspiration to the TV series *Mission: Impossible* when that show debuted in 1966. Still it's hard to call these genuine boners when not caring about reality and the time-space continuum just adds to the boobs-and-boner-driven buffalo stampede of fun.

In summation—or "cummation"—anyone viewing *Screwballs* once will love it forever the way Melvin Jerkovski loves his bowling ball. I still wonder if the Academy Award-winning 1995 thriller *The Usual Suspects* didn't crib its essential plot hook from *Screwballs*—namely, "You don't put five guys like that alone in a room together." If so, somebody owes Linda Shayne and Rafal Zielinski an Oscar to go with their giant inflatable wiener.

SECOND TIME LUCKY [1984]

DIR. MICHAEL ANDERSON; W/DIANE FRANKLIN, ROGER WILSON, JON GADSBY, ROBERT MORLEY

VIRGINS 📼 COLLEGE PARTY 📼 ROCK BAND 📼 DIANE FRANKLIN NAKED

This plot has been made into at least three romantic comedies: God plans to destroy humanity forever, but an ethereal persuader successfully begs for one last chance—if one particular young woman and young man can successfully merge to make an idiotic and annoying couple. The saga was performed with spectacular stupidity by Olivia Newton-John and John Travolta in *Two of a Kind* (1983); then extra pretentiously by Ewan McGregor and Cameron Diaz in *A Life Less Ordinary* (1997); but not before going through the Diane Franklin–Roger Wilson wringer in this movie.

The devil (Robert Helpmann) makes a wager with God (Robert Morley) that if the Lord starts mankind over from scratch, with a new Adam and Eve, that Old Scratch could tempt them all over again into falling from grace—only this time, even worse! God takes Satan's bet and dispatches the angel Gabriel (Jon Gadsby) to find heterosexual innocents pure enough to become cosmic guinea pigs. Cut to a schlocky college bash where Gabriel spots two conveniently named prizes: handsome but nerdly Adam (Wilson) and sweet coed Eve (Franklin). Eve is lovely, and her hymen is intact. Good enough.

The fates dump Adam and Eve into the Garden of Eden. Once the supple-bodied origins of our species appear naked, you can get up and leave right then. Afterward Adam and Eve just travel through time, continually going gooey for one another in cheap, crappy approximations of ancient Rome, World War I, the roaring 1920s, and the shitty-rock-band 1980s. *Second Time Lucky* is a bet the audience loses.

Secret Admirer [1985]

DIR. DAVID GREENWALT; W/C. THOMAS HOWELL, LORI LOUGHLIN, KELLY PRESTON

VIRGIN ▣ LAST DAY OF SCHOOL ▣ TOPLESS BACK SEAT SEDUCTION ▣ ANGRY COP DAD

On the last day of junior year of high school, a secret admirer slips a gushing love note into the locker of Michael (C. Thomas Howell). Understandably, Michael hopes the mystery missive is the doing of radiantly blonde campus heartthrob Deborah Anne Fimple (Kelly Preston, who gets nude here, but not as nude as in the same year's *Mischief*).

Our secretly admired protagonist presents the amorous epistle to nearly everyone he knows: his goofball buddies Casey Siemaszko, J. J. Cohen, and the always welcome Courtney Gains; his kid brother (Corey Haim, who's funny, especially when dousing his Froot Loops with Bosco); and Toni (Lori Loughlin), his best friend in the whole wide world, who just so happens to be a mousy brunette (that this matters speaks volumes as to the main character's priorities). While Michael tries to unravel its author's identity, his note falls into the hands of his mother, Connie (Dee Wallace), who mistakes it as a come-on from Lou Fimple (Fred Ward). Lou is Deborah Ann's father, and he's a *Dirty Harry*–level angry cop. Connie is *not* upset while under this misimpression.

Secret Admirer is slight and obvious and innocuous, with the exception of Fred Ward's fully committed performance that goes repeatedly from slow burn to nuclear boil. Ward is hilarious, visibly popping more veins in fury than one would suspect a normal human head could hold.

By the end, Michael unmasks his hit-and-run pen pal; somebody somewhere might be surprised that this leads to him and Lori Loughlin making out just before the end credits roll. No spoiler alert is necessary for anyone familiar with narrative motion pictures.

Senior Trip [1981]

DIR. KENNETH JOHNSON; W/SCOTT BAIO, FAYE GRANT, RANDY BROOKS, MICKEY ROONEY

HICKS IN THE CITY ▣ SEX PROS ▣ NERDS ▣ JOCKS ▣ VIRGINS ▣ CLOSET CASE

The CBS TV movie *Senior Trip* follows a school bus filled with lucky last-term high students from Youngstown, Ohio, to the heart of New York City. One of the kids is gay. Another is burned repeatedly while trying to score weed and hookers in Times Square. A theater chick auditions on Broadway for Mickey Rooney. Eventually, a goofy couple embarks on a sped-up, slapstick subway jaunt set to silent movie music. The harried class chaperone just can't keep up with any of these antics.

Scott Baio, as one of the visiting teen Buckeyes, wears John Lennon glasses to indicate seriousness. He's a hemophiliac, but nobody should laugh when he cuts himself on glass from a broken door—nothing could be funny about that when he's bedecked in such somber eyewear.

However muted and melodramatic this *Senior Trip* may be, even a TV movie remains infinitely preferable to the excremental 1995 big-screen bust, *National Lampoon's Senior Trip*. This *Senior Trip* was also a Quinn Martin production, and thus shares lineage with crusty '70s cop shows on the order of *Barnaby Jones*, *Cannon*, and *The Streets of San Francisco*. Although in those shows, kids seemed to have no problem scoring weed and hookers, particularly in Times Square.

Senior Week [1987]

DIR. STUART A. GOLDMAN; MICHAEL ST. GERARD, GEORGE ROBERT KLEK, ALAN NAGGAR, BARBARA GRUEN

SPRING BREAK ▣ DAYTONA BEACH ▣ ROAD TRIP ▣ NERD ▣ VIRGINS ▣ PRANKS

Senior Week busts out the 1987 comedy goods. The packed convertible on the movie poster is loaded with a cool dude from New Jersey waving his diploma; a fat guy pumping his fist; a com-

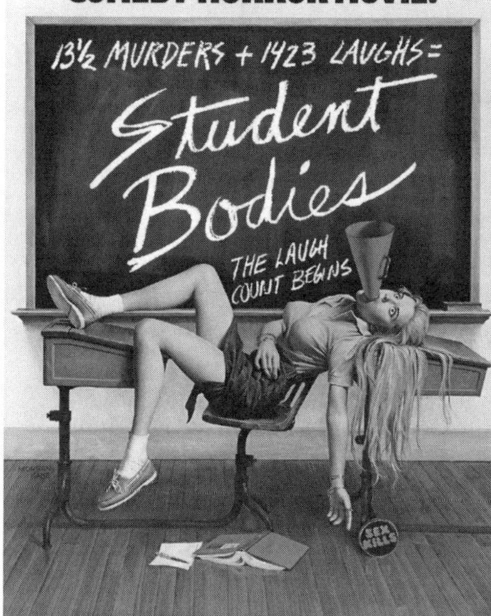

Clockwise from top left: The Student Body *(1976) is a women-in-prison film gone to college;* Student Bodies *(1981) slays as the most hilarious horror comedy of all;* Seniors *(1978) showcases Priscilla Barnes just prior to* Three's Company; Second Time Lucky *(1984) casts Diane Franklin at the heart of a cosmic battle between God and Satan.*

puter nerd attempting to keep it together; and a good-time gal decked out in a bikini bottom and a "Party Naked" half-shirt. All those characters actually appear in the movie, alongside a plethora of other seaside celebrants, many of whom, indeed, party at least half-naked.

The most important and historically distinguished dish *Senior Week* brings to the '80s teen sex comedy table was a behind-the-scenes scandal covered by the *New York Times* under the tremendously "tsk-tsk"-y tabloid-esque headline "Nude Film Shot in School Is Rated F."

The problem was that Palisades Park High School principal Nicholas S. Rotonda rented his learning facility to the makers of *Senior Week* to shoot classroom and campus scenes. Once the movie came out, all the local prudesters dove for their fainting couches as they realized how many naked bodies had been filmed on-site. Rotonda was suspended, even as he pled ignorance. Fair enough—movies like *Senior Week* plainly prejudice the public to mistrust the word of a guy from New Jersey with a mitt full of greenbacks and a name like Nick Rotonda.

Almost as if participating in some lame teen sex comedy, the real-life Palisades Park students rallied behind their besmirched educator, demonstrating en masse and chanting, "Forget the flick/We want Nick!" After an investigation, Mr. Rotonda was fully vindicated and reinstated. Unlike in the movies, the students possibly remained clothed at this point.

As for the actual movie at the center of all these university hijinks, the film earns better-than-passing grades. The opening scene is a dream by cool guy Everett (Michael St. Gerard), imagining a classroom full of actresses in their twenties trying to pass themselves off as teenagers, along with one pretending to be a teacher and definitely not pretending to get topless.

His dream ends rudely as his real teacher, the shrewish Miss Bagley (Barbara Gruen), rouses Everett to tell him that he must turn in a final paper after spring break if he wants to graduate. Since Everett is hell-bent on driving from New Jersey to Daytona Beach during the break, his solution is to drag along brainy nerd Jamie (George Robert Klek) and have him pound out the assignment in a motel room. Jamie's keen on the idea, boosted by the prospect of catching some sexual leftovers. With tub-of-fun party animal Kevin (Alan Naggar) weighing down the convertible, off they go. Miss Bagley is hot on their tails, however, chasing the lads from the Garden State to the Sunshine State to make sure Everett writes his work himself.

Senior Week's story is consistently amusing. Michael St. Gerard's uncanny resemblance to Elvis Presley soon nabbed him Elvis roles in *Great Balls of Fire* (1989) and the curious ABC series *Elvis* (1990). He dresses retro enough here for viewers to imagine the movie as a time-warp post-*Porky's* teleport of Elvis from *Fun in Acapulco* (1962) and *Clambake* (1967). Barbara Gruen debuts here as a battle axe from hell. She pumps her all into Miss Bagley, a nightmare teacher whom anyone would drive a thousand miles from Palisades Park to Daytona Beach to flee. By the end, all involved, plus the movie itself, come away with proper commencement honors.

The Seniors [1978]

DIR. ROD AMATEAU; W/DENNIS QUAID, LOU RICHARDS, JEFFREY BYRON, PRISCILLA BARNES

COLLEGE ▣ NERD ▣ AMATEUR BROTHEL ▣ GORILLA SUIT ▣ SOFT ROCK

The Seniors stars Paul Newman, Robert Redford, Al Pacino, Burt Reynolds, Ryan O'Neal, Robert DiNiro [*sic*], Clint Eastwood, and Charles Bronson—at least the opening credits claim so, until a funny little animated cartoon professor rearranges the letters into the names of the actual stars. That ballsy gag sets a tone to which *The Seniors* mostly adheres. Priscilla Barnes soon appears topless, and the film lumbers awkwardly into a freshly hatched 1978 forecast of what teen sex comedies would become during the ensuing decade. Thanks to the movie's public-domain status, genre fans have already had many chances to snag the movie from the dollar bin, filling in the grainy picture of the roots of teen movie hell.

The seniors in question here are Steve (Lou Richards), Alan (Dennis Quaid), Larry (Jeffrey Byron), and Ben (Gary Imhoff). They reside blissfully in a house near campus where glowing, golden-haired goddess Sylvia (Priscilla Barnes, just prior to *Three's Company*) lovingly cooks, cleans, and drains various veins for them without speaking a single word. Small wonder they are all soiling their shorts in dread over the imminent prospect of school graduation.

Harpo-haired dorkus Arnold (Rocky Flintermann) visits to drool over Sylvia, and offhandedly suggests the guys apply for a study grant so they can get paid to stay in school. Overjoyed, our gallant heroes tell Arnold that if he makes study grants happen, he can marry Sylvia. Arnold sets about making the study grants happen, pronto.

Working to create a "super-mosquito," wiggy scientist Professor Heigner (Alan Reed, the voice of Fred Flintstone) backs the lads, and they soon receive $50,000 to establish Phantom Research. In theory, their brainless think tank will someday issue a report titled "Sex and the College Girl." Their research commences with them paying twenty dollars per intercourse session to liberated coeds. The guys bed subjects until the point of sheer exhaustion; then they broker their female charges to high-paying businessmen, rapidly turning Phantom Research into a megabucks prostitution corporation.

Eventually *The Seniors* becomes crazily bogged down with plot, as though screenwriter Stanley Shapiro (*Pillow Talk, Dirty Rotten Scoundrels*) and director Rod Amateau (*The Many Loves of Dobie Gillis, The Garbage Pail Kids Movie*) decided to attempt satire. That unwise decision culminates with our protagonists plotting to murder Professor Heigner while corrupt investors plan, in turn, to murder the young men. After all that, a bunch of bad guys are crushed by a falling car and the four leads graduate. Arnold the nerd dies, but first he has sex with Sylvia, so everything turns out okay in the end.

Seven Minutes in Heaven [1985]

DIR. LINDA FEFERMAN; W/JENNIFER CONNELLY, BYRON THAMES, MADDIE CORMAN

FRIEND ZONE ▪ TEEN RUNAWAY ▪ SCARY OLDER GUY

Named for a next-level spin-the-bottle variation involving dark closet make-out sessions, *Seven Minutes in Heaven* is a movie made possible by the advent of John Hughes, but, refreshingly, not influenced by him. Written and directed by women, *Seven Minutes* effectively juggles heartfelt emotions with funny gags and strikes a winning balance.

Civic-minded fifteen-year-old Natalie (Jennifer Connelly, the same year as Dario Argento's splatter fantasia *Phenomena* [1985], aka *Creepers*) is mature enough that her single dad allows her to stay at home unsupervised while he leaves town for a week. This situation allows Natalie to take in runaway pal Jeff (Byron Thames), splitting from a bum trip at home. Turning it into a chummy threesome—but not that kind—is Polly (Maddie Corman), a chirpy semi-outcast who has been bitten by the my-virginity-is-a-disease bug.

Love, lust, jealousy, and other unavoidable coming-of-age atrocities drive the story onward. Each of the leads performs memorably, and the film's sexual frankness is all the more effective for not being bolstered by leering exploitation elements. This one is a keeper well after the egg timer dings.

She's 19 and Ready [1979]
aka Sunnyboy and Sugarbaby

DIR. FRANZ JOSEF GOTTLIEB; W/SABINE WOLLIN, EKKEHARDT BELLE, CLAUS OBALSKI, GINA JANSSEN

VIRGIN ▪ LOVE TRIANGLE ▪ SEXY COUSIN ▪ RICH UNCLE ▪ FAT GUY ▪ PRANKS

The German-made *She's 19 and Ready* is all about Eva (Sabine Wollin), a captivating lass courted by both athletic Stefan (Ekkehardt Belle) and doofy prankster Claus (Claus Obalski). Each guy has full knowledge of the other—and then some. Eva wonders out loud about which one to make her "steady" as she awakens from a nude slumber between the two dudes. As she ruminates, her suitors dress her together from the panties up. Scenes like this throughout *She's 19* supply some unexpected attention-grabbing moments. After sending all their prudes off to America a hundred years earlier, Germany was on some next-level sexual frankness in the 1970s.

When a rich uncle leaves Eva some Hong Kong properties, the trio wings off to the exotic Far East. There they hook up with worldly young Britta (Gina Janssen), Eva's sexually experienced cousin. A typical Euro-softcore cavalcade of fuzzy-focused sightseeing and hairy flesh flaunting ensues. The highlight is costumed Teutonic disco glee club Dschinghis Khan blasting out their non-U.S.-dance-floor megahit, the eponymous "Dschinghis Khan."

By adventure's end, Eva decides she has a big enough heart and more than enough body to go around for everyone, so status quo reigns and she keeps both teen lovers. Everybody wins until the 1980s come knocking a couple years later.

She's Out of Control [1989]

DIR. STAN DRAGOTI; W/AMI DOLENZ, TONY DANZA, CATHERINE HICKS, LAURA MOONEY

UGLY DUCKLING ▪ UPTIGHT DAD ▪ BIKINIS ▪ SCHOOL TRIP TO EUROPE

Ami Dolenz, real-life daughter of *The Monkees'* Micky Dolenz, stars as Katie in *She's Out of Control*. She's a bespectacled, brace-faced dorkette supreme who turns fifteen and submits to a relatively provocative makeover. Katie's widower dad Doug (Tony Danza) proves ill-prepared for his offspring's sudden tempestuous transformation. He frantically attempts to stamp out Katie's budding sexuality, interfering with her attempts to date and running seaside in proto-*Baywatch* slow-motion while she's bouncing everywhere in a curve-hugging swimsuit. Yes, relations between this on-screen dad and his daughter redefine "awkward" with near pornographic intensity.

As the spastically flustered Doug, Tony Danza is pure capicola ham. The role is essentially an extension of Danza's contemporaneous run on the ABC hit *Who's the Boss*, where he starred as a widowed father coping with his little girl blossoming into Alyssa Milano. *She's Out of Control* adds a smutty component, and, like Tony, the film itself really can't deal. In the end, the lesson nobody ever wanted to learn is that teen sex comedies focusing exclusively on parental discomfort instead of teen fun are somehow more perverse than all those old tapes in the curtained-off section of the video rental store that had "Taboo" in the title.

Six Swedes on a Campus

[1979] aka Six Swedes in a Boarding School

DIR. ERWIN C. DIETRICH; W/BRIGITTE LAHAIE, NADINE PASCAL, FRANCE LOMAY, DANIELLE TROGER

BOARDING SCHOOL ▪ SWEDES ▪ BAD TEACHERS

Sunny, upbeat, and as close to hardcore as the soft stuff comes, *Six Swedes on a Campus* loads ninety sweet minutes with exactly what the name promises. A sextet of bodacious blondes—Greta (Brigitte Lahaie), Inga (Nadine Pascal), Kerstin (France Lomay), Lil (Danielle Troger), Astrid (Kathleen Kane), and Selma (Elsa Maroussia)—show up at boarding school to live, learn, and lust under the tutelage of Fräulein Klein (Anne Libert).

The slinky headmistress appears to be the only faculty member at the institution, until gym teacher Mike Montana, as "Martin, der Sportlehrer," appears. He tutors one of the honeys in a manner similar to that later practiced by fisherman Eric Falk as "Karl, der Angler"; woodsman Edgar Del Ponte as "der Förster"; and peeping tom Roman Hubler as, simply, "Peeping Tom."

Capitalizing on the rage for Scandinavian sin so succinctly summarized by Daniel Ekeroth in his book *Swedish Sensationsfilms*, this movie was made nowhere near Sweden and seems to contain zero Swedes—a half-dozen less than promised. It's one thing to pass off thirty-year-olds as teenagers, but bogus Swedes is really going too far. Nonetheless, this lighthearted film is a watchable exception to the typical Euro-schlock pumped out by video label Private Screenings, which was often weirdly downbeat or even violent. The struggle was real once, youngsters, as even fake Swedes and their woodsman friends can tell you.

SIXTEEN CANDLES [1984]

DIR. JOHN HUGHES; W/MOLLY RINGWALD, ANTHONY MICHAEL HALL, JUSTIN HENRY, GEDDE WATANABE

NERDS ▣ VIRGIN ▣ SHOWER PEEPING ▣ CHEERLEADERS

Sixteen hot takes on Sixteen Candles*:*

1. *Das Darf Man Nur Als Erwachsener*, **the German released title, translates to** *One May Do That Only as an Adult.*

Nothing else in any way attached to the film is remotely as cool as that proclamation.

2. **John Hughes debuts here fully formed as "John Hughes, Filmmaker."**

Sixteen Candles is exceptionally well written and well cast, and presents such a distinct point of view that it instantly begat its own genre. That alone is admirable, even if many of the specifics might be despicable (although the value of three-plus decades of having something to kvetch about should be properly noted).

3. **John Hughes also debuts here as "John Hughes, Class Warrior—for the Bad Guys."**

With its upper-class suburban luxury, maniacal focus on materialism, and, above all, an infuriating sense of teenage presumptuousness treated as "the way things really ought to be," *Sixteen Candles* sows the radioactive seeds of snobs-against-slobs counterrevolution that would reach full global thermonuclear impact four years (and three Hughes movies) later with *Ferris Bueller's Day Off*. Money and the kids who have it are what matters in the Hughesiverse.

4. **Molly Ringwald emerges as "Molly Ringwald."**

As protagonist Samantha Baker, Molly Ringwald lives the role as organically and inevitably as John Belushi does Bluto in *Animal House* (1978); Tom Cruise does Joel Goodson in *Risky Business* (1983); and even as much Eddie Deezen does Menlo in *Surf II* (1984). Hers was a welcome return to the screen after appearing as "Molly" on the first season of *The Facts of Life*.

5. *Sixteen Candles* **expanded the gender component of "sex" in "teen sex comedies"—but not for the first time. Rich preppy John Hughes doesn't deserve all the credit.**

Much praise has been retroactively heaped upon *Sixteen Candles* for providing a female vantage point in a genre previously overwhelmed by horny adolescent dudes. Fair enough—and *Sixteen Candles* certainly helped open doors for *Clueless* (1995), a bona fide work of genius from director Amy Heckerling. Yet Heckerling had already put teen girls front and center in her previous masterwork, *Fast Times at Ridgemont High* (1982). The same praise is due Martha Coolidge's *Valley Girl* (1983). Curiously, John Hughes seems to often receive the cultural accolades for this girl-power progression.

6. *Sixteen Candles* **made the first decisive cut to remove the crucial "sex" from "teen sex comedies."**

In the process of downplaying aggressive male idiocy, *Sixteen Candles* filed off the sharp edges that made post-*Porky's* youth comedies the era's only mainstream cinema of rebellion. The move is the celluloid version of how Disneyland removed the menace of the midway and the sleaze of the sideshow to create a perfectly safe and sanitary carnival experience. Though Disneyland coexists with traveling fun fairs; *Sixteen Candles* effectively forced unhinged horny teenager farces into oblivion.

7. Surprising levels of PG-13 nudity and F-bombs abound.

In 1984, the fledgling era of home video, bare bodies on the big screen still sold movie tickets—even in movies rated PG-13. That explains the unflinching shower-room interlude during which Samantha jealously eyeballs naked pom-pom hottie Caroline (Havilland Morris). Language-wise, when Sam realizes the central plot conceit early on, she loudly declares: "I can't believe this! They *fucking* forgot my birthday!" Later on, casual usage of an *f*-fronted slur against homosexual men is used as a synonym for "not cool."

8. The nerds are NOT cool.

Farmer Ted (Anthony Michael Hall) is not merely uncool in *Sixteen Candles*; his character is referred to simply as "The Geek"—a nasty insult in those pre-*Wired* magazine days. *Sixteen Candles* beat the redemptive *Revenge of the Nerds* to theaters by several months; even a "nerd" was far better than a "geek" in 1984.

9. Anthony Michael Hall actually did make uncool kids cool in the long run.

While *Revenge of the Nerds* did much to alter the status of the dork set, Anthony Michael Hall set the change in fast motion; first as Farmer Ted in *Sixteen Candles*, and then as Brian Johnson in *The Breakfast Club*. John Hughes himself explained Anthony Michael Hall's dynamism thusly: "Every single kid who came in to read for the part did the whole stereotyped high school nerd thing. You know—thick glasses, ballpoint pens in the pocket, white socks. But when Michael came in he played it straight, like a real human being. I knew right at that moment that I'd found my Geek."

Sixteen Candles recognizes that nerds were severely castigated social pariahs. Their demimonde of comic books, role-playing games, superhero crap, and stupid *Star Wars* would get them immediately wedgied, swirlied, and stuffed inside a locker. The idea of such things ever being "cool," let alone the defining component of all-around popular culture, could only have been described as insane. Thirty years later, CEOs decorate their penthouse offices with *Ghostbusters* Lego. What a world.

10. Underage drinking looks awesome—and it is awesome.

Everyone getting trashed at the great party at Jake's house—and then, in turn, trashing Jake's house—is under the legal drinking age. *Sixteen Candles* presents this bacchanal as not just as a solid fact of teenage life, but as big, crazy, fun. Of course, high school students drank and took drugs back then, and they still do now. The difference these days is the heightened awareness of the consequences. Too many fatal or otherwise tragic outcomes have dimmed this topic as one that should be presented lightly. Still, there was nothing like an '80s keg party when somebody's parents went out of town. Now it's all, "Don't drink and Instagram, kids."

11. Actual teenagers portray teenagers, and the grandparents actually look like old people.

Molly Ringwald and Anthony Michael Hall were both fifteen while shooting *Sixteen Candles*. The other kids in the cast were also kids. This jolt of reality upends a tradition typified by thirty-four-year-old Stockard Channing as Rizzo in *Grease*, and it proved to be minor-league revolutionary.

Often today, you'll hear that sixty or even seventy is "the new forty." Back in the '80s, that metric was the exact opposite. Thirty counted as middle-aged. By age fifty, most people were grandparents—and the years seemed to wear on them harder. When Sam's grandparents come off as hyperbolic mummies, they are a nice reminder of the natural order of things.

12. Fat, nasty kid brother Justin Henry rules.

In 1979, adorable, eight-year-old blond moppet Justin Henry won audience hearts and earned a Best Supporting Actor Academy Award nomination for his work in the acclaimed divorce drama, *Kramer vs. Kramer*. He played the sweet, precocious son at the heart of a custody battle between

Dustin Hoffman and Meryl Streep, and seemed destined to grow into long-term stardom. *Sixteen Candles* viewers were treated to Henry as Samantha's porky, mean-mouthed, proto-Eric-Cartman brother. The transformation oddly reflects a similar shock seven years later when audiences at *Edward Scissorhands* took notice of that film's mean, beefy bully: "*That's* Anthony Michael Hall? Yowza!"

13. Debbie Pollack as Lumberjack Marlene rules even harder.

Marlene is redwood tall, she's Sasquatch strong, she slow-dances with the Donger, and she makes brilliant use, on a front both amusing and arousing, of her B-52 bomber tree-toppers.

14. The music stinks hard.

Hughes ham-fistedly comments on the stupidity of young Americans by playing David Bowie's "Young Americans." Nothing wrong with Bowie or the song itself, but playing it while Samantha's foolish and uncool family members rush about making sure her young American older sister has a pleasant wedding day sends the message that those simps ought to be showering Sam with a sports car instead. She insists, and Hughes could not possibly agree more.

Except for a few other anvil-subtle choices ("Rebel Yell" during Farmer Ted's big cool come-around; the Stray Cats cover of the title song), the rest of the music is still more class warfare ammo. Samantha's room, reportedly decorated by moneyed L.A. showbiz kid Ringwald herself, is plastered with posters of Euro-fop synth-mince new wave artists. In 1984, that's what rich kids liked, so the detail is accurate, but, as always with Hughes, the message is coming downward on the audience that his world is better than yours.

15. The date-rape issue will never go away.

So far as I can tell, Farmer Ted does not rape Caroline. Watching closely, they don't have sex at all; she just thinks they did—since she was deliriously drunk, she "remembers" it as being great. That stated, the scene where Samantha's crush Jake (Michael Schoeffling) "gifts" the passed-out Caroline to Ted is simply hideous. Why it took decades for this to crop up in public discourse as an example of unacceptable attitudes and behavior is a very good question.

16. *Sixteen Candles* itself will never go away.

For a few years, *Sixteen Candles* remained a constant, because the masses bought what John Hughes was selling. Then *Sixteen Candles* became an object of nostalgia. In our present realm of virtuous misery and righteous shaming, *Sixteen Candles* is an emblem of what was crushingly offensive about times past. That argument has a point. However, the typical follow-up notion that such relics require censorship should only ever be argued *against*.

The very day I wrote this review, an article cropped up online under the headline: "So *That* Happened; Anthony Michael Hall Date Raped Jake's Girlfriend in *Sixteen Candles*." It contained a link to a story in the *New York Post* (of all places) titled "*Sixteen Candles* Is Racist and Sexist—and Needs to Be Retired."

How far we've come. Whether that direction is up or down depends on your own loudly touted personal branding, as hindsight dictates all perception at present. It didn't always. From the late 1960s into the 2000s, audiences often laughed at bad behavior and antisocial ideas precisely *because* such things were wrong. Such appalling attitudes and activities played out on-screen or in print provoked laughter over the sheer awfulness of any such real-life prospects. *Can you imagine?*

That's exactly how shock humor made the leap from the underground realm of R. Crumb comics and *Pink Flamingos* to mainstream movies and TV, rolling forward from the sudden surprise of Monty Python's silly walks to the loaded discourse of *All in the Family* to the prime-time assaults on proper taste of *South Park* and *Family Guy*. Along the way, *Sixteen Candles* fits, too.

Regardless of one's stance on matters political, laughter in the 2000s is perceived *only* as an endorsement. It's a phenomenon once perfectly

Brrrrrrr! Clockwise from top left: Ski School *(1990) stars Dean Cameron of* Summer School (1987) *and fell on European slopes as* Ski Academy; Snowballing *(1984) is a wipe-out;* Ski Party *(1965) moves the Frankie-and-Annette beach formula from sand to snow.*

described by late-night TV host Seth Meyers as "clapter," and has become an era-defining societal reflex.

The exception is mean-spirited laughter solely at approved objects of ridicule, as a declaration of "owning" whomever one perceives as the cause of the world's—meaning *your*—problems. Fox News and *The Daily Show* share the blame for creating a reality where audiences no longer guffaw involuntarily until they cry, but instead laugh with careful calculation in order to elicit and savor the other side's "tears."

Humor itself is lost. It's a situation worth crying over. And if you want to debate that topic, you can just fucking forget my birthday, too.

SIZZLE BEACH U.S.A. [1981]
aka MALIBU HOT SUMMER

DIR. RICHARD BRANDER; W/KEVIN COSTNER, LESLEY BRANDER, ROSELYN ROYCE, TERRY CONGIE

BEACH HOUSE ▣ BIKINIS ▣ DUDE RANCH ▣ COWBOY DWARF

Released as *Malibu Hot Summer* in 1981—although filmed what looks to be the better part of a decade earlier—the motion picture most familiar to Kevin Costner completists as *Sizzle Beach U.S.A.* is a dazed pastiche of fairly glorious hippie-dippie nonsense, mostly taking place at the shore but sometimes on a dude ranch, where young Costner plays a hunky hired hand.

Petite party gal Dit (Lesley Brander), Farrah-feathered blonde Cheryl (Roselyn Royce), and leggy convertible driver Janice (Terry Congie) crash at a beach house. The three friends swim, sun, frolic with a dog, and display a consistent aversion to clothing. They have talent, too. Acoustic-guitar strummer Janice proves to be an astonishing lyricist: "A world's creation dies of cancer/a tender rose hides its thorns/Breasts of Destiny hold no answer/against feelings of scorn." One thing is certain: *Breasts of Destiny* would be a wonderful alternate title for this book.

Aside from Costner's pre-fame appearance and an overall likeable air of stoned delirium, *Sizzle Beach U.S.A.*'s real must-see feature is rootin'-tootin' slickster/hard-ass Pete (Peter Risch), a Verne Troyer–proportioned little person who dresses and carries himself like Hank "Bocephus" Williams Jr.

Roselyn Royce later underwent wrestling training for an episode of TV's *The Fall Guy*, and used that know-how to create her softcore catfight video line, *Golden Girls*.

SKI PATROL [1990]

DIR. RICHARD CORRELL; W/ROGER ROSE, YVETTE NIPAR, T. K. CARTER, MARTIN MULL

SKI RESORT ▣ BIKINI MODELS ▣ NERD ▣ PRANKS ▣ JAPANESE STEREOTYPES ▣ EVIL DEVELOPER

Actor and comedian Roger Rose momentarily achieved enough fleeting late-'80s stardom as a VH1 video jockey to win the lead role in *Ski School*. The movie is an attempt by *Police Academy* producer Paul Maslansky to launch another slapstick franchise where everybody could wear the same wardrobe from movie to movie. Roger Rose, in theory, was poised to become the Alpine version of Steve Guttenberg.

As quick-wit ski pro Jerry, Rose leads a Benetton-ad diverse assemblage of slope jokers in defending their treasured Snowy Peaks resort from evil land baron Maris (Martin Mull), who wants to buy it from kindly old Pops (Ray Walston) so it can be turned into—well, a better ski resort, apparently. Backing up Jerry are African American hotshot Iceman (T. K. Carter); Mexican demolition expert Eddie Martinez (George Lopez); nerdburger Stanley (Paul Feig); schizophrenic suicide snowboarder (Sean Gregory Sullivan); and pint-size power-mouth Murray (Leslie Jordan). Not amusingly, they all launch into celebrity impressions, the most woeful being either Lopez busting out his Spanish-accented Rodney Dangerfield or Feig (future director of *Bridesmaids* [2011] and the *Ghostbusters* remake [2016]) belting it out as Tina Turner during the lodge's talent show.

Ultimately, Rose's snooty "I'm-too-handsome-to-be-here" VJ persona while introducing clips by Milli Vanilli and Will to Power might have worked better for a bad-guy role in a goofy sports comedy. No *Ski Patrol* sequels followed. Rose has since done pretty well as a voice-over performer. Steve Guttenberg remains irreplaceable.

Ski School [1990]

DIR. DAMIAN LEE; W/DEAN CAMERON, DARLENE VOGEL, MARK THOMAS MILLER, TOM BRESNAHAN

SNOW BUNNIES 📼 RICH JERKS 📼 FLASHING 📼 PRANKS 📼 HOT TUBS 📼 THE BIG SKI RACE

High school. College. Summer camp. Spring break. Without question, these are the four most totemic settings for teen sex comedies of VHS vintage. However, slaloming close behind in terms of frequency, is a fifth locale: the ski resort.

Free from parents, teachers, and other vanguards of buzz-killing responsibility, winter resorts have proven to be holy mounts for youth romps starting with the proto-powdery Frankie Avalon jaunt *Ski Party* (1965), through the piney peaks of *Hot Dog...The Movie* (1984), all down the hill to the 1990 showdown between *Ski Patrol* and this borderline watery, but undeniably well-remembered Canadian snobs-vs.-slobs saga.

Cool-dude-with-a-cocked-woolen-hat Johnny Roland (Tom Bresnahan) arrives at British Columbia's famed Whistler Mountain winter sports facility. He quickly falls in with party-hearty snow bum Dave (Dean Cameron, Chainsaw from *Summer School*); his sidekick Fitz (Stuart Fratkin of *Valet Girls*); and their untamed assemblage of downhill racers known as Section Eight. The gang's rich dick rivals, headed by snooty blue blood Reid (Mark Thomas Miller), are called Section One. Thank the creators of *Ski School* for making things easy to understand.

The two factions square off a lot. One dude with an earring will make a wisecrack to another dude with a fake Hah-vahd accent, then they'll both yank down their face masks and go careening down the side of a mountain—again and again.

As with *Hot Dog*, devotees of Warren Miller–style ski documentaries will find loads of worthy B-ski-roll, much of it set to heavy jams by Tom Morello's pre–Rage Against the Machine group Lock Up. The rest of us will just wait for the next skin-packed hot tub soirée.

Ski School also delivers entertaining, logistically impossible pranks between all that ski footage. The funniest gag climaxes with a sauna-set mass lambada dance. Later, a huge snowball fight inside the lodge's cafeteria grows and grows into something kind of scary. By the end, *Ski School* tumbles across the finish line before viewers go cold. Go slush yourself.

Ski School 2 [1994]

DIR. DAVID MITCHELL W/DEAN CAMERON, HEATHER CAMPBELL, BRENT SHEPPARD, WILL SASSO

SKI RESORT 📼 RICH JERK 📼 PRANKS 📼 LESBIAN LEATHER BAR 📼 THE BIG SKI RACE

In the original *Ski School* (1990), Dean Cameron had aged a bit from his breakthrough turn as Chainsaw in *Summer School* (1987). By the time he reprised his good-time-snow-bum role as Dave in *Ski School 2* in 1994, he was as sorely lacking in prime spryness as the '80s teen sex comedy genre itself.

Dave returns to his ski resort of yore for the wedding of his ex-squeeze Beth, who now owns the whole mountain. She's engaged to sleazy creep Steve (Brent Sheppard). Naturally, greedy cad Steve only has eyes on swiping the entire enterprise away from Beth. Somehow, this gem of a sweetheart is the only one who can't see this. Just leave it to Dave, his human-beer-keg party machine sidekick Tomcat (*Mad TV*'s Will Sasso), and various snow bunnies to save the day. As the bawdy boys declare before crashing a snooty soirée, their mission is to "untighten asses."

As with the first *Ski School*, winter sports fans will delight at endless footage of stunt doubles doing their downhill stuff. One concession to the 1990s comes after pranksters push sleeping Dave's bed out onto a hill and he rides it down the mountain like a snowboard. Meanwhile, *Playboy* model Wendy Hamilton, as lusty lodge lingerer Lola, misunderstands the concept of "painting a nude" and thus paints *in* the nude. That puts a sprightly spring in the movie's wintery step.

Sky High [1985]

aka Sky High: Summer of Fire

DIR. NICO MASTORAKIS; W/DANIEL HIRSCH, CLAYTON NORCROSS, FRANK SCHULTZ, JULIE SIMONE

COLLEGE BREAK ▣ EUROPE ▣ CRUISE SHIP ▣ EGG FIGHT

Mangle-brained B-movie maestro Nico Mastorakis (*Ninja Academy* [1989]) crossbreeds a comical travelogue about three UCLA pals on holiday in the director's native Greece with an incomprehensible spy thriller. Yes, he blows it all *Sky High*!

While visiting the Acropolis, a dying KGB agent slips a top-secret formula for a drug called "sky high" to bespectacled computer dork Lester (Daniel Hirsch). In short order, a squad of KGB killers hunts down Les and his hunk buds Bobby (Clayton Norcross) and Mick (Frank Schultz), leading to a chase that lasts essentially the rest of the movie. The most memorable sequence involves our boys racing away from the KGB thugs in rickshaws that happen to be loaded with eggs, thereby providing them with handy projectiles. Lush scenery along the way includes Grecian wonders, natural and otherwise, along with nude beaches, and a bikini-top-optional Mediterranean luxury liner.

Sky High is actually fits with two other Mastorakis action comedies that flirt with teen flick dynamics. *Glitch!* (1985) concerns a pair of dolts who crash an absent stranger's mansion and pretend to cast a movie, only to run up against a gay ninja and secret agent Ted Lange—Isaac, Your Bartender, of TV's *Love Boat*. *Terminal Exposure* (1987) follows two teen creeper shutterbugs who shoot pics of Venice Beach bikini babes and accidentally end up photographing a mob hit executed by a female assassin with a telltale shapely caboose. Each warrants a curious peek.

Slumber Party '57 [1976]

DIR. WILLIAM A. LEVEY; W/DEBRA WINGER, RAINBEAUX SMITH, JANET WOOD, JOE E. ROSS

VIRGINS ▣ PILLOW FIGHT ▣ SKINNY DIPPING ▣ DRIVE-IN MOVIE ▣ BIKERS

Debra Winger, the Academy Award nominated thespian of *Urban Cowboy* (1981), *An Officer and a Gentleman* (1982), and *Terms of Endearment* (1983) portrays the main character, conveniently named "Debby," in this agreeably imbecilic and smashingly sleazy period piece. She's not just background dressing who hit the big time and then had her name forced above the title on the video box. In her capacity as star here, Winger proclaims one of the movie's many memorable kinky outbursts: "Getting spanked by my dad sure does kinda hurt...but it's also kinda hot!"

At the height of the "'50s," as continually reconfirmed by an oldies soundtrack dominated by hits from the '60s, six high school gal pals gather for an all-nighter at Debby's house while her parents are out of town. Among the sleepover companions are cult icon Cheryl "Rainbeaux" Smith (*The Swinging Cheerleaders, Massacre at Central High*) as Sherry, and jubilant Janet Wood (*The Centerfold Girls*, Russ Meyer's *Up!*) as Smitty. First things first, everyone strips to their undergarments and hops in the backyard pool. Yanking down one another's panties becomes the name of the game. After that, our sextet wraps in towels and, one by one, each lass opens up about how she lost her virginity. The stories play out on-screen.

Hayseed Bonnie May (Bridget Holloman) recounts a Bonnie-and-Clyde-style car chase where she and her moonshine-running boyfriend Silas (R. L. Armstrong) elude redneck justice by ducking into a drive-in theater. They do it in the backseat while Boris Karloff reigns in *Cauldron of Blood* above them (that 1970 movie goes right along with the anachronistic music score).

At her sixteenth birthday party, Grinch-grinned Angie (Noelle North) slinks to her bedroom with Harold Perkins (Will Hutchins), her father's fortysomething pal. Sex happens, whereupon Angie's ogre of an old man kicks in the door and seethes, "You little cunt!" He throws the naked girl over his knee and barehandedly whacks her butt red as she beams an orgasmic smile.

Debby recalls visiting a beach, where she suggestively mouths a banana and inspires her beau to beat up menacing bikers. Sherry triumphantly drag races against a Mexican cholo named Dope Fiend (Rafael Campos) but gives him the real prize. Then, in a return to intense familial intimacy, Smitty hops on stable boy David (Bryan Englund) while his naked sister Hank (Janice Karman) watches from a haystack and masturbates. "I felt liked I'd died and gone to heaven," Smitty coos.

Finally, Hollywood hopeful Joanne (Mary Appleseth) makes it with movie star Rex Parker (Victor Rogers) on the set of a jungle flick, whereupon "ooga-booga"–style natives toss her into a giant pot of boiling water with vegetables for their cannibal feast. The kink keeps coming!

After the flashbacks, five of the girls' horned-up male classmates crash the bash, and an all-out orgy erupts. All the ladies admit they fabricated their vivid previous accounts. Everybody loses their virginity, this time for real.

Slumber Party '57 also includes a mid-flick threat from a cat burglar that prompts a cameo from *Car 54, Where Are You?* funnyman Joe E. Ross as the responding police officer. The once-and-forever Gunther Toody looks in even more cardiac peril here around young female flesh than he does in *Gas Pump Girls* (1979).

The filmography of *Slumber Party '57* director William A. Levey could start and end with this madness and *Blackenstein* (1973) and he would be a trash film legend. Astoundingly, Levey also made *Wham! Bam! Thank You, Spaceman!* (1975); *The Happy Hooker Goes to Washington* (1976); *Skatetown, U.S.A.* (1979); *Monaco Forever* (1984), in which Jean-Claude Van Damme makes his movie debut as "Gay Karate Man"; and *Hellgate* (1989), the only known motion picture to contain the naked ass of Ron Palillo, aka Arnold Horshack from TV's *Welcome Back, Kotter*.

Snowballing [1984]

DIR. CHARLES E. SELLIER JR.; W/ALAN SUES, MARY BETH MCDONOUGH, P.R. PAUL

SKI RESORT ▣ SENIOR TRIP ▣ HOT TUBS

There is something vaporously Christian about *Snowballing*, maybe even Mormon. No actual proselytizing or anything even vaguely religious happens in the movie, but the connection stems from the unique crappiness of Christian cinema, the kind of movies that play in churchyard tents and can be rented via services like Pure Flix (not a good place to find the titles in this book).

The Jesus-flick genre is best known for Book of Revelations sci-fi (*Left Behind* [2000]) and Biblical boy band manifestos (*God's Not Dead* [2014]), but if the makers of *A Thief in the Night* (1972) and *Kirk Cameron's Saving Christmas* (2014) met in the middle to approximate an '80s teen sex comedy—yes, replete with their own version of teens, sex, and comedy—*Snowballing* would seem to be the result.

Accordingly, an unmistakable air of amateurism and prudishness sours this PG-rated puffball. The standard ski lodge senior trip looks murky, sounds even murkier, and contains no actual sex or nudity, even with all those hot tubs. The buzzkill extends to *Snowballing*'s casting decisions, as well. *Laugh-In*'s resident flaming funny queen Alan Sues—who's normally a one-man combination of a laff riot and the Stonewall riot—shows up only to be hampered with the role of the straitlaced chaperone (as if!).

Don't mix *Snowballing* up with the 1971 *Québécois* non-teen bunny-humping slope spree *Snowballin'* (aka *Aprés Ski* and *Sex in the Snow*) or the 1974 Bavarian softcore pole-puller *There's No Sex Like Snow Sex*. Also, don't fall for the absolutely criminal marketing campaign that pushes

Snowballing as a virtual companion piece to *Hot Dog...The Movie*. In short, try to have nothing to do with *Snowballing*. As a matter of fact, stop reading this review right now.

Some Girls [1988]

DIR. MICHAEL HOFFMAN; W/PATRICK DEMPSEY, JENNIFER CONNELLY, SHEILA KELLEY, LANCE EDWARDS

CHRISTMAS BREAK ▣ CANADA ▣ FUNNY FAMILY ▣ WACKY GRANNY

Some Girls offers a detailed "meet the parents" plot that sounds quirky enough, but emerges in a watered-down haze of late-'80s crappiness. Patrick Dempsey stars as college dude Michael. On Christmas break, he travels to Canada to meet with the moneyed, intellectual family of his girlfriend, Gabriella d'Arc (Jennifer Connelly). The d'Arcs are warm and welcoming, but also snooty and more than a bit odd. Mr. d'Arc (Wallace Shawn), for example, walks around nude, explaining that he can only write his treatise on French philosophy while free of clothing.

Gabrielle's coquettish sisters Irenka (Sheila Kelley) and Simone (Ashley Greenfield) are bent on seducing Michael. Gabi not only seems okay with that, but she's possibly the mastermind behind the scheming. *Some Girls* is no sardonic, bourgeoisie-skewering sex roundelay, though. The movie explicitly announces its lowbrow nature when a tempted Michael breaks free from Simone's come-on, runs outdoors, and stuffs his dick into a pile of snow.

Despite several attempts at planting mysteries, the only intriguing elements of *Some Girls* are its ties to the art-house classic, *My Dinner with Andre* (1981). In that esteemed exercise, celebrated playwrights and thinkers Wallace Shawn and Andre Gregory share 110 minutes of enthralling conversation over a meal, and the camera treats us to their talk.

As mentioned earlier, Andre Gregory plays Mr. d'Arc here opposite college-age Patrick Dempsey in *Some Girls*. Three years earlier, Wallace Shawn memorably spouted off about lust as a lisping monk to youthful parishioner Patrick Dempsey in the Catholic high school comedy *Heaven Help Us*. Somewhere in the balcony of the great beyond, Gene Siskel and Roger Ebert—the original and most vociferously outspoken champions of *My Dinner with Andre*—are smiling side by side in their ethereal aisle seats.

Some Kind of Wonderful [1987]

DIR. HOWARD DEUTCH; W/ERIC STOLTZ, LEA THOMPSON, MARY STUART MASTERSON, CRAIG SHEFFER

RICH GIRL ▣ TOMBOY ▣ LOVE TRIANGLE ▣ PUNKS

Some Kind of Wonderful gives *Pretty in Pink* a sex change so that screenwriter John Hughes could use the initial ending for his previous smash. In the original *Pretty in Prink* script, Hughes had lower-class art-girl Andie (Molly Ringwald) choose plucky nerd Duckie (Jon Cryer) over handsome preppy Blaine (Andrew McCarthy). Fortunately, director Howard Deutch listened to audience feedback (and perhaps his gut instinct) and reworked the ending so that the cool chick opts for the rich dude. It's a bold reflection of, you know, how teenagers actually work. Alas, that blot of high school truth apparently did not sit well with Hughes, so he cashed in all his post-*Pretty* clout to whip up *Wonderful*. The latter movie was also a hit, but proved to be the Waterloo of Hughes' teen movie juggernaut. After this, he switched to first-graders (*Home Alone* [1990]) and big dogs (*Beethoven* [1992]).

In *Wonderful*'s inversion of *Pretty in Pink*, blue-collar painter and sculptor Keith (Eric Stoltz) subs for sub-working-class fashion designer Andie. Tomboy rocker Watts (Mary Stuart Masterson) takes the place of flashy Duckie. Moneyed suburbanite Amanda (Lea Thompson) is the girl version of moneyed suburban Blaine. The other main character, a rich creep who wants to befoul the budding across-the-tracks romance, gets to stay male. In *Pink*, he's Steff (James Spader); here, he's Hardy (Craig Sheffer);

Pretty in Pink director Deutch returns to the chair and essentially re-creates his previous effort beat-for-beat, right up to the through-the-looking-glass finale when it changes so that Amanda tells Keith she likes him so much she wants him to be with Watts, who loves him more than anyone else ever could—and Keith goes home with Watts.

Debate goes on regarding Duckie in *Pretty in Pink* being gay. Ringwald says she thought he was. Cryer says no. Hughes died before this became an issue he needed to address. Mary Stuart Masterson's Watts, on the other hand, seems as lesbian as lesbians can lesbianically be. Freed from all these Hughesian high school jerks in her immediate future, it's easy to envision a liberated adult Watts being allowed to find some *real* kind of wonderful.

Something Special [1986]

aka Willy/Milly; I Was a Teenage Boy

DIR. PAUL SCHNEIDER; W/PAMELA ADLON, PATTY DUKE, SETH GREEN, JOHN GLOVER

MAGICAL SEX CHANGE ▪ WHEELCHAIR KID ▪ NONSTOP PENIS AND VAGINA JOKES

As an adult, Pamela Adlon is best known for vocalizing young Bobby Hill on the animated TV series *King of the Hill*, and for portraying Louis CK's dark muse on his pre-scandal sitcom *Louie*, and her own sort-of spin-off, *Better Things*. As a teenager, though, Pamela Adlon magically sprouted a penis in the alternately bold and gentle adolescent gender-confusion comedy, *Something Special*.

Pamela stars here as Milly Niceman, a fourteen-year-old tomboy who's perpetually scolded by her mother Doris (Patty Duke) to act more "girly." Seeking peace wherever she can find it, Milly visits a supposed witch who promises to cast a spell that will make the teenager's deepest desires spring to life. The next day, Milly wakes up with a full-grown wang and loaded ball-bag dangling atop her vagina.

On the advice of her weirdly understanding father (John Glover), our freshly hermaphroditic heroine decides to go with this below-the-belt development. Milly declares herself male, takes on the name Willy, transfers to a new school, and sets out to enjoy life's specific excitements that come with sporting a complete complement of fully functioning human genitalia.

Willy beats off bullies (no, not like *that*), befriends an "out" gay kid in a wheelchair (a unique character at the time), and ultimately decides that, at her core, she's a girl who wants to date boys. So, by the end, Willy reverts back to being Milly, but she's enriched with the lessons of living as another sex classification. Plus—who knows?—maybe she'll dude out again or end up somewhere on the gender spectrum thirty years hence.

Equally known by its overseas moniker, *Willy/Milly*, the movie takes a prescient approach to the subject matter. The adolescent gender questioning is far more relevant to present-day thinking than other mid-1980s takes on the subject, the best (and meanest and grossest) of which was John Hughes' savagely hilarious one-two *National Lampoon* short-story combo, "My Vagina" (1978) and "My Penis" (1979).

In addition, *Something Special* may have also inspired *Cleo/Leo* (1989), a bawdy, low-budget flesh farce directed by Chuck Vincent (*Preppies* [1984], *Summer Camp* [1979]), about a womanizer who becomes womanized in the sense that his dick mysteriously morphs into a slit. Vincent, in turn, maintained that legendary Hollywood filmmaker Blake Edwards borrowed heavily from *Cleo/Leo* by making the Ellen Barkin junk-swap comedy *Switch* (1991). Ultimately, it becomes hard to keep all these gender-bender burlesques *straight*—but maybe that was the point all along, sweeties.

Sorority Babes in the Slimeball Bowl-O-Rama

[1988]

DIR. DAVID DECOTEAU; W/LINNEA QUIGLEY, MICHELLE BAUER, BRINKE STEVENS, GEORGE "BUCK" FLOWER

SORORITY BABES ▫ NERDS ▫ PEEPING ▫ BOWLING ▫ HORNY PUPPET

Sorority Babes in the Slimeball Bowl-O-Rama is the ultimate *USA Up All Night* basic cable movie. Boasting the quintessential self-celebratory "schlock" title, *Slimeball* casts huge-haired, well-past-college-age '80s scream queens as first-year Greek house pledges, and champions campus dorks dressed in party store nerd costumes as heroes after they team with a bedraggled old character actor to defeat an evil hand puppet. Happily, *Sorority Babes* only wobbles occasionally off the beam separating legit B movie from "look how wacky we know we are" worthlessness (i.e., Troma).

As Delta Delta Delta pledges, Taffy (Brinke Stevens) and Lisa (Michelle Bauer) endure naked ass paddling and naked whipped-cream coatings at the wicked mitts of Rhonda (Kathi O'Brecht), Frankie (Carla Baron), and mean girl in charge Babs (Robin Rochelle, RIP). Afterward, they shower, attracting the prying peepers of dweebensteins Calvin (Andras Jones), Keith (John Stuart Wildman), and Jimmie (Hal Halvins). Just prior to sneaking over to the Tri-Delt house, the trio had been leafing through jackoff magazines while splatter movies played on TV in the background. This film clearly knew its audience, intimately.

The nerds are busted and forced to join the pledges on a caper to break into the local bowling alley and pilfer a trophy. Upon arrival, the heist seems easy since the janitor (prolific cult actor George "Buck" Flower) has locked himself in a closet, seething, "Fuck! That's stuck tighter'n a nun's cunt!" Then slinky, spandex-encased cat burglar Spider (Linnea Quigley) turns up amidst the oiled lanes and rental shoes. She wants to swipe the cash register, but she's happy to help the college kids with their own breaking and entering.

The invaders nab a trophy, inadvertently drop it, and unleash a gremlin-esque rubber puppet that calls itself the Imp (and is voiced by Haunted Garage front man Dukey Flyswatter). The creature says he can make wishes come true; as usual, none of the robbers think carefully before wishing. The results include a prom dress that turns into garbage bags; uncomfortable sex in the bowling alley's seemingly massive locker room; and the queen bee Tri Delts mutating into rampaging monsters imbued with the power of fatal lesbianism.

Sorority Babes ends up being as pleasingly punchy as can be expected from a hybrid of mid-'80s teen sex comedy tropes and late-'80s self-consciously smirking horror crap. I regret not catching the movie during its blip of a theatrical run, but I am glad I saw it on *Up All Night*, where it always truly belonged.

Sorority House Party

[1992] aka Rock and Roll Fantasy

DIR. DAVID MICHAEL LATT; W/ATTILA, APRIL LERMAN, KIM LITTLE, AVALON ANDERS

SORORITY ▫ HOUSE PARTY ▫ ROCK STAR ▫ HAIR METAL ▫ STRIP POKER ▫ HOT TUB

The sorority house party in *Sorority House Party* happens right after a baffling opening credits sequence setting up a familiar 1980s pay cable "erotic thriller." Loud rock 'n' roll powers up on the soundtrack (yes, definitely rock 'n' roll, a singer even drones the words "rock...and...roll.") We view a hodgepodge of beer chuggers, skinny-dippers, strip-poker players, bad dancers, and mirthless cutaway gags on the flimsiest collegiate movie set this side of a porn production.

The big bash breaks up, and curly-haired campus cutie Alex (April Lerman) rescues passed-out long-haired heavy metal hunk Jamie Z. (the single-named Attila). Luckily for Alex, Jamie Z. is her very favorite rock star. She spends the rest of the movie embroiled in a comic caper about Jamie's employers putting a hit on him. Alex's blonde BFF Bre (Kim Little—not Lil' Kim) helps out.

Sorority House Party, filmed under the more accurate appellation *Rock and Roll Fantasy*, is about as inessential as such a promising daydream can get. The movie succeeds mainly as a hideous spray-tan blast from the early '90s, represented here by male lead Attila, a model who here combines the lesser traits of Fabio and Type O Negative's Peter Steele for a performance worthy of a cigar store wooden Indian statue. Which reminds me: Local tavern proprietor Indian Jim (Jay Phillip Ghazal) is a white guy dressed as a Native American tribal chief who speaks with an Apu accent. Laugh at that or don't, but, either way, please don't take to Twitter about it.

Soul Man [1986]

DIR. STEVEN MINER; W/C. THOMAS HOWELL, RAE DAWN CHONG, JAMES EARL JONES

COLLEGE ADMISSIONS MADNESS ▣ RACE RELATIONS

Even in 1986, the premise of *Soul Man* was stupefying; C. Thomas Howell affirmative-actions his way into Harvard by overdosing on tanning pills, then spends the rest of the movie in blackface. When *Soul Man* was actually made and then commercially released, instead of the expected coast-to-coast protests the only known demonstration against it was a single-day rally at UCLA. Instead of receiving widespread condemnation, the movie proved to be a minor hit in theaters and a popular cable TV staple. The '80s were different, everybody!

Soul Man amusingly makes necessary points about racial inequality on and off college campuses with a spoonful of shoe polish to help the medicine go down. Howell is deft in the lead, as is Rae Dawn Chong as the actual minority scholarship candidate he beats out for his position. Howell and Chong subsequently married each other in real life, a testament to *Soul Man*'s power to unify humanity that few other cinematic endeavors can claim.

Even the MTV tie-in music video is confusing. Six years after *The Blues Brothers* turned the song "Soul Man" into a schoolyard staple (probably paving the way for this movie), *Soul Man* revisited the familiar Sam and Dave classic with the help of Sam (Moore) himself and Lou Reed (yeah, *Lou Reed*). The clip intersperses scenes from the movie with lip-sync cameos by Bruce Willis, Gumby, Elvira, Ray "Boom-Boom" Mancini, Jamie Farr, and Ron Reagan Jr. You can assume that half of those oddballs would have bolted if they were told the premise of the movie.

Splitz [1982]

DIR. DOMONIC PARIS; W/ROBIN JOHNSON, PATTI LEE, DOM IRRERA, SHIRLEY STOLER

SORORITY ▣ ALL-GIRL ROCK BAND ▣ NERDS ▣ NEW WAVE ▣ HYPNOSIS ▣ MOBSTERS ▣ STRIP BASKETBALL ▣ LINGERIE WRESTLING

"We wish this movie was about sex, drugs, and rock 'n' roll," claims the tagline of *Splitz*, "but two out of three ain't bad!" The quip nails *Splitz*'s attitude (or, better still, "RADitude") and nicely sells a cut-rate, jokes-a-poppin' music comedy in the vein of those made by Allan Arkush (*Rock 'n' Roll High School, Get Crazy*), with Robin Johnson, lead Garbage Girl of 1980's *Times Square* instead of the Ramones.

As tough-talking, axe-shredding Gina Napoliani, Johnson fronts the female new-wave power trio Splitz, backed by bassist Joan (Patti Lee) and drummer Susie (Barbara Bingham). When the members of Splitz hear their pals at Hooter College might lose their sorority house, the band pledges to do whatever is necessary to help. In addition to performing three pseudo-music-video numbers (one of them shot at CBGB), "whatever is necessary" includes lingerie wrestling, strip basketball, and taking showers six girls at a time.

Johnson is the same hard-ass, hotheaded Brook-

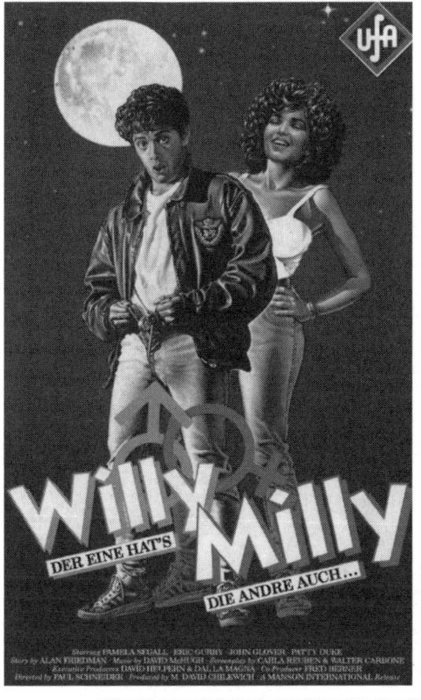

Clockwise from top left: Something Special *(1986), aka* Willy Milly, *the teenage hermaphrodite hit of the decade;* Sixteen Candles *(1984), perhaps you've heard of this film initially pitched to teens as coming "from the man who brought you Mr. Mom";* Slumber Party '57 *(1976) stars Debra Winger;* Splitz *(1982) delivers rock 'n' raunch revelry—and one of a handful of sideways VHS boxes from the home video boom.*

Clockwise from top left: The Sure Thing *(1985) college rom-com bliss;* Screwballs *(1983) fully rules (ask Mr. Skin); Spring Break* (1983), *a major frontline victory in fun bikini maneuvers;* Swim Team *(1979), the curiously crappy post-*Animal House *return of both Flounder (Stephen Furst) and Greg Marmalarde (James Daughton).*

lyn Italian she portrayed in *Times Square*, and several marinara-soaked subplots involve her mobster father (Raymond Serra) and her dimwit hypnotist cousin Vinny Mamabasta (stand-up comic Dom Irerra). As Hooter College's malevolent Dean Hunta, cult actress Shirley Stoler (*The Honeymoon Killers*) deftly hams it up en route to a big, campy cabaret routine at the end.

Splitz first played theaters in 1982, and didn't reach VHS until 1984, the year that the PG-13 rating was created. Even spliced down to PG-13 length and standards for home video release, *Splitz* boasts an eye-bulging abundance of nudity. Enjoyable in either incarnation, *Splitz* remains fairly funny, delightfully dated, and reasonably rockin'.

SPRING BREAK [1983]

DIR. SEAN S. CUNNINGHAM; W/DAVID KNELL, PERRY LANG, STEVE BASSETT, CORINNE WAHL

SPRING BREAK ▫ FLORIDA ▫ WET T-SHIRTS ▫ RICH JERKS ▫ CUSTOM VAN ▫ VIDEO ARCADE ▫ THE BIG BELLY-FLOP CONTEST

In 1980, director Sean S. Cunningham assembled the horror juggernaut *Friday the 13th* by placing select moments from the slasher movie deluge following 1978's *Halloween* onto a basic template scripted by the relatively obscure 1971 Mario Bava shocker *A Bay of Blood*. In doing so, Cunningham built a perfect exploitation beast and struck the B-movie motherlode.

Cunningham does the same thing with *Spring Break*, switching genres to fuse together mid-'60s beach party flicks and post-*Porky's* raunch. *Spring Break* didn't make even a fraction of the impact of *Friday the 13th*, but the movie is a swell if surprisingly mellow stretch of sun, shore, and college students with a one-week license to impair their livers and unleash their libidos. Plus the title track by Cheap Trick is absolutely killer.

When dorky nice guys Nelson (David Knell) and Adam (Perry Lang) arrive at the Breeze N' Sea motel in scenic Fort Lauderdale, they discover their room has been double-booked. They'll have to share bunks with a couple of spaghetti-breathed Brooklyn goombahs named O.T. (Steve Bassett) and Stu (Paul Land). Why outer-borough New York Italians repeatedly figure into these films remains a mystery, but teen movie hell is awash in leftover '70s passion for the Pacino/De-Niro/Stallone/Travolta stable and nods to Frankie Avalon beach parties. In this case, Cunningham racks up his good-time guidos on the list of essential active ingredients alongside wet T-shirts, teeny bikinis, belly-flop dives, graphic banana consumption, and a montage of swimsuit frolicking set to "Hit the Beach" by Big Spender.

On-screen, the shy Midwesterners and the show-off East Coasters become best pals pronto. Nelson charms Susie (Jayne Modean) by showing her some tricks on a Galaga video game. Fearing bad publicity from such arcade prowess, Nelson's a-hole, jelly-bean-gobbling, politician stepfather, Ernest (Donald Symington), sends goons to kidnap our hero. Furthermore, Senator Jerk Dad wants to foreclose on the Breeze N' Sea Inn immediately. He dispatches crooked building inspector Eddie (Richard B. Shull, looking like a balloon-animal Walter Matthau).

Meanwhile, O.T. eyeballs sex bomb songstress Joan (*Penthouse* Pet of the Year Corinne Wahl) as she belts out "Do It to You" while fronting her smut-rock combo, Hot Date. She can't resist his Bensonhurst bravado. *Spring Break*'s product placement is even less subtle. Everybody exclusively drinks Miller beer in every frame, except for when Susie brings Nelson back to her hotel and pointedly asks him to get some Coca-Cola. He hits the truck-size Coke machine in the lobby, then realizes he forgot the room number, so he wanders the halls with couple of cans pointed straight at the camera to while .38 Special's "Caught Up in You" leads him home. A Chipwich umbrella cart turns up several times, too.

The good times roll forward until the kidnappers whisk Nelson away to Senator Jerk Dad's yacht. Luckily, everybody else saves him and the Breeze N' Sea at the same time. Party on, dudes and dudettes!

Spring Break is a genuine blast of nostalgia. Corinne Wahl is especially great as Joan, while Jayne Modean's eight-pack abs actually look strange among all those other Miller-and-Coke-fed '80s bodies. Look for Jeff Garlin—yes, Larry David's sizable sidekick from *Curb Your Enthusiasm*—as the Big Gut-Gut, a wordless mondo basho beast who chews open a beer can and moons a crowd before splashtastically decimating all other contenders in the big belly-flop contest.

Spring Fever [1983]
aka Sneakers

DIR. JOSEPH L. SCANLON; W/SUSAN ANTON, CARLING BASSETT, SHAWN FOLTZ, FRANK CONVERSE

SPRING BREAK · FLORIDA · TENNIS · COUNTRY CLUB · MALE STRIPPERS

In teen movie hell, *Spring Fever* commits what amounts to the crime of the century. The painted poster image depicts two deliriously gleeful, super-shapely bikini babes—one blonde, the other brunette—holding a shirtless Speedo hunk in scuba flippers upside-down on the beach and dousing his crotch with a freshly cracked beer. "Your big chance to go totally crazy!!" announces the tagline, emphasizing everything already on display with double exclamation points.

Nothing in this movie rates even a single exclamation point. *Spring Fever* contains no bikini babes, no beer, no upside-down flipper-footed Speedo hunk. The movie turns out to be a Canadian tax write-off kiddie sports saga, first known as *Sneakers*, about the budding friendship of thirteen-year-old Junior Women's Tennis Tournament players K.C. (Carling Bassett, whose name sounds like a verb and a noun placed together) and Missy (Shawn Foltz, whose last name sounds like a noun and a verb at once).

The girls meet in Florida for the event and become just the bestest of pals despite their disparate backgrounds. Karen's mom, Stevie (Susan Anton), is a voluptuous Las Vegas showgirl, while Missy's prissy old lady Celia (Jessica Walter) is a moneyed snob. The height of *Spring Fever*'s "crazy" occurs when Karen and Missy lock arms and skip around Busch Gardens.

What *Spring Fever*'s infamous poster truthfully represents is a nefarious Canuck plot to confuse and preempt audiences into believing this film was actually Columbia's highly touted *Spring Break* (1983), which *Spring Fever* beat into theaters by a few weeks. *Spring Break* proved to be a hit, but petered out far short of the studio's phenomenal *Porky's*-level expectations. Inquiring minds can only wonder how much of a diverting role *Spring Fever* played in that weak showing, not to mention what those crafty low-budget movie producers to far north of Florida might be scheming right now.

Squeeze Play [1979]

DIR. LLOYD KAUFMAN (AS SAMUEL WEIL); W/JENNIFER HETRICK, JIM HARRIS, RICK GITLIN

SOFTBALL · FLASHING · VIRGIN · WET T-SHIRT CONTEST · FUNNY ALCOHOLIC

The low budget, but high-profile success of the deliriously dopey sports comedy *Squeeze Play* made New York schlock house Troma Films a proper trash-culture brand name. By 1979, Troma had already bounced about in the sexploitation ball-pit and produced the beyond-extreme horror classic *Bloodsucking Freaks* (1976). With *Squeeze Play*, company heads Lloyd Kaufman and Michael Herz cannily promoted the studio itself as the film's real star.

Bizarrely, *The New York Times* took Troma's bait, giving *Squeeze Play* a rave review ("Zesty!" critic Janet Maslin proclaimed twice in her writeup), and then dispatched a reporter to lovingly profile Kaufman and Herz. Since then, the B-movie powerhouse has continued to plop out lazy, self-aware crap on film while coyly cooing, "Ain't it adorable how all we plop out is crap?"

Perhaps because it got there first, *Squeeze Play* is one of Troma's least despicable efforts. Shot in 1976 and not released until 1981, the dated-on-arrival slop depicts a gaggle of young, foxy New

Jersey "softball widows" who organize their own team, the Beaverettes, to get in on the action that keeps drawing away the attentions of their boyfriends. They raise funds by putting on a wet-T-shirt contest, where one doused cotton top bears the words "Support the ERA."

Equally amusing, at one point a guy drops his drawers and catches a line drive with his ass. "She really cracked that one!" the announcer says. "They're going to have to call for a clean ball!" Although not quite teenaged in taste, *Squeeze Play*'s surprise big box-office home run did rally a youth audience that shortly thereafter made blockbusters out of other raunch-driven, independent studio sex comedies, most notably *Private Lessons* (1981) and, of course, *Porky's* (1981). When Troma tried to directly cash in on that craze, they gave us *The First Turn-On* (1983) and it sucked and so did the studio, and it still does, suckily compounded by four subsequent decades of suckitude.

STARHOPS [1978]

DIR. BARBARA PEETERS; W/DOROTHY BUHRMAN, STERLING FRAZIER, JILLIAN KESNER, DICK MILLER

ROLLER-SKATING WAITRESSES ▣ DRIVE-IN RESTAURANT ▣ EVIL CAPITALIST ▣ SAVE THE BUSINESS

Starhops mines familiar exploitation terrain filled with young girls in scanty outfits who pump new life into a limping business; e.g., *Gas Pump Girls* (1979), *Lunch Wagon* (1981), *Valet Girls* (1987), and, from the porn side of the tracks, *Hot and Saucy Pizza Girls...They Deliver!* (1978). "Starhops" is a drive-in burger joint that starts the film as "Jerry's." The place is a money-bleeding mess, as is Jerry himself (Roger Corman go-to Dick Miller). After he reluctantly fires his beloved carhops Angel (Jillian Kesner) and Cupcake (Sterling Frazier), the girls, perhaps realizing names like those must control their destinies, seduce a bank officer into forking over a loan. They buy their employer out and give the greasy spoon a makeover.

Angel and Cupcake hire sensuous French chef Diane (Dorothy Buhrman), and together they aesthetically pizzazz the dump into a retro-future hot spot. Come opening day, the new proprietors, along with some other freshly hired hotties, don warp-speed-inducing space-chick swimsuit uniforms to service customers.

Starhops is an instant smash. The roadside eat-and-ogle attraction proves so popular that megalomaniacal oil baron Carter Axe (Al Hopson) hatches a greedy plan to turn it into a gas station. Nothing doing, say the ladies, and, from there, *Starhops* rolls into slapstick battle mode, pitting the benevolent babes against the crass old capitalist. You won't be shocked by who wins, but you will be unpleasantly surprised by the dearth of sex and sin in a supposedly R-rated film marketed as a softcore fun farce.

Like the eatery on-screen, *Starhops* is the product of a female creative team that clearly understood the commercial allure of sexploitation. Director Barbara Peeters previously made the rape-and-revenge ass-stomper *Bury Me an Angel* (1974) and helmed the rape-and-run-wild monster masher *Humanoids from the Deep* (1980). Screenwriter Stephanie Rothman directed *It's a Bikini World* (1967), *The Student Nurses* (1970), *The Velvet Vampire* (1971), the barbaric *Terminal Island* (1973), and *The Working Girls* (1974), wherein Cassandra "Elvira" Peterson debuted the very pair of pumpkins that continue to hornify every Halloween season. As renegade drive-in filmmakers, Peeters and Rothman were sisters doing it for themselves, creating memorably weird and inventive cinematic experiences for male audience members who were undoubtedly doing it *to* themselves.

Stewardess School [1986]

Dir. Ken Blancato; w/Donald Most, Brett Cullen, Mary Cadorette, Wendie Jo Sperber

Flight Attendants ▣ Training Academy ▣ Bikers ▣ Punks ▣ Hookers ▣ Peeping

If Steve Guttenberg in *Police Academy* (1984) is a few clicks south of Tom Hanks in *Bachelor Party* (1984), just imagine how far down you have to turn the dial to reach Donnie Most—"Ralph Malph" from TV's *Happy Days*—in *Stewardess School*.

The fact is that *Donald* Most, as he's billed here in an amusingly misplaced grab at big-screen respectability, didn't become the beloved joke-a-minute Mr. Malph because he wasn't funny. Leading-man charismatic he is not, but casting *Donald* in the top-billed role just adds charm to a way-under-the-radar, R-rated training academy raunch romp.

Most plays George Bunkle, the party-hearty yang to the straight man yin of Brett Cullen as Philo Henderson, his best friend. Philo is a handsome hero type who dreams of being a major airline pilot. He's hampered by the fact that, without contact lenses, he's almost entirely blind. Calamitous slapstick and mega-magnifying Coke-bottle-eyeglass gags ensue.

After George and Philo are booted from a pilot-training program, the best buds enroll in "Stew School" (also the title of the movie's theme song), the spacious, ivy-covered flight attendant breeding ground Weidermeyer Academy. Among their fellow students, blonde goody two-shoes Pimmie Polk (Julia Montgomery of *Revenge of the Nerds* [1984]) shows up all smiles. Constant klutz Kelly Johnson (Mary Cadorette) crashes in after literally getting her ass bounced out of a kettle drum gig with the local philharmonic. Professional wrestler Wanda Polanski (Sandahl Bergman of *Conan the Barbarian*) trades the squared circle for the friendly skies to mend a broken heart. Rich-girl punk rocker Cindy Adams (Corinne Bohrer) arrives on the hog of her beastly biker boyfriend Snake (Dennis Burkley). Charmingly chubby Jolean Winters (Wendie Jo Sperber) shows up to supply the movie with a welcome dose of Wendie Jo Sperber–isms.

Recently jail-sprung sex pro Sugar Dubois (Judy Landers) makes the funniest entrance. The bodacious blonde is dropped off by her Cadillac-driving benefactor, Harry (Teddy Wilson, familiar to fans of the sitcom *What's Happening!!* as Al Dunbar, the music bootlegger on the one-hour Doobie Brothers episode). After Sugar gripes about going to Stew School, Harry says, "Look, Sugar, I'm your parole officer, not an employment agency!" She accepts her fate and tells him, "Don't take any wooden pickles!" Later, Sugar supplies the movie's most outrageous moment. As a panicking airline passenger is forcibly confined to his seat by an entire flight staff, Sugar calms the man by kneeling before him and covering his lap with a blanket, which we then see bobbing unmistakably up and down.

Stewardess School keeps the riotous raunch coming fun and furiously. Solid sidesplitters include the ladies allowing Philo to shower with them since he can't see, and a kid in a cowboy outfit blasting the permanent grin from Pimmie's pretty face by aiming his toy pistol at her and saying, "How would you like your tits shot off?" The sex-drenched silliness all builds to a semi-suspenseful climax during which our crack class of graduates must contend with a mad bomber and a knocked-out cockpit crew at 35,000 feet.

The inevitable happy ending could only have been made happier with the addition of one or seven sequels. *Stewardess School*'s final image is a freeze frame of beaming Mr. Most flanked by two good-time gals who are planting smooches on each of his cheeks. There he is—the Donald we can all endorse.

Stitches [1985]

DIR. ROD HOLCOMB (AS ALAN SMITHEE); W/PARKER STEVENSON, ROBIN DEARDEN, GEOFFREY LEWIS, EDDIE ALBERT

MED STUDENTS GONE WILD ▫ PRANKS ▫ PEEPING ▫ SEXY NURSES ▫ PUNKS ▫ DRAG ▫ EVIL DEAN ▫ BOOZE MACHINE

Stitches opens big, bold, and bare-assed. A med school instructor leads a class of students into the morgue to perform their first-ever examinations of human cadavers. The stiffs lie on slabs before them, covered by sheets. On the instructor's direction, the students remove the sheets and three bald, male specimens immediately stand out. One of the stiffs smirks. Another reaches over and squeezes a female intern's plump rump. The third not-so-dead guy jumps up and whoops like Curly from the Three Stooges, signaling the other two bogus bodies to leap up and freak out the unsuspecting class members. The pranksters then loudly scramble out of the room, running wild and naked all over campus to the tune of the supremely '80s-movie theme song "Sometimes You Win" by Henry Small.

After that audacious beginning, *Stitches* keeps the hostile energy going strong. Crash-landing Hollywood star Parker Stevenson, thirty-three at the time and clearly with no shinier offers on the table, fully commits to the role of Bobby, leader of a trio of wild-and-crazy med students who run the school. More than once, they do so with their dicks swinging in the open breeze.

Frequent Clint Eastwood costar (and father of Juliette) Geoffrey Lewis costars as Ralph Rizzo, a seemingly brain-damaged delivery man who rigs up a booze machine called "Alkie" and assists the future doctors in various schemes. For fun, they lead a parade of lunatics adorned in extravagant body organ costumes through town. Eddie Albert, as prickly Dean Bradley, keenly reworks a role he perfected as the evil warden in the 1974 Burt Reynolds classic *The Longest Yard*.

Stitches is punchy, smutty, and popping end-to-end with ludicrous nudity. One memorable table-turning prank involves peeping on fifteen topless female classmates; those same peeped-upon students and resident nurses are keeping a horse-hosed bodybuilder under observation for weeks over a "possible hernia" that requires constant checking.

Turn-your-head-and-cough procedures rival only rectal exams in frequency as far as *Stitches*' bawdy fodder is concerned. When the females get their full revenge, a flaming florist impersonates a *trés* handsy cock-and-balls specialist in a scene that is not only hilarious, but borders on homosexual pornography. *Stitches* really holds it together with something for everybody.

The Stöned Age [1994] aka Tack's Chicks

DIR. JAMES MELKONIAN; W/MICHAEL KOPELOW, BRADFORD TATUM, CHINA KANTNER, RENEE GRIFFIN

STONERS ▫ NOSTALGIA ▫ WILD PARTY ▫ PSYCHO DAD ▫ THE BIG CONCERT

On-screen, it's the 1970s, the "stoned age." Two heavy metal longhairs on summer break from high school, pimply redhead Joe (Michael Kopelow) and mildly menacing Hubbs (Bradford Tatum), tool around scenic Torrance, California, on one scorching night in search of beer, babes, weed, or anything resembling a worthwhile evening out of the house. Nothing seems doing until they pick up local fast-talker Tack (Clifton Gonzalez Gonzalez), who promises to guide their VW station wagon ("the Blue Torpedo") to a swinging soirée that he *swears* is just erupting with wanton young ladies aching to blaze the bongs of dirtbag catches like Joe, Hubbs, and Tack.

Throughout their ensuing wild booze-and-cooze chase, our hesher heroes fight about Blue Öyster Cult and fuck up at every turn. They don't quite know what to do once they actually come across females in the form of *Playboy*-beautiful Lanie (Renee Allman), who slips out of her own BÖC tee; and sweet hippie honey Jill (China Kantner), who keeps her tie-dye on tight. When these likeable sad sacks finally do arrive at a get-together that may be Tack's mythical bacchanal, a volcanically pissed-off dad bursts inside and busts up the shindig by single-handedly (and hilariously) beating the unholy piss out of every teenage boy within punching, strangling, and pummeling distance. As he's suffering violent comeuppance, Joe spiritually communes with a laser-shooting eyeball that blew maybe more than just his mind during a BÖC concert.

Even while still in production (under the names *Tack's Chicks* and *Teenage Wasteland*), *The Stöned Age* unfortunately found itself stuck in the shadow of the more mainstream *Dazed and Confused*. Enough room exists for film fans to love and laugh at two rich, clever, quotable, and endlessly rewatchable early-'90s movies that reflect on the gloriously wasted youths of the mid-1970s.

While *Dazed and Confused* is the more "important" of the two films, let's all still throw some horns to the loose, scrappy, arguably more laugh-out-loud funny *Stoned Age* for packing its pipe with sweet skin and some genuinely gnarly heartache. Watch for climactic cameos, both by Blue Öyster Cult and by the teen movie heartthrob that got this whole cinematic beach ball rolling in the first place, Mr. Frankie Avalon.

Student Affairs [1987]

DIR. CHUCK VINCENT; W/TRACEY ADAMS, JIM ABELE, VERONICA HART, DAVID F. FRIEDMAN

MOVIE SHOOT ▫ VIRGIN ▫ NERDS ▫ CHEERLEADERS ▫ PRANKS ▫ SEX TAPE

Student Affairs is exploitation auteur Chuck Vincent's *8 1/2*—and not because there's a joke here involving that number followed by the word *inches*. As with the overall approach of Federico Fellini's superlative 1963 meditation on what it is to be a filmmaker during the making of a film, *Student Affairs* takes place within the halls and classrooms of an actual 1980s high school while a movie crew mounts the complicated shoot of *Oakwood High*, a 1950s teen sex comedy.

Off-camera complications intermingle with footage from the movie-within-a-movie. "Norman," the dorkiest, most picked-on dweeb in *Oakwood High*, for example, is portrayed by the fictitious production's top-billed, highest-paid actor, an overbearingly egotistical Hollywood prima donna named Andrew Armstrong (Jim Abele). Vincent keeps such character contrasts clear and maintains compelling parallel storylines: the behind-the-scenes drama works (in an agreeably cheesy B-movie way) while the *Oakwood High* T&A antics slam home the salable elements (in a magnificently cheesy B-movie way).

The cast layers another "meta-" factor. Chuck Vincent made his bones by directing numerous classics of the theatrically released hardcore porn era. He went on to stud his R-rated productions with XXX performers, most notably his muse Veronica Hart. She does double duty here as a hot *Oakwood High* teacher, and the actress playing her, "Veronica." Adult-entertainment fixture Tracey Adams, who worked with Vincent a year earlier in *Wimps*, plays the female lead of both *Student Affairs* and *Oakwood High*. The poster's tagline refers to her like so: "In this school, the student body is 36-24-36!"

Vincent also packs the screen with male smut-biz figures. B.C., the director, is portrayed by acclaimed X-rated filmmaker Henri Pachard (*The Bizarre Ones* [1968], *The Devil in Miss Jones Part II* [1982]). Rex, the bratty screenwriter, is played by Andy Nichols, best known as sinister master of ceremonies Max Melodramatic in the hardcore midnight movie *Café Flesh* (1982). The big boom, though, comes from grand grindhouse sex-and-gore pioneer David F. Friedman—producer of sordid gems from *Blood Feast* (1963) to *The Erotic Adventures of Robin Hood* (1969) to *Ilsa: She Wolf of the SS* (1975)—who shines here as the money man behind *Oakwood High*.

Now, if only somebody had thought to shoot a documentary about the making of this making-of-a-movie movie, the mad spiral of *Student Affairs* could have gone on forever.

STUDENT BODIES [1981]

DIRS. MICHAEL RITCHIE, MICKEY ROSE; W/KRISTEN RITER, MATTHEW GOLDSBY, JOE FLOOD, THE STICK

HORROR SPOOF ▪ VIRGINS ▪ NERDS ▪ JOCKS ▪ PEEPING ▪ THE BIG GAME

Scripted by Woody Allen's writing partner Mickey Rose and directed, at least in part, by Michael Ritchie between *The Bad News Bears* (1976) and *Fletch* (1985), *Student Bodies* is the product of comedy movie royalty. One shorts-soaking guffaw at a time, it lives up to its gut-busting bloodline. This, not *Class Reunion* (1982), is the horror spoof *National Lampoon* should have released after *Animal House.*

The gags in *Student Bodies* keep flying at us a mile a minute amidst a standard plot from any of a million "dead babysitter" movies. Laugh-wise, the hit-to-miss ratio is spectacular—especially the moment, which will not be spoiled here, when the nudity-and-gore-free movie earns its R rating.

Student Bodies offers three supreme comic creations. First, there's the Breather, voiced by producer Jerry Belson as "Richard Brando." He's a clumsy, seemingly asthmatic stalker, and we see each homicidal setup and murder through his eyes. He neurotically talks to himself the whole time, and constantly steps in wadded-up chewing gum ("I'm gonna kill the kid with the gum!" he snaps at one point). The second gift from the comedy gods is shop teacher Mr. Dumpkin (Joe Flood), who looks like his name sounds. He relentlessly repeats the words *horsehead bookends* so often that, once you see the movie, that phrase will be branded on the haunches of your mind forever. Finally, the movies delivers the absolute freak show of a janitor Malvert, portrayed by an actual freak show of a stand-up comedian who went by the name "the Stick." His signature line—"Sometimes Malvert pees red"—is not even close to the creepiest thing about him.

Student Bodies prevails over other horror comedies of its day because it's really a teen comedy decorated with fright film flourishes. Each frame is packed with gags in the style of a *Mad* magazine illustration (e.g., the black balloons bobbling around at a cheerleader's funeral; a prissy virgin's increasingly sizable "NO!" buttons that are exposed each time she takes off a layer of clothing). I still won't reveal why the movie is rated R, but here—help yourself to some fucking horseheads bookends.

THE STUDENT BODY [1976]

aka CLASSROOM TEASERS

DIR. GUS TRIKONIS; W/JILLIAN KESNER, JANICE HEIDEN, JUNE FAIRCHILD, WARREN STEVENS

COLLEGE ▪ WOMEN IN PRISON ▪ PREPPIES ▪ NERDS ▪ POOL PARTY ▪ MAD SCIENTIST

Viewers must marvel at the ingenuity and flexibility of marketers tasked with selling the interchangeable genre films in teen movie hell. The madcap poster for *The Student Body* declares, "A secret campus experiment...from inmates to classmates to playmates." When this same movie was reissued as *Classroom Teasers,* the tagline also transformed: "They bend every rule to turn on the school!"

As *The Student Body*, this movie was sold as a rah-rah raunch romp; as *Classroom Teasers,* the pitch was pure, steamy sexploitation. Neither angle really fits the strange reality—a women-in-chains poster would have been just as appropriate, but also off the mark.

The action here begins near Kansas City, with a full-blown female prison riot so brutal and berserk that its three main instigators are offered early parole if they agree to submit to a drug trial and behavioral experiment at a nearby university. The trio at hand consists of ferocious Carrie (Jillian Kesner), bratty airhead Mitzi (June Fairchild), and nymphoid nookie-junkie Chicago (Janice Heiden). Posing as college students, the jailbirds move into the residence and laboratory of Dr. Blalock (Warren Stevens), who dopes and analyzes them as part of a grand scheme to transform hardened ex-cons into harmless coeds.

The trouble is, his methods don't work at all.

Violence and lunatic-level lack of impulse control prove to be the true order of *The Student Body*. Carrie turns out to be a genius, but she largely loses her mind while hunting down the sponsors of Blalock's experiment (might be the military, or maybe the rotund fuck in the basement who keeps constant watch on the girls via hidden cameras). Mitzi smashes a store's plate-glass window so she can make off with a four-foot stuffed penguin. Chicago's amorous feelings for a fellow quickly explode; she attempts to rape him, then beats the tampons out of the guy's girlfriend in a back alley. Afterward, she exhales, "Christ! I'm freaked!"

Maniacal as all that, *The Student Body* is too slipshod to jell into an off-the-wall madcap success. Unlike Chicago, you'll come away un-freaked—until, like Carrie, you really *think* about the whole thing. Unless you have a four-foot stuffed penguin, you won't feel akin to Mitzi at all.

The movie's alternate title, *Classroom Teasers*, is a calculated knockoff of the skinternational 1975 Gloria Guida teen sex hit, *The Teasers*. Director Gus Trikonis boasts a commendable run of drive-in trash, also gracing us with *Five the Hard Way* (1969), *Supercock* (1975), *The Swinging Barmaids* (1975), *Nashville Girl* (1976), *Moonshine County Express* (1977), *The Evil* (1981), and *Take This Job and Shove It* (1981).

SUMMER CAMP [1979]

DIR. CHUCK VINCENT; W/JOHN LAUGHLIN (AS JOHN C. MCLAUGHLIN), LINNEA QUIGLEY, RAY HOLLAND, VERKINA FLOWER

SUMMER CAMP 📼 PRANKS 📼 VIRGINS 📼 FOOD FIGHT 📼 PANTY RAID 📼 CUSTOM VAN 📼 THE BIG TURD-MEASURING CONTEST

In the depths of teen movie hell, *Summer Camp* boasts one of the most fertile premises (a down-and-out owner of woodland facility invites former campers back for a post-puberty reunion); one of the absolutely most provocative and ass-kickative posters (a gorgeous knockoff of Rick Meyerowitz's "captured chaos" *Animal House* imagery, centered on a human pyramid of youth flick archetypes); and is the creation of one of the genre's most reliably energetic and compelling filmmakers (the esteemed Mr. Chuck Vincent).

Somehow, *Summer Camp* falls short and ends up feeling closer to 119 hours than its actual 119 minutes. Much like mythical Icarus with his waxen wings, here is a down-and-dirty slapstick T&A youth farce that dares to soar too high, too fast, and too close to the flying nuclear furnace at the center of its universe of nude boobs, absent parents, beer bashes, shower peeping, and power pranks. *Summer Camp* just kind of sucks, best described for genre fans as a must-see that quickly and sloppily degenerates into a must-not-ever-see-again.

Camp Malibu is the ramshackle outdoor getaway of the title. Proprietor Herman Samuels (John F. Goff) and his late-'70s classy old lady Sharon (Brenda Fogarty) summon a dozen or so nearly grown ex-campers under the guise of a fun time in nature, just like when they were little kids. Now that they're able-bodied young adults, he plans on bamboozling them into fixing up the dump with a series of "boys against girls" competitions while hitting up their parents for money.

Slammed-together set pieces cover the essential ingredients: shaving cream vandalism; charging a dollar to spy on the girls' shower sessions; a comically overaggressive panty raid; a pseudo-toga party with a "Nights of Arabia" theme; and way too many overlong sporting contests. That last misstep really burns, and it's a common sin in teen movie hell; too often filmmakers pad their flimsy reels to required feature-length by splicing in football matches, relay swims, and other such crap that we avoid by watching idiocy like this in the first place.

Standout characters include Belushi-clone Horse (Ray Holland), who really does give his all; curvy virgin Muffy (Verkina Flower); hideous-haircut salami hound Jerry (George Mills); and the more-or-less constantly topless Ginny (Alexis Schreiner), who seems angry about being horny.

Meanwhile, nymphomaniacal dragon lady Kim (the single-named Valdesta) pisses off one dude after another by fucking them, and Mrs. Camp Owner pursues an extramarital romp with one of the interchangeable dullards from the boys' bunk.

In the entire Chuck Vincent filmography, *Summer Camp* is the sole occasion where he seems lost. The revolting disco soundtrack doesn't help. Such was the fate of these flicks in the post-1978 wake of *Saturday Night Fever*; generic soft rock with pretty harmonies and gentle grooves was shoved aside for thunder-popping basslines and shrieking strings. What a relief it was when new wave arrived a year or two later. *Summer Camp* ultimately holds one big surprise: toward the end, a gooey couple walks off into the woods and emerges on an ocean beachfront. Where the fuck did that body (of water) come from?

Summer Job [1989]

DIR. PAUL MADDEN; W/SHERRIE ROSE, JAMES SUMMER, AMY LYNN BAXTER, CARI MAYOR

SUMMER JOBS ▣ BEACH RESORT ▣ SURFER ▣ COWBOY ▣ FLASHING ▣ RUBBER CHICKEN

This woeful softcore is rendered worse by an inspired VHS box cover that looks to hail from the plum teen movie hell era of 1981–83. Underneath the dandy threads, *Summer Job* is a breast implant–display video that embodies the worst of the decade's terrible tail end, rolling out all the cosmetic surgery boondoggles of the glam-metal-groupie-type cast and little else.

Sherrie Rose, as limp as she was in *Lauderdale* (1988), stars as Kathy, a supposed college student who lands a summer job at a seaside resort with her supposed college pals. The gang's mutual interests include partying, getting naked, and claiming to be at least ten years younger than they really so visibly are.

Summer Job deserves one begrudging nod for the sheer strangeness of ELO offshoot Orkestra turning up as the movie's super-cool rock band. A second nod is due to vintage plus-size burlesque star Fannie Annie, who barrels on camera to motorboat a lecherous old bartender. Otherwise, every actor in *Summer Job* is as bad as the writing and directing. A rubber chicken–cooking prank and a fat guy wears who wears a phony beer gut under his Hawaiian shirts can't carry a feature-length movie on their own.

Summer of '42 [1971]

DIR. ROBERT MULLIGAN; W/JENNIFER O'NEILL, GARY GRIMES, JERRY HOUSER, OLIVER CONANT

OLDER WOMEN ▣ VIRGIN ▣ NOSTALGIA

Fifteen-year-old Jewish city pals Hermie (Gary Grimes), Oscy (Jerry Houser), and Benjie (Oliver Conant) vacation on Nantucket Island in *Summer of '42*. While the self-proclaimed "terrible trio" clowns around and pines for girls their own age, Hermie falls hard for his *shiksa* war bride neighbor, Dorothy (Jennifer O'Neill). When she's consumed by fear about her pilot husband flying into high-risk combat, Dorothy turns to Hermie for comfort, which turns into him getting bar mitzvah'd all over again in the bedroom.

Summer of '42 is achingly sentimental, matching the somber, grandiose tone of author and screenwriter Herman Raucher's runaway best-selling memoir. In an odd turn, Raucher wrote the screenplay first, then adapted it into a book, which hit stores ahead of the movie.

Fashion model and champion horse-rider Jennifer O'Neill became a huge star for a while after *Summer of '42*. She actually beat out Barbra Streisand for the part of Dorothy (think of *that*, Hermie!). Previously, O'Neill had broken her neck in three places and, in 1982, she accidentally plugged herself in the gut with a .38 caliber handgun. Her 1999 autobiography is titled *Surviving Myself*. Who wouldn't instantly fall in love with a pistol like Jennifer?

SUMMER SCHOOL [1987]

DIR. CARL REINER. W/MARK HARMON, KIRSTIE ALLEY, COURTNEY THORNE-SMITH, DEAN CAMERON

SUMMER SCHOOL ▣ COOL TEACHER ▣ TEEN PREGNANCY ▣ FOREIGN EXCHANGE STUDENT

A more inherently, instantly, and indelibly likeable film than *Summer School* simply may not exist in this book or anywhere at all. Writer Jeff Franklin (creator of TV's *Full House*) and director Carl Reiner (creator of TV's *Dick Van Dyke Show* and much more) craft a free-and-breezy romp that's the good-time cinematic equivalent of leading hunk papa Mark Harmon's snazzy aloha shirts—or, better still, the red Wayfarer sunglasses that repeatedly land on the snout of his party pooch, Wondermutt.

Harmon stars as surf bum turned cool-dude high school gym coach Freddy Shoop. His Hawaiian vacation is nixed gets when "bite in the ass" vice principal Phil Gills (Robin Thomas) threatens to sink Shoop's pending tenure if the jovial jock doesn't teach warm-weather remedial English. Come day one of the summer session, Shoop meets his ragtag charges: daydreaming surf babe Pam (Courtney Thorne-Smith); squeaky neurotic Alan (Richard Steven Horvitz); gridiron grunt Kevin (Patrick Labyorteaux); knocked-up Rhonda (Shawnee Smith); dyslexic bad driver Denise (Kelly Jo Minter); and narcoleptic Larry (Ken Olandt), who turns out to be an underage male stripper by night.

Anna-Maria Altobello adds spice as newly arrived French student Fabiana. Kirstie Alley looms romantically large as Robin Bishop, the sophisticated lady who's teaching AP history in the beachfront classroom next door. Towering African American Jerome (Duane Davis) splits to use the bathroom early in the movie, and only returns to deliver one of *Summer School*'s most charming gags.

The immediate cast standouts are *Summer School*'s unique and altogether glorious Dave (Gary Riley) and Chainsaw (Dean Cameron), a raucous two-man underachievement crew on the order of Bill and Ted, Wayne and Garth, and Beavis and Butt-head. The crucial difference is that Dave and Chainsaw predate those dunder-headed duos by years. Rather than lazily explain their idiot savantism through heavy metal music (Chainsaw's Iron Maiden shirt notwithstanding), the movie makes them very, very *accurate* horror movie fanatics, complete with homemade gross-out mutilation latex effects.

Summer School's plot plays out as a zesty and never-insulting amalgamation of after-school-special themes and slobs-vs.-snobs farce. Neither element harshes the other. The kids learn to respect themselves, and Shoop catches on that there's more to his job than just getting July and August off. The message works thanks to the actors; that includes the leads, the kids, director Carl Reiner himself as a burnt-out teacher who bails, and, above all, Wondermutt. *Summer School*'s casting is the very picture of perfect.

Though there's no raunch to speak of, *Summer School* at least earns a PG-13 with naughty language and unexpected gory fright gags. Plus, Rhonda claims the father of her baby is either David Lee Roth or Sean Penn. Back in 1987, that really rang some bells.

SUNSET COVE [1978]
aka BEACH BUNNIES

DIR. AL ADAMSON; W/RAY ANDREWS, KAREN FREDRIK, SHERRI COYLE, JOHN CARRADINE

BIKINIS ▣ PRANKS ▣ NERD ▣ MUSCLEHEAD ▣ CUSTOM VANS ▣ SAVE THE BEACH

If any Z-movie operator could out-cheap, out-quick, and inadvertently out-baffle the '70s SoCal beach flick output of Crown International Pictures (*The Pom Pom Girls, The Van, Malibu Beach, Malibu High*), Al Adamson proved to be just the anti-talent to do it. Adamson blazed a unique path through exploitation cinema by way of likeable—occasionally even lovable—inept and insane genre cash-ins. His prolific output drew rapid inspiration from bikers (*Satan's Sadists*), revisionist westerns (*The Female Bunch*), classic monsters (*Dracula vs. Frankenstein*), blaxploitation (*Mean Mother*), women in uniform (*Blazing Stewardesses*), and adults-only fairy tales (*Cinderella* 2000), among others.

Sunset Cove sees Adamson hitting the shore to chronicle the noble cause of local high schoolers defending their favorite beachfront hangout from greedy real estate baron Dexter (Jay B. Larson). He represents, as described on the movie poster, "the condominium machine!" Yuck.

Prank-pulling nerd Mike (Ray Andrews) teams with blob-bellied booger-eater Chubby (Steven Fisher) and the honorable Judge Harley Winslow (Methuselah-esque John Carradine) to work up a legal strategy. More effectively, Mike also unites the often bare-breasted beach bunnies to fight the power by way of sexual blackmail. All of their plots work out great, not only to the misery of Dexter but to the high annoyance of cranky motorcycle cop Kragg (John Durren), who would love to clear the cove of the teenagers he refers to as "birth defects."

Al Adamson's focus of replicating the Crown International formula is so specific that *Sunset Cove* even includes an obnoxious bodybuilding boogie-van pilot named Moose (William Nuckols—on the set, did they call him "Moose Nuckols"?). The character is a focused imitation of Dugan (Stephen Nichols), who appears in two outstanding Crown efforts, *The Van* (1977) and *Malibu Beach* (1979). Before you faint from shock that anybody was paying attention to such details at all—pause and remember the mighty name Al Adamson.

SUPERVAN [1977]

DIR. LAMAR CARD; W/MARK SCHNEIDER, KATIE SAYLOR, MORGAN WOODWARD, CHARLES BUKOWSKI

CUSTOM VANS ▪ CB RADIO ▪ WET T-SHIRT CONTEST ▪ EVIL CAPITALIST ▪ WEED

The star of *Supervan*, of course, is the title character—a futuristic, solar-powered, high-tech, highway-cruising dream machine that can emit a signal to disable speed-tracking radar guns. As designed by George Barris, creator of TV's Batmobile, Monkeesmobile, Munstermobile, and numerous other one-of-a-kind vehicular masterworks, the Supervan is the very four-wheeled embodiment of '70s shag-carpet super-coolness. Plus, its proper name is "Vandora."

Young Clint Morgan (Mark Schneider) quits a dead-end gig at his dad's garage to pilot Vandora to the nation's premier gathering of such vehicles, the International Freak-Out in Kansas City, where a cool $5,000 prize is at stake. Along the way, Clint rescues rich runaway Karen (Katie Saylor) from, as she puts it, "friendly bikers on their way to a rape." He later runs afoul of Mid American Motors honcho T. B. Trenton (Morgan Woodward), who aims to quash Vandora's environmentally friendly fuel system—*and* who turns out to be Karen's father. Slapstick-spinning and irate Highway Patrolman Banks (Len Lesser, *Seinfeld*'s Uncle Leo) gives chase throughout.

Most of *Supervan* consists of uneventful, home-movie-caliber footage of souped-up "rolling bedrooms" traversing the bucolic byways of Missouri and Kansas. CB radio slang and soft rock dominate the soundtrack. All of this is even more pleasant than it sounds.

The Freak-Out, where Vandora ultimately triumphs, features a cheap-jack wet-T-shirt contest prominently attended by leering, groping, orangutan-bodied booze-shtick literary giant Charles Bukowski. The esteemed Poet Laureate of Liver Failure's own lump-hugging tight, white T-shirt reads "Wet T-shirt Contest Water Boy." Ask somebody who still refers to Bukowski as "Hank" to tell you why they think that's cool; then, while they explain, just imagine those cool vans rolling around the flat Midwestern highways. It's a cool trick, and works when subjected to almost any kind of dead-end dialogue.

The Sure Thing [1985]

DIR. ROB REINER; W/JOHN CUSACK; DAPHNE ZUNIGA; ANTHONY EDWARDS, NICOLETTE SHERIDAN

ROAD TRIP ▫ DREAM GIRL ▫ MOONING ▫ FLASHING ▫ FRAT PARTY ▫ BEERS

At the dizzying crest of the competition by mid-'80s teen flicks to out-boob, out-puke, and out-gross one another, *The Sure Thing,* director Rob Reiner's follow-up to *This Is Spinal Tap* (1984), stood coolly out on the veranda by itself. The movie stems from an era far before *Porky's,* the age of vintage Hollywood romantic comedies such as the 1934 Clark Gable–Claudette Colbert classic, *It Happened One Night.*

Such relatively highbrow aspirations certainly did not guarantee a good movie, but Reiner's deft hand guides an ideal cast of up-and-comers through a witty script. *The Sure Thing* eschews the guaranteed easy thrills found in other youth fare of the day in favor of something sweet and meaningful. That also sums up the journey of the two leads, Walter "Gib" Gibson (John Cusack) and Alison Bradbury (Daphne Zuniga), as they travel, one comical mishap and misery after another, from a snowy East Coast college campus to various promised landings waiting for them in sun-splashed Los Angeles.

The long-distance motivation for party-hearty, fly-by-the-seat-of-his-one-pair-of-sweatpants Gib is a vision of string-binkini'd blondeness and sexual guarantees referred to solely as "the Sure Thing" (Nicolette Sheridan). No-nonsense honor student Alison is making the schlep to reunite with her stiff-upper-everything lawyer-in-training boyfriend Jason (Boyd Gaines). Over the course of three thousand miles, each is royally annoyed by the other while simultaneously absorbing positive qualities. Prudent and prissy Alison, for example, responds to a drive-by mooning by impulsively flashing her chest at the pranksters. Glib Gib allows to Alison go off with a potentially violent pervert, but then he then rushes to do the right thing, rescuing her from a potential sex assault by proving he can "out-psycho" the would-be perpetrator

Cusack lapses into a Bill Murray impersonation on occasion, but that's fine. Zuniga embodies Alison so completely that her post-loosening-up scenes with square-beyond-square Jason go from merely amusing (Gaines plays it perfectly) to hilariously wince-inducing. Nicolette Sheridan, whose actual function here is to simply preen, works the role so intently that she immediately becomes the exact type of celebrity she has remained ever since. As Gary Cooper ("But not the dead Gary Cooper!"), one half of a dork couple that first drives Gib and Alison west while insisting they all sing show tunes, Tim Robbins overplays the part in the manner of an *SNL* sketch; he's more believable as a jacked-up jock asshole in the same year's *Fraternity Vacation.*

Unlike the 1930s gems that inspired it, *The Sure Thing* has not aged into something universal and timeless. Instead, it remains a uniquely engaging and endearing time capsule—which is plenty sparkling enough.

Surf II [1984]

aka Surf II: The End of the Trilogy

DIR. RANDALL M. BADAT; W/ERIC STOLTZ, CORINNE BOHRER, JEFFREY ROGERS, EDDIE DEEZEN

SURFERS ▫ NERD ▫ VALLEY GIRLS ▫ PUNK ZOMBIES ▫ THE BIG GROSS-OUT EATING CONTEST ▫ EDDIE DEEZEN

About ten minutes into *Surf II,* a sequence occurs of such inspired wit and deft execution that, if it happened in a movie starring the Marx Brothers or Woody Allen or Peter Sellers (or even Cheech and Chong or Adam Sandler), critics and admirers would still marvel at the moment as a landmark of satirical filmmaking. Adjust your bearings, this is serious talk. Yes, we're discussing the Eddie Deezen vehicle *Surf II*—and, no, there never was a *Surf I.*

Here's the moment of revelation: Two elementally identical suburban kitchens appear side by

Surf II

The movie that gives insanity a bad name.

A HILARIOUS LOOK AT THE NIFTY 50'S

Sweater Girls

"SWEATER GIRLS"

HARRY MOSES • MEEGAN KING • NOELLE NORTH • KATE SARCHET
CAROL SEFLINGER • TAMARA BARKLEY • JULIE PARSONS • MICHEAL GOODROW
WILLIAM KUX • JACK O'LEARY • STEPHEN LISS • SKIP LOWELL as JIM

R RESTRICTED

THE STUDENT BODY ALWAYS SCORES with

SUMMER SCHOOL TEACHERS

DELL 8348 1.25

The nationwide bestselling novel . . . now an unforgettable motion picture.

SUMMER OF '42

HERMAN RAUCHER

'SUNSET COVE'

Clockwise from top: Surf II *(1984), a mad milestone in hilarious, brilliant idiocy; in* Sweater Girls *(1978), look hard for Charlene Tilton;* Sunset Cove *(1978), proves you can flash city hall!;* Summer of '42 *by Herman Raucher, paperback source of the 1971 hit film;* Summer School Teachers *(1974) scores with Candice Rialson.*

side on the screen, each mirroring the other, left and right. In both rooms, a middle-aged grump puffs a cigar and does paperwork at a table (Morgan Paull on one side; Biff Manard on the other), while a 1950s homemaker mom prepares breakfast (on the left, *Laugh-In*'s Ruth Buzzi; to the right, *Fridays*' Brandis Kemp). SoCal surf bums Chuck (Eric Stoltz) and Bob (Jeffrey Rogers) enter the scenario: These are their parents and these are their homes. The characters, in unison, speak the same perfectly synchronized dialogue in the same perfectly synchronized tones to one another before setting out to experience the same perfectly synchronized lives. This moment of sublime comedic grace is a lofty strain of funny to find in teen movie hell, but, then again, *Surf II* is full of surprises.

Eddie Deezen, nerdom's most nerdastic nerd of nerd's nerds, stars as Menlo Schwartzer, a mad teenage megalomaniac who once suffered humiliation at the hands of wave-riders. He now exists to exact his revenge via Buzz Cola, a vile concoction he brews in an undersea lab. Up on the beach, Chuck and Bob's dads peddle the swill to thirsty surfers. Trouble is that the smoking, oozing, volcanic concoction transforms all who drink it into mindless punk-rock zombies in black leather and freaky face paint. The only locals who won't touch the stuff are Chuck and Bob; their Valley girl gal pals Cindy Lou (Corinne Bohrer) and Lindy Sue (Lucinda Dooling); and their behemoth-bellied best bud Johnny Big Head (Joshua Cadman). Mr. Big Head, let it be noted, is one of slob cinema's all-time champion human bulldozers and garbage disposals; he bites through chain-link fences and punctuates his victories by dropping his voice and bellowing, "Bow-Bow!"

Astonishingly, *Surf II* repeatedly surpasses itself with sheer lunacy and avalanches of hilarity. The movie never slows down and never lets up. Jokes fly at tsunami speed and volume, with everything perfectly delivered by comedy pros who go admirably all-in on absurdity. Cleavon Little, the sheriff from *Blazing Saddles* (1974), plays high school principal Mr. Daddyo. Each time he appears, everyone on-screen yells, "Hey, Daddy-O!" Tom Villard, aka Clay Stork in *One Crazy Summer* (1986), puts on a killer pantomime performance as zombified beach bum Jocko. Terry Kiser (Bernie from *Weekend at Bernie's*) and Carol Wayne (Johnny Carson's buxotic "Tea Time Movie Girl") camp it up as Villard's surf shop-owner parents. The local cops are Chief Boyardee (Lyle Waggoner from *The Carol Burnett Show*) and Inspector Underpants (Ron Palillo, Arnold Horshack from *Welcome Back, Kotter*).

Rip-roaring dance parties and comic confrontations explode out of nowhere, always delivering gut-busting gags. Dubiously named actors Fred Asparagus and Jim Greenleaf are a rotund riot as accurately named characters Fat Boy #1 and Fat Boy #2. To them go the honors of *Surf II*'s grossest interludes. First they stuff their blubber into wet suits and bend over. Their suits split open and we get close-up shots of their actual assholes. Later, they boogie with a beach babe who pops out of her top and punches each Fat Boy in the face with one nude knocker apiece. Pow and pow!

Other wow-lights include a garbage-eating contest between Big Head and Pondo that's as stomach-turning as any 1970s Italian cannibal flick; a zombie autopsy that extracts self-aware detritus from other beach movies; a ferocious surf soundtrack featuring everything from Dick Dale to the Circle Jerks; not to mention a concert appearance by ska-punks the Untouchables.

Surf II is unique, but at the same time deeply indebted to the original Frankie-and-Annette beach party movies. Even at the dawn of the surf movies, surreal asides and story devices such as diabolical teen-hating scientists were typical stock-in-trade. Writer-director Randall Badat infuses that formula with punk bluntness, heavy metal barbarism, and other active ingredients that weren't available back in more innocent times. Namely, he delivers the goods in the form of swimsuit-free physiques and, boy howdy, Eddie Deezen.

Swap Meet [1979]

DIR. BRICE MACK; W/JON GRIES, RUTH COX, DEBORAH RICHTER, DANNY DEVITO

NERDS 📼 PRANKS 📼 MOONING 📼 CUSTOM VANS 📼 HIPPIE CHICKS 📼 HOOKERS 📼 SKATEBOARD 📼 SEX IN A VOLKSWAGEN BUG

At the swap meet, yeah, we got that special buy / At the swap meet, guaranteed to satisfy / At the swap meet, come on along, we gonna make you high!

The theme song to *Swap Meet* even includes the movie's tagline, "where fifty acres of junk is worth a fortune in fun!" but not everything you hear in a teen movie theme song is true.

Here's what really happens at the swap meet: High school hotshot Doug (Jon Gries) and his knuckleheaded henchdudes Buddha (Loren Lester) and Billy (Dan Spector) sell potted plants and hit on the ladies. Hippie chicks Nancy (Ruth Cox) and Susan (Deborah Richter) push live turtles. Nerdling swap-meet manager Ziggy (Danny Goldman) panics nonstop while hoping to romance homeless hottie Annie (Cheryl Rixon), who, in turn, aims to find a husband among the heaps of trash for sale. Danny DeVito turns up as wacky auto mechanic and Rhea Pearlman plays a shoplifting mom.

Shot at the Roadium, a real-life swap-meet location in Torrance, California, *Swap Meet* looks and feels promising as it runs through one Saturday in the life of various peddlers, purchasers, and pranksters in the Los Angeles sun. Much like the garbage-with-price-tags on-screen, though, the movie proves worthless to the point of wasting the potential of *Penthouse* Pet Cheryl Rixon. She and the general location are scenic, but nobody's idea of a celluloid escapism is a teen comedy about desperate people peddling garbage.

Sweater Girls [1978]

DIR. DON JONES; W/HARRY MOSES, MEEGAN KING, JULIE PARSONS, CHARLENE TILTON

VIRGINS 📼 NERD 📼 DRIVE-IN 📼 SLUMBER PARTY 📼 FOUL-MOUTHED OLD LADY 📼 UNDERAGE DRINKING 📼 BUMBLING COP 📼 1950S

Sweater Girls begins and ends with an ersatz doo-wop tune of the same name performed by some sadists billed as David Somerville and the Head Tones. Between the start and the finish, the song appears a distracting number of times, so much that it hurts. There's a lot else about *Sweater Girls* that's maddening.

Newsreel footage establishes the year as 1956, and a gaggle of high school honeys appear in order to pledge to maintain their sexual purity. They defy this oath of chastity visually by all wearing pink, curve-gripping angora sweaters. Yes, these are "the Sweater Girls."

The hot-and-bothered hijinks commence as hot-to-trot Joella (Julie Parsons, *Hometown U.S.A.* [1979]) joins the fluffy-jugged club and they all gather for a sleepover at the home of one gal's absent grandma. Fetishists of Jayne Mansfield–type bullet-brassieres may not survive the sleepover scenes, as the girls continually try on and take off one another's sweaters.

The girl's male classmates appear to be fatal alcoholics. Early on, they get cirrhosis-drunk at "the lake," a smaller puddle of slush than any of them will soon be puking. Once these teen lushes are sufficiently soused, they get behind the wheel and invade grandma's house. With a few clicks in another direction, this moment could have rendered *Sweater Girls* akin to some of director Don Jones's other grindhouse gruel sessions, specifically *Schoolgirls in Chains* (1973) and *The Love Butcher* (1975). When one lass says she sees someone sneaking outside a window, another shrugs, "It's probably just a rapist."

A fumbling fatso cop (Jack O'Leary) gives chase to the underage drinkers-and-drivers. Sweater

Girl Lynne (Tamara Barkley) doffs her woolen pullover to steal her boyfriend's car and drive around topless. Literally three minutes before the movie ends, Charlene Tilton shows up in white cha-cha pants to declare herself the new girl in town. She vanishes immediately with one of the male beer addicts. By the time *Sweater Girls* hit home video in 1983, Tilton had become an international star via TV's *Dallas*. Now just guess *who* had her name and picture plastered above the title on the *Sweater Girls* VHS box?

Swim Team [1979]

DIR. JAMES POLAKOF; W/JAMES DAUGHTON, STEPHEN FURST, JENNY NEUMANN, BUSTER CRABBE

SWIM TEAM ▣ NERD ▣ SHARK ▣ BIKINIS ▣ SPEEDOS ▣ CUSTOM VAN

The swim team of *Swim Team* is a coed Southern California squad that hopes a comically hardheaded new leader, Couch Ouchowski (Guy Fitch), can reverse their soggy performance record. Out of the water, pretty blonde team member Erin (Jenny Neumann) ignites a romantic rivalry between erstwhile tight bros Danny (James Daughton) and Johnny (Richard Young). When those dudes aren't duking it out, everybody is partying poolside. Erin expresses existential angst that goes nicely with her series of bikinis.

Couch Ouch falls prey to a pool prank with a plastic shark, and buoy-bellied teammate Bear (Stephen Furst) makes quite the literal splash. During one race, Bear's bulk slams the water with such impact that the waves displace his rivals and he reaches the finish line uncontested.

Nineteen thirty-two's Olympic swimming gold medalist Buster Crabbe, who starred as both Flash Gordon and Buck Rogers in those eponymous old-time movie serials, cameos as a swimmer's dad. Similarly gracing this amateurish (albeit reasonably enjoyable) nonsense with their presence are Furst and Daughton, fresh off big-time breakout performances in *Animal House*, where they portrayed good guy Flounder and villainous Greg Marmalarde, respectively. Considering that Furst's next role was in the execrable *Getting Wasted* (1980) and that Daughton didn't return to the big screen until *The Beach Girls* (1982), maybe this type of poolside foolishness was just their thing.

The Swinging Cheerleaders [1974] aka H.O.T.S. II

DIR. JACK HILL; W/RAINBEAUX SMITH, JO JOHNSTON, ROSANNE KATON, COLLEEN CAMP

COLLEGE FOOTBALL ▣ SCHOOL PAPER ▣ HIPPIES ▣ BAD COACH ▣ BAD COPS ▣ BAD TEACHER

The uncovering of President Richard Nixon's criminal Watergate hijinks by doggedly determined *Washington Post* reporters provided endless grist for comedians high and low in the 1970s. Only *The Swinging Cheerleaders*, however, applied radical journalism and the subversion of ruling authority to the naked pom-pom genre. The movie tosses a nod to Tricky Dick, plastering his smiling face on a dartboard in the college newspaper press room. Man, *everybody* had Dick Nixon to kick around back then.

Mesa College campus newspaper reporter Kate (Jo Johnston) announces to her sour, clown-haired boyfriend and editor Ron (Ian Sander) that she's going incognito to infiltrate the school's cheerleader squad. She wants to blow the lid off acoustic megaphone exploitation or something. Kate is so fully committed to the ruse that she even puts on a bra—don't worry, those things come off pretty easily when necessary.

Succumbing to a common peril of undercover journalism, Kate rapidly becomes best friends with her cheer team subjects. Chief among the roster are doe-eyed virgin Andrea (Cheryl "Rainbeaux" Smith); African American sophisticate Lisa (Rosanne Katon), who's sleeping with her statistics professor; and flouncy rich chick Mary Ann (Colleen Camp), who just wants her star quarterback beau Buck (Ron Hajak) to pop the question—when all he's interested in is popping something else (*rah!*).

Kate comes up with a sizzling scoop. She discovers the "I-thought-you-were-cool" stats teacher is a bookie working in cahoots with the school's evil dean and the football team's even more evil coach. Together, the cunning cabal throws games and makes big bank fixing bets. While running down her leads, Kate fucks Buck, which hurts Mary Ann and infuriates scuzz-fro'd Ross. He retaliates by conjuring a cluster of hate-hearted hippies to sexually beset upon poor Andrea. Nobody yells, "Go, team, go!"

Further heaviness arises when the corrupt authorities pressure Buck to throw a big game. When the quarterback refuses, thuggish cops plant weed on him and kidnap him on play day. Buck's teammates storm in to rescue him from the pigs, igniting a madcap locker-room brawl complete with sped-up film and ragtime music. Just when the hilarity hits a high note, somebody actually gets shot. Sis-boom-*blam!* Thanks to some forced vomiting (for real), a happy ending saves the movie in the final seconds.

Gang rape and gunplay might seem out of place in a film titled *The Swinging Cheerleaders*, but, for teen sex comedies of the mid-'70s, similar rushes of sudden, life-threatening, and even gruesome violence weren't that weird at all. Such were the T&A times—when it came to ass, gas, grass, blades, bullets, and severe beatings, nobody rode for free.

Quentin Tarantino refers to director Jack Hill as "the Howard Hawks of exploitation movies." Just as Hawks's Hollywood classics ranged from screwball comedies to film noir to musicals, Hill scored defining knockouts in disparate grindhouse genres such as freak horror (*Spider Baby*), women in prison (*The Big Doll House*), and blaxploitation (*Foxy Brown*). *The Swinging Cheerleaders* is Hill's contribution to '70s pom-pom pictures. Like the rest of the films in Jack's canon, *Cheerleaders* delivers every specific for which its audience clamors while also achieving a state of cracked grace.

Champions of *The Swinging Cheerleaders* further hail the movie as a rejection of monogamous male supremacy, praising its one-of-a-kind revolutionary tirade on behalf of feminism. Maybe. I can kind of buy *The Swinging Cheerleaders* as an intentional hard-left softcore political tract, but just possibly the lesson from this surprisingly tough pep squad flick is that revolution only ever really happens the hard way.

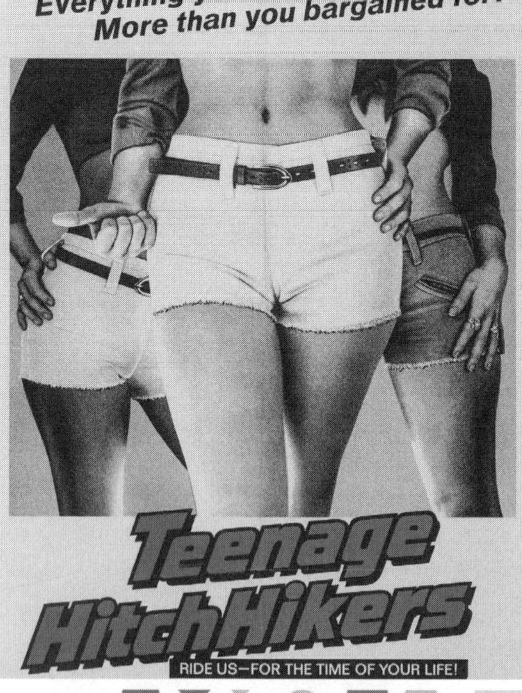

Clockwise from top left: Teen Wolf *(1985) deals with a different sort of hairy palms;* Teachers (1984) *is amazingly known in France as* Flush the Teachers!; Teenage Hitchhikers (1974) *gets a thumbs up; the raunchy sequel* The Teasers Go to Paris *(1977) answers questions left open by* The Teasers *(1975).*

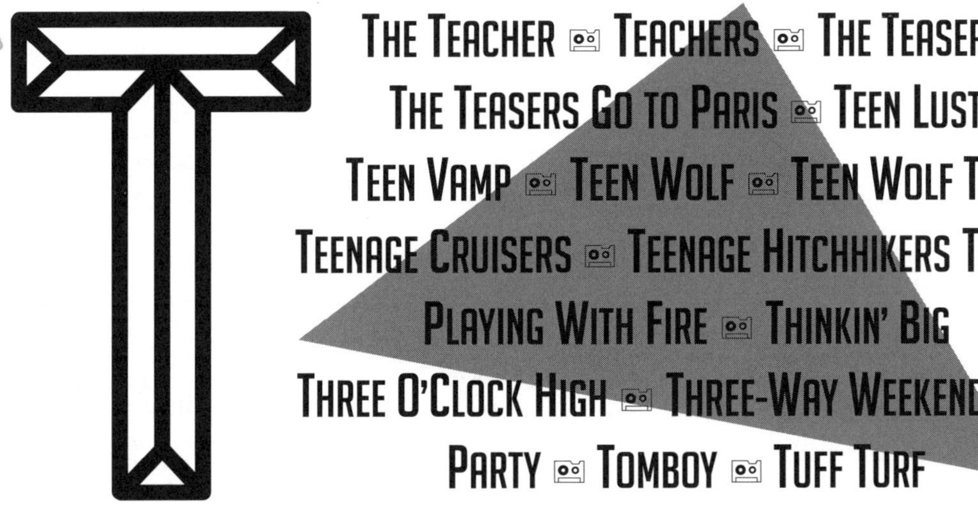

The Teacher ▭ Teachers ▭ The Teasers The Teasers Go to Paris ▭ Teen Lust Teen Vamp ▭ Teen Wolf ▭ Teen Wolf Too Teenage Cruisers ▭ Teenage Hitchhikers They're Playing With Fire ▭ Thinkin' Big Three O'Clock High ▭ Three-Way Weekend Toga Party ▭ Tomboy ▭ Tuff Turf

The Teacher [1974]

DIR. HOWARD AVEDIS (AS HIKMET AVEDIS); W/ANGEL TOMPKINS, JAY NORTH, ANTHONY JAMES

BAD TEACHER ▭ VIRGIN ▭ PEEPING

She corrupted the youthful morality of an entire school!

Her best lessons were taught after class!

Voted most popular by her male student body!

Angel Tompkins is *The Teacher!*

The Teacher utilizes not one but four killer taglines to sell its tawdry wares from the agreeably gnarly drive-in flick pumphouse Crown International Pictures. At least on the fourth count, nobody can argue false advertising: Angel Tompkins really *is* The Teacher.

Tompkins remains beloved in '70s roughneck cinema for her turns opposite Lee Marvin in *Prime Cut* (1972), with Bo Svenson in *Walking Tall Part II* (1974), and facing a gaggle of midget gangsters in the mega-grossly titled *Little Cigars* (1973). Here she ably portrays Diane Marshall, an abandoned wife who, at the ripe old age of twenty-eight, is the older woman who makes all the young dudes on campus go gaga. Some go more gaga than others.

Before Ms. Marshall can properly corrupt the youthful morality of an entire school, however, somebody has to suffer. Badly. As in permanently. That's how it goes with many of these Crown International movies; a typical setup for a fun-loving escapade centered on pubescent poking can only come loaded with doom, nastiness, and strangely integral violence. *The Teacher* doesn't waste time in taking us to those dark spots.

High school horndogs Sean (Jay North) and Lou (Rudy Herrera, Jr.) climb a water tower to spy on the sunbathing Ms. Marshall. Lou's thuggish older brother Ralph (snake-faced character actor Anthony James) shows up with a knife. A sibling shoving match turns severe, and Lou slips to his death, pooping the peeper party. After that—well, school's out! Time for Sean to get laid!

After denying to the people that he has any knowledge of how Lou bit it, Sean falls liltingly in love with Ms. Marshall over the course of the summer. After a series of incognito dalliances, the taboo twosome take a risky step by dining together in public, inviting disapproval from a pair of tongue-clucking matrons called Gossip Lady 1 and 2. Weirdly, the Gossip Ladies are played by Katherine Cassavetes, mother of filmmaker John Cassavetes, and Lady Rowlands, mother of actress Gena Rowlands, John Cassavetes's wife and creative partner.

Thanks to the sensibilities of the 1970s, *The Teacher* dares not wrap without a final dose of unpleasantness. Ralph returns to permanently silence Sean regarding slippery-shoes Lou. If a blade won't do the job, then Ralph's nauseatingly gaudy yellow windbreaker just might. Also, nobody's been raped on camera yet, and that bears correcting, complete with a gory, almost simultaneous, revenge. Nobody's happy at the end, but at least one character can still breathe.

Notably, Jay North, the grown-up star of the early '60s sitcom *Dennis the Menace* stars as Sean. North seems pent-up and edgy throughout, as though perhaps worried that his notorious stage-parent aunt might suddenly show up and force-bleach his hair again like she did when he was a kiddie TV star.

Israeli-born director Howard Avedis later revisited a similar bad-teacher-gone-lethally-rotten scenario in 1984's way crazier *They're Playing with Fire*. Should one ever ponder in what directions young Howard's mind wandered while daydreaming over female faculty members at Tel Aviv High, I'd wager these celluloid specimens speak volumes.

TEACHERS [1984]

DIR. ARTHUR HILLER; W/NICK NOLTE, JOBETH WILLIAMS, RALPH MACCHIO, CRISPIN GLOVER

BAD TEACHERS ▫ PRANKS ▫ ABORTION ▫ SCHOOL SHOOTING

Porky's dicked over a couple of movies really badly; *Heaven Help Us* (1984) is one, and *Teachers* is another. Each long-in-development film had been a seriocomic labor of love intended to provide thoughtful, substantive meditation and commentary on adolescents caught in the machinations of the American education system. While *Heaven* contends with early-'60s Catholic institutions, *Teachers* takes on the blighted urban public-school crisis of the 1980s. Had either picture reached the screen a decade earlier, they would likely have emerged as their creators intended—heavy, heartfelt, sardonic, and very '70s. Instead, each had to answer to the ongoing tits-and-zits comedy box office bonanza of 1982, which forced the final products, Play-Doh Fun Factory style, through dirty-joke tubes and lusting-leer gears, out of which they emerged on the other side as unrecognizable mush.

Heaven Help Us absorbed its quotient of raunch more successfully. The movie remains very funny with several moving moments. *Teachers* is almost a total botch. What was clearly created to be a Paddy Chayefsky–style decimation of the U.S. high school system (director Arthur Hiller even made the harrowing 1971 Chayefsky howler *The Hospital*) comes off instead as a series of comedy sketches and *ABC Afterschool Special* histrionics interspersed with Nick Nolte in perma-hangover mode as a burnt-out educator. Nothing gels.

Teachers drops us off on a typical Monday morning at John F. Kennedy High School, a crumbling youth warehouse in an unnamed city. We see adult staffers coming to blows, students stabbing one another in the hallway, and a recent graduate suing because he isn't able to read. Funny stuff? No, but it could have been.

A sense of humor is sorely needed to jolt the budding romance between Nolte as a "cool teach" and JoBeth Williams as the attorney handling the illiterate kid's lawsuit. Smiles are missing altogether when Nolte mentors shutterbug student Ralph Macchio, turning him into an amateur photojournalist documenting the ineptitude and indifference of school authorities. Furthermore, pitch-black humor could have made legendary a sequence where a callous-prick gym coach knocks up a sophomore (Laura Dern), and she can only turn to Nolte for a ride to the abortion clinic. The same sardonic suggestion goes for when a schizophrenic youth (Crispin Glover) escalates a routine locker search into suicide-by-cop.

At the same time, all this seriousness in *Teachers* could have been played straighter, theoretically resulting in a hard-hitting, gritty contemporary drama. The movie doesn't go that route either; viewers end up nauseous from the careless clash of humor and pathos on the screen, roughly the cinematic equivalent of the mixed scoops of unrefined slop that pollute the school cafeteria lunch trays.

The one element of *Teachers* that works is the same one that knocks the rest of the movie furthest off course. Richard Mulligan (rubber-faced Bert Campbell from TV's *Soap*) plays an escaped mental patient who disguises himself as a history teacher. His spirited reenactments actually get his kids to love learning. Mulligan as George Washington astride his desk as he lectures about crossing the Delaware with various young hooligans paddling alongside, for example, is hilarious. As funny as the Mulligan interludes are, though, they stop the movie cold and only tease the serrated-edged satire that *Teachers* might have been.

Teachers is not remembered today for any of the aforementioned elements, nor for the minor radio and MTV hit theme song, "Teacher, Teacher," by .38 Special. The movie's small degree of enduring notoriety emanates instead from a climactic incident of shock nudity. JoBeth Williams, fresh from playing the mom in *Poltergeist* (1982), responds to Nolte's metaphorical challenge to "strip away" her prejudices and "roam the school halls naked" by putting her money where her mound is. She peels down completely bare and charges, Lady Godiva–like, through a crowded JFK High corridor, ringing bells wherever she roams.

The Teasers [1975]

aka La Liceale; Sophomore Swingers

DIR. MICHELE MASSIMO TARANTINI; W/GLORIA GUIDA, GIUSEPPE PAMBIERI, RODOLFO BIGOTTI

VIRGIN ▪ BAD TEACHERS ▪ SKINNY-DIPPING ▪ HITCHHIKING ▪ HOOKERS

Italy's supremely glamorous Gloria Guida burst into international sexploitation stardom via *The Teasers*, known in its original tongue as *La liceale* ("The High School Student"). Guida, who was twenty at the time, plays sexually aware sophomore Loredana. Taking cues from her free-love-espousing parents, she tempts and taunts her teachers during the school day, while longing to find love. She's aching to lose her virginity, which we learn whenever she's speaking to anyone who'll listen.

Loredana skinny-dips with a jockish male classmate, and she poses nude for another who claims to be a painter, but her much-vaunted virtue remains unsullied. Finally, she goes gaga for worldly professor Dr. Marco Salvi, and the sullying begins. They get it on, Loredana discovers he's married, and a succession of bummers brings things to a philosophical close.

The Teasers packed theaters worldwide, whether sold by various overeager B-flick promoters as a rowdy teen sex blast or a tawdry potboiler. Despite comic moments, the movie is largely a downer. Gloria Guida is undeniably appealing, but *The Teasers* gives her a hard time.

It's surprising, then, that *The Teasers* begat four official follow-ups, three of which also feature Signora Guida: *La liceale nella classe dei ripetenit*, aka *The High School Student in the Repeating Class* (1978); *La liceale, il diavolo e l'acquasanta*, aka *The High School Student, the Devil, and the Holy Water* (1979); *La liceale seduce i profressori*, aka *The High School Student Seduces the Professor* (1979); and *La liceale al mare con l'amica di papa*, aka *The College Girl on Vacation* (1980). Even a total rip-off flick hit big: *The Teasers Go to Paris* (1977).

The Teasers Go to Paris [1977] aka Sophomore Swingers

DIR. MAX PÉCAS; W/SYLVIA CHAMARANDE, DOMINIQUE JUBELIN, JEAN-MARC LONGVAL, VANESSA VAYLORD

PUBLIC NUDITY ▫ PILLOW FIGHTS ▫ BIKINIS ▫ THREESOME ▫ MUD IN FAT GUY'S FACE

Seven sporty American high school lasses decamp to a European boarding academy in *The Teasers Go to Paris*, a French follow-up in stolen name only to the 1975 Italian teen sex hit *The Teasers*. Upon arrival, the Yanks peel off their Adidas tracksuits and more or less maintain that status through a series of comic interludes that all start ("Let's have sex!") and end ("That was fun sex!") the same way. Come to think of it, this is almost exactly the same movie as *Six Swedes on a Campus* (1979), with exactly the same number of Swedes: zero.

Aside from horrendous dubbing that might feel nostalgic to some vintage VHS renters and traumatic to others, the most intriguing aspect of *The Teasers Go to Paris* is its poster, painted by master pulp artist Robert McGinnis. Two years prior, McGinnis created a tawdry original one-sheet for *The Teasers*, but for *Go to Paris*, he largely repurposed the stunningly raunchy doggy-style artwork he created for the big-budget Burt Reynolds–Kris Kristofferson Hollywood football comedy *Semi-Tough* (1976). Nobody called foul.

What connects these European softcore trifles to the American teen sex comedies of the 1970s is that the old-world exploitation mavens were aiming to cash in on the global box office sensations being made by the SoCal-spawned likes of *The Swinging Cheerleaders* (1974) and *The Pom Pom Girls* (1976). Alas, the country of Jean-Paul Sartre proved inherently incompatible with the surfer-dude mentality, and neither Milan nor Munich can pass, in any sense, for Malibu. As a result, all these Euro-teen crotch operas exude both more explicit carnality and more existential oddness, and thereby stand out as a sort of parallel category. Still, these films were marketed worldwide to be confused and/or billed with red-white-and-boobs goofapaloozas like *Cherry Hill High* (1977) and *H.O.T.S.* (1979), so they all fall under the grand *Teen Movie Hell* beach umbrellas.

Teen Lust [1979] aka High School Teasers; Police Academy Girls

DIR. JAMES HONG; W/KIRSTEN BAKER, PERRY LANG, LESLIE CEDERQUIST, GEORGE "BUCK" FLOWER

BEER ▫ WEED ▫ DRAG ▫ FLASHING ▫ PEEPING ▫ BUMBLING COPS

During the course of a 1978 obscenity trial, a Cincinnati prosecutor blasted *Hustler* magazine as "the wet dream of a homicidal maniac." Writer-director James Hong's *Teen Lust*, while definitely not as graphic as *Hustler*, does play like a fevered fantasia equally worthy of that colorful summation. Even *Hustler* publisher Larry Flynt would have to half-drool in awe.

Teen Lust opens normally enough. A pack of good-looking, good-time high school pals cheer and jeer at 8mm home movies of their summer vacation. They mug for the camera, hit the beach, do headstands, flash some tit, de-pants a pal doing pull-ups; the usual fun stuff. Upon parting ways, the film's two lead blondes, Carol (Kirsten Baker) and Neeley (Leslie Cederquist), go to their after-school junior police officer training program. Stop and note that, right there, *Teen Lust* turns unusual—and from there, things just keeps turning.

Carol's chaotic home life is dominated by a fatally alcoholic mom (Dalene Young, billed as Dolly Carolla), an incestuously grabby dad (Stan Kamber), and Dustin (Michael Sloane), the destructive mental defective next door who stands to inherit a pile of money. He claims Carol is his fiancée, and maybe he's on to something.

Terry (Perry Lang) is Carol's off-and-on boyfriend. He pals around with gearhead Hotrod (Richard Singer), while half-heartedly fending off sexy town floozy DeDe (Lee Ann Barnes). Viewers learn that not every unhinged young male reacts well when an open and forthright woman freely states her sexual desires. Instead of being properly squired to the nearest den of iniquity, DeDe soon finds herself topless and trapped in the trunk of Hotrod's speeding cruiser, basted in the face with whipped cream, and tossed nude by the side of the road. The sadism here comes fast and furious.

Carol's gal pal, ethereal beauty Neeley, has much greater success with the gruntier sex. She dates Hotrod, hops into bed with Carol's brother Ted (Michael Allyn), and bangs her own hairy-backed, comb-over-headed, unhappily married police program mentor. As Neeley, Cederquist fills the screen with Rainbeaux Smith–like allure; unfortunately, *Teen Lust* appears to be her only credit.

The supporting players here add to the anarchy. Obese lass Bambi (Liza Stanley) stuffs her face nonstop, despite repeated lightning-fast pimp slaps across the kisser from her nasty mother (Ernee Simpson). Carol's perma-stewed mom takes to copulating with salty cowboy-pirate-biker-plumber Mr. Sykes, played by B-movie legend George "Buck" Flower. Even with a filmography that includes *Sex in the Comics* (1972), *Ilsa: She Wolf of the SS* (1975), and *Drive-In Massacre* (1977), old Buck only consented to be billed as "Sherman Backus" in *Teen Lust*.

Before long, Carol poses as a prostitute as part of a police sting, only to be aggressively propositioned by her own brother. This is a *wacky* comedy, folks. The movie's madness peaks in a sequence that starts with Carol and Terry necking in a parked car. Off in a woodsy field, the handsome young couple kisses and snuggles in Terry's convertible with its top down. Nearby, a cluster of preteen boys play ball in the sunshine. In a flash, everything goes all *Lord of the Flies* meets *A Clockwork Orange*.

The kids attack the car with rocks and mud-bombs. They beat Terry in the face, smash the car's lights and windows, and pull Carol out of the passenger seat. Worried more about his sweet ride than about his imperiled girlfriend, Terry fires up the engine and zooms away, leaving Carol to the band of ten-to-twelve-year-old marauders. The boy-beasts shred Carol's shirt, but she breaks away for a chase set to Alan Stanley Tew's "The Big One," aka the theme from TV's *The People's Court*. Just as the savage lads catch Carol and pin her to the dirt, a handsome cop who's had an eye on her swoops in and shoos away the junior sex criminals. Those nutty rapscallions saunter away, flipping the bird and snorting, "Oink! Oink!"

Teen Lust's maker, James Hong, is just as fascinating as his bizarre film. Best known for roles in *Blade Runner* (1982) and *Big Trouble in Little China* (1986), and as the Chinese restaurant maître d' on *Seinfeld*, Hong spans seven decades of parts as a character actor. New generations love him as Mr. Ping in the *Kung Fu Panda* movies. Hong also directed X-rated martial arts mash-up *Hot Connections* (1972), the fun monster schlock-fest *The Vineyard* (1989), and *Singapore Sling* (1999), aka *Scandalous Behavior*, a Shannon Tweed softcore epic.

Perry Lang, the most familiar face among the *Teen Lust* ensemble, went on to star in *Spring Break* (1983). Kirsten Baker appears here during a hot streak that included *California Dreaming* (1979), *Gas Pump Girls* (1979), *Midnight Madness* (1970), and *Friday the 13th Part 2* (1981). Dalene Young, whose performance as a chronically intoxicated housewife would have fit perfectly on the late-night soap satire *Mary Hartman, Mary Hartman*, wrote the screenplays for the underage prostitute TV movie classics *Dawn: Portrait of a Teenage Runaway* (1976) and *Alexander: The Other Side of Dawn* (1977), as well as that of the beloved big-screen race-to-lose-your-virginity gem, *Little Darlings* (1980).

On its own, *Teen Lust* feels like a vortex gateway to some lunatic other dimension. Coupled with the backgrounds of its cast and creator, you can rest assured, it is exactly that. Proceed without caution.

Clockwise from top left: Thinkin' Big *(1986) takes spring break to big old Texas;* Teen Lust *(1979) starts with titillating role reversal on its video box, then enters "a vortex gateway to some lunatic other dimension"; long before Twilight, there was* Teen Vamp *(1988); nobody in* Three-Way Weekend *(1979) resembles a young Jack Nicholson—unless maybe he's the Nixon-obsessed creep wearing a gorilla mask?*

TEEN VAMP [1988]

DIR. SAMUEL BRADFORD; W/CLU GULAGER, KAREN CARLSON, BEAU BISHOP, ANGIE BROWN

NERD 📼 **VIRGIN** 📼 **VAMPIRE PROSTITUTE**

Swiping obvious inspiration for its title and plot from *Teen Wolf* (1985), this cockeyed stink-show may or may not be set in the 1950s. Cars and fashions change at random over a thirty-year range extending to the year the movie was made.

Hormone-hopped high school zilch Murphy (Beau Bishop) unwittingly picks up an undead prostitute, gets fanged hard, and—*voilà!*—the adolescent bloodsucker of the title is born. The newly vampirized Murphy transforms from loser to lady-killer, beguiling hottest-girl-on-campus Conny Sutton (Angie Brown) and beating the jockstrap off any bully who previously gave him grief.

When Murphy's mom notices a difference in her son's complexion, she calls on the Reverend (prolific cowboy actor Clu Gulager) to perform an exorcism. That plot point proved very funny in *Zapped!* In *Teen Vamp*, it's just... *Teen Vamp*. The power of watching anything else but this will compel you.

TEEN WOLF [1985]

DIR. ROD DANIEL; W/MICHAEL J. FOX, LORIE GRIFFIN, JAMES HAMPTON

LYCANTHROPY 📼 **THE BIG BASKETBALL GAME** 📼 **NERDS** 📼 **JOCKS** 📼 **PROM** 📼 **CHOLOS**

The origin of *Teen Wolf* begins with *Valley Girl*. While a spate of action films produced post-*Val* by parent company Atlantic Releasing tanked, the outfit's 1983 Deborah Foreman–Nicolas Cage teen sex hit just kept on hauling in cash. By 1985, Atlantic was demanding another dirt-cheap adolescent comedy with a super-exploitable premise. Ah-whoo... *Teen Wolf*.

Against a budget of $1 million, *Teen Wolf* grossed $80 million in theaters alone, thereby validating the Atlantic strategy. Clearly the 1980s were still shaking off the 1950s, and many scenes in *Teen Wolf* self-consciously reference portions of pioneer-era teen sex comedy *American Graffiti* (1973). What really lined up the crowds, though, was *Back to the Future*, the year's biggest blockbuster, playing just across the multiplex, and starring *Teen Wolf* headliner Michael J. Fox. *Ah-whoo*... cha-ching.

This movie is pretty funny, too. Fox portrays a high school basketball player who discovers that he hails from a long family line of amusingly Sasquatch-like lycanthropes. The sight of the transformed Fox's ropey brown fur flying in his yellow basketball uniform during slow-motion dunks and such—coupled with how his fellow students so inclusively embrace and cheer for "The Wolf"—is involuntary crack-up material. *Ah-whoo*... ha-ha-ha.

Teen Wolf's comedy is what matters, and highly indicative of what teen culture meant in the mid-1980s. In 2009, MTV launched a "dark" *Teen Wolf* spin-off series "with a greater emphasis on romance, horror, and werewolf mythology." *Ah-whoo*, the 21st century is so stupid.

TEEN WOLF TOO [1987]

DIR. CHRISTOPHER LEITCH; W/JASON BATEMAN, KIM DARBY, JOHN ASTIN

LYCANTHROPY 📼 **THE BIG BOXING MATCH** 📼 **COOL PROFESSOR** 📼 **SPAZZY DANCING**

Before zipping up the fur suit in place of original howler Michael J. Fox in *Teen Wolf Too*, Jason Bateman became revered for starring in one of the most subversive, inventive, and uproarious sitcoms ever aired on TV. Long before *Arrested Development*, young Bateman hit the NBC roster as a high school con man in *It's Your Move*, a single-season (1984–85) cult favorite. Bateman's character met his match in viciously scheming, equally underhanded teacher David Garrison, who lived next door and was dating Bateman's mom on the show (Caren Kaye of *My Tutor*).

After *It's Your Move* proved just too cool to live, its creators went on to make *Married*...

With Children. Bateman got a shot at movie stardom via *Teen Wolf Too*. All involved delivered commendably. Here he plays the college freshman cousin of Michael J. Fox's character, except instead of basketball, his sport is boxing. The movie's big laugh arrives with Bateman's first, spazzy "wolf-out" on a crowded dance floor. It's a riot. There is also a surprise werewolf on the university faculty—but, surprise, it's not Dean Dunn, played by John Astin, aka Gomez Addams of TV's *The Addams Family*.

Teenage Cruisers [1977]

aka Cruisin', Young Hot 'n Nasty Teenage Cruisers

DIR. JOHNNY LEGEND; W/JOHN HOLMES, SERENA, WILLIAM MARGOLD, CHRISTINE DE SHAFFER

CAR CRUISING ▪ VIRGINS ▪ GREASERS ▪ ROCK BANDS ▪ PIE FIGHT ▪ DONKEY SHOW

The theatrical adult-film industry attempted to knock off (and knock up) *American Graffiti* (1973) through a multitude of X-rated efforts, none more brain-boggling than *Teenage Cruisers*.

Writer-director-star Johnny Legend is a Rasputin-bearded, jubilantly enthusiastic trash-culture guru who has subsisted since the mid-1960s by promoting rockabilly dances, B-movies, pro-wrestling cards, cheap local TV, novelty records, and honky-tonk hell-raising. *Teenage Cruisers* represents Legend's rebel taste run orgasmically amok, incorporating each of those hellzapoppin' callings plus hardcore sex among big-ticket porn stars, all splattered among relentless gag-valanches in the vein of *The Groove Tube* (1974) and *Kentucky Fried Movie* (1977).

The action centers on a horny high school brigade hitting the main strip in their shiny cars, tuning into DJ Mambo Reaves (Johnny Legend), and falling into various encounters and corporeal combinations that all end the same way—i.e., with the couples at hand looking the way everybody else does toward the end of the movie's big, comical pie fight.

Bulking up the overall bizarreness of *Teenage Cruisers*, Johnny Legend also claims that he shot the "donkey show" segment at Spahn Ranch, a former cowboy set location and HQ of the Manson Family. On top of that, Legend maintains, actual Mansonites supplied the animal! Accordingly, the *Teenage Cruisers* rockabilly soundtrack is connoisseur quality, as it was mostly assembled by legendary X guitarist Billy Zoom. Rhino Records released the vinyl LP, and music is generally still available through iTunes and other online streaming services.

An R-rated cut of *Teenage Cruisers* allegedly played drive-ins and the midnight circuit, and that very possibility warrants the movie's inclusion among the more lighthearted fare here in teen movie hell. The single known revival screening, at the Nuart Theater in L.A., was hosted by the fragrant-as-ever Legend himself, and all the full-penetration bow-dee-oh-doe remained intact.

Teenage Hitchhikers [1974]

DIR. CLAUDE GODDARD (AS GERRI SEDLEY); W/SANDRA CASSELL (AS SANDRA PEABODY), CHRIS JORDAN, NIKKI LYNN, RIC MANCINI

HITCHHIKING ▪ VIRGIN ▪ ROCK BAND ▪ HIPPIES ▪ USED-CAR SALESMAN

Teenage Hitchhikers follows the tellingly named title duo, Mouse (Chris Jordan) and Bird (Sandra Cassell), as they stick out their thumbs, peel off their tube tops, and hustle across various highways and even bi-ways of America.

The girls party with rock group Energy Crisis, pull a three-way with traveling lingerie salesman Dick Daggert (Peter Carew), and save underage runaway Jennie (Nikki Lynn) from an escaped rapist (Ric Mancini). They also flash for food, yell "Faggot!" at drivers who won't stop for them, and agree to go home with moneyed lesbian Toni Blake (Claire Wilbur). The sophisticated sapphist quickly gets Bird in her bathtub; Mouse sets out to pocket some valuables but gets distracted and masturbates instead. For the big finish, free love reigns at a hippie orgy.

Sandra Cassell famously played teenage victim Mari Collingwood in Wes Craven's *The Last House on the Left* (1972). She has a lot more fun here as a teenage hitchhiker.

They're Playing With Fire [1984]

DIR. HOWARD AVEDIS; W/SYBIL DANNING, ERIC BROWN, ANDREW PRINE

BAD TEACHER • YACHT SEX • DORM SEX • FAT GUY • POWER BALLAD

What's funny about *They're Playing With Fire* is that it's not even remotely a comedy. Ever-savvy Roger Corman's New World Pictures sold the movie as a raucous return to form for Eric Brown, who starred in their 1981 older-woman-meets-horny-virgin money machine *Private Lessons. Fire*'s ads clearly implied it was yet another "bad teacher" farce, maybe even a kind of *Private Lessons* sequel.

In the previous movie, Brown scored with international sex film siren Sylvia Kristel (*Emmanuelle*) as his saucy French tutor. This time, his maiden escapade is with B-flick glamazon Sybil Danning (*Chained Heat, Howling II*) as his cherry-popping college professor. Playing university freshman Jay Richard, Brown gets it on with Danning, who plays married Shakespeare scholar Diane Stevens. They do it on her yacht, and in his dorm room. Then Diane cajoles the smitten idiot into executing a dastardly criminal plot that hinges on elder abuse. Very quickly *They're Playing With Fire* reveals itself to be a mean-spirited caper film.

Things grow frighteningly more serious after Jay unsuccessfully tries to scare the mother and grandmother of Professor Stevens's husband into signing over their sizable fortunes. A masked killer breaks into their house, slaughters the two old ladies, and pins the crime on the college student. Suddenly, *They're Playing With Fire* is a slasher movie! Running amok with this new direction, *Fire* then features a mystery machete slitting throats, a poodle that is bound and gagged, and the unknown murderer donning Santa Claus garb and grabbing a baseball bat to bash a comely coed into crimson eggnog. While terror mounts, Sybil Danning reveals her naked mastery of the full-body suntan.

One comic element carried over from *Private Lessons* is that the lead's best pal is a jocular fat slob. Glenn (Dominick Brascia) cracks wise, belches, pees a lot, and loads his pizza with mustard and anchovies. He's good, but the cartoon-voiced killer is still better.

One more dangling *Private Lessons* connection compounds this insanity. The 1969 novel *Philly* by Dan Greenburg, on which the *Private Lessons* screenplay is based, is also not a comedy but a crime thriller that delves into horror. Somewhere, somehow, all these wires are crossed. The good news is that, as a result, humanity receives two eminently memorable cinematic experiences in *Private Lessons* and *They're Playing With Fire.*

Thinkin' Big [1986]

DIR. S. F. BROWNRIGG; W/BRUCE ANDERSON, NANCY BUECHLER, RANDY JANDT

BEACH RESORT • WET-T-SHIRT CONTEST • TOPLESS CAR WASH • KARATE • MOBSTERS

Over the course of just five releases, Texas-based regional filmmaker Sherald "S. F." Brownrigg branded his indelible mark on drive-in cinema. Three Brownrigg efforts are brooding, brutal experiences that generated millions on the trash-flick circuit: *Don't Look in the Basement* (1973); *Don't Open the Door* (1974); and *Scum of the Earth* (1974), aka *Poor White Trash II.* A fourth film, *Keep My Grave Open* (1976), is less renowned, but still a lurid dive worth taking.

A decade later, here came *Thinkin' Big,* a movie not afraid to remind us that everything is bigger in the Lone Star State and that bigger is always better. The story begins with a sno-cone truck hurtling down the highway with four teenage buds inside. Either the Texas sun is harsh on male skin, or these actors all reached the thirty-candle threshold on their birthday cakes long

Clockwise from top left: Three O'Clock High *(1987), it's Buddy Revel's world, we just cower in it*; Tomboy *(1985) with Betsy Russell*; They're Playing With Fire *(1984), student, teacher, sex, and suspense*; Teen Wolf Too *(1987) takes the Jason bait, man.*

ago. Now they are beating a path to the sunny beaches of South Padre Island on the Gulf of Mexico.

At some point, virtually every human who appears on camera declares the need to "think big." Two characters matter most: Pud (Bruce Anderson), a morbidly obese good-time glutton; and Wong (Randy Jandt), described as "the Oriental sno-cone king." Wong speaks with a "ching-chong" accent, practices martial arts, and owns and operates the aforementioned sno-cone truck. In a delightful subversion of stereotypes, though, Wong's wang is a wondrous whopper.

After endless references to Wong's trouser dragon, viewers are treated to seeing it in silhouette as he does karate stuff on the shoreline at dawn. If things are bigger in Texas, they appear to be absolutely monstrous in Asia. Endlessly impressed to the point of tying a brick to his own pricklet, Pud asks his Wong how he, too, might expand his one and only non-gigantic appendage. Wong replies—get ready: "Think big!"

Nudity abounds during skinny-dipping, wet T-shirt contest, and topless carwash segments, all of which Pud "thinks big" about. Then, in an oddly serious turn, mobsters threaten everybody's carefree and clothes-free nice time until one goombah gets shot in the head. No more thinkin' big for him.

S. F. Brownrigg himself may have thought a little too big about *Thinkin' Big*, as the film runs a needlessly long one hour and thirty minutes. Still, the whole thing is a hoot flecked with entertaining idiosyncrasies. As with Bert I. Gordon making *Let's Do It* (1982) and *The Big Bet* (1985), it's great to see how one of vintage exploitation cinema's unique visionaries witnessed the teen movie hell of the '80s T&A flick explosion and thought: "Grab a camera, I need in on this idiotic gold mine!"

Three O'Clock High [1987]

DIR. PHIL JOANOU; W/CASEY SIEMASZKO, ANNIE RYAN, RICHARD TYSON, STACEY GLICK

NERD · BULLY · CHEERLEADERS · JOCKS · BAD TEACHER · THE BIG FIGHT

Director Phil Joanou whips the little-guy-vs.-big-bully comedy *Three O'Clock High* into a firestorm of visual acrobatics and editing pyrotechnics. His camera swoops, dives, and storms the action from every jolting and unexpected angle, as the film stock speeds up, slows down, and warps all sense of time, scale, and perspective. These whirlwind technical demonstrations properly convey the mind-strangling terror experienced by every teenager who has felt like a mouse walking straight into an appointment with the biggest, meanest, and most famished cat in town.

Casey Siemaszko stars as anxious high-school everydude Jerry Mitchell. After a bad start to the day, Jerry accidentally runs afoul of Buddy Revell (Richard Tyson), a recent transfer student who happens to be the most behemoth and homicidal teenage bully yet produced by mammalian evolution. Buddy announces that he will pummel Jerry in the school parking lot at three o'clock, and the movie warps into a manic vortex tracking each moment as the hours tick away toward the confrontation.

The big beat-down happens on schedule. The expected outcome, however—does not. Jerry ultimately triumphs over Buddy Revell by way of dirty fighting to a point that could become deadly. Maybe that dramatic choice says something about the era, or maybe human nature snaps into action as Buddy so effectively chills us to the bone with recollections of our own bullies. Once the opportunity arises to witness our stand-in pound the beast into tomato consommé by any illegal and unfair means necessary, our biology commands that our blood boils over with the righteous excitement of wanting to see it happen.

Siemaszko is appropriately cipher-like in the lead, while Tyson creates nothing less than a cinematic icon. He's funny while never coming off as likeable or vulnerable. While it's impossible to root for Buddy Revell in the midst of *Three O'Clock High*, viewers will cheer the performance. Even his moniker packs a wallop.

Fist Fight is a 2017 remake of *Three O'Clock High* starring Charlie Day in the Casey Siemaszko role and Ice Cube as an updated Buddy Revell—except they're *teachers*. The mere thought of this makes me want to challenge Hollywood to a fight at 3 p.m. Who's with me? Brass knuckles for everybody on our side!

THREE-WAY WEEKEND [1979]

DIR. EMMETT ALSTON; W/TREY WILSON (AS DAN DIEGO), JODY LEE OLHAVA, BLAKE PARRISH, JERRY ZANITSCH

CAMPING ▫ PEEPING ▫ WEED ▫ DIRTY OLD MEN ▫ GORILLA MASK ▫ NIXON MASK

During the dozen or so years leading up to this motion-picture monstrosity, no single icon exerted a more omnipresent influence on comedy than disgraced U.S. president Richard Nixon. His ski-slope nose; the quaking *V*-for-victory hand signs; and the jowly "I am not a crook!" declaration spiced up nearly every commercial comic undertaking during the Watergate scandal and for way too long afterward. *Three-Way Weekend* is an example of "way too long afterward." But for many a desperate teenager in the 1980s, crap like this hit the mark as the dirtiest possible VHS tape available to rent.

The first of two Tricky Dick addicts in the film is Harland Glend (Jerry Zanitsch, also the movie's producer), a hard-boiled right-wing park ranger who hunts communists and longs for the return of Spiro Agnew—Nixon's first vice president and the butt of so many jokes in *Mad* magazine that even *The Simpsons* noticed. Before long, a head injury combined with a cheap Nixon mask convinces Glend he *is* the former president.

The second Nixon-on-the-noggin protagonist is Howard Creep, an outdoors-dwelling voyeur and ex-member of the 1972 administration who can only cure impotence by donning a gorilla mask. As *Three-Way Weekend* opens, Creep wears the ape face and nothing else while spying on a pair of young campers (Jody Lee Olhava and Blake Parrish) going girl-girl wild in the woods. Creep's personal pull-yourself party is pooped when Ranger Glend busts the sun-kissed sapphists for being in "a known pervert area" and warning them of "big commie cocks" on the loose.

Portraying Mr. Creep under the nom-de-poon "Dan Diego" is character actor Trey Wilson (best known as the unpainted-furniture baron in the Coen Brothers' *Raising Arizona* [1987]). Wilson also produced *Three-Way Weekend* and composed and performed its bawdy sing-alongs, for example, "My cock's a rock / And that's no crock!"

A marginally Nixon-related subplot involves grizzled war vet Lester Popsicle (Richard Blye) and Kim San (Karen Stride), the "Korean whore" he's brought stateside and married. (As Kim looks to be in her early twenties, she must have come from a "specialty brothel" during the 1950–53 military conflict.) Lester continually explains to Kim that she is his wife, as she repeatedly insists, "You number one G.I.! You give ten dollar, we go boom-boom long time!" and "No tickee, no nookie!" Adding to the insult, actress Karen Stride is a white woman wearing just the barest "Asian" makeup. The couple's exploits provide respite from the Nixon humor when Kim and Lester get "stuck like dogs" while making shower boom-boom, due to her professional sex skills.

Long before its 85-minute running time is up (about 84 minutes prior, in fact), *Three-Way Weekend* collapses under the burden of its imploded I.Q. The movie bombards the screen with the dirty-old-man-fantasy fulfillment of teenage orgies, the passing of hoagie-size joints, a Jimmy Carter photo used to repel an ersatz Nixon like a cross to a vampire, and, ultimately, comical pig-fucking. Should you make it without fast-forwarding to *Three-Way Weekend*'s final credits, you will have passed quite a challenge as a devotee of lowest-of-lowbrow comedies.

Toga Party [1979] aka *Pelvis*

DIRS. ROBERT T. MEGGINSON, ANDY MILLIGAN; W/LUTHER "BUD" WHANEY, MARY MITCHELL, CINDY TREE, BOBBY ASTYR

TOGA PARTY ▣ GROUPIES ▣ SPAZZY DANCING

The toga party in *Toga Party* consists of lumpy, libidinous, middle-aged 1970s New York City swinger types running amok on an almost bare set, hoping to create wedged-in content that can siphon a few bucks from the box office juggernaut of *Animal House* (1978). At random intervals in *Toga Party*'s ongoing plot, we see the actual toga partiers scream, flail, smoke cigarettes, dance like cattle-prodded epileptics, paint one another's bodies badly, and make sandwiches from a gruesome deli tray.

Lording over the rambunctious revelers is Snake, played to the cigar-puffing hilt by Catskills-style comic and hardcore-porn star Bobby Astyr. The character, a Manhattan nightclub owner, serves as the sole link between the ersatz Roman orgy and the rest of *Pelvis*, a pre-existing 1977 film into which the separately shot toga material is crammed with the grace of a Caligula's fist. The end result reached screens in 1979 under the supremely marketable title, *Toga Party*.

The action follows horse-hung farm boy singer Purvis (Luther "Bud" Whaney) on his upward jaunt to rock stardom in New York City, where Snake successfully markets the rube as a glam rock take on Elvis Presley. His stage moniker, naturally, is "Pelvis."

Overall, *Toga Party* is more than a mere eyesore; it's actually closer to a bedsore—but one on your brain. Still, just try not to laugh Pelvis's songs, from the country ballad, "I Knew a Man Who Screwed a Chicken" to the tuneful plea for racial harmony, "My Little Wetback Maria" to the driving anthem of ambition, "Suck My Way to the Top." Funniest of all is "Nazi Girl," which Elvis croons while accompanied by on-screen follow-the-bouncing ball lyrics.

As poverty-rotted and plug-ugly as the "Pelvis" portions of *Toga Party* look, the toga stuff is indescribably worse. Please note that this wretched violation of celluloid is the handiwork of notorious grindhouse guttersnipe Andy Milligan. The seedy director of biologically unwatchable trash flicks (*Fleshpot on 42nd Street* [1973]; *The Rats Are Coming! The Werewolves Are Here!* [1972]), Milligan is also the subject of the highly recommended *The Ghastly One: The Sex-Gore Netherworld of Filmmaker Andy Milligan,* by Jimmy McDonough (Chicago Review Press, 2003).

Tomboy [1985]

DIR. HERB FREED; W/BETSY RUSSELL, GERARD CHRISTOPHER (AS JERRY DINOME), KRISTI SOMERS, ERIC DOUGLAS

BATTLE OF THE SEXES ▣ RICH JERK ▣ THE BIG RACE

In terms of exploitation movies, 1985 really was Betsy Russell's year. She took on the "honor student by day, Hollywood hooker by night" title role in *Avenging Angel*; she outshone a populous young cast in the stranded-on-an-island teen adventure *Out of Control*; and she turned the lightweight *Flashdance*-with-race-cars knockoff *Tomboy* into her own bona fide star vehicle.

The tomboy herself is Tomasina "Tommy" Boyd (Russell), an East L.A. auto mechanic who falls for stock car racer Randy Starr (Gerard Christopher). Comic relief comes from Eric Douglas as a Junior Leeds, an arrogant and sleazy racing promoter; and Kristi Somers as Seville Ritz, Tommy's ditzy and often nude best friend, who dreams of dance stardom.

After Tommy and Randy fall out of love, they square off against another in a high-stakes car race where the winner will earn a spot in the Daytona 500. Even though a sequel on the order of *Tomboy Goes to the Daytona 500* never materialized, Betsy Russell was not free from teen movie hell yet, soon appearing in *Cheerleader Camp* (1988) and *Camp Fear* (1991) before assuming the continuing role of Jill Tuck, wife of the Jigsaw Killer, in the *Saw* movie series.

Tuff Turf [1985]

DIR. FRITZ KIERSCH; W/JAMES SPADER, KIM RICHARDS, ROBERT DOWNEY, JR.

NEW KID ▫ GANGS ▫ PUNKS ▫ GRAFFITI

Immediately following his villain turn in *The New Kids* (1985), James Spader handles hero duties in *Tuff Turf.* Spader stars as new kid in town Morgan, a high-speed bicycle enthusiast whose family downgrades from civilized Connecticut to savage L.A. In California, his new graffiti-splattered high school is lorded over by a loudly fashionable teenage outlaw organization run by thuggish Nick (Paul Mones) and Nick's feather-haired main squeeze, Frankie (Kim Richards).

Right away, Morgan thwarts a robbery being committed by the cabal, which is no way to make friends. Frankie informs him that his "ass is grass." Before long, though, Morgan and Frankie fall for one another, and they discover the hard way that, as a contemporary pop song suggested, love is a *battlefield.*

Tuff Turf is a rousing, extremely of-its-moment binge-and-purge of star-crossed romance, juvenile delinquent hyperbole, and music video overkill courtesy of director Fritz Kiersch, who managed to whip up this whirlwind between crafting two other cult benchmarks, *Children of the Corn* (1984) and *Gor* (1987).

Atypically cast as the good guy, Spader rocks pretty hard, although not quite as hard as Robert Downey Jr., who portrays Jimmy Parker, Morgan's new wave drummer best friend who ends up slamming skins shirtless at an underground punk club for *Basketball Diaries* author and art rock legend Jim Carroll! The hip literary cameo seems to underline the movie's unlikely premise: what if Holden Caulfield was plopped down into the dumb, violent world of *Colors*?

Kim Richards makes a scrappily unique antiheroine, and not just because of her ridiculous maxi-crimped hairdo. The love scene involving Spader and this former *Witch Mountain* kid and future *Real Housewife* (as well as actual aunt of Paris Hilton) stars one of the most hilariously obvious body doubles in cinema history.

Tuff Turf proved to be the most lasting of '80s teen cinema's varyingly violent action subgenre, at least in part because its title is so fun to say out loud and even just to think about. The movie zooms along with a likeable sense of humor, a trait not shared by other entries in this field such as the Sean Penn juvie-hall nightmare *Bad Boys* (1983), the Linda Blair rape-and-revenge crossbow adventure *Savage Streets* (1984), or Adam Baldwin as a one-man leather-jacket wrecking machine in *3:15* (1986). Those are terrific films in their own right, but in the cheeky depths of teen movie hell, *Tuff Turf* is king of the mountain.

Clockwise from top: *James Spader and costars Robert Downey Jr. and Kim Richards are plenty tuff (and plenty crimped, in Richards's case) in* Tuff Turf *(1985); it's Buddy Revel's world, we just cower in it;* Toga Party *(1979) is what happens when you splice toga party footage into the genuinely weird preexisting grindhouse comedy* Pelvis *(1977).*

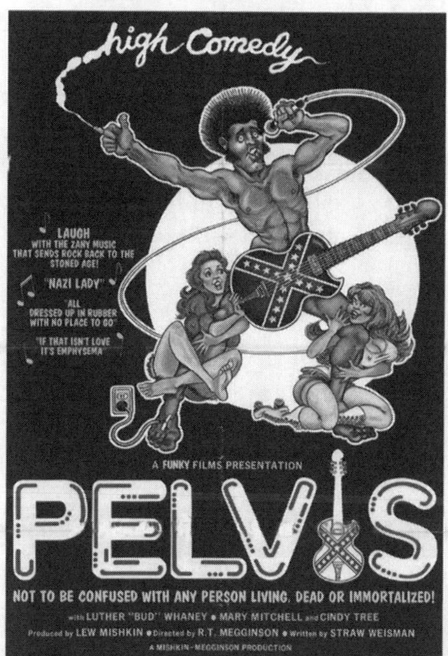

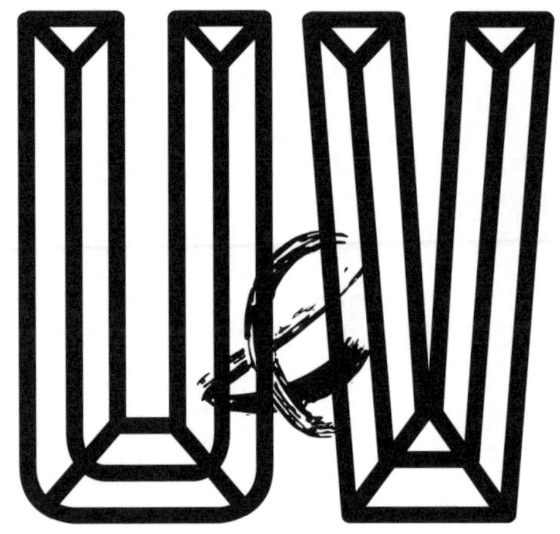

Up the Academy ▫ Up the Creek ▫ Ups & Downs ▫ Valet Girls ▫ Valley Girl ▫ The Val$ ▫ Vamp ▫ The Van ▫ Van Nuys Blvd. ▫ Virgin High ▫ The Virgin Queen of St. Francis High ▫ Vision Quest

Up the Academy [1980]

DIR. ROBERT DOWNEY SR.; W/RON LEIBMAN, RALPH MACCHIO, BARBARA BACH, ANTONIO FARGAS

MILITARY SCHOOL ▫ FAT GUY ▫ ARAB SHEIKS ▫ MOBSTERS ▫ FASCIST AUTHORITY

The 1980 motion picture released as *Mad Magazine Presents Up the Academy* represents one of the great tragedies in all of cinema history. Not only was the film a creative botch, but its financial decimation cost humanity the opportunity to witness a full-blown "*Mad* movie" representing the magazine's golden era while its cherished "Usual Gang of Idiots" were all still operating in peak form.

Up the Academy slaughtered and buried a long-in-fitful-development *Mad* film project that would have allowed viewers to bask in the projector glow of Alfred E. Neuman, Spy vs. Spy, Don Martin's rubber-limbed wonders, Al Jaffee's "Snappy Answers to Stupid Questions," and Dave Berg's "Lighter Side" hippies and squares. Picture Sergio Aragones's "Drawn Out Dramas" playing out on the margins of the big screen, and imagine what 35mm could have done for the *Mad* Fold-In! Instead, we got *Up the Academy*. The world still mourns.

It happened like this. After *National Lampoon* begat the blockbuster *Animal House*, Warner Brothers, which owned *Mad*, naturally sought to tap its in-house humor periodical for movie bucks. *Mad Magazine: The Movie* at last was fast-tracked. First, though, Warner wanted to test the brand's drawing power. They slapped *Mad Magazine Presents* above the title of *Up the Academy*, a pre-existing military-school lark directed by iconoclast Robert Downey Sr.

As a visionary cinematic satirist of the '60s counterculture, Downey created the blistering classic *Putney Swope* (1969), a serrated send-up of race relations and advertising industry that still stings brilliantly.

Alas, Downey was an unreliable hitter when it came to Hollywood projects. While *Up the Academy* percolates with fine and funny ideas, the end result is ill-paced and clumsy. Some unneeded F-bomb dialogue earned the picture an R rating, thus making ticket sales to *Mad*'s

Clockwise from top left: Valley Girl *(1983) poster featuring Nicolas Cage and* not *Deborah Foreman;* Up the Academy *(1980)* torpedoes *hopes for a proper* Mad *magazine movie;* The Virgin Queen of St. Francis High *(1987);* Valet Girls *(1987), they deliver.*

preteen audience impossible. Full-color *Up the Academy* ads in Sunday newspaper funny pages left eleven-year-olds nationwide heartbroken, that big "R-Restricted" logo at the bottom piercing age-appropriate *Mad* fanatics everywhere like a hot knife.

Up the Academy bombed atrociously at the box office, and its toxic financial fallout permanently annihilated any possibility of the *Mad* movie proper. The best thing that resulted from the whole boondoggle was the actual parody in Mad magazine, titled "Throw Up the Academy."

The setup brims with promise. Five amusing walking teenage stereotypes with behavior problems are shipped off for correction to the Sheldon R. Wienberg Military Academy. Viewers meet mobster spawn Chooch (Ralph Macchio); African American son of a preacherman Ike (Wendell Brown); oil sheik scion Hash (Tommy Citera); scandalous political offspring Oliver (Hutch Parker); and, way best of all, bombastically funny fat guy and compulsive arsonist Rodney Ververgaert (Harry Teinowitz).

Rodney rules. In fact, in bringing Youngman Ververgaert to such unique, vivid life among *Up the Academy*'s multitude of misfires, Teinowitz deserved to break into stardom. His psychotic chuckle rates a proper honor in All-Time Hall of Hilarity in teen movie hell.

Standing out amidst the Wienberg faculty are bombshell weapons instructor Miss Bliss (Barbara Bach); effete pimp-slick Coach (Antonio Fargas); flamingly boy-crazy Master Sergeant Sisson (Tom Poston); and secretly kinky dictatorial Dean of Discipline Major Vaughn Liceman, portrayed by esteemed New York actor Ron Leibman with unrelenting commitment to fascist fury.

The previous year, Leibman played the male lead in the iconic Sally Field union drama *Norma Rae*, and he then starred on the popular CBS lawyer series, *Kaz*. Once Leibman got a whiff of the completed *Academy*, he removed his name from the credits, and, for about a week, was billed as the movie's "secret star." His repeated command—"Say it AGAIN!" barked as one syllable—is an extremely low-ranking but durable catchphrase.

Ultimately, *Up the Academy* did enrich the universe with two artifacts of value. The first is a life-size brass statue of *Mad*'s "What, Me Worry?" mascot, Alfred E. Neuman, in full military dress, which has since resided in the lobby of *Mad*'s MADison Avenue office. The other is an awe-inspiring, more-than-mildly chilling, cartoon-realistic Alfred E. Neuman mask worn by a lucky unnamed actor in the movie's opening and closing credits. Sometimes eternally lasting art emerges from the most unlikely wellsprings.

Up the Creek [1984]

DIR. ROBERT BUTLER; W/TIM MATHESON, JENNIFER RUNYON, DAN MONAHAN, STEPHEN FURST

BIG FAT PARTY ANIMAL • NERD • SORORITY • FUNNY DOG • THE BIG RACE

Up the Creek is a crassly calculated Frankenstein, a stitched-together '80s teen sex comedy that just barely floats. The movie stars Tim Matheson and Stephen Furst (Otter and Flounder from *Animal House*) along with Dan Monahan (Pee-Wee from *Porky's*) as college fuckups at a school named after a legendary fart performer, Lepotomane University. John Hillerman (Higgins from TV's *Magnum, P.I.*), doing his own take on *Animal House*'s Dean Wormer here, blackmails the trio into competing in a bikini-friendly whitewater rafting competition. The female lead is Jennifer Runyon (heartthrob Gwendolyn Pierce from *Charles in Charge*).

Lepotomane U., better known as "Lobotomy U.", faces rival teams including obnoxiously preppy Ivy Leaguers, sexy sorority sisters, and gung-ho wannabe commandos from a military academy. With such a setup, overseen by exploitation legend executive producer Samuel Z. Arkoff, how could *Up the Creek* not have made a bigger splash?

The admirably cheap opening credits feature slides of white words against a black background in the style of a Woody Allen movie. Instead of jazz or silence, though, the background music is the massively infectious title song by Cheap Trick. Viewers will long to see equally cheap footage of roaring rapids, wasted riverside antics, and topless flotation devices.

As team captain Bob McGraw, Tim Matheson seems to reprise Otter at age thirty-seven, the actor's actual age. Stephen Furst, while ideal as Flounder, never convinces as party monster and "human garbage disposal" Gonzer. Though plenty fat, he lacks the dangerous sexual powder keg potential of Gross-Out from *King Frat* (1979) or McDorfus from *Joysticks* (1983), let alone Bluto Blutarsky. Dan Monahan as Max offers little besides a *Porky's* connection. Sandy Helberg manages to be one of this genre's few unmemorable nerds.

The supporting players are better. John Hillerman's slow-seething style perfectly fits Dean Burch, as does the pipe-clenching a-hole bravado of James B. Sikking, (the arrogant SWAT team commander on *Hill Street Blues*) as Tozer, leader of the military squad. Jennifer Runyon is funny and diverting. Best of all is Jake as Chuck the Wonder Dog, who, in *Up the Creek*'s big laugh-out-loud scene, points the heroes toward a kidnapped comrade by acting out charades.

Playboy model Lori Sutton appears as a flasher at an RV rally, and Swedish Bikini Team standout Peggy Trentini is a celebratory sorority sister. Both do what they were hired to do. Between obvious bouts of belching and body-baring, *Up the Creek* even works in a subtle running gag: instead of just ordering beer, the characters repeatedly enter bars and order antiquated libations like Harvey Wallbangers and Brandy Alexanders.

Once the whitewater raft race starts, it never ends. The sequence is well shot, and every so often one team's act of sabotage against another livens up repeated scenes of big, yellow, inflatable boats on a roaring river. Mostly, when confronted by yet another round of race footage, the idle thought arises: "Okay, put a pin in it."

UPS & DOWNS [1981]
aka PREP SCHOOL

DIR. PAUL ALMOND; W/ANDREW SABISTON, COLIN SKINNER, LESLIE HOPE, ALISON KEMBLE

PREPPIES 📼 **VIRGIN** 📼 **ROCK BAND** 📼 **SCHOOL DANCE**

Six years before Canada graced the world with *Degrassi Junior High*, the Great White North explored adolescent hosehead-ism on national airwaves with the TV movie *Ups & Downs*. Unlike *Degrassi*, with its public campus, *Ups & Downs* focuses on a coed private boarding school.

Ups starts with promise as class cutups Chip (Andrew Sabiston) and Drifty (Gavin Brennan) wager against Arthur "Sherlock" Holmes (Colin Skinner) that they can break every major rule of the school without getting busted. Sherlock takes the lads' action, and onward they graduate to some gentle lessons about growing up.

For some inane reason, *Ups & Downs* favors the second half of its title. Bummed out mathlete Mouse (Alison Kemble) has issues with her boyfriend, the school's big-shot soccer team captain and also leading rugby star; a more Canadian double threat is hard to imagine. Artsy outcast Emmie (Sandy Gauthier) is bullied by campus mean queen Penelope (Leslie Hope). Chip and Drifty, in a defilement of their most excellent outlaw names, are repeatedly busted during every attempt to go rogue. Even when the bad boys form a rock group for the big dance, they blow it by composing a song about being considerate of other people's feelings. Party on, dudes.

VALET GIRLS [1987]

DIR. RAFAL ZIELINSKI; W/MERI D. MARSHALL, APRIL STEWART, MARY KOHNERT, JACK DELEON (AS CHRISTOPHER WEEKS)

PARTY GIRLS 📼 **PRANKS** 📼 **MADONNA WANNABE** 📼 **SLIMY MUSIC BIZ EXECS** 📼 **NEW WAVE**

Valet Girls is the name of this busy jaunt, and also of the workplace where the film's Hollywood hopeful heroines don skimpy tuxedoes and start parking cars around Tinseltown. Southern belle Carnation (Mary Kohnert) longs to be a movie star. Spunky new-waver Lucy (Meri D. Marshall) fronts a rock band; she is determined to meet record mogul Alvin Sunday (Michael Karm). Tall and authoritative Rosalind (April Stewart) aims to conquer show business in all forms through sheer force of her female will.

When the Valet Girls show up to provide parking for guests at the fiftieth birthday party of big-shot actor Dirk Zebra (Jack DeLeon), they prove themselves amply equipped to the orgiastic task at hand. Drunks run amok, nostrils hoover coke, old lechers leer at young revelers, and the pool overflows with skinny-dippers.

In the course of the bacchanal, Lucy performs in front of Alvin Sunday, but he will only talk contracts with her if she agrees to a threesome with a Madonna wannabe actually billed in the credits as "Madonna Wannabe" (Kim Gillingham). This pre-#MeToo scenario results in a rather stupefying physical brawl between the young singer and the evil music exec. Lucy triumphs. Perhaps this scene means *Valet Girls* is ripe for a cathartic Hollywood reboot?

Compounding the chaos, dwarf caterer Sammy (Tony Cox of *Bad Santa*) repeatedly hurls his three-foot-tall body in harm's way. Withered womanizer Lindsey Brawnsworth (Jon Sharp) loses both his dentures and his toupee to scorned former conquests Grueling Greta (Elizabeth Lamers) and Egypt Von Sand Dunes (Rebecca Cruz). Finally, the Valet Girls' male car-parking rivals crash the soirée in chicken costumes, igniting smoke bombs and bombarding the revelers with live spiders, lizards, and other flesh-crawling pests. In the end, the Valet Girls line those lads up bare-assed against the actual Hollywood sign for a punitive humbling.

Four years passed between director Rafal Zielinski's teen sex comedy breakthrough *Screwballs* (1983) and *Valet Girls*, his farewell to the form. Since four years is often enough time to complete high school, it makes sense that, after this, Zielinski left teen movie hell behind.

VALLEY GIRL [1983]

DIR. MARTHA COOLIDGE; W/DEBORAH FOREMAN, NICOLAS CAGE, ELIZABETH DAILY, MICHAEL BOWEN

VALLEY GIRLS ▫ NEW WAVE ▫ PUNK ▫ MALL ▫ FOOD FIGHT ▫ CRUISING

The *Romeo and Juliet* of '80s teen comedies—note the initials of lead characters Randy (Nicolas Cage) and Julie (Deborah Foreman)—*Valley Girl* arose from a pop culture craze set off by, of all trendsetters, Frank Zappa and his daughter, Moon Unit Zappa. The family duo scored Papa Frank's only Top 40 hit with 1982's "Valley Girl" (it peaked at number thirty-two), a blast of bass over which Moon imitates the aggressively airheaded tone and rapid-fire slang of her peers from the San Fernando Valley. Suddenly "Valspeak" phrases such as "gag me with a spoon" and "grody to the max" entered the lexicon virulently enough to warrant a youthsploitation movie cash-in.

Back in 1983, a *Porky's*-style cavalcade of pranks and perversions titled *Valley Girl* would not have barfed anybody out. Impressive, then, that writers Wayne Crawford and Andrew Lane instead teamed with director Martha Coolidge to deliver a heartfelt star-crossed high school romance that also supplies ample hilarity.

Julie lives—where else?—in the Valley, where she patrols Sherman Oaks Galleria Mall and bops along to new wave on KROQ-FM with fellow "Vals" Loryn (Elizabeth "E. G." Daily, Dottie in *Pee-Wee's Big Adventure* [1985]), Suzi (Michelle Meyrink, Jordan in *Real Genius* [1985]), Stacey (Heidi Holicker). Julie dates handsome Tommy (Michael Bowen), and works at a health food restaurant owned by her aging hippie parents, Steve (Frederic Forrest) and Sarah (Colleen Camp).

Meanwhile, Randy, a rough-and-tumble punk rocker straight out of the L.A. scene documented in *The Decline of Western Civilization* (1982), catches Julie's eye at the beach. Soon after, Randy crashes a Valley party with his pal Fred (Cameron Dye), only to disgustedly announce,

"That techno-rock you listen to is gutless!" Julie can't help but be impressed. She grabs Suzi, and together they join the punks for a Saturday night cruise on Hollywood Boulevard. They ends up at a rock dive where power-popsters the Plimsouls are performing "A Million Miles Away." The musical movie moment is great, although it's fun to imagine what could have happened if roots-punks X—Martha Coolidge's original choice—hadn't pulled out after unsuccessful negotiations. (In 2018, a friend of X front man John Doe said the band never seriously considered taking the gig, because, as Doe allegedly put it, "our fans would have killed us.")

Passions rise, subcultures clash, a famous "falling in love" montage occurs to "I Melt With You" by Modern English, and Suzi's hot stepmom Beth (Lee Purcell) seduces Suzi's crush Skip (David Ensor). The high school prom looms. Will Julie choose as her escort Tommy, with whom her friends are pressuring her to reunite; or Randy, the leather-vested, snaggle-toothed rebel who drives the 101 Freeway of her heart? The film's prom-night resolution takes multiple clever turns, and features the movie's funniest scene: Julie's dad Steve sneaking a joint in the john because his mind is blown that *he's got a kid going to the prom, man.*

Among the almost flawless cast, *Valley Girl*'s big revelation is Nicolas Cage. Randy is the first of many characters Cage would play from odd, unpredictable angles, and the movie set him on a fast path to stardom. Deborah Foreman, at the heart of everything, is surrounded by cascading fountains of charisma. She's just a pretty pool of *okayness,* not unlike, as its multitude of haters will tell you, the San Fernando Valley itself. Compare her lacking central girl power to the brilliance that director Martha Coolidge coaxed from Alicia Silverstone in *Clueless* a dozen years later.

Los Angeles teenagers reacted to *Valley Girl* like traffic passing through a massive freeway interchange, either taking route A: "Bitchin'! That's me up there!" or route B: "Fuck this fucking bullshit thinking it knows me and telling the world that's how I am!" Regardless, *Valley Girl* survives as a flash-frozen capture of a particular time and place that was lost when California's distinct new wave youth culture was transformed for national consumption by MTV.

Says costar E. G. Daily: "Martha Coolidge was a newer director and very, very good at what she did. We had a blast. She'd sit on the floor with me before a shot and we'd talk about things. There was a moment when I was frustrated about the topless scene, but we talked about it and she was very sensitive to me. I have a lot of respect for her. This incredible little movie blew up to become an iconic cult hit."

However of-its-moment *Valley Girl* may be, the film's legacy has evolved with the times. In 2009, MGM greenlit a musical remake of *Valley Girl*. After nearly a decade of stops and starts, the studio announced in 2016 that director Rachel Goldenberg (*Lady Time, Snackpocalypse*) would soon deliver the totally tubular goods.

Alas, in December 2017 costar Logan Paul, a hunky YouTube influencer (the twenty-first-century version of a *Tiger Beat* pinup), ignited freak-outs worldwide after he posted a video of his trip to a Japanese "suicide forest" and filmed a real corpse dangling from a tree. Paul's requisite torch-and-pitchforking by a grodied-to-the-max public not only led to his YouTube channel being removed, it also, according to the Hollywood news site *Deadline,* prompted MGM to pull *Valley Girl* from the roster in search of "another release date." In other words: Don't gag yourself with a spoon waiting for this remake.

Counterpoint by Christina Ward:

I hate *Valley Girl*. I hate the movie you love. *Valley Girl* is ninety-nine minutes of sanctimonious nice-guy cult programming, and the movie is the guilty progenitor of every John Hughes milquetoast fantasia. *Pretty in Pink* (1986) is *Valley Girl* with the gender roles reversed, and is equally terrible. That would be reason enough to topple *Valley Girl* from its dubious pedestal, but the film is guilty of even greater crimes.

Romeo and Juliet it is not. The plot features an unlikeable cute girl who is worried about her social status and disenchanted with her wholly terrible yet somehow popular boyfriend. When Terrible Boyfriend fails to serve her narcissism, she dumps him. Ego bruised, the suntanned Svengali humiliates and manipulates her friends. She then finds herself attracted to Randy the Nice Guy, Nicolas Cage in his hairy glory, rendered benign in an after-school-special version of a Hollywood punk. Of course, Nice Guy is nice to her. And of course, she rejects him for the Terrible Guy. Nice Guy decides he's made enough nice deposits and begins stalking her and beating up Terrible Boyfriend at the prom.

Deborah Foreman, as Julie the Cute Girl, tries to embody a real girl, but the limits of the plot and writing sapped the fine totality of her powers. Julie never had a choice: She is the object, the prize to be won. It's telling that after hearing Pa's sincere advice to "follow her heart," Julie is unable to make a decision. Because she has no heart, no autonomy. She was never meant to have a heart, or a brain, or anything resembling an emotional interior life.

Director Martha Coolidge, the leader of the Sonderkommando on this woman-hating production, can't do enough to disguise the fact that Julie is a banal blond hotsie-totsie, bikini-wearing teenage wet dream. I get it; satisfied viewers of *Valley Girl* are misunderstood punk outsiders listening to 7-inches of French-Mongolian aggro jazz-core obtained from trading away a pair of Steve Albini's underpants. Never mind that this girl in no way represents real women. This pastiche of the girl next door is the culmination of your fevered masturbatory reveries, and she is owed to you.

I have no problem with male fantasy. *Porky's* is a delightfully raunchy romp around the tits and ass circus. Women easily recognize (and dismiss or enjoy) the overt crassness of teenage sex comedies. *Valley Girl* is different. *Valley Girl* is insidious. Disguised as a romantic comedy, *Valley Girl* is propaganda that built the dreaded Nice Guy myth for the punk generation. This is the stuff of "involuntary celibates" dogma—that if Nice Guy makes enough Nice with any girl, every girl, then she *owes* him sex and affection.

I'm not surprised that punk boys fell for this poser crap. But I am incandescent with rage that girls claim to love this Stockholm syndrome of a movie. Post–*Valley Girl*, the Randys of the world realized that they were just as entitled as the jocks to as much sex as they wanted. Underneath the Mohawks and leather coats, they were predatory Nice Guys with chips on their shoulders and a patriarchal sense of entitlement. With *Valley Girl*, they received a powerful tool to convince previously unattainable girls to put out.

Oh, and the soundtrack sucks too.

THE VAL$ [1983]

DIR. JAMES POLAKOF; W/JILL CARROLL, GINA CALABRESE, ELENA STRATHEROS, SONNY BONO

VALLEY GIRLS ▫ FRATERNITY ▫ FAT GUY ▫ NEW WAVERS ▫ BEER BONGS ▫ COCAINE ▫ SHOPPING MALL ▫ LINGERIE STORE

First, any title that switches out the letter *s* for a dollar sign ($) is an instant party. Compound that decision with a buoyantly bubble-brained cash-in on the early-'80s Valley girl craze, littered with grizzled Hollywood vets (John Carradine! Chuck Connors! *Sonny Bono!*), and *The Val$* registers "cha-ching" in terms of non-grodiness to the totally tubular mega-max.

San Fernando sisters-in-spoon-gagging Sam (Jill Carroll), Trish (Elena Stratheros), Beth (Michele Laurita), and Annie (Gina Calabrese) cruise the mall, party with frat guys, and discover beer bongs courtesy of rotund party animal David (Jim Greenleaf, aka McDorfus from *Joysticks*). The "Vals" also contend with their snooty rivals from Beverly Hills, the "Bevs," in a car race "for pinks." Tragically, Trish loses her Mercedes convertible and, more importantly, its "TUBUL R" custom license plate.

Between giggles and jiggles, the girls scramble to raise money for an orphanage run by saintly Old Man Stanton (Carradine, looking older than Dracula). At the same time, they also battle greaseball cocaine dealers.

Ah, cocaine. That very '80s, very L.A. narcotic factors substantially into the *The Val$*. Trish's TV producer father (Connors) snarfs lines and babbles like a madman. Frat president Mike (Tony Longo) lectures on the chemical components of "the devil's dandruff." The name of Sonny Bono's character says it all: "'Spaced-Out' Musician." Furthermore, the overall slapdash pacing and peripatetic plotting of *The Val$* also capture the, let's say, "energy" of the powder at hand.

Director Jim Polakoff previously made *Swim Team* (1979). *Playboy* model and B-movie superstarlet Tiffany Bolling (*The Candy Snatchers, Kingdom of the Spiders*) turns up as Trish's saucy, sultry mom. And the overall takeaway message of *The Val$* rings as true now as it did back when the movie came out and Rick James was still alive and sniffing: "Cocaine is a hell of a drug."

VAMP [1986]

DIR. RICHARD WENK; W/CHRIS MAKEPEACE, GRACE JONES, ROBERT RUSLER, DEDEE PFEIFFER

VIRGINS ▪ FRATERNITY ▪ SEXY VAMPIRE ▪ STRIPPERS ▪ BIKERS

Vamp is a hyperstylized horror-comedy answer to Martin Scorsese's one-mad-night-in-Manhattan misadventure *After Hours*. Amidst sets and costumes that scream mid-'80s NYC art market excess, fraternity pledges Keith (Chris Makepeace of *Meatballs*), AJ (Robert Rusler of *Weird Science*), and Duncan (Gedde Watanabe of *Sixteen Candles*) hit the big town to corral strippers for a campus party.

The movie's dark heart belongs to trapezoid-coifed, panther-eyed, razor-smiled nightclub sensation Grace Jones. In *Vamp*, Jones follows her big-screen adventures as a barbaric Conan cohort and a vexing James Bond villain by throwing herself full throttle into the role of Queen Katrina. She's an undead predator who peels onstage at a nudie club that serves as a front for her cabal of bloodsuckers.

The college virgins and the succubus strippers soon encounter one another. Half-human Amaretto (Dedee Pfeiffer) takes a sympathetic shine to the frat dopes and guides them through the city's anything-goes underground; in the case of ghouls who nest in a sewer, that description is literal. Elevated by the aforementioned Scorsese influence, *Vamp* is consistently clever, but also one of its era's most instantly dated eye-bleeders.

Even in 1986, *Vamp* looked too 1986 for its own good. As the only figure ferocious enough to inspire greatness from both Andy Warhol and Dolph Lundgren alike, Jones herself embodies this aesthetic overkill. She prowls the dance stage in body paint, slinking over a throne designed by downtown pop-art icon Keith Haring. The effect is brilliant, but in such an intensely concentrated dose, it all comes off a bit rich. As you take in *Vamp*'s visual firestorm, don't be surprised if a neon Swatch suddenly materializes on your wrist, and you find yourself gripping a stranger's mitt as part of Hands Across America. You'll either enjoy revisiting that very specific moment, or frantically try to book a seat on the space shuttle *Challenger*.

THE VAN [1977]

DIR. SAM GROSSMAN; W/STUART GOETZ, DEBORAH WHITE, DANNY DEVITO, MARCY BARKIN

CUSTOM VAN ▪ HIGH SCHOOL GRADUATION ▪ WEED ▪ DRAG RACING ▪ BIKINIS ▪ PINBALL ▪ HOOKERS ▪ BEER

The van is the thing in *The Van*. The vehicle in question is an absolutely primo custom model, decked out with a CB radio, a refrigerator, a toaster, an 8-track hi-fi, several TV sets, a mirrored ceiling, and—oh, yes—a waterbed. No wonder they named the movie after that monster. The van belongs to recent high school grad Bobby Hampton (Stuart Goetz), who forgoes college to focus on the aesthetic perfection and amorous possibilities of his new prized possession. Mostly, the action follows Bobby's freewheeling sexual misadventures, but, as is weirdly typical of this time and these movies, some side plots go darker than sanity would dictate.

Bobby's car-wash boss Andy (Danny DeVito) sidelines as a bookie, and gangsters beat him pissless. A couple of Bobby's horny pickups turn out to be hookers, and one girl's terrifying pimp bursts into the van to demand his fee for services rendered. After Bobby's coworkers run his convertible through the wash with its top down, he spikes their beer with liquid laxative.

Bobby is also not above attempted date rape; nor is an Amazonian, badonka-butted waitress named Bertha (Lillian McBride) beyond forcing herself on Bobby. In fact, she does so with such impact that the waterbed bursts. Afterward, Bobby notes that he never knew intercourse could be so "physical."

The Van also introduces Steve Oliver as greaseball bully and fellow van enthusiast Dugan. Bobby and Dugan race for pink slips during the climax. Watch the movie to see who wins. Dugan returns the following year in Crown International Pictures' follow-up frolic, *Malibu Beach*.

After being an early "Skinemax" favorite at the dawn of the '80s, *The Van* aired regularly on cable movie channels deep into the 1990s. More recently, *The Van* surpassed Crown International's previous cult champ, *The Pom Pom Girls* (1976), as the go-to midnight movie for revival theaters looking to showcase primo pet-rock-era SoCal teensploitation. Such theaters could do a lot worse.

The funniest thing about *The Van* is a sonic screwup. The movie's delightful soft rock theme song, "Chevy Van" by Sammy Johns, became a '70s radio staple, hitting number five on the *Billboard* pop chart, and selling more than a half-million copies. It's astonishing for such high-profile success to emanate from such lowbrow source material. What's not astonishing is the filmmakers' lack of attention to detail. Sammy clearly sings about a Chevy Van; in the movie, Bobby drives a Dodge.

Van Nuys Blvd. [1979]

DIR. WILLIAM SACHS; W/ BILL ADLER, CYNTHIA WOOD, DAVID HAYWARD, MELISSA PROPHET

CUSTOM VANS ▪ CRUISING ▪ DRAG RACING ▪ CHEERLEADERS ▪ BIKINIS ▪ ARCADE

Van Nuys Blvd. is an unmistakable knockoff of the 1962-set *American Graffiti*, even though it takes place in 1970s Los Angeles. The most direct *American Graffiti* lifts come from Bobby (Bill Adler) obsessively cruising the ten-mile San Fernando thoroughfare of the title behind the wheel of his custom Chevy dream machine, which we first glimpsed in *Malibu Beach* (1978; when Bobby was simply credited as "Vanner").

Once on the strip, Bobby teams up with the mightily mustachioed Chooch (David Hayward), a brash grease monkey who pilots an exposed-engine hot rod and joyfully bays at pedestrians, just like Paul Le Mat in *Graffiti*. The movie also employs drag racing and a mysterious dream girl in a passing car, à la Suzanne Somers.

Aside from the nostalgia difference, this movie splits from *American Graffiti* in that it's loaded with naked bodies. Rather than a nonstop soundtrack of hits, one song plays over and over again. "Van Nuys Blvd" by Ron Wright is not even so much a song, but a thumping disco nightmare composed almost entirely of headache bass, whispering backup singers, and a maniac repeatedly bellowing, "Van Nuys!" at Chinese-water-torture intervals. It is *heinous*.

Otherwise, *Van Nuys Blvd.* runs like a dream. Everybody hits an arcade, an amusement park, and a beach, where a pig named Reggie cruises the sand. There's a comical love scene that hinges on smearing a burger, fries, and milkshake combination platter all over nude carhop Wanda (Tara Stroheimer). Bobby's sidekick Greg (Dennis Bowen) lands in the hospital after an attempt to devour a huge submarine sandwich leaves him with lockjaw. The Kansas City Kings Glitter Girls cheerleaders shake themselves silly during an infernal disco dance number.

Dana Gladstone, as cruiser-bruiser Officer Al Zass, pulls off the scary cop part well. Cynthia Wood, *Playboy*'s 1974 Playmate of the Year, delivers on the promise of her playing a character named Moon. Di Ann Monaco is dangerously alluring as the mysterious Motorcycle Girl. Also, Chooch rules.

Virgin High [1991]

DIR. RICHARD GABAI; W/RICHARD GABAI, TRACY DALI, BURT WARD

CATHOLIC GIRLS' SCHOOL ▪ VIRGINS ▪ NERDS ▪ PREGNANT NUN

In *Virgin High*, writer-director-star Richard Gabai does for Catholic girls' academia what he did for college frat life in his *Assault of the Party Nerds* movies. He turns the subject into *USA Up All Night* rerun fodder that's utterly unimaginable in any other context.

As usual, Gabai dons his "nerd" costume (i.e., eyeglasses) as Jerry Kaminski. Tracy Dali costars as his girlfriend, Christy Murphy. At the time of filming, Gabai was twenty-seven and Dali was twenty-five. Under micro-budget lighting, both actors look even older. Naturally, Jerry and Christy are passed off as high-school sweethearts.

Due to a screwup, Jerry delivers Christy home past curfew, and her hothead pop (Burt Ward) ships her off for correction to nun-run boarding school the Academy of the Blessed Virgin. Once there, Christy tangles with wicked dormitory queen bee Kathleen, played to the hilt by horror flick scream queen and frequent Gabi coconspirator Linnea Quigley. The esteemed Ms. Quigley was thirty-three at the time.

Virgin High's comedy largely concerns Jerry donning priest's vestments and attempting to penetrate the Academy as Father Güüs ("It's Swedish!"). Not one to waste wardrobe, Gabai retained the same frock—and premise—for his follow-up, *Hot Under the Collar* (1992).

The Virgin Queen of St. Francis High [1987]

DIR. FRANCESCO LUCENTE; W/STACY CHRISTENSEN, JOSEPH R. STRAFACE, LEE BARRINGER

VIRGIN ▪ NERD ▪ CATHOLICS ▪ SEXUAL BET ▪ LAKESIDE RESORT ▪ SYNTH-POP

A late entry into both the 1980s teen sex canon and the Canadian-tax-shelter filmmaking boom (*Porky*'s, anyone?), *The Virgin Queen of St. Francis High* at least takes place in the nation *National Lampoon* scribe Anne Beats once labeled "the [R-word for "mentally challenged"] giant to our north." Finally, a little honesty in lakefronts has arrived!

We know we are in Canada straightaway, because the high school characters openly hang out in a bar. They casually down Mooseheads and Molsons as though they were downing malteds at Pop's Chock'lit Shop in Riverdale. The Great White North's legal drinking age remained eighteen long after the U.S. went "uncool" about it.

Among the saloon regulars are nerdy Mike (Josef R. Straface) and studly Randy (Lee Barringer). When peppy blonde class queen Diane (Stacy Christensen) sashays into the barroom, Randy snarls, "There she is, the Virgin Queen of St. Francis High. Know what she reminds me of? The Matterhorn. She's never been conquered and she never will." As only makes sense, Mike bets Randy $2,000 that he'll be the first explorer to scale Diane's maiden peak.

This plot may seem like an '80s teen flick staple, but the premise of a bet hinging on some mook betting he can score with an unattainable girl didn't really run completely rampant until the late '90s with *10 Things I Hate About You* (1999), *She's All That* (1999), and assorted knockoffs. Maybe Hollywood screenwriters were reading the back of the *Virgin Queen* VHS box cover for plot inspiration. Nobody took anything else from this muddy-sounding, unprofessionally acted snooze.

On the plus side, Stacy Christensen in the title role packs more depth into her character than necessary. Also, Mike dons a welder's mask and claims to be "an Elephant Man" whom the Virgin Queen is dating out of charity (she's, of course, not really dating anybody). That's the movie's one good joke.

Vision Quest [1985]

DIR. HAROLD BECKER; W/MATTHEW MODINE, LINDA FIORENTINO, MICHAEL SCHOEFFLING, MADONNA

WRESTLING ▭ OLDER WOMAN ▭ VIRGIN ▭ MINIMUM WAGE JOB ▭ THE BIG MATCH

One of the most enduring and affable coming-of-age films of its era, *Vision Quest* is also a sports classic. Though not exactly a teen sex *comedy*—it's included as an honorary visitor to the locker room of teen movie hell.

High school wrestler Louden Swain (Matthew Modine) is fixated on beating the state champion, at least until Carla (Linda Fiorentino), a sultry drifter in her twenties, shows up to rent a spare bedroom in his family home. After that, Louden is fixated both on winning the big match *and* on falling in love with Carla.

Modine makes a great hero, and Fiorentino exudes a vivid worldliness mixed with intriguing sad-eyed mystery. Ronny Cox, as Modine's dad who never recovered after losing the family farm and his wife, is moving and memorable. Invigorating comedic moments come from Louden's fellow wrestler Kuch (Michael Schoeffling), who sports a Mohawk haircut and proclaims himself the hero's "half-Indian spiritual advisor." Kuch teaches Louden about the Native American concept of a "vision quest," which the two athletes apply to their training methods.

Vision Quest takes place in the unusual setting of Spokane, Washington, where Louden works after school as a hotel bellhop. Much care went into making the movie reflect the authenticity of lower-middle-class reality at the time, drawing from the 1979 Terry Davis novel on which the movie is based.

Possibly even more meticulous attention went into making the *Vision Quest* soundtrack match what actual teenagers listened to in 1985. Madonna makes two cameos as a barroom singer. She belts out two numbers that went on to become Top 40 and MTV monsters—the ballad "Crazy for You" and the rocker "Gambler." As you might expect, she's MX-missile-level charismatic.

The rest of the soundtrack accurately simulates a mixtape that a real-life Louden may well have given to a real-life Carla. The movie opens with Louden running to "Only the Young" by Journey. When Louden comes back from bad news to break a personal record in the gym, the thrilling moment is perfectly set to "Change" by John Waite. From there, the song roster incorporates heavy metal ("Hungry for Heaven" by Dio), new wave dance pop ("No More Words" by Berlin), Euro-synth sophistication ("Shout to the Top" by Style Council), arena stomp ("I'll Fall in Love Again" by Sammy Hagar), and a jock jam supreme that was just waiting to be discovered ("Lunatic Fringe" by Red Rider). This is the sort of musical mixed bag that defined adolescence when music was mostly discovered by endlessly spinning the radio dial.

Davis ended the *Vision Quest* novel on a surprising note: after a rousing lead-up to the final match, Louden takes the mat against his white whale of an opponent as the crowd roars—and that's it. We don't know if he wins or loses: What matters is he completed his vision quest. No movie studio could have possibly allowed a teen sports movie to go out on that enigmatic note, so we see Louden pin the state champ while Carla watches from the side. The movie clearly implies that she'll be slipping out of the gym right afterward and rolling on to wherever life takes her next. Even that degree of heartbreak was daring, though, and sends *Vision Quest* out on top.

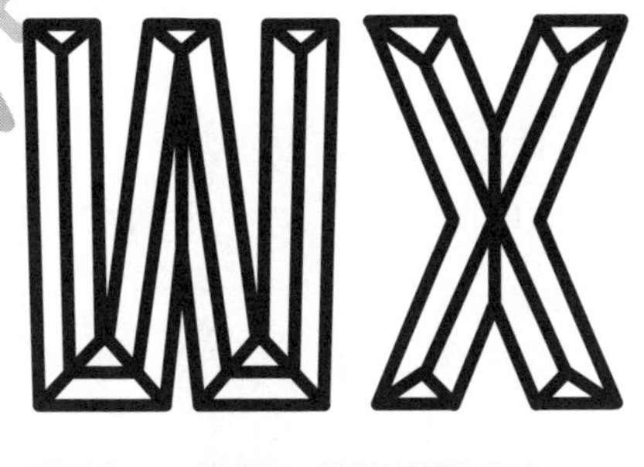
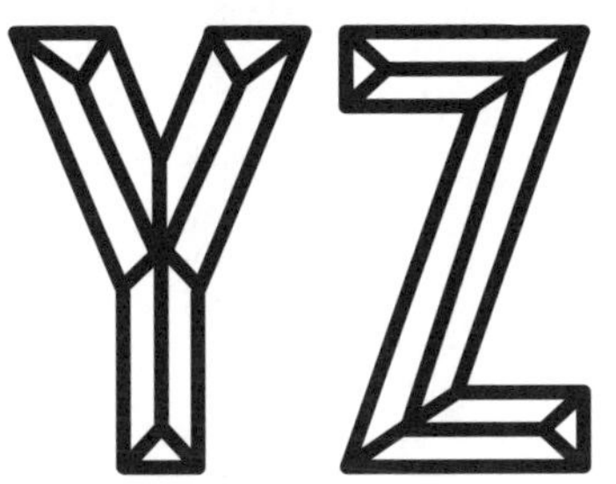

Wacko · Weekend Pass · Weird Science
Welcome to 18 · Where the Boys Are
Where the Boys Are '84
The Wild Life · Wildest Dreams · Wimps
Young Gangs From Wildwood High
The Young Graduates · Young Lust
Zapped! · Zapped Again! · Zero for
Conduct The Zoo Gang · Zuma Beach

Wacko [1982]

DIR. GREYDON CLARK; W/JOE DON BAKER, JULIA DUFFY, ELIZABETH DAILY, ANDREW DICE CLAY

PROM · SLASHER PARODY · ITALIAN STEREOTYPES

Five years after *Satan's Cheerleaders* (1977) and just before *Joysticks* (1983), director Greydon Clark helmed this *Airplane!*-style teen horror send-up that ranks just below *Student Bodies* (1981), right alongside *Pandemonium* (1982), and way above *Class Reunion* (1982). When planning a film festival, show those movies in that order.

Julia Duffy of TV's *Newhart* stars as virginal Mary, a high schooler prepping to attend the Halloween night Pumpkin Prom with a date named Norman Bates (Scott McGinnis). Thirteen years earlier, Mary witnessed her sister fall prey to the pumpkin-headed "Lawnmower Killer"; guess who bolted from the local loony bin just in time for the big dance?

The jokes are relentless. Even when *Wacko*'s gags miss, it's on the level of Jeff Altman playing a character called "Harry Palms," so no complaints here. Andrew Dice Clay does what he does, hilariously, as Tony Schlongini (Dice's improvised Tony Schlongini doo-wop theme is quite an experience). Elizabeth "E. G." Daily (*Valley Girl*) is one of the younger faces in a gruff-and-tumble cast including Joe Don Baker (*Walking Tall*), Stella Stevens (*The Nutty Professor*), George Kennedy (*Cool Hand Luke*), and Charles Napier (*Harry, Cherry & Raquel!*). If *Wacko* itself were just one gray hair more self-aware, it would contain a wisecrack about the per diem Greydon Clark had to shell out to the cast for Geritol.

Weekend Pass [1984]

DIR. LAWRENCE BASOFF; W/PATRICK HOUSER, CHIP MCALLISTER, HILARY SHEPARD, PHIL HARTMAN

SHORE LEAVE · NERD · VIRGIN · AEROBICS · STRIP CLUB · MOTEL · PUNKS

Weekend Pass is the most notable U.S. Navy spin on the teen sex comedy genre. A crew of wet-behind-the-zippers swabbies hits Hollywood on a 72-hour break from their San Diego naval base. While each sailor has his own plan of

Clockwise from top: *Promotional 8 x 10 for* Up the Creek *(1985), a different set of fraternity paddles;* Weird Science *(1985)—"She's alive!";* The Young Graduates *(1971), summa cum laude, the commencement of teen make-out genre.*

action, all involve partying with female civilians. Blond hunk Webster (Patrick Hill) and regulation black pal "Bunker" Hill (Chip McAllister) track down a couple of old flames. Ship cutup Fricker (D. W. Brown) aims to make ladies loopy while performing as a stand-up comic. Nerdy bespectacled virgin Lester (Peter Ellenstein) just aims to get his barnacles blasted.

Weekend Pass plays out like a generic-malt-liquor-budget Los Angeles 1984 travelogue with some agreeably sleazy stops along the way. Viewers will visit a strip club, a massage parlor, and an aerobics studio; pass by some adult bookstores and porn theater marquees; and arrive at Venice Beach just in time for colorful punk rockers to show up. Finally they reach a comedy club where the emcee is future *SNL* legend Phil Hartman.

Nothing really interesting or funny happens in *Weekend Pass*, but the footage is all there. Somehow, this movie earned more than ten times its budget while playing in theaters. Anchors aweigh, somebody.

WEIRD SCIENCE [1985]

DIR. JOHN HUGHES; W/ANTHONY MICHAEL HALL, ILAN MITCHELL-SMITH, KELLY LEBROCK, BILL PAXTON

VIRGINS ▣ BULLIES ▣ DREAM GIRL ▣ SCIENCE ▣ HACKERS ▣ MUTANT BIKERS

With *Weird Science*, writer-director John Hughes took a momentary breath between Molly Ringwald fetish exercises *The Breakfast Club* (1985) and *Pretty in Pink* (1986) to unleash the closest cinematic equivalent to his outrageously funny *National Lampoon* short stories "My Penis" and "My Vagina." *Weird Science* is not as good or as dirty as those stunners, but the movie presents sex-on-the-brains, jerk-off jokes galore, a shit monster, and Michael Berryman of *The Hills Have Eyes* (1977) as a Satan-spawned motorcycle maniac.

Highly skilled high school computer dorks Gary (Anthony Michael Hall) and Wyatt (Ilan Mitchell-Smith) catch *Frankenstein* on TV and conspire to apply their hacker powers to the highest purpose conceivable: their boners. Concocting their notion of a "perfect woman" online, the pent-up doofs hack a government computer, hook electrodes to a Barbie doll, and...whoomp, there she is.

English supermodel Kelly LeBrock materializes as Lisa, Gary and Wyatt's wet-dream-by-committee. In a turn the nerds couldn't have foreseen, however, the savvy, sophisticated, and fully self-realized Lisa also embodies "dangerously sexy." To a commendable degree, *Weird Science* subverts the expectations of both the horny hackers and its intended audience. The movie's woman of wonders is no mere Frankenstein's fuck doll, but a perilous force of chaotic human potential.

Lisa prompts Gary and Wyatt to charge forward into their most debilitating sources of fear: football team bullies Ian (Robert Downey Jr.) and Max (Robert Rusler); Wyatt's spectacularly ass-holic older brother Chet (Bill Paxton); and, most perilous of all, female classmates Deb (Suzanne Snyder) and Hilly (Judie Aronson). In a moment of expertly executed cringe humor, cigarette-puffing Lisa asks Gary's mother, "Have you ever wondered how sad it is that your son's only sexual outlet is tossing off to magazines in the bathroom?" In panicked response, Gary blurts, "I was just combing my hair!"

Before her work is done, Lisa turns Chet into an immobile fecal frog creature and initiates a mighty parent-free house party to end them all, proclaiming, "There's going to be sex, drugs, rock 'n' roll, chips, dips, chains, whips! Just a couple of hundred kids running around in their underwear, acting like complete animals!" The climactic blowout proves so cataclysmic that it conjures mutant bikers from hell and possibly Armageddon itself—in a PG-13 kind of way.

Lessons are soon learned. The apocalyptic showdown smacks too much of producer Joel Silver's erstwhile mega-budget action endeavors (*Predator*, *Die Hard*), so all that's in order remains in order. Whatever. *Weird Science* is frequently laugh-out-loud funny, and almost the entire cast performs perfectly. LeBrock and Paxton, in particular, elevate their characters to icon status. As in *The Wild Life* (1984), the rub remains Ilan Mitchell-Smith, with his squeaky-hinge voice and general air of undescended testicles.

Oingo Boingo's title track never charted, but new wave radio stations like L.A.'s KROQ and Long Island's WLIR played it repeatedly, turning the song into an '80s hit of unique distinction. A spin-off TV series on the USA Network, with Vanessa Angel (*Kingpin*) in the role of Lisa, ran for eighty-eight episodes between 1994 and 1998. That the show has been so largely forgotten seems pretty weird and quite unscientific.

Welcome to 18 [1986]

aka Summer Release

DIR. TERRY CARR; W/COURTNEY THORNE-SMITH, MARISKA HARGITAY, JOANN WILLETTE

SUMMER JOBS ▪ DUDE RANCH ▪ VIRGINS ▪ SHOWER SCENE ▪ WEED

Three friends turn eighteen and are sprung from high school. Together, they spend the months before college working on a dude ranch where they get a little wasted, get a little laid. This PG-13 coming-of-age-in-the-great-outdoors saga racked up a brief but notable cult following due multiple cable airings. Scrappy dudette Mariska Hargitay eventually became a household name via TV's *Law & Order: Special Victims Unit*, although Courtney Thorne-Smith was *Welcome to 18*'s first breakout star as a result of *Melrose Place*. Costar JoAnn Willette has worked consistently as a character actress.

If only they could reunite on a dude ranch somewhere for a movie called *Welcome to 48*. Alas, this movie remains the sole writer and director credit of Terry Carr, who died in 2005. Carr also served as production manager on kid-in-the-walls TV-movie *Bad Ronald* (1974), the ludicrous Dino De Laurentiis version of *King Kong* (1976), the franchise-ending *The Bad News Bears Got to Japan* (1978), and the ultimate rockin' New Year's Eve comedy, *Get Crazy* (1983).

Where the Boys Are [1960]

DIR. HENRY LEVIN; W/DOLORES HART, GEORGE HAMILTON

SPRING BREAK ▪ VIRGINS ▪ ROCK BAND

The very first teen sex comedy as we came to know teen sex comedies debuted huge in 1960, establishing at least twenty archetypal plot components for all teen sex comedies to follow. Let us count the active ingredients:

This MGM megahit starts when four decidedly different college coeds (1) flee their frozen campus (2) for the swingin' shenanigans (3) of spring break (4) in Fort Lauderdale, Florida (5). Once there, the gung-ho party girl (6), the sheltered neurotic (7), the clumsy darling (8), and the sassy, brassy songbird (9), who's played by an actual pop star (10), meet up with a handsome rich guy (11), a slightly bumbling romantic (12), and a zany joker (13) who's also a musician (14). Romance blooms (15), jokes get pulled (16), heartbreak happens (17), and everyone involved learns something (18), including, for a select few, what actual intercourse feels like (19). The title song became a mammoth worldwide hit (20).

That elemental twenty-point formula, widely and deeply imitated ever since, was laid out by *Where the Boys Are* a solid quarter-century—and a million years culturally—before the likes of *Spring Break* (1983), *Fraternity Vacation* (1985), and *Lauderdale* (1989).

Where the Boys Are '84 [1984]

DIR. HY AVERBACK; W/LISA HARTMAN, LORNA LUFT, LYNN-HOLLY JOHNSON, WENDY SCHAAL

SPRING BREAK ▪ THE BIG HOT BOD CONTEST ▪ BIKINIS ▪ FLASHING ▪ MALE SEX DOLL

The original *Where the Boys Are* (1960) crystallized a moment of baby boomer perfection—in Technicolor and CinemaScope—with its tale of northeastern coeds hitting Fort Lauderdale for spring break. The landmark hit signaled the brewing sexual revolution by addressing such previously taboo topics as premarital relations, affairs with older men, and even date rape. Costar Connie Francis scored an immortal pop standard with the soaring title ballad.

Where the Boys Are '84 features Lorna Luft—Judy Garland's non-Liza daughter—participating in a "hot-bod contest." Lorna, age thirty-two during filming, costars as one of the updated romp's pretend college girls going wild, alongside similarly suspect-in-the-age-department Wendy Schaal (thirty), Lynn-Holly Johnson (twenty-six), and top-billed Lisa Hartman (twenty-seven). They go to Fort Lauderdale, where Lisa ends up in a love triangle with a classical pianist and a dipshit rocker. Freakishly chaste partying rules the beach until hundreds of spring breakers crash a formal banquet at the mansion of one girl's snooty aunt.

Except for the title, nothing connects *Where the Boys Are '84* to its predecessor, nor is there sufficient sex appeal to play into the drooling hopes of its youth audience. Metaphorically, the most risqué moment occurs when a male blowup doll deflates after Lisa bites it too hard on the nipple.

In reality, *Where the Boys Are '84* comes off as the botched fever dream of executive producer Allan Carr, the delightfully flamboyant, corporeally overstuffed Hollywood Nero type who shepherded *Grease* from Broadway to the big screen in the late 1970s with blockbuster results. He then promptly annihilated his ensuing mogul status by backing the Village People boondoggle *Can't Stop the Music* (1980). *Where the Boys Are '84* didn't turn that around for him.

THE WILD LIFE [1984]

DIR. ART LINSON; W/CHRIS PENN, ERIC STOLTZ, LEA THOMPSON, ILAN MITCHELL-SMITH

PARTY ANIMAL ▪ NEW WAVE ▪ PUNK ▪ HEAVY METAL ▪ VIETNAM VET

The Wild Life is to *Fast Times at Ridgemont High* (1982) as *Shock Treatment* (1981) is to *The Rocky Horror Picture Show* (1975); an indirect follow-up to a surprise classic youth culture phenomenon. In each case, Hollywood studios gave the creators of the initial films carte blanche for a sequel. Both filmmakers delivered undercooked, less accessible variations on the originals. As a result, both *Shock Treatment* and *The Wild Life* bombed and were fast forgotten, though each abandoned stepchild has its merits.

Fast Times screenwriter Cameron Crowe deemed his script for *The Wild Life* a "spiritual sequel" to his breakthrough effort. The movie inhabits the same SoCal suburban haze, dealing with life outside of high school, hanging out, and the emergence of adult concerns. All the kids work typical teenager jobs, in a touch that the John Hughes films would soon eliminate from teen movies by focusing on the domestic lives of pampered brats.

Nice guy Bill Conrad (Eric Stoltz) oversees the lanes at a bowling alley with best bud Tommy Drake (Chris Penn). This peroxide blonde, perpetually wasted, party-hearty wildman and wrestling team beast is modeled so exactly on Jeff Spicoli that he could only be played by Sean Penn's brother. Anita (Lea Thompson) slings sugar at an all-night donut shop. Punk-coifed Eileen (Jenny Wright) hustles new wave fashions at the mall. Only Bill's kid brother Jim (Ilan Mitchell-Smith) is unemployed, but he's only fifteen and busily obsessed with the Vietnam War.

The loose-limbed plot puts each character on a path toward a housewarming bash at Bill's apartment. Bill is the first among his peers to move out of his parents' house, landing in a singles complex where comely flight attendants hang out en masse by the pool. Anita, Bill's ex, contends with David (Hart Bochner), a married, semi-psycho cop with whom she's having an affair. Eileen swats off her smitten boss Harry (Rick Moranis). Jim takes a pal to see brain-bombed 'Nam vet Charlie (Randy Quaid), who, in a shock scene out of a 1930s narcotic scare film, roars at the boys as he shoots dope on his toilet ("Everything about that guy is cool!" the other kid says). Drake, meanwhile, meticulously assembles the rager to end all ragers—but first he and his boys stop at a strip club to catch the bazooka-impact burlesque stylings of Russ Meyer movie glamazon Kitten Natividad.

The climactic blowout falls somewhere between the riots of other '80s comedies and realistic high school parties where too much stuff gets broken. Drake and his pals expand the dance floor by knocking down a wall to open up the (occupied) apartment next door. Lee Ving, front-man of punk marauders Fear, is very funny as Bill's brew-guzzling cable guy. Rolling Stone Ron Wood inexplicably turns up among the revelers, a relic from Cameron Crowe's years as a *Rolling Stone* journalist. The next morning, the apartment complex manager looks around at the debris, and departs after one word: "Lawsuit."

Ultimately, *The Wild Life* falls short of its title, but not by much. The music score by Eddie Van Halen is a scorcher. Seek out the instrumental "Donut City." Chris Penn is a hoot, too, imitating Spicoli as literally only a brother can; for five seconds or so his catchphrase—"It's casual!"—became enough of a thing that it turned up as a caption in my sophomore yearbook.

WILDEST DREAMS [1990]
aka BIKINI GENIE

DIR. CHUCK VINCENT; W/JAMES DAVIES, HEIDI PAINE, TRACEY ADAMS, SCOTT BAKER

NERD ▪ GENIE ▪ VIRGIN ▪ HAREM ▪ HORNY HOUSEWIFE ▪ EVIL PROFESSOR

Exploitation director Chuck Vincent pumped out four films in 1990, the year before AIDS took him from us at age fifty-one. Of those, *Wildest Dreams* comes closest in spirit to his most vibrant teen sex comedies (*Preppies, Wimps*). The action follows young Bobby Delaney (James Davies), a dorkadocious antique shop employee who takes a moment off from rubbing himself to rub an old lamp. A sexy blonde spirit with the engagingly dumb name Dancee (Heidi Paine) escapes the artifact after a 2,000-year imprisonment, and immediately offers Bobby three requisite wishes. The movie's original and infinitely superior title was *Bikini Genie*.

Longing only for his one perfect girl, Bobby stumbles through a series of carnal crack-ups before he recognizes that Joan Peabody (Tracey Adams), his sweet, shy, brick-house-built coworker has had a crush on him the whole time. The actors are fine, especially erstwhile porn starlet Tracey Adams as the busting-to-bloom wallflower. Vincent's direction is also on the money, but as magical-sex-sprite farces go, *Wildest Dream* doesn't really hold a 2,000-year-old lamp to its main 1990 competition, the lusty leprechaun opus *Getting Lucky*.

WIMPS [1986]

DIR. CHUCK VINCENT; W/LOUIE BONANNO, TRACEY ADAMS, JIM ABELE

VIRGIN ▪ NERDS ▪ FRAT ▪ INITIATION ▪ SECRET ADMIRER ▪ STRIP CLUB

From its first frame, *Wimps* is unmistakably the work of porn-director-turned-teen-exploitation-visionary Chuck Vincent. Petite, distressed, arch-browed Francis (Louis Bonanno) appears in a freeze-frame close-up while several opening credits run and a crowd jeers on the soundtrack. Such weirdness immediately begets more such strangeness.

Suddenly, Francis launches into a monologue about the futility of existence, and the camera pulls back to reveal him suspended in his tighty-whities above a table with other frat pledges about to endure a sadistic swinging spaghetti-consumption initiation rite.

A series of montages follows, masterfully edited by Vincent to rapidly convey the amusing and appalling reality of Francis's condition; he can't shit in peace, he can't jack off in peace, he *can* be forced to don the garments of a classic English maid and serve food to the upperclassmen, and so on. Vincent's montage rhythm never abates. Whether wittingly or not, the director taps into the death knell of humanity's post-MTV attention span. *Wimps* is essentially a series of quick-cut highlights, enhanced musically either by consciously trumped-up college marching band bombast or a cheapo synthesizer approximation of romantic melodies.

Unique mad genius filmmaking style aside, *Wimps* is a dead-on embodiment of the circa-1986 snuck-into-theaters-just-before-VHS teen romp. The flick notably predates Steve Martin's *Roxanne* (1987) in reworking *Cyrano de Bergerac* in a modern setting. Neurotic Francis wins protection and friendship from his big-man-on-campus roommate Charles (Jim Abele) by writing love letters for him to a sophisticated coed named, you guessed it, Roxanne.

Among the most admirable hallmarks of the Chuck Vincent canon is how the director provided the starlets from his X-rated films with shots at *Wimps*-level legitimate acting gigs. For example, Roxanne is played here by the talented, glamorous X-rated siren Tracey Adams, credited as Deborah Blaisdell.

As Francis's sexual education in the film often involves professionals, several porn stars enjoy shining R-rated moments. Chief among them is Jane Hamilton, aka Veronica Hart, a riot as a prostitute in a fancy restaurant who orders Froot Loops and douses them with beer. Also on hand is sex activist Annie Sprinkle as a strip-club peeler who yanks off Francis's hardworking Fruit of the Looms and actually finds the skid marks therein to be cute. A wimp can dream, can't he?

Young Gangs From Wildwood High [1978]

aka Team-Mates

DIR. STEVEN JACOBSON; W/KAREN CORRADO, MAX GOFF, JAMES SPADER, ESTELLE GETTY

GIRL ON THE FOOTBALL TEAM ▣ VIRGIN ▣ LOCKER ROOM ▣ HOUSE PARTY

After a post-drive-in drop into utter obscurity, 1978's *Team-Mates* made its way back to theaters in 1983 as *Young Gangs From Wildwood High*. There are no gangs, young or otherwise, in *Young Gangs*. Instead, the movie is about peppy student Vicki (Karen Corrado) catching her quarterback boyfriend cheating on her, and exacting her revenge by becoming the first female member of Wildwood High's football squad.

Young Gangs requires a description beneath "low-budget," beneath "amateur," and perhaps even beneath "possible." Consider that a bookshelf in the back of a classroom is actually just wallpaper with images of books on it. Consider that the cast members seem to flub more lines of dialogue than they get right. Just don't consider not seeing *Young Gangs From Wildwood High*. Anything this insane is a must!

James Spader and Estelle Getty completists will be interested in witnessing their idols' respective motion picture debuts as good-time dude Jimmy and a priggish history instructor simply billed as "Teacher." The pair would reunite in *Mannequin* (1987). On that set, do you think they reminisced about good ol' *Wildwood High*?

The Young Graduates

[1971]

DIR. ROBERT ANDERSON; W/PATRICIA WYMER, BRUNO KIRBY, DENNIS CHRISTOPHER, JENNIFER RITT

HIPPIES ▣ BIKERS ▣ ACID ROCK ▣ CUSTOM VAN ▣ PREGNANCY ▣ DUNE BUGGIES

The Young Graduates primarily concerns one young graduate-to-be, Mindy Evans (Patricia Wymer). Worried that she's become pregnant by her married teacher (Steven Stewart), Mindy and gal pal Sandy (Marly Holiday) dune-buggy off to Big Sur. Amidst glorious sun-soaked scenery and flashback-inspiring early-'70s fashions, the girls tangle with bikers and skinny-dip with hippies. The psychedelic far-outness explodes into dimensions that cannot be measured.

Wonderfully dated, *The Young Graduates* impressively balances a stone groove vibe with a rumbling air of a post-Altamont bummer trip. The bikers pummel flower minstrel Pan (Dennis Christopher) to a floppy-hatted pulp, and, before the upbeat conclusion, a full-blown revolutionary riot occurs. Even fun times had to be heavy back then. A bazillion extra points go to the tagline: "The hot pants generation is loose!"

YOUNG LUST [1984]

DIR. GARY WEIS; W/FRAN DRESCHER, MEWS SMALL, TERRY KISER, MARY WORONOV

YOUNGSTERS ▣ LUSTFULNESS

Young Lust is an unholy Holy Grail among 1980s teen sex comedies, a genuinely lost film directed by early-era *Saturday Night Live*'s brilliant documentary-short maker Gary Weis. Paramount reportedly put *Young Lust* into production as early as 1981, but the finished product may not have ever been delivered. An elite cadre of cinematic seekers have pursued the truth about *Young Lust* ever since.

Loin-tingling, laugh-launching *Young Lust* poster art depicts a shapely female from behind with the film's title on her back. She passionately embraces and sucks face with multiple partners, at least one of which is a donkey. Hee-*haw!*

Fran Drescher headlines with support from cult stars on the high order of Mary Woronov (Principal Togar in *Rock 'n' Roll High School*), Dey Young (Kate Rambeau in *Rock 'n' Roll High School*), and Terry Kiser (Bernie in *Weekend at Bernie's*). The catch is that *Young Lust* may be a mere legend. Still, like that aforementioned Grail, the Arthurian quest to unearth it continues.

ZAPPED! [1982]

DIR. ROBERT J. ROSENTHAL; W/SCOTT BAIO, WILLIE AAMES, FELICE SCHACHTER, HEATHER THOMAS, SCATMAN CROTHERS

NERDS ▣ SUPERPOWERS ▣ PRANKS ▣ WEED ▣ EDDIE DEEZEN

Zapped! is the telekinetic teenage T&A rampage comedy toward which all previous telekinetic teenage T&A rampage comedies led and from which all subsequent telekinetic teenage T&A rampage comedies have proceeded. It's a short list, but that's beside the point. What matters here is simply the greatness.

With perfect stupidity, *Zapped!* spins the sci-fi-tickled saga of Scott Baio as Barney Springboro, a high school science geek who develops the power to move objects with his mind after an accidental lab explosion. Gag by gag, in one scene after another of Baio cocking his eyebrow and sending shit flying around the room, *Zapped!* revels in all the slapstick and smutty possibilities of its premise. Few films in teen movie hell could be said to more deeply and directly respect their audience.

The phenomena starts with Barney slamming doors from across a room and unfurling a classroom map from his desk because he doesn't want to stand up and reveal his boner. Things escalate when Barney manipulates baseballs during the Big Game; spins Tilt-A-Whirl cars at an amusement park to make drunken bullies puke; and pops the buttons off a number of blouses.

The movie's apocalyptic prom sequence delivers laughter of appropriately Armageddon-size proportions. This climax is a sprawling, fearless parody of the teen horror classic *Carrie*, tracking Barney as he unleashes his mind magic against the assembled faculty and students. While poor Carrie was cruelly doused onstage with a bucket of pig's blood, Barney is conked on the noggin with a watermelon, and ends up with a bra stuck to his face. The prurient possibilities of Barney's powers, of course, served as *Zapped!*'s big selling point. The movie promised on-screen gratification to leering young males who grew up tantalized by the dress-penetrating possibilities of the X-ray specs advertised in comic books—and then got burned by the reality of ordering them. Consequently, the whole thrust of *Zapped!* has aged about as well as any actual pair of X-ray specs anybody ever really bought.

Beyond the obviously unacceptable tearing off of clothes by invisible forces (an awful idea in the real world that maybe induced laughter because it was so awful—and impossible), the rest of *Zapped!* is a riot. One monumentally dumb comic conceit after another lands a direct depth-charge to the funny bone, ranging from underwater mice in deep-sea diving suits, an out-

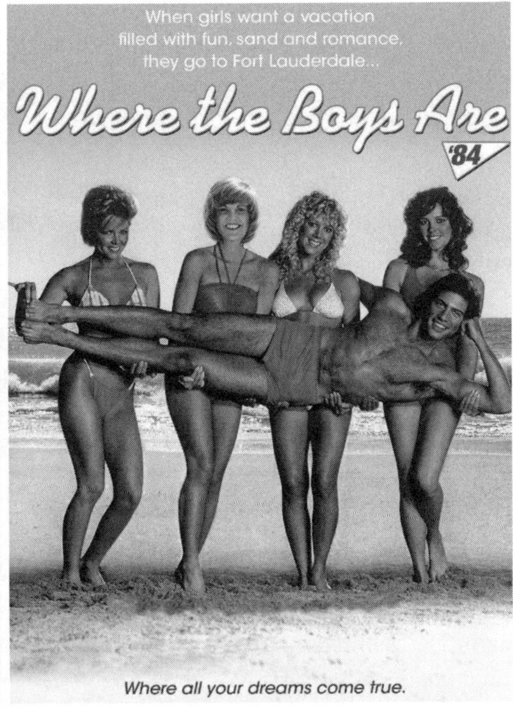

Clockwise from top left: *Spicoli's brother Chris Penn in Cameron Crowe's* Fast Times *follow-up,* The Wild Life *(1984);* Where the Boys Are '84 (1984)*, is not where a watchable movie* is; Zapped! *(1982), telekinetic teen mayhem played for lust and laughs.*

of-nowhere *Star Trek* spoof set in a fish tank, and Barney chasing off exorcist priests with a floating ventriloquist's dummy.

The cast sells it without mercy, beginning with Baio in his final stretch as Fonzie's cousin Chachi on *Happy Days*. His high-rolling best bud Peyton is played by Willie Aames, shortly after winding up his run as Tommy Bradshaw on TV's *Eight Is Enough*. Barney's bookworm love interest Bernadette is Felice Schachter, previously best known as Nancy, one of the first-season-only characters alongside Molly Ringwald on *The Facts of Life*. Robert Mandan, aka Chester Tate on *Soap* from 1977 to 1981, highlights the movie's main subplot as horny high school principal Walter J. Coolidge. Scatman Crothers absolutely slays as beleaguered gym coach Dexter Jones, a part he clearly had a blast playing. Dexter's wife, who shoots salamis at him from a bazooka during a pot-induced hallucination, is LaWanda Page, Redd Foxx's hothead church-lady nemesis Aunt Esther on *Sanford and Son*.

Heather Thomas, who plays the school's resident blonde bombshell, parlayed *Zapped!* into a costarring run on TV's *The Fall Guy*. During the end credits, an on-screen declaration makes clear that a body double "was used for Miss Thomas in her nude scene and photograph." Just so everybody knows.

Merritt Butrick appears sporadically as Gary Cooter, a goombah version of his new wave Johnny Slash from *Square Pegs*, the CBS sitcom about first-year high school outcasts that premiered the same month *Zapped!* opened in theaters. In a category of his own, as always, über-nerd Eddie Deezen cameos unforgettably as a roulette player clad in a T-shirt that declares him "God's Gift to Women."

Baio and Aames continued as a comedy team on TV throughout the 1980s via the series *Charles in Charge*. Each played essentially his same *Zapped!* role, with Baio as a studious nice guy and Aames as a happy-go-plucky hedonist. Why mess with perfection?

Director Robert J. Rosenthal brings quite a teensploitation pedigree to proceedings, having served as second unit director on the *The Pom Pom Girls* (1976), scripted *The Van* (1977), and then both written and directed *Malibu Beach* (1978). He transitions here into the 1980s exceptionally well.

ZAPPED AGAIN! [1990]

DIRS. DOUG CAMPBELL, JAKE HOOKER; W/TODD ERIC ANDREWS, KELLI WILLIAMS, LINDA BLAIR, LYLE ALZADO

NERDS ▫ JOCKS ▫ CHEERLEADERS ▫ SUPERPOWERS ▫ THE BIG RACE

After downing some deep-stashed bottles of Relaxo prune juice discovered in the Ralph Waldo Emerson High science lab, dorkus Kevin Matthew (Todd Eric Andrews) develops the same top-popping telekinetic powers boasted by Emerson alumnus Barney Springboro (Scott Baio) in the 1982 classic *Zapped!*

The movie is terrible. Let's make that clear. It's not funny, it's not odd, and it's not even alleviated by an unquestionably enjoyable array of nameless student nudity. In addition, suffering through lead actor Todd Eric Andrews's flailing attempts to channel Robin Williams at his most antic will leave you feeling incredibly empty and sad. As noted cartoonist Greg Fiering (*Migraine Boy*) is fond of saying: "*Zapped* was good the first time, why do it again?"

Zapped Again! does deserve a half-cocked eyebrow of appreciation for stunt casting. Pro-football steroid fatality Lyle Alzado grunts effectively as a gym coach, while '70s superstarlet Linda Blair turns up as a hot home economics instructor and Karen Black is a saucy sub.

Zapped Again! is also weirdly committed to being a legitimate sequel. Much is made of Barney's mind-over-mammaries impact on Emerson High in the first movie. Sue Ann Langdon reprises her role as a teacher from the original. Blair further reveals that she was Baio-as-Barney's classmate, just before her skirt is magically blown upward to reveal fancy old-timey garters—and if that doesn't possess you and get your head spinning, make your own *Exorcist* joke.

Zero for Conduct [1933] aka Zéro de Conduite

DIR. JEAN VIGO; W/JEAN DASTÉ, ROBERT LE FLON, LOUIS LEFEBVRE

NERDS ▣ PRANKS ▣ FAKE-BEARDED DWARF

The French milestone *Zéro de conduite* is the movie that taught the world how to make teen comedies. This 44-minute film by French provocateur Jean Vigo contains no sex, per se, but plenty of epic pranks, cleverly mounted outrage, and adolescent blows against the empire of adults, laying down the first paving stones on the road to *Porky's* and *Revenge of the Nerds.*

At a strict boys' boarding school, three tough students—Caussat (Louis Lefebvre), Colin (Gilbert Pruchon), and Bruel (Constantin Goldstein-Kehler)—team up with brainy Tabard (Gérard de Bédarieux). Together they wage gag wars against the buzzkills in charge, especially the principal *du collège* (the single-named actor Delphin), a fake-bearded dwarf who seems to be in a permanent rage.

The gang says the word *shit*, enacts a colossal pillow fight, and even mock-crucifies a jerky faculty member by tying him to his bed and standing it upright so they can make fun of him. In real life, France banned the "subversive" *Zéro for Conduct* until 1946. That's thirteen years—just about the age of the heroes of the movie.

The Zoo Gang [1985]

DIRS. PEN DENSHAM, JOHN WATSON; W/JASON GEDRICK, TIFFANY HELM, MARC PRICE, JACKIE EARLE HALEY

ROCK CLUB ▣ FIXER-UPPER MONTAGE ▣ AEROBICS ▣ HOMELESS TEENS

Throughout the first half of the 1980s, homeless, runaway, and cast-off teens figured as a major public concern, inspiring earnest TV movies (*Off the Minnesota Strip* [1980], *The Children of Times Square* [1986]), art films starring Kevin Bacon as a young hustler who sells a soon-to-die boy to an old john (*Forty Deuce* [1982]), the acclaimed 1985 documentary *Streetwise,* and myriad episodes of *Donahue* and *Oprah.* Then came *The Zoo Gang,* which decided to have a little fun with the national tragedy.

Only a couple of the *Zoo Gang* kids are in fact homeless, but they solve their own problem by teaming up with bored townies to rent a beat-to-shit old nightclub called the Zoo from a hothead drunk named, yes, Leatherface (Ben Vereen). After a requisite new-wave fix-it-up montage, the Zoo reopens as a local youth center, rock 'n' roll hot spot, and indoor residence for underage drifters. The Zoo's success unfortunately also attracts the wrath of local thug clan the Donnelys, led by sinister, sneering Little Joe Donnely (Jackie Earle Haley).

Tensions accelerate to the level of slapstick warfare. After a requisite training montage, the Zoo gang defeats the Donnelys with thumbtacks, marbles, and other improvised weaponry. The good guys get to dance at the end.

Despite being shoddy and dull, *The Zoo Gang* stands as a milestone in cinema history as the first film to register the MPAA rating "PG-13." The commie-stomping teen action favorite *Red Dawn* (1984) actually reached theaters first, but *The Zoo Gang,* released about seven months later, will always count as the first motion picture to be given the mark that ruined movies forever.

Zuma Beach [1978]

DIR. LEE H. KATZIN; W/SUZANNE SOMERS, MICHAEL BIEHN, P. J. SOLES, ROSANNA ARQUETTE

BIKINIS ▣ LIFEGUARDS ▣ SURFERS ▣ MYSTERY BLONDE ▣ ROCK STAR

The NBC-made piffle *Zuma Beach* is a bouncing, flouncing relic of network broadcasting's "jiggle TV" era that stars no less abundant an eyeful of that moment than *Three's Company* shirt-stretcher Suzanne Somers. The movie itself is a pleasant summer trifle, with Suzanne as aging rock songbird Bonnie Katt (the actress was thirty-two at the time). She slips away for a solo day of seaside recuperation at the lush locale of the title, only to become enmeshed in the hassles of local teenage swimmers, surfers, and barely bikini-clad sunbathers. Some no-biggie consumption of marijuana also bespeaks *Zuma Beach*'s late-'70s pedigree.

However unmemorable *Zuma Beach* is plot-wise, the cast is like a grand finale drawing stars from throughout the many decades of decadence displayed in teen movie hell. Among Bonnie's young surfside admirers are Perry Lang (*Teen Lust*), Michael Biehn (*Hog Wild*), and Timothy Hutton (*Young Love, First Love*), while her dune-bunny protégés include Rosanna Arquette (*Gorp*), P. J. Soles (*Rock 'n' Roll High School*), Kimberly Beck (*Massacre at Central High*), and Tanya Roberts (*California Dreaming*). Seeing them flicker across the screen is like seeing a dream montage of countless nights lost at the drive-in, pressing rewind on the VCR, and mashing buttons on the basic cable box.

Then the coda: *Zuma Beach* aired just a few weeks before the 1978 horror landmark *Halloween* opened in theaters. Both films feature screenplays written by John Carpenter, who thereby reinvented the two genres that would define the adolescent moviegoing experience for the next decade and beyond. That's right, in 1978, John Carpenter was the world's oldest, and most prescient, teenager. What a scream!

The great Curtis Armstrong, manifesting Dudley "Booger" Dawson in Revenge of the Nerds II: Nerds in Paradise *(1987)—leaving us to burn in teen movie hell while pondering a conundrum for the ages. Illustration by Corinne Halbert.*

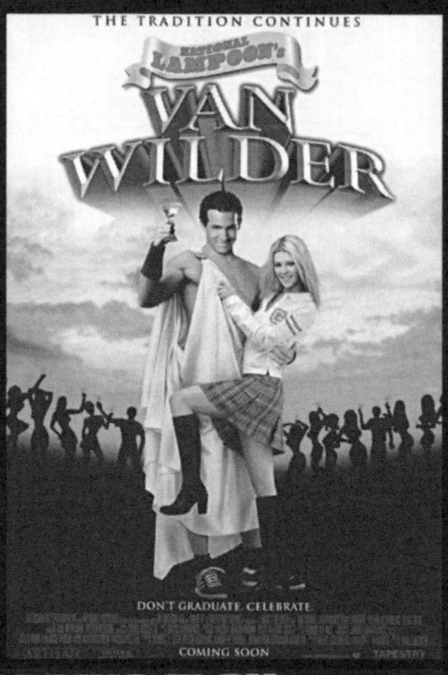

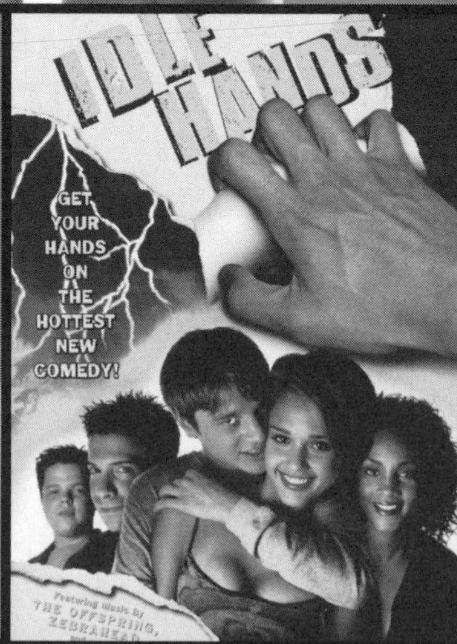

Clockwise from top left: National Lampoon's Van Wilder *(2002) juiced the mag's movie brand; pom-poms and masks in* Sugar & Spice *(2001); Emma Stone cutes hard in* Easy A *(2010); Kirsten Dunst and Mila Kunis in* Get Over It *(2001); a thumb up for* Idle Hands *(1999);* But I'm a Cheerleader *(1999)* satirically socks homophobia; *teenage dirtbags in Loser (2001); Dunst again in the great* Bring It On *(2000).*

Return to Teen Movie Hell
Retro Teen Sex Comedies of the 21st Century

By the end of the 1990s, rising wisps of 1980s nostalgia consolidated and hit gale force. That's what happens. Just consider that in 1973, *American Graffiti* asked, to the tune of millions of dollars, "Where were you in '62?" So with Generation X aging fast toward marriage-and-baby phases, the end-of-the-century cultural question became, "What did you *see* in '83?" The answer, of course, was slasher movies and teen sex comedies.

However, "it's all been done" cynicism ruled the Lollapalooza Decade, thereby eradicating the inherent all-around naiveté required by genres as dopey as slashers and teen sex. Still, nobody ever went broke peddling someone else's memories to the public. Thus, Hollywood adapted and churned out reconstituted takes on teen trash flicks of the recent past, creating booms still in the process of their own re-reinvention (and re-re-reconsumption).

Director Wes Craven and screenwriter Kevin Williamson's hyper-sentient *Scream* (1996)—originally titled *Scary Movie*—cleverly deconstructed slasher tropes in part by naming them along the way. Two all-star sequels followed, along with scads of imitators (*Disturbing Behavior* [1998], *I Know What You Did Last Summer* [1998], etc.), as well as, right on schedule, a 2015 MTV series.

In terms of teen sex comedies, the savvy, well-made *Can't Hardly Wait* (1998) emerged as the first '90s high school movie that was wholly aware of '80s high school movies. Come early 1999, *Varsity Blues* hit big with its whipped-cream bikini and teacher turned stripper, thereby tapping the keg in preparation for *American Pie* to gush forth. After *Pie* in 1999, the late-'90s/early-2000s revival of '80s-style teen sex comedies was on.

Visible semen jokes aside (thank you, *There's Something About Mary* [1998]), no true going back in time could actually take place. Societal attitudes had long since shifted away from the post-1970s practice of treating teenagers as junior-league adults. Teen audiences were now treated like extended-season children, presumably to be marketed toward and herded into theaters simply by pushing a series of preinstalled red stimulus buttons on their foreheads.

Some of the postmodern neo-*Porky's* rehashes worked, and some didn't. Nothing anarchic and unpredictable like a *King Frat* (1979) or a *Surf II* (1984)—or really, even a *Porky's*—arrived in the calculated and largely contrived bunch. But a mini-boom was measurable, thanks to the tremors that follow.

Can't Hardly Wait [1998]

A substantive "night-in-the-life" comedy about a high school graduation party gone amusingly berserk, *Can't Hardly Wait* is a real achievement. Writer-directors Deborah Kaplan and Harry Elfont commingle huge laughs with heartfelt moments by way of multiple "star is born" performances from a cast that includes Jennifer Love Hewitt, Seth Green, Lauren Ambrose, and Ethan Embry. Particular praise must go to the wordless, sticky-fingered work of Chris Owen as the running gag character, "Klepto Kid."

10 Things I Hate About You [1999]

Shakespeare's *The Taming of the Shrew* agreeably and amusingly goes to high school with Julia Stiles and Heath Ledger, who both emerged stars.

Varsity Blues [1999]

The '90s teen sex comedy boom credited to *American Pie* actually hit theaters a few months earlier in the form of *Varsity Blues,* a hybrid that combines small-town Texas high school football drama in the vein of *All the Right Moves* (1983), with party-hearty pranksterism and naked mayhem. Ali Larter scores an important cinematic touchdown with her whipped-cream bikini.

American Pie [1999]

The makers of *American Pie,* all *Porky's* generation escapees from teen movie hell, specifically sought to re-create the spirit of horny high-schooler farces of their own high school years. Go stick your pecker in the pastry of the title—they did it.

American Pie owns its corner of coming-of-age cinema as steadfastly as any previous juggernauts, and deservedly so. It coined the term MILF, introduced the phrase "This one time at band camp...," and, in Seann William Scott's Steve Stifler, contributed a unique loony-goon character to the all-time canon. *American Pie 2* (1999), *American Wedding* (2003), and *American Reunion* (2012) followed on the big screen. They're all funny.

Paramount also spun off "American Pie Presents" as a "National Lampoon's"–style brand with a series of (mostly) unrelated direct-to-DVD college comedies: *Band Camp* (2005), *The Naked Mile* (2006), *Beta House* (2007), and *The Book of Love* (2009).

But I'm a Cheerleader [1999]

Stretching the confines of teen movie hell a little, *But I'm a Cheerleader* is a thorny indie flick send-up of Christian "gay conversion therapy" with teen prank knee-slappers. Our heroes are a couple of pom-pom girls, and if the '80s were all about adolescent male voyeurism, the '90s seemed to be all about coming-of-age female bisexuality. Natasha Lyonne and Clea Duvall costar as the unmistakably homosexual pep squad members.

Cruel Intentions [1999]

Ostensibly a drama based on the 1782 novel *Les liasions dangereuses, Cruel Intentions* is a riot. Working a camp angle so masterfully that we can never be sure if he's kidding or not, writer-director Roger Kumble brews up a wicked potboiler of Park Avenue prep school monsters out to fight, fuck, and financially flagellate one another into oblivion.

As an on-screen presence, male lead Ryan Phillippe conveys roughly the effect of Wite-Out, yet his cipher status perfectly serves the storm brewing around him. Sarah Michelle Gellar is his cackling Cruella DeVille Jr. of a sister. They bet whether or not Ryan can deflower the headmaster's daughter (Reese Witherspoon), who has publicly declared her intention to save her virginity for marriage. Ryan wagers his vintage

Jaguar; Sarah puts up the promise of scorching incestuous sex. Selma Blair works into the mix as a lisping nerd to whom Sarah administers sloppy French-kissing lessons in Central Park. It all ends tragically—hilariously.

In 2000, Fox attempted a weekly TV spin-off titled *Manchester Prep*, but a preview clip of teen girls having public orgasms stirred sufficient outrage that the show was hastily recut into the direct-to-video sequel, *Cruel Intentions 2*, followed in 2004 by *Cruel Intentions 3*. A new *Cruel Intentions* series is still in the works.

Drive Me Crazy [1999]

Melissa Joan Hart goes to the prom with Andrien Grenier and they end up as stepsiblings. Britney Spears provides the smash title track.

Election [1999]

Indie film provocateur Alexander Payne established his "normal people are objects to ridicule" aesthetic with *Election*, an unsubtle satire about, you know, Nebraska or something. As a maniacally ambitious future Republican politician running for high school class president, Reese Witherspoon is phenomenal; as the schmendrick liberal teacher who's moved to destroy her, Matthew Broderick is Matthew Broderick. You're either on board with transplanted big-city sophisticate Payne's look-and-point mockery—or you're a tolerable person. Vote wisely.

Idle Hands [1999]

Horror fans and retro-'80s enthusiasts would do well to discover this flop fright comedy loaded with gore, nudity, sick jokes, and teen lust. Devon Sawa's right hand becomes demonically possessed, so he cuts it off, and the thing runs rampant all over his high school.

Jawbreaker [1999]

This late-'90s swing at a *Heathers*-style black comedy stars Rose McGowan, Rebecca Gayheart, and Julie Benz as mean girls who accidentally choke to death one of their own with the candy ball for which the film is named. Judy Greer is Fern Mayo, a hopeless nerdette who knows their secret and gets a makeover to stay silent, then out-means even the meanest of them. The cult of *Jawbreaker* has grown strong in recent times, which is sweet.

Never Been Kissed [1999]

Copping a move from Cameron Crowe's *Fast Times at Ridgemont High* (1982) experience, Drew Barrymore plays a young-looking newspaper reporter who goes undercover as a high school student—and gets to relive her teen experience and do it right this time. It was a big hit; but the *21 Jump Street* movies handle a similar premise far more outrageously (and amusingly).

She's All That [1999]

An absolute charmer with a possibly repulsive message, *She's All That* stars Rachel Leigh Cook as a shy, bespectacled teenage painter who longs for an art school scholarship and becomes the subject of a nasty wager. Star jock Freddie Prinze Jr. bets he can turn any girl on campus into the prom queen in six weeks—so his friend challenges him to take on freaky Rachel.

Their sham romance blossoms into the real deal and it's all actually quite well done, as embodied by the famous moment of Rachel descending the stairs in her prom finery to the soundtrack hit, "Kiss Me" by Sixpence None the Richer. Still, the final moments seem to hammer home: Quit being a weirdo because it's more important to make out with the football hero.

Bring It On [2000]

One of the sharpest, most inventively funny teen comedies ever made, *Bring It On* works as a straightforward saga of cheerleader competitiveness, cafeteria cliques, and teenage race relations, while simultaneously functioning as a satirical hot-footing of all of the above. Kirsten Dunst leads a flawless cast, with Eliza Dushku standing out as a goth gymnast and Upright Citizens Brigade cofounder Ian Roberts injecting uproarious absurdism as cracked choreographer Sparky Polastri.

Though hilarious, if any film ever screamed out to blast past its PG-13 constraints, it's this one. A raw dash of R-rated rah-rah raunch and a hard pinch of slapstick sadism would elevate *Bring It On* from cult favorite to undisputed classic status.

Universal Studios went another direction, converting *Bring It On* into a tween brand with four direct-to-DVD follow-ups that essentially function as remakes: *Bring It On Again* (2004), *Bring It On: All or Nothing* (2006), *Bring It On: In It to Win It* (2007), and *Bring It On: Fight for the Finish* (2009). Basic cable keeps those kiddie flicks in constant rotation, but the original's legacy lives on in the 2010s' extremely funny and unexpectedly edgy *Pitch Perfect* movies, which are to *Bring It On* what *American Pie* was to *Porky's*.

Road Trip [2000]

Director Todd Phillips warmed up for his blockbuster *The Hangover* with *Road Trip*, a sex-soaked slapstick saga of four college buds frantically driving cross-country to prevent an accidentally mailed sex tape from reaching one guy's girlfriend. MTV's Tom Green stays behind and periodically offers his Tom Green shtick. Prior to shooting her nude scene, Phillips pep-talked Amy Smart by telling her how much Phoebe Cates's *Fast Times* bikini-top pop had meant to his entire generation. She proves to have been properly inspired.

Get Over It [2001]

Kirsten Dunst shines in this punchy, unjustly unsung rom-com set around the mounting of a high school musical, *A Midsummer Night's Rockin' Eve*. In one of the film's highlights clearly descended from *Bring It On*, Martin Short is a riot as the control-freak drama teacher creator of the show. This is a minor gem worth unearthing. Get on it!

Loser [2001]

Fast Times and *Clueless* director Amy Heckerling says she envisioned *Loser* as "a teenage *Marty*," referencing the classic 1950s drama about an overweight butcher who finds love after a lifetime of loneliness. The studio pressured her to cast *American Pie*'s Jason Biggs in the lead as a college freshman über-dork, and he's fine. So's the movie.

Not Another Teen Movie [2001]

By 2001, enough neo-retro puberty laffers had come down the pike to warrant a gag-a-minute-style spoof largely inspired by *Airplane!* (1980) and updated to great success in *Scary Movie* (2000). *Not Another Teen Movie* specifically razzes *American Pie, Bring It On, Cruel Intentions, She's All That, Varsity Blues,* and other contemporary hits, as well as '80s faves like *Fast Times, Risky Business* (1983), and the John Hughes movies. Molly Ringwald cameos at the end and drops an F-bomb.

Sugar & Spice [2001]

An all-star cast of budding young starlets play felonious cheerleaders in *Sugar & Spice*, donning cool ersatz-Barbie masks applying their impeccably choreographed pep rally routines to the robbing of banks. The premise is great, but the movie is undone by attempts at shock humor that thud on arrival ("I'm as happy as a Make-a-Wish kid at Disneyland!")

Van Wilder [2002]

National Lampoon's movie division came back—albeit way briefly—with *Van Wilder*. Ryan Reynolds is perfect an seventh-year college senior and "party liaison" who runs all the fun on campus, until, setting the inevitable comic disasters in motion, his dad, Tim Matheson (Otter from *Animal House*), says Van has to graduate or get cut off. *Van Wilder: The Rise of Taj* (2006) is the sequel. *Van Wilder: Freshman Year* (2009) is a prequel.

Sorority Boys [2002]

Sorority Boys survives as a jolting reminder that, just before the world went woke, a noxious wave of "just kidding (but no, really, I'm serious)" wannabe alpha-machismo scorched the culture in the form of "guy humor." Think back to *Maxim* magazine, *The Man Show*, and Tucker Max. From that douche heap of history arises *Sorority Boys*.

Harland Williams, Barry Watson, and Michael Rosenbaum star as members of Kappa Omicron Kappa (KOK), which is regularly protested by the feminist sorority Delta Omicron Gamma (DOG). The KOKs bombard the DOGs (get it?) with dildos. They also use a secret camera to record themselves having sex with chicks from the campus hottie house, Pi Pi Pi (the Tri-Pi's).

Now, 2002 is still not 1982, so once the KOKs dress up as women and infiltrate the DOG house, they learn valuable lessons about being nicer to females, even those they deem "unbangable." The hijinks all lead to the movie's final scene, depicting a life raft loaded with Tri-Pi's adrift on the ocean. There's no land in sight and no help is on the way. The implication is that these young women will all die at sea. It's a joke! Laugh, bro!

Easy A [2010]

In keeping pace with what goes on outside the movies, the teen sex comedy mutated considerably across the eight years that separate the mirthful, male-bonding misogyny of *Sorority Boys* from the underdog female empowerment of *Easy A*. Consider that the time it took for society to achieve both high school and college degrees of greater understanding while majoring in entertainment about minors.

Emma Stone broke through to stardom with *Easy A*, a very 2010 spin on *The Scarlet Letter*, complete with webcam narration and a PG-13 rating. Stone plays Olive, a high school senior who lies about losing her virginity, only to have the fake news snowball into wild exaggerations all over town.

In response, Olive embraces her new "dirty skank" label and, taking a cue from the source book, stitches a bright red *A* onto all her clothing. She also works the badge of dishonor into a sort of sexless prostitution: Olive agrees to let any guy in school claim he slept with her, in exchange for gift cards (again: very 2010).

The final image, with Olive and her actual new boyfriend kissing as they ride off on a lawnmower, is a visual homage to the closing moments of the 1987 Disney teen-for-hire comedy, *Can't Buy Me Love*.

The To-Do List [2013]

With *The To-Do List*, writer-director Maggie Carey gender-flips an age-old teen movie hell trope by having Aubrey Plaza as pent-up high school senior Brandy Klark itemize a set of goals she hopes to achieve before graduation. At the top of the list is sex with Rusty (Scott Porter), the hottest college dude in town. Also, Brandy's never had an orgasm.

The To-Do List's own roster of vulgar transgressions is impressive. Brandy gets a lifeguard gig at the local pool, assumes a floating brown log is a riff on *Caddyshack*'s Baby Ruth gag, and then literally eats shit in front of her crush. When Brandy finally does get busy with a guy in lover's lane, she ends up peering in on her parents having sex in the next car over. The movie ends with Brandy having sex in her college dorm room. The exact moment she achieves her very first orgasm, her dad walks in on her. Cue credits.

Daddies' Girls [UNRELEASED]

In 2015, original *Porky's* (1981) cast members Tony Ganios (Meat) and Cyril O'Reilly (Tim) announced they would be producing a screenplay they'd cowritten under the title *Daddies' Girls*. The premise was that the all-grown-up Porky's posse must presently contend with the adolescent awakenings of their own daughters.

Working under the tagline, "Payback is a *bitch...,*" *Daddie's Girls* was touted as the return of *Porky's* stars Dan Monahan (Pee Wee), Mark Herrier (Billy), and Scott Colomby (Brian); along with cult actors Jeffrey Combs (*Re-Animator*), Leslie Easterbrook (*Police Academy*), and William Forsythe (*The Devil's Rejects*).

Despite the horror pedigree, the movie was touted on its defunct production web site as: "The very first 3-D teen sex comedy...to feature confident, sexually aggressive teenage girls in lead roles, instead of the usual complement of goofy, oversexed teen boys...We'll show you a brave, spiteful new world where bouncing breasts and flying female fists are the order of the day, and where frustrated fathers learn that despite their most hilarious efforts to defend their little angels' virtue, not only are they powerless to stop their daughters from growing up, but, come what may, the bonds between dads and *Daddies' Girls* can never be broken."

Ganios announced a Kickstarter campaign to fund production costs, but that effort was delayed, and the movie web site was soon shuttered.

The DUFF [2015]

The title of *The DUFF* is an acronym for "Designated Ugly Fat Friend" and the movie is all about a teenage girl who finds herself cast in that role alongside her two popular, confident best pals. Can you believe, then, that *The DUFF* doesn't have a mean bone in its body?

Adapted from a popular young adult novel of the same name, written by seventeen-year-old Kody Keplinger, *The DUFF* is a witty, bravely unflinching deep dive into puberty blues circa 2015. The film depicts the daily disappointments and even humiliations that befall Bianca Piper (Mae Whitman) without ever exploiting her with ridicule or elevating her to martyr status.

Instead, Piper learns that life can be a bummer. Her heart can and does get broken, but there will always be another first-period bell tomorrow bringing unknown chances to maybe make something cool happen. By the end of the movie, Piper has made a lot of cool stuff happen. She's also riotously funny. In the lead, Maw Whitman is perfect. She was twenty-five at the time, but what else is new? Welcome, *The DUFF*, to teen movie hell, we've been waiting for you.

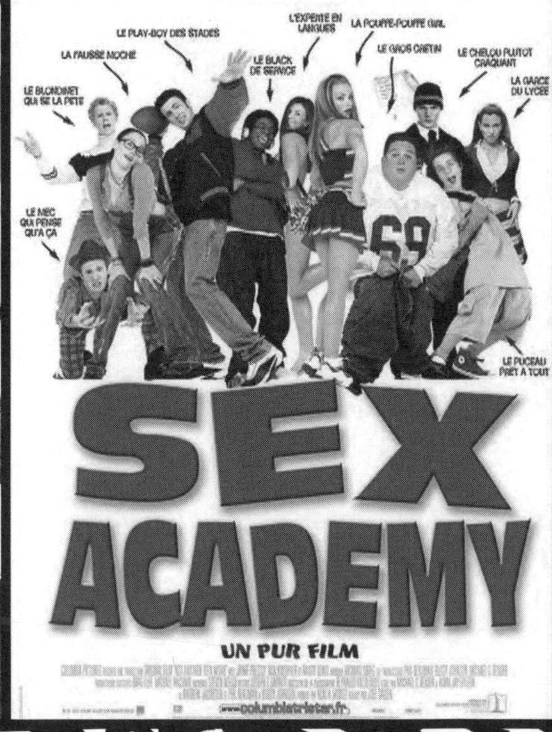

Clockwise from top left: *Blue ribbon retro teen-sex blockbuster* American Pie *(1999); writer-director Maggie Carey's cult favorite* The To-Do List *(2013)*; American Pie *and its imitators soon spawned a popular parody,* Not Another Teen Comedy *(2001) aka* Sex Academy; Road Trip *(2000) successfully wedged MTV star Tom Green into a funny college farce.*

FRANKLY! IT'S HER MOST PROVOCATIVE!
The shocking revelations of student–teacher affairs.
BRIGITTE BARDOT
in The Infatuation Story of a Stage-struck Girl
"School For Love"
JEAN MARAIS and MISCHA AUER
An N.T.A. Pictures Release

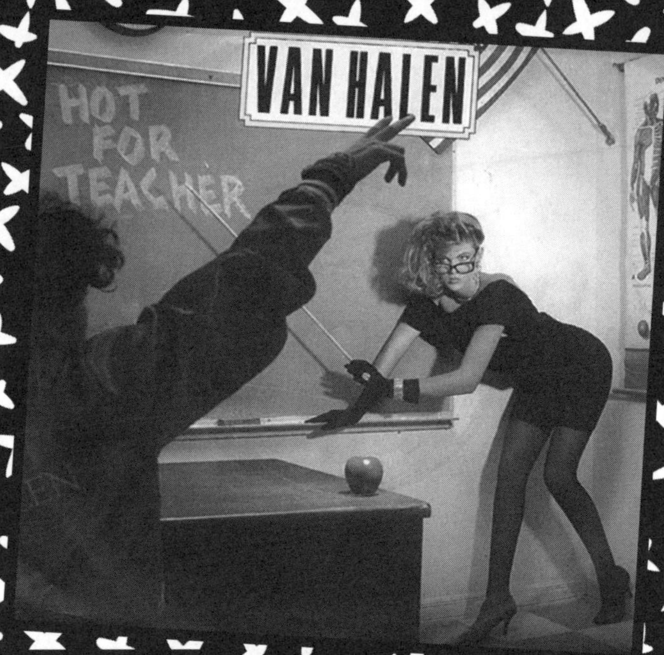
VAN HALEN
HOT FOR TEACHER

They can teach you a lot...Enter their course!
"I teach sex-ed my way!"
"I can't resist the student body!"
"What I do after school is my business!"
"I give very private lessons!"
SEX-ED LAB
THE STUDENT TEACHERS

ENZO BORIA presenta
CARROLL BAKER
LEZIONI PRIVATE
ROSALINO CELLAMARE · LEONORA FANI · EMILIO LO CURCIO
LEOPOLDO TRIESTE · FEMY BENUSSI · RENZO MONTAGNANI
CARLO GIUFFRE · VITTORIO DE SISTI

HER BEST LESSONS WERE TAUG AFTER CLASS
THE TEACHER
SHE CORRUPTED THE YOUTHFUL MORALITY OF AN ENTIRE SCHOOL!
COLOR

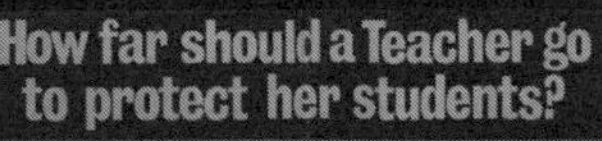
How far should a Teacher go to protect her students?

TRIP with the TEACHER
They forced her to commit the ultimate sacrifice!
A CROWN INTERNATIONAL PICTURES RELEASE · COLOR

THE STUDENT BODY ALWAYS SCORES with
SUMMER SCHOOL TEACHERS
A NEW WORLD PICTURE

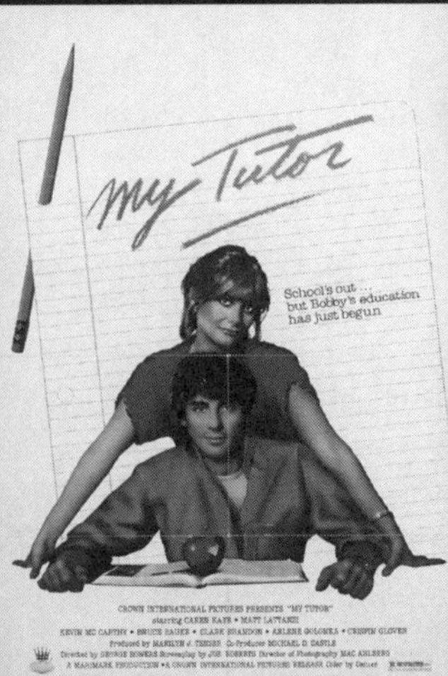
my Tutor
School's out ... but Bobby's education has just begun
CROWN INTERNATIONAL PICTURES PRESENTS "MY TUTOR"

Hot for Teacher

Student-Teacher Relations in Teen Sex Comedies

by Kier-La Janisse

I was an overly ambitious kid who wanted to be involved in everything, and by grade seven I had already obliged three requests from classmates to join them in the student talent show. First I was cast in a male role in a ballet showcase by my friend Jenny. Then I performed an early breakdance routine set to the Newcleus song, "Jam on It." My windmill was impressive enough that we took home the prize, which speaks to the breakdancing standards in my all-white Catholic school. The third time around, my friend Mora and I opted for a dramatic performance of Van Halen's "Hot for Teacher." Mora played the sexy teacher, and I was the horny student; I remember wagging a pencil like Groucho Marx with his cigar. We thought nothing of it, but our classmates were perceptive enough to sense the embarrassing and inappropriate dimensions of the song.

Educational culture has always been full of student-teacher liaisons. In the 1970s, when I grew up, such pairings were common in post-secondary environments. Though we are now wary of gender and power imbalances that play out in the classroom microcosm, as author Jo Keroes writes in *Tales out of School* (Southern Illinois University Press, 1999), an undeniable connection exists between teaching and sexual politics. The "lessons" imparted from on-screen representations of those relationships have real-life consequences for women.

It's No Crush, I'm in Love

Unlike the narrative from the Van Halen song, which shows a bikini-clad female teacher gyrating in front of a class of ten-year-olds, statistics show that relationships between *male* teachers and *female* students are the most common in real life. For a long time, these relationships seemed to be normalized. Sheila Cavanaugh points out in *Sexing the Teacher: School Sex Scandals and Queer Pedagogies* (UBC Press, 2007) that, until the late-20th century, it wasn't uncommon for male teachers to marry female pupils after graduation. In the early Brigitte Bardot vehicle *School for Love* (1955) her teenaged character embarks on a romantic relationship with her singing teacher. In *The Prime of Miss Jean Brodie* (1969), set in 1930s Edinburgh, the title character is preparing one of her sixteen-year-old students for an affair with her own rejected lover, an art teacher at the school. After the sexual revolution, these relationships no longer required a marital destination; the young female student's simultaneous physical experimentation and intellectual awakening by an older, wiser male teacher was seen as something of a rite of passage in the 1970s; only to become before a pathetic cliché in the 1980s, when culture-steering magazines like *Playboy* began to show their age.

In the most innocent films tackling such relationships, the male professor might be oblivious to a romantic fixation on the part of his student, as was the case in the ABC Afterschool Special *It's No Crush, I'm in Love* (1983). Cynthia Nixon (*Sex and the City*) stars as a pre-teen who falls for her new teacher due to his resemblance her favorite soap opera actor. In *Little Darlings* (1980) and *Summer School* (1987), the girls try in vain to seduce their teachers (swim coach Armand Assante and summer school stand-in Mark Harmon, respectively), who break the girls' hearts as gracefully as possible. Note that when female students aim to seduce their teachers in coming-of-age comedies, the motivation is never simply unbridled lust, as is overwhelmingly the case with their teen male counterparts. Most often, the girls are loaded with romantic yearning fed by teen magazines.

This puppy love can affect quite young characters, too. In the Mexican coming-of-age comedy *La Lucha con la Pantera* (1975), a trio of what appear to be eleven-to-twelve year-olds struggle with varying neuroses. One is in love with her brother, another has violent rape fantasies, and a third wants to go to bed with her teacher. Only the last succeeds in her goal, and quite easily. She writes a poem called "The Woman with the Burning Soul" and delivers it to him; he likens her to his own "Annabel Lee" and off to a hotel room they go. Rather than let their love fade and die, she stabs herself with scissors. The professor, found next to her naked, bloody body, is immediately arrested for the rape and murder of a child. Did I mention that this movie is a comedy?

In other cases, seduction of a teacher is merely part of a blackmail plan, as in *Malibu High* (1979) and *How to Seduce Your Professor* (1979). It's arguable whether *Malibu High* even is a comedy, as the film offers very few laughs except the nervous ones that spring from inappropriateness and audacity. *Malibu High* rivals exploitation cheapie *Bat Pussy* (1973) for the sheer amount of on-screen bickering. Ultimately the seduction of her teachers is one stop in a trajectory of empowerment that ends with the protagonist becoming a hitwoman for the mob. *How to Seduce your Teacher* is significantly lighter fare (as signaled by the presence of Italian comedy buffoon Alvaro Vitali). Prompted by her friends, Guida sets her sights on the history teacher (Fabrizio Moroni) for a blackmail scheme. The two find themselves in love by the end, without facing judgement from their community.

In all cases, the films reinforce the inevitability of sexual relations between girls and their male teachers, with most girls easily encouraged by the slightest attention. Whether those relationships are consummated or not, the male teacher's experience and wisdom are validated and his irresistibility confirmed.

The Sexual Revolution

In American sex comedies, sexy teacher storylines often involve male students vying for the sexual attention of a female teacher. How the female teacher becomes the object of romantic or sexual fantasy is related to cultural myths that change over time; studying their portrayal in the teen sex comedy is especially revealing. Historically, the female teacher existed somewhere between a nun and a stewardess. If not living with older relatives, she often boarded at the school and was forbidden from marrying, so teaching was a vocation suited to widows and spinsters, as well as young women not yet married. (*Little House on the Prairie*'s Laura Ingalls began teaching at age sixteen, but gave it up to marry Almonzo Wilder two years later).

Some women found immense freedom in teaching (and in working as nuns and stewardesses, for that matter), as they were able to travel, experience culture, and satiate a thirst for knowledge while having surrogate children in the form of their pupils. While Maggie Smith's character in *The Prime of Miss Jean Brodie* often comments on the "sacrifice" she made to remain single and devoted to her "Brodie Girls," she clearly values the cultural freedom her position affords her.

With the advent of pop psychology in the

1950s, the spinster teacher was suddenly seen as a suspicious, corrupting influence—and not only because they might lead their students to flights of fancy as in *Miss Jean Brodie*—but because it was discovered that sequestered female teachers would experiment with lesbianism. Non-pornographic films addressing lesbian student-teacher relationships are rare; two examples are *Mädchen in Uniform* (1931) and the 1987 *Degrassi High* episode "Rumour Has it" where Caitlin questions her sexuality after having an erotic dream about her teacher.

Overall, the female teacher's sexuality has always been something heavily monitored and controlled, conveying an anxiety about female sexuality in the classroom that isn't extended to male teachers. According to Sheila and Mikee Deloney's essay "Professional Paradox: Teachers in Film and Television," the sexualization of the female teacher on film and TV had an important milestone with the 1963 *Andy Griffith Show* episode "Andy Discovers America" in which he meets Opie's history teacher "Old Lady Crump" and discovers that she is, in fact, a fiery young woman.

After the sexual revolution, the fantasy of the female teacher was unleashed and proliferated in teen sex comedies. An interesting comparison of conflicting values for male and female sexuality is Roger Vadim's first English-language feature *Pretty Maids All in a Row* (1971), scripted and coproduced by *Star Trek*'s Gene Roddenberry (based on a book by Francis Pollini) and starring Rock Hudson and Angie Dickinson as a pair of teachers who see the hot-blooded students of a California high school as fair game for testing the waters of the sexual revolution—even as a serial murderer is creating a body count on campus of Hudson's nubile conquests. The killer is revealed to be Hudson's character himself, a pathological Don Juan, a pied piper who leads the students to their deaths under the auspices of encouraging their freedom, thus undermining the light comedy with a deep strain of misogyny. Many viewers found the movie troubling, because of its punishment of sexually liberated girls and the unbalanced power dynamic between the Hudson and Dickinson characters. There is a euphoric beauty to the film, but its All-American sunshine doesn't engage with the morality of student-teacher sexual relations as much as it focuses on how the school prioritizes the status quo, represented by a football game, over the safety of its students. This was meant to be Roddenberry's criticism of the school system, even though the film's salaciousness frequently overrides any intended satire. In one scene created by Roddenberry, Hudson's character says:

In a typical high school it would be difficult to invent a system more destructive of a child's natural creativity. Only in the most backward penal institutions does one discover equally oppressive rules of silence, restriction of movement, constant examination of behavior.

However, the film's sporadic attempts to address issues of institutional oppression feel shoehorned. Vadim himself said the appeal of directing the film was that it was "completely immoral," and by all accounts he and Roddenberry did not share the same goals.

While Angie Dickinson's role as pedagogical seductress is certainly one of the most smoldering examples ever seen on-screen, two Julie Corman-produced pictures of the early 1970s, *The Student Teachers* and *Summer School Teachers*, remain the sex comedies of this era that offer protagonists who truly act as advocates for their students' creativity and healthy exploration of sexuality. They also most directly engage with the zeitgeist of second-wave feminism in asserting their female leads' erotic agency both within the school and without. (Corman alum Joe Dante synopsized them more dismissively: "Women take their clothes off, get in trouble, and say left-wing things.")

The Student Teachers, directed by Jonathan Kaplan (*Over the Edge*) has feminist and civil rights agendas, with an emphasis on promoting alternative models of education. It presents freewheeling, sex-positive teachers, and breaks down boundaries between students and teachers (helped by the fact that they are presented as not being that far apart in age). The sex ed classes are the best example here of a teacher asserting her authority while also engaging the students in a non-traditional way, one aligned with changing social mores. Part of her authority comes from the fact that she's seen to be sexually active and that her knowledge is not gleaned from textbooks, unlike the uptight coach played by Corman staple Dick Miller, an example of what happens when sexuality is stifled: he becomes the school rapist.

Corman's followup, *Summer School Teachers,* this time directed by Barbara Peeters (*Humanoids from the Deep*), furthers the feminist mandate with Candice Rialson as the coach who initiates their school division's first-ever girls football team, much to the chagrin of the boys' coach Dick Miller, returning from *The Student Teachers* to again play a despicable male chauvinist. The film's most overt misstep, undercutting its feminist theme, is having one of the teachers fall for the school juvenile delinquent after he assaults her in class. He grabs her tightly by the collar and kisses her forcefully, establishing that her authority does not extend to him. While at first shaken, she negotiates this unfair dynamic by insisting on helping to extract him from some of the external pressures affecting his education—namely a local petty crime ring that has him on a leash, and a school administration that sees him as an easy scapegoat. The feeling that she might be the one to get through to him manifests as sexual arousal, and two share a psychedelic love scene, followed by a hilarious car chase.

In real-life Canadian teacher Heather Ingram's memoir *Risking it All: My Student, My Lover, My Story* (Greystone Books, 2013) she writes about her own student lover's delinquency, and admits that he responded to her lessons because of a sexual attraction which she exploited to get him to learn. She gave the troubled boy someone to talk to, which is virtually identical to how the teacher ends up romantically involved with her student in *Summer School Teachers.* "I feel myself falling into the seductive illusion of being needed," writes Ingram, "of being important enough to make a difference in someone's life."

As with male teachers who seek attention from their female students, there is a need for validation. Wrapped in a feminist framework, this is presented not as an abuse of power but as exercising or regaining power that the woman has previously been denied. But this is a precarious sort of power, one that can be stripped from her whenever it becomes a threat to the institutions that monitor and control her place in the world.

Lessons Are So Cold

Referring to John N. Smith's *Dangerous Minds* (1995) in his essay "Indecent Proposals: Teachers in the Movies," D.M. Bauer labels the classroom as "an eroticized zone, supercharged with violence, disrespect for authority and moral chaos." His description recalls not only the scene in *Summer School Teachers* where things could go horribly wrong, but also Fernando Di Leo's *Naked Violence* (1969), in which a young female teacher is gang-raped by her students and left dead on her desk in the classroom; and *The Private Lesson* (1975), an Italian pseudo-comedy starring Carroll Baker that takes a left turn into blackmail and humiliation.

The 1973 murder of New York City school teacher Roseann Quinn—a crime known as "The Goodbar Murder"—put an effective halt to the notion of the sexually active schoolteacher as a feminist icon. She was not murdered by a student, but by a one-night stand who she met at the neighbourhood pub, one of many places she frequented outside of school hours. Her final night's conquest was just one of a succession of men she took home in the years leading up to her death. The media painted her murder as a warning to sexually liberated women everywhere, and the evnt became ground zero in decades' worth of discussion around victim-blaming. In Judith Rossner's best-selling novel *Looking for Mr Goodbar* (Simon & Schuster, 1975), the fictionalized version of Quinn had been deflowered by a teacher, a cold and demeaning college professor who only bolstered feelings of shame over a spinal deformity left over from childhood polio. This woman wasn't a strong-willed free spirit like her counterparts in the Corman-produced films, she was just a lonely woman in a big city.

The book's fictional backstory of a married male professor seducing and ruining a younger woman is truly a morality play aimed at controlling the sexuality of young women. Likewise, another book relatively contemporaneous with Quinn's murder—Lacey Fosburgh's *Closing Time* (Delacorte Press, 1977)—also allowed for speculation as to why Quinn "invited" her own death.

In 1973, the year of Quinn's murder, Susan Brownmiller (author of pioneering anti-rape treatise *Against our Will*) pointed out that the lifestyles of several murdered young career women—including Quinn, stewardess Cornelia Crilley, schoolteacher Emily Hoffert, and her roommate, *Newsweek* researcher Janice Wylie—were being used by the media as cautionary tales against the advancements of second wave feminism. They were being punished for their independence, their audacity, and their vanity. The *New York Daily News* headline about Quinn's murder said as much in chilling terms: "Teacher Victim of Sex Slaying Battered with Statue of Self."

While Julie Corman's 1970s teacher films propped up their feminist protagonists as in control of their own narratives, the reality of such outspoken women in the school system was much more regulated. The French student riots of May 1968 provided the backdrop for a famously tragic pedagogical encounter: that of high school teacher Gabrielle Rossier and her sixteen-year-old student Christian Rossi, which formed the basis of the acclaimed 1971 Andre Cayatte film *Mourir D'Aimer*, starring Annie Girardot as the fiercely independent and hip teacher. Her affair is seen as a violation of her "position of public authority," but she refuses to heed the principal's insistence that she stop seeing her student. Not only is he a tall, bearded, committed political activist who appears much older than he is, but the atmosphere of revolution has broken down many social boundaries, among them that of student and teacher. "In May, all kids thought they were men," says the judge, "but the law remains the law!" In this milieu, our heroine is made an example of; she is sent to prison, while her young lover sent to a mental hospital and medicated beyond belief. The possibility of a normal life together becomes so remote that when his parents begin a campaign to send her back to jail, she commits suicide.

After Roseanne Quinn, the sex life of the on-screen schoolteacher evolved further and further removed from reality into a cartoonish fantasy. Female teachers became more naïvely desirable without the "political bummer" of feminism attached to their sexuality. This became a way to avoid the reality of what happens to women who participate in the fantasy that teen sex comedies propagate. They go to jail. And some end up dead.

I Think the Clock Is Slow

It makes sense that the American sex comedies of the 1970s feature feminist protagonists so prominently, given that America was at that time the hotbed of radical feminism. Julie Corman in particular excelled at a brand of exploitation that offered a platform for seemingly incongruous feminist ideals. But the sex comedies of the 1980s are more derived from the tradition of bawdy European sex comedies, in which women are comparatively objectified.

After the soul-searching, sexually fluid 1970s, the 1980s was an era where America returned to more conservative values. It's no coincidence the first teen sex comedies of the era (*Lemon Popsicle, Animal House, Porky's*) were set in the 1950s and pre-revolution early 1960s.

Gone were the feisty, feminist protagonists of the 1970s Corman films, replaced by a decade-long parade of horny male teenage protagonists led around by uncontrollable libidos. While there's no denying the 1980s films became enjoyable comfort food for a certain generation, they're easily several degrees dumber than their 1970s counterparts. In his book *Pretty in Pink: The Golden Age of Teenage Movies* (St. Martin's, 1999) Jonathan Bernstein calls them "tits n' zits movies."

In Bob Clark's Canadian tax shelter classic *Porky's*, considered the English-language prototype for the '80s teen sex comedy (even though Boaz Davidson's hugely successful 1978 German-Israeli production *Lemon Popsicle* came first), guffaws are elicited from the contrast between the lithe, oversexed gym teacher Miss "Lassie" Honeywell (Kim Catrall)—so called because of her ear-splitting howl when satiated; and sexually repressed, heavy-set gym teacher Beulah Balbricker (Nancy Parsons), who is the constant butt of sexual jokes, including the film's famous "tallywhacker" scene. While the film is progressive in other ways—namely its race politics and its non-judgemental approach to promiscuous student Wendy Williams—both gym teachers are presented as extreme comic book stereotypes already several decades old.

While *Lemon Popsicle* clearly intended to ride the nostalgia wave propagated by the success of *American Graffiti*, *Porky*'s launched its own 1980s teen sex comedy tsunami. The dick-in-the-shower gag became a template for the subgenre's emphasis on absurd hijinks. This type of gag—for instance, a boy in drag trying to infiltrate a girls' dormitory—was certainly a staple of foreign sex comedies in the 1970s, from Germany's *Schulmädchen-Report* films (1970-1980) to Italy's fifty-plus Decamerotics (mostly 1971-1975). *Porky*'s seemed to be the gateway for North American audiences to embrace that hybrid of teen nostalgia and silly sex comedy that formed the backbone of the German and Italian film industries in the 1970s.

In *Loose Screws*, the sequel to z-grade Canadian sexploitation comedy *Screwballs* (of which Jonathan Bernstein wrote: "This one's really a relic from the rollicking days before date rape became a consideration"), a group of horny boys divided into clearly demarcated "types" (the hunk, the nerd, the fatso—only BFFs in fantasy films like this) are sent to summer school where they immediately begin a campaign to sexually humiliate the young French teacher. She is constantly being tricked into situations where she is caught nude; one of the teens dons all manner of disguises to trick her into disrobing, a transgression for which he is made to write lines on the blackboard such as: "I will not make sexual advances towards the female teachers of this institution." Eventually she is humiliated at a school ceremony by having a film screened of her sexual exploits with the principal. Then, drugged, she performs a striptease in front of the entire school, faculty, and parents. Her treatment of the boys never warrants this, she is but an innocent bystander to their feud with the principal. This revenge seems merely a mean-spirited punishment for not succumbing to the boys' advances.

The sexy teacher is also presented as a contrast to the droning professor ("Bueller...Bueller...") Sexualizing the teacher becomes, for bored kids, a way to pass time that isn't necessarily meant to progress beyond harmless fantasy. *In Grease 2*, French teacher Connie Stevens seems perfectly aware but unconcerned that her male students can't keep their eyes off her bosom. "I'd like to see all of you in drama class this year," she says to the loitering T-Birds. "I'd like to see all of *you* in drama class this year!" says head T-Bird Johnny Nogarelli (Adrian Zmed), to which she replies flirtatiously, "You just might!" It's clear that the film's position is that such exchanges are unthreatening, and even cute.

Sexy teacher films are an extension of the trope in sex comedies (and coming-of-age film) of the loss of virginity to an older, more experienced woman, such as *Private Lessons* (1981) and *The Big Bet* (1985)—both starring *Emanuelle*'s Sylvia

Kristel, who also appeared as "Miss Copuletta" in *Private School...for Girls* (1983). The presence of Kristel in these films further signals their debt to the European sex films of the '70s. While in Europe the Edwige Fenech *School Teacher* series that began in 1975 was immensely popular ("she gave him private lesions," stated one poster's erroneous tagline), in North America the most famous of the classic '80s student/teacher sex comedies is probably *My Tutor* (1983), in which Karen Caye plays a French teacher (the most common kind of teacher in these fantasies) hired by rich Yalie Kevin McCarthy to tutor his son, Matt Latanzi (who in 1984 married Olivia Newton-John, ten years his senior). Since Caye is a freelancer, the student-teacher boundaries are not as pronounced, and the line are broken down further by the fact that she lives in a guest house on the property and swims in the nude after dark. Their affair begins after she catches Latanzi spying on her. The previously unattainable girl his own age starts to notice him after his deflowering, acknowledging that something about him is "different"—a newfound confidence instilled by the affections of his older tutor. As he ends up with his classmate in the bittersweet ending, the affair with the teacher is reinforced as a short-lived but necessary rite of passage. Now he can enjoy a more fulfilled life as a sexually active teenager, and a more considerate lover for girls his own age. However, while Kaye's character has shades of her feminist counterparts from the 1970s Corman era—she dumps her cheating boyfriend and spurns her employer's advances after her own self-confidence is bolstered by the "tutoring" of her inexperienced young lover—the film ultimately centralizes the boy's journey into manhood over any examination of female power.

While the voluptuous or sexually liberated female teacher is a staple of these films, the taboo of student-teacher relations occasionally manifests on-screen as the subversion of the uptight teacher's authoritative role through sexual tension. *Three O'Clock High* (1987) is highly stylized male wish fulfilment that sees the nerdy, anxious protagonist suddenly becoming irresistible to his tightly-wound English teacher. She is wooed by his book report on "Honey Goes to Hollywood," after which he plants one on her in front of the whole class ("Now that's what I call a book report!" exclaims one of the fellow students).

The repressed teacher receiving a sexual awakening from her student probably reaches an apex in *A Night in Heaven* (1983), starring Leslie Ann Warren and heartthrob Christopher Atkins as her student-by-day, stripper-by-night. In spite of the Bryan Adams music throughout, the movie is a solid, steamy drama (with *Dance Fever*'s Deney Terrio in a small role!) However, *A Night in Heaven*'s point-of-view favors the middle-aged adults—the female teacher whose sexual repression is highlighted by the unrepentant sexuality of her student, and her husband, who is trying to hold onto his idealism in a corporate environment. By the end of the film, the status quo is reinstated and the wayward teacher's marriage is salvaged. Not many women teachers can escape living out this fantasy unscathed.

Since the Mary Kay Letourneau case in 1997, in which Letourneau had a sexual relationship with her thirteen-year-old student (she gave birth to their first child in prison, and they were married upon her release), female predators in the school system have been given higher profiles in the press than their more numerous male counterparts. But in the teen movies of the 1980s, and largely in real life at that time, the word "predator" was not used to describe women who embarked on relationships with their students. Conflicting messages are thus imparted through these films; on the one hand they safely explore the common fantasy of sex with an authority figure, but on the other hand they trivialize the real-life consequences of these transgressions. They normalize these relationships as a privilege or a rite of passage for very young teens, with the inherent power dynamic projected as a turn-on rather than a problem.

As David Lee Roth's diminutive double says at the end of Van Halen's "Hot for Teacher" video: "Funny, I don't *feel* dirty."

Bobby couldn't make it...
till he went
Fun-Truckin'!
CROWN INTERNATIONAL PICTURES
presents
THE VAN
R RESTRICTED

GET THAT
FREE WHEELIN'
FEELIN'
WATCH YOUR DONKEY...SMOKEY'S GONNA GETCHA
SUPERVAN
IT'S ONE MEAN MACHINE!
COUNTY JAIL
STARRING
MARK SCHNEIDER • KATIE SAYLOR • MORGAN WOODWARD
Produced by SAL CAPRA • Directed by LAMAR CARD • Executive Producer NOLAN RUSSELL BRADFORD
Music by Andy DeMartino, Mark Gibbons & Bob Stone • Performed by "Vandora Express"
Color by DELUXE • An Empire Releasing, Inc. Presentation
SPECIAL SCREEN APPEARANCE By The "King of the Kustomizers" GEORGE BARRIS
Creator of the Solar Powered "SUPERVAN"

Young bodies on
the prowl...
they
pay
by
the
mile!
Blue Summer
ALLAN SHACKLETON
presents a film by CHUCK VINCENT
starring DARCEY HOLLINGSWORTH - BO WHITE with JOANN STERLING
- MELISSA EVERS and CHRIS JORDAN - original music by SLEEPY HOLLOW
cinematography by STEPHEN COLWELL - IN COLOR -
A MONARCH RELEASE

The Greatest Cruisin' in the Land
Takes Place on the Street –Where it all Began...
VAN NUYS BLVD.
Starring
BILL ADLER • CYNTHIA WOOD • DENNIS BOWEN • MELISSA PROPHET
DAVID HAYWARD • Executive Producer NEWTON P. JACOBS
Produced by MARILYN J. TENSER • Written and Directed by WILLIAM SACHS
Director of Photography JOSEPH MANGINE Associate Producer MICHAEL D. CASTLE
Edited by GEORGE BOWERS • Music by KEN MANSFIELD and RON WRIGHT
A CROWN INTERNATIONAL PICTURE
R RESTRICTED UNDER 17 REQUIRES ACCOMPANYING PARENT OR ADULT GUARDIAN

Cruising Beyond Vansploitation

Fast Times and Sweet Rides on Van Nuys Blvd.

by Samm Deighan

Vansploitation movies are the vehicle that zoomed 1970s drive-in teen sex comedies into the more conventional 1980s. In an early moment of William Sachs's *Van Nuys Blvd.* (1979), a neon sign that reads *Pleasure* illuminates the Los Angeles night, implying that this will be a film about hedonism, with characters seeking carnal delights while cruising the streets in tricked-out vans and muscle cars. As a fictional portrait of a particular time and place, the film captures a fantasy world of sexual freedom and teen rebellion, while depicting the end of that dream. Like other transportation-themed films from that period, the road itself—and the vehicles that cruise along it—represents a yearning for freedom beyond the confines of conventional society and its rules, regulations, and expectations.

The loose plot of *Van Nuys Blvd.* follows Bobby (Bill Adler), who, on a whim, leaves behind his boring small town life—including his naked and horny girlfriend (Susanne Severeid)—and points his van towards Van Nuys Boulevard, home of drag racing and adventure. The beautiful Moon (Cynthia Wood) challenges him to a race, but they are promptly arrested by a local ballbuster, Officer Zass (Dana Gladstone). During a night in jail, Bobby bonds with Moon, her friend Camille (Melissa Prophet), and boisterous redhead Greg (Dennis Bowen), who has a crush on Camille and has allegedly been dreaming of her. The two couples are soon taken under the wing of the older Chooch (David Hayward), and have a series of carefree adventures throughout the city as the group—including Chooch and his new girlfriend, Wanda (Tara Stroheimer), a waitress at the local drive-in—grow closer.

The film's theme song suggests that Bobby's van is a "love machine," and that he has his "wheels in motion" to find some sexual companionship. Ultimately, though, the film is revealed to be about settling down and growing up, with just a few zany sex scenes limited to the first act. Such is the transportational power of *Van Nuys Blvd.* a forerunner in the "Vansploitation" film subgenre of comedies about young adults searching for freedom while riding in custom vans. Other entries include films like *Blue Summer* (1973), *The Van* (1977), and *Supervan* (1977).

In Jason Coffman's 2015 essay for *Medium*, "Freedom, Fun and Fine Transportation: A Brief Guide to Vansploitation Cinema," he writes: "The roots of the van movie reach back most obviously to the 1950s...fast cars, open roads and dangerous games of "chicken" both signified a potentially hazardous teenage freedom and (even better) they made the squares nervous. B-movies about teens driving recklessly all played expertly on the growing sense of unrest and rebellion in the youth of America.

Coffman notes that motorcycle films as far afield as *The Wild One* (1953) and *The Wild Angels* (1966) set the blueprint for Vansploitation films. In those revved-up outings, frustrated, bored, and sometimes lawless teens guzzle gas in the name of a powerful search for freedom *The Wild One* establishes its protagonist's need to break from conventional society and form a community of his own. The majority of similar productions—whether the protagonists ride motorcycles, cars, or vans—are concerned with a similar foundation of communities outside the conventional "adult" middle class world.

Van Nuys Blvd. was made for Crown International Pictures, an independent company that produced low-budget, B-grade and exploitation films in the '60s, '70s, and '80s, including a variety of vehicle-related cult fare like *Hell on Wheels* (1967), *The Hellcats* (1967), *Wild Rebels* (1967), *Pick-Up* (1975), *Trip with the Teacher* (1975), *The Van*, and *Burnout* (1979), among others.

Director William Sachs actually planned *Van Nuys Blvd.* to be a satire of the other Vansploitation films, which possibly explains its lighthearted tone, and the quickness to touch upon broader themes of the subgenre. Furthermore, the characters actually get away from the vans that bookend the film.

Coffman writes, "The vans in Vansploitation films are a symbol of the characters' sense of freedom, usually their main leisure activity is driving the vans...the engine that drives the plot forward and/or provide the stage in which the action of the plot actually takes place...In short, most van movies are about getting laid (in a van) and winning road games or other competitions (also in a van)."

In Vansploitation films, the majority of the screen time takes place in or around vans. In *Van Nuys Blvd.*, the group goes to an amusement park, a nightclub, the beach, a racetrack, an arcade, and other good-time venues. In a sense, the characters are already moving away from their obsession with vans and cruising the strip: drag racing is more or less a plot device that places Bobby in Los Angeles and brings he and Moon together.

Unlike the more nihilistic motorcycle films, van movies as early as *Blue Summer* generally show a gradual movement away from teen rebellion and towards stable adult life. *Blue Summer* starts as a party on wheels, where anything goes, but it ends as a colossal bummer drenched in the downpour of the inevitable responsibilities of adulthood.

Van Nuys Blvd. Director William Sachs (*The Incredible Melting Man, Galaxina*) discussed influence of the surrealist movement on his work in an interview with Sam Weisberg on *Hidden Films,* citing in particular his love for Luis Bunuel's *The Discreet Charm of the Bourgeoisie* (1972). In that film, a group of middle-class friends attempt to dine together, but they are interrupted by increasingly bizarre events.

Similarly, *Van Nuys Boulevard* relies on a series of vignettes. Though they move in chronological order, they are effectively disjointed and become increasingly absurd, such as a segment in which the redhead Greg gets lockjaw from attempting to eat a large sandwich. Another sequence, where Officer Zass is stranded on the beach, also takes on a surreal tone, as he has a number of strange encounters—first with a vindictive biker, later a dog.

While *Van Nuys Blvd.* lacks elements of emotional cruelty or nihilism that mark other '70s and '80s teen comedies, the movie is gently firm with its ultimate moral: eventually, you have to leave the fantasy behind and grow up and join the real word.

Although Van Nuys Blvd. is a real road running through the San Fernando Valley, its depiction in the film is a fantasy; a nostalgic, rose-colored view of cruising in the 1960s and 1970s, created some years after the lifestyle it depicts had faded away. In this sense, the film borrows heavily from a quintessential teen comedy, George Lucas's *American Graffiti* (1973), which follows a group of high school students in the early 1960s on the very last night of their summer vacation before college begins. The night is primarily spent drag racing and saying goodbye to friends as they all prepare to depart for different schools.

American Graffiti served as the blueprint for countless later coming-of-age teen comedies. Though *Van Nuys Blvd.* doesn't explicitly follow teens on their last day of high school—a trope that would recur in later comedies like *Dazed and Confused* (1993) and *Can't Hardly Wait* (1998)—there is a finality in the adventure.

The movie is a snapshot of the last day of frivolity and immaturity for the group. Even their oldest member and nominal leader, Chooch, reverts to his birth name (Leon), finds a wife (Wanda), and sells his car (to Officer Zass). Though the film closes on a hopeful, even romantic note, with all three couples happily paired off, the closing credits revert to a melancholic and undeniably nostalgic tone, once again depicting the freedom of nightly cruising on the boulevard.

Like *American Graffiti, Van Nuys Blvd.* is deeply concerned with nostalgia and a surprising amount of whimsical innocence for an R-rated sex comedy. The film's tagline—*The Greatest Cruisin' in the Land Takes Place on the Street—Where it all Began...*—refers to this mythical state of mind.

Made just a year after the similarly themed, but far less ribald *Grease* (1978), *Van Nuys Blvd.*'s attitude towards sex is surprisingly wholesome, ultimately depicting stable romance as the true end goal for male as well as female characters. For example, Chooch, the most experienced of the characters, is revealed to be incredibly awkward around Wanda; he is vague about the number of girlfriends he has had and she initiates sex between them.

Van Nuys Blvd. definitely differs in this way from a number of similar films. Certain teen sex comedies from the period, like Israel's *Lemon Popsicle* (1978) and its American remake, *The Last American Virgin* (1982), portray sex as frustrating and difficult—only the selfish, mercenary characters have active sexual relationships, and those are implied to be superficial and manipulative. The "cool" character seduces a teen girl, takes her virginity, and impregnates her, immediately discarding her once he learns this bit of news.

Other Vansploitation films, such as *Supervan* (1977), include sexual assault and the manipulation of female characters as a recurring theme. Unlike some other Vansploitation films such as *Blue Summer* or *C.B. Hustlers* (1976), which boasts a van brothel—sex is not commodified in *Van Nuys Blvd.* in the same way.

Vansploitation movies and the vans they exploit did not last into the Reagan era. The sensibility and realities of the California streets were fundamentally different in the 1980s. Many of the Los Angeles-based erotic dramas and thrillers released just after *Van Nuys Blvd.* have a nihilistic tone and can generally be thought of as exploitation films: titles like *Vice Squad* (1982), *Body Double* (1984), and *Savage Streets* (1984) frankly confront topics like sex work, rape, and the abuse of women.

Van Nuys Blvd. treats female characters with surprising equality. Women always have the upper hand in sexual situations. Wanda is sexually manipulative, but saves herself from rape at the hands of Officer Zass. She tricks him into disrobing, handcuffs him to his own police car, and leaves him stranded on the beach. She also has a softer side, and is quick to settle down with Chooch once she realizes what a decent guy he is. She goes so far as to conceal her freewheeling sexual history from him.

Likewise, Moon is Bobby's equal—she's not just a girlfriend, but a drag racer herself, with her own van. In fact, they ride off together in her vehicle at the end of the film, after Bobby destroys his own van in a demonstration of his love for her. He no longer needs his freewheeling independence in this movie.

Remember, *Van Nuys Blvd.* is ostensibly a sex comedy. The beginning of the film establishes what turns out to be a somewhat deceptive tone, rife with ribald sexual encounters. When Bobby pulls up to the drive-in in the first place, Wanda takes his order and then has impromptu sex with him in the back of his van. The two spray condiments all over one another, a sure sign of hilarious lusty interludes to come.

Similarly, Greg becomes stranded after his car is smashed by a rival for Camille's affections. He hitchhikes a ride with a biker babe (Di Anne Monaco), who drives him to a wild party, has sex with him, then returns him to the same gas station where he was initially stranded. Suspiciously, *Van Nuys Blvd.* seemingly rejects the general Vansploitation rule of the van as a mobile space for sex and freedom, as the majority of sex occurs in a parents' home, an adult apartment, or a boat on the beach.

In this film, vans bring six friends together for companionship and community, a sort utopian preemptive solution to the often bleak punk teen film problems that quickly followed in *Over the Edge* (1979), *Times Square* (1980), and *Out of the Blue* (1980). *Van Nuys Blvd.* is basically a celebration of youth culture without drugs—aside from a scene on a rollercoaster at Magic Mountain where Bobby lights up what seems to be a joint.

The lighthearted sequence in *Van Nuys Blvd.* set in a disco is worlds away from the slightly earlier *Saturday Night Fever* (1977), with its hard themes of working class turmoil, family tension, date rape, young pregnancy, and suicide. Aside from spending a night in jail, the most rebellious exploit of the group is driving around using vast amounts of gas for no real reason other than seeking some fun during the tail end of a serious gas crisis.

Leaving the mayhem and anarchy of the 1970s in its rear-view mirror, *Van Nuys Blvd.* points the audience to the forthcoming John Hughes films and their suburban values, preoccupied with forming families. Marital relationships are established here over pinball and shuffleboard. Bobby and his friends reject the middle class of their parents, but the carefree, fun lifestyle they espouse is really just a ruse for settling down and establishing themselves on their own terms. Welcome to the 1980s.

Madonna, whose breakthrough movie, director Susan Seidelman's Desperately Seeking Susan *(1985), is one of the last motion pictures to heavily exploit the awesomeness of a custom van—in this case a punk band's tour vehicle. Illustration by Corinne Halbert.*

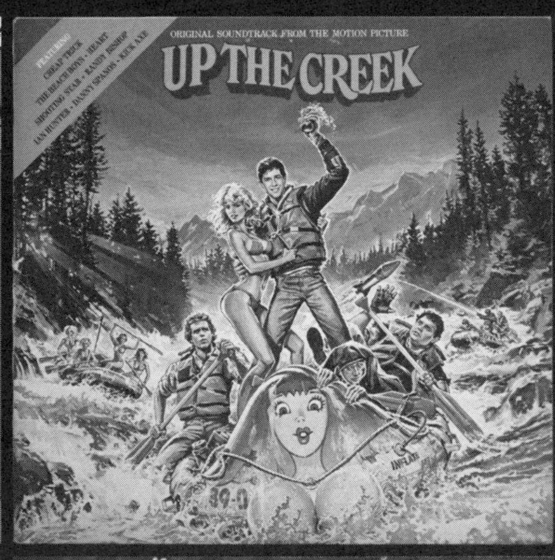

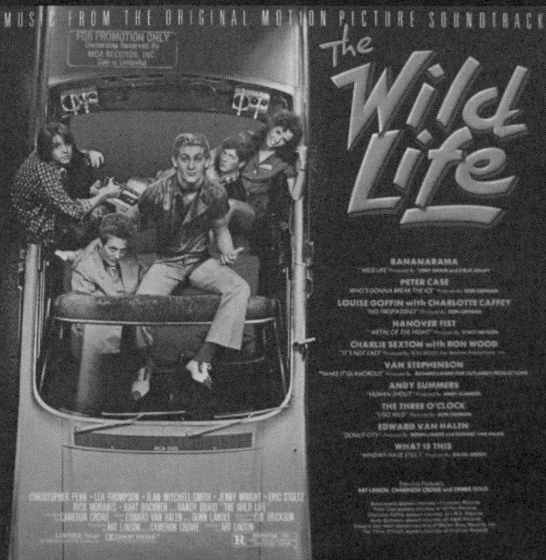

The sounds of Teen Movie Hell, *now available on LP, cassette, 8-track, compact disc, VHS, Betamax, LaserDisc, and your friendly neighborhood multiplex and pay cable channels.*

Teen Music Hell
The Official Teen Movie Hell Mix Tape

Forget about "Don't You Forget About Me" by Simple Minds from *The Breakfast Club*; "Old Time Rock-'n'-Roll" by Bob Seger from *Risky Business*; "Oh Yeah" by Yello from *Ferris Bueller's Day Off*; and "In Your Eyes" by Peter Gabriel from *Say Anything*—at least *try* to forget the most worn-out "classic" tunes from vintage teen comedies and listen to me now.

Within the following teen sex comedy anthems, every note is a keg tap, every groove is a food fight, every solo is a spring break bacchanal—even the mellow ones. This is your *Teen Movie Hell* mixtape. Construct it carefully and use it *extremely* unwisely.

CHEAP TRICK

"Up the Creek," from *Up the Creek*

An a capella chant of the chorus intros "Up the Creek" in headphone-swirling stereophonic grandeur. A blast of silence then cascades naturally into a four-chord tidal wave upon which the S.S. *Cheap Trick* effortlessly sails, our journey with these sharp-dressed Midwest cutups fueled by masterfully timed gushes of pop whimsy and hard dips into the craft's party-metal reserve tanks. As a single, "Up the Creek" got a big record company push at the time (including a "Too Hot for MTV" music video), and it really did deserve *Billboard*'s top spot. Instead, it sank after reaching #36. It's a pleasure, then, to rank "Up the Creek" number one here.

KEANE

"Trying to Kill a Saturday Night," from *Zapped!*

A bouncing piano opens "Trying to Kill a Saturday Night" and makes a sound that's at once giddy, nervous, and just a little bit freaked out, thereby matching the exact emotions that go into prepping for an adolescent weekend evening outside your bedroom (for once). In 1977, brothers John and Tom Keane flopped as *Tiger Beat* heartthrobs (despite their own CBS summer variety series) and then flopped again as a rock duo early the next decade. That was a shame—twice—as proven by the Keanes' wicked eyebrow-cocker that plays under the title credits of *Zapped!*

GLEAMING SPIRES

"Are You Ready for the Sex Girls?"
from *Last American Virgin*, *Revenge of the Nerds*, and *School Spirit*

Art-rock weirdness so nice, classic *Teen Movie Hell* soundtracks had to include it thrice. *Revenge of the Nerds* incorporates this new-wave noodle-bender most effectively and School

Spirit actually showcases the Gleaming Spires in action, but give *The Last American Virgin* the nervy credit for popping the song's cherry.

LEGION

"Totally Awesome Video Games," from *Joysticks*

Just as an argument can be made that *Joysticks* is the perpetual main attraction in teen movie hell, the same could be said about the film's gloriously idiotic (vidiotic?) theme song, "Totally Awesome Video Games." Higher praise than that exists nowhere in all eternity.

BLOW-UP

"Kickin' Up a Fuss," from *Up the Academy*

Punk energy explodes out of a solid pop-rock construct in "Kickin' Up a Fuss" by forgotten L.A. basement show brawlers Blow-Up. The same goes for *Up the Academy* itself, as well as for the movie's entire remarkable soundtrack, which also features burly new-wave oddities by Lou Reed, David Johansen, Cheeks, and Pat Benatar, along with primo bare-knuckled cuts by the Stooges and Eddie and the Hot Rods.

ADAM ROTH AND HIS BAND OF MEN

"I Just Wanna Have Some Fun,"
from *Beach House*

From the gleaming, grimy, glorious dawn-of-the-decade moment when the Ramones constituted "surf rock" along the coastlines of Long Island and the boardwalks New Jersey, Adam Roth and His Band of Men infused the goombah-accented boogie-board grandeur of *Beach House* with a perfect rock embodiment of that highly localized zeitgeist. As indicated in the film by the decal letters on their bass drum, Roth and the BOM plug in classed-up gear from the Pleasantville Music Shoppe and pump out Garden State greatness built on whatever three fuzzy chords are immediately at hand and a youth of AM-radio bubblegum structures bopping around their brainpans. Each number rips at a tempo intended to knock the swimsuits off any revelers within earshot—successfully. HoZac Records is slated to put out a proper *Beach House* soundtrack album in 2019. Crank it up now and see who loses what.

PENNY ALEMIAN

"King Frat," from *King Frat*

The undercooked meth nursery rhyme title theme to "King Frat" hinges on a staccato chorus with an unnatural syllable break—"King Frat, King Frah-[pause]-aahht." Hear it once and it owns your brain forever, just like how, in the movie, Grossout Grombowski owns all challengers at every major-league professional fart contest.

BILLY SQUIER

"Fast Times (The Best Years of Our Lives),"
from *Fast Times at Ridgemont High*

Billy Squire's signature AOR swing-funk gets muscled up by marching-band horns in a booming zoom of a song that soaringly underscores *Fast Times*' football sequence. Billy's big beats provide rousing accompaniment to infuriated Charles Jefferson (Forrest Whittaker) as he assassinates Lincoln High players all over the gridiron.

CHEAP TRICK

"Spring Break," from *Spring Break*

Even if the song "Spring Break" sounds like Cheap-Trick-for-hire, it's still Cheap freakin' Trick that *Spring Break* maker Sean S. Cunningham hired. Rick Nielsen's lead riff (probably played, somehow, on all six necks of his specialty guitar at once) is a charging bull of a party beast matched by lyrics that could actually have been scrawled on the sands of Fort Lauderdale between mega-barfs and bottomless beer cup refills (consider the chorus: "I need a break! Gimme a break! I need a spring break!").

THE WIGS

"Fire," from *My Chauffeur*

Pitched from an ideal point between early-'80s power pop and late-decade hair-metal power ballads, "Fire" slings savvy melancholy that moves your feet and sticks where you can feel it. The very same year the Wigs got to play onscreen in *My Chauffeur*, front man Marty Ross departed the Wisconsin combo to costar in the syndicated TV shit-show *The New Monkees* (a thing that actually was). Nobody's career made it out alive.

KRAK

"Hardbodies," from *Hardbodies*

"Hardbodies," the song, pulls off being the sonic equivalent of both the movie's poster and the movie itself. It sounds like electro-rock created by a Texas Instruments computing device and performed by unemployed actors who showed up at an audition to play a rock band by wearing long-hair party-store wigs. It's also, somehow, semipornographic. So, yeah: This is way the right song for the right movie at hand (and glands).

JEFF ALAN BAND

"Losin' It," from *Losin' It*

Suppressed desperation floats closely around the synthesized Farfisa and preprogrammed beats of "Losin' It." So that's to say the music very much matches the movie. The sing-along chorus is a keeper, too, especially since it's so dubiously credible—"Losin' it!/Confusin' it!/ Abusin' it!/Havin' the time of our lives!" Yeah, sure you are, Jeff Alan Band. Us, too.

IAN MATTHEWS

"Shake It Baby," from *Little Darlings*

It's smutty, this shimmering bon-bon of dry-docked yacht rock by the former front man of Fairport Convention, and it's directed toward a female subject addressed only as "Baby." It also vividly conjures a '70s NoCal fern bar, fragrantly (and flagrantly) exuding that milieu's associated sensations with unmistakable accuracy: sauvignon-blanc-spritzer breath, Virginia Slim finger stains, Rorer 714 eyeball glaze, and cocaine's promise of a better next three-and-a-half-minutes until exactly three minutes and thirty-one seconds later. So even though it's all about "Baby," this open-toed-espadrille-tapper is patently adult, which makes it the absolutely perfectly inappropriate theme song for the absolutely perfectly inappropriate *Little Darlings*. Let Ian Matthews shake you, babies. Forever.

BONE SYMPHONY

"One Foot in Front of the Other,"
from *Revenge of the Nerds*

This bubbling synth-pop confection that plays during the nerds' charmingly slapstick, high-speed extreme frat-house makeover is an instant spirit booster and booty-mover. Grab a broom, do the robot, and just let it happen.

VIXEN

"Computer Madness," from *Hardbodies*

In 1988, Sunset Strip glam foursome Vixen nabbed heavy rotation during MTV's high hair-metal era with "Edge of a Broken Heart," an accomplishment denied them four years earlier when they portrayed seaside rockers Diaper Rash in *Hardbodies*. Who's to say that Diaper Rash's "Computer Madness" wasn't at least as deserving of the group's later platinum sales? After you hear the prognosticating number and its prescient lyrics ("The machine is taking over/that thing he used to call work/What's he gonna tell the wife and the kids?/They'll think that Daddy is a jerk!), that naysayer won't be you.

JIMMY BUFFETT

"I Don't Know (Spicoli's Theme),"
from *Fast Times at Ridgemont High*

If you didn't know going in that "I Don't Know (Spicoli's Theme)" was by Jimmy Buffett, you'd never guess it and, in that ignorance, you'd allow yourself to embrace the bliss brought on by this sweet, midtempo new-wave sway that rotates like a boardwalk carousel, complete with ups-and-downs, and ends with you, like Spicoli, feeling gleefully dizzy. Listen without prejudice.

MISSING PERSONS

"Mental Hopscotch," from *Lunch Wagon*

As leaders of the group Missing Persons, married veterans of the Frank Zappa war machine Dale and Terry Bozzio generated a couple of the most unique and enduring concoctions of the new-wave era with "Words" and "Destination Unknown." Equally deserving of immortality is the Missing Persons single "Mental Hopscotch" a video-in-the-process-of-killing-the-radio-star rip-roarer that also serves as the effective theme song of the slapstick T&A romp *Lunch Wagon*. Weirder still is that Missing Persons star in *Lunch Wagon* as a band called Teddy and the Rough Riders, but their songs are credited to U.S. Drag. In this one case, you can accept all substitutes.

JOSIE COTTON

"Johnny Are You Queer?" from *Valley Girl*

The *Valley Girl* soundtrack is appropriately applauded as one of the decade's essentials, and it generated two touchstone tunes that will be forever connected to the film: "I Melt With You" by UK tech-wavers Modern English and "A Million Miles Away" by Cali power-popsters the Plimsouls. Each does what it does without flaw and you can (and will) hear both in the general ether of existence at any time.

One *Valley Girl* barb that sticks, though, is that for all of Nicolas Cage's punk-rock bravado on-screen, no actual punk songs made it into the movie. Attitude-wise, "Johnny, Are You Queer?" by Josie Cotton comes closest. It's a spiky retro-'60s send-up that fit in swell on big-city new-wave stations between "The Dominatrix Sleeps Tonight" by Dominatrix and "Teenage Enema Nurses in Bondage" by Killer Pussy. Life used to be fun, you know.

RICK SPRINGFIELD

"The American Girl," from *Private School*

Rick Springfield's 1981 breakout LP *Working Class Dog* is a power-pop masterpiece that doesn't always get properly lauded as such because, ironically, its pop proved too powerful. After "Jessie's Girl," there was simply no way TV's Dr. Noah Drake could just remain a cult figure on par with Nick Lowe and Dwight Twilley. "The American Girl," Springfield's deft donation to the *Private Lessons* soundtrack, is pure Rick for Phoebe Cates People, and the song's adroit underscoring of a leeringly photographed outdoor aerobics class only compounds everything that's great about Rick, Phoebe, the movie, the moment, and all other things that, with great power, go pop—greatly.

WILLIE NILE

"That's the Reason," from *Private Lessons*

The *Private Lessons* soundtrack is a shockingly unhip lump of preexisting adult contemporary hits. That doesn't make it bad, per se, and it even makes it kind of impressive.

On the one hand, the song selections were likely what the movie's game show maven producers Jack Barry and Dan Enright imagined "kids today" really grooved to. Then again, it's no leap to imagine *Private Lessons*' central dork Philly (Eric Brown) swooning to "Lost in Love" by Air Supply, attempting (and failing) to rock out to "I Need a Lover" by Johnny Cougar (pre-Mellencamp), and experiencing every glossily overproduced emotion supplied by a trio of Rod Stewart AM-radio staples.

Private Lessons' sole musical venture past the parts of the Casey Kasem countdown your mom would hum along to is "That's the Reason," a retro rocker by Willie Nile, who emerged from the same post-Springsteen NYC folk-rock swirl that got his peers Steve Forbert and Marshall Crenshaw some mass media airplay. Nile never did get his own hit song, but he'll always have placement on the *Private Lessons* tie-in LP alongside Randy Van Warmer ("Just When I Needed You Most") and Crazy Horse minus Neil Young attempting to sound like Crosby, Stills, Nash & Young minus Neil Young ("I Don't Want to Talk About It").

Y&T
"Summertime Girls," from *Real Genius*

Sugar-rush pop meets headbanging heat in "Summertime Girls," the signature smash of Bay Area hair-metal marauders Y&T. Deservedly, the song remains one of rock's all-time great salutes to the season when school's out and swimsuits go on (in hope of later taking them off).

Real Genius recontextualizes "Summertime Girls" in fittingly smart fashion, by having it underscore a joyful moment when the science majors make it snow inside their dorm hallway and an impromptu winter carnival results.

CIRCLE JERKS
"Moral Majority," from *Surf II*

For a movie so outrageously original, the *Surf II* soundtrack is disappointingly retread-heavy, even when it blasts reliable righteousness by way of '60s surf punks (Dick Dale, the Ventures), their '80s progeny (the Deserters, Jon & the Nightriders), and/or solid KROQ briquettes (Talk Talk's "Talk Talk" and Wall of Voodoo's "Mexican Radio" both feature here).

The two boldest picks of *Surf II* pack are the amyl-nitrate-inflamed Kraut-stomp "Fan Fan Fanatisch" by Berlin electro-shockers Rheingold, and "Moral Majority" by SoCal lords of hardcore Circle Jerks. Either tantrum works in terms of wrapping up the *Teen Movie Hell* mixtape, but let's err on the side of the 55-second discharge of skate-rage over not needing "some dumb schmuck" to dictate "what we can watch and read." Front man Keith Morris made that statement in 1982, but the sentiment hits even harder in 2019. The more things change, the more they stay so lame.

Extended Plays: Disco Dance Tracks for Mandatory Body Movement

DONNA FEIN
"Midnight Madness," from *Midnight Madness*

Back around the time that the Disney movie *Midnight Madness* came out, Disney Records hawked the album *Mickey Mouse Disco* via nonstop after-school TV commercials. Among the touted tracks were "Macho Duck" and "Watch Out for Goofy (He's a Disco Demolition)." The infectious "Midnight Madness" belonged on that LP back then, and it belongs on your *Teen Movie Hell* comp tape forever.

NILE
"Pink Motel," from *Pink Motel*

Pink Motel, the motion picture, contains three points to recommend: its bizarrely effective '50s-style poster art, the fact that it stars elderly funny folk Slim Pickens and Phyllis Diller, and this emergency siren of a theme song. To play it once is to sing for the rest of your days, "PIIIIINK Mo-tel/Nobody kiss n' tell!"—sometimes just inside your head, and sometimes very much not.

KATHY BROWN
"You're My Tutor," from *My Tutor*

This 5-minute, 14-second pump-up is all things Aerobicizable in sonic formation. Your heart will pound in time to the Casio drum setting, your loins will thrust along with the slap bass, and your brains will liquefy further with each screeched lyric, mixing with sweat and blissfully oozing out into your XL neon headband. Heed hard whatever lessons you come away with from there.

Instrumentals

TANGERINE DREAM

"Love on a Real Train," from *Risky Business*

The song that people remember from *Risky Business* is the Bob Seger dad-rump-shaker that Tom Cruise boogies to in his skivvies. The musical moment that truly makes the movie, however, belongs to German synth wizards Tangerine Dream. "Love on a Real Train" gleams like the steel rails on a Chicago El track and swells and pulsates and melts in the manner of what Cruise and Rebecca De Mornay do onboard the Pink Line headed toward O'Hare.

EDDIE VAN HALEN

"Donut City," from *The Wild Life*

EVH's solo contribution to Cameron Crowe's "spiritual sequel" to *Fast Times at Ridgemont High* is a bit of thump-and-grind that serves just fine as a connector between scenes, songs, or both. The music sounds weirder than Eddie's other 1984 soundtrack effort, but that one's wins in contextual strangeness: it's the score for then-wife Valerie Bertinelli's blackjack-addict housewife TV movie, *The Seduction of Gina*.

Essential Bonus Track

THE WAITRESSES

"Square Pegs," from *Square Pegs* (TV series)

In the early '80s, the Waitresses, a female-fronted art-snarl combo that emerged from the same Akron, Ohio, freak storm that also forged Devo, showed potential rock star promise by way of their sassy exercise in new-wave sarcasm, "I Know What Boys Like." Alas, the group is now best remembered only in December when their irresistible "Christmas Wrapping" lights up holiday playlists.

Come 1982, though, the Waitresses staged another pop culture coup by providing the theme song to *Square Pegs*, a daring CBS sitcom about high school outcasts, that actually outperformed the show itself in perfectly crystalizing the grotesquerie of the Generation X teenage experience.

"Square Pegs," the song, hinges on a chant of the title, around which aloof-like-a-fox lead singer Patty Donahue deadpans inner-monologue truth-bombs such as, "I'd like it if they'd like us, but I don't think they like us," and, "Yeah, I'd be cuter without gum in my braces."

Square Pegs, the TV show, created by brilliant *National Lampoon* editor Ann Beats, should have been the greatest thing that ever happened. It wasn't. The Waitresses' brilliant title track, however, is absolute greatness in and of itself, and lest ye doubt, just consider Patty's deepest gut-punch observation: "You know, our school colors should be black and blue." Did you attend classes on that campus, too?

About the Author

The volume you've just read is, itself, a teenager. In 1999, I penned an epic-length proposal for *I Lost It in the Locker Room,* a reference guide to teen sex comedy films. The book was almost published, and I'm glad it wasn't. We all needed time to grow up. So here it is at last, still drinking underage many iterations later—old enough to know better; too young to give a flip.

Aside from my maniacal passion for cinema in general and its knucklehead naked-nipple youth farce variations in particular, my life has been uncannily in step with *Teen Movie Hell.* These films punctuated the highlights of my own puberty. *Porky's* opened widely in 1982 just as I wrapped up junior high. *Fast Times at Ridgemont High* premiered that fall on the first actual Friday of my freshman year of high school. *Sixteen Candles* arrived in 1984 just as I turned sixteen. Right before I started my senior year, I lost my virginity on a lakefront to a blonde cheerleader so she could test a theory expounded by *Revenge of the Nerds.* Seriously.

My previous book, *Heavy Metal Movies: Guitar Barbarians, Mutant Bimbos, and Cult Zombies Amok in the 666 Most Ear- and Eye-Ripping Big Scream Films Ever!* (Bazillion Points) drew from the splatter horror, apocalyptic action, and other berserk notions of entertainment I devoured as a teenager while knocking around the grindhouse theaters of 42nd Street in mid-'80s Manhattan.

When it came to R-rated teen sex comedies, though, I caught the bulk of them either at local theaters in Brooklyn, where I grew up, or on the Jersey Shore, where I spent summers with my grandparents. Cable TV didn't come to Brooklyn until 1986, the year I graduated high school. That didn't stop me. Almost daily, I'd rent VHS tapes from mom-and-pop video shops, often to watch with other horny bozos in parent-free TV rooms as smuggled Budweiser shot forth from our noses in mirthful response to whatever idiocy the VCR provided.

Yes, I watched a lot of movies as a teenager. No, I did no schoolwork. My proper education—along with what the blonde cheerleader showed me—was gleaned from what came in blocky, colorful cardboard boxes from the video store, and *Teen Movie Hell* is my dissertation of playing doctor. I hope you will award it a Ph*T&A*. Thank you for reading.

Illustrations by Corinne Halbert.

Contributors

KAT ELLINGER ("The Ellinger Code," page 13) is editor-in-chief of *Diabolique* and cohost of the *Daughters of Darkness* and *Hell's Belles* podcasts. She has written for the British Film Institute (BFI), *Sight & Sound, Fangoria, Senses of Cinema,* and *Scream,* and is the author of *Daughters of Darkness* (Auteur) and *All the Colours of Sergio Martino* (Arrow Films).

WENDY MCCLURE ("The Free Clinic Isn't Free," page 21) is the author of the memoirs *The Wilder Life: My Adventures in the Lost World of Little House on the Prairie* and *I'm Not the New Me.* She has contributed essays and stories to *BUST, The New York Times Magazine,* and *This American Life.* She lives in Chicago with her husband.

KATIE RIFE ("Modern Girls," page 25) is an editor at and contributor to *The A.V. Club.* She is a programmer at Chicago's Cinepocalypse festival, a former contributor to *Daily Grindhouse* and *Mr. Skin,* and an unabashed lover of puns.

HEATHER DRAIN ("Blue Summer," page 54) is a freelance writer whose work has appeared in publications and web sites ranging from *Diabolique, Video Watchdog, Dangerous Minds, Art Decades,* and many, many more. Read more of her work at mondoheather.com.

RACHEL MCPADDEN ("Foxes," page 95) is a former '90s zinester, music critic, and XOJane writer, and current legal partner of Mike McPadden, dog mom, and clay enthusiast.

LIZ MASON ("Girls Just Want to Have Fun," page 104) is the manager of Quimby's Bookstore in Chicago. She publishes zines and does massive amounts of preposterous dancing. Find her at: LizMasonIsAwesome.com.

LISA CARVER ("Night of the Comet," page 184) is the author of fourteen books. Her latest, *I Love Art,* is available from TigerBee Press.

CHRISTINA WARD ("Valley Girl," page 301) is Vice President, Feral House Publishing. She doesn't want to read your manuscript.

KIER-LA JANISSE ("Hot for Teacher," page 329) is a film writer and programmer, owner/artistic director of Spectacular Optical Publications, founder of the Miskatonic Institute of Horror Studies, and author of *House of Psychotic Women.*

SAMM DEIGHAN ("Cruising Beyond Vansploitation," page 337) is associate editor of *Diabolique* and cohost of the *Daughters of Darkness* podcast. She's the editor of *Lost Girls: The Phantasmagorical Cinema of Jean Rollin* (Spectacular Optical). Her book on Fritz Lang's 1931 film *M* is forthcoming.

CORINNE HALBERT lives and works in Chicago, conjuring all manner of unholy mayhem via eye-popping zines and infernal artwork. Follow her on Instagram: @corinnehalbert

SCOTT R. MILLER is a Chicago-based artist, zine publisher, and outstanding mustache bearer. Follow his Instagrams: @scottare and @printsploitation

McBeardo Thanks

Rachel McPadden—first, last, and all points in between. You are my fox of all *Foxes*, my dearest of all *Little Darlings*, and without you, I'd merely be a (non-Fabulous) Stain. Every day, Rach, you reinvent a life beyond my wildest dreams (and I've had dreams about the *Surf II* gang crashing the *King Frat* house at Camp Northstar!). I love you.

Ian Christe of Bazillion Points.

Aaron Lee. This book began in 1994 as a conversation with Aaron that has continued nonstop ever since. On occasion, we digress.

Scott R. Miller, an incomparable illustrator, collaborator, friend, and mustache.

Jim "Mr. Skin" McBride (you've accepted that this partnership is permanent, right?).

Heroic contributors Kat Ellinger, Kier-La Janisse, Katie Rife, Samm Deighan, Heather Drain, Liz Mason, Wendy McClure, and Lisa Carver.

Special thanks to the contributors whose pieces fell prey to size limits: Christine Colby (the greatest boss I've ever had), Salem Collo-Julin, Jo Weldon, and Katie McPadden Mullaney (yes, I cut out my own sister).

Corinne Halbert, a visual sorceress whose heart is as warm as her artwork is wicked.

Christina Ward of Feral House, an endless wellspring of inspiration and support.

Liz Mason (again!) and Quimby's Bookstore. Anne Elliot and Cheri Gutierrez, and their witchy wonderland at Sideshow Gallery. Jennifer Kilgore and Grant McKee at Bucket O' Blood Books and Records.

Mark Johnston, formerly of Shocking Videos, who supplied me with out-of-print laugh riots. Bill Van Ryn of Groovy Doom and Lana Revok, who materialized multiple mind-melting movie ads. Odd Obsession Video in Chicago.

Jimmy McDonough, Eddie Deezen, Greydon Clark, Allan Arkush, Gilbert Gottfried, Dara Gottfried, Frank Santopadre, E. G. Daily, Jon Abrams and Mike Vanderbilt of Daily Grindhouse, Zach Sokol of Merry Jane, Allan MacDonell, Joe McGinty, Heather Buckley, Paul Fishbein, Danny Wolf, Mathew Klickstein, David J. Moore, Clint Weiler, Brian Abrams, Benjamin Howard Smith, Jordan Runtaugh, Archie McPadden, and Zelda McPadden.

Finally, a salute to the late Adam Parfrey, founder of Feral House and creator of the 1990s-that-mattered. We all live in weirder times as a result of Adam's vision and efforts. See you in Feral Heaven.